For
Sir Michael Eliot Howard
Friend, mentor, scholar, and teacher

CONTENTS

LIST OF ILLUSTRATIONS

LIST OF MAPS

ACKNOWLEDGMENTS

I MET SIR MICHAEL HOWARD WHEN I WAS A GRADUATE student at Yale, but I knew of him long before that. Browsing as a child through the legendary Johnny Appleseed Bookstore in Manchester, Vermont—haunt of Pearl Buck and Robert Frost—my parents made me a generous offer: choose any book you like. I chose Michael Howard's *The Franco-Prussian War*—probably more for its striking cover than its stirring prose. I was, after all, ten years old. Years later, as a graduate student, I was asked by Paul Kennedy to assemble a file to support Yale's attempt to hire Michael Howard as the first Lovett Chair of Military and Naval History. In the ensuing weeks I read and reproduced articles and reviews for the file and began to appreciate all that Sir Michael had accomplished as a student, decorated officer in the Second World War, founder of the War Studies program at King's College London, stalwart of Chatham House and the International Institute of Strategic Studies, organizer of the immensely valuable Liddell Hart Centre for Military Archives, translator and editor of the world's standard English edition of Clausewitz, Chichele Professor of the History of War, and then Regius Professor of Modern History at Oxford.

Naturally I was awed by all of this, and all the more awed by his gracious and diligent reading of my dissertation drafts. When Sir Michael started at Yale, I was actually in Vienna researching in the

Austrian archives. In that last period before email, I would trudge to the Technical University in the Karlsplatz, print chapter drafts on recycled paper with faded toner, mail them to Professor Howard, and wait. Eventually they would come back, lavishly marked up with corrections and suggestions. When I returned to Yale to write up the dissertation, he was no less helpful. He was also the first professor to insist that I lecture to his class. He was teaching an upper division course on Modern European warfare and thought it would be foolish for me not to teach the unit that overlapped with my dissertation research. As easy as that seems to me now, it was forbidding then, but essential for my development as a scholar and teacher.

We've been friendly ever since, and he has given me all manner of good advice—on career, history, politics, travel, writing, and the ups and downs of academic life. I've enjoyed his generous hospitality in New Haven and England and have learned much from him over the years. I dedicate this book to Sir Michael and to his salutary influence on the study of military history, which he expanded from the study of battles to the study of war and its intersection with politics, society, culture, business, and diplomacy, and its relevance to contemporary defense studies.

Any book on this scale requires the assistance of so many people. I must thank the archivists everywhere I researched: in the French Defense Archive in Vincennes, in the British National Archives in Kew, in the UK Parliamentary Archives in Westminster, in the Bavarian War Archive in Munich, the Austrian War Archive in Vienna, and, of course, in the US National Archives in College Park, Maryland. In Vienna, I must thank my friend and colleague Rudolf Jerabek, who helped me identify the Austro-Hungarian divisions that fought the Americans and the best sources on them. In College Park, Tim Nenninger was a great help, constantly suggesting document collections and later helping me secure the images for this book.

I am grateful to my colleagues in the History Department at the University of North Texas for their support, and especially to my close friend, Mike Leggiere, who helps me run the Military History Center at UNT. The College of Liberal Arts and Social Sciences provided critical research funds that paid for archive visits in Washington and Europe, as well as a tour of the American battlefields in France. On that tour, from Paris through the Aisne-Marne salient, into the caverns of the Chemin des Dames, along to Reims and the Blanc Mont, then to Saint-Mihiel and the Meuse-Argonne, I enjoyed the company of my good friend, Jim Dutchik, who thought the prospect of tramping through woods and hills, peering into moldering bunkers, and studying row upon row of war graves and memorials well worth the drive from Düsseldorf (where he works) to Château-Thierry (where my tour of the battlefields began). The US Army kindly awarded me a General and Mrs. Matthew B. Ridgway Research Grant to use their collections in Carlisle. In London, I was able to spend considerable time in key British archives because of the kindness of David and Caroline Noble, who put their Battersea flat at my disposal and—to their delight—that of my two sons in the summer of 2016. In Washington, close to the National Archives in College Park, I benefited from the generous hospitality of my good friends, Steve and Vicky Connors, who very kindly let me use their house in Chevy Chase while I did the preliminary research for this book. In Dallas, I am grateful for the friendship of Cici Sepehri, who is always fun, supportive, and, as the Germans say, "someone to steal horses with."

My editor at Basic Books, Lara Heimert, is a joy to work with. She has a light touch but never hesitates to recommend course corrections that have always turned out well. She, for example, has titled my last two books—patiently waiting until the titles I had chosen slipped from my exhausted grasp. Lara, as usual, has assembled a great team to help produce this book, including Erin Granville, Liz Wetzel, Allie Finkel, Kait Howard, Melissa Veronesi, and Katie Lambright. My thanks to Mike Morgenfeld and his team for doing the maps. Tina Bennett is a wonderful agent—full of good advice and encouragement, from beginning to end.

Research like this yields fascinating discoveries and acquaintances. In the latter category, I must mention the mayor of Souilly—Madame Christine Habart. I was returning to Paris from the Meuse-Argonne battlefields and thought I'd detour through the little village of Souilly, where Pétain and Nivelle had directed the Battle of Verdun and Pershing had commanded the Battle of the Meuse-Argonne. I arrived after the *mairie*—the town hall that had served as the French and then American headquarters—had closed. Moments later, as I stood on tiptoe in the twilight peering through the darkened windows to catch a glimpse of history, a car skidded to a halt behind me, and out of it stepped the mayor, wondering what I was doing. I explained my interest, and she insisted that I come inside and see everything for myself, including the very desks, chairs, and battle maps used by Pershing and his French allies. It was exceedingly kind of her, and it made a great impression on me and this book.

I must also thank my family: my dear mother, Judith Stoughton Wawro, still soldiering on with vigor, grace, wit, and selflessness in her 95th year; my six siblings—Peter, David, Mark, Jill, George, and the memory of Robin, who passed away too soon to see this book but, living most of her life in Normandy, awoke in me on my regular visits a great love of Europe, France, and history. My sister Jill has been an especially great confidante and friend in all areas. David and Mark were good enough to read the first draft of the book and give me valuable feedback. Finally, my thanks to my beloved sons, Matias and Winslow, who are my proudest legacy and who bring me so much happiness.

INTRODUCTION

THE SHEER VARIETY OF AMERICANS WHO WENT TO WAR IN France in 1917–1918 to defeat the Germans and "make the world safe for democracy" was striking. A short list includes professional athletes at the peak of their careers. Eddie Rickenbacker was a race car driver selected—in a rare case of the army fitting a man to his calling—to be General Pershing's chauffeur. Finding that too dull, he transferred to planes and became the greatest American ace of the war, with twenty-six kills. Famous baseball players went, like Christy "Matty" Mathewson of the New York Giants, statistically still one of the top three pitchers to ever play the game. Branch Rickey, president of the St. Louis Cardinals, went, commanding the chemical warfare unit that killed Mathewson (accidentally) and employed other baseball stars, including Ty Cobb, who still holds the record for highest career batting average (.367), and "Gorgeous George" Sisler, whose record of most hits in a single season (257) endured until finally broken by Ichiro in 2004.

Phillies pitcher Grover Cleveland Alexander—still in possession of the record for most wins by a rookie starting pitcher (twenty-five)—served in France in the field artillery and was gassed, shell-shocked, and rendered an alcoholic for the rest of his shortened life. George Halas served in the US Navy during the war, returning home to found the Chicago Bears and coach them for forty seasons. Seventeen-year-old

Tommy Hitchcock Jr., one of the best polo players in America (and the model for Tom Buchanan in *The Great Gatsby*), dropped out of St. Paul's School to fly planes in the war. Gene Tunney, who twice beat Jack Dempsey and was world heavyweight champion after the war, was a Marine during it and, hardly surprisingly, the US military's best boxer.

Politicians and the sons of politicians fought. Being a "senator's son" in 1918 may have made your appearance in the trenches more, not less, likely. All four of former president Theodore Roosevelt's sons went. Ted Jr., Archie, and Kermit served in the 1st Division; Ted Jr. and Archie were both severely wounded. Quentin, the baby of the family, joined the Air Service and was shot down and killed in the Marne salient at the age of twenty, a loss that hastened the death of his father. Hamilton Fish III, a Harvard All-American football star who would go on to a twenty-five-year career in Congress, chose to serve in the segregated African American 369th Regiment (the Harlem Hellfighters) to make the point that black soldiers were as good as white ones. Henry L. Stimson, who would serve in the cabinets of Hoover, FDR, and Truman and who had already been President Taft's secretary of war, enlisted "for the duration" at age fifty and served in the field artillery in France.

Herbert Hoover, a forty-year-old Quaker when the war erupted in Europe, ran the US Food Administration during the conflict. To "Hooverize" meant to save food for the hungry Allies in Europe. Franklin Delano Roosevelt, assistant secretary of the navy during the war, insisted on going to France to inspect the 4th Marine Brigade, contracted the flu and pneumonia, and nearly died. Two of FDR's future Republican opponents—Alf Landon and Wendell Willkie— served in the army during the war, as did Leverett Saltonstall, the future governor and senator from Massachusetts. The thirtieth vice president of the United States, Charles Dawes, went, rising from major to brigadier general in the supply service. Hugo Black served in the 7th Division's field artillery before returning to a career in the Senate and a seat on the US Supreme Court. Thirty-four-year-old Captain Harry S. Truman, commanding a battery of field artillery in the Missouri National Guard, fought bravely in the Meuse-Argonne.

Everett Dirksen, the Illinois senator known for the saying "A billion here, a billion there, pretty soon you're talking real money," flew observation balloons over the Western Front. "Wild Bill" Donovan was wounded three times in the war, then went on to found the Office of Strategic Services (OSS)—forerunner of the CIA—during World War II. New Yorker Fiorello La Guardia left a safe seat in Congress to become a major in the US Army Air Service in France and Italy. Frank Knox, who'd be Alf Landon's running mate in 1936 and secretary of the navy under FDR, fought in France with the field artillery. Teddy Roosevelt's secretary of state, Robert Bacon, served as chief of the American military mission at British headquarters on the Western Front. New York City's thirty-eight-year-old progressive Republican "Boy Mayor," John Purroy Mitchel, lost his reelection bid to the Tammany machine in 1917, joined the Air Service, went up on a training flight, fell from the cockpit, and plummeted five hundred feet to his death in a Louisiana swamp. Sam Ervin, who chaired the Senate Watergate hearings in 1973, fought in the 1st Division—the storied "Big Red One"—and, like Ted Roosevelt Jr. and thousands of other Americans, was wounded at Soissons in July 1918.

Among the career soldiers, Dwight Eisenhower and Omar Bradley didn't make it to France. But most of the greats of World War II did, including George C. Marshall, George Patton, Douglas MacArthur, and Mark Clark. James Van Fleet, who would lead the assault on Utah Beach in 1944 and command UN forces in Korea, was a captain commanding a machine-gun battalion in the 6th Division during the Battle of the Meuse-Argonne. Terry de la Mesa Allen and Clarence Huebner, who would overlap as 1st Division commanders in World War II, overlapped on the crowded roads of the Saint-Mihiel salient in 1918. Allen was shot in the face there; Huebner was the most rapidly promoted second lieutenant in 1918, rising to the rank of lieutenant colonel in a few months for conspicuous bravery and effective leadership. Courtney Hodges, whose First Army would bear the brunt of the German attacks at the Battle of the Bulge, commanded an infantry battalion in the 5th Division in 1918.

US airpower in the war suffered from infighting between its chief proponents, Billy Mitchell and Benjamin Foulois; they both served in France, usually at each other's throat. A young lieutenant named Jimmy Doolittle served on their tumultuous staff. Captain Carl "Tooey" Spaatz, who would command US Strategic Air Forces in Europe in World War II, ran the army's flying school in World War I. Lieutenant Lemuel Shepherd, who would command the 6th Marine Division at Okinawa, was wounded three times in World War I, twice in Belleau Wood and once in the Meuse-Argonne; John Lejeune, "the Marine's Marine," was his commanding officer. Troy Middleton, who would famously hold Bastogne against the Germans in 1945, fought with such distinction with the 4th Division at Château-Thierry and the Meuse-Argonne that he became the youngest colonel in the American Expeditionary Forces at the age of twenty-nine. Major Leslie McNair, who would be killed by friendly fire in July 1944 after organizing a US Army of ninety divisions, proved so indispensable in 1918 that he became the army's youngest general at the age of thirty-five.

Both Walter Short and Husband Kimmel, the general and admiral who would be overwhelmed by the Japanese sneak attack at Pearl Harbor in 1941, participated in World War I, Short commanding the US Army's machine-gun school at Chaumont and Kimmel serving aboard the USS *New York* with the British Grand Fleet at Scapa Flow. Jonathan Wainwright, who would surrender the Philippines to the Japanese in 1941, was a staff officer with the 82nd Division in 1918, helping to locate the Lost Battalion in the Argonne Forest. Walter Bedell Smith, who would be Eisenhower's chief of staff in World War II, was wounded leading a platoon of the 4th Division during the Second Battle of the Marne. Future admirals (like Kimmel) also cut their teeth in the war. William "Bull" Halsey commanded a destroyer in Ireland, escorting convoys and hunting German U-boats in the Atlantic. Marc Mitscher began work on naval aviation. Lieutenant Commander Harold "Betty" Stark led a flotilla of destroyers twelve thousand miles from Manila to Gibraltar to assist in the blockade of the Central Powers and the submarine war.

Famous professors fought, like the diplomatic historian William L. Langer, who asked to be an interpreter and was assigned to chemical warfare instead. Harvey Cushing Jr., the greatest neurosurgeon of the twentieth century, served in the Medical Corps. The astronomer Edwin Hubble crossed the Atlantic as an infantry officer with a division that never saw combat. In his spare time, he was rumored to have lent his doctoral expertise in curved space and time to help direct long-range artillery fire.

Musician James Reese Europe, the leading composer in the African American music scene in New York, fought and led the band in the Harlem Hellfighters. Writers like Ernest Hemingway, e. e. cummings, Robert Hillyer, and John Dos Passos served as ambulance drivers. Twenty-one-year-old William Faulkner—ever the Anglophile—left a dissolving love affair in Mississippi for Canada and joined the Royal Air Force. He joined too late and was still in flight school in Toronto when the war ended. Poet Joyce Kilmer was shot between the eyes by a German sniper near Château-Thierry. Archibald MacLeish, the Pulitzer Prize–winning poet, drove an ambulance and then joined the field artillery. The novelist John Marquand served, as did the great sportswriter Grantland Rice, who popularized athletes like Bill Tilden, Babe Ruth, Knute Rockne, and Red Grange. Rice coined memorable phrases like the one describing Notre Dame's Four Horsemen—"They were known as Famine, Pestilence, Destruction, and Death; these are only aliases"—and served in the 37th Division's field artillery.

Some famous newsmen covered the war and others chose to fight, like Captain Walter Lippmann, who served as an intelligence officer in Pershing's headquarters and drafted Wilson's Fourteen Points. Robert McCormick, the publisher of the *Chicago Tribune*, served as a colonel in the 1st Division's field artillery. Frederick Palmer, America's most famous war correspondent, who had covered wars in South Africa, the Philippines, and the Balkans, served as Pershing's press officer during the war. Harold Ross and Alexander Wolcott wrote for *Stars and Stripes* and then went home to found the *New Yorker*.

Movie directors like William Wellman fought, as did artists like Horace Pippin, the greatest African American folk painter. Edward

Steichen, the highest-paid photographer in the world, who made portraits of Rodin and J. P. Morgan, supervised the Air Service's Photographic Section, which carried cameras aloft to photograph German trenches before an assault. Humphrey Bogart served in the US Navy, returning demobilized Americans from France to the United States. Walt Disney arrived in Paris late in the war and drove an ambulance at the front for the Red Cross. Rin Tin Tin was a puppy saved by Corporal Lee Duncan from German trenches near Saint-Mihiel. Buster Keaton went across with the California National Guard and later made a film called *The Doughboy*, a tribute to the US troops in the war, who called themselves "Doughboys" or "Doughs." The nickname had circulated since the Mexican-American War seventy years earlier, possibly a corruption of Mexico's ubiquitous *adobe*, whose dust clung to the "Doughboys," or a reference to the sweaty, dusty appearance of the US infantry—like deep-fried doughboys rolled in sugar. Whatever its provenance, "Doughboy" caught on, and it would be the nickname of the American combat infantryman until World War II, when "GI" became the preferred moniker.

Wealthy executives and entrepreneurs went, men like Robert Lowell Moore, who would found the Sheraton hotel chain after the war, and Howard Johnson, who would go on to franchise the HoJo chain, with its twenty-eight flavors of ice cream. Stephen Bechtel, heir to the San Francisco construction business, served in an engineering battalion. Conrad Hilton, who would expand his father's hotel chain after the war, commanded a labor battalion of the 79th Division. Kingdon Gould, grandson of the billionaire robber baron Jay Gould, served as an interpreter in the 79th Division and saw combat in the Argonne. Jay Hormel served in the 88th Division until his meatpacking expertise earned him a transfer to the supply service, where he saved space on supply ships by boning and freezing meat in the States before shipping it to Europe. Frederick Weyerhaeuser, who would run the family lumber company, flew bombing missions with Major Fiorello La Guardia on the Italian front.

Most of these men survived. Whereas 90 percent of Civil War soldiers served in combat, only 40 percent of the Doughs did. Most

Being a "senator's son" or any other young man of privilege made your appearance in the trenches more, not less, likely in 1918. Healthy American men felt shame for not serving in France. Here, robber baron Jay Gould's grandson Kingdon Gould— shown in slouch hat, carrying a bag—arrives with a cohort of recruits at Camp Dix, New Jersey. At the time, young Gould sat on the boards of Western Union and three Gould railroads and was a champion polo player. He'd be cited for bravery twice in the Meuse-Argonne. (National Archives)

Americans served in relatively safe jobs behind the lines, as what the combat troops called "fountain-pen soldiers." The 117,000 Americans killed in the war were not so fortunate. They were slain in their youth and rendered silent by a history that hasn't given them their due. Why, exactly? Well, the war ended abruptly, a year sooner than expected, because of the German Empire's internal collapse. Faced with mounting rebellion against the long war and its misery, the German fleet mutinied on October 30, 1918, and the German people, appearing in the streets, forced Kaiser Wilhelm II's abdication and the appointment of a socialist government on November 9. The German army, still three million strong and defending positions in France and Belgium behind the Meuse River, decided to ask for an armistice, not because it had been beaten by the British and French—who seemed incapable of beating the Germans in 1918, or arguably ever—but because it was beaten by the Americans, who broke through the eastern bastions of the Hindenburg Line, advanced on both banks of the Meuse, and surrounded the German army in France. Field Marshal Hindenburg, Hitler, and the next generation of German soldiers were quite correct when they said that the German army in 1918 had been "stabbed in the back." It had been—not by the communists, Jews, and other "November criminals" indicated by Hitler, but rather by a US Army that stabbed the Germans in the gut on one bank of the Meuse while stabbing them in the back on the other.[1]

The war had nearly ended in German victory in the spring of 1918, when the Germans had shattered both the British and French armies. American troops, entering battle in large numbers for the first time at Belleau Wood and Château-Thierry, stopped the German advance on Paris and commenced the long counterattack that pushed the Germans back to the Meuse. The British, commanded by Field Marshal Douglas Haig, spent much of their dwindling manpower breaching the Hindenburg Line in the late summer of 1918. The French, who had generally renounced the offensive after their army mutinies of 1917, followed the British advance cautiously, in many cases "conquering" ground that the Germans were abandoning to shorten their lines.

The Germans retreated in 1918 for many reasons. They'd exhausted their assault divisions in five offensives in the spring and summer of 1918; they needed to shorten their defensive perimeter; they needed to buy time to train school-aged recruits in Germany. But the principal reason they retreated was because of American pressure on their "vital pivot," the narrow zone between French-held Verdun and German-held Sedan. There the German army's main Western Front supply line had to be squeezed into a dangerously thin space just north of the Meuse-Argonne battlefield. This vital pivot was well known. The great bulge of German-occupied France and Belgium narrowed temptingly above Verdun, and the French, who'd lost the ground in 1914, had launched annual attacks to recover it until 1916, when they gave up attacking because the German defenses in the Meuse-Argonne—the eastern stretch of the Hindenburg Line—were

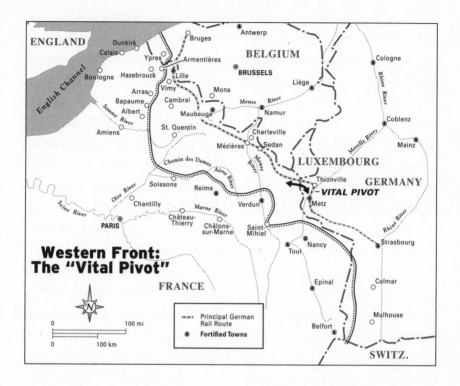

Western Front: The "Vital Pivot"

too strong and the French casualties too high. Had the Americans not entered the war and deployed two million troops to France, the Allies would almost certainly have lost. They'd have lacked the will and manpower to drive the Germans back to the Rhine. Germany would have ended the war in possession of Alsace-Lorraine and much of northern France and Belgium. The global balance of power would have tipped heavily in Berlin's favor.

The war's abrupt and surprising end in November 1918 made it possible for the flagging French and British to claim that, after all, they'd won it, and that the American contribution had been marginal. Field Marshal Haig called the war's successful conclusion in 1918 "a miracle," as if the hand of Providence had rescued the Allies. But it was the hand of America. Naturally, the proud, scarred Allied governments and militaries couldn't admit that. America's war dead, after all, were less than a fifteenth of Russia's, a tenth of France's, an eighth of Britain's, a quarter of Italy's, and less even than Serbia's. Total American casualties were just 1/55th of the total Allied loss.

Crediting the Americans with victory would have diminished the achievements of the Allied militaries as well as the doleful culture of remembrance that evolved after the war to honor the massive casualties: forty-one million killed and wounded. It would also have given the United States—already making trouble with its empire-threatening Fourteen Points—too much leverage at the peace conference after the war, for if the Americans had been acknowledged to have won the war, they'd have had to be conceded the right to shape the peace. And so the great charade began—conjuring an Allied victory won by the Allies, not by America. Unfortunately for America, the charade was facilitated by its nebulous president, Woodrow Wilson, who tried to "change the world" at Versailles by substituting a League of Nations and a world army and navy for the instruments of national power that had actually secured the Allied victory.

Wilson wasn't the man to emphasize America's role in winning the war, because he was in such a hurry to outlaw war. He was not the man to cement America's global mastery with new alliances and security arrangements, because he hated those vestiges of the "old diplomacy." The "new diplomacy" of the League and one-world internationalism was everything to him. Handed this respite by an American president who was fuzzy on strategy to begin with and became fuzzier after a stroke in 1919, the Europeans shaped the postwar order with a revenge program of war guilt, reparations, annexations, and imperial expansion—the very things an increasingly distraught Wilson had vowed to prevent. The US Senate, far more practical than Wilson, tried to anchor the peace in something tangible—rejecting Wilson's expansive vision of the League—but stalemated on the issue with an intractable White House.

Without presidential leadership, the United States drifted into the Roaring Twenties, forgetting its losses and lessons in the European war. Edward Streeter, who had composed the popular Dere Mable letters during the conflict—the *Willie and Joe* verse of the First World War—noted the speed of forgetting. It began the moment the troops returned from France in 1919: "And as the hobnailed feet clattered down the gangplanks, the cry arose 'The war is over. The next duty of every patriot is to forget it.'" Streeter, who'd grown to love the Doughboys as a journalist, resented the speed of forgetting the war and its significance: "The great days of mud and filth and fatigue and laughter and death" were replaced by musings on "the Younger Set, Prohibition, raisin recipes, trans-Atlantic flights, the high cost of remaining alive, Russian vaudeville, hold-ups and the quaint spectacle of extravagant gaiety spending its idle hours enthusiastically censoring itself."[2]

American isolationism was the inevitable response to this forgetfulness. Isolation battened also on renewed acrimony in Europe that struck Americans as little different from the acrimony that had ignited World War I. Faced with an incorrigible Europe, Americans looked inward. The Wall Street crash, the Depression, the Nazis, and the Second World War came on in a rush, effectively erasing memories of World War I by shifting attention to World War II and its aftermath.

Then came the historians. The history of 1918, of the "Hundred Days" that carried the Allies to victory in the summer and fall, has been largely interpreted as a British and French victory. From the classics to the newer accounts, the Doughboys are acknowledged but generally assigned marginal importance. It was the British, French, and Italians who won the war (and the two million Russians who had died on the Eastern Front). The Americans merely provided financial and economic aid and a "morale boost" on the battlefield. Other historians have argued that the Germans were defeated by their own bloody offensives in 1918, which left them with little to stem the Allied counteroffensive. And yet such a view neglects the fact that the Germans wouldn't have launched those offensives if the Americans hadn't intervened in the war. They'd have dug in even deeper in occupied France and Belgium—where they extracted most of the fuel they consumed in the war—and dared the demoralized, half-defeated French and British armies to attack their trenches and forts and drive them out. It never would have happened, as readers of this book will discover from eavesdropping on real conversations in the headquarters of the British and French commanders and in the war cabinets in Paris and London.

Even after the monstrous casualties the Germans suffered in their 1918 offensives, they would, in all likelihood, have stemmed the Allied counteroffensive if the Americans hadn't outflanked the Germans at Sedan and severed their line of retreat. American histories have tended to focus on the American Expeditionary Forces (AEF)—as the army sent to France was known—and its campaign in the Meuse-Argonne. British and French histories have tended to focus on their national armies. What's been lost is the critical synergy that existed between the surging US Army and the crumbling British and French armies. It was generally acknowledged in 1918 that Haig was battling toward the Meuse with "Britain's last army." London either lacked or would not give—the War Cabinet always obfuscated the question—the manpower to replace Haig's casualties. The French, with the highest per capita casualties among the great powers and a modest population, had already scraped the bottom of their demographic barrel. The French soldier, or *poilu*, had become defeatist and demoralized by 1918.

Simply put, it was American power delivered to the battlefields in France that made it possible for Haig to risk "Britain's last army"—much of which was killed and wounded in the Hundred Days—and for Pétain to take the offensive with an army that was frankly gun-shy. The synergy of the British and French offensives allied to the American offensive in the Meuse-Argonne ended the war, but not until the Americans surrounded the Germans at Sedan and delivered what British war correspondent Charles Repington called "the matador's thrust." Without that thrust, the German army would have stopped the British and French at the Meuse, or even south and west of it. This interpretation may surprise some historians as much as it surprised me. I began my research with standard accounts of 1918 in mind and only changed my thinking as I worked successively through American, British, French, German, and Austrian archives and began to appreciate what a muddy understanding we have of how World War I actually ended.

Sons of Freedom seeks to rescue the Doughboys from this purgatory. Using multiple archives, it meshes American intervention in the war with Allied strategic deliberations, initially without the Americans and then with them. It weaves together the Allied offensives in Flanders, Picardy, and Champagne, and the American battles in the Aisne-Marne salient and the Meuse-Argonne, revealing their crucial teamwork and in particular the American blows that saved Paris, bought time for the British, demoralized the German home and fighting fronts, and then delivered the thrust that killed Hindenburg's army at Sedan. It re-creates the tension and indeed panic that overtook French and British headquarters in 1918 as the German offensives hit and the Allies saw themselves losing the war—out of men and pleading for American help. It portrays the dilemma of the AEF commander, General John J. Pershing, who was pressured—even by influential Americans—to give US troops to the British and French to use as replacements in their own shattered armies. Pershing insisted on keeping the US Army together, under American command, and taking over an independent sector of the Western Front above Verdun to achieve an *American* victory that would underscore America's new role as a global power. His commander in chief, President Wilson, supported Pershing but wavered whenever the German guns neared Paris or Calais in the first half of 1918. For this reason and many others, Pershing aged visibly during the relatively short campaign. The stresses were tremendous, leading to wise and unwise decisions, all described in this book.

The Doughboys, of course, are the heart of the book. These citizen-soldiers, who were drafted, shipped to France, and sent against German artillery and machine guns at a time when Allied armies shrank from such attacks, won World War I. There was nothing elegant about it. They were hastily trained and equipped, their technology lagged, and their tactics were appalling; their operational art was in its infancy, their staff work deficient, and their levels of desertion high, but the hundreds of thousands of Americans who fought did so with courage and selflessness that will awe the reader and, at last, give full voice and credit to the men whom poet Archibald MacLeish called "the silent slain."

1

DOG DAYS

WORLD WAR I BEGAN IN AUGUST 1914 WITH A GERMAN invasion of Belgium and France and an Austro-Hungarian invasion of Serbia and Russia. Britain, which had hesitated to join the war despite its alliance with France and Russia, did, shipping an army to Belgium and France to beat back Germany's bid for European mastery. "Army," of course, was a generous overstatement. The British Expeditionary Force (BEF) of 1914 contained only six divisions. The Germans had more than two hundred divisions. Long reliant on the Royal Navy for its security, Britain would need two *years* to assemble and train the men for just sixty divisions. This fact, combined with French tactical blundering, permitted the Germans to seize and hold the most advantageous ground in Belgium and northern France in 1914 and focus their fire on the armies of Russia and France, inflicting crippling casualties.

The great powers assumed that the war would be short, blasted to a quick finish by new technologies like machine guns, quick-firing artillery, and high-explosive shells, but the opposite occurred. On every front, the fighting bogged down in trench lines. Multimillion-man armies, paralyzed by defensive fire and barbed-wire entanglements, stared at each other across cratered landscapes called "no-man's-land." The intervention of hitherto neutral states—Italy and Rumania on the side of the Allies, Turkey and Bulgaria on the side of the Central Powers—did nothing to move the lines. German submarines ("U-boats") mocked British hopes that a naval blockade would strangle the Central Powers. The U-boats sank Allied ships faster than the Allies could build them and threatened the food supply in Britain. In the spring of 1917, with the World War entering its third year, France dispatched its most famous soldier to tour the United States and advocate for immediate American intervention in the war. Without America, the Allies saw no way to win World War I.

For the Allies, or Entente Powers, the situation was dire. The lines drawn and the fronts created by the German invasion of Belgium and France in 1914 weighed on them as never before. True, the German effort to engulf Paris with five armies arrayed from Strasbourg to Liège had been stopped at the Battle of the Marne in September 1914, but the German invasion's strategic effects had never been reversed. Retreating from the Marne in 1914, the Germans had settled into prepared positions along the Aisne River and the steep ridges of Picardy and Champagne that enclosed the principal mineral resources, strategic railroads, and industrial zones of Belgium and France. In 1915, France, which had lost a million men in 1914 (300,000 killed), had lost another 1.9 million troops (350,000 killed) trying to push the Germans out of this space. Farther east, where the left-hand armies of the German invasion force had failed (barely) to take Verdun in 1914 and had also receded, the Germans retained and fortified the east bank of the Meuse and, west of the river, the Saint-Mihiel salient, a bulge in the line that projected between the French forts of Verdun and Toul, and cut the main French road and rail communications with the eastern fortress of Verdun. This liability weighed on the French every year. Without Saint-Mihiel, Verdun was always at risk, and if Verdun ever fell, important cities like Nancy and Châlons-sur-Marne would fall too, and the Germans, masters of the Meuse, would be able to resume a broad-front assault on Paris without danger to their left flank.

France had wasted 14,000 men in futile efforts to retake Saint-Mihiel in 1914, 40,000 more in 1915, and then France and Germany had spent the entire year of 1916 fighting for Verdun itself, and France had barely held on, at the cost of 340,000 casualties. The Pyrrhic victory there ripped the heart out of the French army, killing what remained of its best troops and doing nothing to dislodge the Germans from their Saint-Mihiel bridgehead. There they remained, with one foot across the Meuse, awaiting their next chance.[1]

There would be more chances. Germany had nearly twice the population of France, and the German people, with their galloping birth rate, were young. The French, their birth rate stagnant for a century, were old and unable to absorb casualties on the scale of Verdun. In a war that was increasingly about the ability to find effectives—able-bodied men to fill up the depleted ranks—France had tragically wasted its most robust manpower in the first three years of the war. By the end of 1917, France's total of dead and wounded would surpass three million. Thereafter, France would rely on frightened boys and wary middle-aged men to replace casualties; these were the least effective effectives. They were certainly not, in the parlance of the Great War, "attacking troops."[2]

Britain's attempt to relieve pressure on the French at Verdun had also misfired. General Douglas Haig's Somme Offensive, launched in July 1916 with many of those sixty new divisions of volunteers raised after the destruction of the BEF two years earlier, had drowned in a bloodbath. British divisions had been cut to pieces plodding into German artillery and machine-gun fire. The fifty-six-year-old Haig had underestimated the durability of the German defenses and overestimated the impact of the British artillery and assault formations. Britain and France lost another 620,000 men in a battle that lasted four months and gained just six miles of largely worthless ground. Haig had promised victory and a dash to Berlin; instead he crippled the British army, hollowing it out for the duration of the war. Haig's failure on the Somme, which he would reprise in the mud of Passchendaele in 1917, caused the collapse of Liberal prime minister Herbert Asquith's government. Asquith's secretary of state for war, David

Lloyd George, took the reins of government but, thanks to a split in his own Liberal Party, was forced to govern in coalition with the Conservatives, who distrusted the wily, silver-tongued "Welsh wizard."

Lloyd George's rise triggered a full-blown civil-military feud in London between Haig's supporters (who insisted as a condition of joining the coalition that Lloyd George retain Haig as army commander) and the new prime minister. For the duration of the war, Haig would try to operate freely—trusting his Conservative backers in Lloyd George's coalition government to protect him—and Lloyd George would try to reduce Haig's powers and the troops at his disposal, worrying that any reserves or replacements sent to Haig would be wasted in crude assaults on hardened German positions.[3]

Haig was, as one analyst put it, "the distilled essence of Britain," not a genius, but the embodiment of Britain's normal virtues and defects: calm, unimaginative, and possessed of "a serene faith that all will come right in the end." Sadly, that determination—"which when beneficial was called tenacity, and when harmful was called obstinacy"—persuaded Haig to launch reckless offensives, men against concrete and steel, merely hoping that things would "come right." They didn't. His casualties came in indigestible lumps: 420,000 on the Somme, 300,000 at Passchendaele. By the end of 1917, Haig's casualties in the war would total two million, threatening Britain, like France, with the exhaustion of its manpower. Lloyd George called Haig's command "the military Moloch," a reference to the Canaanite god who consumed his victims with fire. The prime minister had promised "total victory," but could he get it, with *this* military leadership, before British manpower ran out?[4]

Taking in all of this, as well as the deteriorating situations on the war's other fronts, the Allies convened at Versailles in November 1916 and vowed to win the grueling war the following spring with a flurry of synchronized offensives. Russia agreed to attack the Austro-Hungarians in Galicia and the Turks in the Caucasus; Italy would pierce Austria's southern border with an offensive across the Isonzo River; and Bulgaria would be crushed by the Greeks, Serbs, and Rumanians, plus a dozen British and French divisions. The

Turks would be driven out of Mesopotamia and Palestine by British offensives there. The Germans, the beating heart of the Central Powers, would be knocked out by a massive blow delivered in France by the combined British and French armies. The British, who held one hundred miles of the Western Front—one-fourth of the total—would attack between Bapaume and Vimy, the French from the Somme to the Oise, rupturing the German line in France and driving the Germans all the way back to the Meuse and, if the other Allied offensives succeeded too, maybe even out of the war.

The Allies deemed a big push in early 1917 critical. Russia had already lost five million men in the war. Its living standards were plummeting, and it trembled on the brink of revolution. France also flirted with revolution, with Socialist deputies like Pierre Laval (who would reprise his defeatism during the Vichy regime) and Joseph Caillaux demanding peace at any price. The French army, lacerated by the yearlong Battle of Verdun in 1916, stood on the brink of mutiny. Defeatism and drunkenness coursed through its ranks. General Philippe Pétain called the two conditions an "epidemic" and warned France's minister of war in February 1917 that "pacifist intrigues and propaganda" threatened to destroy what remained of the army. The shaggy French infantry of the line, called *poilus* (bearded ones), were increasingly "making apologies for Germany and affirming the impossibility of victory," said Pétain. A British official in Paris warned that "France is very, very tired," and "at a psychological moment when discouragement may lead to any sort of acquiescence in any sort of peace rather than continue the war." Revolution was in the air, he said. "The crust is very thin just now."[5]

Marshal Joseph "Papa" Joffre, the avuncular French commander who'd led the French armies until the last hour of Verdun, was kicked upstairs and replaced with a dynamic new man, General Robert Nivelle, who exuded confidence. Nivelle pledged to win the war and silence the grumblers with one last offensive, modeled on new tactics he'd successfully wielded against the Germans at Verdun. He tore up Joffre's plan from the Versailles Conference and wrote his own, a more ambitious one, for a broader front north and south of the Oise River.

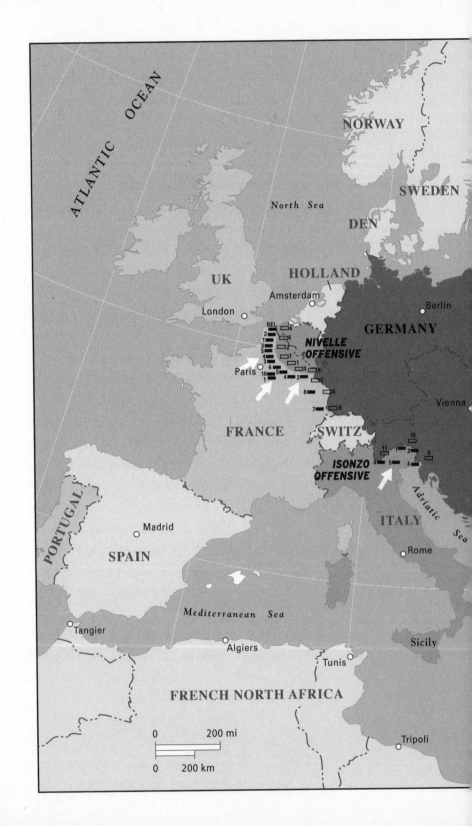

The "War Winning" Allied Plan for 1917

While the British delivered their attack between Bapaume and Vimy, Nivelle would freeze the Germans with the attack between the Somme and the Oise and then gore them with a three-army attack between the Oise Canal and Reims that would surge up and over the Chemin des Dames—a twenty-mile-long limestone ridge overlooking the Aisne—into the flank and rear of the German armies fighting the British. According to Nivelle, the Germans would either have to fight a desperate last battle, surrounded on all sides, or retreat out of France. This Nivelle Offensive *had* to succeed. If it didn't, the already-demoralized French army might dissolve in anger and hopelessness.

While the Allied armies waited for the spring weather that would dry the roads, clear the skies, and permit operations, things began to go wildly wrong. Revolution broke out in Russia in March, fanning more "pacifist intrigues" in the French army and casting real doubt on the new Russian government's ability to contribute its own offensive to the Allied plan for 1917. On the Western Front, the German commanders, Field Marshal Paul von Hindenburg and his staff chief, General Erich Ludendorff, saw the Nivelle Offensive taking shape and took measures to defeat it. On the critical sixty miles of front facing the looming British and French attacks, the Germans abruptly pulled their lines back fifteen miles and devastated the ground they evacuated, poisoning wells, razing villages, cratering roads, tearing up railways, and blowing up bridges. They did it so efficiently—two weeks of vandalism in March that confirmed their reputation as "Huns"—that neither the French nor British had time to organize a pursuit.

When Nivelle and Haig did finally attack, on April 9, the great offensive, touted by the Allies as a "war winner," foundered immediately. The British made limited gains and the French, their morale impaired by the Russian Revolution, made none. The roads they'd hastily built across the desert created by the German withdrawal dissolved in April showers, and the troops fell back under withering defensive fire.

Nivelle had assured the poilus that he would mass an unprecedented number of guns to blast them through the German lines with minimal casualties. But the Germans, installed in steel-and-concrete bunkers inside the limestone quarries of the Chemin des Dames, survived the bombardment, then emerged from their shelters to inflict 187,000 more casualties on Nivelle's attacking troops. The poilus were also victims of "defense in depth," the new German practice of leaving just a quarter of their troops in the front line to slow the enemy's attack while the bulk of the defenders sheltered just beyond the effective range of the attacker's artillery. The poilus might sweep over the thinly manned German front line, but two or three miles farther on, they'd stagger wearily into the main German force: entrenched, rested, their quick-firing artillery and machine guns zeroed in and ready to fire. The Germans called this the "spring-coil defense"—luring the French (or British) deep into a cunningly prepared "battle zone" and then snapping back like a coiled spring to annihilate them with counterattacks.[6]

Nivelle never even had the chance to slide his "army of maneuver" into the gap created at the Chemin des Dames. There was no gap. The poilus, who'd been assured by Nivelle that their total casualties wouldn't exceed ten thousand, mutinied in rage and frustration. Since 1914, over a *million* French soldiers had been killed in battle. Nivelle had told his troops that he had a plan to break the German line and win the war in forty-eight hours. The plan failed wretchedly, and 49 of France's 113 divisions mutinied. French infantry now refused to go into the line; they occupied train stations so that reserves couldn't be summoned; they sang the socialist anthem "L'Internationale"; they appointed delegates to negotiate with their officers; and they passed leaflets through the trenches: "We Are Men, Not Beasts," "Down with the War," "Death to the Culprits," the last a reference to politicians and industrialists, or any officer witless enough to order another attack. In the resulting repression, 554 French soldiers were condemned to death, and even the American e. e. cummings, a volunteer ambulance driver (like Ernest Hemingway and John Dos Passos), was arrested by the French and jailed simply for being the friend of a man who'd praised the mutiny in his letters.[7]

A horrified French government replaced Nivelle with Pétain, but the damage had been done. France's military fiasco coincided with shortages of food and fuel, a cost of living 80 percent higher than before the war, and a wave of strikes in the war factories. Prime Minister Paul Painlevé's government fell, the premier declaring that France was "at the end of its resistance." The US Army's general staff concurred, noting that, for however much longer the war lasted, the French would be unable to undertake any operations "involving large losses." Their will was broken. Thirty-six-year-old Captain George C. Marshall, a fast-rising staff officer, grimly noted that "the fiasco and hideous losses had destroyed the aggressive spirit of the French infantry."[8]

The timing of Nivelle's defeat couldn't have been worse, for it coincided with an accelerating revolution in Russia. Tsar Nicholas II had been ousted in March, and the new Provisional Government in Russia seethed with internal divisions. "The whole of Russia is no more than a vast heap of maggots," the German chief of staff in the East said with a smile. With Russia teetering, the combat power of its 223 divisions annihilated by repeated German offensives, and a blockade of its most accessible ports, France, Britain, and Italy looked queasily to the future. If Russia fell—and it looked like it would fall—the Germans would be able to transfer most of the seventy-eight German and twenty-five Austrian combat divisions, now on the Eastern Front, to the *Western* Front, at a moment when the French had exhausted their manpower and the British, who had lost another 160,000 men in their part of the Nivelle Offensive, had nearly exhausted theirs.[9]

It was against this grim backdrop that France's most famous soldier, Marshal Joffre, alighted in America in April 1917 to discuss US intervention. For the Allies, the math of the Great War had become bleaker than ever. The Germans already had 150 divisions on the Western Front against 170 French and British divisions. If they could bring west just 60 of the 103 German and Austrian divisions facing Russia, it would be the end for the Allies. With 62 divisions (1.5 million troops) on the Western Front, the British were at maximum strength. Unless they successfully introduced conscription in Canada, Australia, New Zealand, and Ireland, they too would run out of men. And because the Dominions were self-governing and unwilling to implement a draft—they were as sickened by the war as Britain—and because Ireland was restive and unreliable, Britain *would* shortly run out of troops. The British army's chief function, the American general staff noted, was a sharply limited and entirely negative one: to gnaw away at German strength and "prevent Germany from collecting a reserve of new men for offensive use in 1918" through bloody "wearing-out battles," like the one the British began in 1917 at Passchendaele in Flanders to buy time for Pétain to rebuild the French army.[10]

But if the Germans were able to release a horde of *new* troops to the Western Front from the Eastern Front, the exhausted British—who were as worn out by Haig's "wearing-out battles" as the Germans—might not hold. The French war minister's talking points, prepared for Joffre's visit to America in April 1917, laid bare the predicament: "English army at maximum strength and weakening; Italian army focused on Italy; Russian army? No one knows what 1917 holds for them. For the French army, 1917 marks the exhaustion of our recruiting resources. In 1917, the French army will fight its last campaign with full power." And yet even now "full power"—an estimated 1.25 million poilus—was an illusion, a sleight of hand achieved by reducing French divisions from four regiments to three, permitting a spurious "increase" in the French army from 109 to 118 divisions in 1917. This was clearly the end; French planners predicted a decrease of two hundred thousand recruits in 1917 and a further decrease of four hundred thousand in 1918. The war had killed and maimed too many, an average of 3,638 French soldiers every *day* in the war. The French had begun the war with an army of men in their twenties. Now the only men left were middle-aged or teenagers—the roughly 250,000 French boys who turned eighteen each year. The army eyed them more greedily than ever. By 1918, in other words, the French would have to reduce their number of divisions and essentially give up on the total victory needed to reclaim Alsace-Lorraine, annexed by the Germans in 1871, and all of the additional territory in northern and eastern France occupied by the Germans since 1914.

With sixty-two divisions on the Western Front, the British also planned to reduce, not augment, their strength. Haig would sacrifice another three hundred thousand troops in the mud of Passchendaele in 1917 to gain just two miles—an appalling waste of men. He wanted to seize the Belgian Channel ports to relieve pressure on British shipping and defeat the German U-boats, but he instead defeated himself. The battle was so ineptly conceived and executed that a large percentage of the British deaths were from drowning in mud that Haig's own shellfire had churned into quicksand. British tactical railways, needed to supply the push, were literally engulfed in rising mud, one general observing his locomotives sinking into the morass. Haig was the unimaginative, authoritarian type who rose to the top in a British army that still valued "men who ride straight at their fences," without guile or subtlety. Two million Tommies—short for "Tommy Atkins," the nickname of the British soldier since Wellington—had been killed or wounded on Haig's watch. The cream of the British army—the smart, young, healthy men who'd volunteered in 1914—had been wasted on the Somme in 1916. Many of those who survived were killed off at Passchendaele, leaving a demoralized rump.[11]

Thanks to the reckless tactics of Haig, Joffre, and Nivelle, the Entente, which had begun the war with two million more troops than the Central Powers, emerged in 1918 with no advantage at all. Their profligate offensives had leveled the playing field for Germany. None of the good Allied troops could be adequately replaced. British draft requirements for height, weight, and mental fitness dipped as the BEF conscripted the dregs of society to maintain the divisions in Flanders and Picardy. The extent of France's manpower shortage was glimpsed in the case of twenty-year-old future serial killer Marcel Petiot. Arrested before the war for assault, vandalism, and burglary, Petiot was deemed mentally unfit for the French army in 1917 and 1918—"obsessions, phobias, depression, melancholia"—yet the army drafted him anyway, twice, and sent him into the trenches until he finally shot himself in the foot and earned a diagnosis of insanity. By 1918, "Dr. Satan," as Petiot would eventually be known, was the sort of recruit the French army was forced to conscript. With nine hundred French soldiers killed every *day* in the 1,564-day war, the best men had long since been wiped out. Italian losses in 1917 approached seven hundred thousand, and Italy's sixty-one withered divisions—which lost 250,000 men and three thousand guns in October 1917's Battle of Caporetto—found themselves checked by just forty-nine mediocre Austrian divisions. Russia alone had manpower reserves—two million men of military age still available—but they'd never be called if the antiwar Bolsheviks, already sharing power in Petrograd, took control of the Russian government and Russia's 223 divisions really *did* crack and drop out of the war, as most now assumed that they would.[12]

"These would be the benefits of a U.S. intervention in the war," the French war minister concluded in his secret instructions to Joffre. "*Only America holds the solution*; U.S. intervention would remedy the certain decrease of French manpower; it would compensate for Russia's defeat and maintain the military power of the coalition." The British took the same view; Prime Minister David Lloyd George's senior policy adviser Maurice Hankey suggested to the War Cabinet after the failure of the 1917 offensives that the Allies could no longer *win* the war. They could hold—maybe—but they couldn't defeat the Germans without the Americans, who'd become, before they arrived or even formed into an army, the indispensable "strategical reserve" of the Allies. "We have succeeded in checking the enemy but not in overthrowing him," Hankey told the War Cabinet. Now only the Americans could defeat the Germans, he bluntly told his colleagues. "America *must* lead the way," for "Russia has failed [and] our armies and those of France, good as they are, have proved inadequate. Our resources and those of France are strained. America must bring fresh ideas and increased energy and determination, and supplies of men." Only the Americans could "deliver the knock-out blow." Without the United States, the best London and Paris could hope for was "stalemate and an inconclusive and unstable peace." Washington alone was the "guarantee of final victory."[13]

To the beleaguered French, the United States, with its one hundred million citizens, was the indispensable nation, *le peuple transatlantique*—"the transatlantic people." America had at least ten million men of military age—twenty-one to thirty—and many more millions if the age range were extended in either direction. The US Navy was growing fast, nearing three million tons. Behind these men and ships stood "factories, shipyards, arsenals, thousands of trained workers, and forests and fields." US banks had billions of dollars available for war loans. US industry had so much capacity that it could double, triple, or even quadruple Allied war production as needed. Armed intervention would develop and deliver all of these American resources to the Allied side.[14]

American intervention would also alleviate France's financial crisis. The French government was guaranteeing American loans not only to itself but to France's towns and war industries as well, and borrowing from the British too. French purchases of American war matériel had increased from $30 million a month in early 1916 to $58 million a month in early 1917. All of this had to be financed by loans, meaning that French debt service costs in 1917 were $218 million a month, 60 percent of this to the New York banks, the rest to the British. Credit was no less exhausted than manpower in France. The nation's debt ratio was soaring and the French public had stopped buying war bonds, making costly American loans—short-term, at rates as high as 8 percent—the only recourse. British loans to France were also drying up, as London too was overextended to American banks. America was the only great power with the confidence and reserves to go on lending to the beleaguered Allies, and if America could be persuaded to join the war, the dollars would flow in a low-interest, long-term torrent.[15]

The celebrity dispatched by the French to secure that maximum American effort in April 1917 was a great bear of a man. Sixty-four-year-old Marshal Joffre had masterminded the "Miracle of the Marne" in 1914, when the French had hurled back the German pincers encircling Paris but had been undone in 1916 by the yearlong bloodbath of Verdun. The stupefying French casualties there had made him finally vulnerable, and he'd been dismissed to assuage the grief and disappointment of the French public. Still, Joffre remained a symbol of French resistance and an international figure. During his weeklong passage to America, he remarked that he was in good spirits because he was leaving bloodstained Europe for "the Land of Optimism."

There could have been no better emissary to the Land of Optimism than Joffre. When Joffre's ship anchored in Hampton Roads, Virginia on April 24, after a nervous passage through waters patrolled by German U-boats, he was acclaimed. Admiral Henry Mayo fired a salute, welcomed Joffre, and called the shipboard meeting on the USS *Pennsylvania* "the greatest honor of my life."

Joffre landed to be greeted by the US Army chief of staff, General Hugh Scott, and the assistant secretary of the navy, Franklin Delano Roosevelt. They sailed together on the presidential yacht *Mayflower* to Washington, where the boat was met by Secretary of State Robert Lansing, the commander of the US Atlantic Fleet, Admiral Frank Fletcher, and a British delegation led by Foreign Secretary Arthur Balfour. Balfour, remembered for his line "Nothing matters very much and few things matter at all," surely recognized that American intervention in World War I mattered a great deal. As the official party drove into the capital city, one hundred thousand Washingtonians lined the streets, including twenty thousand schoolchildren who'd been released early to catch a glimpse of the "Victor of the Marne." Shouts and cheers in French welled up. "Joffre! Joffre! Vive l'armée française! Bravo la France!"

Groups of Civil War veterans saluted the passing French general, crying, "He's all right! Hooray for the marshal!" Government agencies, shops, and factories closed to swell the crowd. The *New York American* captured the exultant tone of the press: "Just as Lafayette symbolized France for millions of Americans before, now Joffre symbolizes France for millions of Americans today."[16]

Over the following days, Joffre, joined by former French premier René Viviani, met with American secretary of war Newton Baker, Secretary of State Lansing, and General Scott and officers of the general staff. Meanwhile, Balfour and Joffre's British counterpart, General George Bridges, gave a presentation at the US Army War College at Washington Barracks "about the most important changes in modern warfare," nearly all of which—heavy artillery, rolling barrages, tanks, aviation, poison gas, modern assault tactics, and deception—were entirely unknown to the small and inexperienced US Army, which hadn't seen serious combat since the Spanish-American War of 1898, when none of these things had even been invented. Joffre capped his visit with a meeting at the White House with President Woodrow Wilson and Vice President Thomas Marshall, the latter most famous for his declaration that "what this country needs is a really good five-cent cigar." He would have had occasion to smoke one with "M'sieu Joe," who loved American cigars and carried boxes of them back to France in his luggage.[17]

There was urgent business behind Joffre's high-profile visit. German submarine attacks and meddling in Mexico had prompted a US declaration of war just before Joffre's arrival, but up to now the impact was purely symbolic. With the World War in its third year, the US Congress was still stalemated on the vital question of conscription. America in 1917 had only 150,000 troops under arms; to build a true great-power army, capable of intervening against Germany's army of five million, a draft was needed. But in the Senate, 40 members supported conscription, 38 opposed it, and 18 were "doubtful." In the House, there were 218 for, 186 against, and 28 undecided. President Wilson needed Joffre to whip up enthusiasm for the war and the draft.

He did. On April 27, Joffre met with the US Army leadership and then emerged to deliver a blockbuster speech widely reported in the press: "After more than one hundred years we are Allies again! I hope to have you soon beside us on the battlefields of Europe." Meeting with reporters, Joffre asserted that "America and France will fight shoulder to shoulder in defense of liberty." The effect was electrifying. Unwilling to hear paeans to war from their own leaders, Americans listened raptly to Joffre's. The next day, the House voted 397–27 for conscription, the Senate 81–8. Interventionist newspapers used the marshal's visit to insist on the draft: "What does the victory of the Marne prove? It proves that democracy *must* be armed and that every citizen *must* serve." America will "send its flag to France." With its vote for the draft, "Congress has played the funeral dirge of Germany."[18]

Onlookers were astonished by this eruption of war fever in a country that only days before had been pacific and neutral. Joffre's delegation reported that "in the course of a single week, war sentiment here in America has made remarkable progress." A "French fury" attended Joffre everywhere he went. In theaters, audiences cheered whenever the word "France" was uttered, and orchestras struck up "La Marseillaise" repeatedly during shows.

After ten days in Washington, Joffre entrained for Chicago on May 4. Chicago was America's metropolis, the hinge between East and West. Forty percent of American railroads crossed through the Windy City. With three million inhabitants, Chicago was the capital of American agriculture and a hotbed of immigration, and no great American political movement could flourish without the city's support. Chicago was now in a fighting mood: three hundred thousand Chicagoans turned out to welcome the marshal, shouting, or trying to shout, his name, which came out variously as "Joff, Joaf, Joffrie, Joffer and Joffrey." At press conferences, Viviani was forced to sound out his name phonetically for the journalists: "Vee-vee-ha-nee." The *Chicago Herald* headline of May 5 read: "Joffre Captures Chicago." The paper published an editorial in French that day, posing stark alternatives; America must choose between *la démocratie* and *l'autocratie*; America must "draw its sword to impose the will of the democratic peoples" against Germany. Illinois governor Frank Lowden spoke at the Chicago Club and warned his listeners of what awaited a democracy that didn't draw its sword: the Germans would "wipe it off the map of the world."

From Chicago, the French party took the rails to Kansas City. Every station they rattled through was draped with French flags or tricolor bunting. Women could be glimpsed in the fields wearing tricolor smocks or aprons and waving to Joffre's passing train. The *Kansas City Star* credited France with "fighting America's battle" since 1914, standing up for "all free peoples in the struggle to safeguard democracy in the world."[19]

A Danish journalist in America tried to make sense of the abrupt shift in US opinion. It was one thing to capture "cosmopolitan places" like New York and Washington, quite another to win the places Jof-fre was now enrapturing: "the vast West, the enormous fertile plains from the Allegheny to the Rockies, where the *real* Americans live." Those "real Americans" lived provincial lives, having nothing to do with Europe and even less to do with world politics. Few of them had ever seen the two great oceans that were America's first line of defense, and most of them were indifferent to foreign affairs. "The distance from New York to Omaha is as great as the distance from Copenhagen to Rome," the Danish journalist observed. "This fact alone tells you how unlikely the average American is to leave his home and invade a foreign country." And yet it was precisely America's iso-lation and indifference that constituted its greatest strength, for, the Dane observed, "America fights *despite* itself: not for special interests, but for Good against Evil."[20]

In St. Louis, Joffre's party filed into the vast hall of the Missouri Athletic Association for a breakfast banquet. The menus on each table featured crossed American and French flags and the injunction: "St. Louis salutes noble France and is ready to aid France in the struggle for justice, right and liberty." The assembled dignitaries sat beneath a placard hung from the ceiling that advertised 150 years of Franco-American political cooperation:

> *1776: Lafayette-Washington*
> *1803: Napoleon-Jefferson*
> *1917: Poincaré-Wilson*[21]

The message was clear: just as George Washington had teamed with Lafayette to secure American independence and Jefferson had ar-ranged the Louisiana Purchase with Napoleon to expand America's frontiers, Wilson would join French president Raymond Poincaré to slay German militarism and make the world safe for democracy. Joffre's visit had made intervention seem almost easy—an invincible flood of inspired American brawn would overpower the Germans. But American brawn would need soldiers, weapons, and tactics. In their meetings with French and British officers in the spring of 1917, the leading minds of the US Army had heard about technologies and techniques that few Americans had ever even contemplated in anything other than a newspaper or a book. The United States was now at war with Germany. Within twelve months, its army would be in action in France, expected to proceed with confidence and precision. Would the troops rise to the challenge, muddle through, or fail? All of that remained to be seen.

2

"TOO PROUD TO FIGHT"

NONE OF THE EUROPEAN POWERS REALLY UNDERSTOOD THE United States in 1914. America was as dynamic and complex a society as could be found anywhere in the world. A country that had counted just three million inhabitants in 1780 and fifty million in 1880 numbered one hundred million in 1914. A country that had been 60 percent "British" and 35 percent "German" in 1860 had been transformed by twenty million immigrants who'd arrived in the two decades before 1914. A largely Anglo-Saxon, Protestant country had abruptly become a "melting pot," now 11 percent British, 20 percent German, 30 percent Italian and Hispanic, and 34 percent Slavic. "Just look at the U.S.A. now," an Austro-Hungarian diplomat marveled in 1917. "Yankees are now a minority; the new majority is America's first generation of foreign-born immigrants." The French called Americans the "transatlantic people," for most Americans hailed from Europe, and many of them quite recently. These were the "hyphenated Americans"—Irish, Italians, Poles, Jews, Ukrainians, and others. The Germans contemptuously called them "half Americans." They'd inevitably complicate American efforts to intervene in World War I.[1]

No group would complicate US intervention in the war more than the twenty million German Americans, who read 1,100 German-language newspapers, joined pressure groups like the German-American National Union, and were concentrated in cities and states with political clout and electoral votes. German Americans and Irish Americans were the core of the 2.5 million–strong American Neutrality League, which insisted on "true neutrality," favoring neither alliance in the war. The Germans loved Germany and the Irish loathed England. They circulated clever antiwar propaganda like *The Archives of Reason*, a tract discouraging American intervention: "Dig a trench shoulder high in your garden," the pamphlet enjoined. "Fill it half full of water and get into it. Remain there for two or three days on an empty stomach. Hire a lunatic to shoot at you with revolvers and machine guns at close range. This arrangement is quite equal to a war and will cost you much less."[2]

Former president Theodore Roosevelt, who desperately wanted America in the war on the side of the Allies, railed against the "dual allegiance" of German Americans, and he wasn't entirely wrong. Many memoirs of the war would mention the surprise American soldiers in France felt when they took German prisoners on the Western Front who'd left their American homes to enlist in the kaiser's army. Captain George C. Marshall, for example, recalled his shock when he called out to a column of German prisoners near Verdun, "Do any of you men speak English?" and one of the passing Germans said, "I do, I'm from Detroit," and another said, "I'm from Brooklyn and I'll be glad to get back there." And there were plenty of German Americans who didn't put on the uniform but worked hard for the Reich in other ways, like former Pennsylvania governor Samuel Pennypacker. He told a Philadelphia newspaper in 1916 that America must work for a *German* victory in the war: "If the British win, they will tighten their hold on the seas, where they even now threaten New York and the coasts. The Russians will be in Constantinople and Berlin, and the Japanese will be crossing the Pacific. What good will *this* do America?"[3]

That was one way to look at it. Another was to view the war as a convenient way to weaken Germany. Militarily, Berlin was on the verge of conquering Europe. Economically, Germany was America's chief competitor; its lower wages and superior technology gave it a viable formula for challenging America's otherwise invincible economies of scale. Most alarming of all, the Germans showed no respect for the Monroe Doctrine and Pan-Americanism. They had inserted military advisers into Mexico and colonists into Brazil, and they were making inroads into Argentina and Chile as well. If they weren't stopped in Europe, they could be expected to challenge American primacy in Latin America and the Caribbean, where many locals valued the Germans as a check on US hegemony.

Gearing up for a presidential run in 1916, Teddy Roosevelt toured the Latin American republics in 1914 to win them for Pan-Americanism and was received coolly everywhere. In Mexico, Honduras, Argentina, Chile, and Brazil, leading politicians and papers asserted that Pan-Americanism was really just lipstick on the pig of gringo monopolies like Standard Oil (Mexico), the United Fruit Company (Central America), the Chicago Packing Trust (Argentina), and the big railway companies (Brazil.) "The Latin American republics *hate* Americans," the Brazilian ambassador declared to a colleague in 1914. "There are only two ways open to us—accept American control or enter into open conflict." A German victory in World War I might overthrow the Monroe Doctrine and Pan-Americanism, offering new choices to Latin American and Caribbean leaders.[4]

Political and economic strains compounded the ethnic complications of intervention. In 1914, America was still nursing the wounds of the Civil War. The Republican Party—the Grand Old Party, the Party of Lincoln—remained an eastern and midwestern organization. It had lost its Lincoln-era zeal for Reconstruction, leaving America's nine million blacks in a state of limbo. Backed by heavy industry, the trusts, and the millionaires, the Republicans were expansionist and imperialist. They'd held power since Lincoln, with only a single Democrat winning the White House between Lincoln's death in 1865 and Woodrow Wilson's election in 1912. In 1898, President William McKinley, a typical Ohio-born Republican, had declared war on Spain to ensure that America—not Britain or Germany—secured Madrid's colonies in Cuba, Puerto Rico, Guam, and the Philippines.

Against this Yankee juggernaut, Democrats extended their base from the South to the new states of the West. Their platform aimed to combat the centralization and corruption of Washington and stop the quest for new colonies. The Great Republic, after all, had been forged in revolt against the British Empire. How could Washington in good conscience "play the imperial game," as Mark Twain put it? Yet play Americans did, acquiring Alaska from Russia and forcing the French out of Mexico in 1867, going to the brink of war with Britain in 1895 over the border between Venezuela and British Guyana, annexing Hawaii, Guam, the Philippines, and Puerto Rico in 1898 and then taking Cuba under American "protection" and interfering in Colombian internal affairs to create the breakaway state of Panama in 1903, which would give Washington control of the Canal Zone until 1977.

By 1895, the Monroe Doctrine had acquired new meaning. It had initially been risk-averse and defensive, committed to nothing more than excluding the European powers from Latin America and the Caribbean in the interest of freedom and independence. Under successive Republican administrations, the Monroe Doctrine added an offensive mission: American control of the states of Latin America and the Caribbean basin through "dollar diplomacy," which was foreign policy backed by overwhelming military power and economic pressure. The Democrats were never comfortable with this domineering instinct, which they called "big brother policy." They'd have traded away the Philippines or given the colony its independence, but they feared the loss of prestige in the world and among American voters. The Republicans embraced imperialism. Teddy Roosevelt's Big Stick policy made Washington the policeman of the Central American republics and the Caribbean islands, where Marines and warships would be sent whenever instability (or European intervention) threatened. TR dismissed as craven Woodrow Wilson's payment in 1914 of $25 million in "damages" to Colombia for the American seizure of the Panama Canal Zone. When asked if he'd trade the Philippines for the British Antilles, Teddy Roosevelt answered simply: "We shall have them both."[5]

The presidential candidate of the Democrats from 1896 until 1912 was the "Great Commoner," William Jennings Bryan. His attacks on the Republican-backed gold standard—immortalized in his "Cross of Gold" speech at the Democratic National Convention in Chicago in 1896—began from the premise that gold favored eastern banks and its scarcity drove up the cost of living and left southern and western farmers chronically short of capital and vulnerable to the regular panics that shook the American economy and pitched it into recession. The Democrats were for bimetallism—gold and silver currency—to give their rural constituents easier access to cheap money and to solve the chronic deflation and stagnation that clung to the gold standard.

The Democrats also combated trusts, the vast price-fixing conglomerates run by American billionaire families like the Rockefellers, Fricks, Carnegies, Armours, Fords, and Vanderbilts. The Democrats opposed high tariffs, which had been protecting American industry and agriculture since the Civil War but which increased the cost of living for ordinary consumers. William McKinley's victory over Bryan in the presidential contest of 1896 represented victory for the eastern, Republican position on gold, tariffs, trusts, and imperialism. Bryan would lose four successive presidential elections to the GOP. He was, as even a sympathetic British journalist remarked, "just a good-natured old idiot with nothing in him but hot gas." For Democrats, there seemed to be no way to turn the tide.[6]

With the wounds of the Civil War still raw, America now suffered new divisions: eastern and midwestern Republicans against southern and western Democrats; establishment Republicans, willing to cut deals with Democratic machines like New York's Tammany Hall, against uncompromising reformers variously called Mugwumps, Liberals, or Silk Stockings. American blacks, demeaned by segregation and discrimination, had begun to seek economic, political, and social equality under the leadership of men like Booker T. Washington and W. E. B. Du Bois. Militant labor unions like Samuel Gompers's American Federation of Labor agitated for better pay and work conditions. America also had Socialist candidates for the first time and experienced a rift in the Republicans when Teddy Roosevelt bolted the big-business GOP to form the Progressive Party in 1912, dedicated to a fair shake for the little man, clean government, and environmental protection. Roosevelt's third-party run did far more for the Democrats than Bryan had accomplished in four campaigns. Helped by TR's bolt, the Democrats, under the former governor of New Jersey and Princeton professor Woodrow Wilson, finally took the White House in 1912.[7]

Wilson's secretary of state, a rejuvenated William Jennings Bryan, asserted that the election gave a mandate to America's "peace vocation." Bryan pledged that so long as he sat in Wilson's cabinet, America wouldn't enter a European war, or any other. "The times are past," Bryan thundered, "when kings can sacrifice their people in dynastic wars." The "power of the people," he argued, "will *force* governments to pursue peaceful policies." British commentators were aghast: "He's an absolutely inefficient man. His ignorance about foreign affairs is quite appalling and shows what a shallow mind he has. The truth is that an orator of his quality is really an actor and how seldom the best actors show any glimmering of brains."[8]

This was the befuddled state of America when World War I broke out in August 1914. Before the war, America's foreign policy had been inconsistent—tough in Asia and the Americas, relaxed and disinterested in Europe. In the Pacific region, American policy was expansive: "Big Stick and Dollar Diplomacy," as it was known. In 1899 President Theodore Roosevelt's secretary of state, John Hay, had issued the Open Door Note, which insisted on unfettered international access to China at a time when the European powers and Japan were trying to carve China into colonial enclaves. After 1899, the United States—with its new Pacific bases in Guam, Hawaii, and the Philippines—became the toughest advocate of Chinese sovereignty and territorial integrity. President Roosevelt hosted the peace talks that terminated the Russo-Japanese War in 1905, in large part to dampen

Japanese efforts to grab a Chinese hinterland and threaten American access to the Pacific Rim.

During the first years of World War I, Japan, not Germany, was viewed as the number one threat to America. There had been a war scare in 1913, when the California legislature passed a bill banning Japanese American citizenship and landownership. That measure had been so controversial that President Wilson and Secretary of State Bryan had pleaded with the California governor not to sign the legislation, at least not until the brand-new Panama Canal was ready to move American battleships from the Atlantic to the Pacific. As it was, the US Navy had no battleships on the West Coast, just four cruisers against the dozen dreadnoughts of the Japanese war fleet, which loitered five thousand miles from San Francisco while the US Atlantic Fleet, not yet able to traverse the canal, was twelve thousand miles away.[9]

The world war that exploded in 1914 shifted America's attention to Europe, but only intensified Washington's rivalry with Japan in Asia. Japan, whose authoritarian political system resembled Berlin's far more than London's, nevertheless intervened on the side of the Entente in 1914 to seize the German colonies in China and Micronesia. Tokyo's new island chains—the Marshalls, Marianas, and the Carolines—physically separated the Philippines from Hawaii and the Panama Canal. The strategic message was clear: Japan could cut America's communications with Manila at any time. Moreover, the hostile treaty that Japan forced on China in May 1915 was a total rejection of America's Open Door policy. Japan occupied one of China's richest provinces and then declared its intention to direct China's economy, foreign relations, and internal affairs. The Wilson administration, which had ordered US banks out of China to protest the predatory lending practices of foreign banks there, smoldered at the insult, but with a world war on and Japan opportunistically allied with Britain, France, and Russia, there was little Washington could do. The showdown would have to commence after the war.[10]

American policy in Europe remained one of isolation and neutrality, rejecting alliances or even ententes with the European powers, which had been US policy since President James Monroe. When war broke out in August 1914, America reacted as if it had been blindsided. No one in Washington understood why this rather typical European crisis—the slaying of an Austrian prince in the Balkans—had exploded into real war. Wilson took the position that America "had neither concern nor interest in a European quarrel" and instructed Americans to be "neutral in thought as well as in deed." He was on solid ground, as an American journalist affirmed: "What did it matter to Brattleboro, Keokuk, or Walla Walla, already safe for democracy, which European Power held Alsace-Lorraine, Trieste, Belgrade or Przemysl?"[11]

American attitudes toward the belligerents reflected this strategic apathy. Germans had been among America's most admired nationalities before the war. There were an estimated twenty million German Americans, and they were respected for their wealth, education, and stature. Many professors at American universities were Germans, and many Americans had studied in Germany before the war. Turning the nation against Germany—casting Berlin as "the enemy of civilization"—would be a hard sell even for a president as eloquent as Wilson. There'd be an outcry from America's powerful German communities if Wilson pushed too hard. As for Austria-Hungary, America had absorbed millions of its emigrants too, many of whom were glad to be away but were still connected to their old fatherland through family and friends. Far from breaking up the Austro-Hungarian Empire, the Americans—to the extent they even discussed these remote things— hoped to convert it into a Swiss-style federation after the war.

Some Americans viewed the Germans as immensely threatening, all the more so in view of America's military unpreparedness. General Leonard Wood, the US Army's chief of staff until 1914, then commander of its Eastern Department, earned the odium of President Wilson for constantly emphasizing the German threat. In Wood's correspondence with John Strachey, the influential editor of London's *Spectator*, the two men agreed that Germany, once finished with Europe, would turn its guns on the United States, the Panama Canal, the Latin American sphere of influence, and the Philippines:

"If Germany is not utterly beaten in this war and comes out of it half-beaten it is certain that she will try to recoup herself for her losses by an attack on America. . . . Germany's predatory leaders will say 'we've got iron and the Americans have got only gold.' Then will follow the destruction of the American fleet, the seizure of the Panama Canal and the occupation of the desirable ports of South America. If the Americans object, the coast cities will be held to ransom." Germany would claim billions of dollars from the US on the grounds that Washington had supplied the Allies with the loans and munitions that had killed so many German troops and prolonged the agonies of the German home front. If the Americans refused to pay, German battleships would bombard America's coastal cities until Washington coughed up the money.[12]

Ambivalent about the Central Powers, Americans were largely hostile to the Allies. Though sympathetic to France, which was regarded as America's oldest ally, having helped secure American independence during the revolution against England, there was little American affection for Britain. Having attacked the US in the Revolutionary War, the War of 1812, and the American Civil War, when Britain backed the Confederate bid for secession, England was widely resented in America and still viewed as America's "hereditary enemy." America and Britain had nearly gone to war during the Civil War, when London had considering extending diplomatic recognition to the Confederacy, British officers had served in the Confederate army, and British yards had built armed ships for the Confederacy, inflicting damage on the Union's merchant fleet so severe that it still hadn't recovered in 1914. Only in the last year of the war did Britain, realizing that the South would lose, withdraw its support of the Confederacy. What this meant in 1914 was that the British were despised in the North *and* the South. Southerners still felt the sting of London's desertion, and Northerners recalled how close the US had come to war with England over its supply of arms and commerce raiders to the rebels.

Meanwhile, the East Coast's big Irish American communities—one million in New York, five hundred thousand in Boston—despised Britain for its failure to concede home rule to Ireland and its bloody suppression of the Easter Rising in 1916. To the Irish, the status quo in British-ruled Ireland was intolerable. As one American journalist wrote, "The Irish always have a stone in their pockets to throw at you in times of peace." In times of war, they were even more troublesome, which made the White House and Congress nervous. Irish rioters had seized New York City for three days during the Civil War to protest conscription; more than a thousand New Yorkers had been killed in street fighting before the Irish American rioters were put down by two Pennsylvania regiments rushed to New York from the field at Gettysburg. Who could say the Irish wouldn't riot again if the US allied with England in *this* war?[13]

Editorials in US papers ran solidly against London. New York's *Daily Mail* asked why America should go to war to roll back German conquests when the British Empire—already possessing a quarter of the earth's population and land mass—could settle the matter by divvying up its own surplus territory: "Surely England, which owns more of the earth's surface than any other nation, will not grudge Germany a few extra square miles." Public intellectuals campaigned fervently against American involvement in the war. Nicholas Butler, president of Columbia University and a director of the Carnegie Endowment for International Peace, wrote a series of articles under the pseudonym "Cosmos" in which he called for an end to empires. The world, Butler argued, must be governed by a "league of nations," with a league fleet that would combine all of the world's great navies and use them for peacekeeping. David Jordan, president of Stanford, argued that peace-loving, principled America could pursue no policy other than neutrality and pacifism.[14]

Russia was another obstacle in the path of American intervention. Ten million emigrants had fled Russia for America—Jews, Poles, Ukrainians, and Russians—and now were opposed to any military support for the empire of secret police, poverty, and pogroms. To them, war in alliance with the tsar, to whom American banks had already advanced $188 million for the purchase of war supplies, was supporting bigotry and autocracy, not democracy. The Italians, French analysts discovered, were as "obnoxious to Americans as the

Germans and Austrians" because of their designs on Ottoman and Habsburg territory, ambitions "that seemed as brutal, unscrupulous and obnoxious to America as Russian designs on Constantinople." If diverse America believed in anything, it was democracy, the principles of manhood suffrage, national self-determination, and the rights of small nations, none of which the Allied powers seemed ready to acknowledge.[15]

Overall, American sympathy for the Allies was dampened by the realization that none of the Allies really accepted democratic principles. England and France aimed to subjugate German colonies (and their own existing ones) after the war. Italy and Russia also planned to extend their domination of foreign peoples. To the American onlooker, World War I was simply a war of clashing empires, certainly not a crusade for liberty and democracy. Joseph Choate, a former American ambassador to Britain, described the dilemma succinctly: "Our hands are tied and must remain tied." With New York and Pennsylvania alone containing one-quarter of the population of the US—and much of the immigrant population—it was easy to see why neutrality was essential. As the politicians said, "Votes is votes," and US involvement in this accursed war wouldn't win a lot of them. When Fiorello La Guardia ran for Congress from East Harlem during the war, he campaigned in five languages—English, Italian, Croatian, Yiddish, and German—which hinted at the irreconcilable array of political sympathies in that district alone. By 1915, the most popular song in America was "I Didn't Raise My Boy to Be a Soldier." Its verses demanded negotiation, not war, and concluded, "It's time to lay the sword and gun away":

> *I didn't raise my boy to be a soldier*
> *I brought him up to be my darling boy*
> *Who dares to place some musket on his shoulder*
> *To shoot some other mother's pride and joy.*

Selling the war in America, in short, seemed impossible. President Wilson's declaration of neutrality in August 1914 enjoined "every man who really loves America to act and speak in the spirit of true neutrality." This was as much to keep the peace inside America as to keep America free of foreign entanglements. "The people of the United States are drawn chiefly from the nations now at war," Wilson said. "It is natural and inevitable that there should be the utmost variety of sympathy. . . . Some will wish one nation, others another, to succeed in the momentous struggle. It will be easy to excite passion and difficult to allay it." Wilson pleaded with Americans to avoid "camps of hostile opinion, hot against each other," for that would weaken America in its duty of "impartial mediation, as the one great nation at peace." Just as Teddy Roosevelt had brokered an end to the Russo-Japanese War a decade earlier, Wilson hoped to bring all sides to the table in the World War. It would be the highlight of his career. Wilson was so determined to remain neutral that he rejected calls to arm from the "Plattsburg movement," whose leading minds were former president Roosevelt and former army chief of staff Leonard Wood. General Wood and TR had organized a summer camp in Plattsburg, New York in 1915 for civilians to get military training in case of war. By 1916, the voluntary camps had spread across the country, opposed but tolerated by Wilson, who viewed them as elitist Republican hotbeds that duplicated the work of the National Guard.[16]

The Germans increasingly viewed Wilson's neutrality as a sham. They noted that the neutral policy of Secretary of State Bryan was continually undermined by Wilson's personal envoy to the Entente—Texas-born, fifty-seven-year-old Colonel Edward House, a confidant of the British foreign secretary and a friend of the Allies. Neutral policy went out the window altogether when Bryan resigned in 1915. His office was taken by Robert Lansing and his functions by Colonel House, whose colonel status was an old-time southern honorific, not a military rank. Wilson's distrust of the orotund Bryan had been so complete that the president had come to rely entirely on House anyway.

John Strachey, editor of London's *Spectator*, judged Colonel House in April 1915 "the most influential man in America, in fact, he is 'It' in Washington, the President relies entirely on his judgment." In the public mind, House was "the silent man in the black coat behind the throne who never appears himself but pulls the strings." The real House—Strachey affirmed—was less a gray eminence than "a man of quiet steady brains who would size up a situation promptly and report on it free from all exaggerations, a man who in Pope's fine phrase 'would not be awed by rumor, nor again be grave through pride nor gay through folly.'" House, raised in Houston and educated at Cornell, sidestepped quarrelsome government departments and got things done.[17]

Edward Martin, editor of *Life* magazine, called House "Wilson's indispensable man." The president was windy and professorial, in love with his own voice, and dismissive of critics. "Wilson has clear ideas and a strong will," Martin wrote, "but is a green hand at national politics, with almost no political friends, and few close friends. House was the fingers to his political hand. He pointed, he picked, he placed. But always as a helper not a dominator."[18]

The problem, immediately detected by the Germans, was that House got his information from the British and was an Anglophile. He'd point, pick, and place more in the interest of the Allies than of neutrality. Wilson compounded the problem. More interested in broad humanity than narrow national interest, he never articulated a hard-nosed strategy in the war, whether to destroy German power, reform Russia, or manage the decline of the British and French empires. "Delphic" was the word most pundits used to describe his policy utterances. "His flowery speeches," Melville Stone of the Associated Press remarked, "are of such a type that no two men can agree on what they mean." He began projects—"to fix Russia," for example, in the midst of its revolution—and then quietly dropped them when the difficulties mounted. Another high-placed critic noted the president's "clammy self-complacency" and his preference for sanctimony over strategy.[19]

The British-led blockade of all trade with the Central Powers was hugely controversial. To protect civilians of all nationalities, the great powers in 1909 had clearly defined *contraband* and set strict limits on what naval powers could blockade and what they couldn't. The British, however, unilaterally extended the definition of *absolute contraband* to include food and other critical supplies, effectively walling off the German, Austrian, and Ottoman economies, which, basing themselves on the 1909 agreement, had assumed that, even in the worst case of Britannia ruling the waves, they could be supplied with whatever they needed through neutral "windpipes" like the US, the Netherlands, Denmark, or Sweden. Indeed, the German army's Schlieffen Plan had originally designated the Netherlands and Belgium as invasion routes into France in 1914, but the Netherlands had been spared at the last minute—and the German army's logistical problems augmented—to leave Holland as just such a neutral windpipe.[20]

But the British had sealed off *everything*, the Central Powers and the neutrals. They risked a major clash with Washington but assumed that the Americans could be talked around to the British point of view. In this gamble, London was aided by American naval weakness. The US had the world's third-biggest navy, after Britain and Germany, but in 1914 it was in no shape to tangle with the war-ready British. Forced to cannibalize itself by a fiscally prudent Congress (filled with "Little Navy" men who wanted no more than a coast guard), the US Navy had just auctioned two of its cruisers to Greece in order to pay for a new dreadnought battleship. America's fleet had no aircraft, no submarines, and no ammunition reserves, and it would need to recruit five thousand additional sailors just to operate the ships that it had. The army's coastal artillery, the last line of defense around American ports, possessed ammunition for only thirty minutes of fire.[21]

In view of these facts, Wilson chose not to challenge the British naval blockade, despite the insult to American pride, trade, and neutral rights. Wilson traded exclusively with the Allies and waved off legitimate German protests with the explanation that he could do nothing else because Allied warships were blocking access to German and Austrian ports. The Americans did constantly protest against the British "blacklist"—London's ban on overseas trade by any American violator of the blockade—and war censorship, but they shrank from confronting Britain in the midst of London's war with an arguably more menacing Germany. An American analyst summarized the situation in 1915. America was not "a unit." It consisted of three camps: "1. A majority for the Allies; 2. A minority for Germany; 3. A harassed Government trying with too much caution to maintain neutrality and 'protesting' only when forced to do so by some injury to the actual interests of a few American citizens, yet keeping silent about matters that seem to most of us far larger, although open to difference of opinion between the majority and minority in America." The "far larger" matters were German crimes against humanity like the "rape of Belgium" and violations of international law like the brazen attacks on neutrals and civilians and, indeed, the decision to trigger the war in the first place, when Berlin, worried about the shifting military balance, had used the pretext of the assassination of fifty-one-year-old Austrian archduke Franz Ferdinand in Sarajevo to ignite a world war.[22]

In February 1915, in retaliation for the British blockade of Germany, the Germans designated the waters around Great Britain a war zone. How, the Germans said, could they do otherwise? The war was just getting started and the US had already shipped $300 million worth of weapons and munitions and $240 million worth of food to the Allies. As the Austro-Hungarian ambassador in Washington put it: "The massive increase in war material shipments from the U.S.A. will be one of the decisive factors in the outcome of this war. It is our duty to interrupt or stop these shipments." Anything transiting through the "war zone" was fair game for German U-boats.[23]

Three months later, in May 1915, the Germans sank the Cunard passenger liner RMS *Lusitania*, killing 1,198 aboard, including 128 Americans. Although the ship had been ferrying munitions for the British army along with the martyred passengers, that fact was suppressed, and many expected American intervention then. Henry Lee Higginson, the founder of the Boston Symphony Orchestra, who had links to the music worlds of Berlin and Vienna, could scarcely believe that the Germans had done something so utterly self-defeating. "Of all the untoward acts, I never saw one more calculated to hurt Germany and to do the Allies good than that," Higginson sputtered. He had reason to be aggrieved. He'd retained German and Austrian musicians and a German music director to make the point that the Germans weren't barbarians. The slaughter on the high seas suggested that they were. "I never saw our public feel as it did about the *Lusitania* since the outbreak of our Civil War," Higginson, who'd lost control of the BSO for refusing to play "The Star-Spangled Banner" before every concert, now conceded. "Germany could not have done anything worse for her cause." Liners sailing the same route the next day reported the horrors of the sinking to a disbelieving public: wreckage as far as the eye could see, "boats, oars, chairs, bodies in plenty, and some boats picking up the bodies."[24]

But President Wilson still hesitated to take the US into such an unpopular and vicious war. Voters east of the Alleghenies, he told a journalist, would support war with Germany, but those west of the mountains wouldn't. He accepted a German pledge to stop targeting passenger ships and kept the peace. His critics exploded. Strachey deplored those "frigid and pompous Notes," like the one Wilson wrote to the Germans demanding a halt to the attacks, and his "inhuman indifference" to the German atrocities. There is, Strachey wrote, "something ghastly in the way he declares that one side in this fight is as good as another, and makes no attempt to place Germany under a ban for her crimes against international law, humanity and the comity of nations."[25]

Campaigning for the Republicans against Wilson, who was seeking reelection in 1916, Teddy Roosevelt was interrupted by a Wilson supporter at one of his rallies. "Three cheers for Woodrow Wilson," the man yelled. "Yes," Roosevelt yelled back. "Cheer for him, and cheer for the murdered babies on the *Lusitania*!" This affair, TR scoffed in a withering aside, "is going the way of all the rest. Words and words and words—*vox et praeterea nihil*," which means, "a voice, and nothing more," "a threat, not carried out." Roosevelt excoriated "the professional pacifists, poltroons, and college sissies" gathered around the "peace-at-any-price" president. Elihu Root, who'd led the War and State Departments under Roosevelt, joined the clamor: "If," Root said in a speech, "the President wishes to know the will of the people, let us cry aloud our desires in this matter of war. Tell him that we *want* it."[26]

The salvaged peace of 1915 was an uneasy one. The Germans were relieved by Wilson's forbearance but still furious at the rate of American shipments to the Allies. Kaiser Wilhelm II's advisers remained split between hawks and moderates, the hawks insisting that Wilson was bluffing. Would Americans, they reasoned, deeply divided by the war, hostile to England, and overwhelmingly opposed to intervention, really agree to fight for the right to supply the Allies or to defend passenger liners like the *Lusitania* that were knowingly sailing into harm's way? Hadn't the German consulates in America taken out newspaper ads and placarded the docks to warn Americans not to sail into British waters? Those who had traveled despite the warning had done so at their own risk. In the pause between German submarine campaigns, US trade with the Entente surged again. From New York alone, in December 1915, American firms shipped $3 million worth of military supplies to the Allies every *day*: shells, cartridges, explosives, rifles, planes, cars, trucks, as well as raw materials like steel, cooper, lead, and industrial lubricants. The Americans almost single-handedly solved Britain's "shell crisis" early in the war, shipping 70 percent of the shells fired from British guns until new British factories opened in 1916.[27]

German grievances against America now rained into four barrels that were already brimming over. First, despite being officially neutral, the US was supplying 25 percent of the guns and munitions consumed by the Allies in their battles with the Germans and Austrians. Second, the US financed the Allied war effort; by year-end 1916, American banks had advanced the Allies $12 billion, alleviating a financial burden that might otherwise have crushed the Entente. Third, the US blocked, with its threats of intervention, German efforts to break the British blockade with submarine warfare. To Germany, this was illogical. The Allied navies were literally starving the Central Powers; U-boats were the only weapon that had proven effective against the blockade, yet the Americans threatened intervention unless the Germans discarded submarine warfare. Why did Washington—if it were truly neutral—not force the British to relax their blockade and let America trade with *both* sides in the war?

In 1812, America had declared war on Britain over this very issue: the Royal Navy's attempts to restrict American trade with Napoleonic France. Why was America not insisting on its neutral rights *now*? Fourth, the Germans considered America's submission to the British blockade, trading with the Allies but not the Germans and permitting the British to seize German mail and dispatches from American ships, to be itself a gross violation of neutrality. Much of Wilson's vacillation on intervention had to do with these same issues. He was as aggrieved as the Germans by British high-handedness and suspected that the British blockade was being used not only to beat Germany but to secure British trade dominance and an expanded empire when the war ended.[28]

And then there was the fraught question of Mexico. America's southern neighbor of fifteen million people had been torn by revolution since 1910; this posed a chronic strategic threat to the United States. Whereas the US could and did intervene regularly in places like Haiti and Nicaragua to prop up American economic interests and secure the newly opened Panama Canal, Mexico was too big to fail or even manage. Every one of Mexico's regular civil wars cost American investors millions of dollars and filled American consulates with refugees, yet it was the one place Washington dared not "send the Marines" on anything more than a token scale. To stabilize Mexico, the US government estimated that at least three hundred thousand troops and years of effort would be needed. No American president would recommend such a course and no American Congress would authorize it, so Mexico loomed, as a diplomat put it in 1913, "as the great incalculable in American policy." It bordered the US and was dangerously "close to the Canal, but intervention there would involve huge costs and casualties that must be avoided."[29]

Mexico's chronic revolutions—there were two in Wilson's first term alone—gave foreign powers easy access to the country's contending parties and regions. Mexico could be manipulated by an American rival—such as Britain, Japan, or Germany—to threaten the US and the Panama Canal. Mexican internal chaos—driven by *caudillos*, warlords with private armies—could also spill over the border into America, as actually happened in March 1916, when Francisco "Pancho" Villa and one hundred guerrillas raided Columbus, New Mexico, and killed twenty-three Americans in reprisal for the Wilson administration's support of a Villa rival. Wilson had admired Pancho Villa, who seemed like a true democrat interested in fair elections, not the sham ballots that victorious caudillos employed to make themselves presidents for life after dispatching their rivals. But the suspicion lingered that Villa was, as one canny journalist put it, just another greedy warlord who'd "made the rich poor and all the poor, who did not serve in his army, poorer." Wilson also believed, as the same journalist added, that "although elections might be farces in Indo-American countries, and that was their own business, we had a tutorial right to demand that local constitutional forms be observed." To end the turmoil, Wilson had thrown his support behind a dictator, Venustiano Carranza, in 1915, hoping that Carranza and his army of fifty thousand would stabilize Mexico and revert to those "constitutional forms." Carranza was pro-American and inclined to let US oil companies drill and produce freely in Mexico. Villa, who'd recently been an honored guest of General John Pershing's brigade on the Mexican border, was quietly dumped, prompting his 1916 cross-border raid to humiliate Wilson and grab horses, guns, and ammunition for his renewed struggle with Carranza.[30]

Thus, while World War I raged in Europe, Wilson ordered Pershing to lead a ten-thousand-man Punitive Expedition into Mexico to find Villa and bring him to justice. President Carranza authorized Wilson's Punitive Expedition to pursue Villa inside Mexico, but a year passed and the Americans remained, squatting in a sprawling army post in Chihuahua. Moving in cars and wagons along primitive roads, US troops were constrained by strict rules of engagement even as they took fire from elusive guerrillas. Logistics were a nightmare. The 1,200-mile-long Mexican border was 1,000 miles from the nearest American industrial zones and poorly served by railways. Trying to support the expedition from the sea was futile; what ports existed in Mexico were shallow and not linked to Chihuahua anyway. The American troops, nicknamed "Doughboys" for the *adobe* dust that powdered their sweaty uniforms, were miserable: "The sky was cloudless, the thermometer at 120 and the water not fit to drink. Everything seemed ready to stick or sting us." To no one's surprise, Pershing's expedition failed, and that failure in Mexico compounded America's doubts about the wisdom of intervention in Europe. So weak was the US regular army that 125,000 National Guardsmen had to be summoned just to pursue Villa. So weak was the National Guard in the poor southern states that the Guard units had to be summoned from the only places where they existed in division strength: New England, New York, New Jersey, and Pennsylvania. It became a massive, costly undertaking that accomplished nothing.[31]

The whole Mexican expedition—intended to show America's teeth—proved toothless. Reginald Wright Kauffman wrote a poem about it titled "Mexico." The last stanza sums up the futility of the campaign, at a time when American attention was pivoting to Europe.

> *Fifty miles from Carrizal: half-past time to die—*
> *We don't mind the dying, but we'd like to know the why.*
> *If we weren't sent here to shoot (and we weren't, it's clear),*
> *Tell us, Mr. President, why in Hell we're here.*
> *What's the use of bluffing when the Greaser's got us right?*
> *He's no kind of talker, but he's not too proud to fight!*

"Not too proud to fight" was a reference to President Wilson's speech in May 1915 after the *Lusitania* sinking. The twenty-eighth president had defended continuing neutrality with the words, "There is such a thing as a man being too proud to fight. There is such a thing as a nation being so right that it doesn't need to convince others by force that it's right." The infelicitous phrase became, as a journalist put it, "the byword for a craven weak pacifism." Teddy Roosevelt had immediately assailed Wilson, calling the president a coward and a weakling: "As for shame, he has none, and if anyone kicks him, he brushes his clothes and utters some lofty sentence." The presidential campaign of 1916 was hotly contested against this backdrop of stark choices. What to do about the war in Europe and on the seas? What to do about

Mexico? What to do about a US economy that was being warped by insatiable overseas demand for American products?[32]

Wilson was vulnerable in 1916. The Germans had made him seem weak at the time of the *Lusitania* affair, which was small comfort to the large number of Germans, Irish, and others in the US who'd have reviled him if he'd appeared strong. He was trapped in a quagmire in Mexico. Only his insistence on continuing neutrality in the World War was popular. Most Americans still wanted to keep out of it at all costs. When Wilson promised, "We want no war nor will there be any war," Americans felt reassured. But could Wilson keep his promise?[33]

After the intraparty feud of 1912, when the Republican vote had been fatally split between William Howard Taft and Theodore Roosevelt, the Republicans in 1916 nominated fifty-four-year-old Supreme Court justice Charles Evans Hughes, a former law professor and governor of New York, whose conservative and progressive credentials unified the party again. Roosevelt had sought the nomination, but the Republican establishment, furious at Roosevelt for the damage he'd done to Taft four years earlier, had refused to recognize TR's Progressives except through a compromise candidate, which was Hughes. Roosevelt gamely agreed to campaign for the nominee.

Roosevelt and his protégés—like Massachusetts senator Henry Cabot Lodge—had also been stifled at the Republican convention in Chicago by the GOP's strong German American faction. They threw their support behind Hughes, expecting him to be pro-German, or at least genuinely neutral. The German American press openly boasted of this, claiming Hughes as "their" candidate. German Americans resented Roosevelt but hated Wilson for shipping munitions to the Allies and crippling German naval strategy with his scolding diplomatic notes.[34]

Hughes, who would have to tiptoe around this full-throated German support, opened his campaign with a speech accepting the Republican nomination at Carnegie Hall in July 1916. He had to be regarded as a heavy favorite, Wilson having won in 1912 only because Taft and Roosevelt had split the always-dominant Republican vote. Hughes now announced his major themes for the campaign, attacking Wilson for his lack of results in Mexico and his weak-kneed diplomacy in the World War. The *Lusitania* had been sunk because of American weakness. The Germans had brazenly threatened the attack, buying ad space in New York papers to warn Americans not to sail to Europe. Wilson had stood by passively while the tragedy unfolded and the Germans "destroyed American lives." Hughes insisted that *he'd* have warned the Germans *not* to sink the liner. Wilson, "the talker in chief," had never been firm or menacing enough. Hughes called for "unflinching maintenance of *all* American rights on land and sea."[35]

This was a delicate way of saying that the Republicans would stand up not only to the Germans but to the British and their aggressive blockade and war censorship too. The British tightly controlled information, permitting only staff reports and the heavily censored accounts of just a dozen accredited correspondents. "It is too horrible, too muddy," Britain's secretary of state for war explained to an American journalist. "There is nothing for you to write about, nothing cheerful to report." And so journalists, eager to describe the reality of the war to an American public that might soon be in it, were left, as reporter Frederick Palmer put it, "sitting on the steps of the War Office watching the buses pass."[36]

This was not a minor nuisance; war information was critical so that citizens could make sense of the war and brace themselves for its ghastly realities. When Palmer gave a talk on the nature of the war in Toronto in 1916—describing the conversion of a "fresh battalion, surcharged with war spirit" to "blood-stained, mud-stained shadows of men wondering how it was they were still alive"—women actually fainted, and many had to be helped up the aisles and out of the hall. "War fever," such as would strike America in 1917, arose in places where the realities of war were hidden. Wilson had tolerated this blockade of information as passively as the blockade on shipping. Though a professor himself, a graduate of Brown University and Columbia Law School, Hughes delighted in mocking Wilson's professorial side. The president's frequent diplomatic notes were filled with "brave words," but "it is not words, but the strength and resolution behind the words that counts." Wilson had been "too much disposed to be content with discussion."[37]

Mexico, Hughes alleged, had degenerated into "a confused chapter of blunders" on Wilson's watch. There, the US Army had revealed nothing but weakness. "Preparedness" was a Teddy Roosevelt mantra, and Hughes repeated it here for the old lion's benefit. "We are shockingly unprepared. *All* of our available regular troops are on the Mexican border or in Mexico; we've needed to call the National Guard and summon all movable military forces just to prevent bandit incursions." Hughes demanded "adequate national defense." The regular US army was too small; "we need to build a bigger army and not be afraid of it." This was an era when politicians of both parties feared big armies for their cost as well as the threat they might pose to democratic institutions. But Hughes declared that antimilitarism was no longer tenable. "With a population of 100 million, we need to be surer of ourselves. . . . National isolation is no longer possible."[38]

Hughes was swimming against the tide. Wilson, after all, had been trying since the war erupted to increase US defense spending, arguing in 1915 that "if our citizens are ever to fight effectively upon a sudden summons they must know how modern fighting is done." But even his modest proposals—to add ten new infantry regiments and four artillery regiments and to offer a two-month training exercise to 133,000 men a year—had been rebuffed by Congress. His naval requests—ten new battleships, sixteen cruisers, fifty destroyers, and "a great merchant marine"—had been trimmed, the *Washington Post* opining that raising American taxes to pay for a bigger military was a nonstarter everywhere: "Taxpayers have already been assessed more than a generation's share." *This* generation of Americans had already paid for the Panama Canal and subsidized the Republican tariff to the tune of $100 million. Asking them to dedicate "huge additional sums to pay for the military" simply wouldn't fly in an American system that still prided itself on fairness and balanced budgets. As the British embassy noted, "Republicans attack Wilson for his 'lack of patriotism,'" but "the immense majority of Americans are absolutely determined to keep out of the war as long as possible."[39]

A curiosity of the campaign was that German Americans overwhelmingly supported Hughes—who'd lived for two years in Germany as a young man and had explored the country on a bicycle—despite the fact that, as the British ambassador put it, "nothing in Hughes' utterances shows that he is for or against either of the belligerents." That's how unpopular the war was in America. Neither candidate dared take a stand for either of the European alliances. The British embassy judged Mexico a bigger issue than the European war in the presidential race and concluded that either candidate would serve British interests, for "both candidates will follow U.S. interest without 'racial sympathy.'" Neither pro-German nor pro-Entente factions would prevail. William Jennings Bryan, who'd served in Wilson's cabinet until he resigned in 1915 to protest the president's tilt toward the Allies, now campaigned effectively for Wilson as the candidate of peace; so did industrialist Henry Ford, whose well-funded peace movement endorsed Wilson.[40]

The usually reliable Teddy Roosevelt became a poisoned chalice for Hughes. His speeches spoke of "German caste militarism" and "international barbarity" that threatened America's "national honor and vital interest." German depredations, like taking workers from conquered countries and using them as "state slaves," were as wicked as any since the Thirty Years' War, said Roosevelt. TR breathed national pride and indignation at every meeting. He called Wilson "the infernal skunk in the White House" who treated "elocution as a substitute for action," who "dwelled in the realm of shadow and shame," who pursued "national emasculation" and wished to "Chinafy the country and reduce us to the impotence of Spain." At a rally in Lewiston, Maine, in August 1916, TR thundered that "Wilson has lacked the courage to lead this nation in the path of high duty." Yet few besides Roosevelt actually wanted to take up the high duty of saving Europe.[41]

The American economy was also an issue in the campaign but not one that Hughes, with his ties to Republican financial and industrial elites, could properly exploit. What eventually changed the American attitude toward the war, according to the French, who studied the American scene closely, was less the "rape of Belgium" or German submarine attacks than the severe economic disturbance that the war brought to America's shores and interior. Shipping $20 billion worth of goods to the Allies during the war, America's trade surplus increased fivefold: from a $475 million prewar annual average (1910–1914) to a $2.6 billion average (1915–1922). This was too much of a good thing. Exporting billions to the Allies and importing little in return, America suffered a crisis of raw materials; by 1916, all of the Allies—the Russians, British, French, and Italians—were ordering textiles, steel, copper, munitions, and food from America; the prices of those raw materials surged. American small businesses could no longer even afford them, concentrating the war business increasingly in the hands of the big producers. The prices of cotton and copper tripled; the price of steel doubled; wages for skilled workers shot up to twelve dollars a day. Only the conglomerates could afford these prices, but even they were beginning to quail.[42]

In late 1916, the US actually weighed a ban on the export of food and munitions to Europe. The prices of bread and sugar in America had risen tenfold since 1914. Costs were so high that the exports were decreasingly profitable, and they were running up the cost of living in America at a time when new taxes to pay for national defense—a personal income tax, a luxury tax, and an 8 percent tax on all train tickets—were already causing hardship. American food was being sent to Europe in such quantities that Americans were being asked to reduce their consumption of wheat, meat, and sugar. Loans to Britain—$400 million by J. P. Morgan alone—might become a shattering liability if the Allies lost, but also if they won, Wilson's treasury secretary fearing that the British might be spending those loans on building up their navy and colonies to oppose American interests after the war. Coal was being exported so rapidly that Americans had to go a day or two every week without heat or light, and America's war factories occasionally had to suspend operations. Freighters loaded with ammo and other supplies for the Allies swung idly at anchor for a week or more as they too awaited coal deliveries. The Federal Reserve Board actually urged a ban on war loans to the Allies, reasoning that only an embargo on American credit would stop the punishing exports of food and raw materials.[43]

And yet, with European demand and prices so high, war exports soaked up everything in America. What industrialist could resist margins like these? Remington, which shipped rifle cartridges and shrapnel fuses to the French army, earned $1.8 million in pure profit on every shipment of one hundred million cartridges and $2 million of profit on every ten million shrapnel fuses, which the plant made for a nickel each and sold for a quarter. Remington took a French order for a billion cartridges in June 1915 that netted the company a profit of $20 million in a single transaction. British observers were struck by the avidity with which the Americans got into the arms business. Until 1914, there'd been no American arms industry. What weapons had been needed by the little US Army had been manufactured in small quantities in government arsenals. In a few short months, American ingenuity had triggered an explosion in production. New factories were built, a labor force trained, machines and tools designed, scarce raw materials stockpiled, and production begun to exacting specifications.[44]

With raw materials focused on weapons production, nothing was left for the domestic market: no rails, no girders, no agricultural machinery, no copper for power plants. "The internal development of America has been halted for the profit of a handful of Eastern bankers and producers," one analyst wrote. He concluded that "the U.S. has nothing to gain from the continuation of this war." The conflict was a "disaster, that must end fast, to return the U.S. economy to a normal footing and to save European markets—critical to U.S. exports—that are headed to ruin."[45]

American farmers, meanwhile, left their fields and headed to town to find factory work, causing a plunge in US food production at the very moment when more food was needed to feed America and the Allies. In 1915, American farmers had produced twenty-eight million tons of wheat; that number plunged to twelve million tons in

1916, driving the price of wheat from one dollar to fourteen dollars a bushel in a single year. Wool for military uniforms disappeared into the holds of Europe-bound ships, forcing the Wilson administration to intervene and purchase a $25 million stockpile just in case America did go to war.[46]

German Americans exploited hardships like these to try to stop US trade with the Allies. In 1916, before the election, German American groups sought an embargo on exports of wheat and flour "to protect the American bread consumer." Hughes as president would have come under severe pressure from German Americans to stop bank loans and food and munitions sales to the Allies. German American votes would have been decisive in a Hughes victory. They nearly were. As the editor of a Minneapolis paper put it in November 1916, German American lobbyists would have argued that they'd been "sufficiently powerful to defeat Mr. Wilson," and a President Hughes, "threatened with their disfavor," would "have been in no position seriously to oppose them against the desire of a subservient Congress alive to the demonstrated might of the German-American vote."[47]

Americans were feeling this economic pinch when Wilson sent his Peace Note to all of the belligerent capitals in December 1916. The US president decried the "disturbing effects" of the World War and demanded that the European powers state their war aims clearly and meet to negotiate a peace and stop the brutal "slow attrition." America needed peace and would impose peace on Europe by peaceful means, or by military intervention if necessary, "lest the situation of neutral nations, now exceedingly hard to endure, be rendered altogether intolerable." French military intelligence summarized the note thus: "The U.S. may have to intervene to end the deep internal disturbances caused by the war and to restore normal living conditions." Germany's resumption of unrestricted submarine warfare in February 1917—sharpening America's transport crisis by sinking more scarce hulls—would trigger US intervention, but the logic of intervention as a way of stabilizing the American economy was already in place during the presidential campaign of 1916.[48]

In his run against Wilson, Hughes—beholden to the Republican Party's big-business and banking interests—didn't dare analyze America's predicament in the way the French did. He merely pointed out that the boom in the parts of America that mattered most to him and his backers was owed entirely to "the unhealthy stimulus of the European war" and thus was "built on sand." In a speech in Springfield, Missouri, in October 1916, Hughes warned that the "fabulous" export boom wouldn't last; when the millions of Europeans in uniform returned to work, the "happy dreams" and "intoxicated fancy" of the Wilson years would dissolve and American exports would "fall tremendously." The *New York Times* reported the speech under a man-bites-dog headline: "Hughes Assails Prosperity of War."[49]

Hughes ultimately failed to make a solid case for Wilson's removal. The president won reelection, chiefly on his isolationist slogans: "America First" and "He Kept Us Out of War." German American support for the Republican candidate backfired, one newspaper editor calling vocal German support for Hughes "the strongest factor in accomplishing his defeat." Voters who would normally have selected the Republican challenger voted for the Democrat to thwart the German lobby. In Minnesota, an overwhelmingly Republican state where German Americans always voted Democratic, they voted this time for the Republican, and yet Hughes carried the state by fewer than four hundred votes, proof that legions of Minnesota Republicans had voted for Wilson to deny Hughes. The GOP had deployed Teddy Roosevelt, known for his hostility to German Americans, to allay fears of Hughes's alleged "pro-Germanism," but it hadn't been enough. An analyst concluded that voters, especially in the West, where TR was popular, "fully realized that a ballot for Mr. Hughes was a ballot in favor of German-American propaganda, which they despised."[50]

Woodrow Wilson's reelection had strategic consequences for Berlin. An emboldened American president now took a cautious step away from isolation and toward belligerency: "We are provincials no longer," Wilson declaimed at his second inauguration. The world

At this fateful meeting at German army headquarters in Silesia in January 1917, Hindenburg (left) and Ludendorff (right) persuaded Kaiser Wilhelm II (center) to resume unrestricted submarine warfare against American shipping bound for Europe, even at the risk of American intervention. "We have our hands full with England in this war," a German diplomat warned. "We will never exhaust America." The German generals ignored the warning. They planned to defeat the faltering Allies before American troops arrived in France. (National Archives)

might have to be "made safe for democracy," a presidential doctrine aimed squarely at the Central Powers. Would the Germans feel compelled to negotiate, or would they renew the submarine war to sever the transatlantic connection? The first phase of German unrestricted submarine warfare—designed to stop American exports to the Allies—had nearly provoked war over the *Lusitania* in 1915 and again in March 1916, when a German U-boat had sunk the passenger ship *Sussex* with several Americans aboard. To forestall US intervention in the war, Kaiser Wilhelm II had suspended the unrestricted submarine campaign.[51]

On January 9, 1917, the kaiser chaired a momentous meeting at German Great Headquarters in Silesia with his chancellor and military chiefs. They discussed Wilson's reelection and whether to unleash a new campaign of submarine warfare. Under pressure from the generals and admirals, Chancellor Theobald von Bethmann Hollweg caved with the memorable words, "Your Majesty, I cannot counsel you to oppose the vote of your military advisers." Bethmann glimpsed the certainty of American intervention in the war if the attacks resumed, but the kaiser's military advisers insisted that Europe-bound American shipping *had* to be attacked to cut off food and arms for the Allies.

The German military advisers were their usual overweening selves. They ignored warnings from their own diplomats in America, one of whom wrote: "Our government still doesn't fully grasp the American situation. We have our hands full with England in this war. We will never exhaust America." The chiefs of the German army didn't care. They were confident that they could win *before* the Americans could become a decisive military factor. Sixty-nine-year-old field marshal Paul von Hindenburg inquired how the Americans—if they did react to the submarine campaign with a declaration of war—would even reach Europe if German U-boats blocked their passage. Admiral Henning von Holtzendorff swore on his "word of honor" that "not one American would land on the Continent." Hindenburg's deputy, fifty-one-year-old general Erich Ludendorff, assured the kaiser that even if they did, the Americans would never be a factor in the war. Their army was too small and inexperienced and would take too long to expand and deploy. The German leadership agreed to resume unrestricted submarine warfare against all ships, belligerent and neutral, that approached Allied ports.[52]

Wilson, still pursuing his vision of a "peace without victory" in Europe that would satisfy all sides, read to Congress in January 1917 a declaration stating the conditions under which the war might end. These would become the Fourteen Points. Wilson's attempts to end the war through mediation having failed, he now stipulated America's aims in the conflict. Generally, Wilson was for "peace without victory and peace between equals, recognizing the rights of all, including the weak." Specifically, he was for decolonization, freedom of the seas, free trade, limited armaments, no annexations, open diplomacy, a League of Nations, and an international police force to prevent conflicts. The French and British (privately) judged Wilson's conditions "chimerical," but they were diplomatically vague on the matter. German ambassador Johann Heinrich von Bernstorff's reply, after a week's reflection in Berlin, was most notable for the insolent irony of its preamble. Berlin would accept only a peace *with* victory: retention of Alsace-Lorraine, control of Belgium, annexations in Poland and Ukraine, and the return of all of the German colonies lost in the war to predators like Japan and England.[53]

Apprised of the new German submarine campaign, Wilson finally broke diplomatic relations with Berlin in a speech to Congress on February 3. Yet the president refused to take military action without congressional approval. "I have called the Congress into extraordinary session," he said, "because there are serious, very serious, choices of policy to be made, and made immediately, which it was neither right nor constitutionally permissible that I should assume the responsibility of making." Wilson recommended the immediate extension of new credits to the Allies and a US Army of at least five hundred thousand men chosen by a draft. The German government, Wilson asserted, had "put aside all restraints of law and humanity," making "neutrality no longer feasible or desirable where the peace of the world is at stake and the freedom of its peoples." These were not the phrases of a presidential speechwriter. Wilson wrote his own speeches on a typewriter, and he was the first chief executive since John Adams to appear in person before Congress, infusing, as one journalist put it, "dry state documents with human interest."[54]

With the Germans sinking a half-million tons of British shipping every month and with just six weeks' supply of grain in their silos, the British deplored Wilson's appeal to Congress for war powers: "And so he is *not* going to fight after all!" Prime Minister David Lloyd George spat. "He is awaiting *another* insult before he actually draws the sword." Increasingly frantic about the effects of the British blockade—many Germans by 1917 were subsisting on turnips and bread made of grass and sawdust—Berlin turned a deaf ear to the rumblings on Capitol Hill. On February 6, the Germans sank without warning the US-flagged merchant vessel *Housatonic*, then the *Lyman M. Law* ten days later.[55]

Worse was still to come. On January 16, 1917, German foreign secretary Arthur Zimmerman had sent a coded message to Ambassador Bernstorff in Washington. Zimmerman's telegram, which Bernstorff was instructed to forward to the German minister in Mexico City, was a German offer of alliance to Mexico. The Germans would provide "generous financial and diplomatic support" for Mexico to reconquer the territory in Texas, New Mexico, and Arizona that Mexico had lost to the United States seventy years earlier. Having broken the German diplomatic codes, British naval intelligence presented the text of the Zimmerman telegram to the US ambassador in London on February 24. Two days later, Wilson divulged the plot to Congress. Again, he stressed the need for bipartisan unity and congressional consent in matters of war "so that neither counsel nor action shall run at cross-purposes between us."

In this way, the separate Mexican and European issues that had infused the presidential campaign of 1916 were merged by the remarkably tactless German government. Wilson had never wanted war, but he was all but forced into it. Moviegoers in America now ignored the notice run before every film—"The President has called for strict neutrality; please do not hiss"—and lustily hissed Germany. "Drummers," the traveling salesmen who gave rural Americans their war news, doubled down in their condemnation of the kaiser, summarized thus by a seventeen-year-old boy from West Texas: "We all felt that the Kaiser was going to invade America. . . . Then we'd hear how they were riling up the Mexicans so they'd want to fight us. I thought I better go over there and fight so I wouldn't be no slave to any foreign country."[56]

On March 18, three more American ships were sunk by German U-boats. On March 20, Wilson's cabinet voted unanimously for war. At a joint session of Congress on April 2, 1917, just a few short months after his reelection on a peace platform, Wilson requested a declaration of war on Germany. The attacks on American shipping and the German attempt "to stir up enemies against us at our very doors" had to be answered with force. Wilson predicted "many months of fiery trial and sacrifice" as America came to grips with "the most terrible and disastrous of all wars." The president contended that "civilization itself [was] in the balance" and that certain rights were "more precious than peace," chief among them "democracy—the right of those who submit to authority to have a voice in their own governments." Before the first American soldier had even deployed, Wilson was already reaching for the League of Nations and a new world order after the war. He was an ideologue and a political scientist who thought in terms of perfectible systems, not flawed humans. Small nations, he pledged, would be protected from the strong. Democracy would be strengthened "by a universal dominion of right by such a concert of free peoples as shall bring peace and safety to all nations and make the world itself at last free." Wilson demanded an all-out effort: "To such a task we can dedicate our lives and our fortunes, everything that we are and everything that we have." He left the capitol to stormy applause, returning in silence to the White House, where he lay his head on the table in the Cabinet Room and wept. "My message today was a message of death for our young men," he groaned to his chief of staff. On Capitol Hill, the Senate voted 82–6 for war, the House 373–50.[57]

To the last, Wilson was careful not to ally too closely with the European powers. Rather than join the Entente, America would fight as an "associated power." The president hoped that this distinction would leave him a free hand after the war to assert American principles and shape the peace. Nevertheless, opponents blasted the president for embarking America on a savage war that would embroil the US in world affairs, now and forever. "Upon the passage of this resolution we will have joined Europe in the great catastrophe and taken America into entanglements that will not end with this war," progressive Republican George Norris of Nebraska told the House. Those entanglements, he predicted, "will live on and bring their evil influences upon many generations yet unborn." Democrats saw Republican industrial and financial interests at work, what Norris called the "command of gold," men determined to go to war and "put the dollar sign on the American flag" at any price, indeed the higher the price the better. Republican senator Warren G. Harding, an ally of big business, voted for the war but damned Wilson's idealism: "I want especially to say that I am not voting for war in the name of democracy," Harding declaimed. "It is none of our business what type of government any nation on this earth may choose to have. I am voting for war tonight for the maintenance of just American rights." There were still many in America who, like Harding and Norris, preferred realism or isolation to engagement. Wilson was not one of them. The war, he believed, was a vehicle for a new world order—"not a balance of power," as he put it, "but a community of power, not organized rivalries, but an organized common peace." On April 6, President Wilson signed the resolution, and America was at war with Germany.[58]

3

SLEEPING SWORD OF WAR

Congress's declaration of war landed with a dispir-iting thud in the War Department. Although the World War had been raging for three years, Wilson's cabinet and general staff hadn't even bothered to draft a plan for intervention. The general who would eventually command US forces in the war later commented in his memoirs that "figuratively speaking, the pigeon-hole was empty." Literally speaking, there was also nothing: "The War Department was face-to-face with the question of sending an Army to Europe and found that the General Staff had never considered such a thing."[1]

The old US regular army—sized for garrison duty in the American West under a small, somnolent general staff—was entirely inadequate for a world war against fully armed great powers. A mass army would have to be built from scratch, at a time when the entire active-duty strength of the US Army was just 120,000 troops, with 80,000 in reserve. Pushed to its limits, in other words, the US Army in April 1917 could eke out 200,000 troops. Throwing in the nation's two Marine regiments raised the total to just 207,500. To this pitiful number, the president could add America's 382,000 National Guardsmen, few of whom were considered competent, but even assuming that they were, a 600,000-man army wasn't much for a nation of one hundred million at a time when the Allies in Europe were wielding multimillion-man armies against the ten million troops of the Central Powers.[2]

And what an army it was—old, drunk, and stagnant, forged in the doldrums of peace. "All you need in the US Army," the saying went, "is a strong back and a weak mind." Company commanders were fifty years old, and some ran through one or two bottles of whiskey a day while reminiscing about their exploits in Montana or the Philippines. Generals and colonels had never directed fighting like that on the Western Front; American officers had no experience of modern, combined-arms battle, what was called "major war," as opposed to the small wars America had been waging against weak opponents since 1865. Efforts by the McKinley and Roosevelt administrations to professionalize an army that had looked improvised in the Spanish-American War had yielded a war college in Washington and a staff school at Fort Leavenworth, but, given the small size of the US Army and its limited responsibilities, those schools had educated a paltry number of staff officers with more knowledge of irrelevant case studies like the Franco-Prussian War than of the savage war of attrition now consuming Europe. Confidence and real-world experience were so low that the US Army named the force it would send to France the American Expeditionary Forces (AEF), a pallid imitation of the British Expeditionary Force (BEF) already there.[3]

Casting about for someone to command the AEF, President Wilson made an inspired choice: fifty-six-year-old General John J. Pershing, who'd recently commanded the Punitive Expedition to Mexico. Pershing was young and energetic. He'd proven himself in combat—against the Plains Indians in the 1880s; in the Spanish-American War, where he'd charged up San Juan Hill with his regiment of black Buffalo Soldiers (and earned the sobriquet "Nigger Jack," later amended by journalists and historians to "Black Jack"); and in action in the Philippines against Moro rebels in 1913, when he'd been recommended for a Congressional Medal of Honor. He'd also experienced "major war," President Roosevelt having sent him to

To command the AEF, President Wilson chose the best man for the job: 56-year-old General John J. Pershing. Pershing had fought in the American West, Cuba, and the Philippines; he'd served as an observer in the Russo-Japanese War; and he had commanded the Punitive Expedition in Mexico. Teddy Roosevelt, who'd served with Pershing in the Spanish-American War, called him "the coolest man under fire I ever saw in my life." (National Archives)

Manchuria in 1905 to observe the Russo-Japanese War (and earn fast-track promotion). Teddy Roosevelt had served in Cuba with Pershing during the Spanish-American War and said of him: "I have been in many fights but Captain Pershing is the coolest man under fire I ever saw in my life."[4]

To Roosevelt's patronage, Pershing had added that of the chairman of the Senate Military Appropriations Committee, whose twenty-four-year-old debutante daughter the forty-five-year-old Pershing had married in 1905. That same year, President Roosevelt, having tried and failed to persuade the army to promote Captain Pershing to the rank of colonel, had used his prerogative as commander in chief to make Pershing a brigadier general, skipping three ranks entirely and vaulting him over the heads of 862 of his superiors. Pershing was mentally tough. He had to be, given the envy he now attracted. Some said that the nickname "Black Jack" reflected his cold implacability more than his past command of African American troops. And things had become exceedingly black for Pershing when his wife Helen and their three daughters were killed in a house fire in the San Francisco Presidio while he was serving on the Mexican border in August 1915. Pershing had endured the pain, collected his six-year-old son—the sole survivor—and returned to Texas. He'd dealt with that cup of tragedy as coolly as he dealt with all of the taunts about "Nigger Jack" or his political connections. He hid them in compartments behind his impassive face and did his job. Officers called him the "Iron Commander," or simply "JJP."

The job Pershing now faced was as daunting as any in American military history. Despite America's great size, its army was small and fragmented. By May 1917, the US expected to have just four divisions of the regular army trained. These would be joined by a dozen trained National Guard divisions in July 1917 and four more trained Guard divisions by September. But this was a drop in the bucket by European standards, and the National Guard, derived from the state regiments and militias of the Civil War, was noted chiefly for its relaxed discipline and poor officers—many of them political appointees with no military aptitude. National Guard troops tended to be men who used the obligation, as one put it, "to get away from an overworked housewife" for the weekend.[5]

General Leonard Wood declared the American predicament to be analogous to Russia's—huge reserves of manpower but far too few trained officers and noncommissioned officers (NCOs) to make good troops on short notice. "We are sleeping the sleep of fools," Wood wrote, "lulled by the words of those who last year said the war was over, and now say that this is the last war." Wood, whose brilliant career was stopped cold by President Wilson for caustic comments like this, added: "We have been cursed with a 'peace at any price' man as an orator on too many occasions. . . . I refer to no particular man"—of course he did—"but to a type, the sort of man who goes around and takes the plugs out of the life boats and renders disaster certain if things go wrong." Wood called America's twelve Plattsburg-style camps—created by Wood and Theodore Roosevelt in 1915—an effort "to punch holes in Wilson's theories." Wood acknowledged to friends that, as he put it, "I am skating on thin ice, but I am going to skate." Inadequate as Wood's camps were, they may ultimately have been the difference between success and failure, as Wood noted: "Had it not been for the Plattsburg Training Camps, we should have had practically nothing to start with; for it was only the 30 or 40 thousand men we got hold of directly and the hundreds of thousands we had reached through the Universities and the millions of people they had preached to on the subject of universal service which sent our Conscription over with a rush, and without complaint or protest."[6]

Pershing inherited this mess: regulars, National Guardsmen, Marines, and the improvised Plattsburg camps. To create a European-sized army, Congress passed the Selective Service Act on May 19, 1917. It was controversial, the Democratic Speaker of the House leading a rebellion against the president. Missourians, Speaker Champ Clark railed, see "precious little difference between a conscript and a convict." But Republicans in Congress crossed the aisle to vote with Wilson, calculating that if the war went well they'd benefit, and if it went badly Wilson and the Democrats would absorb the blame. The ensuing draft of men aged twenty-one to thirty-one contained some fascinating subplots. Wilson pushed it hard in part to prevent his rival Teddy Roosevelt from raising a volunteer corps for service in France. Roosevelt and Leonard Wood had planned to lead a corps of twentieth-century Rough Riders to Europe, and Wilson feared their eventual success at least as much as their more likely failure. Reserving all young men for the US Army would deprive TR of his battalions.[7]

As for those battalions, America was a young nation, recently swelled by a horde of European immigrants, many of whom hadn't yet naturalized. One in three Americans was either foreign-born or had foreign-born parents. Since federal authorities looked at total population—native and foreign-born—to arrive at state draft quotas, the northern states were more heavily burdened because they contained so many immigrants, many of whom weren't citizens. In some northeastern states, resident aliens amounted to a third of the population. In the economically stagnant South, the foreign population was 1 percent or less across the board. With each state required by the Selective Service Act to draft 9.32 percent of its draft-aged men, the northern states faced a far heavier liability if aliens were counted in the population but excluded from the draft, as everyone supposed they would be.

Connecticut senator Frank Brandegee claimed that the cities of his state "had been boosted far beyond their actual population" by the assumptions of the Selective Service Act. Massachusetts senator Henry Cabot Lodge and Ohio senator Atlee Pomerene had the same complaint: "Northern and Western cities have been credited with much bigger populations than they possess." They assumed that Wilson's administration, filled with southerners like the president, had done this deliberately to favor Dixie. It had. "The South is clearly in the saddle," presidential adviser Colonel Edward House noted, "both in Congress and the Administration." Staunch defenders of states' rights, southerners generally opposed the draft and the shipbuilding program needed to convey an army to Europe as dangerous expansions of federal power that might never be reversed. The resulting delays in the shipbuilding program would have massive military effects. America's supply of oceangoing ships in 1917 was the same it had been in 1812—one million tons. The Germans in 1917 were sinking that much tonnage every sixty days. Yet serious American naval expansion wouldn't begin until the summer of 1918, which meant that any American troops bound for Europe would have to be crammed into British and French ships and be forced to sail without tanks, aircraft, artillery, motor transport, or even machine guns. All of that would have to be claimed, in insufficient quantities, from the British and French.[8]

To make the big northern drafts more palatable, the Senate Military Committee took the extraordinary decision in July 1917 to draft citizens *and* aliens into the US Army. To have left aliens undrafted would have demoralized the citizens who were drafted. American boys would have been shipped off to fight Germans while immigrants from Russia, Germany, Austria-Hungary, Ireland, and Italy took their vacant jobs in America to toil in profitable safety. In places like Brooklyn, New York, more than a quarter of military-aged males were new immigrants from Russia. None of them suspected that Wilson would draft *them*. They looked at their draft board, a witness recalled,

The Selective Service Act of May 1917 drafted American men between 21 and 30 years of age, many of them foreign-born aliens. Here, a typical group of draftees departs New York City for basic training on Long Island. In August 1918, the draft would be extended to all men 18–45 years old. Nearly 3 million Americans would be drafted during the war. (National Archives)

shrugged, laughed, and said, "What are you going to do about it?" They'd be drafted, that's what. As the British embassy put it in July 1917: "A feeling has grown up here that if U.S. citizens are compulsorily drafted, it is not fair that their wages would be earned at home by able-bodied subjects and citizens of the Allied powers, who have shirked their duty to country and remained in the U.S."[9]

Much of this anxiety was whipped up by William Randolph Hearst's media empire; Hearst, who owned the nation's largest chain of newspapers, railed against job-poaching "foreign slackers" in the US. Hearst demanded that America's resident aliens be located, drafted, and sent to fight in Europe alongside native-born Americans. This would explain the bewildering names in the American war cemeteries in France—names like Ottavio Fiscalini, Aleksandr Skazhkows, and Thorwald Knutson—and the curiosity that nearly 20 percent of American troops in World War I were foreign-born aliens.

US Army censors would have to read their mail in forty-nine different languages. Teddy Roosevelt, always worried about the patriotism of "hyphenated Americans," felt certain that there'd be no better school of the nation than the AEF: "The military tent where they will all sleep side by side will rank next to the public school among the great agents of democratization."[10]

Taking no chances, Wilson pushed for emergency powers to repress the activities of hyphenated Americans and any other dissidents who might oppose conscription and US intervention in the war. In June 1917 Congress approved Wilson's Espionage Act, which gave the president the power to fine and imprison opponents of the war—anyone who "obstructed military operations" or used the mail to inform and rally antiwar agitators. American Socialists, who'd garnered six hundred thousand votes in the 1916 presidential election, were the first to feel the heavy hand of the act, which jailed their leader and presidential candidate, Eugene V. Debs, and suppressed their newspapers and mailings, effectively crippling the Socialists as a movement. Wisconsin senator Robert La Follette, an antiwar Republican progressive, was reviled by many of his Senate colleagues as a "traitor" and a "German agent." Teddy Roosevelt suggested that men like La Follette "ought to be hung." As revolution spread in Russia, Wilson feared that European radicalism would flow through the "hyphenated Americans" to the United States. "Any man," the president said, "who carries a hyphen about with him carries a dagger that he is ready to plunge into the vitals of the Republic." Speech too was controlled, by the Sedition Act, which was appended to the Espionage Act six months later. Violating the First Amendment, the Sedition Act forbade all "disloyal language" about the United States and its government, Constitution, flag, or armed forces. Wilson tolerated the gross abuses that flowed from his two powerful Texans, Attorney General Thomas Gregory and Postmaster General Albert Burleson, who vowed to hunt down dissidents: "May God have mercy on them, for they need to expect none from an outraged people and an avenging government," Gregory growled.[11]

The Wilson administration outlawed dissenting views on the war with its Espionage and Sedition Acts. Often crowds took matters into their own hands. Here, during a military parade in Springfield, Massachusetts, men who refused to bare their heads when the flag passed are accosted by their more patriotic fellows. (National Archives)

Every US attorney became, as one observer put it, "an angel of life and death clothed with the power to walk up and down in his district, saying, 'This one will I spare, and that one I will smite.'" Gregory employed twenty-five thousand informants across the country to spy on friends, colleagues, and neighbors, and he encouraged the spread of vigilante groups like the American Protective League, which threatened opponents of the war. Gregory sought the broadest application of the Espionage and Sedition Acts, jailing for three years a journalist in New Hampshire who'd merely written—in regard to J. P. Morgan's massive loans to the Allies that effectively made the bank too big to fail—that "this is a Morgan war, not a war of the people." A man was jailed in Montana for grumbling about food rationing. Burleson denied use of the US Postal Service to so many publications that Wilson felt compelled to ask him to exercise more "caution and liberality."[12]

Burleson ignored the president. Wilson, after all, had set the tone with his declaration that too many aliens born abroad but living in America "under its generous naturalization laws" had "poured the poison of disloyalty into the very arteries of our national life." Wilson himself had vowed to "crush them out." How could his law enforcement officers do any less? They suppressed or censored papers and mailings that contained anything even mildly critical of wartime policy. Burleson's list of abuses was long: punishing a newspaper for writing that Britain should make Ireland a republic, censoring another that called for the British to give independence to their colonies, and suppressing a paper for arguing that the American war effort should be financed by taxes, not borrowing. Two thousand Americans were tried under the acts during the war, and more than two-thirds were convicted. The Supreme Court, "locking the doors after the Liberty Bell was stolen," would review none of these cases until after the war.[13]

To make a positive argument for the war, Wilson created a Committee on Public Information (CPI) and entrusted it to forty-one-year-old George Creel. Creel deplored the heavy hand of Burleson and Gregory, noting that Americans responded better when "the desired compulsions proceed from within than from without." Censorship and repression, Creel thought, were European mechanisms; America just needed to be inspired. Creel had been a progressive politician and muckraking journalist before working on both of Wilson's presidential campaigns. He now knitted together a formidable propaganda program. The composer of "Take Me Out to the Ball Game" was induced to set "What Kind of American Are You?" to the same tune. It demanded immigrant loyalty: "If the Star-Spangled Banner don't make you stand and cheer, / Then what are you doing over here?" Creel employed seventy-five thousand "Four-Minute Men" to prowl the theaters, schools, union halls, and main streets of America, touting the benefits of intervention. Creel printed bulletins in multiple languages explaining the war, and provided newspapers with ghoulish press releases recounting German atrocities. He created "loyalty leagues" inside America's immigrant communities. The goal, largely achieved, was to keep "patriotism at white heat" and hasten the "Americanization" of recent immigrants.[14]

Many had worried that the draft would provoke Civil War–style draft riots—that, as a Missouri senator put it, the streets would "run red with blood." Instead, it went off smoothly, President Wilson taking pains to put draft boards in the hands of civilians instead of military officers, who invariably alarmed draftees with their severity. Local draft boards, of course, didn't miss the opportunity to exempt the best men from service. Skilled industrial workers were particularly prized and kept back—millwrights, tool fitters, sheet-metal workers, electricians, engineers, machinists, riveters, boilermakers, and welders. The Selective Service's "work or fight" order meant that the least skilled men were going to fight; those with skills would remain home to work. Married men were regularly exempted, leading to a wave of sudden marriages. Southern draft boards often exempted whites and shoveled blacks into the service. In Fulton County, Georgia, 526 of 815 whites were exempted while all but 6 of 202 blacks were conscripted. Overall, the Jim Crow South was flummoxed by the whole question. Blacks, 10 percent of the population, composed 13 percent of draftees, but the temptation to shunt the burden on to African Americans was undercut by the fear, expressed by Mississippi senator James Vardaman, that to do so would place "arrogant strutting representatives of black soldiery in every community."[15]

And so the American draft lumbered ahead unevenly in ways that were often comical despite the approaching bloodbath. An Irish immigrant in Pennsylvania described his interview with the draft board:

> An' the little Jew major-man, he says to me, "In what shtate was you born?" An' I give him the answer from the catechism. "I don't mean that," says he. "I mane in what shtate of the American Union was you born?" An' I says, "In Antrim, sor, but I shpint the innocent years of me childhood in Delaware, U.S.A." . . . "An who thin is the governor of the shtate of Delaware?" he shouts at me. "Ah, now major," says I, "shurely ye wouldn't expect a sane man to know

that," I says. And so he just turned to the clerk and says, "Mark him Highly Intilligint."[16]

Modern mass armies, the norm in Europe since the 1870s, had long since concluded that men in their midtwenties were the optimal recruits. They were young enough to have illusions of immortality and mature enough to accept discipline and hardship. Men in their twenties were considered "attacking troops" because they were willing to go over the top and seek danger. The Europeans had run through their populations of men in their twenties and were now being forced to recruit teenagers and middle-aged men, neither of whom were ever regarded anywhere as suitable attacking troops. Pershing was pleased with the demographics of his new army—the average age of draftees was twenty-five, and 82 percent of the US troops who served in World War I were between twenty and twenty-nine years old—but he was disappointed by their level of education. The "work or fight" order, the massive number of exemptions, and segregation meant that what remained to the army was poorly educated—an average of just seven years of schooling for American whites, five years for immigrants, and fewer than three years for blacks.[17]

Twenty-five percent of American draftees were illiterate. Too many of them, Pershing said, were "physically defective or partially defective men." In some camps one-quarter of the draftees had to be rejected for physical disabilities. Pershing was struck by "the high rate of venereal disease existing among the young men of the country." At one camp that trained men from a dozen states, 10 percent of the whites who reported suffered from acute venereal disease. This was the average at all camps for whites, and the percentage was higher among blacks. Poor language skills and meager education posed serious military problems. Pershing remarked on "the large number of men of alien birth who had no knowledge of English," making them "unfit for use in combat organizations" that were increasingly technical. Among black troops, the problem was especially severe. In one day's review of 1,500 black draftees, only two were found who could read. When illiterates and non-English speakers were combined, Pershing put the percentage of "unfit" draftees at 40 percent. He lamented the "large number of effectives that had to be left behind to care for, develop, and instruct this pool of mediocre material." Pershing had boldly declared that the standards of the AEF would be "those of West Point." He had a long way to go.[18]

Ten million Americans registered for the draft in the six months following passage of the law. Fourteen million more would register in 1918. Many, like Seward Strickland of Hartford, Connecticut, went gladly "as the best and only way to uphold our American Flag and this Christian nation." But patriotic duty wasn't universally felt. John Dos Passos, who graduated from Harvard during the war and went to France to drive an ambulance, alleged that "they had to run special trains to get the intellectuals to Washington, they were in such a hurry to run to cover." Many Americans did work their connections to find cover. Twenty-eight-year-old Joseph P. Kennedy Sr., father of the thirty-fifth president and already a wealthy businessman, found his cover in the offices of Bethlehem Steel. Thousands of less well-connected Americans simply refused to go; in all, 337,649 men failed to report, of whom 170,000 were still at large two years after the war. Wilson's Justice Department conducted "slacker raids" in cities like New York, Boston, Pittsburgh, and Chicago to catch draft dodgers. A raid in New Jersey netted thirteen thousand of them, giving the lie to some of Creel's more flowery paeans to American nationalism. In some states, 90 percent of draftees sought to be exempted, few successfully.[19]

In his own study of Americans sent to train with the French, General Philippe Pétain noted the immense difficulties. Americans would eventually arrive in France having done little in the States besides "gymnastic exercises, close-order drill, and some rifle fire." They were, as one observer put it, "making military bricks with the very minimum of straw." American inexperience was only worsened by doctrinal confusion. Pershing and his lieutenants appeared to suffer a "cult of the offensive" not unlike the one that had destroyed the French and British armies early in the war—a wooden belief, as expressed in the army's *Field Service Regulations* of 1914, that "decisive results are obtained only by the offensive." Pershing hankered after the "open warfare" the Germans were unveiling in Europe after three years of trench warfare, but he didn't seem to grasp that open warfare could only be practiced by seasoned troops precisely trained in combined arms warfare—the knitting together of artillery, infantry, armor, and aviation in a coordinated package. Pétain, who understood Pershing better than any other Allied general, saw the yawning gaps in America's military education but cautioned his trainers to "avoid an attitude of superiority" toward the Americans: "They have an extremely high developed sense of *amour-propre*, based on their pride in belonging to one of the greatest nations in the world." He reminded French officers that their chief mission was to give the Americans "the benefit of our dearly bought experience," a reasonable-enough statement across which Pershing later scribbled: "An experience that has made them *timid*."[20]

The French, desperate for American troops, pretended not to notice this bumptiousness. They requested forty thousand American officers for immediate training in the "new warfare," *la guerre actuelle*. Despite Pershing's doubts, the Americans would need it. More than 90 percent of the two hundred thousand American officers who served in the war entered the army in 1917–1918. Most of these officers would arrive in France with just three months' training and an exam; they were the original "ninety-day wonders." Most of them were youthful survivors of a process that failed half of the candidates. One of them recalled introducing himself to his platoon in France when a furtive voice called from the back: "And a little child shall lead them." A career officer pronounced the US Army's situation "worse than 1898," that is, worse than it had been when called on to fight impoverished Spain. How would they ever match the Germans?[21]

The British had sent their own mission to America at the time of the Joffre visit. Led by Arthur Balfour, the British mission's military affairs were managed by General George Bridges, the man who'd briefed the US Army War College on the new warfare in May 1917. Bridges didn't bother to conceal his contempt for American backwardness; he saw no other solution than to "amalgamate" or combine the British and American armies, that is, use America's vast draft pool to build new British divisions and bring the shattered ones back up to strength. That would save time and lives, for the Americans would only have to train soldiers, not headquarters staff, and their recruits would serve under experienced British officers, who might avoid the disasters that inexperienced American commanders would almost certainly blunder into.[22]

Britain's own experience in the war weighed on everyone in London and Washington. The two powers were so alike. Both relied on their navies for their security and began the war with small regular armies—just eight divisions each. Britain's first taste of major warfare in 1914, at bloodbaths like Mons, Le Cateau, and the Marne, had been horrific, all but wiping out the BEF. Britain's replacement army, built first from volunteers and then from conscripts, hadn't been judged ready for great offensive operations until 1916. "It took the English, who had a powerful colonial army, two entire *years* to create and lead an army on the Western Front battlefield that was capable of measuring itself against the Germans," the French general staff reflected. "It seems obvious that it will take the Americans more than two years, for they are not a military people."[23]

The draft presented the US Army with masses of new manpower. But how exactly would they be employed? With just thirty infantry regiments and six artillery regiments, the regular army didn't have enough units to absorb the influx, and so an entirely new organization was adopted. The regular army was increased to 300,000 men and instructed to form ten divisions. The National Guard was increased to 425,000 men and authorized to form twenty divisions, though the National Guard, with its short periods of exercise and mediocre officers, was never an imposing deterrent. The 7th New York National Guard Regiment, for example, was essentially a social club for Manhattan's "four hundred families." The men in the "Kid Gloves 7th" were WASPs with old-money names like Astor, Van Cortlandt, and Roosevelt. They wore West Point grays, drilled in Central Park under the eyes of admiring debutantes, and held elaborate balls. Few of them—as one recruit to their ranks put it—had "ever lifted anything heavier than a set of golf clubs." Overall, the French were charmed but unimpressed. "These are poor units. They lack discipline. They include lots of bankers and business types, who are political appointees with poor physical conditioning."[24]

But beefing up the National Guard was viewed in the White House as critical to persuading "disinterested states" to take an active interest in the war. Southern whites (and their governors), for example, particularly valued the National Guard as way to promote themselves and bar blacks from public service. Wilson had suffered the indignant resignation of his secretary of war in 1916 over this very issue. On hearing of Wilson's intention to use the National Guard as a reserve army, Secretary of War Lindley Garrison wrote a letter to the president seeking to dissuade him—"such a system cannot be used to create a homogeneous army"—and then resigned rather than involve himself in what he considered "a betrayal of the public trust." Relying on the Guard would be foolhardy: "The nation will be forced to depend on a military force for which it cannot recruit, it cannot name officers, it cannot train and over which it has no authority."[25]

Garrison resigned in February 1916, and by June the truth of his prophecy was clear. The National Guard units mobilized for the Punitive Expedition against Mexico were not only incompetent; they cost the federal government five times more to deploy than regular army units and cratered morale across the force. Federalized Guards sent to Mexico received two pensions—federal and state—and had to be paid eighty dollars a month (thirty dollars to the troops, fifty dollars to their families), whereas regulars were paid just sixteen dollars a month, with a single pension, a discrepancy that had the regulars loathing the Guardsmen for more than just their poor military performance. In Mexico, 30 percent of the Guard troops in any given unit were classed "unfit for service." This was because governors had sent raw recruits to the front to meet their quotas and qualify for federal dollars. Those recruits, arriving from Pennsylvania, New York, New Jersey, Connecticut, and Massachusetts (the only Guard formations judged fit for service), still needed two months of instruction before they could be trusted with even the most basic tasks. When the New

President Wilson never selected advisers who might overshadow him. In 1916, with the United States weighing intervention in the European war, Wilson named a former student, 44-year-old Newton Baker (above), a man with no national security credentials, to be the US secretary of war. In Washington, Baker was judged a pacifist and was best known for introducing a three-cent streetcar fare as mayor of Cleveland. The French expressed astonishment: "The Grand Republic is in a deplorable situation. Can *he* be the man to rescue *this* situation?" (National Archives)

York Guard proposed to march ten miles, the exercise had to be canceled because the troops couldn't hack it. The French were stunned: "Events in Mexico catch the U.S. *in flagrante delicto* of military unpreparedness. This great, careless country is fortunate that it has no nearby enemy that can pose a serious threat."[26]

Secretary of War Garrison's replacement wasn't reassuring. He was forty-four-year-old Newton Baker of Cleveland, chosen entirely for his Buckeye origins, Ohio being a critical swing state in national elections. Baker was small and unassuming. General Robert Lee Bullard, seeing the new secretary of war standing beside a general at a meeting, assumed that Baker was the general's "secretary or stenographer." Baker "looked as though he was about something which he did not understand," Bullard added. He was. Nothing had prepared Baker for the great task ahead. He'd once studied under Professor

Woodrow Wilson at Johns Hopkins University and had served as mayor of Cleveland, but, by his own admission, he "had no military competence." His most notable accomplishments as mayor had been instituting a three-cent streetcar fare and founding the Cleveland Symphony Orchestra. As a Quaker and a Democratic politician, he had always campaigned *against* military spending and had once refused the presidency of the Ohio Boy Scouts on the grounds that the organization was too militaristic. The press referred to him as a pacifist. Taking stock of the Baker appointment, the French were again struck dumb with amazement: "The Grand Republic is in a deplorable situation. Can *he* possibly be the man to rescue *this* situation?"[27]

Baker was less of a problem than the War Department itself. The US Army had never bothered to organize itself efficiently. Dramatic Prussian victories over Austria and France in 1866 and 1870–1871—triumphs of organization as much as strategy and tactics—had forced every great-power military to shift critical functions to the general staff, but not in the US. There, old fiefdoms had been allowed to survive and flourish, often overwhelming the more modern structures, like the general staff, that had been intended to replace them. The old US Army bureaus of the engineers, quartermaster, ordnance, and the adjutant general continued to compete with each other and the general staff because they'd never been tamed by a military leadership that rotated faster through its jobs than the bureau chiefs did theirs.

The chief of the general staff in 1917 was sixty-four-year-old General Hugh Scott, who'd earned his stars fighting the Indians. As a young lieutenant in the 7th Cavalry, Scott had been sent to recover and bury Custer and his dead at the Little Big Horn. By 1917, he was an old general and had reached the army's mandatory retirement age when America began to mobilize. His intellect wasn't prized. "Everybody's talking about the Battle of the Marne," Scott called to an aide one day. "What happened at the Battle of the Marne anyway?" Hard of hearing, Scott spoke in "grunts and sign language," hardly the man to whip the US Army into shape. His deputy chief of staff, sixty-four-year-old General Tasker Bliss, was also on the brink of retirement. Bliss, the son of a college librarian, was an unimposing introvert unlikely to achieve what Pershing felt was essential: the "absolute supremacy of the general staff and the complete recognition of that supremacy by the whole service." That, Pershing said, is "a *sine qua non* of efficient organization." Bliss's pedantry was notorious. In 1912, he'd commanded the combined maneuvers of the Connecticut National Guard and some regular army units and had caused a sensation by halting a column of troops on the rut of a wagon wheel. The long, dusty, perspiring column shambled to a halt until Bliss, inspecting the vanguard, noticed that they'd stopped on the wrong rut, a yard in front of the one he'd indicated. They were on a vast field, it hardly mattered, yet Bliss made the entire column shuffle three feet backward.[28]

Secretary of War Baker and Generals Scott and Bliss wrestled in 1917 with the manpower question—what to do with the draftees—and arrived at what seemed to be the only feasible solution. Since there was no space in the regular army for so many men, and since no one had any faith in the weekend warriors of the National Guard, the bulk of the American draft would be directed into an entirely *new* body, which was given the name "National Army." In this they were following in the footsteps of the British. London too had begun the war with a derisory army of just eight divisions, geared like the US Army for colonial service. The Germans had immediately mauled the six divisions of the "Expeditionary Corps," forcing London to raise a mass army for the long war ahead. Like the Americans, the British had created a third structure outside the regular and territorial armies, supplementing their eight regular divisions with twenty-eight brand-new "Kitchener divisions," named after Britain's secretary of state for war, Field Marshal Herbert Kitchener, who'd supervised the expansion until his death in 1916.[29]

America's first draft yielded 500,000 men, who began training in August 1917. The French gaped at the almost limitless supply of American manpower. This was just America's first slice. Another draft of 570,000 men would be trained by May 1918. Whereas France's reserves were exhausted—it was down literally to its last cohorts of healthy military-aged men—America swarmed with fresh troops. "U.S. intervention is now a necessity due to the attrition of

French effectives," France's war minister reminded his liaison officers in America. But he cautioned French diplomats and officers to conceal this desperation. The last thing Paris wanted was for the Americans to deploy to Europe in the eleventh hour of this hellish war and reap all of the credit for a victory that might need American power now but that had been purchased with three years of Allied sacrifice. "In no case can you let slip that France has need of American help. Assure the Americans that France is capable with her own resources of liberating territory and dictating peace; U.S. intervention is needed only to *hasten* the end of the war." Privately, the French admitted that they were in fact wholly reliant on American manpower and couldn't possibly win without it: "The Russian reservoir has dried up. We must now gain access to the American reservoir."[30]

In the hastily expanded US Army, the regulars would be divisions 1 through 10, the National Guard divisions would take the numbers 24 through 42, and the National Army would replace losses in regular divisions and form its own divisions, numbered 11 through 23 and 43 through 102. All divisions were made up of one thousand officers, twenty-seven thousand troops, and a brigade of field artillery. They were "square divisions," with two brigades of two regiments each. Pershing later excoriated this improvised system. "We had in France," he wrote, "four separate organized forces—regulars, Marines, militia, and national army. They had three sets of traditions, customs, regulations, and methods operating concurrently." Pershing noted that even if all of the units had been highly efficient—they weren't—they'd have been degraded by the "bureaucracy festering in this hybrid army." Units and staffs had too much "overhead," and the combat formations had no training in modern warfare. National Guard officers were "consistently below standard, with deficient education, political and local affiliations, and an unwillingness to enforce discipline." What success the Guard would have in the war would be due to the rare extraordinary higher officer—not because of his training, but in spite of it.[31]

Marshal Joffre, advising the French government on military affairs, had wondered in May 1917 how long it would take to get large numbers of trained American troops to France. By the fall, the answer was taking shape. Because of the French crisis at Verdun in 1916, Britain's green Kitchener divisions had been committed too soon at the Battle of the Somme and had been mauled. Pershing refused to let the desperate Allies stampede him into a similar disaster. His headquarters frankly admitted that the AEF "cannot be considered as a real combat factor before June 1918." Even then, the AEF would be capable of only "minor offensive operations." Nothing large-scale and "decisive" would be attempted until the spring of 1919. The French and British protested this business-as-usual attitude—when they were bracing for a potentially war-ending German offensive—but Pershing saw no other way. If the AEF were committed too soon and failed, the impact on American morale and public opinion would be devastating.[32]

The US Army's officer deficit would be addressed in fifteen training camps hurriedly established after the declaration of war. There American officer candidates took a three-month course, yielding sixty thousand new officers in every cycle; candidates under twenty-seven generally went into the regular army, those between twenty-seven and forty-four to the National Army. The National Guard units would have to find and train their own officers, virtually guaranteeing chaos in that arm. (Officer material was so urgently needed that thirty-three-year-old Harry Truman, legally blind in his left eye and nearly blind in the other, was judged fit to command an artillery battery in Missouri's 35th National Guard Division.) Yet chaos was virtually guaranteed in the regular and National Army too. Visiting the officer-training camp at Fort Myer, near Washington, DC, France's military attaché, General Louis Collardet, observed that "the program of instruction wasn't shaped by actual war." There was "no practical instruction, no use of grenades, no trench work, no use of mortars or machine guns, and no practice of open-order." Artillery officer candidates had "never fired a cannon or even seen one being fired."[33]

Despite a dumbed-down curriculum, half of the US officer candidates washed out (and were sent to the Signal Corps as enlisted men, doubtless a cause of *its* epic problems in 1918). The rest were commissioned according to age and experience as lieutenants, captains, or majors. All promotions above major were reserved for the regular army. Across the army, there remained a critical shortage of staff officers and NCOs, as all effort had been focused on conscripting an army and training field officers. Working in the army's Eastern Department when Congress declared war, Captain George Marshall described the months that followed as "the most strenuous, hectic and laborious in my experience." Training camps were packed and inefficient, especially when the War Department made inscrutable decisions like sending the 369th Infantry, the only African American regiment (of four in the army) that had black officers, to Spartanburg, South Carolina, for training. Black officers of this storied New York unit—originally the 15th Heavy Foot—were accosted in town, called "dirty niggers," and thrown off streetcars and evicted from hotels and restaurants. Black enlisted men were shouldered off the sidewalks and beaten. Unable to train in South Carolina, the 369th traveled back to New York to train with the 42nd Rainbow Division on Long Island. The Rainbows, however, contained the 167th US Infantry, better known as the 4th Alabama, whose men bullied the black troops day and night, so frequently that the black troops had their ammunition seized lest they fire on their tormentors. (In Houston, thirteen black soldiers were hanged by the army for killing white civilians who'd harassed them in this way during training.) The other three African American regiments, none of which had black officers, received none of this attention. "The different attitude toward Negroes still under white masters was one for psychologists, not soldiers, to ponder," a veteran recalled.[34]

Pershing gave a talk at the Army War College in August 1917; he projected that America would have one million trained troops for a 1918 offensive and three million troops for what he expected would be the decisive, war-winning offensive of 1919. For 1918, he wanted an American army of five corps, each containing six divisions, four of combat troops and two of replacements. But the French, whose fate hung on the speed of the American transatlantic deployment, heard the Pershing speech with agonized disbelief; new officer candidates were being authorized slowly and trained even more slowly. The general staff needed at least 310 new officers yet had begun training only 112. "Overall, it's difficult not to be unfavorably impressed by the torpor of the American military administration and the retrograde spirit of its chiefs. I very much doubt that the U.S. Army can be ready to strike in the spring of 1918," a French military attaché in Washington scribbled.[35]

It was easy to see why the French were worried sick. Their own losses were enormous, and they were down to literally their last recruits. Russia, whose reservoir of manpower had always diverted a large fraction of the German army, was tottering. The Provisional Government of revolutionaries had ousted the tsar in March 1917. Their leader, the thirty-six-year-old chief of the moderate Socialist Mensheviks, Alexander Kerensky, had pledged to honor Russia's alliances and fight on to "defend the revolution" and defeat the Germans and Austrians. Initially pleasing to America—Wilson was relieved to be allied at last with a democracy in Russia—Kerensky's government wilted in the summer heat. Russian offensives, which the French government had hyped to bolster France's own fading morale, faltered, and the army dissolved.

In November 1917, Lenin's communist Bolsheviks seized power and announced their intention to conclude a separate peace with Berlin and Vienna and exit the war. While that was happening, an Austro-German offensive smashed the Italian army at Caporetto and all but removed Italy from the war. By early December 1917, the Italian army had lost nearly seven hundred thousand troops and half of its artillery. Most of the Italians had surrendered without a fight. The Italians, who'd pinned down the bulk of the Austro-Hungarian army since 1915, were no longer capable of offensive operations. Meanwhile, the Bolsheviks had conceded the Germans and Austrians a truce in the East pending a final treaty of peace. All fighting on the Eastern Front ceased.[36]

On the Italian front, things were so grim that both Britain and France, which needed every available rifle, had to send a half-dozen divisions to stiffen the Italians. The American general staff concluded that Italy was as good as dead—the Germans and Austrians could conquer it easily and hadn't done so only because such a campaign would subtract essential troops from the decisive blow in France. Now the Germans and Austrians could take the bulk of the 1.4 million troops they had on the Eastern Front and the divisions deployed in Italy and send them west to finish off the decimated British and French armies. The British had lost three hundred thousand men in their witless attacks on Passchendaele in Flanders in 1917. The French had lost nearly two hundred thousand troops in their fruitless attacks on the Chemin des Dames, north of the Marne. Now the Germans, who were moving fifty divisions from east to west to finish off these demoralized Allied armies, also enjoyed an advantage in artillery for the first time since the outbreak of the war. It was like the Schlieffen Plan in reverse, only this time with good chances of success.[37]

On November 11, 1917, General Erich Ludendorff convened a meeting of Germany's senior staff officers on the Western Front. Meeting at the headquarters of Crown Prince Rupprecht of Bavaria in Mons, Belgium, the Germans pored over maps to choose the spot for their great, war-winning offensive in the spring of 1918. Ludendorff expected victory, but he knew that time was on the Allies' side because of the American buildup and the tightening of the British blockade. He also knew that the Germans *had* to win in just one throw of the dice. They'd have more than two hundred divisions and one thousand heavy guns to break through and tear up the British and French armies. Once that strength was spent, there'd be few reserves to replace it.

Three targets for attack presented themselves: the British sector in Flanders, the hinge of the British and French armies along the Somme River, and the area around Verdun. Ludendorff chose the Somme. Flanders was arguably better because it would allow the Germans to crush the narrow British sector and seize Field Marshal Haig's Channel ports, effectively destroying the British and isolating the French. But rainy Flanders would be a quagmire till the summer, and Ludendorff wanted to go no later than early March; Verdun was too far from Paris to be decisive. Only the Somme offered good ground for an attack in the spring and the ability to rupture the connection between the British and French and either curl north to destroy the British or plunge south to beat the French and take Paris. Ludendorff named the operation "Michael"—after the Archangel Michael, who had led the forces of God against Satan's armies. Ludendorff concluded the meeting with a warning: "We must strike at the earliest moment, before the Americans can throw strong forces into the scale."[38]

In November 1917, while the Bolshevik Revolution removed Kerensky's army from the war, the Italian army retreated behind the Piave River, and the Germans planned Operation Michael, the British, French, and Italian leaders met at Rapallo and decided that urgent new measures were needed to coordinate and synchronize the coalition. They created a Supreme War Council that would set up shop outside Paris at Versailles and include political and military staffs from the US, Britain, France, and Italy. The US Army's chief of staff, General Tasker Bliss, would take the American seat at Versailles, creating tension with Pershing's AEF headquarters, for, as war correspondent Frederick Palmer put it, "Allied leaders might seek to gain a point over Pershing by appealing to Washington through Bliss."[39]

As the Supreme War Council composed itself, the French prime minister who'd gone to Rapallo fell after adverting his willingness to negotiate with the Germans. Now, France faced a stark choice. The battered nation was torn between two candidates. The first, fifty-four-year-old Joseph Caillaux, wore his defeatism like a badge of honor. *L'homme de la défaite*, "the man of defeat," Caillaux argued that the World War was a titanic waste and grossly unfair, with peasant troops bearing the brunt of combat while the artisan and bourgeois classes did munitions or office work for high wages far from the front. Caillaux, who had strong support in pockets of France, demanded a separate peace and an end to the war. The second candidate, seventy-six-year-old Georges Clemenceau, was a more appetizing figure than Caillaux in terms of character, but less so in his determination to continue a war that looked futile. "He was like a wild animal pacing to and fro behind bars in front of an Assembly which would have done

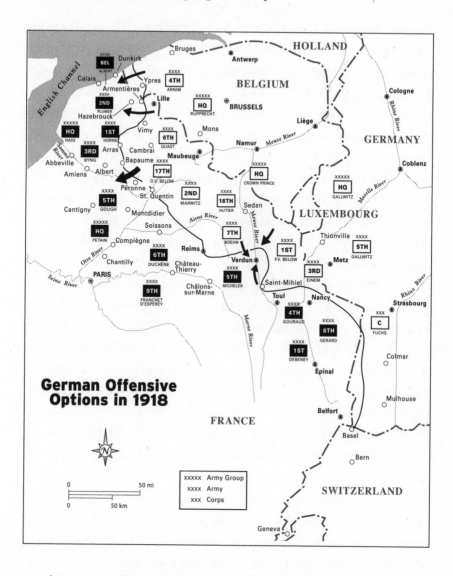

German Offensive Options in 1918

N

| 0 | 50 mi |
| 0 | 50 km |

xxxxx Army Group
xxxx Army
xxx Corps

anything to avoid putting him there," Churchill later wrote. But once appointed premier by President Raymond Poincaré on November 15, Clemenceau dug in, governing from the War Ministry and arresting defeatists like Caillaux—"Neither treason, nor half treason," Clemenceau snarled.[40]

Clemenceau—France's fourth prime minister in the course of 1917—knew that he needed to show results, and for that, he knew he needed American troops. He begged the Americans to accelerate their deployment. Poking around in Washington for the causes of the chronic delays, the French embassy was startled to discover in January 1918 that America's secretary of war had no permanent civilian or military staff. He had to review every piece of paperwork himself. The outgoing general staff chief, Hugh Scott, lacking the energy to manage such a task, had first been packed off to Russia to liaise with the Kerensky government, and then forced into retirement to make way for his deputy, the new general staff chief, General Tasker Bliss. It was hoped that Bliss's bookishness and introversion might result in thoughtful plans. But Bliss was overshadowed by the army's adjutant general, who ruled personnel and promotion. This led to overlapping prerogatives, confusion, and yet another commission, headed by the now retired and presumably no more energetic Scott, to study the problem. Pershing, who'd been given broad authority by the president to organize and lead the AEF, chafed at the unresolved problem of bureaucracy. He had expected the general staff to facilitate his deployment to Europe but instead found Bliss, as General Robert Lee Bullard put it, "displaying and expressing great irritation at what he believed to be the utterly exorbitant ideas and demands of General Pershing."[41]

By hook or by crook, the US Army projected landing between fourteen and twenty-one divisions in France by April 1918; to transport three divisions a month to Europe would require at least five hundred thousand tons of shipping. This unleashed a scramble for hulls, the US government scouring ports at home and abroad for troop transports. Washington impounded all German ships in US ports and seized ninety German merchant ships interned in Brazil as well. The Hog Island shipyard in Philadelphia expanded its facilities and workforce to build fifty transport ships at a time. At least a million tons of new American shipping and scores of borrowed British and French hulls would be needed if America wanted to join an Allied 1918 offensive in any kind of strength.[42]

To make room for more American soldiers on what ships there were, artillery and other equipment would be left behind in the States. The AEF would supply itself with French-made 75mm and 155mm guns in France. Most of the men who'd fire those French guns would sail across the Atlantic untrained. For many of them, that passage to Europe would be their first glimpse of the sea. One Missouri recruit was transfixed by the sight when his troop train set him down on the docks at Newport News.

> If you've been born and brought up in the Middle West, that's a thrill that comes once in a lifetime—your first sight of the ocean. I'd often stood on top of a hill at home where I could see fields of corn, with the wind blowing over them, stretching miles in every direction. I used to wonder if their waves looked anything like the waves of the ocean. I now saw that nothing else in the world could look like the ocean.[43]

4

"LAFAYETTE, WE ARE HERE"

Pershing and his headquarters staff sailed from New York for England on May 27, 1917. Watching them depart, not in uniform but in rumpled suits, Captain George C. Marshall's wife observed: "They were such a dreadful-looking lot of men. I cannot believe they will be able to do any good in France." They traveled via London, where Pershing met with King George V at Buckingham Palace, then crossed the Channel to Paris, where Captain George S. Patton commanded the general's headquarters troop on rue Constantine. In the French capital, Pershing met with the chief of the French general staff, General Ferdinand Foch; France's minister of war, Paul Painlevé; and the two emissaries who'd just returned from America: former prime minister René Viviani and Marshal Joffre. Pershing visited the tombs of Napoleon and Lafayette; at the latter, an aide uttered the famous words ever since attributed to Pershing: "Nous voilà, Lafayette!" (Lafayette, we are here!)[1]

On June 16, Pershing left Paris for Compiègne—sixty miles north of the capital—where he met with the commander in chief of French troops in the field: General Philippe Pétain. The sixty-one-year-old Pétain had emerged as France's leading general after the failure of the

Nivelle Offensive two months earlier. The poilus had mutinied after that debacle, and the avuncular Pétain had been summoned to replace Nivelle as *commandant en chef* of the French armies and to reassure and reorganize them. He had a lot of reassuring to do—even now, two months after the reverse, mutiny and insubordination still seethed in the French ranks. German interrogators were struck by how low the French army had fallen since Nivelle's fiasco. French deserters and POWs seized in May and June divulged every detail of the mutinies: the signs posted by units ("We won't return to the trenches; we'll never attack again"), the hatred of *"ce cochon de Nivelle"* ("this pig Nivelle") that was quickly attached to any officer who supported the chain of command, and the continuing refusal of units to go over the top.

French prisoners told their German captors things like, "In my unit, if the general wants an attack he had better lead it himself," and "We will only attack if the artillery destroys every obstacle." And those were the good troops, those who'd even contemplate attacking again. Others expressed pacifism to the Germans—"Peace at any price"—or revolution: "We fight for the Republic, not for this filthy gang of fools." Many French troops viewed the war as a conspiracy of a "moneyed political élite that takes its orders from England to prolong the war to wring economic advantages from it." The poilus wanted no more of it; German interrogators noted "hatred and rage against England" and a yearning to "compromise with Germany." Hindenburg's headquarters on the Western Front concluded that "anticipated American help is the *only* pillar that is keeping the French government standing."[2]

The US 1st Division—the "Big Red One"—and two regiments of Marines embarked for France in June 1917. Captain George C. Marshall had finagled an assignment with the Big Red One as divisional G-3 (operations) officer. It was just the first spectacular promotion of a career that would carry him to the summit of the US Army in World War II. Watching his troops shuffle up the gangways to their ships under a drizzling rain in Hoboken, Marshall said to the commander of the Port of Embarkation: "The men seem very solemn."

The commander pondered a moment, then replied: "Of course they are; we are watching the harvest of death."

Marshall later recalled that the US Army was so disorganized that the staff of the 1st Division met for the first time aboard ship. None of the officers grasped "the character of the war" they were sailing into. Most of them spent the two-week voyage reading briefing books on the war that had been delivered to the AEF by the French and British military missions in Washington. In Paris, Pershing was only now working out the basic organization of the AEF—from the strength of divisions to the strength of infantry companies and the number of machine guns per brigade. The troops of the 1st Division, the so-called pick of the American army, were anything but. The vast majority of them were new draftees. Marshall observed that "many of the men were undersized and a number spoke English with difficulty."[3]

The 1st Division landed at Saint-Nazaire on June 26. Tramping through the streets of the port, Marshall heard few ovations. The French people were still in shock over the carnage and failure of the Nivelle Offensive. "All of Saint-Nazaire suffered from a deep depression." After a ragged Fourth of July parade in Paris, the Americans departed for the AEF's principal training camp at Gondrecourt-le-Château in eastern France.

The 1st Division was joined at Gondrecourt, sixty miles south of Verdun, by the 2nd Division. The 2nd was pulled together from the two Marine regiments that had sailed with the 1st Division and an army brigade. Then came two National Guard divisions, the 26th Yankee Division and the 42nd Rainbow Division, both considered comparable to regular army divisions because of their service in Mexico in 1916. These "original four" divisions were America's thin green line, the only US units that would spend the entire winter of 1917–1918 in France. The rest of the growing American army remained in camps in the States doing basic training. In truth, the original four were scarcely more competent than those rookies; only a fifth of the men in even these divisions had any military experience. Most were raw recruits.[4]

The Doughboys needed intensive training in the new weapons and methods of the European war. A British colonel attached to Pershing's headquarters at Chaumont, a medieval town on the border of Champagne and Burgundy, recalled a continuous stream of American officers coming to his office at all hours with the most basic questions: "Say, Colonel, when you have to move troops by rail, what do you do?" At Gondrecourt, a sleepy little village of 1,300, US officer and NCO schools were established to create competent platoon and company leaders for the hastily expanded army. All American infantry were given instruction at a "School of Arms" in Langres, where they learned the basics of trench warfare and practiced firing their weapons. The men also charged repeatedly at dummies with the bayonet, not because the weapon would ever be used (nearly all casualties in the war were inflicted by artillery and machine guns) but because bayonet drill taught men to kill in cold blood. As one participant recalled: "Constant bayonet practice was deliberately calculated to overcome any squeamishness about taking human life, and to make a man a hearty murderer."[5]

Machine gunners, neglected till now in the American army, were sent to French and British schools. The American staff college at Langres began instructing general staff officers, who would be needed to coordinate a massive industrial-age army; Langres also gave instruction on liaison and signals, which would be the crucial glue binding together armies, corps, and divisions as well as their all-arms attacks involving infantry, artillery, tanks, and planes. An American artillery school was established at Coëtquidan in Brittany, another at Saumur. American engineers trooped off to Neufchâteau in the Vosges, where French experts gave them a crash course in the construction of trenches and battery positions. Future aviators were sent to Issoudun in the Loire Valley to learn to fly. One aspiring pilot recounted the vetting process:

"I see you went to Williams."
"Yes, sir."
"Graduate?"

"Yes, sir."

"I see you played football."

"Yes, sir."

"Phi Beta Kappa?"

"Yes, sir."

"That's enough; you're in. Let's go have a drink."[6]

The Doughboys chafed at the all-European curriculum. There was a language problem—"My chief success here seems to be that I cause gentlemen from *Oi-o* to fall into deep sleep," a French major from Saint-Cyr intoned one day as he lectured a room of bored Buckeye National Guard officers. But there was also a doctrinal dispute. "Chained to trenches as our Allies had been for so long," General Robert Alexander later wrote, "the importance claimed for these auxiliaries had grown to absurd proportions." Because "these auxiliaries"—the trenches—offered protection, little time was expended on other fundamentals—rifle fire, leadership, discipline, and "the fight in the open" that would inevitably commence wherever the trench line was broken. For that, men and officers had to be trained to direct companies, platoons, and squads under fire, an aspiration that, at this stage, the Allied trainers scoffed at. For them, the trench was all; they saw little independent role for infantry. Infantry would huddle defensively in trenches or maneuver forward in masses to occupy enemy positions already conquered by tanks and an expanding artillery branch. Pershing worried that this conception of war—however logical—would demoralize his troops; they'd lose their attacking spirit. Even Foch agreed, worrying in May 1918 that French infantry had become "deformed" and "paralyzed" by their overreliance on trenches, tanks, and artillery.[7]

Pershing's preference for open warfare was rooted in national character. Seventy percent of his army were recent immigrants whom he considered special men—they had exhibited, as he put it, the "willpower and spirit to seek opportunity in a new world." They were "superior in initiative to those, their relatives, who had remained behind and submitted to the unbearable conditions in the old." Such men only needed to be molded and led. To mold them, Pershing drilled them relentlessly and maintained discipline with military policemen (MPs) and informants who intrusively monitored morale and "vice conditions" among the inflowing waves of "Selective Service men." Troops could "promenade" with women—"native or refugee"—only if the women asked them to. Given the pay of the average Doughboy, a king's ransom in France, many did, and MPs on their beats would constantly observe Doughboys behind trees, up alleys, and sprawled on park benches "engaging in familiarities" with French girls. Bolder ones got rooms in hotels and took the girls there, the well-paid French proprietors, forbidden to rent to transients, looking the other way. At home, nineteen states had already banned alcohol and the country was well on the way to a prohibition amendment to the Constitution, and so spirits were forbidden and only beer, wine, and cider (grudgingly) allowed, when the Doughs were off duty. The troops, few of them "drys," always sought cognac, banging on French doors to get it, and many smuggled bottles of whiskey over from the States in barracks bags. Prostitution was stamped out wherever detected to slow the spread of syphilis and gonorrhea, which could generate as many casualties as a machine gun. If a woman in a village was suspected of venereal disease, an MP was placed at her door, which certainly explains the irony that MPs had the highest rate of venereal disease of any branch in the AEF. "Rather than that the morals of American troops in Le Mans are very low," a snitch wrote his handler at division headquarters, "the wonder of it is that they are not low. Nowhere in America are so many opportunities of a sexual nature thrown open to the men as here."[8]

Pershing's operatives flipped through the paperwork of new recruits and looked for any signs of trouble. Men of "native American stock"—both they and their parents born in the US—were prized, German and Austrian Americans less so. Lists were made of German American recruits and their units. Private Henry Freund, whose qualification card read "Not willing to cross ocean to fight Germans, mother asked him not to cross ocean unless he had to," was placed under surveillance as a likely "defeatist." Fluency in English was anxiously monitored among the immigrant recruits. Italian and Russian

Americans were generally the most incomprehensible and uncompre- hending—"a high proportion of them speak little or no English."

Nearly 4,000 Americans applied for conscientious objector (CO) status in the war; the 1,400 who didn't get it were either court-martialed or coldly sent to France. There they'd be given a perfunctory hearing, their beliefs noted in files but otherwise ignored. If CO status hadn't saved them stateside, it certainly wouldn't save them here: "They can send me up front if they want to and they can make me shoot but they can't make me shoot at the Germans. . . . I have read it in the Bible and I believe war is wrong," one conscientious objector told his hearing. They sent him up front anyway. Free rein was given to prejudice: "The men of this draft are from Arkansas, where illiteracy is greater than any other state. They are mentally sluggish and dull." Immigrants were even more dimly viewed than rednecks: "This man, like all Italians of his class, is cowardly but not dangerous."

Informants circulated among the Doughboys and evaluated their salutes ("lacking in snap, officers seemed bored at having to return a salute"), shaves ("quite a number unshaven"), and eagerness to fight ("all anxious to get to the front"). The whole army seemed to struggle with saluting; most of the men had been in the service for little more than sixty days. They'd salute while seated. They'd salute with the wrong hand. "One officer of the 329th Infantry was observed to salute while his left hand was in his breeches' pocket. One officer had his right hand in his pocket and returned the salute of an enlisted man with his left hand. A soldier saluted from horseback without taking his cigarette from his lips. Officers forget to salute when they meet each other, especially junior officers." Most of the men just wanted to fight. Most of them were wise to the spying and snitching; one sergeant was overheard saying that members of the division's G-2 Intelligence Section "spy upon everybody else and then spy upon each other." All of the new arrivals wanted out of the rear echelons. Informants tended to agree that troublemakers "would make good fighters after they reached the front lines."[9]

Learning how to fight a war like the one on the Western Front wasn't easy. The French, British, and Germans had worked out how to fight after several years of trial and error. They'd learned how to support infantry attacks (or defense) with artillery, tanks, and aviation, and how to coordinate the various arms in the heat of battle. Now the Americans were beginning from a standing start. It was one thing to learn how to fire artillery or deploy infantry but another thing altogether to use them fluidly and effectively *together*. Bright American officers noticed a fundamental problem immediately. Pershing's *Combat Instructions* eagerly anticipated the day when the Germans would be driven from their trenches and subjected to open warfare—artillery, armor, aviation, and infantry working together on the move to pursue and destroy the enemy—but there was no actual training in this. The army's schools in France were separated by branch and specialty, with no teamwork practice between them. In America's rushed, short war, the problem would be hard to correct.[10]

To get the men across the Atlantic to fill the schools and make an army, shipping losses to the German U-boats had to be reduced. Germany's fleet of one hundred submarines was growing. It had penetrated the "safe corridor" the Royal Navy had tried to maintain between British and American waters and torpedoed 852,000 tons of Allied shipping in April 1917 alone. But that was the peak for the Germans. The British and Americans now focused on convoys. They were slow—sailing at the speed of the slowest vessel—but they were safe, as the armed escorts could deter or destroy German U-boats. May 1917 saw Allied shipping losses fall to 500,500 tons; by late autumn they were down to 200,000 tons a month. A surge in US troop shipments to France could now be made in greater safety. Indeed, the Americans would lose only a single troop ship to German U-boats in the entire course of the war.[11]

As the U-boats were defeated, shipments of American troops increased from 60,000 in May 1917 to 250,000 a month a year later. It took twenty 5,000-ton ships to move a single infantry division from America to Liverpool or Brest, ships that would be at sea for

In 1915 and again in 1917, the German navy designated the waters around the British Isles a "war zone" and targeted all civilian and military ships there. Here, a German U-boat patrols at the peak of the German unrestricted submarine warfare campaign— April 1917, when U-boats sank 852,000 tons of Allied shipping in a single month. In the 1917 campaign, U-boats would nearly sever the transatlantic connection between the US, Britain, and France. (National Archives)

six weeks, first dropping the division in England or France and then returning across the Atlantic to pick up a new division. To find troop space for a quarter of a million men a month, the US used every available hull, confiscated interned German freighters, and leaned heavily on British shipping. The AEF would never have made it to France without British shipping, which initially furnished twice as much tonnage as the Americans.

No American division sailed to France or England with its artillery and wagons; those things were left behind, for to have carried guns and wagons would have required a one-sixth reduction in manpower per division. In effect, the AEF could either send a twenty-eight-thousand-man division with its guns and wagon trains, or it could send forty-four thousand men with nothing but the shirts on their backs. Artillery and trains occupied three times more space on board than infantry. Horses were not even contemplated: "We are aghast at the tonnage that must be used if we are to bring horses from America," Pershing's headquarters commented. The manpower crisis in Britain and France was so acute—casualties had wiped out most of the military-aged recruits—that all agreed it would be wisest to send the men alone. British and French industry would provide wagons, artillery, machine guns, and even rifles for the American units. As the shipping became more predictable, it became possible to estimate the timeline and size of the AEF; assuming six divisions of infantry per month (168,000 men), plus casualty replacements at 5 percent (30,000, a number that would soar in real battle) and men from other branches (52,000), the AEF would have thirty divisions in France by July 1918, sixty divisions by December, and ninety by June 1919, when the war was expected to climax in a mighty battle for control of France and Belgium.[12]

Filing off their ships in French ports, the Doughboys, few of whom had ever traveled, were mainly disappointed. One midwestern Doughboy had expected Brest (and indeed all of Europe) to look like ancient Athens or Rome, "with flowers and trees and sculptures scattered around in stone and marble . . . and stately avenues filled with beautiful women." Instead, he was confronted with dirty cow barns, grimy cobblestones, "shapeless women clumping along in wooden shoes," and, most demoralizing of all, French *mutilés de guerre*. "I saw a man who'd lost his arm. Then one who'd lost a leg. And when we passed a man with both legs off I began to feel sick." A lieutenant in the US 28th Division remembered mainly quiet. The French seemed too depressed to cheer: "For the most part there was complete silence, except for the everlasting ring of steel boot nails on hard stones."[13]

Faced with this inflow of raw manpower, Pershing and his general staff chief, fifty-one-year-old General James Harbord, struggled to create a structure that could manage and *use* their swelling army. They were racing against the clock. The Germans were expected to transfer a million troops from conquered Russia to the Western Front in 1918 to strike a decisive blow before the German navy's submarines were neutralized by Allied countermeasures and before the Doughboys arrived in sufficient force to rescue the British and French.[14]

Pershing's instructions from the president and the secretary of war—handed to him the day he sailed for France—were to cooperate with the Allies but to "preserve the identity of the forces of the United States" under their own flag and officers. Unfortunately, the old US Army—now mingled in France with elements of a new US Army—had an incorrigible habit of bureaucracy, with a thin general staff and bloated Washington bureaus for personnel, training, supply, and every other function of the modern army. Keeping this up in wartime would be disastrous, for the modern army had to generate and process massive volumes of information every day. French line officers called World War I *la guerre de papier*—"the paper war"—and *la guerre de petit changement*—"the war of slight changes"—after the daily reams of communications sent and received and the need constantly to amend plans quickly in view of changing circumstances. A single British army headquarters spawned fifteen thousand messages every twenty-four hours, all of which had to be read and applied by reasonably intelligent people.[15]

Pershing and Harbord channeled the flood of paper, creating the army's general staff system that endures to this day. The two men appointed assistant chiefs of staff to bypass the army's meddlesome bureau chiefs and take charge of Pershing's most critical functions. Assigned to one of five sections—G-1 (General Staff 1: organization, equipment, and shipment of troops), G-2 (intelligence), G-3 (plans, strategic studies, combat operations), G-4 (supply, construction, transport, medical), and G-5 (education and training)—these assistant chiefs of staff alleviated confusion and streamlined operations, as they still do today.[16]

By now the British and French had devised a formal division of labor on the Western Front, Haig's BEF holding 100 miles of front in Flanders and Picardy, Pétain's French armies defending the remaining 350 miles from the Somme River all the way east to the Swiss border. With the French suffering the most severe manpower crisis, it made sense for the Americans to take over a piece of the French line, which they now planned to do: the usually quiet sector at the eastern end of the French line, running from the Argonne Forest across the Meuse and Moselle Rivers to the Vosges Mountains. Deployed in this space, the AEF would be optimally positioned to deliver a fatal blow to the German Empire. Even if the British and French remained stalemated on their fronts, the Americans could win the war by swinging into the rear of the German armies facing Haig and Pétain. After recovering Saint-Mihiel, the Doughboys could push the Germans behind the Meuse, seize Germany's vital coalfields in Lorraine, and then cut the German rail line from Metz to Lille and Bruges that supplied the German armies facing the British and French. The entire German war effort in France and Belgium pivoted on the as-yet-unchallenged fortress city of Metz, which the Germans had taken from France in 1871. German reinforcements and supplies had to flow through the city, as would any German withdrawal to the Rhine. If the Americans could advance their lines toward Sedan on the Meuse and Metz on the Moselle, they'd either envelop and destroy Hindenburg's armies or force them to relinquish France and Belgium.[17]

In the months since the carnage of Verdun—where nearly a million men had been chewed up in a battle that hardly budged the lines—the sector between the Meuse and Moselle had gone quiet, with the Germans and the Allies seeking decisions farther west. Pershing hoped to move his army into this now-quiet space and strike at the pivot of the whole German operation in France and Belgium. Construction materials were hauled across the Atlantic for warehouses, wharves, and railways able to shuttle forty-five thousand tons of supply every day in addition to troops and matériel between France's Atlantic ports and the American sector. To tie the four "American ports"—Brest, Saint-Nazaire, La Rochelle, and Bordeaux—to the new US sector, American engineers built supply depots at Tours, Bourges, Dijon, and Chateauroux. Pershing established his headquarters at Chaumont in part because it sat on the rail line from Saint-Nazaire to Verdun, one of the AEF's main arteries.[18]

Even as they worked to stake out an American sector, Pershing and his staff fended off insistent British and French demands that they stop planning independent operations and instead simply "amalgamate" American forces with the already-established armies of Britain and France—that is, use the Doughboys as replacements for battered French and British divisions and not as stand-alone units under US command. This was an old argument that revived every time the Allies came under severe pressure, as they were now.

After his visit to the US in May 1917, Joffre had assumed that Washington would agree to put American units under French command. We must, Joffre said, place the "young shoulders" of America under the "old head" of France. Balfour's British mission in Washington had also pushed amalgamation. Haig too: He told the Supreme War Council in January 1918 that British recruits required fifteen months of training for service on the Western Front. If the Americans didn't give their troops immediately to the Allies, they'd be of no use in any 1918 campaign.[19]

Under a barrage of Allied panic and complaints—the British and French were down to a million troops each at a time when the Germans were building to a strength of three million on the Western Front—General Tasker Bliss, President Wilson's representative on the Supreme War Council at Versailles, intermittently supported amalgamation, embarrassing Pershing, who was trying to lay down a single American line in negotiations with the Allies. General Leonard Wood, who'd been chief of staff of the army under President Taft and was now the choice of many prominent Republicans to command the AEF in place of Pershing, toured France and England in the winter of 1917–1918 and implied to the Allied governments that, were he in charge, he'd amalgamate, only compounding the pressure on Pershing, who knew that war leaders like British prime minister Lloyd George were pressing for Wood to replace him.[20]

Sent by Pétain to observe and report on the US 1st Division in November 1917, French general Auguste Hirschauer was underwhelmed by the "pick of the American army." The Doughboys were progressing in their training too slowly: "They have everything to learn." Their junior officers were of "varying quality" and would be "disoriented by battle." They exhibited little discipline: troops and officers fraternized, drunkenness was widespread, and there was no order whenever they took to the roads. March columns inevitably disintegrated, with pieces of artillery and supply columns jumbled together and every vehicle quickly filled with lazy Doughboys hitching a ride and further retarding progress. Other French officers took the same view: "American troops are arriving in impressive numbers, but they're practically useless—uninstructed, without officers and without a high command skilled in modern war."[21]

France, meanwhile, continued its slide toward the abyss. Nivelle's military fiasco had coincided with a strike wave and a food crisis, for there were no men to sow and harvest. A French wheat harvest that had averaged 255 million bushels before the war was down to just 105 million bushels in 1917. "France," Prime Minister Paul Painlevé declared on the eve of his removal in November 1917, "is at the end of its resistance." Troop morale hadn't rebounded since the mutinies. French staff officers still hadn't resumed wearing their distinctive badges, which made them targets of sneers and even assaults. Covert German subsidies continued to flow to defeatist politicians and newspapers in Paris. It was hoped that the new premier, Georges Clemenceau, nicknamed "the Tiger" for the way he gnawed through his enemies, would turn things around. He certainly *sounded* different from his predecessors. Clemenceau arrested hundreds of defeatists, dismissed weak ministers, and vowed to win. "No more pacifist campaigns, no treachery, no semi-treachery—only war," Clemenceau affirmed.[22]

To wage that war, Clemenceau made regular visits to the American divisions to assess their potential and urge them along. In their own estimate of the situation in November 1917, Pershing's headquarters staff concluded that the war might already be lost. The French army and public now believed that "America had come in too late to be of use." France's "immense weariness" and Britain's growing frustration with the war and its costs made the threat of an Allied capitulation before the AEF became operational real. "The British government and governing class" no longer had the appetite for "extraordinary sacrifices merely to keep France and Italy going." Lloyd George told

US envoy Colonel Edward House in December 1917 that the war was all but lost: "We shall be hard pressed to hold our own and keep Italy standing during 1918. Our man-power is pretty well exhausted. We can only call up men of 45–50 and boys of 17." The British prime minister expected nothing more from his principal ally: "France is done." Only the Americans could "keep the fight going," but they weren't fighting; they were scattered in camps from the North Sea to Switzerland, learning about modern war.[23]

Pershing frantically whipped the AEF into shape. He fired a third of the generals who'd shipped over to France with him as insufficiently aggressive. They were dinosaurs who'd attained the rank of general after decades of toil in the small US Army. The commander of the Big Red One, General William Sibert, an engineer who'd spent the last seven years supervising the construction of the Panama Canal, was among the first to go. Pershing sent him home to the States "in the interest of greater efficiency" and replaced him with General Robert Lee Bullard. Sibert's troops, one officer recalled, "did not seem to re-alize that they were on the verge of a big war." Sibert himself seemed overcome with "pessimism"—the cardinal sin to Pershing.[24]

Bullard was ordered to make attacking troops out of the 1st Di-vision. He immediately set to work removing what he called "incor-rigibles." In January 1918, he ordered "quick and drastic methods" to deal with enlisted slackers, duties so "arduous and dangerous" that they'd become "a subject of fear" among the men. Discipline and efficiency had to be imposed at every level; leaders who failed were sent home, covered in shame. "War is a ruthless taskmaster," Captain George Marshall reflected as he weighed the reliefs and re-placements. It demands "success regardless of confusion, shortness of time, and paucity of tools." Often there was as little justice in reliefs as there was on the battlefield: "One man sacrifices his life on the battlefield and another sacrifices his reputation elsewhere, both in the same cause," wrote Marshall.[25]

For now, no one imagined deploying *this* US Army to the bat-tlefield. It was that bad. Every National Guard division that arrived in the winter mud and slush had its eccentricities and defects. None were exactly comparable in personnel or equipment. Pershing sent Colonel Hugh Drum to inspect the 42nd Rainbow Division for two days in December 1917 as it marched off to train in Saint-Blin. The division's general staff chief, Colonel Douglas MacArthur, already a public relations guru, had conceived the idea—as Newton Baker's military aide—to expand the division from its New York and New Jersey core to embody twenty-six Guard units from twenty-six states and the District of Columbia. The finished product, MacArthur assured Baker, would "stretch over the whole country like a rainbow."

Colonel Drum judged the resulting rainbow "distinctly bad." Important things were lacking because no one had thought to create a supply system. To Drum's amazement, some of the units were still living on travel rations that had been issued to them in New York a month earlier. Unimportant things were piled everywhere, which suggested that for many American divisions, troop space on the ships from America had been wasted, sometimes spectacularly. MacArthur's Rainbow Division had sneaked dozens of washing machines and several hundred five-hundred-pound stoves onto its ships, all of which were now abandoned as useless. Units marched with wagonloads of tent pins and tent poles but no tents. Officers arrived in France with three or more trunks of clothing each. Drum found that every American division he inspected had far too many filing cabinets, desks, and office chairs.

Because only men (and the odd stove and washing machine) had been shipped from the States, the AEF was absurdly undermotorized. The headquarters of the 1st Division had just one car—a Cadillac. Whenever George Marshall used it, even for the most urgent business, he felt guilty for "immobilizing the division." The entire twenty-eight-thousand-man division had a grand total of three cars, three motorcycles, and two trucks.[26]

Troop columns on ruck marches vanished in the cold, foggy backcountry of France. More than once Drum happened upon oblivious sentries standing guard over units that had long since marched away. They wouldn't have gone far; Drum observed the units staggering along beneath the weight of their own equipment as well as that of units that hadn't arrived yet. Those Doughboys already in France were being used as a "left luggage" office for those who weren't, lugging French-issued artillery, machine guns, automatic rifles, ammunition, helmets, field shoes, and gas masks for themselves and for their comrades still in transit from America. Many of the men shivered without overcoats or blankets, those items having been loaded on ships from New York that had turned back. The division's rolling kitchens couldn't be brought on the march because there weren't enough horses to pull them. An entire regiment had to be quarantined with the flu.[27]

The winter of 1917–1918 was brutally cold and wet in France. Morale sagged in every army. The Germans, having already lost five million men and officers in the war, struggled to maintain their legendary military effectiveness with an army whose dwindling manpower wasn't what it used to be. *Der Mann für seinen Offizier und der Offizier für seinen Mann*—"the men for their officer and the officer for his men"—was a Prussian army motto that stressed the organic connection between tough officers and obedient troops. Enlisted men obeyed the officer not because he was liked but because he upheld discipline and led fearlessly from the front. That army was dead, a fact proclaimed by increasingly anxious memos from Hindenburg, Ludendorff, and even the kaiser himself, ordering the German generals to do something about increasingly timid, well-fed reserve officers hated by their hungry, desperate troops, who passed menus filched from the officers' mess through the trenches and gaped resentfully at their delicacies. Hindenburg worried that many German officers, terrified or merely exasperated by the endless war, simply "didn't want to be leaders" anymore. The risks were too great and the rewards too small. Hindenburg assigned "education officers" to every German division; their job was to assemble battalions for invigorating lectures that would make sense of an increasingly senseless war. Just how edifying the troops found these wonkish lectures—"Our 2.5 billion marks of gold reserves have permitted us to increase the notes in circulation"— is unknown, but trench newspapers, cinemas, and concerts, laid on for units behind the lines, were surely welcomed.[28]

For now, not having endured three years of slaughter like the others, American morale was impacted chiefly by the weather. It was the coldest winter in fifty years, and every barracks in the French training areas had signs saying *Pas de bois*—"No firewood"—meaning that troops shivered through the days and the nights in subzero temperatures. Young Men's Christian Association (YMCA) huts, established to provide some comforts of home, were the only places where the Doughboys could warm up. Officers in Pershing's headquarters dubbed it "the Winter of Valley Forge." Captain Marshall called it "the most depressing, gloomy period of the war. . . . When we were not cursed with mud, we were frozen with the cold." Trenches were miserable and dugouts as bad, icy water seeping through the rock and earthen roofs, soaking bunks and pooling on the floors. The disconnect between Pershing's continuing exhortations about "open warfare" and "offensive spirit" and the realities of the frozen front struck American junior officers as insane. Our generals, they said, during evenings around a fireless grate, "have learned nothing since Custer, and apparently can't learn." They insist on the attack "when any fool can see that it's the Germans, and not us, who are going to attack."[29]

The infusion of National Army talent into the mossbacked regular army led to dispiriting showdowns between the "old army" types who taught and the restless new men who learned. "I ain't had a college education, I ain't as fortunate as you, but what do *you* know about providing for the messing of a company," one old-timer said to a group of new 1st Division officers in France. "Winning the war," came the reply from the back of the room, wreathed in sardonic laughter. Italy's defeat at Caporetto in October 1917 meant that precious French and British divisions had to be rushed to northern Italy to hold the line of the Piave River. The rolling stock diverted for that purpose cost the Americans dearly. Forage for their horses disappeared. An officer with the 1st Division recalled watching his famished horses and mules chewing up the woodwork of their stalls and eating their bridles and halter straps. On one exercise, so many American horses dropped dead from hunger that the exercise had to be canceled. With American supplies stuck at the base ports, unable to reach the troops because of the Italian emergency, even shoes ran out. Marshall saw Doughboys on winter route marches and exercises without shoes, limping along with their feet wrapped in gunnysacks. In eighteen years of service, he'd never seen misery like this: "The men frequently stood up to their knees in mud, snow, and ice water for hours at a time."[30]

The British and French looked on impassively. Resentment of the Americans was beginning to seethe in the Allied ranks and head-quarters. Pershing still had only four poorly trained and equipped di-visions in France, yet the Germans were busily shifting fifty divisions from Russia to France for a vast spring offensive with more than two hundred divisions. The Allies read with amazement the text of Pres-ident Wilson's speech to both houses of Congress on January 8. He skipped over the gritty military facts emerging in France and adopted a high moral tone. "What we demand in this war is, that the world be made fit and safe to live in." He ended with a prediction that was most remarkable for what it left out—the US Army's unpreparedness: "The moral climax of this the culminating and final war for human lib-erty has come." Even the sympathetic *New York Times* rolled its eyes. Orate less and fight more, the editors enjoined the president. "Further and satisfactory progress must be made in *fighting Germans*."[31]

But fighting Germans had never been easy, and it hadn't gotten any easier. By March 1918, when the Germans finally concluded their separate peace with the Russians at Brest-Litovsk and seized 90 per-cent of Russia's coal and a third of its population and arable land, the American draft had yielded forty-four twenty-eight-thousand-man divisions. But thirty-seven of those divisions were still organizing themselves in the United States; just three were deployed near combat sectors in France; three others were in France training or debarking in the Atlantic ports; and another—the US 3rd Division—was at sea and scheduled to arrive in early April. These seven bloated American divisions—each the size of three French divisions—might eventu-ally cause the Germans some harm. For the moment, they seemed to be harming only French stationmasters, who complained that it took two or three times as many trains to move an American division as a

French division. The French could only hope that American combat power would catch up to American manpower.[32]

In Washington in January 1918, fifty-four-year-old General Peyton March became the army's third chief of staff in less than a year, its fifth since the war had begun. An artillery officer who'd fought in the Philippines and served alongside Pershing as a US military attaché to the Japanese army during the Russo-Japanese War, March arrived at the War Department wielding a "new broom" to sweep the place clean of old personnel and routines. He was astonished to learn that everyone on the general staff—including his predecessor, General Tasker Bliss—went home at 5 p.m., as if there weren't a war on. Unopened sacks of mail and dispatches lay around the hallways. Even when Bliss had been active, he'd been a problem, spending "hours over things that ought to have been handled in seconds," March sourly noted.[33]

March found the offices of the secretary of war and the adjutant general as deserted as those of the general staff. Secretary of War Baker had an annoying habit of summoning the general staff chief to his office with a buzzer, as if he were a valet. March had an aide rip the wires from the wall. Having studied the methods of the German general staff, March injected discipline and work into the staff, strengthened the intelligence component, and added new departments for innovations like chemical warfare. He pressured the secretary of war to grant him German-like powers in his role as staff chief: "The Chief of Staff must take rank and precedence over *all* officers of the Army." March made many enemies—"One is proud to be hated if it is a consequence of doing one's work well," he liked to say—and would tangle with Pershing frequently, viewing Pershing's autocratic command in France as a violation of the German all-power-to-the-general-staff principle that he (and Pershing) so admired. March also resisted Pershing's cult of the offensive, insisting that recruits in the States be trained for trench warfare, a sound doctrine that had been adopted by the War Department in August 1917. In this bureaucratic struggle, March was hobbled by the simple fact that Pershing had taken the army's best officers with him to France. March, who'd been among those best and brightest taken to France (as Pershing's artillery director) before returning to Washington, was stuck with the dregs, which only heightened his frustration at Pershing's independence. "I wish March was more human," Pershing said after an argument. "He would be happier."[34]

Somehow President Wilson had to accelerate the AEF's deployment to meet the gathering German storm. By the time Peyton March took over as general staff chief in Washington, the Germans had already shunted 46 divisions—700,000 men plus artillery—from the Eastern Front to the Western Front. In early February 1918 the Germans had 174 divisions on the Western Front; in early March, 182; in mid-March, 188, with 20 more on the way. An army that had kept only 137 of its 256 divisions on the Western Front would shortly have 220 of them there.[35]

For the Allies, this combination of German muscle and mobility—so unusual in this creaking, bureaucratic war—was immensely threatening. An enterprising US staff officer found a simple way to compute just how threatening. Taking the 150,000-man Belgian army of 1918 as the basic unit of measurement—1—the American officer calculated the strength of the opposing combat forces on the Western Front thus: Belgium 1, Britain 10.5, France 12.75, America 0.75. With all of their contingents added together, the Allies had a total strength of 25. Germany alone had a strength of 26. But the real German superiority was even greater, because Ludendorff still had fifteen uncommitted assault divisions on the Eastern Front, which could be rushed west for a knockout blow.[36]

Bickering between Pershing and the French, who could feel the massive German spring offensive approaching, intensified. Clemenceau proposed through his ambassador in Washington that American regiments spend some time in a French division until "they became accustomed to actual front conditions." Pershing agreed. He had little choice: what little experience of combat the regular army and National Guard had picked up in Mexico was irrelevant in this theater of industrialized, artillery-intensive trench warfare. It was agreed that American divisions would spend an apprenticeship with

Troops of the US 42nd Rainbow Division—these are the "Fighting Irish" of New York—take over from a French division in the quiet (note the standing trees) Vosges sector. This marked a kind of graduation; from this point forward, these men would be regarded as combat troops who could be deployed at any time in any sector against the Germans. (National Archives)

French or British corps before going into the line as a part of an independent American army in a purely American sector.

The 26th Yankee Division's apprenticeship was the model for all of the others. In mid-February 1918, it was attached to the French XI Corps in a quiet sector of the Chemin des Dames, site of the disastrous Nivelle Offensive the previous spring. There infantry companies of the 26th—the second American division to arrive in France—would alternate in line with French companies. American batteries would fire alongside French batteries to learn their barrage techniques. During this phase, the American division would be under the tactical command of the French. None of this training was without risk. Twenty-two-year-old Captain Mark Clark, who would command Allied forces in the Mediterranean during World War II, became one of the first American casualties of the war when he was

cut down and nearly killed by German shrapnel in his division's training sector in the Vosges. Less exalted figures than Clark died in a
steady drip, the US Army's archives of the war peppered with forgotten tragedies like this: "McColgan and Morgan killed by 105mm at
10 P.M." On the Western Front, as war poet Siegfried Sassoon put
it, "Brother Lead and Sister Steel" were always at work, killing or
maiming men or driving them mad with fear.[37]

In this training phase, the Doughboy had a weird, bifurcated existence, succinctly described by Captain George Marshall: "He sang
French songs and was virtually a Frenchman during the forenoon,
and spent the afternoon being cussed out as an American 'rookie.'"
As the Doughs gained confidence, they'd form larger formations.
Mishaps were frequent, especially when the Germans attacked
with poison gas, which always spooked new units. In the Vosges,
an American lieutenant recalled that the Germans would mass ten
thousand heavy trench mortars—called *Minenwerfer*—to fire ten
thousand two-hundred-pound bombs of poison gas simultaneously
into the American lines. The big gas shells would tumble silently
through the air and explode, usually at night, when many of the men
were asleep without their gas masks. Whole American companies
could be wiped out in this way. The Germans would also use gas to
eliminate outposts, as terse reports to division made clear: "The enemy fired gas projectiles; there were 3 men in one listening post; two
adjusted masks, one stampeded, lost his head, screamed and ran to
the rear without adjusting respirator. He is dead."[38]

Once a degree of terror-dampening experience had been achieved,
the French would be withdrawn and an American division formed of
battle-tested battalions would take over its own sector of the French
corps's area. This marked a kind of graduation, when the American
division would finally be judged ready to fight independently on the
Western Front. American units training with the British first absorbed a course of instruction, then went into the line as battalions,
and then finally as regiments. During the battalion service, the British would send small groups of American officers and troops into the
line for forty-eight-hour periods, then complete platoons for up to

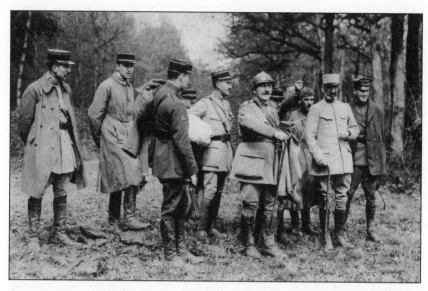

American units arriving in France required instruction in trench warfare from French or British trainers. Here, an unmistakable Colonel Douglas MacArthur (far right), staff chief of the US 42nd Division, observes a practice maneuver of his division alongside his French advisers. (National Archives)

three days, then companies for three days, then whole battalions and regiments for five to six weeks. When the units had learned all that there was to learn, the US division would reconstitute itself and the Americans would take a place in the British line.[39]

Everyone wondered if the US Army could become operational in time to fight in 1918. Doubts about this remained the chief rationale for amalgamation: that the Americans were dangerously ignorant of the strides in warfare that the Europeans had been making in this appalling conflict. Since 1915, for example, Allied and German gunners had been using airplane and flash spotting as well as sound ranging by specially trained observation units to locate and destroy enemy artillery batteries. Planes would fly over enemy lines to map the location of batteries or observe the fall of shells, delivering precise feedback to their side's artillery. Flash spotting revealed the enemy guns, and sound ranging—calculating the exact location of an enemy battery by timing the arrival of its sound wave—permitted accurate counterbattery fire as well as the ranging and correcting of one's own guns. Little of this had been attempted by Americans, much less technical nuances like allowing for wind and temperature changes or distinguishing between the slow "gun wave" and the fast "shell wave"—that is, isolating the all-important sound of the gun from the unimportant sound of the shell using microphones. The US Army's senior artillery officer in 1918, the general who had commanded Pershing's artillery in Mexico, initially refused even to use aircraft for spotting, calling them "no damn good." The AEF's learning curve was going to be steep, and slicked with blood.[40]

Then there was the crushing new emphasis on artillery itself. To soften up German defenses on the Somme in 1916, the British artillery had fired what seemed a breathtaking quantity of munitions at the German lines—1.7 million shells. A year later, when the British attacked in their great Passchendaele Offensive, they fired 4.3 million shells into the German lines before going over the top. This emphasis on artillery reshaped the European armies, which saw their artillery personnel, equal to half the strength of the infantry in 1916, increase to 85 percent of the infantry strength by 1917. British armies advancing or even rearranging their lines in this period were laying 3,300 miles of signal cable every week to handle all of the telephone traffic needed to ensure that British troops went to the right places and British salvos landed on the Germans, not on the British (or French). The Americans were shipping divisions to France constructed with obsolete ratios, technologies, and expectations. They would land in Europe like a man stepping off a moving bus; they'd either slam face-first onto the pavement or, at best, lurch awkwardly down the road till they found their balance. The infantry-centered battle exalted by Pershing seemed to be a relic of the past, crushed to a bloody pulp by artillery and the telephone.[41]

As winter turned to spring in 1918, the great German "Victory Offensive" was imminent. Ludendorff had presided over a meeting of the staff chiefs of the two great German army groups on the Western Front in November 1917. They had studied the field to determine whether to strike west against the British or south against the French. The Germans considered Britain the dominant partner in the Entente thanks to French casualties and demoralization. Ludendorff wanted to knock out the British; if the BEF collapsed, he felt certain that the French would surrender too, rather than continue the war alone.

The problem, however, was that the British were installed on and behind terrain that the Germans had devastated during their strategic withdrawal to the Hindenburg Line in 1917. Devastated is merely a word; actually to witness what the Germans had done was to understand the tactical problems presented. They'd smashed houses down to their foundations, cratered the roads and felled trees across them, burned away all cover, rigged mines and booby traps, demolished bridges, and ruined wells and reservoirs. Their objective had been to delay and hinder any British assault on the new German trench line. But if they now wanted to destroy the BEF, they'd have to cross this desolated landscape themselves. An attack on the French army offered better terrain but was less likely to be decisive, as the French army—unlike the British, which had its back to the English Channel—had almost unlimited strategic depth for a retreat. That had been one lesson of the Franco-Prussian War, when the Germans had exhausted themselves chasing the French army through the vast hinterland south of Paris. Ludendorff concluded the meeting thus: "We must strike at the earliest possible moment . . . before the Americans can throw strong forces into the scale. We must beat the British."[42]

Noting the approach of this German war machine, President Wilson softened his stance toward Berlin, hoping the Germans might agree to peace negotiations *before* they crushed the Allied armies. Speaking to Congress on February 11, 1918, Wilson appeared to retract the Fourteen Points and replace them with just four principles. Now he recast former "demands" like the German return of Alsace-Lorraine and all Russian and Rumanian territory stripped from those beaten countries as mere "suggestions." The Fourteen Points, Wilson now said, were not so much a "pledge" as a "provisional sketch." Sounding like a man frightened by the German juggernaut and determined to wean Berlin from war by any means, Wilson concluded: "I, of course, do not mean that the peace of the world depends upon the acceptance of any particular set of suggestions."[43]

Major Paul Clark, Pershing's liaison in French general staff chief Foch's headquarters, reported in mid-February that the French had definite information that the great German attack would come in early March and would feature the Hutier tactics used to such crippling effect against the Russians in September 1917, when the Germans had crossed the broad Dvina River and taken Riga—a seemingly impossible task—nearly annihilating a Russian army and shortening Berlin's lines on the Eastern Front, the prerequisite for moving troops west. "The essential feature of the new [Hutier] tactics was surprise," leveraged by a stealthy massing of heavy artillery. The victory at Riga had been followed by the no-less-spectacular rout of the Italians at Caporetto. Caporetto paid a triple dividend: it neutralized the Italians, freed up Austro-Hungarian troops for service in France, and increased Rome's demands on French and British manpower and industry. The British had planned a 40 percent increase in their artillery on the Western Front but would fail to meet the target because of the need to replace so many surrendered Italian guns.[44]

The Germans would almost certainly strike on the Western Front between Saint-Quentin and Cambrai, the always-brittle hinge between the British and French armies and a place that the Germans had earlier devastated and yielded and that the French—assuming the Germans wouldn't return—hadn't bothered to fortify as stoutly as other parts of their line. At Cambrai in November 1917, the British had shown that the trench system could be broken by surprise attack with massed tanks, but they'd failed to push their attack home because their reserves had been exhausted at Passchendaele. And they'd hesitated anyway, Ludendorff shrewdly noting that the British had become so reliant on artillery barrages to advance that their "infantry attack had lost all impetus of its own." British platoon and company commanders robotically advanced behind the barrage at the Somme, Arras, Messines, Passchendaele, and Cambrai, but they rarely exploited emerging opportunities.[45]

"It was commonly said that if you took a French or English soldier out of the trenches and into the open he felt like a man stripped of everything," General Robert Lee Bullard noted at the time, and that was certainly the case at Cambrai. This was why Pershing deplored British and French tactics; they were ultimately, as another of his generals put it, a "doctrine of defeat and failure." Ludendorff had no such inhibitions and no such constraints. He was radically revising German tactics to stress initiative and exploitation, and, having beaten the Russians and Italians, he for once had ample reserves. The Germans could burn through a hundred divisions on the Western Front and still have at least fifty assault divisions left over—half a million troops—for a last stab at victory. Clark reported raw fear in French headquarters: "They express their capacity to meet the attack, but there is in their thought a very perceptible amount of anxiety that they may not." The Germans were not only bringing large numbers of troops from the Eastern Front; they were bringing so many gun batteries that they would have artillery superiority in all calibers wherever they wanted it.[46]

Clark also met in February with the British mission to Foch's headquarters: Generals Sidney Clive and Johnny Du Cane. He found them weirdly *yearning* for a German attack. The risks of a German breakthrough to the sea were high but arguably outweighed by the risks of continuing stalemate. Only a German defeat would end "this diabolical murder at such terrific financial cost," the British said. Clive's deputy, Colonel Eric Dillon, warned that "in case the Germans don't attack and the two hostile lines stand in deadlock, facing each other, it's possible that Germany will take the attitude that where our trenches lie is our frontier." In other words, that's how the war would end—the Germans too strong to be driven out of France and Belgium, the French and British too weak to drive them out.

For the French and British, an enemy offensive entailing massive German casualties seemed to be their last best hope, as Clark reported "quite a general acceptance" among the French and British officers that "the Allies are not able to drive the Germans out of France." Whereas the Germans had developed their full manpower and industrial resources early in the war and kept the pipeline full ever since, the British had been so slow to transition from an eighty-thousand-man professional army to a million-man drafted army that what gains they'd made with conscription had been continually eroded by the massive losses they and their Allies had sustained in the first three years of the war when the British, a crucial combatant, were still weak in men, guns, and shells. Haig later judged this the principal reason for the length and futility of the war: Britain had gone off half-cocked, sacrificing first-rate troops to buy time for the training of their increasingly mediocre replacements. The French had no plans for a 1918 offensive if the Germans stood pat; their demoralized troops would probably refuse to go over the top. The French general staff admitted as much: "The army has lost many of its offensive qualities. . . . The day is approaching when a large offensive by us must be curtailed because we cannot fill the vacancies in our units."[47]

Major Claude Rozet, who liaised with American officers at Pétain's headquarters, admitted that the French government no longer believed that it would recover Alsace-Lorraine. Unable to win the war, the French would trade their claim to the "lost provinces" for some of the occupied territory that lay before them now, honeycombed with German trenches and bunkers and crammed with German storm troops. Only German self-immolation—offensives in the open against Allied trenches—and "a final and crushing blow by the American forces" could reset the balance of power and end the war.[48]

For their part, German staff officers interviewed after the war confessed that they wildly underestimated the number of American troops in France and wildly overestimated the deterrent threat of their U-boats. They read the free American press with its (accurate) accounts of American deployments to France and assumed that they were lies. "The openness with which the American authorities announced the number of troops arriving in France each month had absolutely deceived the German Staff as it could not conceive of the Americans announcing the *true* figures." In early 1918, the Germans assumed that the Americans had next to nothing in France. Even at the end of 1918, the Germans would assume that the Americans had no more than fifteen divisions in France, when they actually had forty-two. This overconfidence made Hindenburg even more eager to strike as quickly as possible.[49]

So certain were the Allies that the Germans were about to punch with everything they had that Secretary of War Baker himself sailed for Brest in late February 1918. He arrived there on March 11 to visit with Pershing; meet his French counterparts; tour the American port, supply, training, hospital, and rail facilities; and see for himself the state of the AEF infantry, artillery, and Air Service. Baker, the unbloodied Ohio politician, was bearing no particular expertise. He called his tour a "purely military pilgrimage." He briefed the staff officers at Pershing's Chaumont headquarters and described himself as "a boy who takes apart a watch to see how it is made in order to understand the functions of its parts." On March 19, Secretary Baker traveled to the front, visited with the 42nd Rainbow Division, and went all the way forward to a frontline trench, where he declared: "Now I am on the frontier of freedom."[50]

5

THE KAISER'S BATTLE

O N March 21, 1918, two days after Secretary Baker visited the front, Hindenburg and Ludendorff struck that "frontier of freedom" with 3.5 million troops and seven thousand guns organized in two hundred divisions. This was the long-awaited *Kaiserschlacht*, "kaiser's battle," a series of brutal German offensives intended to divide and annihilate the British and French armies before the Americans could deploy in force. Ludendorff was prepared to expend 1.5 million troops in this effort—"a pretty good packet," as a British war correspondent put it. In fact, it was more than "pretty good." With Pétain's seven armies sharing just thirty-nine reserve divisions and Haig's frontline divisions 25 percent below their normal strength because of the casualties at Passchendaele, Ludendorff's blows were likely to win the war.[1]

The first German offensive was Operation Michael, named for the patron saint of Germany and the archangel of deliverance. Where the German U-boats had failed to bring the Allies down, the German army would have to succeed. As one British analyst put it, "The submarine panacea for victory had been replaced by a military panacea."[2]

Ludendorff's spearhead had seventy-four divisions, with six thousand guns and thirty-five hundred trench mortars. It lined up against just thirty-three British divisions, which were still fully occupied trying to scrape cover and usable roads out of the desert left by the German retreat in 1917.

Ludendorff called this offensive in Picardy—the region surrounding Amiens—a "maneuver of rupture." Unable to flank the Allies, whose lines ran literally into the sea, he wagered everything on shock and awe. "Just make a hole," he liked to say. "The rest will follow." The Germans would break through and then decapitate the Allied headquarters and artillery networks behind the lines, defeating the British and French armies as effectually as they'd beaten the Russians and Italians. Ludendorff would employ the "storm troop" tactics tested at Riga and Caporetto to smash through the center of the Allied armies, separate them, and then roll them up from the flanks thus created.[3]

Ludendorff would have preferred to strike the British in Flanders. He had a contingency plan for that—Operation St. George—in which the Germans would attack along both sides of the Ypres salient and meet at Hazebrouck to trap the BEF, cut its vital north-south railway, and push Haig into the sea. But with fresh memories of the British floundering in the mud of Passchendaele, Ludendorff took up Operation Michael instead. The Germans would still attack the British, but on the firmer ground of Picardy. The attack with three German armies would be anchored in the south, near the hinge with the French army on the Oise River, by General Oskar von Hutier's Eighteenth Army. Hutier would sidestep forward, nudging the Tommies back between La Fère and Péronne while using the Oise and Somme Rivers as shields to block the arrival of the Allied reserve divisions that would presumably hasten north if Haig were on the brink of defeat. The sector thus sealed against any French (or American) reserves, the decisive thrusts of Operation Michael would be delivered by General Georg von der Marwitz's Second Army and General Otto von Below's Seventeenth Army. Driving into the space between Péronne and Arras, seizing the key junctions of Bapaume and Albert, the armies of Marwitz and Below would shatter the fifteen divisions of General Hubert Gough's Fifth Army and the fourteen divisions of General Julian Byng's Third Army, then wheel north to demolish the other half of Haig's BEF.[4]

General von Below, who'd crushed the Italians at Caporetto five months earlier and brought his army here from Italy, commanded Ludendorff's right wing. General von der Marwitz, who'd won the coveted Pour le Mérite fighting the Russians, commanded the Second Army in the center, and General Oskar von Hutier led the Eighteenth Army on the left. Hutier's army had been part of the big strategic shift from east to west, traveling all the way from Latvia, where it had pioneered the new storm troop tactics at Riga. Those so-called Hutier tactics were expected to sweep all before them here. They essentially restored surprise, initiative, and movement to the stalemated Great War battlefield. German artillery and troops were brought up quietly at night; axle boxes were muffled, horse hooves wrapped in gunnysacks, and harness buckles greased to silence the massive nocturnal deployments. These stealthy formations—which were kept thirty miles behind the lines to deceive the enemy and then moved in rapid night marches to the point of attack—were massed before dawn in camouflaged trenches and dugouts. Artillery was concentrated as never before—one gun for every ten yards of front—promising a stunning effect when the cannon and howitzers opened fire.[5]

Colonel Georg Bruchmüller arrived to direct the fire of the six thousand German guns in this sector. The colonel had completely reworked German artillery tactics to extract maximum advantage from Hutier's storm troops. Under Bruchmüller's guidance, the typical World War I multiday bombardment, which alerted the enemy to a pending offensive, was replaced with a short, brutally accurate storm of fire that mixed high explosive, gas, and smoke shells. The fire landed so intensely that it was called "drum fire" (*Trommelfeuer*), because the detonations sounded like the seamless beating of a snare drum. Allied barbed wire would be cut by heavy-caliber *Minenwerfer*, trench mortars that the Germans would smuggle into their advanced positions just before the attack. This was another important advance. Cutting wire with artillery inevitably sacrificed surprise, as

Allied troops feared the German *Minenwerfer* trench mortar more than any other weapon. Its 25cm bombs, shown here, were filled with poison gas or ammonium nitrate—an explosive too volatile to be fired from high-velocity field artillery—and flung silently into the enemy trenches or wire. The British called them "Moaning Minis" for the way they arrived with a barely audible sigh, inflicting devastating casualties. (National Archives)

it would take hundreds of rounds of 75mm or 77mm shells to cut just a five-meter gap in the wire. The 25cm *Minenwerfer*, lobbing what amounted to a massive fertilizer bomb directly onto the enemy wire from short range, did the trick instantly.

German assault divisions would maintain the terrific momentum of an attack by organizing in depth. Ludendorff ended the old infantry practice of assaulting in waves, successive waves of infantry passing through one another to assault enemy lines. When the first wave took the first line, it would rest while a second passed through it to assault the second line, and so on. Now Ludendorff ordered the first group of storm troops to keep going, to the limit of their endurance, to reach and destroy the enemy artillery before it could fire effectively or be moved to safety. Now each assault division refreshed itself from its own reserves and kept going. Two regiments in front, one in reserve, each regiment echeloned in battalions, each battalion in companies, the companies themselves often broken into detachments of a dozen men armed with light machine guns, mortars, and grenades. These storm troops would sprint across no-man's-land, shrouded by smoke shells and dust clouds and preceded by the *Feuerwalze* (fire waltz), a creeping barrage that forced surviving defenders to keep their heads down. The storm troops, hugging the barrage as never before—German assault battalions were trained to run right up to its destructive edge—would sprint through gaps in the wire, drop into the enemy trenches, kill their startled occupants with grenades, knives, pistols, and light machine guns, and keep going. Groups behind the storm troops would set up heavy machine guns, hustle artillery forward, and provide reserves and defense in depth should the stunned enemy ever counterattack. Only the last group would pause to mop up conquered ground while the leading elements raced ahead.[6]

Leadership was emphasized as never before. The risk-averse British and French were neglecting infantry combat and leaning heavily on tanks and artillery. Allied offensives, even when successful, would halt at their objective, awaiting new orders and more fire support. Ludendorff instructed his troop commanders never to content themselves with so little. If successful in their first rush, they had to keep going, to multiply the disorienting effects on the enemy.[7]

The German assault teams carried maps—updated by aerial reconnaissance and prisoner interrogations—that revealed every enemy dugout, machine-gun nest, and gun emplacement. German aircraft would fly overhead to reconnoiter, strafe, and bomb. These tactics were the precursor of *Blitzkrieg*. They aimed to decapitate enemy units by spreading panic, demolishing headquarters, neutralizing artillery, and cutting communications between Allied units. Ludendorff expected his storm troops to advance eight miles on March 21, which would get them into the Allied rear areas, where they could eliminate command posts, capture the enemy artillery, and sow panic. This, the Germans hoped, would be the beginning of the end.[8]

Finding himself at the center of this German storm, General Hubert Gough, commanding the British Fifth Army in the space between

Saint-Quentin and Amiens, struggled to implement German-style elastic defense in a wasteland devoid of cover, roads, and trenches. Haig had given Gough forty-eight thousand laborers to build a three-tiered battle zone, but in the weeks before the German onslaught they'd been entirely occupied rebuilding the cratered roads. Without proper roads—the Germans had destroyed them in 1917—Gough couldn't bring up building materials or communications gear, and so Gough's forward, battle, and rear zones were undeveloped, without sufficient wire, trenches, battery positions, or telephones. The men took shelter in unfinished trenches that they called "blobs"—hastily sandbagged redoubts.[9]

Operation Michael began rolling over the British trenches on March 21, heralded by an unprecedentedly destructive bombardment by six thousand guns along a front of thirty-five miles at 5 a.m. Minister of Munitions Winston Churchill, visiting the British 9th Division when Operation Michael commenced, recalled the fury of the drum fire on the British positions:

> And then, exactly as a pianist runs his hands across the keyboard from treble to bass, there rose in less than one minute the most tremendous cannonade I shall ever hear. . . . It swept round us in a wide curve of red leaping flame stretching to the north far along the front of the Third Army as well as of the Fifth Army on the south, and quite unending in either direction. . . . The enormous explosions of the shells upon our trenches seemed almost to touch each other, with hardly an interval in space or time. . . . The weight and intensity of the bombardment surpassed anything which anyone had ever known before.

Churchill was spared the horrors of the hastily improvised forward and battle zones, where tons of shells and gas landed, collapsing trenches, cutting belts of wire, grinding the "blobs" to dust, cutting whatever phone lines had been laid, slaughtering the artillery's horse lines, smashing artillery pieces and obliterating their crews, and detonating ammo dumps. The German guns shifted their fire from the forward to the battle zone and back again for four and a half hours. For the defenders, many of them new recruits, panic and fear were accentuated by a thick fog welling from all of the waterways in the region, which enclosed them in a narrow hell of gas and shell bursts.[10]

At 9:40 a.m., the German assault divisions went over the top. Racing through the fog, they overwhelmed the British forward zone, sprinting in among the Tommies, flinging stick grenades, and butchering the blinded, coughing, concussed British infantry with light machine guns and flamethrowers. Fog was so thick that the fighting was usually done at a range of fifty yards or less, each startled British outpost blazing away at point-blank range until overwhelmed. The Germans passed swiftly through the forward zone, still shrouded in fog, dust, and smoke. Using maps and compasses, they pushed into the battle zone. Here, the German attack began to meet resistance. At the southern end of the line, where Hutier's Eighteenth Army was attempting to seal the front along the Oise and the Crozat Canal, the fog persisted, and Hutier made better progress than expected. For the defenders in this zone, the Germans appeared out of the mist like ghosts. "I don't remember in the whole war an intenser taste of hell," a British battalion commander recalled.[11]

The three corps of General Gough's Fifth Army were effectively destroyed. North of them, where the storm troops of Below's Seventeenth Army attacked toward Bapaume and Arras, the Germans found that General Julian Byng had foolishly packed the frontline trenches of his Third Army with troops who should have been deployed farther back, beyond the reach of the German drum fire. The storm troops found most of those Tommies dead, wounded, or driven mad by the blasts. British runners carrying urgent messages back to headquarters found the command posts already in German hands. The advance was that fast. Whole British platoons were exterminated by the German bombardment, many of the Tommies killed not by shell splinters but by the hurtling heads, torsos, and limbs of their fellows. Only in the center, where Gough's Fifth Army attached its flank to Byng's Third Army around Albert, did the fog lift. There the real risks of open warfare to the attacker became evident around

11 a.m., when the assault divisions of Marwitz's Second Army loped into the battle zone. With good visibility and over two hours to reorganize themselves after the morning's drum fire, the British slaughtered the German assault units, scything them down with shrapnel and machine guns. But that was the exception. Weather had favored the Germans, and they punched through nearly everywhere.[12]

Ludendorff's master plan had chosen the British over the French deliberately. Haig's Passchendaele Offensive had petered out miserably in November 1917, and his great tank offensive at Cambrai had also misfired, leaving British troop strength and morale low. Songs were despairing—"If you want to find your sweetheart, I know where he is / Hanging on the front line wire"—and the aphorisms were cynical: "Never obey orders—they're already canceled." By 1918 most of the Tommies had been wounded at least once and returned to service. Their daredevil days were behind them; now they just wanted to survive. Nor were British troops trained for fighting retreats, Haig having concluded that such training would erode their offensive spirit. This made the Tommies doubly vulnerable—first in their positions, where they were often packed like targets for the German artillery, then in retreat, where they didn't know how to move and fight.[13]

Ludendorff ordered Marwitz's Second Army in the center to strike at the point where the French and British lines touched near Saint-Quentin, push as far as Péronne on the Somme, then swing north toward Haig's headquarters at Doullens in conjunction with Below's Seventeenth Army. The Somme River, along with Hutier's Eighteenth Army on the left, would fend off any Allied reserves and protect the German flank. If successful, Below and Marwitz would separate the British from the French, surround the BEF, and push it into the sea. The omens were good. The British divisions, already weak because of casualties and the need to exempt able-bodied men for training and the war industries, had been filled up with "B-men," recruits who'd normally never have been admitted to the army because of physical or mental deficiencies. Thanks to the fog, Hutier made better progress than Marwitz and Below, pushing ten miles to the Somme bridges, while Marwitz and Below managed just a few miles and were hung up fighting around Arras.[14]

It was a tribute to the effectiveness of the German attacks in March that they landed just exactly where the Allies expected—on the fifty-mile front between the Sensée and Serre Rivers—and they still succeeded. Indeed, had Ludendorff, whose single-mindedness was, as the American general staff put it, his "besetting sin," only swerved northward into the yawning gap left by the broken British Fifth Army at Saint-Quentin, he might have destroyed Haig's BEF. Instead, he pursued the Fifth Army's rout southwest, into the arms of arriving French reserves. But horrific damage had already been done. In a week of combat, the armies of Hutier and Marwitz had driven from the La Fère–Cambrai line to within artillery range of Amiens— the vital junction of the British and French armies—unhinging the Allies and forcing Haig and Pétain to find scarce reserves to hold a longer, more vulnerable front with suddenly diminished and demor- alized forces. On April 2, the British war correspondent Charles Re- pington noted just how close the British were to defeat: if Amiens fell, the BEF would be amputated from the French army and marooned in Flanders. Haig would be unable to retreat into France and would be too weak to cross the Somme or break through the units Ludendorff would surround him with while he attacked the French army. Re- pington predicted that a beaten BEF in Flanders would either starve or surrender.[15]

It took just four days for the Germans to complete the rout of the British, hammering them back twenty-five miles from their initial po- sitions. Only General Marie-Eugène Debeney's French First Army, which veered into Ludendorff's path, contained the rout. Pétain, who still feared that Operation Michael might be just a feint and that the main German thrust would be toward Paris from Champagne, reluc- tantly sent twelve French divisions to shore up Gough's army, which had retreated to the outskirts of Amiens and dissolved into bands of leaderless men.

Pétain warned Haig that the British army, routed in the south and threatened in the north, was on the verge of being "cornered in open

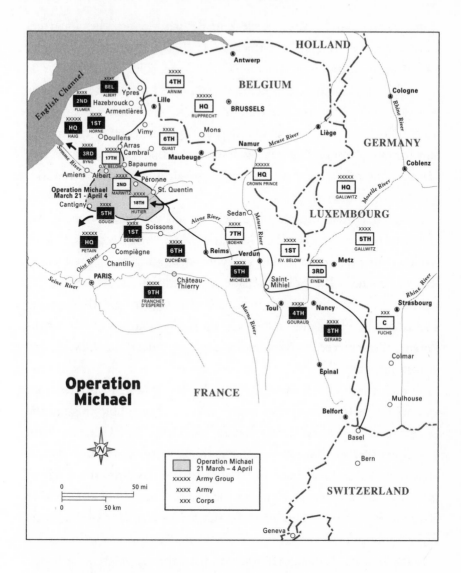

Operation Michael

country." With Haig sending troops south to reinforce the positions around Amiens, he was exposing himself to Ludendorff's planned knockout blow in Flanders: Operation St. George. The German armies took eighty thousand prisoners and 975 guns in the first days of fighting. The British V Corps dissolved, panicked by the hurricane impact of the German trench mortars—17cm guns lobbing 110-pound cans of gas and high explosives into the British trenches—and their first sight of the dauntless German storm troops, easily recognizable by their livery: leather kneepads, satchels of grenades, light machine guns, daggers, and pistols. A clerk in British V Corps headquarters never forgot the panic he witnessed as the Germans methodically sawed through his communications, the corps chief of staff, General Gerald Boyd, clutching the field telephone and trying over and over to reach Haig: "'But the G.H.Q. line?' he kept repeating in an eager voice. This was our last line of defense. As he listened to the reply I saw his face change. If ever I saw despair on a man's face it was on his. 'That's gone too!' he exclaimed with a break in his voice. 'My God, what can we do now?'"[16]

Clearly British officers were not trained to operate outside the chain of command, like the Germans. Boyd's clerk recalled a continuous retreat, night and day, everyone struggling to suppress panic and stay awake: "If I looked outside it was only to see streams of refugees passing by with heavily laden carts or staggering with unwieldy bundles of bedding and household goods. As columns of our troops passed, the refugees jeered at them. This was indeed the darkest hour before the dawn."[17]

German troops advancing on their heels met more resistance from the bad roads than from the enemy. Three feet of rubble clogged the streets, every town and village having been leveled by German drum fire. The rapid German advance sent shock waves as far as America, the *New York Tribune* observing that just three days into the German attack, "New York stood up under the heaviest burden of anxiety that has been hers since she endured the three days' suspense of the Battle of Gettysburg."[18]

The slashing Ludendorff offensive had strained relations between the Allied armies nearly to the breaking point. The French army's chief of staff, General Ferdinand Foch, had shockingly expelled Haig's liaison—Colonel Frederick Cavendish—from his headquarters at Beauvais, declaring, "Je ne veux pas des officiers etrangers ici" (I don't want any foreign officers in here). France was maintaining 103 divisions with a population of thirty-nine million, Britain just 61 divisions from its population of forty-nine million. This was a constant source of tension. The Germans had seized the bulk of France's coal and iron ore deposits as well as its steel production facilities in 1914, and Britain really did have to exempt thousands of miners and workers in order to supply the Allied war effort. But the French nonetheless resented the "blood tax" assigned them and the massive pool of uncommitted military-aged manpower in the UK. "The English lack guts," French officers spat. "Les Anglais manquent de l'estomac."[19]

Nearly everyone appreciated Foch's superhuman calm under pressure, and his magnanimity. Foch was the man who'd sent that legendary dispatch during the 1914 Battle of the Marne: "My center is giving way; my right is in retreat. Situation excellent. I attack." He tolerated bad news or criticism from foreign generals and politicians. Indeed, he'd invariably thump even the most indiscreet visitor on the back and say "Merci, mon cher" (Thank you, my dear friend).[20]

The day the Germans launched Operation Michael, General Pershing and Secretary of War Baker happened to be lunching with General Pétain at Compiègne. They heard the thuds of the German artillery as they anxiously pushed the food around their plates. After lunch, Pershing drove to Versailles for a meeting with General Tasker Bliss, who represented the United States on the Allied Supreme War Council. German siege guns were already hitting Paris from the forward edge of the battlefield, and the French government was weighing a move to Bordeaux. At Langres, where George Marshall was lecturing at the AEF Staff College, "the English instructors on duty became noticeably worried and depressed," all the more so because Marshall was lecturing on "the practical working of a division"—when the British had assumed that the Americans already knew how to work one.[21]

In Washington, the new British ambassador, Lord Reading, met with President Wilson on March 23 and urged him to ignore "past agreements" for an independent American army and ship units as quickly as possible to plug holes in the British ranks. "If America delays it may be too late." The Germans had wrecked the British Fifth Army, cratered British morale, mauled the French reserves sent to fill the resulting gap, threatened the main railroad link between the Allies, and penetrated forty miles. Visiting a French battalion that had been sent to replace a shattered British unit, Marshall noted that it had only two officers. The rest—nearly every company and platoon leader—had been killed or wounded by the German attacks. With Amiens and its rail yards under German gunfire, Ludendorff was poised to divide the British and French armies and beat them separately. President Wilson acknowledged the threat and promised to "do my damnedest."[22]

As Ludendorff's offensive drilled between the Allied armies, the French considered cutting the shattered British army loose and extending their line straight west to the coast instead. With the French digging a new line of trenches well south of the Somme, facing north, the British considered cutting the French loose. In London, Prime Minister David Lloyd George struggled to retain power against a resurgent Herbert Asquith, who'd been dismissed as prime minister after the debacle of the Somme but was making a comeback, criticizing his Liberal rival's conduct of the war. Lloyd George was also drawn into debates with influential proponents of a negotiated peace, men like Lord Lansdowne and the Labour Party's Arthur Henderson, who bluntly questioned the continuing sacrifices on the Western Front and the prime minister's stated resolve "to fight Germany to a knockout." Both powers looked desperately to America, the French staff morosely judging arriving American troops "numerous but practically unusable."[23]

On March 25, Pershing met again with Pétain at Compiègne and found the Frenchman rattled, now preparing to move his headquarters all the way back to Chantilly, on the northern outskirts of Paris. Pershing could feel the vulnerability of the Allies. The Germans were pressing the British back to the sea and the French back on Paris; the two Allied armies were rupturing around the key point of Amiens. Gough's British Fifth Army had been savaged there, and Pétain, determined to shield Paris, hesitated to commit any more reserves to save Gough or Haig. The British were now fighting for survival and the French were focused on defense of their capital. How would they share reserves and coordinate counterattacks under these circumstances? Pershing left Pétain to visit Haig's headquarters at Doullens, a visit that only confirmed his fears that the alliance was disintegrating under the German blows.

The Germans had seized more enemy territory in four days than the Allies had in three years. Had they had tanks or even cavalry, they'd have seized even more through a pitiless pursuit, but the Germans, pinched by the blockade and the need to supply their allies with so much coal, steel, artillery, and munitions, built hardly any tanks in the war, and their cavalry divisions were all in the East, policing the great space of Russia. Even so, the crisis was so extreme that at a meeting of the British and French principals at Doullens on March 26, chaired by French president Raymond Poincaré and attended by French premier Clemenceau, Foch, Pétain, Secretary of State for War Alfred Milner, Chief of the Imperial General Staff General Henry Wilson, and Haig, Haig did the previously unthinkable: he agreed to subordinate himself to Foch, who was given authority to "coordinate the action of the Allied armies on the Western Front." The Allies now had a generalissimo to coordinate all forces.[24]

Still, that wasn't much given the speed of events. Watching Haig depart the town hall of Doullens, a French general nudged Clemenceau and whispered: "There goes a man who will be forced to capitulate in the open field within a fortnight, and we will be lucky if we are not forced to do the same." Major Paul Clark, nosing around Chantilly on March 26 to get information for Pershing, spoke with one of Pétain's colonels, who was decidedly downbeat: "It is nip and tuck, now good news, now bad. There is much doubt whether we are any longer in contact with the British."[25]

Ludendorff's "maneuver of rupture" may have succeeded. Clark noted shock among the French: "Several of the staff look like they had been hit in the belly with a baseball bat." At Compiègne, hastily abandoned by Pétain's headquarters staff, who now huddled fearfully in a train in the station at Chantilly, the German artillery fire was so close that the windows of every house rattled. Compiègne was abandoned, its inhabitants clogging the roads toward Paris in a fifteen-mile-long parade of misery and shattered hopes. The kaiser exulted that day, informing his aides that if the English were ready to surrender, they'd have "to kneel before the German flag for it was a question here of a victory of monarchy over democracy."[26]

On March 27, Pershing, Baker, and Bliss sat down at Versailles to hear a request from Bliss's British counterpart—General Henry Rawlinson—that all future American shipments of troops to France be infantry and machine-gun units that could be slotted into British divisions as replacements. With the British trying to trade British hulls for American troops, Pershing balked, insisting on "rounded divisions" with artillery, supply, and engineers. He was overruled by Bliss, who, stunned by the Allied retreat, agreed to provide American infantry shipments as replacements for the British. Pershing still assumed that the French and British would hold and that a fully trained AEF could add its weight to a war-winning offensive in 1919. Bliss worried that there might not be a campaign of 1919. "The only way to guarantee a campaign of 1919," he wrote Baker, "is to do our utmost in 1918." The new tonnage offered by the British meant that seven Doughboys would be landing in France every *minute* in the months ahead.[27]

Pershing too submitted to Bliss's logic, declaring to Foch, in French, that "at this moment there are no other questions but of fighting—*Il n'y a pas en ce moment d'autres questions que de combattre.* Infantry, artillery, aviation, all that we have is yours; use them as you wish. More will come." In truth, these were just words. Pershing had a law degree from the University of Nebraska, and he now obfuscated with lawyerly skill. Foch believed that Pershing was giving him the 320,000 US troops already in France to deploy wherever needed, but Pershing had no intention of doing that. When he said "All that we have is yours," he really meant "All that we have *might* be yours," when we've finished training and forming complete US divisions. In fact, the first use of American troops in combat would not happen for another sixty days. For the moment, Foch was touched. "A battle won is a battle we will not acknowledge to be lost," he liked to say, and the promise of American troops offered a way not to lose.

Maybe it did; maybe it didn't. The British had already lost 178,000 men to Operation Michael, the French 77,000. The Allies were losing

31,000 men every day to the German attacks. There was a real risk that the Americans wouldn't intervene in time. Foch suggested that he and Pershing step outside to inform Clemenceau of the American commander's offer of assistance. The two generals went into the garden and found Clemenceau walking his dog along a gravel path beneath a cedar tree. Pershing repeated what he'd said to Foch inside and added: "The American people are proud to be engaged in this, the greatest battle of history."[28]

The massive German offensive—90 divisions hurled against 60 miles of front that were manned along their entire 440-mile length by just 155 British and French divisions—had surprisingly stalled. The deeper the Germans pushed, the more their own supply problems increased. The ravaged ground that had hampered the British defense now hampered the German advance, one German officer comparing the waterless, chalky crater fields to a "salt desert." As the Germans had destroyed wells and streams in 1917, there wasn't even water to drink. Troops had to wait for it to be brought forward in carts. When the famished, thirsting Germans captured British supply dumps, they sat down to eat, drink, and pillage all of the items that had been denied them by the British blockade, further slowing the advance.

Although Haig had expected this great German offensive, he had permitted a "business as usual" mentality in his rear echelons, where supplies from Britain had been stacked up close behind the front lines. It was these piles of food and drink that now stopped the Germans more effectively than British counterattacks. German officers raged in vain as their troops stopped attacking and began looting, one battalion commander describing a typical breakdown near Albert: "There were men driving cows before them on a line; others who carried a hen under one arm and a box of notepaper under the other. Men carrying a bottle of wine under their arm and another one open in their hand. . . . Men with top hats on their heads. Men staggering. Men who could hardly walk."[29]

Having made dramatic gains, Ludendorff now stumbled. Unable to dislodge Byng's Third Army from its blocking position above Gough's broken army, Ludendorff stopped his envelopment of the

British and instead unleashed Hutier to pursue the remnants of Gough's Fifth Army and hit any French reserves coming up from the south. Hutier's Eighteenth Army, which was supposed to hold the line of the Oise or the Somme against any Allied reserves, now became the hammer. Tactically, this made a certain amount of sense, but operationally it would be a barren victory unless the Germans could take the vital junction of Amiens, which would unhinge the Allies and facilitate a decisive blow. Thus far, despite the territorial gains—1,200 square miles of enemy territory—Ludendorff had failed to wrest a single strategic hub from the British. He'd driven the British back to their lines of June 1916, but the gains were, as Winston Churchill put it, "Dead Sea fruits," leading nowhere decisive.[30]

With the Germans halted ten miles short of Amiens, Foch sought greater powers, not only to coordinate the defense but to prepare counterattacks that might ultimately break the back of the German army, which he knew was overextending itself. "The trick is to kill as many Boche as possible in the shortest time," one of Foch's aides, Captain Bruneau, told Major Paul Clark. Now more than ever it was a war of reserves. The Germans had committed nearly 50 percent of their available divisions, the French just 25 percent. And the two hundred thousand German casualties among these ninety committed divisions were monstrous, nearly three times as many as the French. The British had estimated that the Germans would accept as many as three hundred thousand casualties to take Amiens, and they were fast approaching the magic number, but without success.[31]

Pershing agreed that 120,000 Americans would be sent from the United States monthly to replenish the British ranks until July. Here was another consequence of American unpreparedness: with the British providing the bulk of the transports, they naturally aimed those transports at the British sector. Pershing made the concession reluctantly. Indeed, the only units Pershing seemed willing to amalgamate under Allied command were four African American regiments that he'd originally planned to combine in a US 93rd Division. Secretary of War Baker had declared during the draft that he had no intention of using the war to address America's "race question." He left

President Wilson made no effort to integrate the US Army. He left in place a segregated army that barred black troops from white divisions and used most of the 350,000 African American draftees as laborers who dug trenches, graves, and latrines, collected the dead, cleared debris, and repaired roads. The men in this picture are digging trenches for a white division. Four black regiments that were intended for an experimental black combat division were given instead to the French, who remarked about their quality: "Excellent morale, appearance, and discipline." (National Archives)

in place a segregated army that barred black troops from white divisions. Pershing now gave the twelve battalions of the four "colored regiments" to the French to do with as they pleased. They were the real "lost battalions" of the war, the only American units that became French units, entirely absorbed into French divisions, with French uniforms and rifles and, a parting touch, a standing order from Pershing's headquarters to the French not to "spoil the Negroes." For the most part, the black troops went gratefully, for the US Army trained them indifferently and used them as laborers, not combatants.[32]

The French used black troops for combat. These four African American regiments arrived in France without artillery, engineers, or signalers and were sent for training with the French and then brigaded with French divisions at the front. All officers above the rank of captain were white; captains and below could be black. Pershing ordered a review of the black regiments he was sending to the French and found them poorly equipped and trained. The 372nd Regiment, which comprised black battalions from the Ohio and DC National Guards as well as companies from Maryland, Massachusetts, Connecticut, and Tennessee, arrived in France without any transport, with Springfield rifles but without artillery, machine guns, automatic rifles, or mortars. Appearance and discipline were rated "fair," health "good," but the unit's preparation for combat in America had been abysmal. There'd been no training in large units, trench operations, machine guns, or grenades. The unit's white field officers were rated "fair," the black company officers "poor." This regiment was given to General Auguste Hirschauer's French Second Army.[33]

Pétain's headquarters, less patronizing about blacks than Pershing's, extolled the African American regiments for their "excellent morale, appearance and discipline." They "showed ambition to outdo white regiments," to "be the best in the American army." Pétain was in the process of breaking up ten French divisions to bring the remainder up to strength. He'd take every available rifle. The black regiments would be armed, equipped, and trained according to French doctrine—so different from American—and would fight as combat troops.[34]

Operation Michael had petered out in the last days of March. Ludendorff's thrust at Amiens with the Eighteenth and Second Armies, slowed by the looting, gorging, and guzzling of the German troops, failed. The BEF had lost 150,000 men in the onslaught, Gough's Fifth Army nearly destroyed, its divisions reduced to 2,000 men, but they'd held. The nearly fatal ten-mile gap that Ludendorff had ripped between Gough's Fifth Army and the French on March 26 had been closed. As the German line lengthened around Ludendorff's new conquests, the Allied line shortened, strengthening the defense and weakening the offense.[35]

Major Paul Clark, Pershing's liaison to Foch, later remembered the moment the tide turned. He'd walked in for dinner late on March 30 expecting the usual long faces and had been met with smiles instead: "Ca va bien maintenant, eh, mon commandant?" General Maurice de Barescut greeted him. (It's going better now, isn't it, Major?) Every officer in the room expressed delight that the Germans had been halted. Pétain had phoned at 5 p.m. from his train to say that the Germans had launched a heavy attack on a twenty-mile front and had been stopped cold. "Our lines stood firm everywhere." Most importantly, the Germans had been stopped short of the vital rail yards at Amiens. Heavy rains were washing out the primitive roads in the sector and forcing all German traffic onto the paved routes through Péronne and Ham, which were jammed with traffic. "Very likely the Boche are not getting enough to eat," Major Claude Rozet snickered as he finished his dinner. The French had lost fifty thousand men in the attacks, but everywhere Clark went, he encountered beaming French officers. "They are stopped; the British front is quiet; we are very much relieved."

The French were under no illusion that this was the end. They all said, Clark observed, that "there will be hard days ahead." They estimated German losses in the offensive at two hundred thousand men, but none believed that Ludendorff was finished, and none saw a way actually to drive the Germans out of France without the Americans. General de Bares of the Operations Bureau threw his arm around Clark and told him that all hinged on the Americans. At best, the French and British could flatten this latest salient; only fresh American divisions could win the war. Major Sérot agreed, telling Clark as they walked to dinner on April 8: "I do not see by what physical power the Boche can be prevented from winning." The British army had been cut up; the French army was too small. Clark was repeatedly asked, "How fast will American troops arrive?" In official meetings with the Allied generalissimo, Clark was badgered about individual units. Could Foch deploy the US 1st Division immediately? Could the 26th, 42nd, and 2nd Divisions be marched immediately into French sectors? How soon would the 32nd Division be ready? Without those American divisions, the Germans simply couldn't be defeated. "The best we can do is hold out till you arrive and finish the job," Captain Davy of the Operations Bureau told Clark on April 8. By now the number of healthy French replacements was so tragically small that it was a closely guarded state secret. "It is so inconsiderable as to be a very important factor in determining the plans and actions of the French," Clark wrote Pershing.[36]

The two sides, panting from exhaustion, regarded each other across no-man's-land. The Allied line was thin, and the roads toward the shrinking British sector were jammed with yet more German assault divisions, war correspondent Charles Repington noting in his diary: "There is going to be the biggest battle ever known, and we stand in a rotten situation." On April 8, British general Sidney Clive stated the obvious to Clark: the next great German offensive would be aimed again at the BEF. "We have enough left for *one* more big battle," he said. Like the French, Clive saw no way for the Allies to win the war without the Americans. "Attacking is a luxury for the Allies at this time. We simply have not got the effectives to do it." All they could do was "hold the Hun and prevent him from getting a positive victory, a negative victory for the Allies is victory of the best kind we can gain at present."[37]

6

"WITH OUR BACKS TO THE WALL"

L UDENDORFF LAUNCHED HIS SECOND GREAT OFFENSIVE—Operation Georgette—on April 9, this time wheeling into Flanders to finish off the British army. "Georgette" was what remained of the original Operation St. George. So much power had been expended in Operation Michael and so many new liabilities taken on—fifty miles of new front to hold—that Ludendorff could only spare eleven infantry divisions to reinforce his Fourth and Sixth Armies in Flanders. In this way, St. George was whittled down to a diminutive Georgette. In operational warfare, which occupies a middle space between tactics and strategy—linking battles to achieve strategic effects, like the annihilation of an army or the capture of a capital—Ludendorff was failing. Yet he appeared to have the British on the ropes. Haig had lost 150,000 casualties thus far and had just scrapped five divisions to bring the rest up to combat strength, mainly with the 118,000 men who'd been on leave or in training when Operation Michael struck.[1]

British will, measured by London's willingness to replace Haig's casualties, was also on the ropes. With seventeen British divisions in peripheral theaters like Palestine and Macedonia, nine divisions in England, and nine million able-bodied men at work in British industry, Lloyd George had plenty of men; he simply refused to pass them along to Haig, whose casualties had surpassed eight hundred thousand in 1917. The prime minister was abetted by Haig's old friend turned rival, Field Marshal John French, who'd commanded the BEF until 1915, when he'd been relieved and replaced by Haig, who'd been one of French's corps commanders. French had been kicked upstairs to command Britain's Home Forces, the very reserves Haig wanted but that Lloyd George now denied him based in part on memos critical of Haig penned by French. Haig, Lloyd George complained, had "smothered the army in mud and blood." The prime minister feared "social revolution" in Britain if the killing continued at Haig's torrid pace. He now began wresting that instrument of revolution from Haig's hands by cutting the flow of infantry replacements and accelerating tank production to reshape the BEF into a smaller, mechanized, and largely defensive force, committed to nothing more ambitious than its own survival. As Lloyd George put it: "Staying power was what mattered most." He ordered the four armies of the BEF to dissolve 141 battalions, a complicated operation that would absorb their entire attention for the month of February, when they should have been training to repel the next German thrust.[2]

The Germans looked piteously at the shrinking BEF. They'd already broken it into "excellent, good, average and mediocre" categories, and any new troops sent to Haig this late in the war would struggle to be regarded even as "mediocre." The only "excellent" and "good" troops remaining to the British and capable of *attacking* were, according to the Germans (who were fighting them, after all), the Guards Division and the other old regular army divisions and any units comprised mainly of Canadians, Australians, New Zealanders, Scots, and Londoners. The rest of the British army was considered adequate only for defense. The French were no better off, summoning the 250,000 seventeen-year-olds of the recruiting class of 1919 early and drafting essential workers from their gun and ammunition factories. There were 600,000 of them and the army wanted at least

200,000. The minister of war would agree to only 50,000. The war of exhaustion was bleeding out.[3]

On April 9, Ludendorff launched Operation Georgette, hitting the tottering BEF astride the Lys River in Flanders with General Friedrich Sixt von Arnim's Fourth Army and General Ferdinand von Quast's Sixth Army. The Germans hoped for decisive results this time. Colonel Georg Bruchmüller, who commanded the artillery in each of the German offensives, shifted his "battering train" of six thousand guns north to gouge a hole in the British line and permit German storm troops to infiltrate between the British armies, take Ypres, and dash to the Channel ports, cutting Haig's lines of supply and retreat. By now Bruchmüller was admiringly known as *Durch-bruchmüller*—"Breakthrough-Müller"—for the devastating results he got with his massed guns. If Arnim's Fourth Army could force the British off the low heights encircling the Ypres salient—ridges like Passchendaele and Messines, which the British had lost tens of thousands of men taking in 1917—it could then converge with Quast's Sixth Army, advancing through Armentières and the even more vital heights southwest of Ypres—Mount Kemmel and the Mont des Cats—seize the crucial railway junction of Hazebrouck and begin pressing Haig back to the coast, which, in these parts, lay only twenty miles behind General Herbert Plumer's Second Army. There were $250 million worth of British supplies and munitions stacked up at Calais. If that cache were taken, the British would be effectively disarmed.[4]

Quast's Sixth Army brushed aside a largely useless Portuguese division (the gunners of England's "oldest ally" were observed cutting out the horses from their cannon and caissons and riding frantically to the rear) and ruptured the British line between the La Bassée Canal and Warneton. The Germans seized the fortified British stronghold of Armentières on April 11. Again the German advance was so rapid that the British had to pull back, fearing an envelopment from the flanks. Everything Haig had gained in his ruinous Passchendaele Offensive of 1917 was lost, the Germans driving a wedge into the British front, seizing Mount Kemmel and the ridges of Passchendaele and

Messines and stopping only on April 18 when more French reserves traveled north to hold the line, which had slid backward six miles under the weight of Georgette.

Having rushed his reserves south to save Amiens, Haig had nothing to plug this latest hole. After bitter wrangling—Haig was still refusing to commit British divisions to an Inter-Allied Reserve—Foch committed a dozen *French* reserve divisions to shore up the British at Armentières and Kemmel, and committed additional reserves to support them at Doullens and Amiens as well. In the meantime, the French were forced to take over more of the British front, pushing up to the Somme River, to permit the British to thicken their lines. German prisoners told their captors that Ludendorff's aim was to destroy the British army and take Calais and Amiens. The Germans were nearly there, and the worst impact of this second German offensive was its continuing drain on the Allied reserves. Georgette killed or wounded another 76,300 British troops and 35,000 French. The two offensives together had subtracted 348,300 men from the Allied ranks. Britain and France no longer had a true strategic reserve—an "army of maneuver"—that could counterattack. Until the Americans arrived in force, they'd have nothing more than a purely defensive reserve to plug holes. "Many," an American study noted, "doubted that it would prove sufficient even for this purpose."[5]

With Georgette stalled in Flanders, the Allied leaders frantically sought clues to Ludendorff's next move. Would he keep pushing toward the Channel ports or shift his attention elsewhere? Traveling to meet Foch at Abbeville, General Tasker Bliss observed frenetic activity as the Allies repaired their defenses and rushed lightly wounded men and any available recruits back into line. The Allies were stretched so thin that wherever Ludendorff's next blow landed, it might well be decisive. Foch held what reserves remained—most of them plucked from quiet sectors of the Western Front—between Paris and Amiens, awaiting the next German push. The fact that the British and French even had reserves at this point was owed in large part to the AEF, which took over France's quiet sectors to free up battle-ready divisions that could now be massed against Ludendorff. At this point, with the

French and British capable of nothing more than "desperate defense," the Americans couldn't arrive fast enough. As John Strachey, editor of London's *Spectator*, put it: "The Germans no doubt feel like a robber who is trying to break the skull of an honest citizen, and sees a rescuer coming along the road, but at a great distance. The Germans realize that unless they can get us and the French smashed before the American aid comes up they are done." But the Americans were still far down the road.[6]

Just how far down the road was revealed in the Doughboys' first combat in France, on April 20, 1918, near the village of Seicheprey in Lorraine, a place whose name briefly became a synonym for American military incompetence. There the 26th Yankee Division had been put in line under French command to complete its education in trench warfare. Some of the Yankee Division's regiments contained colonial-era units like the 1st Connecticut Regiment and the 1st Massachusetts Engineers. The Yankees had been the second US division to arrive in France after the Big Red One and had been trained and then placed in this quiet sector east of Verdun to relieve French units there for service closer to Paris.

Although the 26th Division had been in France since October 1917, had been thoroughly trained, and had spent a month in the front line in the damp, dripping caverns of the Chemin des Dames in February—their bored graffiti still covers the walls a hundred years later—they were nearly overrun in their new positions at Seicheprey. Much of this was due to their commander, the beloved but inept General Clarence Edwards, who incautiously left his troops crammed in forward trenches, not distributed in depth. The Germans, stealing in quietly from the flanks of the Seicheprey salient, easily achieved surprise and overran the division's Connecticut regiment, which lost the town and yielded up 157 prisoners. The Germans used first-class storm troops—*Stosstruppen*—who advanced into the American positions behind a heavy artillery barrage. American outposts were overrun by the Germans, who then bounded into the main American position.[7]

After-action analysis scalded the Yankee Division. Pershing sent his aide-de-camp, Major Edward "Pete" Bowditch, who'd been an

All-American football player at Harvard before the war, to report on the fighting at Seicheprey. Bowditch found that before the battle "there were too many men in the streets doing nothing." When the German attack began, the American phones were instantly cut, and they were never restored. "Good signalers would have restored communication between units almost instantaneously; we need better instruction in liaison." Bowditch also noted bad discipline everywhere and "junior officers not taking enough command." General Edwards, "our Clarence" or simply "Daddy" to his troops and a New England institution, laughed off the criticism. He called it *mucho aire caliente* (much hot air), a phrase he'd picked up in Mexico—only sharpening Pershing's loathing of him. Edwards, who campaigned with his own adoring war correspondent from the *Boston Globe* and was protected by leading Republicans like Henry Cabot Lodge, Warren Harding, and Leonard Wood, could get away with far more than Pershing's other generals.[8]

Another of Pershing's staff officers, Colonel Malin Craig, visited the Yankee Division too and reported that communications between American artillery and infantry had been abysmal and that "many of our casualties occurred from our own artillery fire." There would assuredly have been more friendly-fire deaths had not six American batteries been discovered to be out of ammo before the fighting even started. No one had thought to resupply them. When planes were dispatched to pinpoint the new positions of the advancing Germans, the pilots found that they had no way to communicate with the American infantry on the ground. The casualties were shocking for a raid in a quiet sector: 86 Americans killed, 288 wounded, 240 gassed, and 157 captured. Twenty-seven "shell-shock" cases lay stricken or jabbering in their hospital beds.[9]

A week before the raid, Major Bowditch had seen the whole catastrophe taking shape. The inexperienced Doughboys weren't counterattacking effectively and weren't coordinating with French units on their flanks. A minor German raid a week before Seicheprey—while the bulk of the German army was attacking into Flanders—had cost the 26th Division dozens of killed and wounded; worse, the division

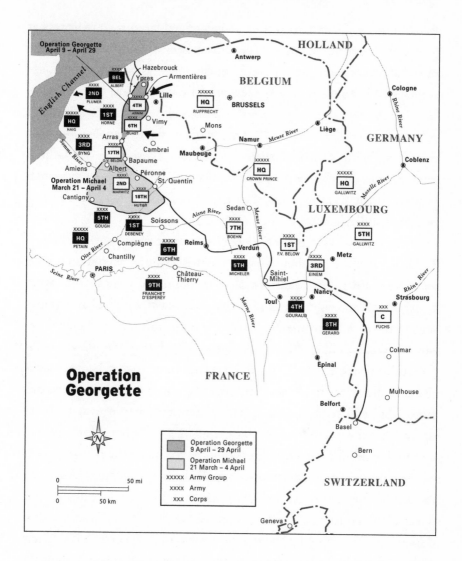

had failed to prevent the Germans from digging in on the boundary between themselves and the neighboring French 10th Colonial Division, effectively rupturing the Allied front. Bowditch, who was there, described scenes of bedlam on the American side. He ducked into the command post of a battalion of the 104th Massachusetts Regiment and found the major in command completely unaware of what his men were doing. They were spread out in the woods before him fighting with grenades and trench mortars, but he had no information on what was happening. While Bowditch sat with the major trying to make sense of the battle, a message arrived from the artillery that it was opening fire on the advanced trenches, which the commander of the 104th, as ignorant of events as the major beside Bowditch, assumed had been taken by the Germans. Bowditch and the major listened to the roar of the guns until a messenger ran into the command post to say that there were still Americans in those trenches and that they were being killed by their own guns. "These men," Bowditch groaned, "are good New England stock, but all of this puts too much burden on the fighting men; the organization must take this burden off of the individual."

Bowditch was struck by the poor communication between the different parts of the division. No unit seemed to know what its neighbor was doing. Every headquarters sat in ignorance of what its men were engaged in. Messages that did arrive were hastily scribbled requests for ammo or reinforcements, invariably with no time on them, so no one knew how old or fresh the request was. Everything else having failed, Bowditch recalled, the division command dispatched a contact plane to fly over the American trenches; the battalion commander from Massachusetts Bowditch had encountered earlier was now ordered to send word to his frontline companies to set out colored panels or handkerchiefs or to fire rockets to show the plane the new positions of the jumbled American troops. Bowditch dryly reported the major's reaction: "The major had no plan of liaison with a contact plane; he'd never expected to have a contact plane fly over his lines." Leaving the dugout and returning up the road to division headquarters, Bowditch added a footnote to his depressing visit. "Trucks with reinforcements were coming up, too fast; it was a dry day, they raised tremendous dust clouds; the Germans could see the dust and would know the reinforcements were coming and would shell the trucks." Seicheprey was a propaganda disaster for the AEF. It gave a fresh new talking point to advocates for amalgamation and a public relations triumph to the Germans. The Germans assembled their mass of American prisoners, photographed them, captioned the photos "Are these the men who are going to win the war for you?" then took the photos up in planes and scattered them over the British and French trenches.[10]

If Haig ever saw one of those leaflets, it would have been the least of his worries. Far to the west, the BEF, having lost an entire army to Operation Michael, was bearing the brunt of Operation Georgette. Having shifted forces to contain the Germans at Amiens, the British had left the all-important approaches to the Channel ports of Calais, Boulogne, and Dunkirk thinly defended. Hindenburg's Fourth and Sixth Armies pressed their grinding attacks along the thirty-mile line from Ypres south to Lens. If the Germans could seize the Channel ports, the British army in Picardy and Flanders would be amputated from its lines of supply and retreat.[11]

American troops couldn't arrive fast enough for Haig, who issued his doleful "backs to the wall" bulletin on April 11: "With our backs to the wall and believing in the justice of our cause, each one of us must fight on to the end." Haig, a British journalist noted in his diary, "is doomed" and "will be the next scapegoat" for Britain's sinking war effort. General William Robertson, who'd just been removed as the British general staff chief, noted that there was now talk of "closing down the continental part of the war and . . . reverting to a maritime war," saving Britain, perhaps, but dooming France. The American newspapers were shocked by Haig's despairing tone. The *New York World* spoke of "dark hours" spent waiting for the latest updates from the front. The *New York Tribune* wondered if the war had not entered its death throes: "Does America comprehend the astonishing changes wrought in three weeks? That Field Marshal Haig now says that the British army must fight with its back to the wall?" Surely, the paper concluded, Pershing's reluctance to commit the AEF to battle in its present state had been "rendered void by the German offensive." Green US troops would have to be rushed into the battle. For now, the British held, stopping the Germans a day's march from Dunkirk, but their casualties continued to mount. One British soldier, sniffing the tang of sea air over the stink of the battlefield, read Haig's "backs to the wall" bulletin and snapped: "What bloody wall?"[12]

With Operation Georgette, Ludendorff had hammered another bulge into the British line, this one twenty miles deep, but again he'd failed to break clean through. Like the victory around Saint-Quentin in March, the one at Armentières in April was barren. Ludendorff took Mount Kemmel on April 25, the last gasp of Georgette, but was stopped short of the Mont des Cats and the rail yards at Hazebrouck. The staff chief of the German armies in the north, General Hermann von Kuhl, expressed frustration. Attacking over open ground, the Germans had lost nearly 57,000 dead and 252,000 wounded since March 21—twice the dead and a third more wounded than the Allies—and yet "no great strategic movement had become possible, and the Channel ports had not been reached. The second great offensive had not brought about the hoped-for decision." Haig, a French general admiringly declared, had somehow "buckled the buckle."[13]

Ludendorff had now exhausted 141 of the 206 divisions he had available, many of them having entered battle two or three times. But the Allies estimated that the Germans had at least 40 fresh assault divisions for another roll of the dice. At this nerve-racking juncture, the kaiser discovered that his Austrian ally had also been rolling the dice, though in a less helpful cause. Operation Georgette coincided with the revelation that Emperor Karl of Austria-Hungary had used his brother-in-law Prince Sixtus of Parma as a back channel to French president Poincaré to work for a separate peace (for Austria) and the restoration of Alsace-Lorraine to France. This was the notorious "Sixtus Affair," and even as they planned their next push, the Germans had to busy themselves with securing the Austrians, recalling the Parma princes from the Belgian front, stopping the influence of Karl's wife, Empress Zita, and taking total control of the flagging Austro-Hungarian war effort. Emperor Karl, a weakling, obediently fired his foreign minister, Count Ottokar Czernin, the author of the plot, then conceded everything to the kaiser. Having withheld Austro-Hungarian troops from the Western Front until now, Karl agreed to send them, bluffly declaring that his answer to Clemenceau's exposure of his double-dealing "will be the roar of our guns in the West."[14]

Such was the Allied "crisis of effectives" after two German offensives that the US 1st Division had to be hustled into line in Picardy faster than anticipated. On April 24, the Big Red One relieved two French divisions that had taken heavy casualties during Operation Michael near Montdidier. Pershing saw the troops off from their billets around Toul with an inspired speech. The Doughboys represented "a young and aggressive nation . . . the mightiest nation engaged" in the war, there "to defend the sacred principles of human liberty on European soil." And yet there were still so few trained American troops in France that the 1st Division was simply referred to as "the combat division." None of the others were, as the fiasco at Seicheprey had amply demonstrated. Pershing's 1st Division was placed under the orders of the French First Army commander, General Marie-Eugène Debeney. It was the first American division to move into a combat sector, but was it too little too late?[15]

The Supreme War Council met at Abbeville on May 1 and 2 to discuss again what Clemenceau and Foch were now, more impatiently than ever, calling *la grosse question* (the big question): When would American troops be sent to the front? The Allied leaders were present, the "black coats"—Clemenceau, Lloyd George, and Italy's prime minister Vittorio Orlando, with Bliss sitting in for President Wilson—along with the generals—Foch, Pétain, Haig, Pershing, and Italy's General Mario di Robilant, best known for losing twelve thousand men at Caporetto. The Italians were feeling as hunted as Pershing; with 1.4 million troops against just 866,000 demoralized Austro-Hungarians, Rome was under constant pressure to send troops north to reinforce the Western Front. For now, the Allies fixed their attention on the United States. Clemenceau, "with his bright shrewd eyes of youth, mouth hidden under his mustache, a tried old blade, razor-edged," opened the proceedings with a razor cut: "What allocations of American troops will be made to the other Allies?" Pershing, whom one contemporary compared to Abraham Lincoln in his refusal to be awed by power—"He recognizes no superior on the face of the earth"—counterpunched: "The other Allies have nothing whatsoever to do with the allocation of American troops." At best, it might be "a subject of agreement," not something for the other Allies to demand or decide.[16]

The relief the Allies had felt in early April had been replaced with renewed fear. The Germans had 128 divisions at the front, with 78 in the rear and 40 of them counted as "fresh." The Allies had just 112 divisions at the front, with 50 in reserve. A third German blow could break through and win the war. Foch, Secretary of State for War Milner, Lloyd George, and Clemenceau took turns badgering Pershing for troops. Some wanted half of the AEF given to the British, half to the French. Lloyd George, who, to Haig's chagrin, viewed the Supreme War Council as a means to shift overall command from Haig to Foch, wanted them all for the British: "Our losses have been greatest," he said. "Ten British divisions have been entirely knocked out; there are no British to refill them."[17]

Pershing bore up under the attacks. The American war correspondent Frederick Palmer, who served in Pershing's headquarters, described the steel Pershing turned to meet every Allied attempt to filch his army. Pershing "might appear with a warm smile of greeting, but canny, watchful, the lips straightening to a thin line, he could be a pillar of flint at the first signal from afar of a plot to purloin any of his men-children whom he knew best how to make into soldiers." Pershing now became that pillar of flint: "I do not understand that the American Army is available for allocation as recruits to either Great Britain or France, nor for any indefinite period. I shall insist on this principle that no parceling out of the American Army shall prevail." He demanded that the Allies forthrightly "declare the principle of an American Army under an American Flag" and stop demanding things like infantry and machine guns only, "which will only defer the organization of an American Army."[18]

Lloyd George hedged. "Yes," he agreed, "but an American Army in the *fall*, after this *present* battle." Foch launched into a harangue, which one of the Americans present described as having "all the atmosphere of clap-trap oratory and sounded more like a 'stump speech' than a discussion." The Allies would be driven back to the Loire, Foch predicted, unless American battalions could be used to replace casualties in French and British units. "Are you willing to risk our being driven back to the Loire?" Foch heatedly asked. "Yes,"

Pershing coldly replied, "I *am* willing to take that risk." Pershing pointed always to the British divisions in England, the Balkans, and the Middle East as evidence that the Allies had ample troops; they just needed to put them in the right places. He saw clearly that his Doughboys needed a clean break from their Allied minders. If not, units like the US 1st Division would be indefinitely annexed to the Allied armies. Foch naturally saw nothing wrong with such a course. He argued that since President Wilson had agreed to his appointment as Allied generalissimo, Pershing *had* to put his troops at Foch's disposal. Pershing acknowledged that President Wilson may have considered amalgamation, but he made clear that he was not the general to carry out such orders: "The American people themselves would not have approved even though the President and his advisers should lean that way."[19]

On May 2, the meeting resumed. Lloyd George stated that it seemed to be the German plan to exhaust the Allied reserves before their own were used up. He announced that the US still had fewer troops in the field than Belgium and asked if "American honor were prepared to lose the war under such circumstances." You can have your independent army in the fall, he said, "but we must get through to the end of August," when French and British recruits now in training would be ready for deployment. Foch, now more heated than before, said that French and British losses were much greater than the two powers could replace. The Germans, he said, can replace that many losses; the French and British could not. He appealed to Bliss and the Supreme War Council to *force* Pershing to turn half a million troops over to him. Pershing kept his cool ("Gentlemen, I will not be coerced") and reminded Foch that "America is an independent nation and the morale of the American soldier depends on fighting under his own flag." America wasn't "a recruiting agency" for France and Britain. As the Allies quarreled, a Doughboy who was training in a French camp nearby later recalled, "rumors from the front kept drifting back, and they were very disquieting. The French were discouraged and pessimistic. Everywhere we heard tales of the great drive that was at last to carry the Germans to Paris."[20]

With Ludendorff bashing bulges into the Allied lines and threatening to break through to Paris and the Channel coast, it was a terrible dilemma, made slightly less terrible by Pershing's sneaking suspicion that the Allied situation was less dire than Haig and Foch described. Pershing suspected that after two mighty offensives, the Germans had shot their bolt. With the French guns and reserves crowded back on Paris, the Germans probably couldn't break through there. With the Bolsheviks slow to accept Berlin's peace terms at Brest-Litovsk, the Germans had been forced to leave thirty-six divisions in the East to pressure the Russians, and also to extract food for the starving German home front. Now that the Allies were adopting German-style zone defense—a weak first line absorbing the German main attack and buying time for strong second- and third-line troops to defend and counterattack—Ludendorff would struggle to break through and exploit wherever he attacked, not least because "a very large percentage" of the surviving German troops were already coming down with the Spanish flu, the global pandemic that would kill fifty million people by 1919. Plus, the Germans needed time to regroup, which would give the Allies time to repair and reinforce their defenses.[21]

Weighing all of this at Abbeville on May 2, Pershing agreed only to ship ten more American divisions to the British army area, where they'd be trained and equipped, along with as many additional American divisions as the British could ship. Victory, as Lloyd George put it, was "to be found in one word, ships, in a second word, ships, and a third word, ships." The British had hulls to spare, the Americans didn't. If Pershing wanted to speed his army across three thousand miles of ocean, he'd have to trade Doughboys for space on British ships. The deal he made this time was this: During training, the US divisions would be available to the British. Once trained, Pershing would move them to the American sector that was taking shape around Verdun. A British officer present at Abbeville recalled that Pershing "argued for hours about the Americans, but nothing much seems to have been settled."[22]

The Allies would have to settle on a plan soon. Senior officials in the British War Office were projecting in early May that if fighting continued at the intensity of March and April, Haig would have to scrap a third of the BEF—twenty-one entire divisions—to bring the rest up to combat strength. The American general staff's Belgian-indexed strength ratios looked even worse in May than they had in March. By the end of May British fighting strength had fallen from 10.5 to 10 and French from 12.75 to 12; the Americans had increased theirs from 0.75 to 2, barely preserving an Allied strength of 25. But by now the Germans had transported thirteen additional divisions from Russia, raising their value to 31. A last German push might break through and win the war.[23]

By now, the British and French governments and commands were at each other's throats, each insisting that it had sacrificed more in the war than the other, each demanding that its ally do more. The British at this point pondered giving up on the offensive altogether and building their own concrete "Hindenburg Line," ten to twelve miles behind their existing line, with an eastward bulge to contain Amiens. Content to preserve a concrete foothold on the Continent, Britain might cede occupied France to the Germans. Swallowing hard, Foch and Clemenceau agreed to release seventeen French divisions that had been held back for the defense of Paris to maintain the frayed connection between the British and French armies. Later, Foch's deputy, General Maxime Weygand, would sing Clemenceau's praises for this brave act: "What other French politician would have been prepared to sacrifice Paris to support the junction between the French and British Armies, which Marshal Foch thought absolutely vital."[24]

On May 19, Pershing met with Pétain at the French commander's headquarters near Chantilly. Pershing had promised Foch in March that "all that we have is yours," but all that Foch really had was that single "combat division," the Big Red One, and it had needed two more *months* to finish its training and move into line. The two commanders agreed that the 1st Division would slide in between divisions of the French First and Third Armies to attack a village called Cantigny on May 28. If successful, the operation would flatten the Montdidier salient and straighten the Allied lines. This would be the first test of a US combat division in a planned offensive.[25]

Lulled by his distance from the front, President Woodrow Wilson was still thinking in terms of a long war that America would win for the Allies in 1919. Speaking in New York on May 18, the president declared that "Prussian militarism" would be crushed, if not by the French and British, then by five million or more American troops. President Wilson would beat the Germans everywhere and not concede them "a free hand in the East to carry out the purposes of conquest and exploitation." He was already thinking in terms of a future peace, in which the small nations of Europe would enjoy the right to organize themselves, free of German, Russian, Ottoman, or Habsburg control. Wilson went before a joint session of Congress nine days later to urge passage of new taxes that would raise $800 million of additional revenue to cover America's ballooning war costs. Three war loan campaigns and the specter of inflation had led Wilson to oppose further borrowing without a tax increase. He appealed to the patriotism of Congress, which would normally oppose taxes just months before midterm elections. Wilson was unapologetic: "The consideration that dominates every other now and makes every other seem trivial and negligible is *winning the war*." The British embassy, which had become accustomed to American vacillation, was struck by the new resolve: "At no time has there been less talk of peace in American papers. . . . Pacifists have not disappeared, but they are hushed and have bowed before the wave of American war enthusiasm."[26]

7

BELLEAU WOOD

O N MAY 27, LUDENDORFF LAUNCHED HIS THIRD OFFENSIVE, this one code-named Operation Blücher, after Prussia's elderly field marshal who'd defeated Napoleon at Leipzig and Waterloo and who shared honors with Hindenburg as the most decorated soldier in German history. Stopped short of his objectives in the first two offensives—Amiens, Ypres, and the Channel ports—Ludendorff now aimed at Paris instead. He still planned to win the war by driving the British into the sea, but he needed to divert those seventeen French divisions sent by Foch into the British sector during Operations Michael and Georgette back to the French sector in order to renew the offensive in Flanders with any hope of success. "The most favorable operation in itself," Ludendorff wrote, "was to continue the attack on the English Army . . . but before we could attack again [at Ypres and Hazebrouck], we needed to make the enemy weaker." He'd make the enemy weaker in the French sector.[1]

He chose his latest target carefully—the Chemin des Dames. This "Road of the Ladies," wending across the crest of a twenty-mile ridge with stunning views of the Aisne to the south and the Ailette, a tributary of the Oise, to the north, had been named for the daughters of Louis XV in the eighteenth century. The Germans had held the ridge—the very point where the Western Front, after running south through the British sector, bent east toward Verdun—but they'd yielded it to the French in October 1917 (after shattering the Nivelle Offensive there) in the course of their withdrawal to the Hindenburg Line. Since then the French had treated the Chemin des Dames as a quiet sector, a place they assumed the Germans had relinquished forever. They placed fatigued divisions there—like the French and British units chewed up in March and April—for rest and rehabilitation. Ludendorff knew this. Stealthily, he moved Durchbruchmüller's "battering train" of artillery there, as well as reserve divisions to beef up General Max von Boehn's Seventh Army and General Fritz von Below's First Army.[2]

Ludendorff struck with a wedge of thirty assault divisions from the Chemin des Dames south, hitting just six British and French divisions sprawled across fifty miles of front between Soissons and Reims. Operation Blücher had two purposes: to steer the French reserves that were sustaining Haig back to the south, opening the door for a decisive German thrust to the Channel coast between Calais and Dunkirk, and to smash open the door to Paris. The sector was thinly defended because the Allies expected the swampy Ailette and the Aisne-Oise Canal to deter any German attack here. If the Germans could overcome the natural obstacles, mass in secrecy, and break through, they'd be well on their way to the French capital.[3]

Fifty-six-year-old General Denis Duchêne, commanding the French Sixth Army in this area, unwisely packed his front line with troops and abjured the cautious, elastic defense in depth preferred by Pétain and the Germans. Duchêne had been Foch's chief of staff early in the war and had absorbed the generalissimo's lust for the offensive and contempt for defensive strategies, without, like Foch, updating that prejudice to take account of reality. The French general crammed his army into the narrow space between the Ailette and Aisne, where the troops had a depth of just five miles. When the German guns opened fire on these compact targets, they literally couldn't miss.[4]

Duchêne's army, holding a critical corridor to the French capital, was first showered with poison gas and then hit with four thousand guns, which played their fire along the slopes, crests, and caverns of the Chemin des Dames for two and a half hours. With the ridge quaking and crumbling under the impact of so many shells—it was the most concentrated drum fire yet—the poilus and Tommies, choking in their ill-fitting gas masks, died in place or ran for their lives. Breaking clean through on May 27, the Germans seized Soissons and its critical railways. They then crossed the Aisne and the rugged ridges behind it (which Duchêne had neglected to fortify), then the Vesle (finding its bridges intact), finally reaching the Marne three days later.

General Pétain, stunned by the speed and the depth of this third German offensive, was forced to throw in the last of his reserves, but they hardly checked the German onslaught. In an attack intended as a diversion to expose Flanders, Ludendorff had swept aside nearly fifty French divisions, taking sixty-five thousand prisoners, two thousand machine guns, and eight hundred cannon, an unmistakable sign of rampant demoralization in the French ranks. At least one Doughboy sympathized with the French: "One got that way. The feeling of utter yearning and despair, the fear of the last indignities ahead, and the knowledge that the war might go on for years and years, brought mental and physical paralysis to the individual."[5]

Demoralized poilus melted away from the front, bawling, "La guerre est finie" (The war is over). General Bullard, whose US 1st Division had French units on both flanks, found them all abject: "The French no longer had élan; their soldiers looked upon counterattacks as leading only to death." Their division commanders "regarded attacks in much the same way." Meeting in Paris, Bliss and Pershing agreed that the French withdrawal had become "a rout." Ludendorff, who'd set limits to this advance in order to facilitate a renewed attack in Flanders, now removed the limits, so certain was he that the French army was cracking. He'd expected that the war-winning breakthrough would be in Flanders; it now seemed that it would be here. His *Ablenkungsangriff*—deflecting attack—had become his main attack. The American press reported "anxiety" in the White House at the "increasingly grave" turn of events. The distance between the German vanguards on the Marne and Paris, New York's *World* reminded its readers, "was just half the distance between New York and Philadelphia." Could France survive?[6]

Foch and Clemenceau considered firing Pétain for the debacle—they even brought a general from the French army in the Balkans to replace him—but ultimately decided that it would be enough to place Pétain more firmly under Foch's authority. Meeting with Foch's British liaison, Major Reginald Benson, on May 28, Pershing's liaison officer in Foch's headquarters, Major Paul Clark, found the Englishman "dirty and tired." Benson had been with the British IX Corps west of Reims and was amazed at how easily Duchêne had let Operation Blücher break through. The French, Benson scoffed, had "dismissed the evidence of an attack at this place with a sweep of the hand," and the next day "the Boche crossed the bridges of the Aisne in columns of squads, marching as though he had nothing to fear. The Hun has gotten this very cheaply. We didn't kill many Boche." This was potentially disastrous. The only advantage that the German offensives conferred on the Allies was the ability to "kill Boche" in the open. Duchêne had let them through unscathed. British troops near Reims, fighting to hold the flank of this latest wedge the Germans were driving into the Allied line, were spat upon and cursed by French stragglers and locals. The French, it appeared, wanted the war over at *any* price.[7]

The Germans raced through virgin French countryside till now untouched by the war, picturesque villages and châteaux bounded by tidy fields green with crops. Surprise was total, for this sector had appeared less promising for the Germans than others. Indeed, in Foch's headquarters, a captain in the operations bureau told his American liaison: "I cannot fathom the object of this new effort. . . . Nothing vital is involved; we will stop him soon." There were only two southbound roads, both terminating at Château-Thierry on the Marne. Logistically, the chief benefit here for the Germans was that seizing Château-Thierry would link the German army's spinal cord in France—the rail line from Metz and Thionville to Lille—to the Marne railroad, which would in turn permit a broader-front German drive on Paris. Attacking across the Marne at Château-Thierry would allow the Germans to chew up the dwindling French effectives and exert psychological pressure on the French people by bombarding their capital, just as they'd done in the Franco-Prussian War. The French Chamber of Deputies panicked. Clemenceau and Foch were reviled for having sent precious reserves to help the British during Operation Georgette. This was the occasion for Clemenceau's famous appearance in the Chamber on June 4, when, to quiet the uproar, he reminded the deputies that there'd be no surrender: "I will fight in front of Paris; I will fight in Paris; I will fight behind Paris."[8]

And yet Ludendorff still hoped to beat the French *and* the British. He had sallied from the Chemin des Dames to force Foch to shift troops there from his reserves at Compiègne; Ludendorff then planned to resume his attack on the British at Arras and Ypres and drive them into the sea. The Allies were fortunate that Ludendorff so consistently lacked focus and operational savvy. Since March, he'd won isolated tactical victories without a single strategic breakthrough. The requirements for a successful breakthrough operation were artillery and troop masses on the broadest possible front, strong flank protection, tanks, and a motorized supply and ammunition column. Because Ludendorff never decided *where* to land the decisive blow—he was constantly shifting between promising alternatives—he never had sufficient masses, reserves, or vehicles at the decisive spot. The wedges he drove into the French and British lines were too narrow and too weak on the flanks to be sustained and exploited. This time, though, Ludendorff seemed to have done the trick. If he could drive this latest wedge forward to join and extend the bulge created by Operation Michael, he'd cleave the French army in half and clear the way to Paris.[9]

The threat to Paris and the Marne was such that Foch had to move reserves from Compiègne to backstop Duchêne, and Pétain had to withdraw the French infantry and artillery intended to support the US 1st Division's attack on Cantigny, which now appeared less

Operation Blücher

	Operation Michael 21 March – 4 April
	Operation Georgette 9 April – 29 April
	Operation Blücher 27 May – 4 June
	Operation Gneisenau 9 June – 12 June
	Peace Offensive 15 July – 17 July
xxxxx	Army Group
xxxx	Army
xxx	Corps

pressing than earlier. Around Reims, the Germans had massed four assault divisions against each Allied division, smothering them in shellfire and then smashing through. French artillery earlier pledged to the American attack at Cantigny now withdrew to positions nearer the Marne, where the German attack was exceeding all expectations. General Max von Boehn's Seventh Army had lunged all the way to the Vesle, installing itself in Braine, Bazoches, and Fismes. Foch yielded the Vesle but resolved to hold on the Marne. If Ludendorff crossed that last barrier, he'd drive the Allies apart and descend on Paris. As stunned by the extent of his success as the Allies, Ludendorff, who'd envisioned the fatal blow in Flanders, now saw that he might land it in the Île-de-France—the lush region around Paris. He hastily drafted a new operation to commence on June 11 and drive southwest from the Aisne. He gave it the code name *Hammerschlag*—"Hammer Blow."[10]

Although Operation Blücher changed everything, Pershing insisted that the attack at Cantigny proceed anyway. Montdidier, the deepest point of the German penetration in Operation Michael—a bulge between Amiens and Compiègne—was the shortest route to Paris, so it made sense to throw the Germans back there, even if, as Marshall put it, "the heights of Cantigny were of no strategic importance and of small tactical value." Pershing's staff also recognized that until they could form an American army—projected for late summer—their only play was to "maintain the morale of [their] Allies, to keep them in the fight by . . . having U.S. troops available to enter critical phases of the fight." The trick was to help the Allies, but not too much. Pershing's priority remained pulling all units out of French and British hands to establish a US First Army in eastern France. Pershing also wanted to test open warfare tactics with an assault on German positions.[11]

Three battalions of the US 28th Regiment took Cantigny with little resistance on May 28. Two hundred and fifty French and American guns had been shelling Cantigny to soften it up. The attack itself was a set piece on a section of German front held by third-rate German units. The American assault battalions came up in trucks from their training area the night before at 11:30 p.m. and were in position by 3:30 a.m. After an hour of artillery preparation, the American battalions attacked at 6:45 a.m., following a rolling barrage that progressed at a rate of fifty yards a minute, the Doughs keeping to within forty yards of it—a terrifying experience even for veterans. They used flamethrowers and a dozen French tanks to clear the Germans out of Cantigny and took 230 German prisoners. At first, the Big Red One met little resistance and no German barrages. Officers on the scene recalled "minor fights" and a village taken with "considerable ease." By 7:20 a.m., Cantigny was in American hands.[12]

Only at noon did the Germans awake to the situation and begin shelling and machine-gunning the Americans. Doughboys lounging in the open to savor the victory were killed by a sudden hurricane of German shells and shrapnel. They hadn't been in the war long enough to recognize the danger of indirect fire. The three battalions were savaged by German shelling, some companies losing a third of their men and most of their officers in this tragic episode. Morale wavered when the Germans brought 210mm guns to bear, George Marshall remarking: "A 3-inch shell will temporarily scare or deter a man; a 6-inch shell will shock him; but an 8-inch shell, such as these 210-mm ones, rips up the nervous system of everyone within a hundred yards of the explosion."[13]

The Germans then launched some half-hearted counterattacks—most of the Germans here were middle-aged reservists, not assault troops—and were driven off by the American artillery. At 6:45 p.m., the Germans launched a serious counterattack from the Bois de Framicourt. This one too was crushed by artillery fire. On May 29, the Germans launched more counterattacks, including a big one at 5:45 p.m., but each time the Germans left the woods around Cantigny, the American guns would throw them back. German rolling barrages were not effective because these troops—middle-aged men of the German 82nd Reserve Division—hung back, 150 to 200 yards behind their barrage, instead of hugging it. Once the barrage passed over the Americans, the Germans, far behind its protective envelope, were gunned down or driven away. Still, nothing here was easy. The French having withdrawn their artillery to the Marne front, the Germans outgunned the Americans, making their stand at Cantigny an unexpected bloodbath. The Americans lost as many men holding the village as the Germans lost trying to recover it.

George Marshall, now a major, later wrote that the horrors of this little battle "exceeded any experience [the troops] were to have later on in the great battles of the war." The Doughboys, in their first battle, couldn't yield the ground, however marginal its importance, "without depressing the morale of our entire Army as well as that of our Allies." On May 30, the 28th Infantry was relieved by the 16th Infantry. Cantigny had been an unqualified success. The 1st Division had gained 1,600 yards on a front of 2,200 yards. It had attacked, consolidated, and fended off hostile bombardments and counterattacks, and killed, wounded, and captured an estimated 1,700 Germans, against 1,600 of its own casualties. It was the war's first American attack delivered with courage and precision, and it was the only Allied offensive operation at a time when the British and French were barely holding on.[14]

Pershing spoke of the "electrical effect" of the Big Red One's "splendid dash." The American press wrung gushing headlines from the little battle, triggering real war fever in a country that had been skeptical before Cantigny. "Our troops are second to none," the *New York Herald* blared on June 1. They, not the Tommies or poilus, would "decide the Battle in France." The Allies were startled by such commentary. More than a year had passed since the American declaration of war and the most the US Army had accomplished was an offensive by a single *regiment*. "The mountainous A.E.F. labored mightily," one historian wrote, "and brought forth a mouse." Marshall allowed that, with thirty-five German assault divisions south of Cantigny, thrusting toward Paris, Cantigny had only marginal significance. "The little village marked a cycle in the history of America," he wrote. The US Army was finally joining the combat in Europe. "Cantigny was but a small incident, while the great disaster further south which was befalling our Allies was hourly assuming more serious proportions."[15]

Ludendorff now converted the intended feint of Operation Blücher into his main effort, a great wedge-shaped push toward Paris in the space between Reims and Soissons. The same French captain of the general staff who'd assured his American liaison on May 28 that "nothing vital was involved" in this latest German thrust had changed his tune two days later. "The situation is very grave. The Boche will be on the Marne and our principal [defense] line will be breached." The French general staff, which had depleted its reserves to shore up Haig, searched frantically for Ludendorff's reserve divisions. "The great, great, great question is WHERE are the Boche reserves?" The French had only identified twenty German assault divisions in this strike, and they knew that Ludendorff had forty more *somewhere*. If thrown in here, they could win the war. This search for German troops had been the essence of the war since the winter. In sectors slated for attack, German divisions would be concentrated, not strung out thinly, as they were in quiet sectors. Each assault division would occupy two kilometers of front, with one division in reserve and a third division behind it to replace the one in reserve when it moved up. All armies had become expert at camouflage and deception, making the search that much more harrowing. "The Boche is after Paris," the French captain concluded. "We must stop him. His advance is so swift that it is more than we can do to fill the holes that he makes on our front."[16]

French staff officers meeting with their American liaison, Major Paul Clark, agreed that the loss of Paris would probably end the war. It was France's indispensable railroad hub and a vital manufacturing center. If the Germans took Paris and the government continued the war from Bordeaux, the French expected the Germans to offer harsh terms and then burn Paris, one arrondissement at a time, until the French accepted. None of the officers believed that the French people would "bear so great a sacrifice" as the destruction of Paris. They would rather submit and end the war. From Foch's perspective, there was only one consolation: "We still hold Reims." Lacking good roads south and west, Ludendorff desperately needed the rail stations at Reims and Soissons to move German troops and ammunition. He now had Soissons; if he could take Reims as well as the rail yards at Château-Thierry, he would connect the German rail hub at Mézières with Paris-bound railways along the Marne. Once in possession of them, he would battle across the Marne and close on Paris from the west. Using divisions taken from the Eastern Front, he hoped either to defeat the French or frighten them into a panicky armistice. If the French yielded, so probably would the British.[17]

On May 30, Pétain again requested American reinforcements to oppose Operation Blücher. The way to beat Blücher was to attack this latest bulge on its shoulders, but the French couldn't; they needed every available man merely to check Operation Blücher's forward progress. The French were so short of manpower that they now contemplated emptying the entire Western Front from Reims to Switzerland—there were thirty-four French and American divisions in that space—and using those men "to fight an open battle for Paris." On the Marne front, there were now thirty French divisions matched against thirty German, but as Major Rozet of the French general staff warned, "Bear in mind that the Boche have a package of 40 divisions *somewhere* and one of our great anxieties is *where* they are going to use them." This, Rozet concluded, "is the gravest situation of the war." A US Marine who was advancing at this very hour with his brigade to relieve shattered French infantry on the Marne noted their poor quality: "They didn't appear to be first-line troops; they were old, bearded fellows of forty and forty-five, territorials; or mean, unpleasant-looking Algerians, such troops as are put in to hold a quiet sector," which was precisely why Ludendorff had hit here. "The fate of the war is in the balance," a French captain assured Major Clark. "Something radical must be done."[18]

After the war, the chief of the French operations bureau, Colonel Duffour, would recall that May 30–31, 1918, had been "the most anxious day of the war." The German push between Soissons and Reims had pinned down all available French reserves, and if Ludendorff had added a thrust on the Compiègne front, "they'd have gone through" to Paris, as there was only a single French reserve division there to oppose them. The French were so low on men that they had no reserve army to swing into the path of any new German thrust. The Germans had by now created three big pockets in the Allied line. The two biggest, the one created on the Somme by Operation Michael and the one just created on the Marne by Operation Blücher, weren't far apart. If Ludendorff could smash down the wall between them—obstacles like Château-Thierry, Belleau Wood, and the Forest of Compiègne—his army could deploy its full strength and take Paris. No wonder Foch was stricken with worry when he met with Pershing on May 30 at the Frenchman's headquarters in Sarcus, southwest of Amiens, near where the French and British armies touched. Pershing recognized the emergency too—all the Germans had to do was bring up more artillery and they'd be over the last hurdle—and agreed that the seven US divisions completing their training with the British and French, which Pershing had intended for an independent US First Army, would instead be rushed to the Marne front for service in French corps.[19]

These American units—the 35th, 82nd, 77th, 28th, 4th, 3rd, and 2nd Divisions—marched immediately, some by foot, others in French trucks. Seventy-five trucks were needed to move a single US battalion, and these convoys, packed bumper to bumper, chugged through the night to deliver the Doughboys to the fighting front. "The head of the German wedge kept coming on," an American report noted, and "finally the Americans were brought up against this head." Pershing ordered the battered 1st Division to extend its lines to the north and double its original front to cover its own Montdidier sector as well as that of the French division on its left that had been withdrawn to oppose the Germans on the Marne. There were still eighty-eight German divisions—1.4 million German troops—massed opposite the British for a final drive to the sea through Hazebrouck. German prisoners and deserters spoke of a looming attack in Flanders. The British army, shrinking and disbanding its divisions, was on track to have no more than thirty of them. At a tense Anglo-French meeting on June 1, Haig suggested that the BEF might fall to just twenty-eight divisions. Foch and Clemenceau were thunderstruck. French staff officers told their American liaison that they wished that the British would "abandon all of the north country and retire to the Somme River" but knew that they wouldn't. The British had bled to defend Calais, Dunkirk, and Boulogne "and would not now consent to the abandonment of those ports."[20]

American opinion hardened perceptibly in this nerve-ripping crisis. President Wilson called for no fewer than three million US troops to salvage the situation in Europe. On May 31, Congress unanimously passed the biggest military budget in American history—$12 billion, the equivalent of $200 billion today—and laid the groundwork for a "No Limit Army," authorizing President Wilson "to draft as many soldiers as he needed" in the fight against Germany. Wilson appointed Wall Street financier Bernard Baruch—nicknamed "Dr.

Facts" and the "Czar of Industry"—head of a War Industries Board to coordinate military and civilian production. Baruch would determine, as the new industrial czar put it, "who gets what and when," the essential basis of a war economy, making clear that civilian needs and wants were not the same thing.[21]

Secretary of State Robert Lansing, previously a voice of moderation, now sounded like a latter-day Sherman: "Prussia shall have war and more war until the very thought of war is abhorrent to the Prussian mind." Former president William Howard Taft wanted to take a big stick to the Germans: "We are fighting the whole German people. We must change their psychological state and perform a surgical operation upon their heads. We need a club, for they have made the devil their god." Senator Henry Cabot Lodge of Massachusetts noted that there was now no other course available to America than the total defeat of Germany. Having conquered Russia and absorbed so much eastern territory at Brest-Litovsk in March 1918—sixty thousand square miles of formerly Russian land from the Baltics down to Ukraine—Germany had to be beaten on the Western Front to save France and England and make Berlin disgorge its Russian annexations. Otherwise, Lodge declared, Germany would become invincible and "the war will have been fought in vain."[22]

Pershing marched the US 2nd and 3rd Divisions to hold the line at Château-Thierry—the 3rd Division would take up positions on the south bank of the Marne; the 2nd Division would advance on its left to fill the space west of Château-Thierry, where the Marne bends southward and runs toward Paris and the Seine. Tactically, this removed the Marne barrier for German troops attacking west of Château-Thierry. They could sweep along the south-flowing Marne toward Paris, the Marne to their left, the Ourcq to their right, an advance that would outflank the French and American forces behind the Marne at Château-Thierry, as well as the British and American forces in Picardy. The only natural obstacle that would impede a German advance here was Belleau Wood, two hundred acres of old-growth trees and ravines—an ancient hunting ground that now assumed military importance.

The Germans marveled at the size of the Americans and at their morale, calling them "healthy, strong, physically well-developed men"—"tall as trees," "fresh," "wide-awake," even "carelessly confident"; "excellent assault quality troops." Here, German POWs march to the rear under the guard of a poilu while Doughboys of the US 3rd "Rock of the Marne" Division march to the front in June 1918.

On May 31, the US 3rd Division—which had just left its training area—took over ten miles of front between Château-Thierry and Dormans. It held the bridgehead over the Marne opposite Château-Thierry against German attacks. Château-Thierry had a desolate look: "A beautiful white city" at the foot of its hills, a Doughboy recalled, "but not a soul could be seen, no wagons on the roads, the railroads only a rusty red line, the towns mere shells." It was "the ghost of a world we were looking at. Everyone had fled." The Doughboys had to struggle just to reach the Marne; the Germans were advancing so quickly that no one knew where to stop the American troop trains, which were chugging up from the south. They didn't want to travel too far along the rails only to glide into German captivity. Lead elements of the 3rd Division finally got off at Montmirail, well south of Château-Thierry. "It was bedlam there," one Doughboy recalled. "French refugees were swarming into town from one direction, and American soldiers pouring in from the other." One of these arriving Doughboys was transfixed by the sight of a departing French hospital train as his unit pulled up to the front line: "That was our first sight of what the war might be going to do to all of us. Of what it would surely do to some of us. . . . It was packed with men. Men lying as still as if they were already dead. Men shaking with pain. One man raving, yelling, jabbering, in delirium. Everywhere bandages, bandages, bandages, and blood."[23]

General Omar Bundy's 2nd Division assembled in Meaux, just thirty-three miles northeast of Paris, and drove in trucks and marched north toward Château-Thierry. The Germans had seized most of Château-Thierry on the north bank of the Marne, as well as Hill 204, which overlooked the town from the west. At Troyes, a group of Doughboys met a train filled with retreating French soldiers. They were, one of the Americans recalled, "a worn and discouraged-looking lot. Some of our men who could talk French called out to them, and they told us that the Germans could not be stopped. They were sweeping everything before them. They would certainly go all the way to Paris. The war was over." When the Americans had joined the war in 1917, an early general staff study had predicted that the war might end this way. The British, the Americans reasoned, probably wouldn't accept defeat. They were the toughest Allied army, with the strongest artillery. The French were the weak link. The Germans probably couldn't and wouldn't actually defeat the French army. It would be enough "to cause the *collapse* of the French Army," by dealing a "psychological blow," such as the one Ludendorff was landing here on the Marne.[24]

Corporal John Barkley of the US 3rd Division recalled that "we heard [the phrase] *la guerre est finie*—the war is finished—so often that we all recognized it." (Within weeks, *fini* would become AEF slang, as in "The food [or ammo] is *fini*.") In Foch's headquarters, French officers expressed the same pessimism: "If we don't do something to inspire the troops with confidence, their present good morale will tumble." If Paris was lost, French fighting capacity, Major Rozet said, "will fall from 10 to 3." Foch's aide was estimating, in other words, a 70 percent drop in already-brittle French morale if the capital fell. "The war would be over in two weeks," he direly concluded. Then the only hope would be a continuing Anglo-American naval war against the Germans to force them to soften their terms to the beaten French.[25]

General James Harbord, who had left Pershing's staff to command the Marine Brigade of the US 2nd Division, was struck by the congestion of the roads between Paris and Château-Thierry. Battered, disorganized French units filled the roads and were joined by hordes of refugees fleeing the German advance: "Men, women, children hurrying toward the rear; tired, worn, with terror in their faces." A private in the 2nd Division was most struck by the silence of the fleeing civilians: "The marchers were too miserable to more than glance at us as we passed and probably thought: 'a few more for the Boches to devour.'" Lieutenant Lemuel Edwards, who would go on to command a Marine division at Okinawa in World War II, recalled the stunned disbelief of the straggling mobs of retreating poilus when they saw American troops advancing up the very roads the French were retreating down. "Retournez, retournez!" the French called angrily. "Go back! Go back! The war is over! The Boche has won!"[26]

Harbord drove as far as Lucy-le-Bocage, near Belleau Wood, on May 31. There he found French troops looting the village as they retreated. Poilus smashed open the doors to wine cellars, rifled through drawers and wardrobes, and slit open parlor sofas and upholstered chairs, looking for hoarded gold and banknotes. The oncoming Germans would do it if they didn't, so why not? The war brought nothing but misery like this to civilians near the front. As one Doughboy put it: "A slight swaying back and forth of the lines meant life or death for many a village." In one such village he met an altogether typical innkeeper: "She is the last woman in the place. Trade is gone and tomorrow she leaves. Her husband and two sons are dead—army, of course—there is nothing to live for. This is the second time in four years that the town has been wrecked."[27]

Operation Blücher's drive southward from the Aisne had driven a bulge as far as the Marne. But the French and Americans still held

Doughboys marching to the Marne and Belleau Wood were struck by the flood of refugees through their columns. "No man who saw that road those first days of June ever forgot it; there was horror in their eyes," a veteran recalled. These people had been turned out of their homes on a few hours' notice with nothing more than what they could carry in their hands. Here, American troops evacuate an elderly French woman. (National Archives)

the flanks and leading edge of the bulge in accordance with Foch's injunction to "dam up the flanks of the enemy in his initial advance." If the German tactical center alone advanced and the wings were stopped, then the whole German position would become untenable—a salient attacked from its flanks and eventually snuffed out. To break out and broaden the advance on Paris, General Max von Boehn intensified the Seventh Army's attacks on Château-Thierry; he ordered General Richard von Conta's IV Reserve Corps to swing into the defenseless space west of the city and then plunge south through Vaux and Belleau Wood to speed the advance on Paris and outflank the Allies' Marne line with five German divisions.[28]

The Germans were straining to press the bulge outward and down on Paris, the Allies straining to hold the flanks of the bulge and halt its forward progress on the Marne. On June 1, the day Château-Thierry fell to the Germans, General Omar Bundy, who'd just brought his US 2nd Division from a training rotation in the quiet trenches near Verdun, summoned his brigadiers to a meeting at his headquarters in Montreuil-aux-Lions, a village between Belleau Wood and Château-Thierry. With the French XXI Corps under General Jean Degoutte commanding this sector, Bundy's 2nd Division was instructed to move into line from Azy-sur-Marne to Gandelu, with Vaux in the center. Bundy had two brigades—one of army and one of Marines—and the Marines now found themselves on the left end of this line around Belleau Wood. Everywhere in this sector—with no Marne to protect them—poilus of the French 43rd Division were bugging out, scrambling backward to reach the road to Paris. The US 2nd Division advanced into their positions.

Lieutenant John Thomason, marching with the 5th Marine Regiment, was most struck by all of the refugees. They thronged Meaux and the Paris-Metz road, essentially the entire civilian population of the territory between the Chemin des Dames and the Marne, "inhabitants of a thousand peaceful little villages and farms, untouched by the war since 1914. . . . No man who saw that road those first days of June ever forgot it. . . . There was horror in their eyes." These people had been turned out of their homes on a few hours' notice with nothing more than what they could carry in their hands. Thomason recalled the variety: an old woman with a copper pot and a string of garlic, rich families in Second Empire coaches with "unreasonable household effects—onyx clocks, bird cages and rabbits," broad-faced peasants in clogs, wealthy bourgeoisie mincing along in delicate leather shoes. Advised by a French colonel to join the flight to the rear, Colonel Wendell Neville, commander of the 5th Marines, replied, "Retreat, hell. We just got here." Thomason recalled that the Marines in his column tramped toward the Germans muttering things like: "Hard on poor folks, war is," "Say, think about my folks and your folks out on the road like that."[29]

While the US 2nd Division marched toward Belleau Wood, the US 3rd Division marched up to Château-Thierry. Corporal John Barkley recalled the forced march from Montmirail through Rozoy and

Belleville to the Grand Forêt growing on the south bank of the Marne opposite Château-Thierry. "And it was hot—damp and sweltering after a rain." It was a forced march, with heavy packs and few halts, but whenever the Doughs did stop, the officers would huddle together and study their maps. "You could tell by the expression on their faces that something serious was going on up there at the front." The fields on either side of the road were filled with more French refugees fleeing back toward Paris: women, children, bearded old men, and crippled French soldiers being carried back by the others. Watchful peasants tried to keep their geese, goats, and cattle in line as they fled. Barkley recalled a mother rushing three little girls along, the girls sobbing, the mother stopping now and then to comfort them. All of the refugees had "a dead look on their faces, as if they couldn't see anything or feel anything anymore." A French speaker in the unit asked what was happening. "*Fini, fini*," they all said. One added: "Don't bother going up there, there's no use for you up there now." On June 3, the Germans seized their first bridge across the Marne near Château-Thierry. They now had one foot poised to cross the river that had thwarted them in 1914 and were just fifty miles from the French capital.[30]

Corporal Barkley was on the hills of the Grand Forêt just south of Château-Thierry. He could see the French retreating and the Germans in field gray coming in pursuit, crossing the two stone bridges beneath him. He focused his binoculars on the bridges and was appalled by the sight. A battalion of forty-eight hastily positioned American machine guns had opened up on the river crossings, covering them with corpses and writhing wounded, the German officers filling the gaps and shoving the columns forward "to certain death at the bridges." Barkley looked as long as he could, then turned away: "They were brave men, those German soldiers. I was learning that early." The battle intensified, German batteries opening up on the American machine guns, newly arrived American batteries countering the German fire. As the German dead piled up on the bridges, the Germans loaded trucks with soldiers and tried to bull their way across through the artillery and machine-gun fire. The Americans aimed at the drivers and the trucks slewed around, crushing wounded men, blocking the bridge, and spilling troops into the Marne. Eventually the Germans retreated, impressing the Americans with their discipline: "They fell back in good order, opening out into formations to lessen their casualties." Barkley, a forward observer, was joined in his post by two French officers, also there to observe the German attack. "America, America!" They laughed. "Vive l'America!" Looking down at all of the German dead and wounded—many of them howling in pain and begging for water—the French officers smiled and kept saying, "Magnificent, magnificent." Barkley was stunned by the casual cruelty, "but I got to understand that better when I'd been in the war a little longer myself."[31]

Belleau Wood also fell to the German 28th Division in the hours before dawn on June 3. The wilderness of trees, ravines, boulders, and fallen timber now acquired larger significance. If they held it, the Germans could push south on a broader front, cross the Marne, outflank Château-Thierry from the west, and seize the Paris-Metz highway, which the Allies were using to shuttle reserves into position. Instead of moving promptly into Belleau Wood and its commanding height, Hill 142, the Americans lay in shallow trenches for three days around Lucy-le-Bocage. They were the last line; if General Richard von Conta's corps smashed through and reached the Marne, just five miles behind them, he'd be able to maneuver the Allied forces at Château-Thierry off the river barrier. An American gun crew had just dug in its battery to support the Marines near Belleau Wood on June 3 when a fat French officer galloped past yelling, "Le Boche! Le Boche! Only two kilometers away. Retreat, fast!" The situation was terrifying—the poilus were retreating in panic, the Germans pursuing relentlessly. Yet each of these American batteries had only two machine guns for defensive fire. The crew carried .45-caliber pistols, which none of these recruits had ever fired in anger. They loaded them and waited, taking care to shorten the fuses on their 75mm shrapnel shells. General James Harbord, commanding the Marine Brigade, gritted his teeth and stood fast. "Nothing doing in the fall back business," he wrote his corps commander, French general Jean Degoutte.[32]

Early on June 6, the Marines, with two army regiments in reserve, decided to take the fight to the Germans. They advanced through rolling wheat fields around Lucy-le-Bocage toward Belleau Wood. They had as their objective the little hills and copses on the fringes of the forest, where they could "hole in" before launching an attack on the wood. Once in position, the Marines would assault Belleau Wood at 5 p.m. Lieutenant John Thomason recalled watching through binoculars the Germans take up positions on the edge of the wood while French walking wounded straggled past the Marines on their way to the rear: "Weary, bearded men, very dirty. They looked with dull eyes at the Americans—*'Trés mauvais, là-bas! Beaucoup Boche, là'*—'It's very bad over there; there are a lot of Germans there.'"[33]

Having seized attacking positions on the fringes of Belleau Wood, Harbord then ordered the Marines to attack into Belleau Wood from the west. Two other battalions would attack the wood from the south and take the tiny village of Bouresches, but at a terrible cost: the Marine Brigade lost 222 killed and 865 wounded on June 6. Witnesses recalled the horror: four ranks of Marines sweeping through the fields, then climbing into the woods themselves. Thomason, leading a company of Marines, deplored the naïve formation, "lines all dressed and guiding true," and was sure that "the old Boche in the woods did not believe his eyes." The Germans, of course, had been attacking, driving the French before them, as they closed on Paris. They hadn't expected a determined counterattack from anyone, least of all the Americans, who were making their first major appearance in the war. Thomason recalled the Germans lying in the underbrush in hastily scraped holes. He remembered the fury of fire, with the Marine waves succeeding each other as the forward lines bowed under the fire. Officers and NCOs yelled, "Battle-sight! Fire at will!" The Marines, making out "green-gray clumsy uniforms and round pot-helmets in the gloom of the woods," fired with their Springfields, and the automatic riflemen brought their French-supplied Chauchat light machine guns into action from the hip, calling back to their ammo carriers, "C'mon kid, bag o' clips!"[34]

Laurence Stallings, another Marine officer, remembered the "opening clatter of dozens of German machine guns that sprayed the advancing lines. Then we heard some shrieks that made our blood run cold." Fighting into the dark wood, the Marines first had to root the Germans out of thickets and wood piles. Woodcutters had recently been through the Bois de Belleau and had stacked up cords of wood in every clearing. Thomason, sheltering behind one of these wood piles with a Chauchat gunner, came under fire from a German machine-gun team at the next wood pile. Hoping to expose the German gunner, Thomason placed his helmet on the tip of a bayonet and poked it into the open. Behind him, he heard the Chauchat gunner discharge one round, then silence. He turned in time to see the Marine die, falling to his knees, still gripping the "sho-sho," as the men called the French gun. Thomason stared in horror: "The man's head was gone from the eyes up; his helmet slid stickily back over his combat pack and lay on the ground," filled with brains. "My mother," Thomason reflected, "will never find my grave in this place." That mad thought gave him courage. He picked up the Chauchat, lay it across the wood pile, and sighted: "Three Boche with very red faces; their eyes looked pale under their deep helmets." He fired the whole clip and they fell dead.[35]

Racing ahead without trench mortars or hand grenades, the Marines overran two-thirds of the forest, rooting the Germans out of their ravines, shallow trenches, and rock piles with nothing more than Chauchats, rifles, and bayonets. They took the rocky, scrubby Hill 142. It was heroic but bloody, all the more remarkable in view of the Marine Brigade's inexperience. The core of Old Timers were seasoned—famous for their accurate rifle fire at eight hundred yards—but new draftees had been needed to bring the brigade up to wartime strength. The navy had purchased land at Quantico for a Marine training area at the time of the declaration of war, but recruits from the Marine boot camps at Paris Island and Mare Island could only be sent to Quantico for assignment to battalions and training as quickly as barracks and other facilities could be built, which had meant a staggered, rushed training program. Indeed, the rifle range at Quantico wasn't finished until a month after the first battalion of Marines had sailed for France. Many platoon leaders had been sent to France with just three weeks of instruction, the Marine Corps judging that their high level of motivation and intelligence—there was "a high proportion of college men and young business men who had left lucrative positions to enlist" before the draft—and "their keenness to reach France to fight" might compensate for their limited instruction.[36]

Intelligence, initiative, and "keenness" were everywhere on display. In no combat in their entire history had the US Marines taken casualties like this. They attacked in the formations they'd been taught by the French—platoons formed in four waves for a short rush, with the expectation that the first three would be lost but the fourth would take the enemy position. "The Marines never used it again," a veteran scoffed. It was unsuited for open warfare and "incredibly vulnerable." Lieutenant Thomason recalled that "it didn't take long to learn better, but there was a price to pay for the learning." All through the day and night the Marines listened, aghast, to the cries of the wounded, "pitiful and thin across the fields," Germans—"Ach, Himmel, hilf! Hilf! Liebe Gott, hilf!"—and Americans—"First aid, this way! First aid, for the love of God!" The screams swelled toward evening as wounds initially anesthetized by shock and adrenaline tortured the men with pain.[37]

Once inside the wood, the Marines struggled to locate themselves and the Germans. There was no trench line, just paths wandering off in all directions and hidden German machine-gun nests in every thicket, ridge, and hollow. Each of the German machine guns was placed to flank the others, meaning every time the Marines attacked one they'd immediately come under fire from other guns on their flanks. In the intervals between fighting, the Marines absorbed bombardments of high explosive and poison gas from Conta's heavy artillery as well as US friendly fire that fell short. The Marines learned to fear the scent of cut grass (phosgene) and onions (mustard gas), which enveloped them during every gas attack. Directions were a nightmare in the wood, and each company had only one map, "exclusive property of the captain." Platoon leaders would hunker around it, memorize as much of it as they could, and then take off with the vaguest directions: "You're here, the objective is that patch of woods a kilometer and a half northeast, about. See?" Most of the Marines in Belleau Wood would go two weeks without a hot meal.[38]

In Foch's headquarters, a better-fed Captain Bruneau observed to Major Paul Clark that "it must be rather a disagreeable realization in Bocheland that not only are the Americans coming rapidly, but that they are fighting well." He was right; German officers questioning their first Marine prisoners were impressed: "From well-to-do classes; they consider it an honor to belong to the Marine Corps; with pride, they resent their assimilation as [army] regiments; they consider themselves 'land and sea soldiers' and are thoroughly acquainted with the glorious history of their regiments during the American War of Independence." A French woman, visiting poilus in a hospital behind Degoutte's Sixth Army, saw a wounded Leatherneck there too, easily distinguishable by his height and clean-shaven face. He'd been injured near the flank where Degoutte's French infantry joined Bundy's 2nd Division and had been picked up and conveyed here by French stretcher-bearers. "Oh," she said delightedly, "surely you're an American." "No ma'am," the casualty answered, "I'm a Marine."[39]

Marine General John Lejeune arrived in France during the Battle of Belleau Wood and visited the French field hospitals near the front, where he was shocked to discover entire battalions of wounded Marines. The fighting in the wood was that intense. "Such ésprit I have never seen," Lejeune recalled. As he walked the halls, the wounded men began to sing the Marines' Hymn—"Its sound grew in volume as man after man took up the refrain"—until the noise was deafening. In Chaumont, after his visit, Lejeune had dinner with Pershing and described the casualties he'd seen around Belleau Wood. Pershing's voice broke as he said: "We must remember, General, that Napoleon said that it is just as impossible to win victories without loss of life as it is to make omelets without breaking eggs."[40]

For Ludendorff, smashing the Marines was important not only to open the road to Paris and outflank Château-Thierry but also to send a message to America and the Allies. The Americans everywhere on the front, he wrote, were "unskillfully led, attacking in masses and failing"—and these were the regulars, the cream of the American crop. France by now was down to 105 divisions. The British had just 50 left, the Belgians 10. America's 40 divisions—equivalent in manpower to 80 European divisions, most of them still behind the lines training—were crucial to Allied survival. Everything now depended on the Americans to hold off the Germans, who could still scrape together 160 divisions for a last push. If the Doughboys could be routed or slaughtered in their early battles, the AEF as a whole might wilt.[41]

The German 28th Division counterattacked in Belleau Wood on June 8. General Conta was under orders to advance through the wood to the Marne on his left. A week of bloody fighting ensued. Harbord, commanding the Marine Brigade, withdrew his troops to safe enclaves on the edge of the wood and then turned his artillery on the center of the forest and "blew it all to hell." On June 10, Colonel Albertus Catlin's 6th Marine Regiment attacked again into the southern edge of the wood. The fighting would advance and stall. Lieutenant Sam Meek, who'd left Yale to join the Marines just a few months earlier, was crouched in a hole, stunned by the din and horror around him. "Morale was at the bottom of the barrel," he recalled.[42]

The 5th Marine Regiment, striving to reinforce the units on the western edge of the forest, penetrated only to find the Germans there as well. The Marines barely clung to the edge. One Marine battalion lost 21 officers and 836 men, nearly its entire strength. The field messaging between the Marines described relentless German attacks and excruciating moments trying to correct American artillery fire, which had trouble differentiating friend from foe in the woods. On June 11 at 5:45 a.m.: "Germans along railway tracks. Request barrage closer." 6:00 a.m.: "Germans attacking with machine guns and infantry." 10:45 a.m.: "Another enemy counter-attack on our left flank. We need barrage immediately along Bouresches-Belleau Road." At 1 p.m.: "Barrage falling short, raise it 200 yards, or more." Many Germans wouldn't surrender because they'd been told that the Americans killed prisoners: "We think we can get more prisoners as lots of them

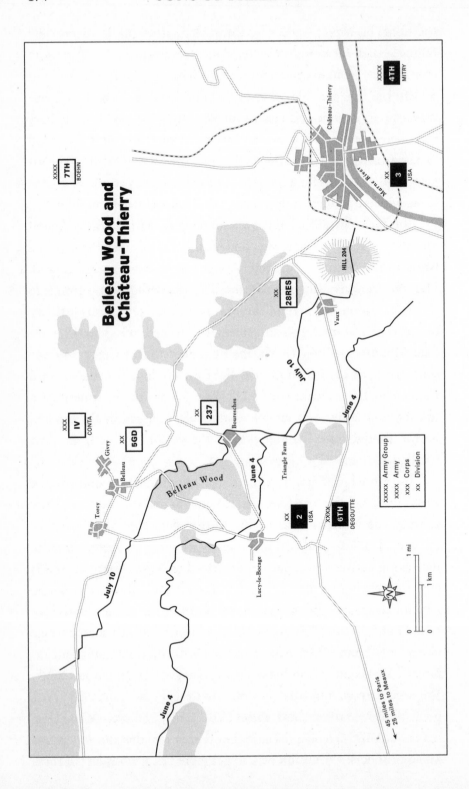

Belleau Wood and Château-Thierry

are hiding afraid to give up, so with German-speaking men we are going to comb them out. We've lost quite a few officers."[43]

Ludendorff's order to Conta's IV Reserve Corps on June 10 emphasized the need to kill and terrorize the Doughboys and Leathernecks the instant they appeared on the front: "The high command orders you to embarrass the formation of the American army in France; it's critical to strike as much as possible the American troops engaged on the front, for those troops are to be the nucleus of new formations." The war was hard everywhere, but Ludendorff ordered it made even harder against the Americans: "To shatter the two American divisions engaged in front of our left wing, use poison gas, heavy bombardment, and raids by storm troops on the Belleau and Bouresches Woods." The Marines fought back viciously. "Bois de Belleau" became notorious in Germany despite the efforts of German censors to suppress its legend. A German machine gunner in the 43rd Regiment never forgot what the Americans did to his company, mainly with rifles and machine guns, in the first ten days of June. "Before then, we had casualties of about 2 percent." The Americans inflicted 80 percent casualties. "American morale was better than any I'd ever seen. Our company strength fell from 150 to 30."[44]

German officers insisted that Paris would certainly have fallen had the Americans not appeared: "Without the Americans, we would have been in Paris by July." Pershing's insistence on rifle fire was not so anachronistic after all. Rifles killed differently from artillery. Artillery was loud and predictable, rifle fire relatively quiet and random. Used to fighting the British and French, Thomason recalled, the Germans had forgotten what "aimed, sustained rifle-fire was, fire that comes from nowhere in particular and picks off men— it brought the war home to the individual soldier and demoralized him." The Marines took a letter off a dead German sergeant in the Bois de Belleau: "The Americans are savages," he'd written. "They kill everything that moves."[45]

It was in this way that Belleau Wood, only half a square mile in extent, became the focus of a vicious battle for nineteen days. Ludendorff had shifted reserves from Flanders to exploit the success of Operation Blücher. He now launched Operation Gneisenau—a fourth offensive, this time with Hutier's Eighteenth Army—into the devastated space west of Belleau Wood, between Noyon and Montdidier. Determined to bash his way to Paris on a broad front, Ludendorff needed to link up the salients he'd created at Château-Thierry (Operation Blücher) and at Amiens (Operation Michael) and remove the V of land and the barrier of the Oise River between them. The French shuddered under this latest offensive. Thirteen rested German assault divisions advanced nine miles and captured thousands of unwounded, demoralized French soldiers. Belleau Wood, which had obstructed the German right during Operation Blücher, now obstructed the German left. In both cases, it lay in the path of the offensive as Ludendorff, attempting to widen the thrust toward Paris and shorten the time between his offensives, pressed south on a broader front.[46]

Needing a decisive counterattack on the Oise, Foch had summoned a general hated by the poilus for his offensive zeal: fifty-two-year-old General Charles Mangin. "The Butcher," as Mangin was known, had been sacked after the Nivelle Offensive and only recently rehabilitated on the orders of Clemenceau. He drove a captured German Opel staff car painted blood red and led from the front. He was fond of saying "Whatever you do, you'll lose a lot of men," and he now lost many more, but he stymied Ludendorff's attempt to link up the two deep pockets he'd driven into the French line, which would have provided a more defensible front in France if the Germans shifted their focus back to Flanders. The Germans broke off Operation Gneisenau on June 12, admitting defeat here as everywhere else.[47]

Everyone was feeling the strain. Together, the armies of World War I had mobilized thirty-five million men. There simply weren't many more military-aged men to be had anywhere in Europe. The British in Flanders had captured many "men" of Germany's 1920 recruiting class, sixteen-year-olds with just twelve weeks of instruction. In Foch's headquarters, Major Sérot crooned like a chanteuse to Clark: "You Americans are our hope, our strength, our life." This was the German estimate too. The Germans were fascinated by the Americans they encountered in Belleau Wood. German staff analyses drafted in the heat of battle marveled that the Americans had somehow become soldiers—"healthy, strong, physically well-developed men"—despite scarcely any preparation, and that their morale was "fresh," "wide-awake," even "carelessly confident." A staff officer of the German Seventh Army interviewed prisoners from the US 2nd Division taken in Belleau Wood and rated them "excellent assault quality troops." They imported the no-nonsense ethos of America, telling their captors simple truths like "We kill or get killed." The Germans had assumed that the US Army, comprised of so many recent immigrants, would shatter into demoralized ethnic pieces if put under pressure. It hadn't. "The majority of them are the sons of foreign parents," but "these half-Americans express without hesitation purely native sentiments," the German staff report concluded. "Their quality is remarkable." They brimmed with "naïve confidence."[48]

Now Ludendorff paused to reconsider his plans. He still had four armies concentrated on the British front, and Haig remained vulnerable. What war correspondent Charles Repington called "the Paris and Channel magnets"—the Allied resolve to defend their key points—meant that France and Britain ceded the initiative everywhere and were always spread thin against stealthily massed German armies. Of the fifty BEF divisions raised in the UK—the rest came from the Dominions—ten were now classed as "exhausted" and eight more were effectively disbanded. The British were losing more men every day to German shelling than the Americans were adding. But there were still sixteen French divisions reinforcing the British sector, and others gathered behind France's left flank on the Somme, prepared to move north in a crisis. Ludendorff needed to push these French divisions away from the British sector to give a renewed thrust to the Channel ports good chances of success. His attack on the Marne, intended to do just that, had stalled. The vast forces he'd accumulated between the Aisne and the Marne were choking on a single railway junction—Soissons. Ludendorff would have to either widen the attack—to capture the critical rail yards of Reims—or get out.[49]

Fighting petered out everywhere except Belleau Wood, which both sides regarded as a critical bastion. William March, a Marine from Alabama, later imagined the letter his commanding officer would have composed to grieving mothers at home:

> Dear Madam, Your son, Francis, died needlessly in Belleau Wood. You will be interested to hear that at the time of his death he was crawling with vermin and weak from diarrhea. His feet were swollen and rotten and they stank. . . . Shrapnel hit him and he died in agony, slowly. You'd never believe he could live three hours, but he did. He lived three full hours screaming and cursing by turns. He had nothing to hold on to, you see: He had learned long ago that what he had been taught to believe by you, his mother, who loved him, under the meaningless names of honor, courage, patriotism, were all lies.[50]

Deaf to March's irony, Degoutte ordered the Americans to continue their attacks in Belleau Wood "to keep the enemy under the impression that he is being threatened" and to suck in German reserves. The kaiser, having promised a rest to the German 28th and 5th Guard Divisions, pulled them out of the wood but then almost immediately put them back in. "We shall have a look at the Americans," one of these tired Germans wrote in a letter home. "We should have been relieved but now the American Division has been identified and therefore our Army General Staff has selected the best of our divisions for use against it." German prisoners revealed that this was part of a deliberate plan to use "picked men"—the cream of the German army—against the Americans "to inflict a morale defeat on them." German officers confirmed that they had orders to "prevent at all costs the achievement of *any* success by the Americans."[51]

The US 3rd Division's 7th Infantry Regiment relieved the Marines on June 16. The Leathernecks hadn't removed their shoes or eaten a hot meal for two weeks, and their companies had been reduced by casualties to platoon strength. Pushing into the wood, the Doughboys recoiled at the stench of death and the rotten odor of mustard gas, which pooled in every hollow and crater. For several harrowing days, they started at every whistle and blast as German heavy artillery pounded the woods, searching for the Americans inside. These men of the 3rd Division were largely draftees—some of them had been in the army barely five weeks and couldn't even work the bolts on their Springfield rifles. "Their sergeants," one of Pershing's inspectors sourly noted, "know less than many privates here in the line." Ordered by Degoutte, who'd replaced Duchêne as Sixth Army commander, to clear the woods with "persistent attacks," the Doughboys wondered how. Like the Marines, they lacked tanks, mortars, machine guns, and hand grenades. One of the 7th Infantry's battalion commanders pleaded with his commanding officer to cancel the attack: the German guns and infantry inside the wood were cleverly placed, "the woods is a thicket and the throwing of troops into the woods is filtering away men with nothing gained." He was ordered to attack anyway, and the battalion was shattered on June 21.[52]

That night, the Marines, resting south of the wood, returned to the forest to relieve the Doughboys. They picked their way cautiously forward, spreading in a line across the northern edge of the wood, where the last German machine guns were concentrated in a rocky amphitheater. On June 23 and 25, the 5th Marine Regiment attacked into the boulders. One company of Marines judged that in advancing twenty yards it had encountered sixteen heavy and thirty-five light German machine guns. The German heavy machine guns were especially hard to eliminate; they had five-man crews—gunner, helper, belt-feeder, and two grenadiers to protect the crew. The casualties were monstrous as squad after squad of Americans dashed forward with the bayonet to overrun the gun crews, only to be scythed down by the traversing machine guns.[53]

The memory of it all was harrowing. One veteran recalled that the lack of American machine-gun and artillery fire in this last struggle meant that there was no roar to drown out the screams of the wounded, making the combat even worse, "the worst afternoon of my life." The same veteran, who lost a leg in the fighting, never forgot the sight of a fellow Marine, on his back, "a kneecap still on its ligaments caught in brambles where it had been shot out of a leg, begging for someone to release it so he might inch back farther." Looking sorrowfully at the wood from his post across the Marne at Château-Thierry, 3rd Division commander General Joseph Dickman said: "The Marines fighting in Belleau Wood are magnificent, but theirs is a useless sacrifice." The goal had been to check the German drive on Paris—already accomplished—not rid Belleau Wood of every last German soldier.[54]

The Marines took the wood, the Germans finally succumbing to concentrated artillery fire and infantry attacks. In the last redoubt, the northern edge rimmed with rocky crests, the rifle pits were jumbled with American and German corpses; these men had fallen struggling for control of the machine guns. Colonel Wendell Neville, commanding the 5th Marines, sent a message to Harbord at 9 p.m. on June 24: "Woods now U.S. Marine Corps entirely." Degoutte gratefully renamed Belleau Wood the *Bois de la Brigade de Marine*, in honor of the five thousand US Marines killed or wounded there in June 1918. The Germans too were impressed. Richard von Kühlmann, the German foreign secretary, went before the Reichstag that day and spoke the obvious: America's intervention on the battlefield meant that "a decision by arms alone, without diplomatic parleys, can hardly be expected." The German troops agreed. "We have fought the Canadians and Australians," a German officer captured in Belleau Wood told his captors. "But you fellows are rougher." The American casualties were certainly as rough as anything experienced by any army. The US 2nd Division had lost nine thousand men, as had the 1st Division in its battles around Montdidier. Each would have to be withdrawn for rest and would have to take in thousands of replacements.[55]

"We're over the worst of the crisis," Foch's deputy General Maxime Weygand wrote on June 22. Ludendorff's attempt to widen Operation Blücher with a fourth offensive in the same area—Operation Gneisenau—on June 8 had been repulsed with the loss of another thirty thousand German assault troops. Allied losses of thirty-seven thousand were easier to replace, now that the Americans were finally entering the line in large numbers. There were now eight hundred thousand American troops in France, with three hundred thousand more sailing every month. Of the twenty-eight American divisions in

France, fourteen were now classed as ready for combat. Eight of the fourteen remained in the quiet sectors of the Western Front east of Verdun, the other six in line or in reserve in the hotly contested space between Reims and Château-Thierry. The fourteen divisions still in training were being rushed to readiness, receiving crash courses in gas drill, trench warfare, rifle training, machine guns, and trench mortars, then being moved forward for their first line experience.[56]

Everyone scrambled to predict the direction of the next German attack. Increased German registration fire portended one at Château-Thierry, as hundreds, sometimes thousands of rounds of high-burst shrapnel, gas, and high explosive came over daily in early July to rake and mark the Allied positions. American scouts swam across the Marne to look around in the night, and listening posts on the riverbank jotted down the sounds that drifted across: "Heavy traffic of wagons, trucks, caissons and rolling kitchens . . . working parties and men digging . . . sounds of iron workers . . . groups forming." It was never easy to conceal an attack. "Trucks," a Bavarian officer recalled, "were the hardest noise to cover up. We had the men sing and yodel when our trucks were driving in big numbers, but really how does one drown out the roar of truck engines?"[57]

The best the Germans could do was hide the work of those trucks. Gradually everything in sight disappeared from view as the Germans erected canopies of canvas and brush camouflage to hide all of their roads, replacing them whenever Allied artillery knocked them down. Continuous harassing machine-gun fire and artillery kept American noses from protruding too far over the Marne. Allied planes, pursued by German fighters, puttered up and down the front, photo reconnaissance aircraft looking for evidence of German infantry and artillery concentration that would reveal Ludendorff's plan. Teddy Roosevelt's youngest child, Quentin, died in this way. Flying his SPAD over Soissons on Bastille Day, he was shot from the sky by a German ace. One thing was clear: Ludendorff was in a tremendous hurry because of the quickening pace of the American deployment. The $1.4 trillion American war economy was finally hitting its stride;

American shipyards were turning out one hundred transport ships every month; the American truck industry was producing two hundred thousand vehicles a year; and Congress had added 2.4 million men to America's draft pool by extending registration from men in their twenties to men aged eighteen to forty-five. If the war dragged into 1919, only America would have the industrial resources and manpower to win it.[58]

8

CHÂTEAU-THIERRY

Ludendorff had wanted to launch his fifth, potentially decisive offensive in August, but now he pushed it up a
month to strike before more Americans entered the line and before
trained French and British recruits, needed to replace the casualties
of the first four offensives, were ready. Fading German public support for the war was being buttressed, for now, by unsustainable lies:
there were no American troops in France; every American transport
had been sunk by U-boats. The lies were so brazen—the German
press would report the sailing of a fictitious American troopship and
then, a few days later, report that it had been torpedoed by a fictitious
U-boat—that they couldn't be maintained forever, even in the face of
a German public cowed into credulity.[1]

The German army still had the advantage on the Western Front,
but it was melting away. Ludendorff had lost nearly a million men
since March and, like the Allies, was rummaging everywhere for replacements. He'd secured a pledge of six divisions from Vienna, but
the Austrian emperor had come up with only four, one of them, the
largely Czech and Polish 106th Landsturm Division, so feeble that
even the Austrians had considered it good for nothing more than

harvesting wheat in Russia. German and Austro-Hungarian units were classified by the youth and quality of their men; regular divisions were the best, followed by Landwehr and then finally Landsturm, the old, broken scrapings of the demographic barrel—men who before the war would never even have been considered for military service. When Austria's 106th Landsturm detrained in France to join General Max von Gallwitz's German Fifth Army, Gallwitz's officers gaped in disbelief. Most of the Austrian troops were barefoot and clothed in rags; German officers called them *sans-culottes*, a reference to the vagrants of Paris during the French Revolution.[2]

Clearly time, men, and matériel were running out for the Central Powers. With mounting desperation, Ludendorff readied what he hoped would be a knockout blow. He'd strike again in Champagne, this time with three armies totaling 2.3 million men. The left and center armies, massing one-third of Germany's entire artillery establishment, would blast into the space between Reims and Verdun. The right-hand army, General Max von Boehn's German Seventh Army, would continue deepening the Marne salient, then cross the river east of Château-Thierry, join with the armies of Generals Karl von Einem and Bruno von Mudra, and battle through the Surmelin Creek valley to gain the highway to Paris.[3]

While Ludendorff planned, Allied aircraft rained ten thousand propaganda leaflets a day on his troops, with messages like this: "German soldiers, come over to us—we don't mistreat German prisoners—here you'll have good food and peaceful quarters." Hindenburg scoffed at them: "If numerical superiority in troops alone won wars," he bluffly assured his troops, "Germany would long since have been smashed to the ground. . . . It's the German spirit that makes us invincible and it's that spirit that the enemy is trying to poison." The reality on the front line was that American units were now capturing German teenagers who hadn't even finished high school, described by one Doughboy thus: "China-faced German boys with purple-ringed blue eyes and grimy, tear-streaked faces." They whimpered when taken, the veteran recalled, or "occasionally bleated a weak-chinned *Kamerad*." When Hindenburg's appeals to "the German spirit"—*der deutsche Geist*—were insufficient, the field marshal told lies: "The enemy will leave you unsheltered in barbed-wire pens, rob you, starve you, beat you, and make you perform hard labor under the ridicule of French civilians."[4]

On July 2, Major Paul Clark, liaising for Pershing in Foch's headquarters, reported that French intelligence indicated that Ludendorff had amassed eighty divisions—half of his remaining force—for a last thrust in Champagne. It was a tribute to German improvisation and resilience that this was the same number of divisions that they had relied on in March, only these were worn down, more than half of them "fatigued" or "reconstructed." Judging from their rail movements, the Germans were expected to attack in three places: Châlons-sur-Marne, Compiègne-Montdidier, and Abbeville-Amiens. A French spy reported that Ludendorff had told his officers that the approach would be the usual: "We are going to make a series of partial attacks and then we will pass to the general attack," with the whole German front advancing when "the partial attacks had sufficiently dislocated the Allies." A Doughboy in the 3rd Division recalled increased German aerial activity over the Marne and German artillery registering targets in the last days of June.[5]

The general attack would be the grand finale, the knockout blow. Ludendorff had decided, Clark summarized, "to go the limit in an effort to destroy the French army." The main thrust would go through the French sector, with Paris as its objective, because, as Foch's intelligence director noted, "the Germans think that if they take Paris it will be the end." Allied aviation reported growing German ammo dumps in Champagne, piles of ammunition in the German trenches there, and "abnormal movements" in the rear, day and night. Burgeoning radio chatter implied a looming attack. German prisoners spoke of fresh divisions in Champagne; one divulged that the objective would be Reims, the hills east of the town, and the Marne, to secure the German left flank. The Germans couldn't launch a "grand attack" on Paris without the railroad through Reims and without resting their left wing on the Marne. The Marne would secure their flank, sharply reducing the number of German troops needed for flank protection and increasing the number available for a thrust at Paris. "The Hun wants Reims," said General Julien Dufieux, "to get more railroads, to split the French army in two, and to draw reserves away from Paris." There were no immediate indications of a German attack on the British front, but one couldn't be ruled out, for even as they planned the massive operation in Champagne, the Germans had twenty-three rested reserve divisions arrayed around Hazebrouck in Flanders. They might attack Haig's withered BEF once the fighting erupted in Champagne and Allied reserves were marching in that direction. Ludendorff was playing his last hand: knock out France, drive the British into the sea, and end the war.[6]

The Germans, in short, were still immensely threatening despite their heavy casualties in the spring. They'd gathered in all that they could from the Eastern Front and had 3.5 million troops available in July 1918. By now, the BEF was down to 1.23 million troops, France down to 1.67 million. The French themselves admitted that their poilus weren't very good: "They lack the punch of fresh new troops like yours," Colonel Rozet told Clark. French offensives were going nowhere; only the tanks were advancing, and the "infantry won't readily follow them."[7] Everyone now looked to the Americans for salvation. Pétain pressed nonstop for American divisions for his armies, which were going to bear the full weight of Ludendorff's next offensive. Foch went to Chaumont on July 8 to meet with Pershing and plead Pétain's case. Many of the newly arrived American units had just two weeks' instruction, but Petain wanted them anyway; he wanted Pershing to plug American regiments into French divisions.

Foch's optimism wrestled with Pétain's pessimism. Foch, "whose accounts of a situation," journalist Charles Repington noted, "were usually rather prophetic than literally accurate," now prophesied the situation to be this: Ludendorff would be stopped and the Allies would soon be presented with a golden opportunity to counterattack the fatigued German assault troops. Foch urged Pétain to "infuse his men with more offensive spirit and audacity" and restore the "élan and abandon we had at the start of the war." Pétain, of course, had heard all of this before; such utopian thinking had blocked his career before the war and, since 1914, had led to mass casualties in every French offensive and the French army mutinies of 1917. Indeed, Pétain had only brought the French army back to life by making broad concessions like fresh bread, ample red wine, prudent tactics, and regular leave that couldn't be canceled, even in cases of national emergency. "Pinard, permission, et croix de guerre," the poilus chuckled (Red wine, leave, and *then* the cross of war). But Foch persisted: with tanks, masses of new artillery, the Americans, and fading German morale, we will win. Pétain remained skeptical. Clemenceau had begun to doubt Foch as well and now considered sacking him. Foch's job as generalissimo, Repington observed, "was easy with success but might be impossible with failure." If he stumbled, he'd be fired, and he looked to be stumbling now.[8]

During the evening of July 14, German intentions finally became clear when a French raiding party captured a German major east of Reims. The officer was carrying Ludendorff's plan of attack for the next morning. Foch couldn't believe his luck; Bruchmüller's desolating bombardment with five thousand guns was scheduled to begin in just six hours, at 12:10 a.m. on July 15. An hour after that, General Max von Boehn's Seventh Army would strike with twenty-eight divisions across the Marne between Château-Thierry and Reims. Between Reims and Verdun, General Bruno von Mudra's First Army and General Karl von Einem's Third Army would thrust toward Châlons-sur-Marne with twenty-three divisions to shatter the French Fourth and Second Armies, and then wheel west toward Paris. Ludendorff's fifth and final offensive aimed to encircle Reims from both flanks, seize its vital rail yards, and extend the salient created by Operation Blücher. The Germans would then pour along the valley of Surmelin Creek, passing through the hills on the south bank of the Marne to threaten Paris in concert with the big German armies turning west from Châlons.

More precious Allied reserves would have to be shifted south and east, possibly permitting Crown Prince Rupprecht of Bavaria to deal Haig a mortal blow in Flanders with his three armies. Berlin was hopeful. Surely *this* offensive would be the decisive one. Hindenburg assured his troops that it would end with a "German Peace," finally rewarding their efforts. At the very least, the drive toward Paris would sever the connection between the French capital and Verdun, causing the fall of the fortress on the Meuse and a rebound in German morale. By now, the French were so worn down that their Second Army, holding the ground at Verdun, had orders, in the event of a German breakthrough around Reims, to abandon its trenches (opening the door to Verdun and Nancy) and strike westward into the flank of the German advance. "This move," the chief of the French Operations Bureau later wrote, "was regarded as the best that could be done to counter the German advance, which was calculated to go as far as Bar-le-Duc and cut the French Army into two parts." Germany's chancellor licked his lips in anticipation. "We expected great things in Paris by the end of July," he scribbled in his memoirs.[9]

But time was running out for the German army. Using the American general staff's Belgian index, British manpower had fallen to 9.5 and French to 11.5, but an American increase to 3 allowed the Allied total of 25 to be maintained. The Germans, meanwhile, had fallen to 30. Foch was insisting that the British keep up 59 divisions, but they were down to 50 and struggling to keep those 50 up to strength. The French were hard-pressed to maintain 105 understrength divisions. The Germans still had an edge—five hundred thousand more troops than the Allies—but American arrivals (and German casualties) were eroding it daily. The Germans had suffered five hundred thousand casualties in their four pushes, including ninety-five thousand dead and thirty-two thousand captured. Storm troop tactics were a two-edged sword: they were fast, but they were risky. The assault battalions couldn't retreat without sacrificing their momentum and effect, and so whenever a serious counterattack developed they were usually wiped out, German officer prisoners (or corpses) found with orders like this stuffed in their pockets: "Not one of your soldiers should dare to withdraw from the combat." Flu was racing through the German ranks. The Germans no longer had enough artillery and shells to launch more than one offensive at a time, which blunted the threat from Rupprecht's Flanders force. This fifth attack—hopefully nicknamed the *Friedenssturm* (Peace Offensive)—would have to crack the Allies. More troubling still, the entry of trained Americans into the line, along with the French recruiting class of 1919 and the British replacements trained since the spring, was about to flip the advantage in reserves from the Germans to the Allies. August 1, 1918, would be the crossover point, when Germany would lose its manpower advantage and never regain it.[10]

On the German right, in Boehn's sector, Ludendorff's fifth and final offensive aimed at General Jean Degoutte's Sixth Army. It curved from Château-Thierry eastward to Reims and contained just one French division, two Italian divisions, elements of the US 28th Division, and General Joseph Dickman's US 3rd Division. The 3rd Division was deployed in the Surmelin Valley, the critical path to Paris. An American officer with the 42nd Rainbow Division—deployed in reserve here—noted that now "the French are really anxious for the Boche to start something, for they've never been so well prepared for an attack, and everyone is confident of walloping them."[11]

Foch ordered every gun south of the Marne to open up on the German positions north of the river at 11:45 p.m. on July 14. This was interdiction fire, intended to hit the masses of German troops and guns that were believed to be filing up to the Marne in the darkness. It worked; the Germans were caught in columns of squads on the banks of the Marne, and one of their assault divisions was nearly wiped out. They absorbed the Allied shells and then fired their own bombardment on schedule at 12:10 a.m. For the French and Americans, the interdiction fire seemed hardly to have checked the fury of the German drum fire, which hammered a space sixty-five miles long and several miles deep for nine hours. Near Château-Thierry, a lieutenant of the US 28th Division watched the impacts under a full moon from half a mile away: "An immense cloud of dust full of lightning and thunder, vast red splashes, fountains of stone and earth, and hurtling trunks of trees."[12]

The German drum fire crept toward the lieutenant in quarter-mile leaps, consuming woods, fields, pastures, and cottages in fiery red whirlwinds. The crash of shells was "world-ending," the American's throat tasted "the choking reek of high explosive." Companies of infantry and batteries of guns deployed in the path of the drum fire were exterminated. In one place where the barrage had passed, the lieutenant saw what remained of a company of men from his own regiment; he knew their faces, or what remained of them: "A couple of hundred men were tossed about, many blown into several pieces, hands, arms and torsos lying about in the forest." When their grief-stricken mothers received the official notification of their demise—"Your son nobly gave his life in the service of his country"—would they ever imagine just *how* these men gave their lives? "To be shelled is the worst thing in the world," the lieutenant added. It is impossible to imagine it adequately." Especially shelling like this, reputed to be the heaviest of the war. "There is a faraway moan that grows to a scream, then a roar like a train, followed by a ground-shaking smash and a diabolical red light." Men simply "lay and trembled . . . some cool, some shaking, some weeping; a few grim jokes, but mostly just dull endurance, a hunching of the shoulders when another comes and the thought—'how long, how long?'"[13]

An American officer near Reims described the same pandemonium there as French and American infantry staggered around in gas masks searching for their dugouts—which "shook like cardboard" under the impacts—while German shells shattered Allied batteries and ammo dumps and German aircraft flew low over the trenches strafing their occupants. Then the Germans launched pontoon boats into the Marne to cross and wrest the south bank from the French and Americans. The Germans were trying to scramble across the Marne at Château-Thierry. This Second Battle of the Marne—the first had been the French and British repulse of the Germans in September 1914—was the first great test of the AEF in France. Eight American divisions were pulled into the fighting to stop the German advance: the 1st, 2nd, 3rd, 4th, 26th, 28th, 32nd, and 42nd—four regular army divisions and four National Guard divisions.[14]

The German X Corps—led by the crack troops of the 2nd Guards Division—attacked General Joseph Dickman's US 3rd Division, which held the Marne riverbank between Château-Thierry and Mézy.

Here the German plan was to surprise the Americans and French on the river, defeat the outposts and "sacrifice units" on the Marne swiftly, then assemble on the south bank behind a creeping barrage at 4:50 a.m. to attack up the Surmelin Valley and wipe out the main French and American lines of resistance farther back. The Germans were now closer to Paris than at any time in the entire war. Criticism of Foch resumed. Clemenceau again was rumored to be on the verge of sacking the generalissimo, a British general remarking: "To outward appearance, [Foch] had been uniformly unsuccessful since taking over the command in France."[15]

At Château-Thierry, the US 3rd Division earned its sobriquet "the Rock of the Marne." The Doughboys stood fast, not behaving like light-footed skirmishers or like the French on either side of them, who prudently withdrew. The French artillery abandoned their guns before the onslaught and Degoutte's sole French division, the 125th, holding the Jaulgonne bend and installed in Varennes, Reuilly, and Cortemont, "absolutely melted and disappeared into thin air," an American colonel informed Pershing's headquarters:

> There is not a single unit of the [French] division in line, except the commander and his staff and I think they have been canned. The only ones who stayed were a regiment of our 28th Division who had been placed with them to prove to the French that we were there. The French abandoned them and less than half of them survived. They were overwhelmed. This despite fact that French were dug in behind the railway embankment and could have done better fighting than trying to get away under the creeping barrage.[16]

One Doughboy recalled sitting down to eat with a battery of French gunners when a messenger appeared and handed the battery commander a slip of paper: "It was like lightning. In less than a minute there was not a single man left in the battery. They mounted the horses left in the woods below them and beat it. They left their supper still cooking. 'Boches coming' was all I could gather, and they were gone," their abandoned guns pointing silently at the Marne.[17]

For the men of the US 28th Division, the battle that ensued was excoriating, an experience, as one veteran put it, "of complete and unmitigated reality." These men would never experience anything so ghastly again. Inner and outer worlds fused. "The sheep or wolf's clothing in which the ego may have wrapped itself are at one and the same time sublimed," a veteran wrote. Men crouched in terror, the "gauze and lace curtains" laid by civilization across the mind ripped away; one saw "clearly by one's naked self for an unforgettable moment blind force operating by pure chance." Doughboys were pulverized randomly by shell fragments and machine-gun salvos, confirming that "living existence is merely the opposite of nothing at all." Survivors were provided "a glimpse of the nature of the end of everything." One had this to say about death: "It has no steps. It arrives."[18]

Dickman's 3rd Division—in similar straits—clung to the Marne's south bank with two 3,500-man regiments and refused to retire. As the French withdrew on their flanks to their main line of resistance, the 3rd Division curled its own flanks backward to hold off persistent attacks from elements of three different German divisions. The Germans, who had taught the Allies defense in depth and could only assume that the Doughs would drop back, were astounded by the American resistance. The Doughboys lay up behind the railway embankment that ran along the river east of Château-Thierry and poured fire into the German assault teams. The fire was so thick that Germans lying flat in the wheat that grew beside the railway called it suicidal to raise one's head "above the ears" in the wheat. A German general, colonel, and major, all sent forward to investigate the delay, were killed this way. The 3rd Division's 38th Regiment took 20 percent casualties, and its 30th Regiment nearly as many, holding the line across the valley between Mézy and Moulins. Pershing called it "one of the most brilliant pages in our military annals."[19]

Of all the carnage, what most impressed Corporal John Barkley of the 3rd Division was the way the German artillery focused its fire on American horses, locating them and then blasting them with gas shells and shrapnel to immobilize the American guns and ammo deliveries. "Wherever there were little open spaces, wounded horses staggered out of the trees, bleeding to death and screaming." The Germans rained shells and phosgene on Barkley's unit: "The woods were going to pieces. Shell fragments were shearing off branches and tops of trees, and whole trees were crashing down as if they'd been felled by an ax." He had his first close call, a heavy shell splinter slamming into the earth an inch from his hand.[20]

A Bavarian officer who struggled to cross the Marne at Chassins and Vincelles described the difficulty of crossing the seventy-yard-wide river against ferocious American resistance. Each time a pontoon bridge was constructed, the American artillery would either ruin or damage it. He remembered crossing a flimsy bridge and stepping over a pile of dead officers in the middle, among them a two-star general; they'd been scythed down by a shell or machine gun while directing repairs. "This memory of a heap of dead officers, the scarlet-striped pants of a general protruding from their midst, still haunts those of us who survived." The German assault troops were so heavily equipped that any who fell into the Marne were dragged to the bottom and drowned by the weight of their packs, bandoliers, and light machine guns. The Bavarian recalled his men "mincing like tightrope artists" along the damaged sections of the bridge; they "crouched fearfully" as they advanced, "for to fall in the river was to die."[21]

Once across, two battalions of the Bavarian 20th Regiment struck into the woods of Condé. They ran into a wounded German captain exiting the wood and asked him where the enemy was. He pointed south: "Keep going in that direction till you contact the enemy, but watch out! The enemy bites too, there are American troops there, and black Senegalese." The fighting in the wood was as bitter as it had been on the riverbank. Senegalese machine-gun nests concealed in the brush spat fire at the German infantry, who had no artillery cover, the German guns taking far longer to get across the Marne than the infantry. A Doughboy entering the wood choked back nausea and despair: "It was full of dead men in all conceivable contortions. Some had been blown to pieces two or three times; others lay as if asleep; some were just torsos. There was a head with glasses still on. The gas masks added the last devilish effect."[22]

The Senegalese machine gunners would let the Germans, stumbling through the underbrush, close to within twenty yards before opening fire, cutting down whole units. An officer of the German 5th Grenadier Regiment recorded the terror the Americans produced in his ranks, which suffered 60 percent casualties. "The Americans kill everybody," German soldiers were heard crying to each other. With their bridges under fire, the Germans tried to cross the Marne in boats and were shot up as badly as the men on the bridges. One Doughboy behind the Château-Thierry railway embankment remembered firing until his rifle was burning hot, the grease boiling out of the woodwork. He had to pour water from his canteen over the rifle and through the barrel. He paused to watch a wounded American officer being carried back with both legs blown off. For men such as this, the Doughs piteously coined the term *basket case*—it referred to a man who'd lost his legs and had to be transported to the rear in a basket. "For God's sake," the captain moaned as he passed, "give me a drink of water or put me out. I can't go back like this."[23]

The night of July 15, an officer in the US 28th Division reflected, was "the supreme crisis of the First World War." Having engaged the German assault divisions on the Marne, he watched them flow past on the roads toward Paris and saw the heads of their columns meet the main American and French lines farther back. The Germans spread out, flattened, and failed to break through. The Peace Offensive had stalled. Overhead, the sky blazed with shellfire—"smears of molten red and white-hot light"—and the Germans, stopped cold, admitted defeat on the Marne and began to extract troops from the south bank back to the north. They'd been undone by Foch's discovery of their plan and Degoutte's Sixth Army, and in no small part by the Rock of the Marne. East of the city, Boehn had managed to get seventy-five thousand men across the river into the space vacated by the French outposts, but those seven divisions were stopped by the intermediate lines of the French Fourth and Fifth Armies and then counterattacked by the French as well as the US 42nd Rainbow Division.[24]

A German captain moving between two assault divisions in this space called it "the most disheartening day of the whole war."

His troops had made easy progress at first and then had run into intact French and American defenses dug into "an endless wilderness of chalk . . . under a merciless sun, the air quivering in a dance of heat." The Rainbows, handpicked by Gouraud for their aggressive spirit, didn't disappoint. "We were tired of all that mustard gas shit, and now we could get our hands on those Goddamned Germans," a veteran snarled. Gouraud had dug new trenches at night, two miles behind the frontline trenches known to the Germans, and when the Germans finally appeared before the new ones, the Americans and French gunned them down. East of Reims, the German effort to reach Châlons-sur-Marne also failed, as the armies of Mudra and Einem were stopped almost immediately by Gouraud's Fourth Army guns, which knew the exact time and place of the German advance.[25]

By now, four months after Operation Michael, the Allies had learned how to defeat German assault divisions. They disposed in depth, placing thinly manned outpost zones in the path of the German storm troops and artillery, and removed most of their infantry and guns to a resistance line beyond the range of all but the heaviest German artillery. If the Germans even reached that resistance line, they'd be so exhausted by marching and fending off artillery, air, and machine-gun attacks that they'd never break through. "At this point," a German colonel recalled, "we all began to suspect that the drive on Paris was no longer feasible." Another German officer noted how demoralizing defense in depth was: "We didn't see a single dead Frenchman, let alone a captured gun or machine gun, and we'd suffered heavy losses."[26]

Boehn was thrown back at Château-Thierry. Advancing American units discovered a German dugout on Hill 204, the height that commanded the town, filled with treasures looted from Château-Thierry: books from Jean de La Fontaine's library, crystal chandeliers, wine, tapestries, and women's clothing. Mudra and Einem were stopped in the chalk wastes and marshy fields on either side of the Marne. They'd shelled French and American frontline trenches that were all but empty for twenty-four hours before attacking. When they attacked, they were, as one observer put it, "herded into lanes by the fire of strategically located strong points, then blinded and butchered by artillery fire that followed them relentlessly." In London, a British general assured Charles Repington over dinner that Einem's loss of fifty thousand men in his initial push must have hit the Germans every bit as hard as the British loss of sixty thousand troops on the first day of the Somme.[27]

Like Boehn, Einem and Mudra called off their attacks on July 18 and retreated back to the north, the American and French artillery shattering their bridges on the way out as effectually as they had three days earlier on the way in. A Doughboy pursuing the Germans back to the Marne noted the devastation all around: "Empty little villages—simply eggshells of houses shelled to pieces." In the bigger towns, "the streets were full of slate and bricks, fires burning, walls full of holes. . . . All windows were smashed, furniture and all manner of articles wasted around, and a kind of breathless air of dead expectancy." He passed a column of French troops, and one of the poilus called to him: "Américains et français, bons camarades!" (Americans and French, good comrades!) There was, the American recalled, "a spirit of rejoicing in the air, a consciousness that the German tide was on the ebb." A French officer filled the American's canteen with wine and patted him on the back: "C'est fini maintenant!" (It's over now!) The American recalled the Frenchman pinching shut his nostrils and laughingly indicating twenty dead horses, all in a row. They were rotting *German* horses; the Frenchman's loathing of the enemy extended even to the animal kingdom.[28]

The Germans retreated past a shattered Reims, described by a visitor as "a deserted city except for a few French gendarmes guarding the ruins," its magnificent cathedral crumbled by direct hits from German artillery, its wasted outskirts "torn up by millions of shells, whole forests destroyed, and town after town reduced to piles of debris." The commander of the Bavarian 20th Reserve Regiment recalled that his men had eaten nothing substantial for three days and that when food was finally delivered on July 18, it was carried into his position by wounded soldiers who'd been released from hospital for this hazardous duty, which certainly suggested the severity of Germany's own manpower crisis. The colonel's regiment had been reduced to 660 men—the strength of a weak battalion. One of his hundred-man companies was reduced to a dozen men when the French or Americans located its rifle pits and fired four massive mortar bombs into them. Four mangled dead and sixteen severely wounded were accounted for, but the other sixty-eight "had simply vanished—blown into thin air."[29]

An American officer surmised that this was the moment when the Germans knew that "the jig was up." All of their roads out of the Aisne-Marne salient were jammed with troops and trains: "The scenes on those choked lines of retreat, as our shells burst on their withdrawing columns, must have been truly infernal. Over the edge of the world, uttering their banshee wails like screams of vengeance, and roaring like express trains, came the messengers of the outraged republics," light and heavy shells, the "bellow of an explosion, arms, legs, trunks of men, death-dealing fragments of jagged steel and whirling wreckage falling for miles along the gray-helmeted, rearward-plodding columns." Against artillery like this, "it was no use to cry '*Kamerad*,' or shriek to *Gott*."[30]

General Dickman's 3rd Rock of the Marne Division had prevented a successful crossing and chewed up two crack German grenadier regiments. German casualties had piled up as they tried to bull their way to Paris. Already on July 16, one of Foch's aides told Major Paul Clark that Ludendorff had lost another "50,000–60,000 men with little result." German prisoners captured in the first days of the Peace Offensive spoke of desperation on the German home front. Troops were being ordered to loot the villages they passed through, to steal clothing and send it back to Germany for the impoverished civilians. The German army was running out of gasoline. The German mark had lost 50 percent of its value. A German officer captured on July 20 had the papers of an enlisted man and the uniform of a lieutenant; when asked to explain the discrepancy he said that he'd been recently commissioned but hadn't been provided with new identification "due to the paper shortage in Germany." Captured propaganda manuals revealed the half-truths German officers were telling their troops to make them go on: the French army was broken and out of reserves; the Americans hadn't arrived in force and "counted for nothing"; the Italians serving on the Western Front "would run as soon as they were attacked."[31]

At his headquarters, Foch predicted psychological collapse in Germany when Ludendorff's ballyhooed Peace Offensive failed. "If he keeps it up, he's a goner. This battle, the biggest of the war, will have a very important influence on military and political opinion in Germany." All of the French officers agreed that the Germans were suddenly on the verge of defeat. Major Aldebert de Chambrun assured Clark that "this is the biggest defeat of the war." General Julien Dufieux called it "the greatest day since the Marne in 1914." Ludendorff had shot his bolt; now was the time to counterattack. "We must keep it up day in and day out till the Boche falls on his knees and begs for mercy." One of Pétain's aides predicted, with astonishing precision, "peace in three months."[32]

But Hindenburg and Ludendorff still had forty-nine reserve divisions north of the Marne, half fresh, half reconstituted. They were still capable of *something*. Having failed again on the Marne, Ludendorff now planned the great blow in Flanders he'd kept postponing while seeking a decision against the French. As the Peace Offensive faltered, he traveled to Mons in Belgium to supervise a resumption of the offensive there. But by now Ludendorff was losing his luster. Five straight offensives having failed, it now appeared that he was just launching attacks—as a colleague put it—"in the hope of something turning up." The Allies anticipated another German push in Flanders but couldn't be sure that the Germans wouldn't double down in Champagne or Picardy again. A brisk debate ensued; counterattack the Germans now, or continue on the defensive until they'd fired their last shot? Major Clark visited General Maurice de Barescut on July 12: "I asked, 'Are you going to attack?' He said, 'We are going to attack, and we will be ready by the 14th. We will put in all we can. We will put in all the Americans we can. It will be launched from the Tenth Army front between Soissons and Château-Thierry, just after the German has committed himself to attack on the fronts of the Seventh and Fifth Armies. If he only attacks in Champagne east of Reims, it will be launched then.'" One of Pétain's aides said much the same thing on July 13: "It will be a tremendous, decisive battle; the Boche will put in 60 to 80 divisions. This is the critical moment of the war."[33]

Ludendorff's thrust in Champagne around Reims had created opportunities for the Allies. The situation in this Second Battle of the Marne was akin to the situation in the first Marne battle of 1914. Then, as now, the Germans had driven a bulge into the Allied line, and then, as now, they'd left the western flank of that bulge—from Château-Thierry to Soissons—weak. With so many Americans now available, the Allies finally had the reserves to attack that weakness.[34]

9

SECOND MARNE

Persuaded by Foch to win the Second Battle of the Marne with a well-aimed counterpunch, Pétain—still worried about Ludendorff's intentions—reluctantly ordered General Charles Mangin's French Tenth Army to spearhead a great Allied counter-offensive against the vital German roads and railways from Soissons to Château-Thierry. Instead of awaiting the last German thrust, Foch wanted to preempt it with his own shattering offensive, just as Joffre had done in the First Battle of the Marne four years earlier. "It was a case of tired troops attacking troops who were more tired," a British observer noted. Eager to be in on the action, Pershing attached General Hunter Liggett's US I Corps, which contained the 1st, 2nd, 26th, 32nd, 42nd, and 77th Divisions, to Mangin's army. General Robert Lee Bullard commanded the US III Corps, which embodied the other American divisions sprawled around the perimeter of the Aisne-Marne salient: the 3rd, 28th, and 32nd. These nine US divisions contained the manpower equivalent of thirty French divisions—a huge injection of manpower at a critical point. They marched into position and, to simplify command and control, were slotted into French corps for the push: Liggett's divisions in the French XX Corps,

Bullard's divisions in General Piarron de Mondésir's French XXXVIII Corps.[1]

Foch saw clearly that after five fruitless offensives, the Germans were vulnerable—at the head of outthrust salients, tired, hungry, and demoralized by their crippling casualties and lack of progress. Soissons presented a particularly juicy target, for every German supply line to Château-Thierry ran through it. If the Allies took it, they might bag the entire German Seventh Army, which was still bunched inside the Aisne-Marne salient. Foch ordered a great Allied counteroffensive for July 18. Needless to say, after all of the setbacks and narrow escapes since March, it was hugely controversial. The Germans were closer to Paris than at any time during the war. They were still attacking, and Pétain was still demanding reserves—for the defense, not the attack. For his part, Haig hesitated to commit four divisions of his scarce reserves to the French front for Foch's offensive.[2]

Foch writhed with impatience. He wanted to smash Ludendorff with a vast Allied counteroffensive before the German could strike again. Foch now insisted on his role as Allied generalissimo, *ordering* an attack along the entire line from Soissons down to Château-Thierry and up to Reims. On July 15, Foch visited General Emile Fayolle, who commanded France's reserve divisions, and asked how arrangements for the counterattack were coming along; Fayolle replied, "We've canceled them and are reinforcing the French front southwest of Reims, where the Germans are still thrusting south." Clearly Pétain was exerting his usual cautious influence. Foch—the chief of the French general staff—insisted that Fayolle ignore Pétain—the commander of the French field armies—and prepare to counterattack. Pétain pushed back; the poilus, he snarled, "can't stand the sight of Foch," who seemed always to be conducting them to their deaths. And yet the deep Marne salient created by Ludendorff's third, fourth, and fifth offensives was ripe for the taking. One of Foch's folksy parables was, "If you arrive at the station two or three minutes after the train has gone, you miss it." He considered the moment ripe to trap General Max von Boehn's Seventh Army before it slipped back to the safety of the Aisne River barrier. "The result of this counter-attack might change completely the history of the war," a British officer wrote from Foch's headquarters.[3]

Though they were American corps commanders—the first since the Civil War—Bullard and Liggett did little more than watch the unfolding battle, which was directed by the French. They lacked staff or even basic familiarity with the terrain, as did their divisional commanders. Fifty-one-year-old General Charles Summerall, the most ruthless officer in the US Army, a perfect fit with "Butcher" Mangin, replaced Bullard as commander of the Big Red One. General Omar Bundy, too pompous and punctilious, even by regular army standards, was removed as 2nd Division commander and replaced by General James Harbord, who'd commanded Bundy's Marine Brigade in Belleau Wood. Summerall and Harbord, who would spearhead Mangin's attack on Soissons, were flung into the line west of Soissons with their troops without explanation. They both hurriedly mimeographed French orders that they scarcely understood, then drove their men through the rain-swept Retz Forest on July 18 to the heights above the Crise River, where their 155mm guns could blast the Soissons rail yards, bustling with German troops and supplies. The plan was simple—kill or capture every German in the space between the Marne and the Aisne.[4]

Foch was in such a hurry to strike that both American divisions nearly missed the battle. The US 2nd Division, on the right flank of the 1st, struggled through the Retz Forest to reach positions commanding the Soissons–Château-Thierry road. Just to reach their positions they had nearly been annihilated by the French Tenth Army staff, which bused one of their regiments on July 16 to a little village named Marcilly, where a French staff officer was to meet the buses and tell them where to deploy. They arrived to find no French officer. After searching the village, the Americans found a French officer sitting in a car on the side of road. "Drive to Fontaine-les-Nonnes for your orders," he said. The regiment drove there, only to find no French officers there either. A search located a French officer in a corner of the village. "Drive to La Plesne," he said. At La Plesne, a French officer said, "Go to Morienval," and placed guides aboard the buses. The buses wended through the night to Morienval, where, the next morning, the French said, "Get off your buses and march back to La Plesne." As the head of the column reached La Plesne, a French officer appeared shouting and waving his arms: "Go to Retheuil," he insisted. Another French officer appeared; "No, no," he said, "march east into the forest of Retz and bivouac there." An hour-long delay ensued while French staff officers counted the Americans, it being French practice to bill the US government for every Doughboy they transported into a French sector. ("They made sure they were not overlooking any single man in the bill to be rendered for moving our troops into the French Corps Sector in which we were to attack," an American officer recalled.)[5]

The exhausted Americans countermarched into the wood and were told to be ready to attack at dawn from its eastern edge. Night fell, and a heavy rain pelted down; it was pitch black, and the Doughs blundered along a muddy track already jammed with troops and equipment. Every battalion dissolved into groups of stragglers who threaded their way past stopped vehicles and guns. The various groups of men arrived in their jumping-off positions just as the attack was beginning at 4:35 a.m. They had to sprint to the starting line, without machine guns or mortars, or even a briefing from their officers. The French meanwhile, whose own primer for open warfare began, "The critical period lies in the transportation of infantry forces up to assaulting distance," sent back snide reports that "the Americans are lost in the woods."[6]

By 8 a.m. on July 18, the US 1st and 2nd Divisions had joined a massive push on Soissons by seventeen Allied divisions and 346 French tanks and had penetrated three miles behind a heavy barrage. But then it took the Americans another five days just to cross the Soissons–Château-Thierry road and take the heights of Buzancy. The German line—ten divisions, nine hundred guns, and nine hundred aircraft in the space around Soissons—had buckled but held, inflicting more casualties on the Allies than they suffered themselves. The Allied force, 70 percent French, 30 percent American, had broken through the Bavarian 11th Division southwest of Soissons but had been unable to exploit the breakthrough, allowing the Germans to recover in new positions behind the Vesle and Aisne Rivers.[7]

Ludendorff was in Belgium, traveling from German general headquarters in Spa to meet with his northern army commander, forty-nine-year-old Bavarian crown prince Rupprecht, at the prince's headquarters in Tournai. They were finalizing arrangements for the projected Flanders offensive—Operation Hagen—when the storm broke. With Foch on the attack, Ludendorff reluctantly postponed Hagen and hustled back to Spa. Hagen was the half man, half elf who'd murdered Siegfried in Wagner's Ring Cycle, and the German generals could see that yet another Ludendorff offensive would only murder what good troops remained to the German army. Back at Spa, Ludendorff met with the commander of the army bearing the brunt of Foch's counteroffensive, German crown prince Wilhelm, the kaiser's thirty-six-year-old son. Wilhelm feared that General Mangin, closing on Boehn's last escape route, was about to inflict "a Sedan" on his army, a reference to Prussia's encirclement and capture of the French army in 1870. A return to the defensive—forcing the *Allies* into the open, where *they* could be slaughtered—offered better chances. With most of the French tanks damaged or destroyed by German fire, it would be easier to stem the Allied onslaught. Easier still because Pétain refused to give Mangin any reserves. The Germans clung to a bridgehead on the Marne and had killed or wounded another ninety-five thousand Frenchmen in the Soissons counteroffensive. It was harvest time, and the ripening grain gave perfect cover for German machine-gun nests. "I know what a seducer you are," Pétain growled to Mangin. "But this time there is nothing I can give you."[8]

With the US 1st Division on the left, the US 2nd Division reached the Paris-Soissons road on July 19, threatening Boehn's principal line of retreat from Château-Thierry. "From that moment," a veteran of the war noted, "the German never took another step forward anywhere in France." Surprised by Foch's offensive, the fury of the American attacks, and his own mounting casualties—another 168,000 Germans killed and wounded in the *Friedenssturm*—Ludendorff now recognized that he'd lost his chance to win the war by flailing at multiple targets instead of driving at one. For the Allies, great opportunities beckoned. The US 1st and 2nd Divisions were attacking the top of the salient, cutting the roads northward, while the US 3rd, 4th, and 26th Divisions attacked the western and southern faces of the salient. Four more American divisions were advancing to attack on the eastern face: the 28th, 32nd, 42nd, and 77th.[9]

The fighting raged day and night, Allied units leapfrogging each other to maintain pressure on the Germans. One platoon leader in Pennsylvania's 28th Division recalled that "a lot of weary men too tired to answer the usual 'What outfit, boys?' soon passed us going to the rear. The platoons looked small. They had been at the front." The Americans pushed up to the edge of the German salient created by Operation Blücher and the Peace Offensive: the 1st Division on the left near Soissons, the 2nd to its right, the 4th and 26th to either side of Belleau Wood, and the 3rd opposite Château-Thierry. Their mission was to collapse the bulge and destroy the Germans inside it.[10]

It was a good thing that the twenty-eight-thousand-man "Pershing divisions" were so bloated with manpower—three or four times the size of a German division—for in its reckless attacks toward Soissons, the 2nd Division suffered 4,300 more casualties fighting for places like Beaurepaire Farm and Vierzy, to add to the 8,000 it had already suffered in Belleau Wood. The 1st Division lost 7,000 troops in its fight for Berzy-le-Sec and the heights above Soissons. Thousands of the casualties were blown to pieces, as the Germans—in compact, prepared position on the plateau of Soissons and the Chemin des Dames—fired masses of preranged artillery into the waves of attacking Doughboys and Marines. Unscathed men emerged with shattered eardrums from all of the detonations. Veterans said that they'd never experienced artillery like this before, or after. "The miracle was not only that any of us survived but that we could keep moving," one wrote.[11]

George Marshall, who was reassigned from the 1st Division to Pershing's headquarters on the eve of the battle, ruefully noted that within seventy-two hours of his departure "every field officer of the infantry, excepting three colonels, had fallen." A colonel, all four

The fighting raged day and night in the summer of 1918, Allied units leapfrogging each other to maintain pressure on the Germans. Here, men of the US 1st Division—the Big Red One—advance through Fresnes in the Aisne-Marne salient. One platoon leader recalled that "a lot of weary men too tired to answer the usual 'What outfit, boys?' soon passed us going to the rear. The platoons looked small. They had been at the front." (National Archives)

lieutenant colonels, and every battalion commander had been killed or wounded in the desperate fighting for the Soissons–Château-Thierry Road. Casualties like this were hard to stomach; they shocked men and strained the bonds of discipline. Colonel Frank Parker, who commanded the Big Red One's 18th Infantry Regiment, accosted Summerall about the casualties. How, he demanded to know, could Summerall have fed the regiment into a battle where most of its men, officers, and NCOs had been killed or wounded? Summerall was unmoved: "Colonel, I did not come here to have you criticize my orders or tell me your losses. I know them as well as you do. I came here to tell you that the Germans recrossed the Marne last night and are in full retreat and you will attack tomorrow morning at 4:30 a.m." A French observer applauded the "wonderful courage" of the Americans but deplored their recklessness: "The only complaint one would make of them is that they don't take sufficient care; they're too apt to get themselves killed."[12]

"Everybody took it on the chin there," a Doughboy of the 1st Division said. "We were never really the same after that fight." Reporting on the fighting of his 26th Infantry Regiment south of Soissons, Colonel J. M. Cullison blamed the "severe casualties" at Ploissy and Berzy-le-Sec on German fire but also on a total lack of mortars, 37mm guns, grenades, and Chauchat ammunition. Every attempt to convey those things to the troops was shot down by the watchful Germans. The Doughboys found that the mortar shells they did have with them were useless because they lacked detonators. New ones couldn't be procured because the Germans swept every path with fire and the mortar shells weighed eleven pounds each anyway, which meant that a man trying to carry shells up to the front line couldn't lug more than four, hardly enough to take out a single target. And so the men—infantry companies and ammo carriers alike—fought with their rifles. "The infantry at all times was amply supplied with .30 cal. ammunition," Cullison grimly noted.[13]

One of Cullison's company commanders, nearer the action than the colonel, reported that things were even worse for his men. They had to use German grenades "picked up along the way." They had to throw away their Browning automatics and fight with service rifles because they'd been given no ammunition for the BARs, which were just being introduced as America's light machine gun to replace the much derided Chauchat. Liaison was appalling—no one knew throughout the fight around Soissons where to find headquarters or even aid stations, and the signals platoons, which were supposed to lay phone lines or flash messages by blinker, failed at both. The blinkers were immediately fired at by the Germans, and each time the signalmen laid phone cable, it was cut by shelling. When finally repaired, it was run over and cut again by French tanks, the regimental signal officer, surveying the tangle of crushed wires, wanly suggesting that "it would be of great advantage to know the approximate route of tanks."[14]

Increasing numbers of wounded, feeling the razor pain of German bullets, cried out for relief, but there was none. Ambulance drivers at the aid stations couldn't drive up to collect the casualties under heavy shellfire. Most of the wounded would lie for twenty-four to forty-eight hours without any care at all. At the point of the spear, the frightened Doughboys "bunched"—instead of keeping ten-pace intervals—and, as the German fire mowed them down, straggling intensified. Colonel Cullison observed "a continuous stream of men going to the rear whose place was at the front," leaving "double duty" for those brave enough to keep going. German machine-gun and artillery fire necessitated breaking up normal "platoon wave" formations—easy to control—into skirmish lines and flanking columns, or "checkerboard formation," with half squads and individuals advancing in bounds like checkers, in theory. In reality, the terrified, unsupervised checkers often disappeared from the board.[15]

But the stumbling attack proved sufficient, with the Germans falling back to their next line of resistance anyway. Summerall famously reprimanded a battalion commander who'd been unnerved by the casualties of his unit and tried to stop the advance: "You may have paused for reorganization; if you ever send another message with the word 'stopped' in it you'll be sent to the rear for reclassification." Threats like this to rank and career usually sufficed to keep even the goriest American assaults going. Between them, the two American divisions captured seven thousand Germans and one hundred guns and advanced eight miles. The German prisoners, denied information by their masters and fed absurd propaganda, exhibited ignorance about everything. When asked by his American interrogators why he thought the United States had intervened in the war, a prisoner confidently answered: "So that the Wall Street brokers can fill their pockets with more gold."[16]

Running out of gold and men, Hindenburg was stymied; at Ludendorff's urging, he'd committed the reserves in the Aisne-Marne battles that he needed for a last punch in Flanders. "This meant the end of our hopes of dealing our long-planned decisive blow at the English army," the old field marshal lamented. Operation Hagen had to be canceled altogether. Crossing to the north bank of the Marne near Château-Thierry, a German officer surveyed those shattered hopes, strewn along both banks of the Marne: "The main roads filled with shattered wagons, dead horses whose carcasses had swollen to the size of gas tanks in the heat, everywhere abandoned material, weapons, equipment, and the unburied corpses of our comrades." He recalled the men in his company breathing shallowly through their mouths until they'd put the Marne behind them, so cloying was the stench of death on the riverbanks. In Berlin, Chancellor Theobald von Bethmann Hollweg resigned and the new German chancellor, Georg Michaelis, a sixty-one-year-old lawyer who'd administered the German grain supply till now, predicted defeat: "We expected grave events in Paris for the end of July. That was on the 15th. On the 18th, even the most optimistic among us understood that all was lost. The history of the world was played out in three days."[17]

But the Germans were far from finished. On the forty-mile arc from Soissons to Reims, the Germans inflicted so many casualties on General Antoine de Mitry's French Ninth Army that it had to be withdrawn from the front. In the Marne salient, the Germans had inflicted brutal casualties on the Americans and given ground, but only as far as the heights above Soissons. They clung to the city and its rail yards, beating back all attacks to facilitate an orderly withdrawal from Château-Thierry to the line of the Aisne. Though German officers often had to force their men back into line at gunpoint, the men did go back to open fire, killing Americans in shocking numbers.[18]

In a US Army where skilled officers were precious—there were no satisfactory replacements—American officers died in droves at Soissons, leading from the front. This was another lesson the Europeans had absorbed in 1914 and the Americans were only learning now. The Big Red One lost 75 percent of its infantry field officers in the week after July 18. The 16th and 18th Infantry Regiments lost every single field officer except the colonel. The 26th Regiment lost every officer including the colonel. The butcher's bill was so high on the American side because of the continuing inability of American artillery to coordinate effectively with infantry. The regular army, National Army,

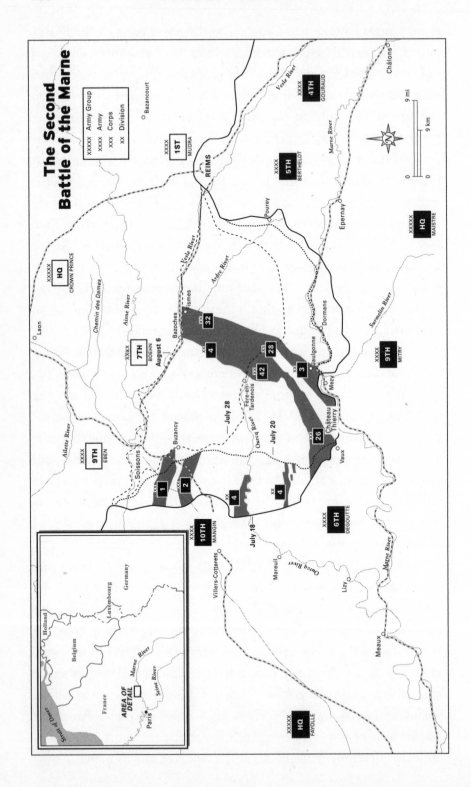

The Second Battle of the Marne

and National Guard had all rushed to add artillery officers in 1917, few of them adequately trained. The French had predicted this even as America mobilized, noting that with only one decent firing range (Fort Sill, Oklahoma) and the need to create twenty times as many artillery officers as existed in the prewar army in a matter of months, good results couldn't be anticipated.[19]

General Max von Boehn, an American veteran recalled, "was the first great teacher of the Doughboys." Ordered by Ludendorff to retreat rapidly out of the Château-Thierry salient with his beleaguered Seventh Army, Boehn instead moved slowly and methodically. Ludendorff had loaded Boehn's army with guns and supplies for the war-winning drive on Paris, and Boehn, confined to a single line of supply, the one from Château-Thierry to Soissons and then back to Laon, was unwilling to abandon those impediments. Generals who lost guns weren't kindly remembered by history. He would use every ridge, stream, and forest between the Marne and the Aisne to slow the American pursuit with interlocked grids of fire; ultimately, he would try to hold along the Vesle, the chalk hills of the Aisne River behind him giving his artillery total command of the Vesle crossings. Backing up carefully, Boehn would try to pivot on Reims and swing his right flank back through Soissons to extricate what remained of his army safely.[20]

The Vesle River, waist-deep and thirty feet wide, swampy on both banks, with no bridges except those American engineers could build under fire, was a natural killing field. Boehn, still hopeful that Hindenburg would launch Operation Hagen with the million troops he had in Flanders, understood that so long as the Seventh Army battled in the Marne salient, the Americans would be unable to reinforce the weakened British. Boehn also saw that Foch, committed to a broad-front strategy and attacking simultaneously everywhere from Flanders to Verdun to prevent Ludendorff from resting and rotating his fatigued troops ("*tout le monde à la bataille*"), lacked the reserves to pinch off the salient in the classical way, by thrusting inward from its shoulders at Soissons and Reims. Instead, Foch seemed to be trusting that the Americans would overpower Boehn simply by bashing their way in from the western and southern faces.[21]

This was assuming a lot. Just to reach the outskirts of Soissons, the US 1st and 2nd Divisions had lost fifteen thousand men. And the French troops who relieved them would manage to advance only five miles over the next two weeks. A British officer surveying the ground conquered by the Big Red One near Soissons was nearly reduced to tears by the sight: in some places the Doughboys had been mown down in skirmish rows, "recalling to him the slaughter of his Camerons, Gordons, and Black Watch at Loos in 1915 and on the Somme in 1916." A German private, who paused to look at a crowd of one thousand American prisoners in Fismes—a crossroads straddling the Vesle between Reims and Soissons—was himself nearly reduced to tears by the sight: "tall as trees, young, healthy guys." The German had been told by his officers that there were no Americans in France. Driving toward the front to rejoin his unit, his sorrow only increased; he'd assumed that, having checked Foch's initial push on Soissons, Boehn would strike again toward Paris. The German private now saw that he wouldn't; there were no German reserves:

From Fismes we drove via Fère-en-Tardenois toward Treloup on the Marne. We'd all been talking about marching with our regiments into Paris, but the further forward we got the more disappointed we became. For such a mighty offensive there had to be great reserves to hand, but all around us we saw nothing—only staffs, baggage, trains and munitions columns. Apparently victory in Russia hadn't freed up enough troops to win in the West after all.

Boehn shifted fluidly from offense to defense, dropping back to the Vesle and planning more slaughters from riverside bastions like Fismes.[22]

General Hunter Liggett's US I Corps, now directing operations under French army command, took aim at Fismes. Pershing had nearly disqualified Liggett for service in France because of the general's girth and appetite. Sixty-one-year-old Liggett had arrived in France with his own Cordon Bleu chef. But Pershing, initially inclined to send him home with underperforming generals like Sibert, had hesitated, and ultimately backed Liggett, a West Pointer and former president of the Army War College, who liked to pat his paunch and say, "There's no fat above my collar." Pershing would find that he couldn't do without Liggett. Captain Mark Clark, attached to Liggett's headquarters, marveled for the rest of his career at Liggett's enduring obscurity: "Hunter was 'old army', all right, but he was one of the great generals of the A.E.F. He had many more men under him than Grant or Lee, [his battles] were bigger than any battle of the Civil War, yet only the real historians can even tell you who he was." Liggett would prove to be the US Army's best general in the war. He ascended the learning curve faster than Pershing and grasped the demands of industrial-era operational warfare—linked, sustainable, robust offensives to achieve strategic effects, like the destruction of an enemy army—in a way that Pershing never did. The Marne salient, however, was Liggett's purgatory, a place where his green army tried and failed to trap the retreating German army.[23]

That purgatory—the bulge hammered by the Germans in May from the Chemin des Dames to Château-Thierry—was formed of green hills, lush pastures, burbling streams, and woods, all of them sculpted into killing fields by the Germans. Unable to crush the salient from the top—the Germans had stopped Mangin's army short of Soissons—there was no other option, or so Pershing was persuaded by a French command that valued American life less than French, than to attack it from the bottom and the flanks. If the objective increasingly was to destroy German effectives, Boehn's army had to be brought to battle and defeated. Otherwise, it would escape across the Aisne and join wing-to-wing with the other German armies crouched along the Hindenburg Line.

Big and little rivers coursed across the salient—the Marne at its foot, the Ourcq and Ardre in the middle, the Vesle and the Aisne at the top, all of them bending as if at the command of German engineers to offer optimal resistance to US and French units that would attack into the salient from its base and both flanks. Between the Marne and the Ourcq, the Allies would have to traverse deep woods

The stench of death was overpowering in the Marne salient as corpses, left behind in the German fighting retreat, swelled and decomposed in the summer heat. These Germans were killed by Alabama National Guardsmen of the 42nd Rainbow Division near Fère-en-Tardenois in August 1918. (National Archives)

and stone farms that the Germans fortified artfully. They'd have to wrest important road junctions like Fère-en-Tardenois on the Ourcq from the Germans and then keep moving to the Vesle, where they'd have to take key crossings like Fismes. That would probably be the end of this Soissons offensive, for between the Vesle and the Aisne the ground rose from the river level to a plateau 50 to 180 meters in height, the slopes steep in places and wooded, cut here and there by winding tracks. If the Germans made it that far, they'd be able to slide into line with the bulk of the German army to fight another day. For the German machine gunners, it was all optimal terrain. The Doughboys would never quite rinse the pervasive stink of the Aisne-Marne salient from their memories. In the heat of the short French summer, it made every man gag in disgust: "There was one thing that was everywhere—the stench of death. You can ask anyone who was there. God, it was awful. All those dead animals, and the men also. Remember, it was July and August. The stench never left you."[24]

To join the hoped-for destruction of Boehn's Seventh Army, General Clarence Edwards's 26th Yankee Division had been moved on July 7 to Château-Thierry from Seicheprey, where it had been savaged by German raids in April. The Yankees replaced a division in Belleau Wood and became the pivoting foot of General Jean Degoutte's French Sixth Army. The US 1st, 2nd, and 4th Divisions would swing like a sickle into the western flank of the Aisne-Marne salient while the 26th Division advanced alongside the 3rd Division at the foot of the salient to anchor the blow and hold the bottom of the sack.

Ordered to advance from Belleau Wood northeast toward Épieds on July 18 to facilitate the attack of the 3rd Division on its right and the 4th Division on its left, Edwards, who'd graduated last in his class at West Point thirty-five years earlier, tried, failed, and then, instead of persisting, walked the entire division backward to regroup and try again. Edwards's method, which endeared him to his men, was to blame everyone above him—usually in the presence of his troops—for his failures. He now pronounced the situation impossible and backed away. The troops, who passed in and out of Belleau Wood, were sickened by gas—the Germans shelled the woods with mustard gas and phosgene—and stunned by the lingering carnage in the wood, especially the decomposing body parts of Germans and Americans still in the trees where they'd been blasted by high explosive a month earlier. They were also stunned by sixty-one-year-old "Gatling Gun" Parker, one of Edwards's colonels, who shouted encouragement like this to the men: "I've brought you over here to get you killed, and that's what I'm going to do!"[25]

With Edwards's Yankee Division in unexpected retreat, Degoutte expressed amazement at the complete disappearance of his pivoting foot. Even General George Cameron's 4th Division, which had just arrived in France and had never been in combat, was advancing to take its objectives around Noroy. "Had I not seen it with my own eyes, I would never have believed that green troops would advance under

General Clarence Edwards (left)—shown here with his staff chief, Colonel Duncan Major, near Belleau Wood—was loved by his New England troops, who called him "our Clarence" or simply "Daddy." Pershing loathed Edwards for his slack discipline, penchant for gossip, and regular insubordination. Edwards, who campaigned with his own adoring war correspondent from the *Boston Globe* and was protected by leading Republicans like Henry Cabot Lodge, Warren Harding, and Leonard Wood, got away with far more than Pershing's other generals in the war. (National Archives)

such fire," a French liaison officer reported. The 4th Division was so green that some of the men had never fired a rifle and the officers had stuffed their holsters with paper because they hadn't been issued pistols yet. Still, the division fought through vicious German artillery and machine-gun fire and took 5,500 casualties, driving the Germans behind the Ourcq.[26]

Pershing, Liggett, and Degoutte made anxious inquiries about the 26th Yankee Division. It appeared that Edwards hadn't only removed his regiments from combat; he'd even moved his headquarters back, losing all contact with the enemy and leaving a yawning gap in the front of Degoutte's Sixth Army. One officer, whose platoon encountered the "disheartened men" of the 26th Division, found that they had "an absolutely fatalistic viewpoint, telling us we would never get through the game." The New Englanders would look piteously at other units coming up. "'Wait,' they said, 'wait,'" by which they meant, just wait and you'll see that we're going to lose.

Liggett, insulated from the worst of this, would later interview the junior officers and NCOs in the Yankee Division to find out why they were so defeatist. It appeared that Edwards had kept too many of his old National Guard buddies in important commands. Suitable, as one historian put it, "as adjutants at ports of embarkation," the weekend warriors broke down completely in battle. "This was the tragedy of misdirected affection, a common fault of the National Guard," a veteran noted. Of three New England regiments advancing on a broad front, only one—the 102nd—had pressed its attack. The other two had shrunk backward, afraid to follow their own creeping barrage into the German lines. The 102nd Regiment—boys from Connecticut, Vermont, and Massachusetts—had been "practically wiped out," its three 1,000-man battalions reduced to 250 men each. The two regiments of the 52nd Brigade that had shied from their rolling barrage couldn't be made to go forward, nor could they even be contacted by the desperate men of the 102nd. "All liaison was lost with them," a staff officer reported. "The 52nd brigade is now a mob. We couldn't make them attack. They are milling around the country, absolutely out of control."[27]

Two days later, prodded by Liggett, Edwards finally took his objective—Épieds—with ruinous casualties. An observer walking around the village afterward thought that the struggle for the place doubtless contributed to the demoralization of the New Englanders: "Whole lines of houses were down, and one could tell by the debris, shells, wrecked machine guns, and machine gun belts scattered here and there what an obstinate hand-to-hand combat it had been. Places were still smoking in the ruins where hand grenades had been used." In a kitchen garden, the observer saw a pile of dead Americans and the snout of the machine gun that had killed them poking through a wall. A German hung suspended from a camouflage screen: "Blown clear off the road, he hung from the sagging wire. Shrapnel had come along afterward and shredded him. He had no head but still cupped his helmet in his rigid hands. He was blood-soaked and his bowels were hanging out." Studying scenes like this, a Connecticut Dough-boy reflected on what it took to keep going: "Hope and kidding your-self helped a lot," for "man doesn't amount to much when H.E. hits him."[28]

Reading the *Chicago Tribune*'s account of the Yankee Division's ac-tion—"The general commanding the division is a leader of men, broad-minded, precise in his orders, of practical mind, who dealt with the operations underway with a mastery which cost dear to the enemy"— Pershing's staff at Chaumont recoiled in amazement. "What do you make of this?" one assistant chief of staff wrote to another. "Good God almighty," he received in reply.[29]

Liggett, commanding the army-sized I Corps, which included the 26th and four other divisions, later praised the courage shown by the men who did attack at Épieds, especially the Yankee Division's chief of staff, Colonel Duncan Major, and Major Greenway of the Engi-neer Reserve Corps, who flung themselves into the cauldron at Épieds to reorganize the troops and lead them into the village. "They saved a difficult situation," Liggett wrote. In the same letter he recommended the immediate relief of every senior officer in the 52nd Brigade: the commanding general as well as every regimental and battalion com-mander in the unit. "They must be replaced," Liggett wrote Persh-ing, "and the division must be retrained and reconstructed." Captain Herbert Bell, sent to interview junior officers of the 52nd Brigade about their travails, reported that "they had plenty to say. Always the same story—frontal attacks on machine gun positions with little or no artillery preparation; the Germans cutting down the men in great numbers. Few prisoners to be had. They seemed a little bitter, think-ing their men were being sacrificed."[30]

The Germans yielded few prisoners because there weren't many Germans to capture; the stay-behind machine-gun detachments comprised just eight men, with ten thousand rounds of ammunition, left to hold back the Americans while the rest of the line withdrew. Those rear guards could be expected to fight to the last man, for they were chosen carefully—close friends, brothers, neighbors, men who could be expected to die together. Captain Bell then met with a 26th Division company commander, "an old friend and <u>very</u> reliable," who said that his "effectives had been cut from 200 to 70 in the last week—practically all killed and wounded." Nevertheless, "the spirit of the men is described as wonderful." The men "most strongly complained of insufficient artillery, poor liaison, and the impunity with which German airmen work."[31]

Colonel Malin Craig, Liggett's chief of staff, had condemned the 26th Division for its slow approach to Épieds, its failure to communicate with corps, and its failure to advance swiftly, enabling the Germans to slither backward out of the sack with all of their guns and supplies intact, "nullifying a favorable opportunity to deliver a blow." Craig, who would serve as US Army chief of staff in the 1930s, declared that the "babying" of the New England division, like so many others, had to stop. We "must bring this fine body of men up to the standard which is demanded of American units." He recommended that the 26th Division be withdrawn for "rehabilitation and training in basic principles of troop leading."[32]

It was easy to see why. Another of Liggett's staff officers toured the Yankee Division's dressing station at Épieds and was struck by what he saw. While gunshot and shrapnel casualties lay untended, the dressing station was clogged with healthy troops claiming to have been gassed. Gas alarms were frequent, and frequently false. They were spread by all means—car horns honking, brass shells beaten, rifles emptied into the sky—and attended by droves of men running to the rear claiming to have been afflicted. The major could scarcely believe his eyes: "These men are lounging and walking around smoking cigarettes in a healthy frame of mind and body. The surgeon in charge suspects that many of them are faking. I've seen these men; one would not suspect that they are bona fide gas cases from their attitude."[33]

The 26th Division proved so dysfunctional that Pershing was forced to send a parade of senior staff officers—sorely needed elsewhere—to sort it out. Lieutenant Colonel Hugh Drum, who would be runner-up to George Marshall for the general staff chief job in World

War II, couldn't even imagine such starry heights from where he sat now. Surrounded by the debris of a broken division, he wondered what to do. Drum wrote General Fox Conner on July 31: "There is no doubt that some radical steps must be taken in the 26th Division to bring it back into shape." Edwards would have to go. "A proper commander and driving power must be placed behind it. It has suffered from ignorant commanders and men of little experience." From his perch in AEF headquarters, George Marshall, now a lieutenant colonel, watched the reliefs of senior officers impassively: "The hurly-burly of the conflict does not permit commanders to draw fine distinctions; to succeed, they must demand results, close their ear to excuses, and drive subordinates beyond what would ordinarily be considered the limit of human capacity. Wars are won by the side that accomplishes the impossible."[34]

This was a side struggling to accomplish the possible. Lieutenant Colonel Drum observed that the bench was so thin in the hastily expanded US Army that General Edwards had been forced to cannibalize his own general staff to lead field units, all but guaranteeing incompetent staff work: "General Edwards had to place his chief of staff, Colonel Major, in command of a regiment, his inspector, Colonel Hobbs, in command of another, and he's asking for another colonel to replace John Henry Parker. Edwards claims that Colonel Parker broke down during the heavy fighting and strain." This was the same "Gatling Gun" Parker—he'd earned the nickname on San Juan Hill in 1898—who'd bluffly vowed to get his men killed in battle. Under incessant German fire, the bluffs and posturing wore thin. These failures of leadership were happening in every American unit, as officers reared in peacetime were struggling to catch up to this fast-moving war. Pershing struggled to find replacements. Sometimes an officer "canned" from one unit would be sent to another, with predictably dismal results. Such men, Drum noted, "can only make bad matters worse." General Robert Lee Bullard, commander of the US III Corps on the east face of the salient, didn't know what to make of his utterly inexperienced staff: "It's the newest thing I ever saw—except what the stork brings."[35]

General Joseph Dickman's 3rd Division, the Rock of the Marne, finally launched its attacks over the Marne near Château-Thierry on July 21, having waited for the attacks on its flanks to dislodge the German defenders on the riverbank. The 3rd Division advanced up the spine of the pocket, reaching Le Charmel by July 24. Doughboys fell along the way in bloody clumps, especially at Jaulgonne, where General Richard von Conta, supervising this section of the front, had placed machine-gun teams in every fold of ground. "There was no safety *anywhere*," a veteran recalled. "If we stayed flat on the ground we couldn't see to fire. And if we made the slightest movement, the wheat betrayed us to the men at those machine guns." The American assault platoons lay motionless; to move or attempt to sit up and return fire was to die.[36]

The Germans "were artists with machine guns," an American NCO recalled. They'd use them at ranges as great as two thousand yards, where the natural trajectory of the bullets would follow down the curve of any reverse slopes the Doughboys were using for cover. You might be sitting with a hill or a berm between you and a faraway German machine gunner, but that gunner, knowing you were there, would aim at the crest of the ridge and fire ten-shot bursts until only one of the ten rounds kicked up dust. With the rest skimming over the crest and plunging down the reverse slope, the German machine gunner would clamp his weapon at that elevation and blaze away, killing and wounding the troops behind the ridge. The same NCO noted that the Doughs, initially stunned by this German finesse, became used to it. They'd sit on the reverse slopes with their heads tucked between their shoulder blades, the bullets passing just over their hunched bodies. Behind cover or in the open, the men experienced hell: "The swish and whistle of high strays, the crack of close misses, and now and then the screech and howl of a ricochet." A Doughboy in the 3rd Division also blamed the French. They were advancing so cautiously on the 3rd Division's flanks and yielding to German pressure so easily that the Americans were constantly being enfiladed by German artillery and machine guns that the French were supposed to have cleaned out.[37]

The French troops who still lusted for the attack were the Algerians. Lying in the wheat, unable to move, Corporal John Barkley of the 3rd Division watched the French colonial troops slither past him on their bellies: "Black as coal, the fiercest looking men I've ever seen." They crawled soundlessly through the wheat, carbines slung around their backs, knives gripped in their teeth. He noticed the shiny bracelets they wore for luck, their scars, their tattooed faces, and their massive size, "all bone and muscle," none of them less than two hundred pounds to Barkley's appraising eye. Whereas the Americans and French were paralyzed by the German machine-gun fire, these men crawled straight through the field, ignoring the bullets snapping overhead. Once through the wheat, they went into the woods. The men of the 3rd Division then heard the German machine guns begin to fall silent. *Tat-tat-tat*, then nothing. Barkley cautiously raised his head and saw Germans running away. When the American assault platoons continued their advance, they saw why the Germans, who never ran, had run: "The ground was full of Germans who'd been carved to pieces. . . . They all had their right ears cut off." The Algerians always cut off the right ear as proof of the kill. Barkley overtook an Algerian later with eighteen German ears looped on a string around his neck.[38]

The aftermath of that episode was less successful and showed why progress was so slow. The Americans surged forward only to run into another web of machine guns. In Barkley's unit, every officer was killed trying to lead the men forward. Companies and platoons were shortly led by sergeants and corporals, most of whom were also killed. The French applauded this courage—"American officers seek danger"—but denigrated its effect: "Unfortunately the losses are very high and at the end of a battle a battalion is left in [the] command of a young officer who faces fire for the first time." In this case, even the rookies were dead or screaming in agony on the ground, targets the German machine gunners left to lure even more victims to their death. Barkley wriggled forward and spied a German heavy machine gunner concealed behind a fallen tree; he was peering toward the Americans, all in holes or ditches or behind trees, just waiting for any of them to make a move, "swinging the muzzle slightly to the right, then to the left, seeking targets," firing bursts whenever he saw one. Barkley was lying in a ditch with a boy from his platoon when a German machine gunner hidden up a tree fired a burst that killed the young soldier. "He yelled as the bullets struck him. It sounded like a baby starting to cry. He was one of the nicest boys in our outfit."[39]

Battalions of the 3rd Division attacked through the Forêt de Fere. In one of its clearings they stumbled upon an American patrol that had been captured and executed by the Germans: "The major's body had been stripped to its underclothing. Several of his wounded men had been shot in the head with rifles at short range. A boy we knew was lying stretched on his back, the whole side of his blond head blown in and one of his eyes lying on his cheek." American interrogations of German prisoners after episodes like these punctured the Allied hope that, faced with a hopeless future, the Germans would give up. They wouldn't. In the first place, Hindenburg kept his army in the dark, and German newspapers lied as boldly as army headquarters about the true military situation. German troops were assured, everywhere they encountered Americans, that the Americans they were fighting were the only Americans in France. "We were herded around like sheep and kept in absolute ignorance of the real political and military situation," a German gunner recalled of this period. "We were closely watched and all of our incoming mail was censored."[40]

Some German prisoners had been so completely gulled that they expressed surprise at meeting Americans; they'd been told that the Doughboys were really British troops wearing the American uniform. Even captured German officers in August and September 1918 estimated, when asked by their interrogators how many Doughboys they thought were in France, that there could only be twenty-five thousand of them, certainly no more than fifty thousand. There were actually one million American troops in France by then. German officers interrogating US prisoners were struck by their resolve and idealism, which the Germans dismissed as naïveté. After questioning Americans captured near Jaulgonne, a German officer praised their courage but scoffed at their rationale for fighting: "They say they've come here to defend their country." For now, ignorance, lies, wishful thinking, and discipline were holding the German army together. "German fighting units are far from the breaking point," Pershing's intelligence office determined in August. "Their psychology is that of a rearguard action with fair confidence in the wisdom of the high command rather than the morale of troops that have been routed and lost faith in their generals."[41]

As the US 3rd Division battled north from Château-Thierry, the 42nd Rainbow Division deployed to its left in relief of the blundering Yankee Division on July 24. Advancing to relieve the New Englanders, the Rainbows, guided by chief of staff Colonel Douglas MacArthur, did little better. The Germans were ready for them, with light machine guns in the trees and heavy machine guns on the ground. Even a man in a shell crater wasn't safe against a German light Maxim firing from the treetops. The Rainbows attacked in dense formations, with five battalions in front and two in reserve, the exact opposite of what should have been attempted.[42]

Moving across open ground against German artillery and machine guns, MacArthur's men were mowed down. Ordered by Degoutte to evict a German division from the fortified Croix Rouge Farm near the Ourcq River, Liggett assigned the task to the Rainbows' 84th Brigade. They'd be assaulting strong rear guards of the first-rate German 4th Division, entrenched in and around the heavy stone farm buildings, with clear fields of fire across open fields in every direction. As the 167th Alabama Regiment moved into position, its colonel protested that the attack, without artillery preparation, would be suicide. Once again, the dead weight of Pershing-ordained "aggressiveness" trumped caution. The colonel was advised that if he didn't attack, he'd be canned and replaced with someone who would. He attacked, and it was suicide. The two battalions of Alabama National Guard that attacked Croix Rouge Farm suffered 225 dead and 600 wounded to German machine gunners who must have gaped at the easy targets. "Our men were literally mowed down," an officer of the Rainbows fairly wept. "The ground was literally covered with killed and wounded. . . . For some distance you could actually walk on dead men."

When the Alabamans finally took the position—today the site of one of the more affecting American memorials in France—they bayoneted every German they captured in cold blood, 283 in all. The Germans would formally protest the atrocity, and the brigadier who'd launched the attack without artillery support was canned and replaced by Colonel MacArthur, who, deftly scaling the ladder of promotion, lauded the "gallantry" of the bungled attack and earned a general's star. The American push paused again as spent units were sent back for rest and replacements while fresh units were pushed forward in their place.[43]

Once relieved, American units went back to rest in tents or old plywood shanties with chicken-wire bunks, many of them built for the French during the last battle of the Marne in 1914. To discourage vice, Secretary of War Baker had invited charitable organizations like the YMCA, the Knights of Columbus, the Salvation Army, and the Red Cross to operate clubs and canteens behind the lines to divert Doughboys from the whores and cognac of French towns. In this pre-penicillin war, France had already lost a million men to syphilis and gonorrhea, and the BEF, at any given time, had the equivalent of two or three full divisions of troops in the hospital with venereal disease. Pershing was determined to prevent similar wastage by encouraging "healthy and moral recreation." The Salvation Army famously introduced the doughnut to lure the Doughboys away from worse forms of vice. Wherever large bodies of American troops were at rest, the YMCA opened canteens to sell chocolate, cigarettes, pens, writing paper, and soap, and "Y-men" intervened continually to discourage whoring, swearing, and drinking, delivering generally unappreciated homilies like this one: "Remember that your women folks, your sisters and sweethearts and mothers are praying for you at this instant." John Dos Passos, who drove an ambulance on the Western Front, described the typical response: Doughboys muttered under their breath things like, "I wish somebody would pray me into a clean shirt."[44]

To discourage vice, Secretary of War Baker invited charitable organizations like the YMCA to operate canteens behind the lines to divert the Doughs from the whores and cognac of French towns. "Y-men"—such as the three pictured here—were widely resented. Many of them had dodged military service and, as one veteran put it, "a religious organization that found its greatest field in purveying stationery, jelly, and ginger snaps behind the lines of battle merited the contempt which it so often received." (National Archives)

Y-men tended to be too old to serve or were physically disqualified. A lieutenant in the 42nd Rainbows recalled running into one of his math professors from Columbia University who was working in the YMCA at Gondrecourt. Normally the Doughboys encountered the Y in mobile canteens that prowled around American divisions in the field. Troops resented having to pay for things they should have been given and having to wait—as one Dough put it—"in the drizzle and manure-soaked water" for the privilege of doing so. "The nature of [the Y's] business, selling gum drops and cakes when civilization hung in the balance, was so petty that they were bound to be despised by the very men for whom they labored," a lieutenant in Pennsylvania's 28th

Division recalled. "A religious organization that found its greatest field in purveying stationery, jelly, and ginger snaps behind the lines of battle merited the contempt which it so often received."[45]

Troops had to bathe in ponds and streams during their rest periods behind the lines. Dos Passos described the arrival of one tired, dirty unit at a pond. The men had stripped off and soaped up when a prissy Y-man appeared, red triangle of the YMCA on his khaki sleeve, "faintly giggling," and told them to crouch in the water: "There are French girls looking at you from the road." Later, pulling on their filthy uniforms, one of the Doughboys said to another: "God, I can't put the damn thing on again, it's like voluntarily taking up filth and slavery again."

The Y-man, "sallow face, pinched nose and chin, neat uniform and well-polished boots contrasting strangely with the mud-clotted, sweat-soaked clothing of the men" coyly reappeared. "Do you call serving your country slavery, my friend?"

John Andrews, a thinly disguised Dos Passos, answered: "You're goddam right I do."

The Y-man cautioned him to choose his words more carefully and reminded him that he was fighting "in a great Christian undertaking," a "voluntary worker in the cause of democracy. You're doing this so that your children will be able to live a peaceful . . . "

"Ever *shot* a man?" Andrews brutally interrupted. "Ever seen what a little splinter of shell does to a feller's body?"

"No, no, I'd have enlisted, I really would. Only my eyes are weak . . . " the Y-man protested.

His swim ruined, Andrews finished buttoning his jacket and sauntered off, nodding in the direction of the Y-man and saying to his buddy, "And *that's* what'll survive you and me."[46]

In the Marne salient, villages like Épieds and Trugny changed hands three or four times as the Germans fought to hold the ground between the Marne and the Ourcq and the Americans tried to break through. Here the Germans actually counterattacked with infantry; elsewhere they seeded the woods and roads with light artillery and machine guns to slow the pursuit. The Germans would block their most important positions with tangles of wire. Into these they'd insert man traps: forty-two inches long, serrated jaws spread twelve inches and cocked. The trap would slam shut on any Doughboy attempting to cut the wire, tearing off his leg with a pressure of three hundred pounds.[47]

Picking their way across ground like this, troops of the US 32nd Division discovered the grave of Quentin Roosevelt, whose plane had been shot down near Fère-en-Tardenois in mid-July. The Germans had buried Teddy's youngest child and marked the grave with a simple monument before withdrawing. All four of former president Roosevelt's sons fought in the war. Archie, who served in the 1st Division with Ted Jr., explained it simply: "Dad always told us, to lead meant to serve." Dad would never recover from the death of twenty-year-old Quentin, the baby of the family. TR would be overheard murmuring "Poor Quenty, poor Quenty" to himself—or howling it out to sea at Oyster Bay—and the twenty-sixth president would be dead within six months, soul-destroying grief probably a greater factor in his demise than the coronary embolism that felled him in his sixtieth year. For now, German propagandists made the most of Quentin's demise: "See! The greatest living American sends his sons to fight against us, yet even they go down before the might of the Fatherland." Not all Germans shared in the exultation: "Quite so," many whispered, "but where are the sons of the kaiser?"[48]

For the Germans, fighting from wood to wood, hill to hill, often without phones or radios, coordinating their fire and supply was everything. They somehow had to maintain their ability to rain accurate fire on the Americans from distant batteries and connect up their machine guns while sparing their own men, who were lying in exposed positions or threading through heavily contested spaces. American veterans all remarked on the constant flash of the German heliographs—mirrors pivoted to catch the sun and flash signals—and the work of German airplanes. The heliographs structured the battlefield for the Germans, allowing scattered units to concert their plans and fine-tune the work of guns behind them in a low-tech way. German planes attacked the

Allies whenever they could but also scoured the ground for friendly units, continually updating their positions.

Captured German codebooks showed how they did this in places like the Marne salient. For their aircraft, German ground troops carried white panels that they'd lay on the ground and shape into letters or symbols to deliver information and instructions. A *T* meant "We are holding the front line." An upside down *T* meant "Cease artillery fire." A *V* meant "We are advancing." A sideways *V* meant "Ammunition required." An *X* meant "Barrage fire needed." And so on. As German planes lost command of the air to the Allies and worsening weather grounded the planes anyway, the heliograph knitted the German army together. The letter *F* alone meant "Commence artillery fire." The letter *R* meant "Enemy penetrated our right" and would alert the guns to pour in fire there. The number 8 meant "Here is a battalion headquarters," which reduced the chances of friendly fire and told troops where their officers were headquartered. German guns adjusted their fire this way: "LKVB" meant "Miss on the left," "WHI" meant "Far behind," and so on. Isolated German troops could obliterate a closing American attack by flashing "FN"—"Bring barrage closer to our own front"—and the sprinting Americans, scenting blood, would suddenly be obliterated by a curtain of shrapnel and high explosive, delivered as if from the hand of an invisible German god.[49]

Foch, in a hurry to win this Second Battle of the Marne and impatient at the lack of American progress, now demanded that the US 42nd Division take Fère-en-Tardenois on the Ourcq River, a railroad junction in the heart of the salient needed by Boehn to shuttle his men and matériel back to the Vesle. The Rainbows took it in a fight that lasted several days and cost thousands of casualties. The fighting here was some of the most vicious of the war. The Ourcq—knee-deep, muddy, and twenty feet wide—ran perpendicular to the American line of advance. The stream and the yellow wheat fields rising from its north bank gave the Germans another strong defensive position from which to delay the American pursuit. With each juddering advance, the US artillery would come forward to shorten its range and hit German targets farther back. One Doughboy paused to admire the work of an American battery here. The lieutenant in charge—"a humorous Kentucky lad"—had the barrels of his guns at a forty-five-degree angle to get maximum range. He'd receive firing data over the phone and blast faraway crossroads and villages inhabited by the Germans. Just then a call came in with map coordinates for a German ammo dump. "Watch this," the lieutenant smiled, pointing at the eastern horizon: "As the shriek of the shell died away, a great flower pot of crimson light shot up into the sky over the horizon. That was the German ammunition dump." The Doughboy watched and pondered the damage, financial—"There was a German bond issue in that umbrella-shaped cloud," and human—"You must imagine some crossroads in the woods over in the German lines with a lot of big shells going off, nitrose powder burning furiously, and darkness finally settling down over some blackened fragments of what had once been men."[50]

General Hunter Liggett's summary of the fighting winced at the sight of places like Fère, Cierges, or the mud road behind the Ourcq, ascending from Sergy to Peuplier: rows of American dead gunned down yards from the German foxholes and tangled rucks of German and American dead in the same machine-gun nest, "testimony of the mutual stubbornness of the conflicts." The Germans either killed with direct fire or, just as often, deployed dummy machine guns on a forward slope to bait American attacks and then killed the Doughboys with indirect fire from the real machine guns hidden on the reverse slope. In the woods of La Fère, an American officer reflected on "the startling quality of our men." Fighting in the woods, cow lots, and villages—"meeting 'Fritz' in cellars, old outhouses, along road ditches, hidden in a tree, coal heap, or haystack"—was "a great man hunt, every little group for itself." It was, he concluded, "the grim common sense of the 'Doughboy' and not our obsolete and impossible tactics that won us ground." Nights, a veteran recalled, were as awful as the days. The hours of darkness were "continually disturbed by the cries of shell-shocked men. Most began with a howling peal of laughter, a laugh to make one's skin creep and hair rise, and ended in a shuddering wail frequently followed by tears. These men had become insane."[51]

A chaplain in the Rainbow Division noted the "desperate courage" of the Doughs, who carried ammunition for their machine guns across fire-swept ground, knowing full well that they'd be killed in the process: "Five feet or so a man might run with it and then go down. Without hesitation, some other soldier would grab it and run forward to go down in his turn. But the guns had to be fed and still another would take the same dreadful chance." Among the Rainbow dead was the poet Joyce Kilmer. Sergeant Kilmer, author of "Rouge Bouquet," a well-known poem that described the extinction of a score of his comrades by German fire in March, now met the same fate. Wriggling forward with elements of Major "Wild Bill" Donovan's battalion to locate a hidden German machine gun, the thirty-one-year-old Kilmer, an editor of the *New York Times Book Review*, raised his head too high and was promptly killed by a sniper, the two-ton blow of the bullet shattering his skull. "There lie many fighting men," Kilmer had written in "Rouge Bouquet." "Dead in their youthful prime, / Never to laugh nor love again / Nor taste the Summertime." He now joined the swelling ranks of dead fighting men. Those still alive to taste the summer buried the gentle young man on the banks of the Ourcq River.[52]

If anyone had asked in what battle Joyce Kilmer died, no one could have said exactly. The grinding three-week slaughter in the salient—later packaged by commanders and historians as the Second Battle of the Marne—was being referred to by Liggett's US I Corps as "the German Retreat of the Marne." Advancing units would crawl past Doughboys killed two weeks earlier and never buried—"shredded by shrapnel beyond recognition, all in terrible condition," their decomposing flesh adhering to their corroded dog tags. "The folly of thinking that all of the dead of the A.E.F. could be brought home is too ghastly to be laughable," one lieutenant reflected. Sights like this, he thought, "must always be a great blow to the lingering belief in personal immortality." The Rainbows alone lost 6,500 men, their Alabama regiment hit worst of all, with 70 percent casualties. Major

Donovan, who always led from the front, was promoted to lieutenant colonel. There was nothing "wild" about Bill, who'd go on to found the Office of Strategic Services (OSS)—forerunner of the CIA—in World War II. He was a prudent leader of men. The nickname was given to many Bill Donovans in America at the time, after the original "Wild Bill" Donovan, a pitcher for the Senators, Tigers, and Yankees before the war, who'd once walked nine consecutive batters.[53]

While Liggett's I Corps attacked the west and south faces of the salient, Bullard's III Corps—which included the 28th (Pennsylvania), 32nd (Wisconsin-Michigan), and 77th National Army Divisions—attacked up the road from Château-Thierry to Fismes, essentially performing the same operation as Liggett's corps, only from the eastern face of the salient. It was hoped that the American pincers would join, killing or capturing the Germans between them. But the Americans struggled to intercept or even locate the Germans. The Doughboys had been so hastily deployed that they lacked key tools like planes and balloons for reconnaissance. Without aerial observation, they relied on men in the field, who couldn't make out anything definite in the lush, rolling country. Still new to the war, they had nothing like the brisk German system of heliographs and blinkers. The Doughboys blundered around as if they were fighting Mexicans in Chihuahua. "We are supposed to have air superiority, but I can't see it," a major in the 28th Division groused. "We're held up by the usual machine gun fire. The French ordered us to advance but we can't move at all."[54]

Coordination between neighboring French and American contingents was tenuous at best. A lieutenant of the US 28th Division attending an attempted Allied council of war in a dugout near Épieds described it thus: "Wrangling ensued. Pennsylvania-ese mated with military French, begetting a strange mule-like jargon. Here was a quarrel about how to fight somebody else conducted in solecisms in which the premises of all parties to the controversy were entirely wrong. It was," he thought, "almost legally magnificent. It was more than that—it was military." The same lieutenant recalled that "cutting out" German machine guns in the Aisne-Marne salient took a particularly heavy toll on "recruit replacements, who nearly always rushed toward one gun and were cut down by the other guns on its flanks. The replacements never lived long enough to learn not to do this." "Thir's always two and sometimes three guns," the lieutenant's top sergeant intoned over and over. Now and then German planes would drop propaganda leaflets on the American troops. "What are you doing in Europe?" the leaflets asked. "Why don't you stand on your Constitutional rights? The capitalists in Wall Street are putting you over here for money!" One Doughboy recalled that the men scoffed at them, except for the always earnest and equitable Swedish Americans, two of whom he once observed studying a leaflet: "Maybe it bane truth," one said to the other. "But what the hell? It's yoost their side of it."[55]

The two great American pincers—Liggett's and Bullard's—converged on the Ourcq. The rolling terrain and rising wheat fields gave German defenders ample room to deploy their machine guns. German artillery was depressingly accurate, finding even the best-concealed trenches and dugouts. This was partly because of German air superiority but also because of the German facility with spies. There were many German Americans with flawless accents who could impersonate American officers, and this they often did, passing through American positions and noting down the location of trenches and rest areas that would then be shelled after the German spy had returned to his lines, usually hitting every target "cold," without warning and with pinpoint accuracy. Every man in a trench would be found dead after the onslaught. A Doughboy from Pittsburgh recalled meeting a pair of German spies in US uniforms, one of whom "was familiar with the streets in my home town."[56]

In the last days of July, the 28th Division attacked alongside the 3rd Division at Ronchères, taking Courmont, Grimpettes Woods, and Hill 192 behind the forest. The attacks were brutal, the German machine guns—"like antediluvian monsters guarding their eggs," as one veteran put it—killing and wounding the Doughboys in swarms as they forded the shallow Ourcq to reach the even more dangerous ground on the other side. A German prisoner taken here "sized up," according to Pershing's headquarters staff, "the psychology of the

Many of the Doughboys had grown up with guns and knew how to use them. "The Americans were always alert and trigger-happy," a German colonel recalled. In the fighting on the Ourcq, wherever a German showed himself—even for an instant—he'd be shot by watchful Americans, like these men of the Rainbow Division at Seringes-et-Nesles, site today of the Oise-Aisne American Cemetery, where over 6,000 Doughboys are buried. (National Archives)

Germans." Asked if German troops still thought they could win the war, he replied: "We don't think about it anymore, but we know we must win." Many of them knew that they wouldn't. The Americans were too tough, as a German officer who'd spent a week fighting the Americans for Chaméry recalled. Many of the Doughboys had grown up with guns and had "gun knowledge," which boiled down to this: "Never shoot at anything unless you have your sights on it," or, put another way, "The most important thing about a shooting iron is the sights." This "hunter's instinct" made every day in this close-in battle a hell for the Germans. "The Americans were always alert and trigger-happy" (*sehr wachsam und schusssicher*), a Bavarian colonel recalled. The instant a German showed himself anywhere, he'd be shot dead or wounded. "Our battalion adjutant, springing for just a moment from a trench to a sunken road beneath it, was shot in the shin. One of our American prisoners, wandering curiously around our position, paid for that curiosity with his life. Corporal Klenk, looking for the unit to our right, was shot in the belly and killed. Private Seidl, who went up a tree to get a better look at the Americans and exposed himself for a split second, fell dead with a shot through the heart."[57]

On August 1, the Americans gave one last heave and drove the Germans off the north bank of the Ourcq. The rear guards of Boehn's Seventh Army now dropped back toward the Vesle, a weary American intelligence report reminding commanders: "Note—it must always be borne in mind that a German division has 400 machine guns. If only one-third of these were used, there would be 130 machine guns in line on a German division front." A German officer seized by the French Sixth Army on Liggett's left had a great deal to say about the Americans. The Doughboys made easy targets. "They march to the attack in close order" and don't spread out, and they approach "without enough regard for bullets, at a slow gait, when they should advance by bounds at racing speed." But overall, the German was awed by the Doughs: their "courage and dash," their growing quantity of cars and trucks, their good-quality uniforms, and their plentiful food. They'd killed every officer in his battalion as well as most of the men. Other prisoners taken in this sector confirmed that they'd been loaned from Bavarian crown prince Rupprecht's army group in Flanders "to permit a counter-offensive against the Americans" and "profit from their inexperience in warfare." The Germans had anticipated an "easy enveloping movement" against the Americans but instead were being enveloped themselves.[58]

Other Germans were most impressed by the lack of American surrenders. Lots of Americans fled to the rear, but those who stayed at the front fought to the finish. "Groups of American soldiers were killed to the last man, instead of surrendering," a German prisoner marveled on August 10. "Most of our men are still completely dumbfounded. They declare that all is lost." No less impressive to the Germans was the comportment of Americans who *were* taken prisoner. German officers agreed that they were the worst prisoners they'd ever taken, exhibiting the irreverence that Americans consider a birth-right. A German interrogator recalled that Americans refused to give information about their units and talked back to the German officers, "much to the annoyance of the officers and the concealed delight of the enlisted men." After questioning some captured Marines, a German officer wrote: "It was impossible to obtain *any* facts. Prisoners scarcely indicated the place they had occupied in the line." American prisoners transported to Germany were even more exasperating: "The Americans were the chief complainers when the food was bad, which was always."[59]

French and American units poked carefully through the ground recently evacuated by the Germans on the Ourcq. The Germans fought dirty. To deploy a machine gun in an area they couldn't safely reach because of American observation, they'd lay the gun on a stretcher, cover it with a blanket, and have the crew slip on Red Cross armbands and carry it, as if it were a casualty, right under the eyes of American infantry and then into cover, where the gun, once installed, would open up on the same Americans who'd let it pass. Every locality the Germans occupied was left riddled with booby traps. The lovely sixteenth-century Château de Fère, sited on a hill in the midst of the Marne salient, was an obvious place for a command post. Taking it over in August, engineers of the US 77th Division nearly blew themselves to smithereens. The Germans had packed the château with 1,300 pounds of ammonium-nitrate explosive and a thousand 77mm shells, all carefully rigged by wires to a door and a hunting rifle in a gun rack on the wall. Had anyone grasped the doorknob or the rifle, the whole palace and its occupants would have been vaporized. General Robert Alexander, commanding the 77th Division, recalled another curiosity of the château. In its park were the graves of several German officers, one of them guarded by a loyal dog, who'd let no one approach the grave of his master. Even Doughboys proffering food were driven off, until the dog, nearly dead from hunger, finally relented.[60]

The 32nd Division relieved the 3rd Division on the Ourcq on August 1. It joined with the 28th Division, took Cierges, and continued to press toward the Vesle. When the 4th Division relieved the 42nd, an officer in the Rainbows observed that "most of the men have not removed their clothes or even their shoes for 24 days, and those in the front line have had no hot food for a week." The fighting was vicious, the American divisions swapping out brigades and trying to maintain momentum, the Germans killing them from the usual web of machine-gun nests and defiladed artillery. A platoon leader recalled the exertions needed to keep his men going. Many of them would go to pieces: "There were three or four maniacs from shell shock whom we had to overpower." The Doughs would advance past their own trenches and dugouts collapsed by German shells and "the faint sounds and stirrings in the caved-in banks were terrible"—the sound of Americans buried alive, suffocating.[61]

Each time a machine-gun nest was encountered, the Doughboys would have to deploy in a particular, time-consuming way. Automatic riflemen would go forward, lie flat, and suppress the machine-gun fire while riflemen with hand grenades would begin a flank movement. Other riflemen would wriggle as far forward as they could and wait to rush the nest. Since each German nest was covered by another, none of this went easily. Capturing prisoners was critical because they could tell the Americans where the Germans were hidden and what they planned to do. Few Germans were taken, but the ones who were displayed a dread of Americans. One said that his company had been told that the Americans kill all prisoners. Another, from the German 1st Guard Division, said that no one in his regiment had even been able to surrender—the entire regiment had been wiped out by American artillery and rifle fire. The mere presence of elite Prussian Guard troops in a rearguard action showed just how tough the Americans were; normally the Germans would have deployed second- and third-class troops for this purpose, but the tenacity of the American pursuit forced them to send in first-line troops to hold the line long enough to evacuate all of Boehn's heavy artillery and ammo dumps.[62]

The Americans were belatedly using heavy artillery, which could reach eight miles behind German lines, to prepare attacks. They were also bringing 75mm and 37mm guns into the front line to shoot up the machine-gun nests. One night, troops of the 4th Division caught a German messenger dog that was racing from a forward unit back to company headquarters with the exact location of the German section in a tube around his neck. They corralled the dog, read the message, and wiped out the German position. North of the Ourcq, the bloody work resumed as the troops now had to fight their way through and alongside a long, narrow forest, the Bois de Dôle. The knolls and gullies of the wood and its hilltop villages offered concealment for German machine guns and artillery, as well as their trench mortars (*Minenwerfer*), which flung a new projectile filled with phosgene gas and tiny pumice stones, the latter increasing the persistency and reach of the phosgene, which, when inhaled, literally dissolved a man's lungs.[63]

On August 4, the 4th and 32nd Divisions finally reached the Vesle. The 4th, advancing between the 2nd and 26th Divisions, suffered one thousand casualties trying to cross the river. Both banks were thickly wired, and every possible ford had been blocked with steel girders and wire hurdles. Doughboys approaching the river even in darkness were cut down, the German machine guns firing at zones and routes of approach with ranges they'd measured in daylight hours. The Doughs learned to dread the German "whizz-bangs"— long-range 88mm and 105mm high-velocity guns whose shells arrived faster than the speed of sound; they gave no warning whistle as they approached, simply a sudden "whizz" and an instantaneous "bang," often the last sound a man heard in his life.

General William Haan, a West Point graduate who'd never maneuvered troops in battle until now, ordered his 32nd Division of Wisconsin and Michigan National Guardsmen to cross the Vesle "at any cost," a ruinous, incomprehensible order. "It was apparent," a colleague dryly noted, "that General Haan had not grasped the dimensions of the problem." Colonel Raymond Sheldon observed the attacks on the Vesle for General Fox Conner, Pershing's chief of operations, and he wasn't impressed: "Coordination was not good, and must be insisted on." Regimental and battalion officers weren't using their intelligence personnel at all to pinpoint the Germans. There was no telephone liaison between the American and French divisions or even between the American divisions, nor was there any lateral communication between the US infantry and artillery. Every unit was just operating on its own, a sin that was all the more striking when viewed against—as Sheldon put it—"all of the superfluous personnel stuffed into every brigade headquarters." Sheldon stuck his head into one American command post in the heat of battle and counted nineteen officers and ninety-five enlisted men. Three divisions were operating in the area; this particular brigade had no idea what was happening around it, yet no one was venturing forth to find out. "Many casualties will result," Sheldon predicted.[64]

French observers with the US 4th Division applauded the courage of the Doughs but estimated that they were needlessly losing about four hundred men a day because the troops refused to scrape shallow trenches when resting and were undiscriminating in their choice of ground, often stopping where they were exposed to German artillery. A platoon leader remembered bandaging some of his wounded near the Vesle: "The feel of human bodies and blood, the quiet patience and confidence of the men, brought a realization of life to me in that hour that I shall never forget. 'This is my body which is given for you.' What that really meant, now I knew." The US 32nd Division—by now admiringly nicknamed "Les Terribles" by the French—attacked Fismes, the 4th Division struck at Bazoches, a few miles downstream. German machine guns still fired stubbornly from nests along the Vesle's south bank while the German artillery boomed away from the north bank, landing 150mm rounds on the Americans. After all that, the 4th Division captured only two German prisoners in Bazoches, one of whom assured his captors that "there is a large concentration of troops north of the river." There seemed no end in sight. Each time the Americans took a river line, the Germans withdrew to the next one.[65]

Some American units broke under the strain, Bullard excoriating one of his (unnamed) companies at Fismette—opposite Fismes—when an officer, broken by the relentless German fire, ordered his men to lay down their arms. Pershing's headquarters exploded in rage—"A person who spreads such an alarm is a traitor or a panic-stricken coward and should be KILLED ON THE SPOT"—yet, in a calmer moment, noted the disturbing fact that "the Germans were able to hold wherever they *wanted* to hold." They held lines like the Ourcq and Vesle as long as they needed them, and they never lost their grip on the all-important shoulders of the salient, around Soissons and Reims, which they held until everything they needed—men, guns, munitions, and supplies—had been evacuated back to the Aisne and the Chemin des Dames, their *real* line of resistance. The Aisne, wide and deep, in a swampy, wooded valley, would stall any Allied attack.[66]

And what stamina the Germans had. Liggett's US I Corps marveled that it had needed three weeks to advance twenty miles and had taken only 674 prisoners and seven guns. Boehn had held the ground between Château-Thierry and Soissons for a month, permitting the withdrawal of his entire army and all of its heavy artillery and, no less important, buying time for the German troops facing Mangin's onslaught around Soissons to withdraw safely. What, Pershing's intelligence section asked, will happen when we have to attack "the pick of the German army" on a line of resistance that they cannot abandon under *any* circumstances? They'd soon find out—on the wooded, fortified ridges of the Meuse-Argonne.[67]

As the last of the Germans retired behind the Vesle, the French proclaimed victory in this Second Battle of the Marne. The vast bulge that Ludendorff had driven into the French line in May had been pushed back to its original position. The Americans had failed to envelop Boehn's army, but the line from Soissons across to Reims was straight again. A deserter from the German 4th Guard Division said that men in his unit were saying, "We must now give up all hope in this war," but for the Americans the bill had been appallingly high. One in six Americans, fifty thousand of three hundred thousand engaged, had been killed or wounded to straighten a line that the Germans should never have bent. Some of the US wounded, questioned in a hospital after the battle, declared that their casualties at Soissons had been so high "because the French had laid down and allowed the Boche to flank the Americans." The French are "fair fighters," they allowed, "but they lie down at times." The French had lost their vigor, although who could blame them after four years of *this*? "They always wait for the Americans to start things." Others, who'd been fighting since May, noted that the quality of the French army was declining: "The new class of Frenchmen used on the line were not as good as the older ones."[68]

It would be no consolation to the dead and wounded that the French generals commanding the sector were punished—Duchêne relieved of command and General Louis Franchet d'Esperey exiled to the French expeditionary force in the Balkans. On August 4, French general Emile Fayolle declared victory in a terse general order: "The Second Battle of the Marne ends, like the first, in a victory. The Château-Thierry 'pocket' exists no more."[69]

In his own report of the battle, General Mangin praised the Doughboys, calling them "troops of attack," a rare commodity on the Western Front. The presence at the front of nine American divisions, he noted, had raised French morale. Germans who'd faced them here were no less respectful. "We'd been told that the Americans were green, untrained and cowardly," a German sergeant told his captors of the 32nd Division. "It didn't take long for my opinion to change." For the Doughboys, all was numbness and desolation here. An officer in the 28th Division recalled the routine of searching dugouts collapsed by German bombardments for casualties:

> We pulled out the men that were smothered in the dirt; some were cut in pieces by the shell fragments and came apart when we pulled them out of the bank. Lieutenant Quinn, a Pittsburgh boy, who had just got his commission a week before, was so mixed with the two men who had lain nearest him that I do not know yet whether we got things right. . . . Quinn's watch was *still going*.[70]

But things were looking up. "The entire aspect of the war had changed," George Marshall, now a colonel, observed from his new position as operations chief in Pershing's headquarters. The Allied push in July had set the table for what would be known as the "Hundred Days"—a vast, enveloping Allied offensive from Flanders around to Lorraine, designed to destroy the Germans in Belgium and France or drive them over the Meuse and the Rhine. General Foch was given a marshal's baton for his stand and counterpunch on the Marne; now he and the other Allied generals dared believe that one last Allied offensive on the Western Front before winter might break the Germans and win the war. The successful push from Soissons to Reims and the flattening of the Aisne-Marne salient had swung the momentum of the war in favor of the Allies.

There were now 1.2 million American troops in France, with a quarter million more arriving every month. In a secret report to the French war ministry in late July, a general on Foch's staff predicted that, if the last push of 1918 didn't decide the war, the Americans would have eighty divisions with 2.5 million troops in France by 1919, at which point the offensive could be renewed and an Allied invasion of Germany could be contemplated. The general predicted that the AEF, amply supplied with draftees, would display none of the French or British hesitation in the attack and thus ensure Allied victory. Even in "very hard fighting," the Americans would probably lose no more than three hundred thousand men a month, which was roughly equal to the number the US Army could ship every thirty days to France. American shipyards were now turning out "standard boats" in six hours, mass-produced ships built with numbered parts that had previously taken three months to build. There no longer seemed any limit to the quantity of troops and matériel America could ship to Europe. For their part, the French would shortly activate their 1919 class and the BEF would receive the replacements they'd begun training in the spring.[71]

Pétain, who'd slow-walked Allied offensive plans till he was satisfied that there were enough Americans on the ground to draw off significant German strength, now joined in the clamor for a great counteroffensive to push the Germans out of France. Artillery was everything in this grueling, dismal war of attrition, and a captured German general staff memo proved what the Allies had only been guessing at: that by the summer of 1918 the Allied artillery, inferior to the Germans in the spring, was now superior. The dreaded German "fire waltz" had begun to collapse in a broken, exhausted heap. Ludendorff noted, in the captured memo, that in a single month, July 1918, Allied artillery had destroyed 13 percent of the German army's artillery in battle. The usually smug German general staff now marveled at the Allied proficiency in counterbattery fire and in systematically destroying German guns, ammo dumps, personnel, and, ultimately, morale. Unanswered Allied cannonades convinced German infantry that the war was lost. Comparing German artillery losses with their own, the Allies discovered that the three Allied armies most heavily engaged in July had lost just 7, 5, and 10 percent of their guns, respectively, and collectively just 1 percent of their heavy artillery. There was light at the end of the tunnel.[72]

"Four years of effort with our faithful Allies, four years of trials, stoically accepted, are beginning to bear fruit," Pétain assured the poilus on August 6. "Broken in his fifth attempt of 1918, the invader is retreating. His effectives are diminishing. His morale is being shaken, while at your side your American brothers, hardly disembarked, are making the enemy, already disconcerted, feel the vigor of their blows. Persevere, be patient, the comrades are arriving."[73]

10

THE HUNDRED DAYS

B y September 1918, the United States dominated the war completely. An awed report by the Central Powers showed just how completely. The Americans now had fourteen million men registered and available for military service. They already had 1.3 million troops in France, and would have three million more on the Western Front by early 1919. America was spending $50 million every day on the war—$12.5 billion so far—and had hiked taxes to pay for it. American farms were exporting $1.4 billion worth of food to the Allies every year. American industry had been organized into a war machine—twenty industrial districts coordinated by the federal government. American plants were turning out 1,500 planes a month for a projected air force of 25,000 planes and one hundred thousand pilots by 1919. Already half of the planes on the Western Front were American. The US had surpassed Britain as the world's greatest ship builder. The British, by 1918, would need five years to build what American shipyards could build in a year. By 1920, the US Navy was projected to exceed the Royal Navy in tonnage. That would be the final hurdle, cementing America's global hegemony.[1]

With the Second Battle of the Marne over and Paris no longer under threat, Pershing was free to move his divisions into the US sector above Verdun and prepare an all-American offensive. The Allies having hammered the Germans back to the Hindenburg Line, Haig argued that the Americans should remain in the space between Soissons and Reims and add their weight to the "convergent" offensives there. But Pershing had constructed a vast infrastructure to supply American armies in eastern France, and he wanted his own sector anyway, one with strategic possibilities—like an attack on the transportation hubs of Metz, Thionville, and Sedan—not one wedged between British and French armies with only contingent possibilities and the likelihood that the war-weary Allies would hang back and rely on American manpower to win their battles.

Foch and Pétain agreed to Pershing's departure to Lorraine. His own army having lost its attacking spirit, Pétain discerned the possibility of winning the war with minimal French casualties. If Haig could be persuaded to continue his attacks eastward from Picardy and Flanders and Pershing could be induced, as a sop to Haig, to make his objective Sedan rather than Metz (to deliver a "convergent attack"), then Pétain's job would be comparatively easy. With the British and Americans pushing a wedge into the German line, the French, advancing cautiously in the space between the two armies, would always be a few steps behind the flank offensives—holding the curve of the salient—thereby minimizing their own casualties, as the Germans ahead of them would be maneuvered out of their positions by British and American progress on the flanks. Journalist Charles Repington estimated France's real strength by now to be just ninety divisions of six thousand men. Every single poilu had become a precious asset. While the British and Belgians would push between Flanders and Amiens, and the French from the Somme River to Verdun, the Americans would attack between Verdun and Nancy—the critical space between the Meuse and the Moselle. Their first target would be the Saint-Mihiel salient, site of so much bloodshed since 1914.[2]

Foch's strategy for what came to be called the "Hundred Days Offensive" was simple: to sustain simultaneous army-sized battles against the Germans in every sector on the Western Front so as to accelerate the attrition of the Germans and to accomplish in one hundred days what would previously have taken years, effectively overwhelming German efforts to reinforce threatened points and replace casualties. Foch couldn't have applied this "general battle" strategy without the guarantee of American manpower, for "general battle" involved appalling Allied as well as German casualties. Of the three great coordinated offensives that comprised the Hundred Days, the American offensive would be the most important, not least because Pershing needed a success to keep grasping Allied hands off his troops. General John Lejeune, who'd just taken command of the US 2nd Division in late July, recalled "the strong pressure" brought by Haig and Pétain to keep American divisions in their armies, not Pershing's. "Even partial failure," Lejeune noted, might cause the redistribution of US divisions away from the AEF and into armies controlled by French, British, and even Italian commanders.[3]

The strategic rationale for Saint-Mihiel was at least as compelling as the political one. After the failure of Hindenburg's midsummer offensives and with decreasing manpower, the German high command decided to make a gradual withdrawal from most of Belgium and northern France. It was their only option. Having spent their advantage in reserves in the five offensives toward the Channel ports and Paris, they had to shorten their lines, pull back their guns and ammunition, and focus all on the defense of Germany and the kaiser's throne. The thinning necklace of five German armies extending from the Channel to Switzerland was down to just 115 divisions. German reserve formations had been cut in half. July 15 had been the last time Ludendorff commanded more reserves than the Allies—81 German reserve divisions to 65 Allied. By September 1, the Allies had 72 reserve divisions against 44 German reserve divisions. No more "victory offensives" could be contemplated in Berlin.[4]

Hindenburg's strategic withdrawal would be a great pivoting movement eastward. Metz would be the pivot, and everything in Belgium and northern France would swing back toward the Meuse and the Rhine on that pivot to achieve a shortening of the German front (and liabilities). Much of the ground that would be taken by the French and British in the months ahead would be freely relinquished by the Germans. "The Western Front may be likened to a door which the Germans were slowly trying to close behind them, as they evacuated their stores of material," an American general observed. "If the hinges did not hold, the door could not be closed. If the hinges were broken, their exit was barred." Pershing's AEF was massing near these hinges of the German door. To succeed in their strategic withdrawal, which sought to buy time for more killing from defensive positions and a negotiated peace, the Germans had to hold the Metz pivot and the line of the Meuse River, including, of course, the railway passing along the right bank of the Meuse through Thionville, Montmédy, Sedan, and Mézières, before bending north toward Lille and Bruges. That single railroad accounted for half the supply and troop-moving power of the German army in occupied France and Belgium. It was the hinge of all hinges. The ground south of it, fortified by the Argonne Forest and the Meuse, lay squarely in the American sector.[5]

Ludendorff turned this all-important sector over to sixty-six-year-old General Max von Gallwitz, who had last fought here as a teenaged artillery officer in the Franco-Prussian War. Gallwitz employed the by-now-usual German method to defend it. He broke his army group—the thirteen divisions of Fifth Army and the nine divisions of Armee-Abteilung C—into "group sectors," each controlled by a corps commander who'd hold that sector with two or three divisions that would be replaced as quickly as they wore out. The commanding general would remain while divisions came and went, ensuring operational continuity. Gallwitz's group sectors, west to east, were Maas-West, Maas-Ost, Ornes, Combres, Mihiel, and Görz. He strung them like a barbed-wire fence across the path the Americans would have to take: from the Argonne Forest to the Meuse at Saint-Mihiel, and then over to the Moselle below Metz. The Germans were utterly confused even at this late date about the American role. Would the Doughboys actually form their own army—everyone knew that they lacked officers, NCOs, tanks, and artillery—or would they agree to be amalgamated in the French and British armies? "In many villages opposite us we observed brown and blue uniforms mixed together," Gallwitz recalled in his memoirs, which implied amalgamation.[6]

But Gallwitz had also been briefed on the rancorous dispute between Wilson and Clemenceau over an independent army. Pershing, who'd performed the surgery separating the Doughboys from the French, suffered no such confusion. "We are engaged in the greatest battle in history," Pershing excitedly wrote. He was determined to amputate the Germans from their lifelines at Metz and Sedan. The British war correspondent Charles Repington would later say that he'd grasped since 1914 the crucial importance of the ground now occupied by the Americans: "An advance down the Meuse by the Allies was the right and decisive strategy when our forces were strong enough to undertake it. It was the matador's thrust in the bull-fight."[7]

Seeking to position the Doughboys to land the killing blow, Foch directed Pershing first to reduce the Saint-Mihiel salient. Without it, the French couldn't be assured of Verdun, and holding Verdun was a keystone of the French war effort, second only to holding Paris. If Verdun and its forts fell, the blow to French morale would be staggering, for Verdun had far more than symbolic significance. Verdun—a road and rail center shielded by a semicircle of forts—threatened the flank of any German drive on Paris and denied the Germans the Meuse as a protective barrier for Metz and their principal railways into occupied France. But Saint-Mihiel, seized and held by the Germans since 1914, posed a constant threat to Verdun; from there the Germans could shell river traffic on the Meuse as well as the railroad along its banks and the other main line through Sainte-Menehould, leaving Verdun supplied by nothing more than a little branch line from Bar-le-Duc. Verdun, in other words, site of the bloodiest battle of the war in 1916, was still vulnerable in 1918 and could be guaranteed only by taking the Saint-Mihiel salient and reopening Verdun's supply lines. The French had fought multiple battles to retake the salient and had achieved nothing but fruitless casualties—140,000 since 1914.[8]

Saint-Mihiel in American hands would also, in Repington's terms, "guard from the side of Metz," the essential preliminary for hazarding an attack down the Meuse to Sedan. The salient was a bastion of Metz and Briey, menacing the Allied flank and shielding German iron deposits and blast furnaces from Allied bombardment. Saint-Mihiel had proved convenient during 1916's Battle of Verdun, when German guns there had poured fire into the flank and rear of the desperate French stand on the Meuse. The Germans would probably abandon Saint-Mihiel as a part of their strategic withdrawal, but they might not. French attempts to retake it in 1914 and 1915 had been so tragic and wasteful that, as a later analysis put it, "their bloody attacks there at Les Éparges, Apremont, and the Bois de le Prêtre—in which 100,000 lives were sacrificed to move a trench line a few hundred meters—must vie in notoriety with such names as Mons, Ypres, Champagne, and Verdun." There was no more succinct proof of France's crippling manpower crisis than this: the Saint-Mihiel salient was thinly held—by just nine weak German divisions holding sixty miles of ground, all of which could be swept by French cross fires—and yet the French after 1915 dared not attack it. When Austria-Hungary's 35th Division arrived to reinforce the salient in August 1918, its officers were shocked to see how feebly defended it was, vast tracts of "group sectors" like Combres around Fresnes entirely undefended by a German garrison whose batteries had been reduced to just two guns and whose infantry companies averaged just fifty men. Yet the French lacked troops, artillery, and a willingness to attack, so they left the Germans in place.[9]

Having fashioned the Saint-Mihiel salient into a three-part killing field—a forward Wilhelms-Zone, an intermediate Schröter-Stellung, and a main line of resistance, the Michel-Stellung, which was an eastern extension of the Hindenburg Line cutting across the top of the salient—the Germans just might remain to kill Americans as efficiently as they'd killed French. If they remained, they'd complicate American operations by driving a wedge into the heart of Pershing's sector and exposing his flank and rear to attack from Saint-Mihiel. The Germans would have to be driven out to give the AEF a straight starting line and secure flanks, roads, and rails. This was part of the overall Allied plan for the Hundred Days—as a British officer in Foch's headquarters put it, "To free the great lateral railway communications of France, clear the mining area in the north, and position the Allies to bring on a serious battle under favorable conditions."[10]

The great Allied counteroffensive that had paused after the Franco-American push toward Soissons in July resumed on August 7. Field Marshal Haig, whom Foch had urged in mid-July to launch a British offensive in Flanders to coincide with Mangin's drive on Soissons, had countered with a proposal to push the Germans back—at least beyond artillery range—from Amiens in concert with as many French divisions as Foch could provide. Haig would direct Henry Rawlinson's Fourth Army, along with Marie-Eugène Debeney's French First Army and parts of Georges Humbert's French Third Army, to attack both sides of the salient the Germans had driven nearly to the gates of Amiens in March and flatten it. This would be the first British offensive since the Battle of Passchendaele in 1917. Many wondered if the British would even be able to attack. Rawlinson's Fourth Army was a formation that had been bled white at the Somme in 1916 and then dissolved after Passchendaele and was only now reestablished to take in the shattered remnants of Gough's now-dissolved Fifth Army. The Tommies were stiffened by the presence of the Canadian Corps and the Australians, all-volunteer units with sturdy morale. They would be needed. Haig's British divisions were filled with raw draftees and rehabilitated wounded. He also had two American divisions—the US 27th and 30th—which Pershing had agreed to leave under British command to alleviate Haig's manpower problems.

Those manpower problems continued to cause controversy. Charles à Court Repington, who'd been driven out of the British army during the Boer War because of an extramarital affair, was chief among the doubters. Lloyd George's War Cabinet, he wrote, was "unconsciously defeatist" in failing to keep up the effectives of the British armies on the Western Front. Repington thought it "really wicked" that Britain struggled to maintain 60 divisions while the French had 100 and America was sending the manpower equivalent of 160 British divisions. He surmised that Lloyd George was seeking a novel way to exit the war. The prime minister would let the BEF wither on the vine, pronounce the country out of men, and then confine British involvement to selling tanks and guns to whoever wished to continue the war. Secretary of State for War Milner remained "unconvinced" that the Allies would win. Writing in the *New York World*, Repington scored London's failure to bulk up for the endgame. Two-thirds of military-aged British men were still not in uniform, the British government insisting that they were needed in the wartime industries. "New facts and a new situation demand new arrangements," Repington exhorted. With their recent victories, "the Allies have beaten the enemy over a front of some 125 miles and beaten him every day."[11]

Foch was less concerned. First-rate German assault troops had been devoured in irreplaceable numbers by Ludendorff's offensives. The survivors were far less capable. The gift of massive American troop deployments since June meant that Haig and Pétain could now worry less about reserves or defeat. So many trained Doughboys were entering the line every month that the Allies, so close to defeat in the spring, now were scenting victory. "Just push hard," Foch directed his British liaison on August 6, "that's all there is to it. All will go well; I promise." Haig agreed to an energetic offensive over the objections of his own headquarters staff, who—an officer recalled—felt tremendous pressure from London about casualties and "were always pulling at [Haig's] coattails to prevent him going on."[12]

For once, Haig saw to it that the British employed the element of surprise. He had telegraphed previous offensives to the Germans with visible laborious preparations. This time he took pains to wrong-foot Ludendorff, appearing to prepare for a strike in Flanders while he shifted his spearheads at night to the firmer ground at Amiens. British raids in the three months before the battle seized all of the good ridges near the point of attack so that Haig could mass his troops behind the lines without being observed. "Ludendorff has shown us how it is done," Captain Cyril Falls jotted. "One thing is clear, if we take the knock this time, we may as well give up."[13]

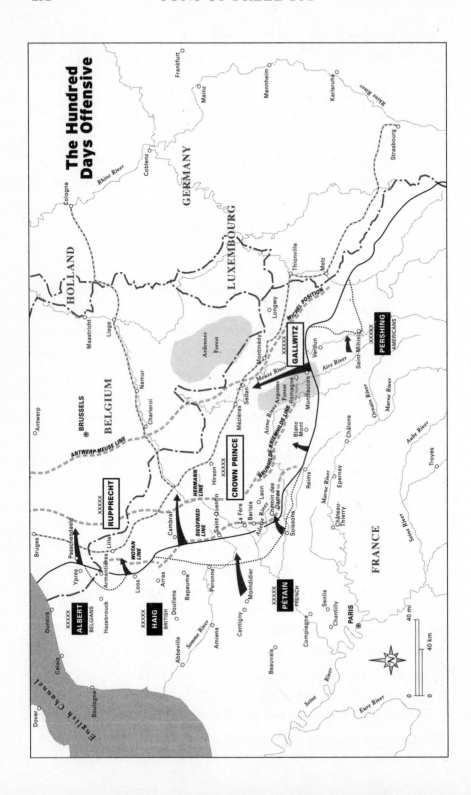

Tanks and aircraft would be critical for a breakthrough. Haig massed eight hundred planes and nearly the entire strength of the Royal Tank Corps—324 fighting tanks—on a fourteen-mile stretch of front at Amiens. To cover the sounds made by this clanking armada, British air squadrons flew "noise barrages" over the German trenches, diving and swooping low with their engines roaring to drown out the sound of the tanks moving into concealment. The tank weapon was vital. With manpower so low, the British increasingly relied on tanks and artillery to cover the deficit in troops and boost morale. Massed tanks would enable the British to pierce a section of the German front and then roll up the main resistance line, killing German men with machines while conducting British infantry forward in relative safety. British and French industry in 1918 assembled tanks as quickly as they could. The tanks revolutionized warfare by restoring mobility to the frozen battlefield. The Germans, their industry crimped by the blockade and the need to sustain their allies, lacked the resources to compete in this game-changing arm, and so German infantry were told to fight tanks with artillery, grenades, or balled-up wads of explosive, none of which seemed equal to these growling, coughing machines.[14]

Spearheaded by its tanks, Haig's army ripped into the unsuspecting Germans on August 7. The initial attacks, led by the Canadians and Australians, succeeded beyond all previous hopes as the astonished Germans were forced to feed in all of their local reserves, none of which could arrest the unexpected Allied push. Amiens and its vital rail yards were freed from the threat of German bombardment, Mount Kemmel was reoccupied, and 110 square miles of German-occupied terrain were liberated. August 8 became notorious as the "Black Day of the German Army." Spooked by the tanks, six German divisions had collapsed—platoons and companies surrendering en masse to single tanks and infantrymen, frontline German troops cursing the reserves sent to relieve them for "sucking up to the Junkers" and "prolonging the war." The British had bashed a fifteen-mile-wide dent in the German front and driven the Germans back to a new line, seven miles east of the Amiens hub. For once, the always-steady German infantry panicked, yielding thirty thousand prisoners in a single day as the Canadians and Australians advanced behind a creeping barrage, leapfrogging tired divisions with fresh ones each time the advance slowed. The British artillery, which now had as many personnel as the infantry—reflecting again the shift from men to machines—fired eleven thousand tons of shells a day to keep German heads down.[15]

Allied morale rebounded as the British secured Amiens and retook the blood-soaked ridges of Messines and Passchendaele while the Americans and French rolled up the last of the Marne salient. The Allied troops felt they were finally winning, after the defeats of the spring. At Baden, the Austro-Hungarian headquarters near Vienna, Emperor Karl told his German attaché that the Habsburg Empire was on its last legs—it might make it through the winter, but no longer. The war had to end. Ludendorff panicked too. He'd spent far too many hours behind a desk and had lost touch with his troops. He rightly cited a decline in German fighting power but wrongly pronounced the army broken. In a military conference at Spa on August 13–14, attended by the latest German chancellor, Georg von Hertling, and the secretary of state for foreign affairs, Admiral Paul von Hintze, Ludendorff appeared to crack, asserting that German victory in the war was no longer possible. Only a "strategic defense" to "paralyze the enemy's war will" offered any hope of success.[16]

Field Marshal Hindenburg was more optimistic. The Germans still controlled most of Belgium and much of France—a space as big as the Netherlands. As yet, there was still no serious Allied threat to German soil. The German army wasn't "broken," but it was badly shaken, having lost so many skilled attacking troops in Ludendorff's failed offensives, whose places would now be taken by boys and old men, grumblers combed out of war factories, and repatriated prisoners from the Eastern Front, many of whom were infected with Bolshevism. But the Germans still had strong positions behind them and the ability to inflict devastating casualties on French and British armies that couldn't afford them and on an inexperienced US Army that might choose to cut its losses if the war bogged down again in unending, hopeless slaughter.

Ludendorff needed to forge the defensive system that would break the Allied will, but he hesitated, reeling in a mental funk, descending toward a nervous breakdown. Two of his generals, Max von Boehn and Friedrich von der Schulenburg, advised a speedy withdrawal to the Antwerp-Meuse Line, but Ludendorff unhelpfully replied that such a "line" hardly existed. He and Hindenburg still wielded absolute power in Germany, and they now, even more unhelpfully, forbade the chancellor and foreign secretary to make any major concessions to the Allies. Germany, Ludendorff insisted, would keep all of its eastern conquests as well as the key parts of Belgium—the Flemish coast and Liège. It would ask for an armistice to reorganize itself—as if the Allies would permit that—and then resume the war if the Allies didn't concede a peace acceptable to the army command. The kaiser, still cowed by his generals, ended the conference with a feeble proposal: that the king of Spain or the queen of Holland be asked to mediate an armistice.[17]

Having paused his Amiens offensive on August 12 to reorganize— the British lacked the reserves to exploit their initial success—Haig resumed his attacks on August 21. The British, Australians, and Canadians bashed their way through Péronne and Mont Saint-Quentin and drove the Germans back to the Hindenburg Line. This chain of fortifications had been planned as an invincible line of defense. Four stories deep in parts, the Hindenburg Line's concrete fortifications stretched from Bruges to Metz and could shelter several hundred thousand troops. The line seemed to ensure that even if the Germans failed to win the war, they wouldn't lose it either.

With most of the AEF concentrated around Saint-Mihiel in Lorraine, Marshal Foch ordered the American troops still lingering on the Vesle to keep attacking there, to prevent Hindenburg from shifting reserves into the path of the British attacks. The generalissimo ordered the divisions of General Bullard's III Corps to fight across the Vesle, root the Germans out of the caves above Fismette, push them back to the Aisne, and free up the Rouen-Reims highway. Fismette and Bazoches were the essential bridgeheads on the north bank, opposite Fismes on the south bank, and the Germans swept both places with fire from the Vesle heights, making every attempted crossing a slaughter.

The Vesle at Fismes was more a creek than a river, clogged with debris and snarls of barbed wire, its muddy banks cratered with shell holes. The Germans had been living comfortably in Fismes all summer and had left in a hurry, leaving graffiti—"names and vile pictures"—scribbled on the walls. One officer recalled the squalor of the region. From a distance, it was beautiful—green woods, steaming fields, and misty valleys—but up close it was noisome: "All those rotten woods were filled with dead horses, dead men, the refuse, excrement and the garbage of armies. The ground must have been literally alive with pus and decay germs. Scratch your hand, cut yourself in shaving, or get an abrasion on your foot, and almost anything could happen."

In a wood near Fismes, the officer found an improvised German cemetery—beautifully wrought wooden crosses wreathed in wax flowers, with legends like "Hier ruht in Gott." "Verily," the Doughboy thought, "these seemed to be the same Goths and Vandals who left their graves even in Egypt; unchanged since the days of Rome, and still fighting her civilization, the woods-people against the Latins." Compared to the French, the officer reflected, Americans were more like Germans, but there was a difference: "Somehow everything German gave one the creeps. It was associated so inevitably with organized fear, that one scarce regarded its owners as men." To the Doughboys, the Germans seemed "like strange, ruthless insect-beings from another planet." Exploring the places Germans had inhabited—trenches, dugouts, villages—was like "waking up at night and realizing that there are rats under the bed."[18]

The US 28th and 77th Divisions wearily renewed the attack at Bazoches and Fismes on August 14. With both armies dug in and the Americans trying to crab their way forward, the whole place, one witness recalled, "had a blank air of utter idleness, a lonesome land full of the sense of impending disaster." The Doughs called the line of the Vesle "Death Valley." The 77th Melting Pot Division, National Army draftees from New York City, contained thousands of recent immigrants from Eastern Europe, Italy, and Ireland. These hardened New Yorkers were, as one who served with them noted, "con-proof." When their general assured them that he'd blast the Germans with two shells for every one they sent at him, the troops of the 77th were observed counting the screams of the German 77s and the counterscreams of the American 75s to make sure that they weren't being deceived. The Melting Pot Division had been through three commanding generals in the last thirty days. The most vivid memory of the war a corporal of the 77th had was huddling in the caves at Fismes, absently watching two lieutenants discuss something when a German shell splinter decapitated one of the two. The one who still had his head took one look at the one who didn't and fainted: "He was shell-shocked to such an extent that he was paralyzed. They had literally to carry him out. I don't know if he ever regained his senses."[19]

Ordered to storm Bazoches on the north bank of the Vesle—a village completely dominated by German artillery on the heights above it—the 77th Division suffered predictably heavy casualties and retreated. The US 28th Division met the same fate in Fismette, "flinging three companies against the German army," as one platoon leader sourly recalled. It was a great controversy of the war, bitterly digested in General Bullard's memoir. Foch and Degoutte, in their distant headquarters, had looked at the map and judged Fismette worth "any sacrifice" in (American) lives. Bullard had obeyed—he claimed—only because he was still under French direction and considered "unity of command" essential. An officer of the 28th Division remarked on the central tragedy of war for men thrown away by generals like Bullard, who would grouse in their memoirs but obey on the battlefield: "The men who had been killed had had their lives wasted after a certain manner, but there is an aphorism about the reticence of dead men who are the only competent witnesses to this kind of fooling."[20]

The 77th Division's third commanding general in thirty days—Robert Alexander—described his troops as "shaken" by their apparently impossible mission. "There was an atmosphere of hopeless gloom about the whole personnel, from the top on down the line."

Alexander could see why. The Doughs of the Melting Pot Division had been barely trained, then rotated through the peaceful Vosges, and then thrown into the savagery of the Vesle front without any real preparation. They were also, in Alexander's view, being used as cannon fodder by Degoutte, who made demands of them that he'd never make of a French division. While the squalid, desultory battle sputtered, Lieutenant Hervey Allen poked through a Catholic seminary in Fismes that had been used as a barracks by the Germans. He picked up a postcard that had been issued to Saxon troops of the garrison. The card featured Saxony's King Friedrich August III, draped flags, children gazing at cows in a pasture, and this caption: "Little ones do without milk so that we can keep our colonies." How that must have appealed to the malnourished children of Germany, Allen thought. He found a print shop where the departed priests had made circulars enjoining the poilus to pray. Allen took one up and scrawled his own invocation across the bottom:

> *The Virgin is plucking asphodels in Heaven with*
> *   little Saint John and the angels;*
> *Mars is walking the meadows of France, cutting the*
> *   throats of God's sheep;*
> *The laughter of children has departed from this town.*
> *   It is bereft forever.*[21]

Enjoying more success on the Somme than Bullard was on the Vesle, Haig was nevertheless cautioned by the War Cabinet to keep his casualties to a minimum as he pursued the Germans eastward from Amiens. He'd lost another 110,000 British troops in the month of August alone, the French another 100,000. "Haig knew with depressing certainty," as one historian put it, "that he was wielding Britain's last army." When these Tommies were gone—and they were going fast—there'd be none to replace them. Secretary of State for War Alfred Milner had already advised Haig that nineteen more British divisions would be dissolved in the months ahead, leaving just forty-two divisions for 1919: thirty-two British and ten from the

Dominions. And that assumed that countries like Australia would continue to maintain their five divisions, which they might not. Haig exploded (to his diary) at this dulling of "the first principles of war," or his conception of them: "What a wretched lot of weaklings we have in high places at the present time."[22]

The great British victory at Amiens was partial. It took hordes of German prisoners—twenty-two thousand in the first push, and then another twenty-six thousand by August 26—but it failed to break the Germans. General Marie-Eugène Debeney, leading the French First Army on Haig's right, had been Pétain's general staff chief in 1917 and had internalized the French commander's caution. His army never pressed its attacks, always lagging hours behind the British spearheads. German reserve divisions, no longer in doubt about Haig's intentions, stopped the Allied advance on the third day, by which time all but sixty-seven British tanks, averaging less than two miles per hour over broken ground, had succumbed to German shells or mechanical problems.

Haig found Debeney "almost in tears" at the unwillingness of his poilus to attack. "To deb" became British army slang for malingering and dawdling. Allied efforts to use their air superiority to bomb the Somme bridges behind the Germans and trap General Georg von der Marwitz's Second Army were thwarted by the famous Richthofen Circus, now commanded by Captain Hermann Göring, which shot down a quarter of the British bombers engaged and saved the bridges. But the initial success at Amiens, compounded by the British capture of Armentières, Bapaume, and Péronne, Debeney's capture of Montdidier, and a successful push by Mangin and the Americans north of Soissons to the heights between the Aisne and the Oise, raised the haul of captured Germans in these offensives to one hundred thousand, took back everything the Germans had seized in their spring offensives, and pressed them back to the Hindenburg Line, the fortified belt that ran from Bruges to Metz.[23]

The British and French paused to study the Hindenburg Line. It wasn't a continuous line but a chain of deep, interlocked fortified *Stellungen* (positions). Even if the Allies penetrated the outer face, they'd have to advance through a deep gauntlet of concrete forts that would repulse their break-in or slow it to a crawl. The Germans had given each *Stellung* a name from German and Norse folklore. The Wotan and Siegfried *Stellungen* faced the British, the Alberich and Brunhilde positions blocked the French, and, farther east, the Kriemhilde and Michel positions blocked the Americans in their new sector.

The French and British resumed their attacks east of Amiens. Using tanks and artillery, they gained some ground on the road to Cambrai. The bulk of Boehn's German Seventh Army, minus the rear guards left to torment Bullard on the Vesle, withdrew to the line Péronne-Noyon to help stem the Allied advance. The Allies paused again and then attacked on the whole hundred-mile front between Arras and Soissons on August 30. Seeking a decisive breakthrough, Foch fed in more and more divisions and tank battalions, but he was stopped again, this time on the fortified line built just west of Cambrai and Saint-Quentin. This was the Siegfried-Zone, the most developed section of the Hindenburg Line, where any Allied attack would be funneled through a ten-mile-deep four-sided system of granite bunkers that would rake the attackers with cross fires.

By pulling back between Arras and Soissons to the Siegfried-Stellung, the Germans had relinquished everything they'd won in the 1918 offensives, but they had thwarted Foch's attempt to smash through, envelop them, and win the war. The Germans called their retreat a *Rückgangsbewegung*—a withdrawing maneuver. There were two great German army groups on the Western Front: the German crown prince's group opposite the French and Americans, and the Bavarian crown prince's group opposite the British. Now forty-nine-year-old Rupprecht, the Bavarian heir apparent, moved his headquarters back to Mons. The German crown prince, thirty-six-year-old Prince Wilhelm, also retreated, pulling Boehn's Seventh Army back from the Vesle, which had run red with American blood in July and August, to the Aisne. Now the Allies would have to regroup again and try to attack across a region in which the Germans had obliterated all villages, roads, rails, wells, and cover.

While the French and British paused, Pershing prepared to pinch out the Saint-Mihiel salient. He had tried to disguise the looming American offensive there, but no amount of secrecy and deception could have concealed the essential fact that the Americans *had* to take it. The Germans knew that Pershing's sector was the space between the Meuse and Moselle, and if the AEF planned to attack toward Metz or Sedan, the essential hubs of the German defense lines in Belgium and France, they, like the French before them, would first have to reduce the Saint-Mihiel salient, which projected across the Meuse into their rear and threatened the flank of any projected American offensive. The thousands of French poilus who had died in futile attacks on the salient and its environs since 1914 testified to that necessity.[24]

Pershing and Marshall took pains to conceal the operation as best they could—moving troops at night and keeping them indoors or under forests during the day—but American secrecy was entirely lacking, as the bored, garrulous Doughboys talked and talked and talked. "Every lorry driver in the American Army, or lift boy in Paris knew, or thought he knew, that the salient of Saint-Mihiel would be attacked by the Americans," a British officer wrote. The American ace Eddie Rickenbacker was in Paris on leave during the first week of September 1918 and was surprised to hear taxi drivers assuring him that *les Américains* were about to attack Saint-Mihiel. They even knew the numbers of the American divisions involved, as did the German press. Field Marshal Hindenburg left Spa to inspect the fortifications at Metz, so certain was he that an American attack on Saint-Mihiel was imminent.[25]

Desperate to sow a degree of uncertainty in Hindenburg's mind, Pershing ordered a ruse. General Omar Bundy, who'd been stripped of his 2nd Division command after Belleau Wood, was given command of a dummy "VI Corps" and sent into the Belfort gap north of the Swiss border to simulate preparations for an American offensive there to fool the Germans. American radio stations filled the airwaves with bogus orders; a handful of American tanks drove up and down the thirty-mile sector at night so that German aviators would photograph their tracks in the morning; and copies of phony

American preparations were left in a Belfort hotel room for German spies to discover. In conversations with German staff officers after the war, the Americans learned that the deception had worked, forcing the Germans to evacuate matériel across the Rhine and send fresh divisions into Alsace as a precaution. Like the French and British, the Americans also busied themselves demoralizing the Germans with leaflet drops that warned of certain defeat: "Your war is hopeless"—"America is here to finish you off"—"Your U-boats are accomplishing nothing"—"We're building more ships than you're sinking."[26]

Pershing had formed his divisions—arriving from training camps or the Marne salient—into the US First Army on August 10 under his own personal command. With Pershing now wearing two hats and operating from two headquarters—Chaumont (AEF) and Ligny-en-Barrois (US First Army)—Foch formally gave him control of the sector from Pont-à-Mousson on the Moselle westward through Saint-Mihiel to a point opposite Verdun on the Meuse. This American sector would be extended across the Meuse to the western edge of the Argonne Forest and would include the French II Colonial Corps and the French XVII Corps, which were already dug in opposite Saint-Mihiel and on the heights above Verdun. If the Saint-Mihiel salient could be crushed out, the Americans could deploy on a broad front to envelop Hindenburg's army.

All too aware of this threat, the Germans had been using French forced labor and Russian POWs to fortify the Saint-Mihiel salient since early 1916, constructing extensive bunkers in the position's wooded heights. The salient was dominated by the Montsec, a lonely hill, visible for miles in every direction, that soared 150 feet above the flat plain of the Woëvre and gave the Germans early warning of any enemy attempt to retake the area. Here, as everywhere on the Western Front, the German plan had been to inflict maximum casualties to demoralize and "bleed out" any attacker, whether French or American. But everything had changed with the failure of Ludendorff's Peace Offensive and the first crushing Allied counterattacks. Now Germans in the salient, at risk of being cut off by Foch's general offensive, were ordered to evacuate back to the Michel-Stellung—the easternmost section of the Hindenburg Line—but slowly.

As elsewhere on the Western Front, the German withdrawal from Saint-Mihiel would be methodical and dangerous. Rear guards, wielding machine guns and laying mines and booby traps, would buy time for the removal of all German war matériel: heavy caliber guns, munitions, railroads, trench weapons, telephone lines, and supply convoys. The German field artillery and infantry would complete the withdrawal covered by rear guards of thirty chosen men from each battalion manning heavy and light machine guns and linked by roving cavalry troops and bicycle platoons. Even as Pershing finalized plans to crush the salient between three great pincers, Ludendorff was issuing orders to empty it out in just three to five days. The Germans always performed their evacuations with maximum efficiency, draining their rear areas of impediments and then streaming the fighting units back to safety, masked by the rear guards. The little rear guards were trained to simulate the activity of full battalions, firing flares at night and shooting rifles and machine guns into no-man's-land, all to give the appearance of full strength. They'd give ground only when seriously attacked.[27]

A serious attack was the one thing that the Americans seemed incapable of. Colonel George Marshall recalled chaos in the new US First Army headquarters. There were five hundred staff officers, yet none of them knew "how to initiate a modern trench-warfare battle," for the simple reason that they'd never done it before. The British and French had done it for them till now. This, in a nutshell, was why Haig and Pétain had pushed so hard for amalgamation. "Here we were," Marshall recalled, "a brand-new staff of a brand-new army, three times the size of a normal army, just entering the line for the first time and approaching its first operation."[28]

Haig, whose own strategic conceptions had been drowned in British blood, still grumbled that the whole operation at Saint-Mihiel was badly conceived: the Germans "would not hold the salient and the American attack would be a blow in the air." Perhaps, but the Germans were evacuating only because the Americans were forcing them out. Having advocated what he called "brash offensives" until the Somme battle, Haig had shifted to a doctrine of "attrition" in 1917 that had unfortunately attritted Tommies as quickly as Jerries. For 1918, Haig was pushing the idea of "converging attacks," and he protested to Foch that Pershing's attack on Saint-Mihiel didn't converge with British and French attacks and, therefore, "could not produce any effect on the enemy opposite him." Like Haig, Foch thought it likely that the Germans would evacuate Saint-Mihiel as their front shrank, but he pronounced himself incapable of talking Pershing around: "General Pershing was obstinate and would not change his opinion."[29]

The Battle of Saint-Mihiel was planned by a weary, overworked Colonel George Marshall. There were nineteen trained and fully equipped American divisions in France by the time Marshall took up his labors at Pershing's headquarters in Chaumont. Half of them were serving in French or British corps or transiting to the new American sector. Six American divisions were immediately available for an assault on the Saint-Mihiel salient. Marshall recalled the difficulty of planning the operation against stout German defenses with fluctuating instructions. First, he was given six divisions. With that number, he planned to push on the salient from its southern face alone. Then Pershing released four more divisions, for a total of ten. Marshall began drafting a new plan. He'd just finished it when Pershing increased his divisions to fourteen. As he finished that plan, he was told that he should plan on having two additional US divisions and six French divisions. Now Marshall began planning a much bigger operation with five hundred thousand US troops, one hundred thousand poilus, and three thousand guns: to pinch out the salient from its base and both flanks and then drive on Metz to the east. The work was grueling: Marshall recalled working from eight o'clock in the morning until two or three o'clock the following morning—eighteen-hour days, at a minimum. "This was not a simple case of an army undertaking an offensive operation," Marshall recalled. Rather, Marshall and his colleagues were literally birthing a new army, providing it with guns, tanks, planes, and munitions, hauling in supplies and services from all over France, and then "plunging this huge infant into the greatest battle in which American troops had ever engaged."[30]

While Marshall toiled, American marching songs began to express boredom: "It's twelve long rainy months or more / I wasted hunting for this damned war." Where was the promised combat? "Oh, we came over to fight the Hun / And all we do is clean the gun." This was the last American army to sing. The GIs in World War II would grumble and wisecrack, but not sing. The Doughboys sang about everything: "The French they had a custom rare, *parlez-vous* / They shit and piss in the local square." The Doughboys especially resented the lack of sex or even alcohol thanks to wartime prohibition, which had reserved grain supplies for food, not spirits or beer: "She ain't here; we want our beer / I don't think we'll get it this year."

Having appropriated "Mademoiselle from Armentières" from the British as their own ballad, the Americans added verses ("The mademoiselle is on the Marne / Fucking horses in the barn"), naming, with intensifying lust, the rhyming mademoiselle of the title first Glycerine, then Vaseline, Lanoline, and, the troop favorite, Analine. Everywhere they went, the Doughboys adapted "Mademoiselle" accordingly: "The mademoiselle from Bar-le-Duc, *parlez-vous* / She'll fuck you in a chicken coop," or "The mademoiselle from Gay Paree, *parlez-vous* / She had the clap and gave it to me." Another greatest hit was "It Takes a Long, Lean, Lanky Gal to Make the Preacher Lay His Bible Down." Everyone's favorite was "Banging Away on Lulu," a tune "as bawdy as the collective imagination of 3,000 horny men could conceive," a veteran recalled. Standard verses like this—"Banging away on Lulu / Banging all day / Where am I going to get my banging / When Lulu goes away?"—were invariably tweaked by the gathered troops into verses calculated to make the Knights of Columbus and the YMCA retreat in horror.[31]

The Y-men of the YMCA continued to supervise whatever respite the Doughs had behind the lines. The War Department had welcomed the Y to France, hoping that it would divert the Doughboys away from the bars and flophouses frequented by the Tommies and the poilus and engage them in healthy recreation instead. Visitors to

Y canteens would see posters and pamphlets with messages like "A German bullet is cleaner than a whore" or "How could you look the flag in the face if you were dirty with gonorrhea?" For men scarred by battle or just military service, it was all a little much. H. L. Mencken later published an acerbic piece about the "chocolate peddlers, soul-snatchers, and doughnut fryers" of the YMCA, these "heroes of the war for democracy." The Doughs razzed them all the time: "They discouraged the amiability of the ladies of France, and had a habit of being absent when the shells burst in the air." The Y-men tried to suppress the favorite songs of the Doughboys—like "There'll Be a Hot Time for the Old Men When the Young Men Go to War," actually banned by the US government—and substitute hymns and prayers in their place. In John Dos Passos's lightly fictionalized account of his own service in the war, he has a typical Y-man order all of the casualties in a hospital ward to stand and sing "Stand Up, Stand Up for Jesus," not noticing that many of them no longer had legs to stand on.[32]

Recruits flowing in from America on the troop transports expressed disgust with the British, whom they blamed, far more than the French, for the Allies' near defeat. Seesawing Doughboy prejudices—the "winter divisions" had liked the British, these didn't—recalled Wilson's hesitation in joining the war at the side of the closest thing the US had to a hereditary enemy, but they also reflected the decline in British fighting abilities. Nobody in America seemed to like England. The arriving troops of the 80th and 83rd Divisions—draftees from Pennsylvania, Ohio, Illinois, Virginia, Kentucky, Georgia, Florida, and Alabama who'd trained in the British sector—expressed "contempt" for the British. The food they'd been served in British transports and camps had been appalling. They thought the English—but not the Canadians or Australians—had "laid down" during the Ludendorff offensives. The Canucks and Diggers (Aussies) fought; they were "regular devils," the men said. The English were "grumblers," better when led by officers risen from the ranks, but poor when led by the British standard, men selected for "wealth and family connections." The more judicious among the Doughs allowed that most of this criticism emanated from the boors of the regular army, "whose favorite sport is to start arguments with Tommy," and that, anyway, the Tommies were bound to complain because they had the strictest discipline and the lowest pay on the Western Front. Others simply noted, after tasting English rations, that "the British would be better soldiers if they were fed more."[33]

Troops who had sailed directly to France on American transports felt no hostility toward the British, proof that exposure to foreign cultures is not always salutary. Most of the American recruits seemed eager to fight, bluffly assuring the snitches Pershing employed in every camp that they were "going to Berlin." Those who didn't want to fight, like Privates Antonio Grillo, Pentaleon Lubinsky, and Otto Ortland, were usually processed this way: "This man is not dangerous, but cowardly, and should be sent to the front." Some, like Lubinsky, who had emigrated from Russia to avoid military service only to be drafted in America, were dismissed with a single word: "Yellow." Being judged "yellow" or "dangerous" was more a curse than a blessing; it might get you sent to a labor battalion, where you'd break rocks or mend roads or bury decomposing bodies. Quick wits correlated with danger: "This man is a coward but as he is well educated it would be well to watch him." Dimness assured immunity from the snitches: "This man has not the intellectuality to be dangerous."[34]

On August 30, the date on which French generals formally handed the forty-mile sector of the Western Front facing Saint-Mihiel over to the Americans, Marshal Foch and his staff chief, General Maxime Weygand, met with Pershing in his new US First Army headquarters at Ligny-en-Barrois, just south of Bar-le-Duc. Foch, like Haig, now had doubts about the efficacy of an American attack on the increasingly peripheral Saint-Mihiel salient. The Germans were going to evacuate it anyway; they had to. If they didn't, they'd lose every man and gun inside it to the surrounding French and American forces. Foch preferred to exploit Hindenburg's withdrawal from Amiens and Soissons by renewing the attack at once, on the entire 250-mile front between Flanders and the Meuse River in Lorraine. The British would press their attack around Cambrai, the French on the Somme and the Aisne. Foch wanted Pershing merely to contain the Germans at Saint-Mihiel and make his main effort between the Meuse and the Argonne, smashing through the Kriemhilde-Stellung and thrusting toward Sedan.

Saint-Mihiel no longer fit with Foch's plan. Instead of attacking eastward toward Metz, Foch needed the Americans to attack northward, into the flank of the shrinking German salient in northern France and Belgium. Sedan and Mézières were now the objectives, not Metz. Pershing might have agreed had Foch left the proposed operation on either flank of the Argonne Forest to the Americans, but instead the generalissimo and Weygand used the change of plan as yet another pretext to seize Pershing's million combat troops for themselves. What they proposed on August 30 was to split the AEF—give half of it to General Auguste Hirschauer's French Second Army for attacks east of the Argonne Forest, and give the other half to General Henri Gouraud's French Fourth Army for attacks west of the Argonne. Foch then proposed that General Jean Degoutte, a man who had wasted American lives in the Marne salient, sit at Pershing's right hand to "advise" the scattered American forces.

Stunned—"Well, Marshal, *this* is a very sudden change"—Pershing naturally refused. He'd already fended off new attempts by Haig to use additional US divisions in his own operations against the Hindenburg Line, as well as a bizarre attempt by the Italian general staff chief, General Armando Díaz, to move two-thirds of the American troops in France to the Italian front. Pershing wasn't now going to hand the AEF over to Foch, Weygand, and Degoutte. "The American people and the American government," he said stiffly, "expect that the American army shall act as such and shall not be dispersed here and there along the Western Front." Foch then *ordered* Pershing to comply—the marshal was the Allied generalissimo, after all—but Pershing stood his ground: "You may insist all you please, but I decline absolutely to agree to your plan." The August 30 meeting was heated and ugly, Foch snidely asking: "Do you actually wish to take part in the battle?" Pershing did, but on American, not French, terms. Here was another benefit of President Wilson's decision to join the

Entente not as an ally but as an "associated power." France and Britain might not be careful with American lives. Having exhausted their own manpower, they clutched greedily at America's.[35]

Pétain arrived at Ligny to broker a compromise. Pershing would have his tune-up operation against Saint-Mihiel, to test the AEF in an American-staffed battle, but would then be expected to shift everything northwest for the more important attack in the Meuse-Argonne space by September 25. Instead of pinching off the Saint-Mihiel salient and then lunging at Metz, a cornerstone of the German position in France and Belgium, the US Army would crush the salient, turn away from Metz, and strike toward Sedan, whose significance was its railway, a railway that could as easily be amputated at Metz and Thionville. An attack on Metz made more sense. It was a critical German fortress, marshaling yard, and communications hub, and its environs included the Lorraine iron ore field, acclaimed by the US Corps of Engineers as "by far the most important in Europe" with its five hundred billion tons of low-cost, easily extractable coal, which furnished 75 percent of Germany's annual needs and powered the kaiser's war machine. The approach to Metz was over the open plain of the Woëvre; the approach to Sedan was through the Argonne Forest, some of the most formidable sections of the Hindenburg Line, and the Meuse itself, which the Germans held in force, right up to the gates of Sedan. If the Germans defended this space as General Boehn had defended the Marne salient, the casualties would be appalling.[36]

Worse, the challenge of launching two widely separated offensives by the same army in quick succession was immense. The Saint-Mihiel and Meuse-Argonne battlefields were sixty miles apart. General Max von Gallwitz's Fifth Army was disposed in such a way as to defend either or both spaces. Gallwitz left the nine divisions of General Georg Fuchs's Armee-Abteilung C to hold the salient—the group sectors of Combres, Saint-Mihiel, and Görz—while the bulk of his army group—the thirteen divisions of Fifth Army—held a line north and east of Verdun that had hardly budged since December 1916. These were the Maas-West and Maas-Ost sectors, *Maas* being the German word for "Meuse."[37]

In Chaumont, Colonel George Marshall continued his labors—trying to figure out how first to fight a great battle at Saint-Mihiel and then quickly shuttle six hundred thousand men, nine hundred thousand tons of supplies and ammo, and 2,700 guns over just three country roads to the Meuse-Argonne. "I remember thinking," Marshall wrote, "that I could not recall an incident in history where the fighting of one battle had been preceded by the plans for a later battle to be fought by the same army on a different front, and involving the issuing of orders for the movement of troops already destined to participate in the first battle, directing their transfer to a *new* field of action." Marshall, driven hard by Pershing, went for a walk, sat down outdoors, and scratched his head. "The harder I thought the more confused I became." He called it "the hardest nut I had to crack in France."[38]

The military risks were hard to measure. If German resistance in the salient were tougher than expected, the American combat divisions would find themselves being stripped of their reserves and artillery in the middle of the fight, and the six divisions of the army reserve, sent away to the Meuse-Argonne before the fighting even began, would be long gone. The roads and logistics were at least as daunting. To move a single American division required nine hundred trucks; artillery and supply carts would jam the roads, all the more because the units would have to wend through Saint-Mihiel, cross the Meuse, and then make their way northwest through an already-bustling French sector.

No one imagined that the Americans might lose the Battle of Saint-Mihiel. Prospects were good. The French provided ample corps and army artillery, giving the AEF superiority in guns of all calibers. The heaviest French and American guns could reach as far as Metz and impede German rail movements. As everyone had expected, Gallwitz ordered the evacuation of the salient on September 8. He'd planned an offensive to exploit American inexperience and disrupt Pershing's preparations but had been pulled back by Ludendorff, who didn't dare risk more precious troops in any great offensive, even against the Americans. Ludendorff ordered Gallwitz to retreat to the Michel-Stellung, the extension of the Hindenburg Line that ran across the top of the salient and was anchored on the Moselle. At the same time, Ludendorff pressed Gallwitz with rising urgency to nail down the AEF's strength and objectives. Were the Americans aiming at Metz, Saint-Mihiel, Sedan, or all three? "I must remind you again of the absolute necessity to do everything in your power to discover the division of enemy forces and his intentions."[39]

The US attack had been planned for September 2 but had to be postponed till September 12 because of heavy rains and slow American preparations. Hitching a ride from Toul to Ligny with General James McAndrew, Colonel Marshall listened as the AEF chief of staff deplored "certain older officers of the Regular Army who were continually slowing down the machinery." They were, in McAndrew's view, "victims of the lifelong routine of our little, dispersed Regular Army." They were too senior and protected to be relieved "in advance of their clearly evident failure," but relieved they would be "once sufficiently tried out to justify their relief." This was the familiar tragedy of every army that promoted on seniority. Troops would be sacrificed to justify the removal of general officers who were already known to be incompetent. With Gallwitz retreating, the Saint-Mihiel operation became more irrelevant than ever. The stable door had been left open too long; the horse was backing out as quickly as he could.[40]

On September 9, the kaiser summoned Ludendorff back to Spa to answer questions from Foreign Secretary Admiral von Hintze about the high command's strategic outlook. The Austrians were falling out of the war, the Bulgarians and Turks too. Drastic new measures were needed to stave off defeat. Ludendorff still clung to the view that "the general idea of the defense is to remain where we are," this despite the dramatic French and British advances and the pending American attack on the Meuse. Retiring would shorten the German lines and free up divisions, but it would shorten the Allied lines and free up their divisions as well. It would also boost the Allies' morale and depress Germany's.[41]

That same day, Haig traveled to London to plead for more troops. Lloyd George and the War Office were still planning on a 1919 campaign with ten thousand tanks, ten thousand tracked vehicles, and thousands of additional aircraft, and they were withholding infantry reserves for all of the usual reasons—chiefly their revulsion at Haig's methods—but also because large numbers of men had to be kept back for the Royal Navy, for key industries, and for training in tanks, artillery, and aircraft. Haig promised a decisive victory "in the very near future" if he were only given the men to do it. London remained skeptical. Haig was notorious for his rosy pronouncements. He'd promised victory on the Somme in 1916 and at Passchendaele in 1917—claiming there, a year earlier, that German morale was broken. Yet he'd broken through nowhere; instead he'd bled the British army white with his frontal assaults. Secretary of State for War Milner warned Haig to hoard what little manpower remained. "Recruiting is bad," Milner explained. "If the British army is used up now there will be no men for next year." Britain's general staff chief, General Henry Wilson, remarked that Lloyd George and Milner felt certain that Haig was far more likely to "embark on another Passchendaele" than win the war. They had reason to be nervous. Once Haig started something, he never relented. The bulk of his total wartime casualties had come in two prolonged spurts—the five months he'd attacked on the Somme in 1916 and the six months he'd attacked Passchendaele in 1917. Each of those sorrowful battles had cost Britain hundreds of thousands of men. Now, in the months since March, Britain was well on its way to losing another half million. Would the latest effort prove as barren as the previous two?[42]

Pershing certainly had the manpower to ensure victory at Saint-Mihiel. The salient formed a triangle between the Meuse and the Moselle, its points at Verdun and Saint-Mihiel on the Meuse, and Pont-à-Mousson on the Moselle. If the AEF crushed it out, then the French-American line would run straight from Verdun to Pont-à-Mousson. Pershing's plan—really Marshall's—was to attack on forty miles of front from Les Éparges around the nose of the Saint-Mihiel salient to the Moselle River. Two American corps—General Hunter Liggett's I Corps and General Joseph Dickman's IV Corps—would assail the south face of the salient while General George Cameron's

V Corps drove east across the salient from its western face to join the troops attacking northward at Vigneulles and trap whatever remained of the German and Austro-Hungarian force inside the bulge. To the French III Colonial Corps would go the honors of liberating the town of Saint-Mihiel. Liggett's I Corps—comprising four divisions, the 82nd, 90th, 5th, and 2nd—had its right on the Moselle at Pont-à-Mousson; its left wing joined Dickman's IV Corps—the 89th, 42nd, and 1st Divisions—in line as far as Xivray, where it joined the French II Colonial Corps, which held the center from Xivray to Mouilly, where Cameron's V Corps—the US 26th and 4th Divisions and French 15th Colonial Division—lined up on the western face of the salient, with orders to clear the three commanding heights of Les Éparges, Combres, and Amaranthe.

The attacking troops mingled veterans and rookies. Liggett's best unit was Marine General John Lejeune's 2nd Division, Lejeune having replaced Harbord when Pershing sent the latter to kick-start a torpid supply service that had assumed that it had until 1919 to prepare the great offensive that was actually beginning *now*. Lejeune noted excellent morale in his division, the troops kidding each other and calling, "Where do we go from here, boys?" as they moved into line, a reference to the popular wartime song by Arthur Fields. And this was a division that had been cut to pieces in Belleau Wood and again at Soissons. "Nothing seemed to depress or daunt them," Lejeune wrote. "They played hard, they worked hard, and they fought hard. They were magnificent." Dickman led two of the AEF's most magnificent divisions; he had the 42nd Rainbows in the center and the 1st Division on the left. The Big Red One had the task of racing north to seize Vigneulles in tandem with one of Cameron's divisions—General Clarence Edwards's 26th Yankee Division, which had stumbled badly at Château-Thierry.[43]

The American and French divisions marched into position at night and hid in the woods by day to achieve some semblance of surprise. Foul weather imperiled the whole operation as a steady rain beat the roads of the salient into mud. The sector had been quiet for so long that the Doughboys bumped into French troops who'd literally been forgotten. Marshall recalled one poilu who'd been assigned to guard a dam near the salient; he'd been there for two years, fishing every day in the lake and sleeping in an abandoned mill. As fresh troops swarmed into the area and battle loomed, the indignant Frenchman appeared from nowhere demanding a transfer elsewhere. Until now, French and German battalions in the sector had held absurdly large territories, two or three miles of front, so certain were they that the other side would never attack here. Patrols had taken pains to avoid any contact with the enemy and to "live and let live." The salient was one of the rare places on the Western Front where one could pass an entire day without ever hearing the sound of artillery. The Germans called Saint-Mihiel the "sanatorium of the West," where battle-fatigued troops were sent to calm their shattered nerves. All of that was about to change.[44]

11

SAINT-MIHIEL

THE QUIET OF THE SAINT-MIHIEL SALIENT WAS SHATTERED at 1 a.m. on September 12, when American and French artillery commenced a million-shell bombardment along the entire forty-mile front. After four hours of artillery preparation by three thousand guns—"the bell-tolling effect of the 75s and the belching of the howitzers, the acrid, thirsty taste of powder in the air"—the seven American divisions in the front line went over the top at 5 a.m., through a thick fog and behind a smoke screen and a rolling barrage. "Inky black, mud up to the knees, and rain," one miserable Doughboy recalled. Before long, three hundred thousand American and French troops were advancing. Tanks driven by French and Americans chugged alongside. Each assaulting division was supposed to make a serviceable road for itself across no-man's-land and beyond, but by noon these hastily built roads were quagmires; by afternoon a hard tangle of men and vehicles had blocked them entirely. Much French and American transport had to be ditched off the side of the road to move the infantry and guns forward. Clausewitz's maxim may have occurred to more than one US staff officer staring helplessly at this mess: "Everything in war is very simple, but the simplest thing is difficult."[1]

The US 3rd Division, the reserve for Dickman's IV Corps, had expected to linger in place while the frontline divisions made contact with the Germans and pushed through. Instead it found itself racing to catch up when the advance went faster than anticipated. None of this was terribly surprising. The US First Army had sixty-four strong battalions in this sector against eighteen weak German and Austrian battalions spread thinly along fourteen miles of front: in other words, sixty-five thousand Americans against eleven thousand troops of the Central Powers. Pershing's prebattle intelligence estimate had identified the enemy divisions in the salient, and they were all third-, fourth-, or even fifth-class Landwehr and reserve divisions, along with the largely Rumanian Austro-Hungarian 35th Division, which, on a good day, might correspond to a fourth-class German division.[2]

Having withheld troops from the Ludendorff offensives, the Austrians could withhold no longer. With the Russians beaten and the Italians quiet, they'd run out of excuses. Vienna reluctantly sent four divisions from Italy to France; first to go was the 10,500-man Austro-Hungarian 35th Division, which embarked with mixed regiments of Rumanians, Hungarians, and Germans for the Saint-Mihiel salient. The idea was to make Austrian units like this one "approximate" German units, with identical tactics and six light machine guns per company, although the Austrians rarely managed more than two despite the German gift of thousands of Lewis guns captured from the British in the spring. These Austrian troops, sent to anchor Gallwitz's Combres group sector, would struggle even to approximate the Germans.[3]

Third- or fourth-class German divisions—and units like these Austrians—had traditionally been used for nothing more demanding than passive defense in quiet sectors. They had been botched together in all manner of demoralizing ways—returned wounded, survivors of annihilated regiments, teenagers of the 1919 recruiting class, or old men of the Landwehr and Landsturm. No first-class German division had set foot in the salient since 1916, except now and then for a period of guaranteed rest. As the Battle of Saint-Mihiel commenced on September 12, these German third- and fourth-raters presented

American roadwork in every battle was deficient. Preparation was inadequate, and rules and right of way were not enforced. Here, soldiers struggle to extricate an ammo wagon from the mud near Saint-Mihiel while a traffic jam forms behind them. (National Archives)

few problems to the young, raw-limbed Doughboys. The Germans retired as quickly as the Americans advanced. One Dough recalled his first sight of a Western Front battlefield. The usually verdant salient had been hotly contested until 1916, and "there wasn't a blade of grass anywhere. . . . The earth looked like soil I'd seen in Texas," turned over so many times that "it was as stripped of life as a desert." The Americans pressed forward, gratefully passing abandoned trenches and dugouts, recoiling at the stench of French and German cemeteries plowed up by the American bombardment: "Little crosses with helmets fastened to them lay here and there; white splinters of bone, occasionally a skull; everywhere the odor of dead things."[4]

The 411 light and medium tanks of thirty-two-year-old Lieutenant Colonel George Patton's 1st American Tank Brigade got nowhere. The primitive machines broke down, stuck in the mud, or fell inside German trenches. The American infantry plodded on without them. Congestion on the roads of the salient—tanks, troops, guns, and supplies—meant that gas for the tanks never arrived. By midday on September 13, the Allied tanks that hadn't succumbed to German fire or mechanical problems were out of gas and out of action. Fuel was eventually dragged forward—around the traffic jams—on sleds, but, with the Germans retreating as quickly as they could to the Michel-Stellung, there was little for the tanks to do.[5]

The leading waves of attacking Doughboys were thin, backed by small columns that mopped up enemy trenches. Thousands of German and Austrian prisoners were taken on the first day; they'd known an attack was coming but had been stunned by the intensity of the four-hour preliminary bombardment, which deluged the German battle zone with gas, high explosive, and shrapnel. Cowering in their dugouts when the Doughboys attacked, the enemy had either died or surrendered without a fight. By mixing gas shells with high explosive—standard operating procedure on the Western Front—attackers forced defenders to pull on gas masks, so ill-fitting and uncomfortable that, as the French liked to say, "an enemy wearing the mask is already two-thirds neutralized."[6]

Lack of experience dogged the Americans everywhere. Though Pershing and his staff chief, General James "Dad" McAndrew, loathed the tendency toward bureaucracy in the Great War armies, they didn't dare unchain the AEF just yet. The staffs and units were so green that they had to be micromanaged; Pershing's divisional instructions for this offensive ran to thirty-three mimeographed pages, plus ten additional chapters of instructions on liaison, phones, radio, telegraphs, balloons, planes, visual signals, carrier pigeons, and cipher codes. Officers would be distractedly thumbing through these fat volumes of paper even as they thrust through the German lines.[7]

American road work was a disaster. No provision was made for two-way travel, up and back. Vehicles moving up roads hogged both lanes; vehicles returning down them had nowhere to go. Teamsters beat their horses so viciously that General Hunter Liggett had to remind the Doughboys of his I Corps that their horses were "public animals," the property of the American taxpayer, and that they must not be "kicked or beaten over the head." Any man caught beating a horse, Liggett warned, would be publicly beaten in the same way.

Some areas were jammed with troops and vehicles, others entirely vacant. "Roads are a *mathematical* problem," McAndrew sputtered. "We know the roads on our side and aerial reconnaissance shows us the roads on the enemy side and so detailed preparation must be made in advance," including which units would use which roads and what work engineers would have to do to move the traffic across enemy trenches, wire, shelled areas, and downed bridges. American units were simply making things up as they went along. Had the Germans been committed to a determined defense of the salient, they'd have slaughtered the immobile masses of stalled American units. "Work must be driven with desperate speed," McAndrew continued, "not in the shiftless manner seen during these operations."[8]

Communications were garbled everywhere. The key phase of the Battle of Saint-Mihiel played out in the dark—the long night of September 12–13, when the relatively seasoned US 1st and 26th Divisions were supposed to join hands across the top of the salient, trapping the enemy inside. But no one's phones worked, and runners, hunting through dark woods for constantly moving headquarters, rarely found them. Mounted messengers weren't used, and motorcycles stuck in the mud. American units blundered around ignorant of themselves and their neighbors. Headquarters lagged too far behind the assault formations. McAndrew noted that at the start of the second day of operations, one American division had its headquarters sixteen miles behind its front line. He hardly needed to add that "it's impossible to command a division properly from this depth."[9]

The commander of the 1st Division's 26th Regiment placed one of his battalion commanders under arrest for requiring eleven hours to advance a mile and a half. The battalion commander's explanation encapsulated the difficulties the entire US First Army faced in a dark salient thinly populated by the enemy. He'd advanced with his headquarters detachment up a dirt track, hearing the rumble of retreating German wagons in the distance, his assault company ahead of him, his support company behind. They arrived at a fork after tripping over two companies of the 28th Infantry sleeping in the middle of the track. In the dark, the poor battalion commander went one way and his companies the other. Hours passed as he sent runners down the paths and through the underbrush "whistling and calling," to no avail. The Germans got clean away, and the major, who'd begun his career as a private in the coastal artillery in 1902, was relieved on the spot. Yet how could he have done any better? he protested. Many had lost their way in the dark; a leaderless machine-gun unit had blundered into his; his troops had been forced to shift from line of combat groups (optimal for fighting the apparently nonexistent Germans) to column of files (optimal for groping through dark woods). The division inspector's verdict was kind but firm: "Major Whitener is a brave man, an energetic man, but it is the consensus of opinion that he is unfit to command a battalion. He has not the confidence of his juniors, his seniors, nor do I believe he has confidence in himself."[10]

It was fortunate that the Germans were retreating, not counterattacking. They were halfway through a total evacuation of the salient when the Americans struck. Gallwitz's Fifth Army was headed for the Michel-Stellung, the eastern extension of the Hindenburg Line, which had been under frantic construction by emaciated Russian POWs since February 1917. Placed on the reverse slopes of a low ridge of hills, the Michel Position threaded through villages like Dampvitoux and Rembercourt and consisted of a double line of trenches, two lines of zigzagged barbed wire, and then concrete dugouts and machine-gun shelters a half mile behind the trenches. German infantry companies were under orders to evacuate immediately to that position, leaving nothing more than seven-man rear guards to slow the Allied pursuit.[11]

The prisoners the Americans and French collared in the salient and on the edge of the German withdrawal position were comically unambitious, hundreds of old Landwehr reservists who explained their decision to surrender in the most unheroic terms: "Prisoner states he was on patrol when shelling began and so he sat down saying he refused to walk into artillery fire." None of these fourth-class men had been trained for assault troop initiative: "Prisoners all state that everything is in a mix-up and that they are told nothing." Captain Walter Lippmann, already a familiar columnist in America, interviewed Germans of various divisions, good and bad, and concluded (in a letter to White House adviser Colonel House) that the Germans held on and resisted American propaganda because of their essential cynicism: the German soldier, Lippmann said, "is a highly trained and technically competent peasant, but fundamentally a peasant in his political relations. . . . Even the most sensitive among them refuse flatly to believe that America has any ideal purpose. They simply do not believe that such things exist between nations."[12]

It's hard to see how the Americans would have taken the salient against real resistance. As it was, the Doughboys staggered ahead. A German Landwehr infantryman, much impressed by the big, brave Americans he saw coming at him in solid formations, nevertheless noted that "we had no artillery in position and that which was in position was almost entirely out of ammunition." He recalled that if his positions had been "powerfully organized," the Americans would have suffered crippling casualties. It hardly mattered that the Allied bombardment, reduced from eighteen hours to four on Pershing's order, failed to cut the German wire. The Doughboys strolled forward and stamped it down with their shoes. Most of it was rusty wire nailed to rotten posts.[13]

"Mopping up" was a critical piece of open warfare like this, but General McAndrew deemed all of the American divisions deficient in cleaning up conquered ground. The Doughs rarely found Germans concealed in farm buildings or brush, nor did they always remember to smash the cartridge guides in the German machine guns they passed so that they couldn't be reused by hidden German rear guards. "Woods and villages were left infested with German troops." McAndrew reported the sad spectacle of one division's first-line battalions attacking a strong enemy position while its second-line battalions, attempting to follow the first line to the front, were being mowed down by a strong line of German machine gun nests that the first wave had passed over and not seen or mopped up.[14]

Here, as elsewhere on the Western Front, the Germans employed machine-gun units as rear guards. Normally, they were sickeningly effective, ambushing enemy infantry with the light machine guns and deploying the heavy machine guns from elevated positions to lay down

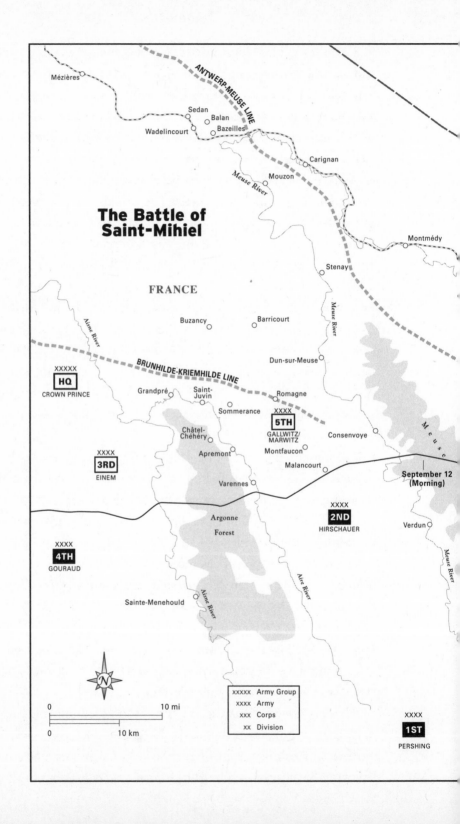

The Battle of Saint-Mihiel

Mézières

ANTWERP-MEUSE LINE

Sedan
Balan
Wadelincourt
Bazeilles

Carignan

Meuse River

Mouzon

Montmédy

Stenay

FRANCE

Buzancy

Barricourt

Meuse River

Dun-sur-Meuse

XXXXX
HQ
CROWN PRINCE

BRUNHILDE-KRIEMHILDE LINE

Aisne River

Grandpré

Saint-Juvin

Romagne

Sommerance

XXXX
5TH
GALLWITZ/
MARWITZ

Consenvoye

Châtel-Chéhéry

Apremont

Montfaucon

Meuse

XXXX
3RD
EINEM

Malancourt

September 12
(Morning)

Varennes

XXXX
2ND
HIRSCHAUER

Argonne
Forest

Verdun

XXXX
4TH
GOURAUD

Aisne River

Aire River

Meuse River

Sainte-Menehould

N

0		10 mi
0		10 km

xxxxx	Army Group
xxxx	Army
xxx	Corps
xx	Division

XXXX
1ST
PERSHING

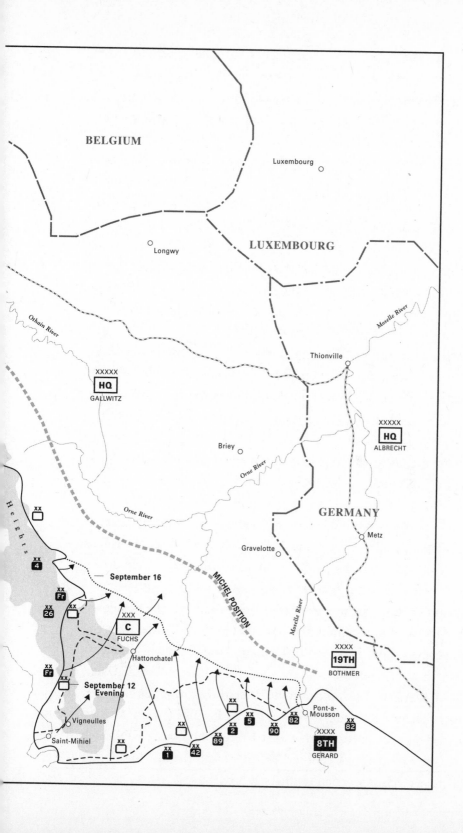

barrage fire. These deadly German tactics—so effectively applied in the Marne salient—would be even more brutally implemented in the looming Meuse-Argonne battle. For now, they were honored in the breach, as unreliable troops posted as rear guards—"sacrifice units" in the German parlance—took to their heels before the Allied advance. Hindenburg sent withering telegrams to Gallwitz as the battle developed—"I warn you now that if I perceive any further weakening of your resistance I will not hesitate to intervene forcefully"—and Ludendorff made frantic phone calls: "Why have you allowed two of your divisions to be crushed?" It was easy to see why. The Americans had so many troops here that they were pushing forward from the tip of the salient and closing in from the flanks. And with all of the German guns reversing out of the salient, these German and Austrian rear guards had little artillery support.[15]

British general Cyril Wagstaff, observing the battle for Haig, noted the absence of German artillery fire or indeed "any long-range artillery reaction at all." Wagstaff spent most of the day in the sector of the US 89th Division. He followed this attack on the base of the salient from a French observation post. "There was practically no opposition in the Boche front line; I only saw about twenty rounds of Boche artillery reaction." A lieutenant in the 89th Division agreed. His platoon had spent most of its time accepting surrenders. One of his sergeants had gone into a dugout with only a pistol and encountered thirty Germans inside, all of whom had eagerly surrendered. Germans would appear from nowhere with their hands up crying "Kinder"— "children"—which meant that they had kids at home. "Naturally, we didn't want to shoot them under those circumstances," the lieutenant added. One of the casualties the 89th Division did suffer was the poet Lieutenant John Hunter Wickersham, killed by shell fragments shortly after going over the top. The men of his platoon recalled that, even as Wickersham bled to death, he dressed their wounds and used his weapon, later receiving a Medal of Honor for his heroism. He had just mailed a poem to his mother that was posthumously published: "The Raindrops on Your Old Tin Hat." It evoked the rain and fog of the salient, as well as worried mothers at home:

And don't you reckon it's her tears, and not the rain,
That's keeping up the patter on your old tin hat? [16]

By 9:30 a.m., Lieutenant Wickersham's body was cold, his mother in Denver may have felt a dreadful premonition, and the Allied gun line was already packing up to advance all the way to Essay. An Austrian lieutenant, hoping to get some information on the breadth of the American advance from an array of observation balloons overhead, watched American planes swoop in and shoot the balloons down, their Austrian observers leaping for their lives from the flaming blimps. Each time the Austrians filled a balloon with hydrogen and sent it up, Allied planes would appear to shoot it down. Over that single Austrian lieutenant, the Allies shot down twelve balloons in the course of the day. In this fight, unlike the ones in the Marne salient or the Meuse-Argonne, Colonel Billy Mitchell, Pershing's air commander, had total command of the skies for the simple reason that, with no other offensives taking place on the Western Front, he'd been loaned hundreds of Allied planes—1,500 aircraft in all.[17]

At the second German line of resistance—the Schröter-Stellung—British observer General Wagstaff noted more German fire from machine-gun holes in front of the German wire, but even here the enemy surrendered readily. Wagstaff saw German officers leading their units into captivity, without fighting on the good lines in the woods or from the pits along the wire. The road and rail junction of Thiaucourt fell at 11:40 a.m. to the US 2nd Division, which captured the entire student body of a German machine-gun school—men from fifty-seven different units who were seized as they tried to board a train out of the salient. Lejeune, commanding the 2nd Division, arrived to inspect the place—"It looked more like a half-destroyed picnic ground than anything else," with its German chalets and cottages scattered in the woods between dugouts. He came across ten dead Doughboys in a perfect row: "They had been killed by machine gun fire as they came over the crest of the ridge" that overlooked the Thiaucourt road. Lejeune never forgot the expressions on their dead faces: "Peace and serenity, not hate and anger."[18]

An Austrian prisoner confirmed that a deep strategic withdrawal along the entire front was under way. He'd seen flatcars loaded with German artillery heading east. He'd arrived in the salient in August and had changed trains in Zabern. That place too had been filled with 10cm and 15cm guns being hauled east. The Germans were clearly preparing for last stands on the Meuse, Moselle, and Rhine.[19]

The Austrians wilted under the American attack. The only direction the Germans gave to the Austrian officers was to "stand fast to the last extremity." None did; the Austro-Hungarian companies simply fled, of their own accord, without orders. Most interesting to the French was the fact that none of the Austro-Hungarians, neither men nor officers, knew anything about German intentions. None of them even knew of the existence of the Hindenburg Line, which lay just to the north. This was remarkable, since German orders captured in the salient spoke plainly of German intentions to evacuate the wedge of territory, anchor the Hindenburg Line "across the chord of the new battle zone," and leave nothing but outposts in the Saint-Mihiel salient to give warning of future Allied attacks. Clearly the Germans by this stage viewed the Austrians as nothing more than sacrifice units—"meat for the guns."[20]

The sheer weight and scale of the American attack with a dozen heavy divisions meant that Saint-Mihiel would never again be a German outpost zone. Had the American attack landed just three days later, it might have been. Ludendorff had planned to evacuate the salient as smoothly and savagely as he'd evacuated everywhere else on the Western Front. Six *Bergetage*, "cleanup days," in which all supplies and artillery would be assembled for evacuation, would be followed by three *Rückzugstage*, "retreat days." The Germans smilingly dubbed these retreat days *Lokitage*, after the cruel Norse god Loki, in honor of all the vandalism that attended any German retreat: villages burnt, orchards girdled, roads cratered, bridges shattered. Touring Thiaucourt on September 13, General Wagstaff saw evidence that Gallwitz had been surprised while transitioning from the cleanup to the retreat phase. Wagstaff saw three brand-new German 8-inch howitzers perched on railroad trucks, THIAUCOURT chalked on their barrels. He also saw eight 120mm guns ready for loading and transport, and neat stacks of shells, spare parts, and engineering stores.[21]

The US 90th Division seized the once-fortified quarries of Norroy that first day with little resistance. One of its casualties was Major Terry de la Mesa Allen, who'd command the Big Red One in North Africa and Sicily in World War II. He was shot through the mouth and jaw, a magical wound that cured him of a stutter.

Observing the ease of the American advance, Colonel George Marshall felt certain that the AEF, if it had continued and not detoured to the Meuse-Argonne front, could have reached the outskirts of Metz by September 13 and "captured the city on the 14th." Maybe, or maybe not. Metz was fortified and lay up the muddy Moselle valley and across the swampy plain of the Woëvre, which could only be efficiently traversed by an army in the summer. The rest of the year, and certainly by now, with the autumn rains pelting down on its clay soil, the plain was a quagmire where shell craters would instantly fill with groundwater and trenches would dissolve. If Pershing's army had bogged down there—pinned between the guns of Metz and those on the Meuse Heights—they'd have been ground down by attrition without contributing anything to the British and French offensives farther west.[22]

The German troops at Saint-Mihiel seemed to have as little fight in them as their Austro-Hungarian allies. A German lieutenant who'd been a Cologne schoolteacher and reserve officer before the war surrendered on September 12. He spoke of a breakdown of discipline among previously unshakeable German officers. The best ones had been killed or wounded. Now, far too many German officers were retirees recalled to service, or mediocre officers dismissed for cause earlier in the war and now recalled because of the manpower shortage. The quality of German enlisted men was also plummeting. The German lieutenant said that a single company of his regiment in 1914 would have performed better than his entire battalion in 1918. German troops that had responded bravely and with initiative

earlier in the war now "needed constant moral and physical prod-
ding." The German officer described this as the army's Achilles heel.
"Our losses in men are the only shortage we are unable to meet." He
spoke of disarray in the German supreme command. The kaiser's
"changeability" had thrown away promising opportunities, like the
U-boat offensive. The troops no longer trusted their government.
Germany's strategy increasingly rested on the hope that "the American people will not have the patience to hold out indefinitely when
confronted by ever increasing losses. If Germany cannot win," he
ferociously concluded, "she is at least out for killing, and will make
the Allies pay so dearly that they will finally have to compromise
with her."[23]

For the moment, the Allies weren't paying dearly at all. The skies
cleared late on September 12, and the sun came out on the thirteenth
for several days, a brisk wind helping to dry the muddy roads. Finally
American and French guns, ammo, and support troops could move
more quickly to the front. I Corps took Thiaucourt, and IV Corps
curved back to the southwest through Nonsard, with the French II
Colonial Corps advancing slowly over difficult ground. V Corps took
its three ridges on schedule, and patrols of the V Corps's 26th Division and IV Corps's 1st Division met at Vigneulles to tie off the mouth
of the sack, unfortunately too late to prevent most of the Germans
and Austrians inside from escaping, many of them up the Bayern-
strasse—a new road through the woods of the salient that wasn't on
anyone's maps. The American attack from the south converged on Vigneulles at the same time that the northern attack was reaching it; the
two pincers accidentally engaged each other, both insisting that they
couldn't advance because of intense fire, which they later discovered
to be their own. It was a good thing that the men were using nothing more lethal than their service rifles, the accompanying artillery,
machine guns, Stokes mortars, 37mm guns, and rifle grenades having
been mostly left behind in the race to the finish line. The Germans,
rushing backward out of the salient, were stepping all over their own
lines of communication, but the Americans took no advantage of this

The American victory at Saint-Mihiel was, as one veteran put it, "more a skillful surprise of mass than a battle." The Germans retreated to the Hindenburg Line and the Americans and French had a relatively easy victory with light casualties. Here, happy American officers drink beer at a captured German canteen in the salient. (National Archives)

owing to the chaos reigning in their own lines. Observing the straggling arrival of the Big Red One at Vigneulles, General Frank Parker, commander of its 1st Brigade, ordered the placement of "straggler squads" behind each of his battalions to sweep up skulkers and keep them in the fight.[24]

The set-piece part of the battle had gone well enough, thanks largely to the weak German resistance. It was more a "skillful surprise of mass" than a battle, a veteran recalled. The American approach march, concentration of guns, and initial assaults had succeeded, but, ominously, the big American force became immobilized after the first twelve hours of combat because it was unable to reorganize under battle conditions. This was the real challenge of open warfare, the ability to *sustain* an advance over broken ground against enemy resistance and still exploit emerging opportunities. Even against light resistance, the Americans had failed.[25]

General George Cameron, the US V Corps commander, later rationalized the failure, noting the obvious: that open warfare worked only until the enemy occupied a new line of defense. Soldiers called this the "period of stabilization." If the enemy was allowed to stabilize, exploitation became impossible and trench warfare resumed. A new set-piece attack on the enemy organization had to be planned in order to break the new line of defense and swarm again into open country. After three days of fighting retreat from Saint-Mihiel, the Germans had taken up new prepared positions and stabilized the front. The American inability to pursue, disorganize, and destroy had consequences here and would pose much bigger problems in the Meuse-Argonne battle. Traveling with American units on the third day, Wagstaff noted sourly that "nothing was done at all." Looking out from high ground at Hattonchatel, he could observe the whole battlefield as far as Metz and Conflans and saw "no sign of anything, just some burning villages, and a constant stream of American artillery moving up the salient."[26]

Saint-Mihiel was an American victory with relatively light casualties—4,100 killed and 5,000 wounded—far less than the 50,000 casualties that had been predicted. This was lucky. Many of the replacements streaming in from the States, shipped in haste during the crisis of the spring and summer, were utterly unprepared. "These men," a typical summary read, "were drafted in May and June from Tennessee, Arkansas, Mississippi, and Iowa. They are for the most part poor farmers without education. They all had one day of preliminary rifle instruction and two days on the rifle range. They've had no gas defense instruction." A batch of recruits from Tennessee had had "no training other than a few hikes"; men from Pennsylvania had had "practically no training, they've fired 10 shots at tin cans near Brest." African American troops, excluded from combat and used as laborers, had even less training. A report on the 539th Colored Engineers noted that they had arrived at Camp Gordon one day and been sent to Hoboken the next, to take ship for France: "A little more than four weeks ago many of these Negroes were working on southern plantations in their bare feet." The report concluded: "It was a wanton waste of life and money to bring them to France, if these Negroes are ever subject to a gas attack they will all be killed."[27]

For now, it was smiles all around. The Americans raked in twenty thousand German and Austrian prisoners and 443 guns, an impressive haul. General Georg Fuchs, the German commanding this sector, had actually summoned four reserve divisions to buttress the eleven inside the salient, only to see them melt away in mass surrenders. A French cavalry division took 3,000 Austrian and German prisoners with just forty casualties of its own. Another French division took 2,500 prisoners and lost only four dead. These were the bloodless conquests preferred by the increasingly gun-shy French army. Austria's 35th Division lost more than a third of its strength in the battle, mostly to mass surrenders. Its commander, General Eugen von Podhoránsky, who'd departed on leave before the battle despite clear indications that an attack was imminent, heard from his subordinates on his return that the unit could no longer be considered reliable. Ludendorff, who'd been pleading for Austro-Hungarian troops since the spring, now saw that they were all but useless.[28]

In an entire day spent crisscrossing the battlefield, Wagstaff counted no more than twenty dead Doughboys along the roads and tracks of the salient. He was impressed by the German prisoners—"a good looking lot, their boots uniformly good and all leather, their uniforms clean, the men looked well." He was unimpressed by the Austrians: "They are a poor lot." General Max von Gallwitz, commanding the German Fifth Army in this space, deplored all of the German prisoners and the lost guns. Such defeatism reflected badly on him, so he shrewdly put it in a broader context that wouldn't have mollified Ludendorff: "As painful as our number of prisoners was, it was all the more painful when viewed beside the fact that elsewhere the Entente had seized more than 128,000 prisoners, 2,000 guns,

A British observer was impressed by the quality of the German officers captured by the Americans in the Saint-Mihiel salient: "A good looking lot, their boots uniformly good and all leather, their uniforms clean, the men looked well." Here, a group of German officers seized by the US 2nd Division are being conducted to headquarters for interrogation. (National Archives)

1,700 *Minenwerfer*, and 13,700 machine guns in the weeks since July 18. We were running out of everything."[29]

The Americans had to pursue the Germans cautiously because of booby traps, which were a problem everywhere the Germans gave ground. The German booby traps here were as ingenious and deadly as they'd been in the Marne salient. They booby-trapped dugouts, draping camouflage netting attached to explosives over the entrances. A Doughboy would sweep the netting aside and trigger the mass of shells or explosive. Inside bunkers or cottages, the Germans would leave a book on a table attached to a thread. When the book was lifted, a powerful charge would detonate. Detonators were hidden in trash heaps and piles of coal and charcoal. Fuses and explosive charges were left in stoves and fireplaces. When cold or hungry troops lit the devices, they'd explode. Shovels and picks—

randomly stuck in piles of coal or dirt—would be attached to mines and would explode when removed. The Germans mined roads with galleries of 150mm and 200mm shells buried beneath the surface. A truck or column passing along the road would depress the detonator. Barbed-wire entanglements were often mined, killing troops trying to cut them or stamp them down. In German dugouts, telephone wires hanging limply from the walls or ceiling were often mine wires. An impatient soldier brushing them aside would detonate a massive charge. The brick and tile floors in houses and stables were usually mined, and many German quarters were smeared with mustard gas.[30]

The Germans used all of the festooned telephone wires around abandoned towns, villages, and bunker complexes to fire mines electronically from a distance. So long as the lines remained uncut, the Germans could blow up bridges, billets, and headquarters remotely. When the Allies began cutting the wires to neutralize the traps, the Germans would suspend a weight from the wire, so when it was cut the weight would fall and ignite a detonator on the ground, killing or maiming the work party. The Germans would load deserted dugouts with two thousand pounds of explosive powder connected to phone wires. Once grateful Allied troops had settled into the shelter, the Germans would explode it. Window weights in houses would be attached to a thread strung across the entrance. When a soldier entered and broke the thread, the window weight would fall on a detonator connected to a pile of explosives. Handrails and banisters in houses and dugouts were often attached to explosive charges. False steps in houses and dugouts would be filled with explosives, and 8-inch shells would be placed in shallow holes under the road surface to detonate when trodden on. Naturally, the Germans poisoned wells and food as well.[31]

Faced with this daily viciousness, Americans had no compunction about robbing German prisoners of their valuables, prompting this (belated) outburst from General Joseph Dickman: "We are in this war to give the world a square deal and we will give it to our prisoners without fail." German POWs spoke of a general desire for peace. Many had served for four years and been wounded multiple times. One said all of his comrades would be glad to be captured "and that the whole war was a fraud." Only food kept them with their units—the army received better rations than the home front—but most now recognized that they'd be better fed as prisoners. A private in this unit declared himself pleased to be captured and disappointed only that his whole starving family in Germany hadn't been captured with him.[32]

Pershing summed up the Battle of Saint-Mihiel: "We established our lines in a position to threaten Metz. The signal success of the new American army in its first offensive was of prime importance. The Allies found that they had a formidable army to aid them, and the enemy learned finally that he had one to reckon with." That was laying it on thick. The British and French remained skeptical of the AEF; they shared intelligence on its performance and didn't conceal their misgivings, British War Office notes worrying that "perhaps the most unfortunate part of an otherwise successful operation was that it confirmed the American High Command in an exaggerated estimate of the efficiency of the American military machine—and of their ability to control it."[33]

For the moment, all doubts were silenced. The US First Army advanced easily and drove the Germans into the Michel-Stellung. Haig had predicted that the Germans wouldn't defend the salient, and he'd been proven correct: "For once the German infantry did not fight." Companies had left small rear guards and beat a retreat. Despite the scarcity of Germans, American souvenir hunters had a field day rummaging through all of their abandoned gear. Officers from every AEF school, headquarters, and office in France contrived excuses to visit the salient, where Marshall saw cars "literally filled with German equipment"—Pickelhaube helmets and Luger pistols were prized most of all—jouncing along the tracks. Dignitaries streamed in to relish the victory. Secretary of War Newton Baker arrived to peer over parapets and watch the Doughboys jog into action. Clemenceau toured the front, as did General Pétain and President Raymond Poin-

After the liberation of Saint-Mihiel in September 1918, dignitaries streamed in to celebrate the American victory. Secretary of War Newton Baker arrived to peer over parapets and watch the Doughboys jog into action. Clemenceau toured the salient, as did General Pétain and French president Raymond Poincaré—shown here with his wife—who could at last visit his nearby birthplace of Sampigny, which had been occupied by the Germans since the first days of the war. Kicking the rubble of his home, Poincaré turned away without apparent emotion. "C'est la guerre," he muttered. (National Archives)

caré, who could at last visit his nearby birthplace of Sampigny, which had been occupied by the Germans since 1914. Kicking the rubble of his home, Poincaré turned away without apparent emotion. "C'est la guerre," he muttered. Pershing's entourage suppressed giggles as the six-foot Pétain stooped to receive the Legion of Honor, and kisses on each cheek, from the French president, who stood five feet four. Pétain spoke to the city fathers of Saint-Mihiel and pronounced their liberation a gift of the United States. Driving across the salient to find suitable ground for an airstrip, Corporal Lee Duncan of the Army Air Service happened upon an abandoned litter of German shepherd puppies. He rescued them and took three of them home to Los Angeles after the war. One he named Rin Tin Tin.[34]

The war suddenly presented tantalizing new options. General Georg Fuchs's Armee Abteilung C, charged with the defense of the critical space between the Meuse and Moselle, had been routed. Five experienced American divisions—the 1st, 2nd, 3rd, 26th, and 42nd—were poised to pursue the Germans into Metz, an operation that would probably have stalled in the mud of the Moselle valley and the plain of the Woëvre but that would have placed tremendous lateral pressure on Ludendorff, who would have had to shift troops sixty miles east to defend Metz while still trying to stem the British and French advance in the west toward his all-important Sedan-Mézières railroad complex. Ludendorff was clearly worried sick. The staff chief of the Austrian 35th Division, retreating into the Michel-Stellung in mid-September, noted the sudden appearance of fresh German first-class assault divisions there. When the Americans didn't press the attack toward Metz, "the assault divisions vanished as suddenly as they had appeared." A German colonel later observed that it was the entirely *unexpected* American attack west of the Meuse, in the Verdun sector, that would "gain the decision for the Allies and bring about the ruin of the German army." Instead of spreading the Germans thin by probing toward Metz, the Americans would drive directly at Sedan.[35]

Not pretty on paper, the plan to attack toward Sedan from the rugged Meuse-Argonne front fit more with Foch's scheme of coordinated, converging offensives than did a diverging strike at Metz. As the principal German railway into France ran north of Metz, through Thionville, Sedan, and Mézières, it made sense to drive on Sedan anyway. That would be the fastest way to cut the all-important German lifeline. Already on September 13, Pershing's fifty-eighth birthday, the AEF commander could begin moving troops to the Meuse-Argonne front, which would be the real American show. There the Germans would definitely make a last stand. Saint-Mihiel was an indefensible bulge. The Hindenburg Line was Germany's last redoubt in occupied France. Averaging seven miles in depth, it straddled the Aisne, Meuse, and Moselle Rivers and wended through the Argonne Forest, across the top of the Saint-Mihiel salient and on to the east. The Germans would have to hold it or surrender their vital roads and railways as well as the great crossroads of Metz. An American veteran recalled that everyone recognized Sedan as the German center of gravity: "If the railroad center of Sedan was captured, the Germans would have no broad way of getting back to the Rhine for a last-ditch stand." The winter trails through the Ardennes Mountains would not suffice to move a big army. As one American officer put it: "Sound reasoning and mature judgment therefore dictated our Battle of the Meuse. Success would mean a catastrophe to German arms—rout, ruin, annihilation and peace. The place between Montmédy and Sedan was the solar plexus. The eventual severance of this German line was one of the outstanding features of the operations on the Western Front."[36]

Pershing's corps and army artillery and reserve divisions—more a hindrance than a help on the choked roads of Saint-Mihiel—had begun to deploy for a battle of the Meuse on a roughly twenty-mile front between the Meuse River and the Argonne Forest. Marshall, who organized the hugely complex change of front from Saint-Mihiel to the Meuse-Argonne, had initially considered it impossible. He had only three roads to work with, and every single division hogged twenty miles of road space. Besides six hundred thousand infantry, Marshall also had to send 2,700 guns and nine hundred thousand tons of supplies and ammunition up those muddy roads. All of the men and matériel would have to pass through the already heavily trafficked zone of the 220,000-man French Second Army, which the US First Army was replacing. The transfer could be accomplished in a night by truck, but horse-drawn vehicles would need up to a week, and because of German artillery and aviation, they could only move at night. For now, those problems lay around the corner. The Saint-Mihiel battle effectively completed the operations that had been planned in July and launched in August and September. The Allies had secured Paris and freed up the strategic railways, and they now had the unexpected opportunity to land a war-winning blow in 1918.[37]

Even if the still-formidable German army didn't crack, it appeared increasingly likely that the German (and Austrian) people would. The effects of the war and the blockade were too dire. The Austrians released a Peace Note in the days after the defeat at Saint-Mihiel that, like the German Reichstag's Peace Resolution of 1917, called for an end to the war through serious negotiations. Hindenburg ignored the Austrian note just as he'd ignored the Reichstag's resolution, ordering his units to fight on and not "go soft." But they were going soft. Gallwitz took one look at a division of Poles and Czechs sent to him by the Austrians on September 22 and recoiled in disgust. These men of the 106th Division were, he sneered, bums, not soldiers. Many of them were barefoot and untrained. More worrisome was the behavior of German troops. A mutiny had broken out in the recruit depot of the German 197th Division on September 14. Twenty-three soldiers had been arrested and imprisoned.[38]

Using the American general staff's Belgian index, German strength had fallen from 31 to 22 by mid-September 1918. The British were down to 8.75 and the French to 10.75, but continuing American troop arrivals raised the US strength to 4.5, maintaining the Allied level of 25. For the first time in four years, the Allies deployed more combat power than the Germans. The ferocity of the synchronized Allied attacks had decreased German strength from a value of 31 to 22 in just two months.[39]

Allied power was being maintained by fresh American divisions. Put simply, the Americans would win the war. France and Britain couldn't. The plunge in German troop morale derived from the American intervention, which, to the average German soldier, made the war unwinnable. Foch frankly admitted in September that Ludendorff had missed a golden opportunity to win the war in the spring. British general Charles Grant dined with Foch and Weygand as the Battle of Saint-Mihiel wound down, and Foch expressed amazement at Ludendorff's "want of judgment." Ludendorff should have pressed hard his attacks in March and April against either the British alone or the junction of the British and French armies. The Allied armies had been disintegrating and "a success which would have separated the British Armies from the French would have been almost irreparable." Foch continued: "If the Germans had taken Abbeville—and this was quite possible—it is difficult to see what could have been done." He concluded: "Je me demande si Ludendorff connait son métier. Je ne le crois pas." (I really wonder: Does Ludendorff know his profession? I don't think he does.) Foch—the believer in convergent offensives—concluded that Ludendorff had been "lured away" by his successes on the Chemin des Dames and around Armentières and had "made those attacks *eccentrically*, the success of one bearing no relation to the success of the other." Meanwhile, the Allies were determinedly making their attacks concentrically, with potentially decisive results.[40]

The Germans appeared to be finished. One last powerful blow might knock them out of the war. Certainly the Germans regretted the loss of Saint-Mihiel. Hindenburg had expected Gallwitz and Fuchs to hold the Americans and French there for many days and inflict demoralizing casualties while the Germans and Austrians dropped back through the three defensive zones. Instead, the Americans had overrun the first two zones in a single day and pressed the enemy into the last one, where Pershing was content to leave them while he shifted his attention to the Meuse-Argonne. Gallwitz's memoirs record the rage of Hindenburg and Ludendorff and even the kaiser at Fuchs's sudden collapse. To satisfy their rage, they fired every divisional staff chief in Armee-Abteilung C and stripped away most of Gallwitz's authority by transferring General Georg von der Marwitz from the Second Army to take command of the Fifth Army. Gallwitz called this the *Sündenbocksystem*, "the scapegoat system"—"punishing generals to improve them." It rarely worked, here or anywhere.

Gallwitz's group had been the least important on the Western Front until now. With all of the action farther west, the best units had been sent there and Gallwitz had been forced to fight with the dribs and drabs he was given. Ludendorff should have ordered him back into the Michel-Stellung earlier. The Germans had received early warning of the American attack. With the troops Gallwitz had, outnumbered four to one, thinly spread, Fuchs owed his survival only to the sluggishness of the American advance. In fact, Saint-Mihiel was just another of Ludendorff's gross errors of 1918. He'd left Gallwitz and Fuchs too far forward and exposed. He should have begun the evacuation a week earlier than he did. The reason the Americans captured so many German guns and troops was that Fuchs had been given no time to evacuate the salient. With everything going badly, the kaiser, Hindenburg, and Ludendorff seemed more intent on salvaging their own reputations than fighting the war efficiently. Gallwitz described pointless confusion in the last days of September: Marwitz brought in as army commander, Gallwitz kicked upstairs as army group commander with diminished powers, and Marwitz forced to fire Gallwitz's seasoned staff—to appease Ludendorff's vanity—and appoint an unseasoned new one. The crushing-out of the salient meant that the German Fifth Army front had narrowed to just three group sectors: Maas-West, Maas-Ost, and Ornes. The Americans had conquered the other two: Mihiel and Görz.[41]

The push had gone so effortlessly that Pershing's headquarters had time to dwell on trivia, like the loss of an assembly line's worth of heavy wire cutters, all apparently flung away by their grateful custodians during the advance. Each pair was investigated and charged to its (disbelieving) owner: "1 pair of wire cutters lost by Private Doll. He does not know where he lost them. He will pay for them. 1 pair of wire cutters lost by Private Hoyt. He gave them to another man but he does not know who. He will pay for them." French villages freed from their wire enclosures by the American attacks around Saint-Mihiel sent thanks to the nearest unit. They were fortunate that the American onslaught had interrupted Gallwitz's methodical withdrawal and prevented the *Lokitage*. Had the German fire gods descended here as they had in Picardy and Champagne, there would have been no villages left to rejoice.[42]

On September 13, the village priest of little Rupt-en-Woëvre wrote to the nearby commander of the New England National Guard division:

Your gallant 26th American Division has just set us free. Ever since September 1914, the barbarians have held the heights of the Meuse, have foully murdered three hostages from Mouilly, have shelled Rupt and on July 23, 1915, forced its inhabitants to scatter to the four corners of France. I, who have remained here upon the advice of my Bishop, feel certain that I speak for the Lord Bishop of Verdun and my parishioners of Rupt, Mouilly and Genicourt in conveying to you the heartfelt and unforgettable gratitude of all. Several of your comrades lie at rest in our Christian and French soil. Their ashes will be cared for as if they were our own. We shall kneel by their graves and bless the 26th Division and all of generous America.

General Tasker Bliss, President Wilson's representative on the Supreme War Council in Versailles, also reflected on generosity and gratitude as Allied stock, buoyed by this American victory, began to rise. Bliss wrote Secretary of War Baker just after the battle:

The European Allies will attempt to minimize the American effort as much as possible. They think they have got the Germans on the run and they now do not need as much help as they were crying for a little while ago. . . . I heard a gentleman in high position here say that the United States was building a bridge for the Allies to pass over; that the time for the U.S. to secure acquiescence in its wishes was while the bridge was building; that after the Allies had crossed over the bridge they would have no further use for it or for its builders.

Bliss was a prophet, as the controversies of the war-ending armistice and the Treaty of Versailles would reveal.[43]

12

MEUSE-ARGONNE: MONTFAUCON

Pershing's flattening of the Saint-Mihiel salient meant that multiple Allied pincers could knife simultaneously into the shrinking German position in Belgium and France. The AEF, its right flank and communications secured by Saint-Mihiel, would attack between the Meuse and the Argonne. Echeloned to the west, the French and British armies formed a tightening noose around Hindenburg's retreating armies. Just west of Pershing was Henri Gouraud's Fourth Army, pushing in the space between the Aisne and the Oise; west of Gouraud was Henri Berthelot's Fifth Army on the Vesle; west of Berthelot was Charles Mangin's Tenth Army on the Aisne heights above Soissons, then, bending round to the north, Marie-Eugène Debeney's First Army, holding the ground between La Fère and Saint-Quentin, then, rising through Picardy and Flanders, the BEF: Henry Rawlinson's Fourth Army, Julian Byng's Third Army, William Birdwood's reconstituted Fifth Army around Arras, Henry Horne's First Army, Herbert Plumer's Second Army in the Ypres salient, and finally the Belgians and a half dozen French divisions holding the ground from Ypres to the sea.[1]

Foch ordered a flurry of Allied attacks at twenty-four-hour intervals to confuse, distract, and stretch the Germans thin. First off
would be Pershing and Gouraud, who would launch the offensive toward Sedan and Mézières on September 26. The next day, the British
First and Third Armies would try to breach the line of the Canal du
Nord and then infiltrate the Hindenburg Line's Siegfried Position
from the north. Twenty-four hours after that, Plumer's Second Army
and the Belgians would attack toward Bruges; and then the next day,
September 29, Rawlinson's Fourth Army and Debeney's First Army
would attack the Siegfried Position frontally. All four pincers would
converge on a tough but dwindling German army; it would be, as
Colonel George Marshall put it, "the greatest battle the world has yet
seen," and to the Americans went "the mission of smashing the vital
pivot" of the entire German line.[2]

The British and French staffs considered the pending American
thrust the most "ambitious" but also the most "decisive." The Germans
could yield ground farther west, but not at the pivot. With its complex
of roads and railways, it was their essential lifeline to Germany. That's
why the Hindenburg Line fortifications in the Meuse-Argonne were
so dense and artfully prepared. That's why the French, no less aware of
the sector's importance, hadn't attacked it since 1916—it had seemed
impregnable until now. Foch described Ludendorff's predicament as
"infernal." He was down to 190 divisions on the Western Front, having dissolved 20 divisions to bring the remaining ones up to strength.
Of these, 149 were in the trenches facing the Allied onslaught. He
had just 41 fatigued German divisions in reserve.[3]

In London, Lloyd George continued to doubt Haig's ability to
achieve more than just another bloodbath. Haig's headquarters too
was sick with worry. Secretary of State for War Alfred Milner and
general staff chief Henry Wilson had warned Haig to limit his casualties, and yet now the field marshal aimed at two bastions of the
Hindenburg Line—the Canal du Nord and the Saint-Quentin Canal. Haig had only two fresh divisions to attack with: the US 27th
and 30th Divisions, which Pershing had left in the British sector.
They were scheduled to join the Australian Corps on September 29

to assault the Hindenburg Line east of Péronne. The operation would be brutal, aimed at evicting the Germans from their positions in the Bellicourt Tunnel of the Saint-Quentin–Cambrai Canal. It hardly seemed just to send green American National Guard troops against this, one of the strongest sections of the Hindenburg Line, where the canal passed through a tunnel under a ridge. But Haig, as usual, was confident of victory. He would fire a million shells into the German line and then take it with the Diggers and the Doughs. Foch assured a nervous London that this would be an all-Allied attack on a broad front, not at all like the one of 1917 at Passchendaele, "pushing through the neck of a bottle."[4]

For the Americans in the Meuse-Argonne sector, the challenge was no less difficult. Whereas the Woëvre plain fanned open north of Saint-Mihiel, the Meuse-Argonne sector to its left was cramped by the Argonne Forest on one flank and the Meuse River on the other. The ridges of the Argonne, rising one hundred meters over the valleys of the Aisne and the Aire, were legendary defensive positions. In 1792, French Revolutionary armies had stopped a Prussian invasion cold here. The Germans had swept over the ridges in 1914, advanced to the Marne, and then retreated back to these heights. The French had spent fifty thousand men trying to take them back in 1915, more in 1916, and then stopped trying for the duration of the war.[5]

The broad German defensive positions running from the English Channel to the Alps narrowed as they reached the Meuse, which meant that the intensity of the defenses facing the Americans (two main defensive lines just ten miles deep) was far greater than that faced by the French and British farther west, where the same two lines would be separated by thirty-five or forty miles, making forward progress between the lines relatively easy. Adding to the difficulty was the fact that the main German supply depots and rail yards lay closer to the Americans than to the British or French. The Germans could yield plenty of ground farther west, but not here at the vital pivot. German troop density in this sector was also optimal. Fifth Army commander General Max von Gallwitz had relied on nine fourth-rate divisions to hold fifty miles of front at Saint-Mihiel. Here, he'd have at least twenty first-rate divisions on a twenty-eight-mile sector. Then there was the ground itself. General Hugh Drum, First Army's chief of staff, called the Meuse-Argonne "the most ideal defensive terrain I have ever seen or read about."[6]

The Americans would have to battle over three heavily defended ridges in the Meuse-Argonne. The French task on Pershing's left was easier. There the Germans had a narrow outpost zone and close-up defense; pressed hard, they would fall back. In Pershing's sector, they were distributed in depth over multiple fortified lines. The first, the Etzel-Stellung, nudged up against Pershing's line of departure for the Meuse-Argonne battle. The second, the Giselher-Stellung, which was the first of two main resistance lines, lay five miles to the north, with Montfaucon—the Mount of Falcons—in its center. Montfaucon so dominated the ground below it that the French despairingly called this line "Little Gibraltar"—as impregnable as the British fortress on the strait between the Atlantic and the Mediterranean. German crown prince Wilhelm had been so impressed by the place that he'd directed the Battle of Verdun from an observatory in Montfaucon. Now it was a fortified outpost of the Hindenburg Line, which lay four miles behind Montfaucon in the Kriemhilde-Stellung, anchored in the Romagne Heights. General Robert Lee Bullard recited the defensive possibilities of this second main resistance line. It's less a line, he said, than a net: "Four kilometers deep. Wire, interlaced, knee-high, in grass. Wire, tangled devilishly in forests. . . . Pill boxes, in succession, one covering another. No 'fox hole' cover for German gunners here, but concrete, masonry. Bits of trenches. More wire. A few light guns. . . . Defense in depth. Eventually, the main trenches. Many of them, in baffling irregularity, so that the attacker cannot know when he has mopped up. . . . Farther back, again defense in depth, a wide band of artillery implacements."[7]

Five miles behind the Kriemhilde Position were the Barricourt Ridge and Buzancy, perfect hilly sites for the last German line before the Meuse—called the Freya-Stellung. Each of these four lines, connected by narrow-gauge railways, bristled with defensive fire: "What bitches they were," a Doughboy said. "Every goddam German there who didn't have a machine gun had a cannon." Taking one line of German bunkers and wire in any of these positions achieved little; it would be covered by a second line of low concrete bunkers with machine-gun openings, which, in turn, was covered by a third line, each of the lines arranged checkerwise to give mutual support and dug in behind three or four coils of barbed wire. Pétain, recalling the bloody French failures to break through here in 1915, looked at his maps and bleakly concluded that the Americans would be lucky to take Montfaucon— only the second of four German lines—by Christmas, so sophisticated were the German defenses. Pétain gave the Americans little chance of breaking through the Kriemhilde or Freya Lines.[8]

The whole sector was a natural fortress—protected in the east by the Meuse River and in the west by the Argonne Forest. Its series of east-west ridges, which undulated over the Meuse, gave the Germans the high ground everywhere and barred the way north. "There was no elbow room," Pershing's operations chief, General Hugh Drum, recalled. "We had to drive straight through." The American III Corps on the right would receive German artillery fire throughout its attack from the Meuse Heights on the east bank of the river. The American I Corps on the left would have to battle through the Argonne Forest and the valley of the Aire River, which were overlooked by the fortified Argonne heights.[9]

Pershing's plan of attack relied on French cooperation. The Argonne was so well fortified that the plan to take it was to advance up the open ground on both sides of the forest, outflanking the German defenders inside. The "French Army Objective" lay west of the wood, the "American Army Objective" east of the wood—a salient dotted with villages, crests, and waterways whose names would become notorious: Apremont, Exermont, Romagne, Cunel, Brieulles, and the Meuse. The "Combined Army Objectives," if achieved, would win the war by pushing the two wedges forward over the Aire, the Aisne, and the fortified ridges and around the Forest of Bourgogne to rejoin above it and cross the Meuse and then take Sedan. The Germans would fight like cornered dogs here; the position was the fulcrum of their line from Flanders to the Meuse. They could retreat any distance farther west, but to remain in France and milk its coal and iron resources and keep the war away from Germany, their flank had to rest on the Meuse. They simply couldn't give ground in the Meuse-Argonne.[10]

German raids increased all along the front in the days before the attack, as Gallwitz struggled to locate the US Army and divine its plan of attack. It was hard to make a million-man army disappear, but Pershing tried. His troops moved between Saint-Mihiel and the Argonne battlefield only at night. When they stepped off their trucks and buses in the dark, they threaded through deserted moonlit villages and filed into wet woods and copses, anything that would provide concealment from the air. There they lived in pup tents and tar-paper barracks, forbidden even to approach the edge of the dripping woods during daylight hours. "At night the noise of wheels was the most characteristic sound of war-time France," a Doughboy recalled. "It sounded like a river in flood, washing and rolling its stones over the jagged boulders of its bed. At dawn all this ceased. The wagons were backed into the nearest *bois*, covered with branches and leaves, and the horses tied to trees. All the men disappeared."[11]

Pershing massed his US First Army on a narrow front and planned to smash his way through the four German lines. He would attack with twelve divisions—equivalent to at least thirty French or German divisions. Heavy tanks were needed, but none were available. It took nearly a year to build a single heavy tank in British plants, and what production trickled out was immediately snapped up by Haig's dwindling army. The Americans would have to rely on the light and medium tanks they could cadge from the French and their massive troop numbers. With the Germans still leaving reserves near Metz, Pershing would initially have 330,000 assault troops against 61,000 Germans.[12]

To be closer to the action, Pershing moved his headquarters from Ligny to Souilly, a town so dank and charmless that the AEF commander decided to live in his train, parked in nearby woods, instead of the place itself, where staff officers crowded into the same dingy homes and offices that Pétain, Nivelle, and their staffs had occupied during the great Battle of Verdun in 1916. There in Souilly, Pershing organized an army reserve of six divisions, giving him eighteen divisions in all for the big push. "We were no longer engaged in a maneuver for the pinching out of a salient," Pershing wrote, "but were necessarily committed to a direct frontal attack against strong, hostile positions fully manned by a determined enemy." Frontal assaults had never worked in World War I, but Pershing naïvely assumed that the sheer mass of American manpower would punch through. "The action was undertaken with the determination to use *all* of our divisions in forcing a decision," Pershing explained. "We expected to draw the best German divisions to our front and consume them, while the enemy was held under grave apprehension lest our attack should break his line, which it was our firm purpose to do." That declaration, written shortly after the war, encapsulated Pershing's failure as a field commander. He foolishly believed that he would "consume" German troops, when, in fact, from positions like these, they would probably consume him.[13]

Flank attacks, the normal means of dislodging an enemy from a strong position, were hard to deliver in this sector, which is why the French had avoided it since 1916. The German guns on the Meuse Heights prevented flanking columns from advancing on either bank of the Meuse, and the German line on the Aisne prevented flanking attacks west of the Argonne Forest, a natural fortress only improved by the Aisne and the Aire Rivers, which curled around the Argonne like a moat. Wedged between the Aisne and Meuse, the Doughboys couldn't outflank the Argonne unless Gouraud's French Fourth Army made rapid progress on Pershing's left or the American center and right advanced fast and deep to force the Germans out of the forest. But would the French attack in earnest? And could inexperienced American units advance quickly in this terrain, against determined German resistance?

Pershing's left wing was General Hunter Liggett's I Corps on the southern edge of the Argonne. It deployed the 77th, 28th, and 35th Divisions in the front line, with the AEF's first African American combat division—the 92nd—tasked with maintaining the connection on the western edge of the Argonne with Gouraud's French Fourth Army. In Pershing's center, a relatively clear area overlooked by Montfaucon, stood General George Cameron's V Corps: the 91st, 37th, and 79th Divisions at the front, the 32nd in reserve. If Cameron took his objectives swiftly or the French advanced rapidly west of the Argonne, the Germans would have to abandon the Argonne Forest. If Cameron's corps bogged down, Liggett would have to fight for the forest. To Cameron's right, exposed to continuous shelling from German artillery on the east bank of the Meuse, were the right-wing divisions of General Robert Lee Bullard's III Corps: the 4th, 80th, and 33rd Divisions, with the 3rd Rock of the Marne Division in reserve. With six divisions in his army reserve, Pershing readied three of them for speedy intervention as needed: the 1st, 29th, and 82nd.[14]

Pershing's three corps—the US First Army—lumbered into position on the night of September 25, replacing French troops who'd held this quiet sector until now. Ludendorff still had only five low-grade divisions in this sector against Pershing's eighteen, for he had to leave his first-rate reserves splayed across the country between the Meuse and the Moselle until Pershing's real objective—Sedan or Metz—became clear. The intensity of Foch's synchronized attacks on the arc from Ypres through Cambrai and Saint-Quentin to Soissons, Reims, and here around Verdun would make it difficult for the Germans to reinforce any one point without exposing another. This was the Foch strategy in a nutshell: a flurry of punches that would pressure the Germans everywhere and prevent them from massing reserves anywhere. For now, Ludendorff ordered the outnumbered troops in the Meuse-Argonne to hold the *Hauptwiderstandslinien*—the main resistance lines—at all costs. There'd be no pell-mell retreats like at Saint-Mihiel. German troops could deploy in depth in the outpost zones but were to mass *all* of their strength in the main lines and not let the Americans through. The Germans were no longer fighting to protect their lines of retreat, which were already too short. They were fighting to hold their positions. First-class assault divisions—still loitering behind the Michel-Stellung—would be moved here when needed to hurl back any American advance. "Gegenstoss nicht Gegenangriff"

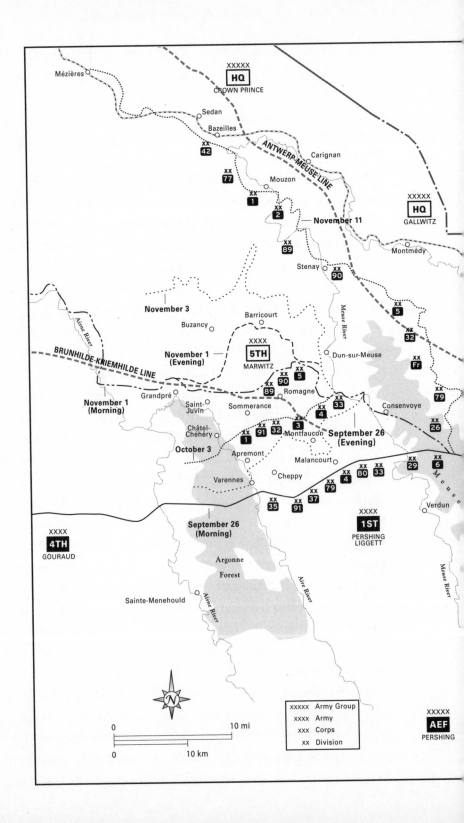

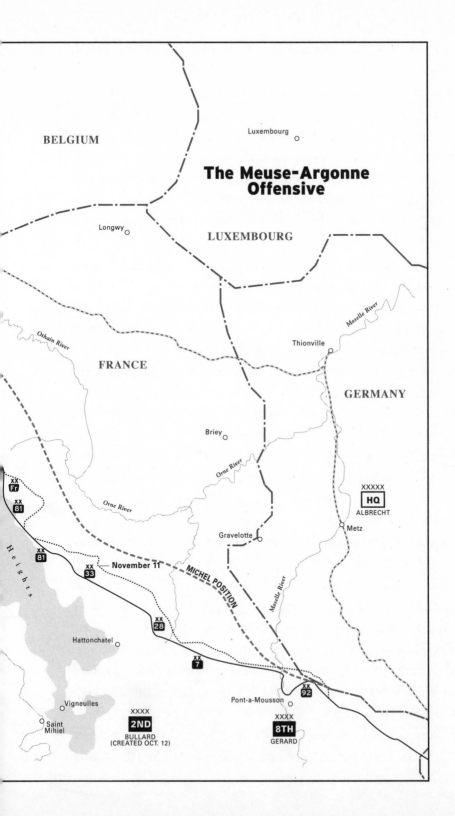

The Meuse-Argonne Offensive

BELGIUM

Luxembourg

LUXEMBOURG

Longwy

Othain River

FRANCE

Moselle River

Thionville

GERMANY

Briey

Orne River

Orne River

XXXXX
HQ
ALBRECHT

Gravelotte

Metz

XX
Fr

XX
81

Heights

XX
81

XX
33 — November 11

MICHEL POSITION

Moselle River

XX
28

Hattonchatel

XX
7

XX
92

Vigneulles

Pont-a-Mousson

Saint
Mihiel

XXXX
2ND
BULLARD
(CREATED OCT. 12)

XXXX
8TH
GERARD

(Counterthrust, not counterattack), a German general reminded his colleagues: don't defend, destroy.[15]

Pershing remained confident; the Germans had a strong position but small troop numbers. He planned to pulverize the Germans with three thousand guns, then send his three corps over the top to overrun the outpost line, swarm over the heart of the first main line of resistance—the three-hundred-foot-high Butte de Montfaucon—and arrive on the threshold of the second main line of resistance, the Kriemhilde-Stellung—eight miles behind the outpost line—on the first day.[16]

He underweighted the main effort: V Corps's push on Montfaucon. Pétain had warned that it might become a prolonged fight, but Pershing thought it would fall easily if he worked around its flanks with I Corps on the left and III Corps on the right. He attached the stronger of his two tank brigades, Lieutenant Colonel George Patton's 142 tanks, to Liggett's I Corps. The weaker brigade of 40 tanks was given to V Corps. Pershing assumed that V Corps would attack Montfaucon head-on and I Corps would work up the Aire Valley—better tank country—to outflank it. Patton worried that the inevitable mishaps on ground like this—"heavily seamed with trenches and pitted with shell-holes"—might give armored warfare a bad name. Still, he agreed to go, in the tones that would later make him famous. Though it would be wiser to hold the tanks in reserve until the infantry had driven the Germans some distance north, where "ground excellently adapted for tanks" began, Patton vowed to use the tanks immediately, through the narrow opening between the Aire River and a little village called Cheppy. He worried—in a memo to Liggett's chief of staff—that if he waited for optimal tank country, "there might be no Germans left to fight." Deploy the tanks at once, Patton advised. To do otherwise would "exhibit selfishness toward the infantry," not by depriving them of armored protection but by "usurping the pleasure of hunting Germans in the open" once good tank country was reached.[17]

Pershing's bombardment of Gallwitz's Meuse-Argonne position began at 10:45 p.m. on September 25. The woods on the southern fringe of the battlefield, crammed with American and French batteries, lit up "and stayed lit with the quivering golden light all night long," one witness recalled. He saw French crews serving big 155mm guns: "Half-dressed, filthy little Frenchmen who worked like wild men, dripping with sweat." The rapid firing of their guns was "like the blow of a lancet on an ear-drum." A sergeant in the US 35th Division—National Guardsmen from Kansas and Missouri—recalled a "greenish-white light to the horizon," quaking ground, and a "solid roof of shells of all sizes going over, the scream of the flat-trajectory 75s and the higher-flying medium and heavy shells rumbling overhead like a train on a trestle." Doughboys who awoke to the shelling ran around and dived into shell holes, confused by the sounds and the strange light effects.[18]

The Germans and Austrians were even more stunned by the bombardment—high explosive throwing "great columns of coal-black earth sixty or seventy feet high in huge geyser-shaped sprays" and a deluge of gas shells forcing the defenders to pull on respirators and lie on the floors of their dugouts. German defense in depth required frontline troops to escape the preliminary bombardment by hiding in shell holes in *front* of their trenches instead of in the trenches themselves, but gas shells—weeping toxins that burned the lungs and eyes, blistered the skin, swelled limbs to twice their normal girth, and seared the hair from men's heads—found these sanctuaries more easily than shrapnel and shell splinters. Mustard gas was feared most of all, the mustard oil releasing a vapor that combined with moisture—sweat, tears, spit, urine, or puddles of water—to make an acid that blinded eyes and burned the skin from mouths, armpits, scrotums, or any body part it touched. "Everything is full of gas," an Austrian officer scribbled as he sent sixty gas casualties from his company to the rear. The Germans attempted counterbattery fire but, faced with such a massive bombardment, quickly shut down: "It was like a penny whistle competing with a steam calliope," a veteran recalled. Two hundred and fifty miles to the north, in the German rail hub of Montmédy, the windows rattled all night long.[19]

The Doughboys attacked at 5:30 a.m. on September 26. Flying overhead, Captain Eddie Rickenbacker looked down at the bombardment and thought that it resembled a winking switchboard in a telephone exchange, gunbursts randomly flashing across the dark space. When the Doughs went over the top, they looked like "ants swarming on gunned molehills." Rickenbacker, no stranger to danger, thought it inconceivable that those men on the ground were anything but "mad with terror." Perhaps Rickenbacker should have been too. On the ground below him an American officer passed an antiaircraft battery, recognized the lieutenant, and called over: "How many planes have you brought down?" "Three," the lieutenant answered. "One was a German."[20]

In the first rush, the Americans took eight thousand POWs; the French, to their left, seven thousand. An American captain recalled taking the surrender of two "spruce, startlingly clean" German officers near Esnes "whose manner reminded me a little of a defeated player in a tennis tournament shaking hands with the victor." German enlisted men were received less nobly. They filed back past the advancing Doughboys stripped of buttons, belts, and iron crosses, all seized by souvenir hunters. These Germans taken in the early going were the dregs of the army, small detachments of fourth-rate divisions left behind as speed bumps in the American path. One American officer recorded his impression of them: "Sallow men with the sickly, greasy white complexion of hotel waiters, slovenly, filthy. Some wore the round caps and some the big bell-shaped helmets. They were not attractive."[21]

In the Argonne, things rapidly fell apart. General Cyril Wagstaff, come from Saint-Mihiel to observe for the British, relayed the news that the US 28th Division had immediately lost touch with the 77th Division on its flank. "Hun machine gun posts held out in the gap," firing into the flanks of both divisions and stopping them cold. In the forest, the Germans placed wire obstacles across every path or defile. When advancing Americans tried to cut them, German machine guns, hidden in the dense woods, mowed them down. Eventually the Americans would cut through, but as they fanned out to outflank the German machine gun, new German machine guns, silent till now and

The Doughboys had a mania for German souvenirs. Pickelhaube helmets, flags, and Luger pistols were the most prized mementos. Here, a sergeant of the US 28th Division, emerging from the fighting around Varennes, grins broadly with one Pickelhaube on his head, another slung around his chest. (National Archives)

hidden on the flanks of the first gun, would open up, killing Americans at a ratio the 77th Division commander estimated at ten to one. The division would lose over two hundred men a day in the woods and get nowhere. The commander, General Robert Alexander, angrily relieved one officer after another, hoping that the new appointments would get his division moving. They didn't, one colonel wondering how his men could advance against "a continuous line of machine-guns which had a good field of fire." Everyone recalled the "dank breath of the Argonne"—the stench of stagnant water, gas, sulfur, and decomposing corpses, new ones and exhumed old ones from years past.[22]

To Alexander's left, the African American 92nd Division went to pieces attacking the ruins of Binarville and ran from the enemy, prompting the division commander, General Charles Ballou, to relieve thirty officers and sentence four black officers to death by firing squad (a sentence later commuted). One (white) battalion commander became hysterical and had to be relieved and led away from his frightened troops. Pershing attempted to give Gouraud the 92nd Division, but Gouraud refused the gift, and the 92nd was withdrawn from the front. Bullard spoke of its extreme "discouragement"—"the most pitiful case I've ever seen among soldiers." But how could it be otherwise? Because of the army's racism—white personnel in every training camp had to outnumber black personnel by at least two to one—the 92nd had never trained as a division. Its various parts had been sprinkled among seven different camps and only met in France, where, as one of the division's black lieutenants recalled, "field officers seemed far more concerned with reminding their Negro subordinates that they were Negroes than they were with having an effective unit that would perform well in combat." The men, black recruits from Pennsylvania, Tennessee, and Washington, DC, never really had a chance. They were poorly led, poorly equipped, and poorly supported. And even well-supported units were making no headway in this death trap.[23]

Assaulting Montfaucon, the US 79th Division—National Army from Maryland and Pennsylvania—also broke down, causing the divisions on its flanks to stop. Technically these men of the 79th were "assault troops," but really they had no answers for the intricate German positions on the Mount of Falcons. German engineers had carved the approaches to the height into lanes enfiladed by bunkers and machine-gun nests. They named these concreted traps—still visible today on the slopes of Montfaucon—the Redoute de Golfe and the Oeuvre du Demon (Work of the Devil). The traps now stuttered into life, lacerating the advancing Doughs with brutally accurate fire. German officers in their bunkers marveled at the innocence of these assault troops. "Swarms of riflemen standing upright were no rarity," a German colonel winced. He had no choice but to mow them down, later counting four hundred dead Americans in front of a single battalion sector. Witnesses saw more panicked troops of the 79th Division running away from Montfaucon than attacking it. Pershing had expected his tanks to smash through the German defenses and open paths for the infantry, but Colonel D. D. Pullen described "slow progress" as the US 3rd Tank Brigade rolled forward with a battalion of French tanks on point. They crossed the first German trenches at 9:30 a.m., clearing out skirmishers and machine guns.[24]

Pausing, they waited for infantry of the US 79th Division to come up and occupy the ground they'd just cleared. They waited in vain, glancing anxiously at their watches as the momentum of the advance ebbed away. The 313th Regiment was skulking, refusing to advance, its officers rather too punctiliously refusing to enter the Bois de Cuisy "without written orders from brigade." Pullen turned to a French officer and asked for the help of his five tanks, to which the French captain magnificently replied: "I don't need written orders. I'm ready to fight anybody anywhere." They motored into the wood, took it, and then looked back to see the Baltimore Doughs plodding reluctantly and cautiously in their wake. Patton had raged against such infantry—"following tanks simply as spectators of the fight rather than using their arms to intensify the fire"—and Pullen now dismounted to confer with the infantry and ask them to intensify the fire. He discovered that the men of the 313th didn't have a single officer with them; the troops were leaderless.[25]

German machine guns opened up from the northeast corner of the wood, and German 77mm guns spat shells at the group from Montfaucon. Pullen glanced toward the sound of the guns, then looked back to deploy what infantry he had, only to see the troops fleeing in panic or throwing themselves to the ground and hiding behind trees. "In a combined attack of tanks and infantry, liaison between the two arms must be accomplished more by mutual understanding than through cut and dried training principles," Patton had averred days before the battle. There was no mutual understanding on this ground, the tankers glaring at the backs of the fleeing infantry. This left the tanks exposed to capture; the French captain turned his vehicle around and drove after the retreating Doughs to rally them or, if all else failed, shoot them. Scouring the ground for officers, Pullen found a "few lieutenants" but noted that "they had no authority over their men." All in all, he concluded, "it would best be described as a mutiny." With no senior officers present at the front and no accompanying guns, the three-thousand-man 313th Regiment had collapsed. When the Germans shelled them, the men of Baltimore had "run like hares." The rest of the division had fared no better. How could they? Pershing's staffs hadn't worked out how to get artillery forward to blast the Germans off Montfaucon. The Doughs, raw draftees beyond the protective envelope of their rolling barrage, were being asked to assault German bunkers and machine-gun nests without fire support.[26]

Colonel Lesley McNair, who'd shortly become the youngest general in the US Army at the age of thirty-five, was with the 77th Melting Pot Division when it attacked in the Argonne on the extreme left of the American line. Like the neighboring 28th Division, the 77th had arrived from the Marne battles unrested and gone immediately into line with infantry companies filled with green replacements. Initially, the chief difficulty was maneuvering in the forest: "It was a lucky platoon leader who could see ten of his men in a line." Some of the units were hit hard, others slipped through gaps in the German line to find themselves among the legendary German pavilions scattered in the forest. These forts—with twenty-foot-thick concrete roofs—doubled as rest camps for fatigued divisions that, in the past, had been sent to the reliably quiet Meuse-Argonne to restore themselves. Outside, the bunker pavilions were done up like Swiss chalets; inside they featured walnut wainscoting, gun rooms, libraries and smoking rooms, mirrored bars, player pianos, bowling alleys, and billiard rooms. The Doughboys of the 77th looted the Bagatelle and Saint-Hubert Pavilions, making off with volumes of Conan Doyle and Rider Haggard and as much wine and schnapps as they could carry in their pockets. They then worked through the dense wood till they were hit with cross fires from the height of Le Chêne Tondu on their right and the hill of La Palette to their left.[27]

McNair followed the 77th Division on the first day of the attack, then moved sideways to follow the other two divisions of I Corps: the 28th and 35th. Mainly with the infantry, McNair also "observed

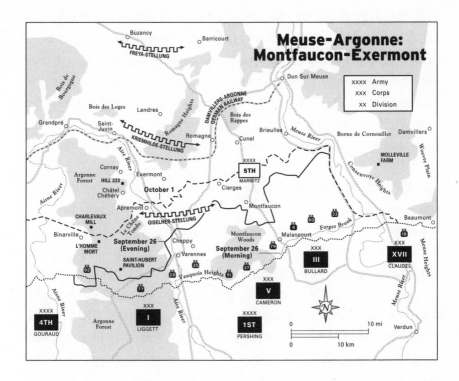

the support afforded the infantry by the artillery." He'd been sent by Pershing to assess the quality of American operations, and his conclusions were damning. Like the 79th Division at Montfaucon, "these three divisions clearly lacked aggressiveness. There was no desire anywhere to push forward rapidly and overcome the enemy by means of numerical and moral superiority." McNair characterized the American assault as "more a follow-up of a retiring adversary than a determined attack." None of the three divisions distinguished itself in any way. The 77th took far too long to reach its objectives. Indeed, it should have taken its objective by noon; instead, the unit essentially stopped in the face of German fire from the eastern edge of the Argonne Forest. The division's biggest ethnic contingent was Italian Americans from New York's Little Italy. Hearing them call to one another, German forward observers assumed that Foch had inserted an Italian—not an American—division here.[28]

McNair deemed the US 28th Division "inert . . . allowing itself to be stopped by machine gun sniping." The men of Pennsylvania's

National Guard division had received no rest since their battles on the Marne and the Vesle; they'd been rapidly shifted here, filled up with replacement troops and officers, and sent into the line. Theirs may have been one of the toughest missions of the day. Half of the division had to attack through the eastern edge of the Argonne, the other half had to attack up the Aire, straddling the river and giving flank support to the 35th Division attacking the Mont Vauquois on its right.[29]

The battalions of the 28th Division shuddered and came to a halt; ten thousand poilus had already fallen assaulting this well-fortified bottleneck, and now hundreds of Americans fell too. The Germans had long since cleared away the French dead and rigged belts of new wire overlooked by interlocking machine-gun and artillery positions. Any platoon leader who tried to lead his men through a gap in the wire was immediately cut down by machine-gun bursts. The Doughs shrank backward from the wire belts, "much Pennsylvania blood and flesh clinging to the rusty barbs." Here as elsewhere on the first day, the terrified Doughboys went to ground, McNair commenting: "A huge mass of reserves was thus immobilized, lying around in sheltered places." Hastily expanded, the AEF had too many men and not enough reliable officers and NCOs. As a result, the units were too big—4,000-man regiments, 1,000-man battalions, 250-man companies—and the US Army, which had begun the war with just six thousand officers, found itself without the ability to subdivide the units, make them more nimble and aggressive, and employ fire and maneuver to dislodge the Germans from strong positions like these.[30]

In all three divisions, American strength plummeted not from casualties but from "skulking"—troops feigning wounds, hiding, or too eagerly leaving their places in line to escort prisoners or carry wounded. McNair personally witnessed two entire regiments dissolve this way. He then listed all of the bizarre combinations that passed before his disbelieving eyes: four Pennsylvania riflemen carrying a single wounded man to the rear; others escorting disarmed POWs who were carrying wounded Doughboys on litters; a rifleman walking to the rear with a wounded Doughboy who was walking without assistance. All of these malingerers went a mile or more back, and most wouldn't rejoin their units until the next day, if then. McNair grabbed at passing skulkers and ordered them to explain themselves. "They said that it was the practice in their company and that they had orders from their captain." It probably was. Officers in National Guard divisions like the 28th were elected by their enlisted men, and they had to keep the voters happy. From this day forward, Pershing's staff would deliberately "break" the National Guard divisions by replacing their casualties not with local boys but with National Army recruits and officers.[31]

As at Saint-Mihiel, McNair in the Meuse-Argonne scored the "faulty use of divisional artillery; it was always too far back." He urged generals to deploy it as far forward before the attack as possible—concealed—then make it move with the infantry, "smooth, uninterrupted, equipped and formed for open warfare." The irony of all this was that the tactics McNair was advocating were not new; they were the German tactics introduced so effectively at Riga and Caporetto and then again in the Ludendorff spring offensives. Just as the Germans knew the strength of these tactics, they also knew their vulnerabilities, and the Americans were giving them no strength and plenty of vulnerability. "It seems not to be realized," McNair scolded, "that the method of attack used at present originated with the enemy. Its difficulties are fully realized by him. He well knows when the attack has progressed to the limit of the range of artillery in its initial position." In passive American hands, this meant that "the overwhelming concentration of artillery" would abruptly cease as guns, stuck in traffic on the muddy roads, were not moving forward to maintain pressure on the Germans. The German "method of resistance is based on these facts." Once the Doughboys plodded beyond the range of their artillery, the Germans settled down to kill Americans, untroubled by American fire superiority. "The solution," McNair concluded, was to "keep the artillery moving forward to maintain the initial artillery superiority. Close artillery support is essential for a rapid advance against serious resistance. Only in this way can a division develop real offensive power."[32]

But the artillery couldn't move forward. With just three roads, Pershing's sector had the most inadequate communications on the Western Front. "They showed on the *Plan Directeurs* as neat little lines but were in reality shell-pitted bogs," an army engineer scowled. Two of the roads were quagmires; the third, the paved *route nationale* from Clermont-en-Argonne north through Varennes, had been a reliable road until Italian troops posted here in May 1918 had exploded an enormous mine under it to discourage German attacks. The road would now slow American attacks, as everything conveyed along the route had to be towed around the Italian crater by tractors. Colonel George Marshall observed that traffic on the appalling roads, which crumbled as quickly as they were repaired because of heavy rains and the weight of tractor-drawn heavy artillery, meant that "accompanying artillery" couldn't actually accompany the infantry and that even the wounded couldn't be evacuated. Ambulances filled with injured men sat for hours in traffic without moving. In their innocent zeal, the AEF assault divisions had brought along too much artillery— twenty-four 155mm howitzers and forty-eight 75mm field guns per division, more than twice the accompanying artillery of a French or British division. Everything now stuck fast in the mud.[33]

Working his way forward with I Corps's 35th Division, Lieutenant B. F. McClellan of Pershing's staff saw nothing but problems. This was the Missouri-Kansas National Guard division that was supposed to use the relatively open ground east of the Argonne to flank the Germans inside, propel the 77th and 28th Divisions through the woods, and give support to V Corps's attack on Montfaucon. Nothing went according to plan. And how could it? McClellan had met the divisional commander, fifty-four-year-old General Peter Traub, the evening before the onslaught and had heard nothing but gloom and doom. Traub, a gray-haired regular army officer with sad eyes, complained that he was everywhere handicapped by "bad personnel." He himself had commanded this National Guard division only since July and had fired both of his brigadiers for lacking "vim and pep." The new ones—Colonels Kirby Walker of the 70th Brigade and Louis Nuttman of the 69th Brigade—had only been on the job for three days and were battling deep resentment stirred by Traub's dismissal of their undemanding predecessors. Traub's chief of staff, Colonel Hamilton Hawkins, had only just joined, as had one of his colonels, Harry Howland of the 138th Infantry. Howland announced that his new command "was low in spirit and training and wouldn't do well." No one, in short, knew anyone, their capabilities, or even their names. McClellan, there to observe and transmit Pershing's guidance as refined by Marshall—"All of the higher commanders must realize that excuses are taboo and that the attack must be driven home"—gaped at the extent of the problem. Traub, always jumped-up on caffeine and cigarettes, was "a conscientious officer prone to occupy his attention with details to the point where they overwhelm him," which they did after just a few hours of combat.[34]

When the troops of the 35th Division went over the top, they had only the ammo on their belts. Platoon leaders told McClellan that they'd been unable to procure grenades or light machine guns. The great disorganized mass plodded ahead until, half a mile south of Varennes and Cheppy, they walked into German machine-gun fire. Six German machine guns were entrenched on a bluff, with two more machine guns in a pillbox halfway down the bluff. This whole area had been fashioned into a killing ground by the Germans since 1914, when they had begun repulsing annual French counterattacks from these same positions. Now the Germans waited till the American mass had closed to within two hundred yards to open fire. The Doughboys fell in waves.

Frantic attempts to dislodge the invisible Germans failed; all of the Kansas-Missouri division's mortars, one-pound guns, and even grenades were back in the supply lines, not forward with the troops where they were needed. The "accompanying artillery," as usual, wasn't accompanying; it was either stuck in traffic or deterred by the spitting German machine guns. The German-held butte was strong, one flank sealed with barbed-wire entanglements, the other resting on the moat of the Aire River. Attempts to turn either flank, over the wire or the river, were hit by more-accurate German machine-gun fire from a second machine-gun position in Cheppy, which covered the butte and the salient of open ground below the village with interlocking fire. Each of the several German machine guns in positions like this was fitted with traverse pins, so that the fire of every weapon precisely overlapped the next one, leaving no seams and wasting no fire. If the Doughboys successfully overran a machine-gun nest, its hidden neighbor—"in its stovepipe water jacket, 7.6-mm nose protruding through its flash screen, and feed-belt cartridges glittering like a rattlesnake's back"—would open up and mow them down, before falling silent again to await the next rush.[35]

Lieutenant Colonel George Patton's tank brigade—small six-ton Renaults with some medium French-crewed Schneiders—was ordered to drive up both banks of the Aire to support the infantry on either side, the 28th Division on the left and the 35th Division on the right. Striving to keep his brigade concentrated, Patton had his tank battalions deploy one company west of the Aire and two east. He commanded the advance from his headquarters, nicknamed "Bonehead," at Les Côtes de Forimont. With the tanks plunging into ditches or shattering under German artillery fire, Patton angrily left Bonehead on foot and began striding toward Cheppy. He was trying to rally 150 terrified skulkers—only six would follow him—when a machine-gun bullet bored into his thigh and exited through his left buttock, leaving a hole the size of a silver dollar. Shocked, Patton was wrestled into a shell hole by his loyal retainer Private Joseph Angelo. While bullets shrieked overhead from two dozen German machine-gun nests, Patton had a vision of himself being borne to an early grave. "It's time for another Patton to die," he thought. He wouldn't die—thanks to Angelo's rescue—but he'd miss the rest of the war. Major Sereno Brett took over from the wounded Patton, but the tanks, thwarted by the broken ground and the German fire, made little progress. Before the battle, Patton had warned about the fragility of the Renaults, counseling American crews to "get maximum effort out of the tanks before they go out of action from mechanical trouble." His tanks went out of action far sooner than expected.[36]

A platoon of Patton's tanks drove into Cheppy and silenced the machine guns there, but the Doughboys were on their own against

"Deploy the tanks at once," Lieutenant Colonel George Patton, commanding the US 1st Tank Brigade, advised. Patton would be wounded in the first day of the battle, and most of his tanks would be knocked out by road hazards or German fire. Here, a column of Patton's American-crewed, French-made 6.5-ton Renault light tanks rolls toward Vauquois and Montfaucon. (National Archives)

the butte below the village. In an advance that was supposed to be rapid—all the way to the German third line in a single day—the entire 35th Division spent four hours trying to assault the bluff from the flanks. Lieutenant McClellan watched in horror as dead and wounded Americans piled up, trying to lumber up the hill without artillery support or even mortars or light machine guns. The division had never been taught how to pass through enemy wire. Troops ran up to the wire, stopped, peered at it, and were slaughtered by the traversing machine guns. The advance didn't resume until 3:45 p.m., when the exhausted Germans finally relinquished the butte and retreated.

The Doughs of the 35th Division shambled up to the Baulny-Very Line, a mile south of Exermont—well short of their objective—and collapsed there till the afternoon of September 27. A squad leader of the 35th Division recalled stepping on what he thought was a half-buried sack of grain. To his horror, it oozed blood, and he leaped away—"It must have been a quadruple or quintuple amputee." This was an inauspicious start. The division had been completely shattered by light resistance. All four regiments were jumbled together.[37]

The 28th Division met a similar fate west of the Aire. The German outposts in the first line—the Etzel-Stellung—had either surrendered or retreated in the course of the morning to the second line, the Giselher-Stellung, centered on the three-hundred-foot height of Montfaucon. The second line was fastened on the right in the Argonne by Le Chêne Tondu and the Bois de Taille l'Abbé, wooded promontories bristling with German guns that commanded the Aire valley and poured fire into every American attempt to flank Montfaucon and break through. When the 28th engaged the Germans there, other German positions to the left and right opened up on them. The whole Giselher-Stellung, from here to Montfaucon and all the way east to the Meuse Heights, was a fortress, with dug-in German machine guns echeloned in depth and German long-range artillery interlocked in batteries to cover every inch of ground the Americans trod. Without artillery support, the Doughboys stopped. General Charles Muir, commander of the 28th Division, was a West Pointer and career officer. He urgently requested that Pershing send him two brigadier generals and two colonels from the regular army to try to get his National Guardsmen going. Pershing complied, with little effect. One of the brigadiers, General Edward Sigerfoos, who'd been commanding the army schools at Langres, was mortally wounded by a German shell, becoming the highest-ranking American KIA in the war. Both colonels were killed trying to lead infantry attacks on Le Chêne Tondu. The surviving brigadier, Pershing's intelligence chief, Dennis Nolan, returned to Chaumont with news of the gory debacle.[38]

Attempts to rally and reorganize the 35th Division also failed. Recognizing that the division had pushed beyond the protection of its own slow-moving batteries (one of which was commanded by Captain Harry S. Truman), the German guns now opened up on it. So ragged and uncoordinated was the US First Army's advance and so poor was the mopping up in the rough country in and around the

Argonne that the German fire came from everywhere: front, flanks, and rear. A sergeant of the 35th Division recalled receiving orders to "move north and develop the new German positions." He asked his lieutenant what it meant to "develop the German positions" and was told, "It's very simple, we just go ahead as usual until we get shot at real heavy. Then we'll know where the Jerries are." Hardly surprisingly, McClellan observed panic among the Doughs, who assumed that they were being shot at by their own guns. They weren't; the Germans simply hadn't cleared out of vulnerable positions because they could see how confused the Americans were and what easy targets they presented. While the division milled around south of the village of Exermont, trying to organize itself, the Germans hazarded a few counterattacks with infantry. They all succeeded. They usually did in the German coil spring defense: the Americans would be lured forward till they'd exhausted themselves and lost whatever liaison they had with their guns, and then they'd be hit by rested German troops, who'd spring at them with field artillery horsed and ready for action.[39]

McClellan remembered pulling together seventy American skulkers, who lied that they'd been sent back to fetch food, and "making them fight." He couldn't find a single officer to help him, so many had been shot down after exposing themselves to fire trying to urge their balky men forward. ("Looked like the war was hard on second lieutenants," said a sergeant of the 35th Division as he stepped over a dead platoon leader near Vauquois and counted thirteen bullet wounds in him.) McClellan saw bigger German counterattacks launched against Chaudron Farm, Baulny, and Charpentry, and he saw the Doughboys in those places "stampeded" by the Germans. General Peter Traub, the already-despondent division commander, rode between the masses of stragglers, trying and failing to rally them. The Germans were holding these villages as long as they could, and far longer than they'd expected to hold them. One reason Montfaucon continued to hold against the three divisions of V Corps was that I Corps, which was supposed to surge forward to outflank the Butte de Montfaucon from the west, was being held south of the line by these light German forces.[40]

Unable to take his objectives, General Traub gave up and re-treated; it was a scandal, an entire 28,000-man US division with-drawing in the face of German rear guards. Traub discovered that his 3,500-man regiments were down to 1,300 or 1,400 men—one of them, the 140th, was reduced to 700 men. Those who survived were more actuarial facts than heroes, the Doughs morbidly affirm-ing that "the last 15 percent are hard to kill." Officer casualties were catastrophic, some regiments losing two-thirds of their officers "due to undue exposure of officers trying to control their commands." The division's medical service performed no better than its combat arms, a witness describing the pitiful chaos of its dressing stations: "Imagine the plight of our wounded. . . . Some were legless; others armless; many with sides torn out by shrapnel. All were in direct pain," and yet there was no care. The men were laid in the open in sleet and rain for thirty-six hours without medical attention. Weeks after the battle, a sergeant in the 35th Division fell into conversation with an-other NCO, who still raged about how misused the division had been: "They oughta be court-martialed and shot, every sonofabitch from Traub down. . . . Shoving us in there against machine guns and artil-lery, getting us butchered like that." He paused and then concluded: "By God they oughta jail those bastards for murder, taking us in there without artillery support."[41]

The kaiser summoned Ludendorff to Spa for meetings on Sep-tember 28. The foreign secretary, Admiral Paul von Hintze, wanted an "unequivocal declaration of military possibilities." Despite the floundering of the Americans in the Meuse-Argonne, Ludendorff saw none. Germany's allies were beaten, and he'd lost faith in his own army. The German home front, cold and hungry, was on the brink of revolution. The German army, Ludendorff argued, would have to yield France and Belgium and try to retreat back to Germany intact. He accused his colleagues of treachery and cowardice, the kaiser of vacillation, the navy of promising too much with its submarines. He lost control, balled his fists, raged at the top of his lungs, beat the table, and then collapsed, hitting the floor with a thud. After Luden-dorff had been gathered up and laid on a sofa, a startled Hintze was authorized to approach President Wilson to ask for peace terms on the basis of the Fourteen Points. Chancellor Georg von Hertling—an elderly cat's-paw of the kaiser and high command—was told to resign. Little pressure was required. Hertling was a seventy-five-year-old Bavarian, and this was no way to spend his golden years. The kaiser would now attempt to mollify the German people with "revolution from above." He'd concede true parliamentary government and replace Hertling with one of his few liberal cousins, fifty-one-year-old Prince Maximilian of Baden. The desperate German generals hoped that Prince Max would be seen as an agent of reform on the home front. He might also impress the American president, divide the Allied coalition, and achieve a negotiated peace.[42]

Though Pershing would have preferred to focus on directing the Battle of the Meuse-Argonne, he instead had to focus on inquiries into each of his stumbling divisions. Tactics had to be reviewed, officers canned, reasons for failure sought. The chief reason for failure was obvious: American troops were being asked to do the impossible—attack machine-gun nests and artillery positions without fire support. Desperate to show progress, Pershing cruelly ordered them to attack anyway, with self-destructive results. Phone every division commander, Pershing seethed to Liggett's chief of staff on September 28, and "tell him that he must push on regardless of men or guns, night or day." Pershing was condemning men to death and punishing officers for, in many cases, their decency and common sense. But he was also hammering his head against a US Army culture that had always bred caution. Having spent their careers in small units or staffs, US Army officers had ascended to colonel or general by skirting the vicious politics of their small peacetime units. They'd gotten ahead not by making decisions but by *not* making them—by offending no one. Such men lacked the killer instinct needed now.[43]

Marshall recalled having to replace senior officer "casualties" on a daily basis, many of which were not due to the enemy. The deposed officers, their careers ruined, would plead for a second chance, anything not to be sent to the army's notorious Officer Reclassification Center in the Loire château of Blois, where they'd be given desk jobs or be sent home to the States. Marshall never forgot the "tragic and depressing scenes" but felt bound to press on with new men in the lead. Too often, competent officers were "blooeyed"—sent to Blois—for no good reason, which only made those still in active command even more fearful and cautious. A Marine lieutenant recalled a typical example of this chariness at Soissons. Ordered to relieve a company of army infantry, a Marine captain went forward with his men. When he arrived, the army officer said: "How can I pull my troops out? I have no orders from *my* people. What do you want me to do, get court-martialed?" The Marine left his Leathernecks with the Doughs and returned to General Lejeune at division headquarters to explain the situation. The general was furious. "Goddamn it," roared Lejeune, "when I give an order I want it obeyed. You're relieved of your command." The Marine captain, a career officer, was sent home in disgrace to command a guard company in a navy yard. "His whole future was ruined by something he couldn't control."[44]

General George Cameron's V Corps made as little progress in the center as Liggett's corps made on the left. How could it be otherwise? The tip of Cameron's spear was General Joseph Kuhn's largely untrained 79th Division—60 percent of its infantry and half of its gunners were draftees with a minimum of training and no combat experience. Somehow they'd been selected to take the all-important Butte de Montfaucon, a fortified ridge bristling with guns nicknamed "Little Gibraltar" by the French.[45]

Thomas Barber, a captain of engineers struggling to clear the ground behind the 79th Division, leaned on a shovel and watched the attack on Montfaucon: "On a high knoll of a distant ridge, with wrecked white masonry shining in the sun and crowned by the shattered arch of a church, stood Montfaucon. The whole town was enveloped in dust, and rocking under our shell fire. There were always four or five columns of dust in the air at once. It was very beautiful."[46]

It was anything but beautiful to the terrified men of the 79th Division, whose units disintegrated during the advance through Malancourt, Cuisy Wood, and the grassy Golfe de Montfaucon, below the hilltop village. Their heavy artillery was still hitting Montfaucon, but their light field guns had failed to keep up on the cratered, muddy roads through the deserted Etzel-Stellung and into the stoutly defended Giselher-Stellung. What progress the fearful Doughs of Maryland and Pennsylvania made here was owed chiefly to lingering fog and smoke screens. Whenever the wind cleared an area, the Germans—dug into the notorious Oeuvre du Demon and Redoute de Golfe—pitilessly gunned them down. One of their victims was Connecticut's Major Israel Putnam—descended from the Revolutionary War general of the same name, who'd swept the British off the slopes of Bunker Hill. German machine guns in the Golfe swept away Putnam and his company, hardly needing to see "the whites of their eyes."[47]

General Kuhn, the very man who'd hosted Joffre and Balfour at the Army War College in 1917 and arranged a lecture by British general George Bridges on the challenges of trench warfare, now experienced those challenges firsthand. He received chiding messages from Cameron all through the night of September 26–27. Pershing had expected Kuhn's 79th Division to sweep over Montfaucon in the morning and reach Nantillois—north of the butte—in the afternoon, to fall into line beside III Corps's 4th Division, which was battling forward in the space between Montfaucon and the Meuse. But the Germans on Montfaucon, looking down from its imposing height on the assaulting troops, remained unsubdued.

Burning with embarrassment (and fear for his career), Kuhn decided at midnight to hazard an attack on the butte with his two brigades abreast in the dark. General Robert Noble's 158th Brigade would now come up on the right of the 157th Brigade and extend all the way northeast to the 4th Division positions around Nantillois. But Noble found that he couldn't locate one of his regiments in the dark. Kuhn, unable to find or even contact Noble once he'd driven off in the dark, did find the missing regiment. Five hours later, as day was breaking, Kuhn found Noble in his brigade headquarters, still insisting that he couldn't find the regiment that Kuhn had passed hours earlier sitting by a road. This was just the sort of offense that got an officer canned and sent to Blois for "reclassification," and Kuhn relieved Noble on the spot and replaced him with one of his colonels. Noble's fate was anything but just. Generals like Pershing might talk about "initiative," but the bureaucracy of the army—poorly adapted to fluid, open warfare—suppressed initiative and left generals like Noble waiting in their offices for the next set of orders from corps and division, which they were required to relay to their regiments and battalions "with all due and timely notice." How could a general show initiative and still sit in his headquarters like a clerk to process incoming orders with "timely notice"? Punctiliousness, in other words, was still valued more than bold acts of initiative. The predictable effect, at this stage, was to keep American officers in their dugouts, by the phone.[48]

The Americans could have taken Montfaucon on September 26 had the 4th Division of Bullard's III Corps on the right combined with Kuhn's 79th Division in Cameron's V Corps sector. Bullard's III Corps—the 4th, 80th, and 33rd Divisions—was having the easiest day of the three corps engaged. "Easy" was relative, of course. The German guns on the Meuse Heights across the river killed so many men on the right flank of the advance that one Doughboy found his squad leader trembling like a leaf, unable to move or speak. The two of them were enveloped by a chorus of agony: "The wounded and dying were groaning and calling for help. 'I'm hit for God's sakes help me,' was the cry. It was almost unbearable. Some were shell shocked and were screaming maniacs." But over a harrowing few hours, III Corps reached its objectives and dug in on the west bank of the Meuse.[49]

The Illinois National Guardsmen of the US 33rd Division anchored the advance on the right, slopping through the marshes of Forges Brook, up to their ammo belts in cold mud, till they reached the Meuse. They took prisoners and secured First Army's right flank, despite a steady battering from German artillery firing into their flank from the far bank of the Meuse. To their left, III Corps's center division, the 80th, also advanced toward the Meuse. The 80th Division was to march to Brieulles and secure its bridge for an attack across the Meuse and into Gallwitz's Maas-Ost group sector, held by Germans and Austrians in the dominating battery positions above Consenvoye. Whereas Pershing was trying to flank the German strongpoints and force the Germans to yield them, the Germans, beneficiaries of an artfully prepared killing ground, were trying to hammer the Americans into a dense mass between the Meuse and the Argonne and funnel them into the teeth of strongpoints like Montfaucon here and the Kriemhilde Line farther back.

Advancing Doughboys could see German signals flashing from hill to hill across their front, calling for converging artillery fire and machine-gun barrages—from Le Chêne Tondu, a wooded outcropping of the Argonne in the west, across to Montfaucon in the center, and then over the Meuse to the right bank, where the wooded Consenvoye Heights and Borne de Cornouiller ("Corned Willy Hill") were carved into German battery positions. These were the notorious Meuse Heights, whose guns had tormented the French at Verdun in 1916 and were tormenting the Americans now.[50]

Those guns on the right bank of the Meuse took two hundred thousand Doughboys under fire for several days. General Auguste Hirschauer's French Second Army on Pershing's right was supposed to silence them, but, here as elsewhere, the poilus hung back. They'd attempt attacks and retreat in the face of resistance. For now, the US 80th Division—men from Virginia, West Virginia, Maryland, and Pennsylvania, the so-called last division of the Confederate army—huddled for three days on "carpets of blood and khaki" along the Meuse, pounded by accurate German heavy artillery. German fire into this little patch increased from five thousand shells on September 26 to sixty-five thousand shells the next day, as the Germans detected the vulnerable targets—they knew that the 80th Division couldn't withdraw from its flank position—and rushed in reserve guns and ammunition to kill as many Doughs as they could. "Tactics," one historian dryly noted, "were easily read in such situations." It was a reprise of the Battle of Verdun, where German batteries in these same positions on the Meuse Heights had pounded the French infantry at Hill 304 and Le Mort Homme. The difference was that the Doughboys had few guns to return fire; they'd given most of their divisional artillery to the 4th Division on their left. The 4th needed every available gun; it was, as one veteran put it, the "latchstring of the gate Bullard was to swing from its hinge at Verdun" to envelop the Germans defending Montfaucon.[51]

General John "Birdy" Hines's 4th Division on III Corps's left fought on the flank of V Corps and pushed five miles to the Bois de Septsarges. But Bullard wouldn't permit Hines to attack into V Corps's sector to assist the still-struggling 79th Division. Hines's orders were to push ahead to the Kriemhilde-Stellung, and he lacked the roads to cooperate with V Corps anyway. Roads were so scarce in this sector that the 4th and 79th Divisions had to share a single road that had somehow been repaired under enemy fire with forty thousand sandbags. Little was moving along the brittle road, and the twenty-eight thousand men of Hines's division would have had difficulty even trying to swing into the trackless sector inhabited by the twenty-eight thousand men of the 79th. Nevertheless, Hines's failure to assist would bloom into a vast controversy. Hines had wanted to take Montfaucon from the flank but had been refused permission by Bullard's staff chief, who worried that Hines's troops would have been hit with friendly fire if they'd turned left toward Montfaucon. The controversy would affect promotions and reputations for twenty years after the war.[52]

Working feverishly to repair the roads, Captain Thomas Barber paused in a ruined village named Haucourt and surveyed the space between the Etzel and Giselher Lines. Nothing was left of Haucourt, just "the broken white rubble of the buildings and a few heavy stone doorsteps." Germans manning outposts here had worn suits of armor to protect against American bullets and shells and then shrugged them off when they fled. Barber's men picked curiously through the piles of metal, "heavy breast-plates and aprons of steel that hung from the shoulders, and huge visored helmets with a curtain of chain mail before the eye-slits." The men gagged from the stench of the battlefield. The opening cannonade had plowed up the ground "and many buried horrors had come back to the light, among them the contents of a German cemetery. Some of the skeletons were scattered, some merely uncovered and lying in their ragged uniforms grinning out from under their pill-box caps." Souvenir hunters went through the pockets of the corpses, looking for anything valuable. They threw notes and letters to the side, and Barber picked one up. It had been written in the summer of 1916 and was still legible. He studied the German graves that had survived the shelling and thought that they "showed the incongruous German sentimentality for the dead." One cross bore this strange legend: "Ein unbekannte Tapfer Frankischer Krieger" (To an unknown, gallant Frankish Warrior). "It would be impossible to conceive of our men writing such an epitaph," Barber jotted.[53]

The Frankish warriors at Montfaucon continued to hang on against all expectations. Having advanced five miles over the ruins of the Etzel-Stellung on September 26, the 79th Division remained stuck short of Montfaucon. Neglecting to mop up, the Americans walked right past German snipers and machine guns in the rubble and gullies of Malancourt only to be shot in the back. Fired at from all sides, the troops frantically dug in around Cuisy and Malancourt, where the Baltimore infantry had refused to follow the tanks forward. Tactically, this was a minor disaster. Cameron's plan was for his 79th and 91st Divisions to outflank Montfaucon on the east and the west, permitting the 37th Division in the center to take the hilly position with minimal casualties when the Germans finally bugged out. But the Germans didn't bug out. They sat at Montfaucon and fired down at the 37th Division, the Ohio National Guard, which approached the hill and then stopped, the Buckeye Division digging in overnight to survive heavy German shelling, "ears pricked for the ker-plop of green-cross shells carrying phosgene gas."[54]

The Germans fought here as they were fighting on the wider battlefield, arresting the American wings with dogged defense, stopping every envelopment cold, and in this way converting every American attack into a brutal, bloody frontal assault across what the Doughboys called "hell's half-acre"—the ground swept by German machine guns. Speed was required to beat German reinforcements to the Kriemhilde Line—positions like the Vauquois Heights and Montfaucon had to be quickly seized or bypassed—but the Americans were not speeding anywhere. Failure to break the Giselher-Stellung on the first day and reach the Kriemhilde-Stellung, as Pershing had planned, meant that the Germans now had ample time to pour in the reinforcements that had been reserved for Metz. Four fresh German divisions would enter the Meuse-Argonne valley late on September 26. Six more would arrive by September 30.[55]

Ludendorff was so worried by the American pressure on the all-important line of the Meuse that he intervened directly in the battle on September 26, ordering General Georg Fuchs's only reserve division out of the Michel-Stellung and over to Dun-sur-Meuse, where it could deploy on either bank of the river. As usual, Ludendorff didn't miss the opportunity to scold Gallwitz: "Why are our reserves always in the *wrong* place?" Things were so bad that the Austro-Hungarian 106th Division was summoned, fitted with steel helmets, and sent into line at Vilosnes, where the Kriemhilde-Stellung crossed the Meuse. That would free up two German divisions to counterattack the Americans west of the river. In this Maas-West sector, General Georg von der Marwitz, now commanding the German Fifth Army, and Gallwitz, his army group commander, urgently interrogated American and French prisoners. They came away with the impression that the best American divisions were here, between the Meuse and the Argonne, and that no serious thrust toward Metz would be attempted before the spring. Nor did the French or Americans seem ready to attack the east bank of the Meuse. German reserves could be safely concentrated between the Meuse and the Argonne. Fuchs's corps could be stripped of its best units and thrown in against the US First Army.[56]

Officers of Gouraud's French Fourth Army, which was echeloned on the left flank of Pershing's First Army, watched incredulously as the American advance halted on September 26 and lapsed into inactivity on the twenty-seventh. The French sent staff officers to investigate; they reported massive failings. Although Pershing railed against the lack of initiative shown by many of his subordinates, the French considered him as guilty as they. He'd unleashed the attacks and then done nothing to follow and fine-tune them. He'd assigned rigid zones of action for each division, which meant that no one exploited opportunity; each unit advanced to the limit of its zone and stopped. Those who didn't reach the limit of their zone stopped anyway. American officers at every level lacked the confidence and experience to exercise initiative. Everywhere they awaited the next set of orders. In the zones themselves, units bunched up and mingled on the muddy roads, causing mass confusion.

With an inexperienced, hurriedly expanded general staff, there was no reliable liaison between American units, so each division operated in a vacuum, cut off from its neighbors as well as from an artillery branch that never seemed to find the fighting. French officers discovered that the American divisions they encountered didn't even know if they were in the first or second line. In one sector, an entire American regiment was reported missing in the line of fire. A desperate search discovered the unit far to the rear. The men had simply strolled individually back to the south to eat. "The American command did not direct the battle," the French observed. "They did not assure continuity of effort, or organize critical services in the rear. Their sole action was this: urge units to attain prescribed objectives." If the objective was attained, the unit stopped, the very opposite of the harrying, thrusting, disorganizing German method that had nearly broken the British and French armies in the spring. In his own after-action analysis, Pershing's staff chief, General James McAndrew, bitterly criticized this lack of initiative and offensive spirit. Whenever American units—like Bullard's—reached their assigned objectives, "there was an immediate relaxation of effort." And yet in many places, away from the key German strongpoints, there was little hostile resistance, just small rear guards; there was still daylight; parts of the divisions were still fresh. "Pursuit to the capacity of men and animals should have been the rule," McAndrew admonished. "But everyone from the division commander down felt he'd done his day's work."[57]

Even allowing for American inexperience, the French struggled to comprehend this ineptitude. Their liaison among armies, corps, and divisions, which they'd been teaching the Americans for a year, was painstaking. As commander of all French armies in the field, Pétain had at his headquarters a liaison officer for each of his armies. These officers kept on their desks the daily situation maps of their own army as well as its neighbors, along with information on the enemy in front of their army. They'd review every order issued by their army as well as every report submitted by their corps and divisions and then cross-check those orders and reports against the most recent instructions of Pétain. If there were any discrepancies, they would reread the orders of Pétain and, finding no exceptions to justify the discrepancies, would then get in a car and drive to their army and ask for an explanation. While there, they'd look around and observe the headquarters in action, making mental notes of its strengths and flaws. Returning to Pétain's headquarters, the liaison officer would explain the situation to the chief of the operations section or to Pétain's chief of staff. A meeting with Pétain would resolve the issue and keep the operation on track. Although Pershing hated the French way of war—too bureaucratic and office-bound, not inspirational in the least—he found himself pushing for just this sort of active liaison at all levels. It was an inescapable necessity of trench and open warfare on the Western Front, where so many lethal machines and men had to be coordinated in crowded terrain. "Liaison," Pershing liked to say, "is team work." In his eyes, not doing it right was "a mark of inefficiency and a neglect of duty." The trick was getting it right, which was difficult in any army, let alone a new one.[58]

The Germans were certainly relieved by the AEF's floundering. Gallwitz wrote late on September 26 that for the next two days "we had no more worries." He'd been given thirty hours in which to speed reinforcements to the Romagne Heights, which anchored the Kriemhilde-Stellung. Pershing's plan to smash through Montfaucon on the first day and advance into the Kriemhilde Line had been defeated. Hopes of seizing the citadel-like village of Grandpré with I Corps to flank the Kriemhilde fortifications and pass Gouraud's Fourth Army quickly up the Aisne Valley were also dashed—just "so many colored pins on staff maps that would hang for weeks on the walls of the town hall of Souilly, Pershing's headquarters," a veteran wrote. That night, as Barber continued work on the critical road from Esnes to Montfaucon, he heard a commotion: *"Asseyez-vous, As-say-eh-vous—till I light a cigarette—or je shoot."* He arrived at the scene to find a Doughboy threatening three frightened German prisoners with a rifle. The Doughboy wanted them to sit while he lit a cigarette, afraid they might dash off in the dark while he tried to strike a match. "Setzen Sie sich" (sit down) Barber said, in the only German he knew, and then said to the Doughboy that there was no point speaking French to German prisoners. "This seemed to confuse him very much. He evidently believed that all 'foreigners' must speak the same language. He lit his cigarette and went on."[59]

Other German POWs weren't so lucky. One approached an American near Malancourt with his hands in the air and the American pressed his pistol against the German's head and killed him. An American machine-gun company in this area took seventeen German prisoners and shot them all.[60]

The British general Cyril Wagstaff, Haig's liaison in Pershing's headquarters, continued his tour of the American front lines on September 27. It was a wet morning as he struck out from Triancourt under a drizzle at 9 a.m., noting approvingly that "the niggers were working on the road, and doing well," which is how US and British officers referred to African Americans in the war. Wagstaff and his little party left the road at La Tour de Paris, on the far left wing of the American position, and walked into the Argonne Forest till they came to a platoon of the 77th Division being shelled by the Germans. Wagstaff recorded what he saw: "The platoon were dog tired—and didn't know what to do, and the wood fighting was being very poorly handled. Line and situation very uncertain. No real attempt being made to beat out the wood." In other words, the Melting Pot Division from New York City wasn't advancing or even mopping up.

Wagstaff and his group reached the front line at Abri Saint-Louis and there too found nothing moving. German machine guns chattered all afternoon, stopping the American advance, which managed barely a thousand yards in the course of the day. To crack open the position at Montfaucon and stream to the Kriemhilde Line, the Americans also had to drive the Germans out of the Argonne, to push the whole line forward. They weren't succeeding. Regaining the road, Wagstaff found it blocked in both directions, which explained the continuing lack of close-in artillery support for the platoons in the

New Yorkers of the US 77th Division shelter in a captured German trench in the Argonne Forest. The division's biggest ethnic contingent was Italian American immigrants from New York's Little Italy. Hearing them call to one another, German forward observers mistakenly reported that they were under attack by Italians, not Americans. Note the density of the forest and the extreme exhaustion of the men, most of whom have fallen asleep. (National Archives)

woods. Wagstaff was struck by all of the loitering. "It seems to take three or four Americans to work one man's job. This results in masses of men being about, making ideal targets. The country was covered with men stargazing or 'resting.' There were hundreds of staff cars about." Wagstaff left as quickly as he could. He had to; the targets the Americans willingly offered the German guns were too combustible. The Englishman stared in disbelief at a stalled column of American trucks carrying shells *and* gasoline. "This seems unwise," Wagstaff deadpanned.[61]

By noon on September 27, Cameron's V Corps had finally taken Montfaucon, shouldering forward to join with the 4th Division in its exposed position ahead and to the right. To their left, the 35th Division strained ahead toward its original objectives but stalled again around Charpentry. Sergeant William "Slim" Triplet described the difficulties, among which was a new regimental commander with no respect for German firepower. Told that his pending attack on German trenches dug into the Montrebeau Woods would be shattered by German machine guns unless American artillery dug them out first, the new commander, sent to this National Guard division from the regular army, scoffed: "By God, my regiment will never be held up by a few machine gunners and to hell with the artillery." The men of the 35th went over the top in a brigade-strength attack and wended through German wire "like ants on flypaper," the German machine guns raking them from the woods: "That infernal cracking, bullets kicking up dirt in front of us, bouncing and howling away." They hit a second belt of German wire, and Triplet saw several men of another platoon snagged in it, "chopped to bloody rags, and two or three cripples crawling away." The attack foundered, the blimpish colonel provided with his baptism of fire on the Western Front, and the 35th Division still far from its objective of Exermont.

Digging in, Triplet noted the harrowing cross fires delivered by the German guns: "A man couldn't feel safe anywhere." Someone in his outfit who'd studied math tried to reassure the others: "You can step between machine gun bullets if you're moving fast. A Jerry bullet travels 2,700 feet per second and their guns fire 600 rounds a minute, or ten rounds per second. That means there's one bullet every 270 feet, that's 90 yards apart." Everyone regarded him as if he were mad. The whole exercise was bathed in futility, enlivened by rare bursts of comedy, as when German American National Guardsmen from St. Louis, their "squad rosters sounding like Hindenburg's staff," wriggled forward and cursed the nearby Germans, sunk behind their machine guns: "Komm' heraus, du shtinkende Schweinhund!"—"Verdammte Gartenzwerg!"—"Schurke!" (Come out, you stinking pig-dogs, yard gnomes, scoundrels!) The Germans never answered, not wanting to betray their positions. Triplet dozed fitfully in a grave-sized hole. "The chaplains tell us that hell is hot. I know better—it's freezing cold and perpetually wet."[62]

On September 28, General Wagstaff, who'd returned to Bar-le-Duc to sleep, attempted to rejoin the US First Army, this time farther east at Esnes, in the V Corps sector, just below Montfaucon. The roads were so clogged that it took three hours for him to drive forty miles. From Esnes, he began to walk toward Montfaucon but got only as far as Malancourt, where the 79th Division had stampeded two days earlier. The road had been destroyed by trucks and troops marching: "Very bad initial work, no bottom, metal all sank into the road which oozed up. Sandbags used to revet it subsided in the rain." Wagstaff met V Corps's chief of staff, General Wilson Burtt, who stared in disbelief at the immovable mass. "There seems to be more men than road here," he sighed.

Wagstaff, coming from the penurious British army, was impressed by the "extravagance of the Americans—both in men and material. For any particular work they seem to have about five-times as much as we do." For now, all of this plenitude availed nothing, for the boggy road was blocked in both directions. Traffic would sit motionless for thirty minutes, grind forward a few inches, and then stop for another thirty minutes. "Lucky there's no Boche aircraft or artillery around," Wagstaff observed. He perceived a lack of energy here among the V Corps. "There were Americans everywhere, scattered over the whole country, but not doing very much. The fighting was poor, hardly any advance was made." General Burtt explained to Wagstaff that "the attacking troops were all new, that they exaggerated the opposition and would not shove on." Burtt also noted that the field artillery, though up, was not firing in close support of the infantry but was instead firing indirect at long ranges, which made the largely unsupported infantry attacks around Montfaucon and in the Argonne "deadly slow." Wagstaff noted "signs of very loose discipline" all around him: "Gypsy-like bivouacs, men stealing bread off ration lorries, men leaving work to raid the Y.M.C.A., every wagon and lorry covered with men who should be walking." There were a lot of staff officers about, "but they all treated the matter in an academic way—and seemed to be out to observe and learn but not to *do* anything."[63]

13

MEUSE-ARGONNE: EXERMONT

Pershing had expected to reach the Kriemhilde Line on the first day; instead, he'd needed two days just to take Montfaucon. He'd confidently issued orders to his engineers to repair roads on the first day as far as Cunel, a place his army would need three *weeks* to reach. Despite the mass of American troops and firepower now crowding into the conquered Giselher-Stellung, progress was hard to detect anywhere, the Germans having fortified the wooded humps that rose between Montfaucon and the Kriemhilde Line. The Germans would defend them in their usual demoralizing way—"long enough to inflict all possible losses." The Argonne remained unsubdued, with the Germans clinging to the Palette Pavilion and the promontory of Le Chêne Tondu, halting progress on either side of the forest. The Kriemhilde-Stellung appeared invincible—dug into two wooded massifs east and west of the village of Romagne. The eastern range, the wooded hills between Romagne and Brieulles, was perfectly situated to block both the V and III Corps, which would have to cross a fire-swept valley to move their lines north. The western range, from Romagne across to the village of Grandpré, blocked

Mopping up: Four men of the US 79th Division pose with captured heavy German machine guns and their crews below Montfaucon. Note that the two Spandau guns are mounted on sleds—the gun and sled together weighed 135 pounds—for ease and speed of movement over rough ground. (National Archives)

Pershing's I Corps, which struggled even to reach Kriemhilde's outworks at Exermont. It was the perfect killing field.[1]

Major Gerald Geiger, a British general staff officer, went forward to observe the stuttering battle with a group of Americans on September 28. They started from Liggett's I Corps headquarters at Rarecourt and drove to the 28th Division headquarters at Varennes and then on to the 35th Division headquarters at Cheppy. From there, where Patton's tanks had crushed resistance on September 26, they walked to the high ground west of Véry. Two days into the battle, Geiger was most struck by everyone's ignorance about everything. At the 28th Division headquarters, "they were ignorant of what their brigades were doing, and there was a noticeable lack of efficient liaison forward and to the flanks." Geiger remarked the incuriosity of American staff officers at all levels: "Very few staff officers from the Corps or Army

staffs go out and see things for themselves; they leave important reconnaissance to young and quite inexperienced officers."[2]

Descending on the US 35th Division's headquarters, still reeling
from its debacle two days earlier, Geiger stayed two hours and "heard
and saw a lot." The whole division had been held in check for two
days by relatively light artillery and machine-gun fire. "When we
got there, *nothing* was known of the position of the forward troops."
The only information that General Traub and his staff were getting
was "a lot of 'windy' reports from platoon and company commanders,
most of which had taken hours to reach divisional headquarters."
Windy was British slang for "panicky." Geiger was struck by the volume of "windy" reports: "They kept coming in." In the British army,
such reports would have been cut off and handled close to the front.
In the AEF, they streamed all the way back to division and corps—
lamenting casualties, requesting tanks, reporting machine-gun and
artillery fire. "It's difficult for me to understand *why* the brigade and
regiment commands sent them through," Geiger noted. The only
matter that technically concerned corps and division was the usual
one: "The infantry was reported to be anxious to get on but would
like more artillery support." In their own attacks farther west, the
British were firing twenty-two thousand tons of shells a day in support of their infantry. The American guns, stuck on the muddy roads,
"were hardly firing at all."[3]

In the predawn darkness of September 28, an American captain
had awakened to hear an entire division nearly dissolve from panic.
Asleep in his tent below Montfaucon, he heard what he described as
"the first inkling that the Division ahead had lost its morale and was
going to pieces." It was the 79th Division, which had struggled up to
Montfaucon and then settled down along the ridge—cold, wet, hungry, thirsty, and frightened. Below them, the captain heard "repeated
cries from the whole line of the front; hundreds of voices scattered all
along the line repeating the same call at once." He strained to make
sense of their garbled shouts. "They were hard to make out, our shells
were roaring overhead. . . . The voices were terrible, they vibrated

with terror, indignation and reproach. . . . Suddenly it took the form of words and the wave of sound swept back to us—'Heavy artillery falling short! Pass it back.'" The men around the captain, spooked just as much as the men above them, took up the cry, which, like a wave in a stadium, was passed back by every unit, all the way back to the faraway guns, the captain hearing it shouted till it died away in the distance. The panic was repeated again before dawn, the captain judging it a "dreadful breach of discipline. That's what phones are for. This can cause a panic," by which he meant the dissolution of an entire combat division.[4]

General Pershing arrived at the front amid this chaos. "It was very fortunate he had not come in an hour earlier," Geiger smirked. Pershing had spent the last twenty-four hours firing officers. He'd now have to fire even more, although there were no obvious replacements. Listening in to the colloquy between Pershing and his generals, Geiger noted that the "chief points of criticism" were poor communication between units and the demoralization of the Doughboys, who weren't receiving the fire support they needed to assault German positions without suffering crippling casualties. Messages between American units were not going through or were taking hours to cross short distances. Pershing learned that there was no liaison at all between the 35th Division and its flank divisions, the 28th to its left and the 91st to its right.

The US First Army was supposed to be rolling forward like a steamroller. Instead, its divisions were fighting singly and blindly, and grinding to a halt everywhere. The German rearguard action here was being undertaken with a few light field batteries and the usual web of invisible machine guns. "No one I spoke to had *seen* any hostile infantry," Geiger observed, yet panicky frontline units kept asking for reinforcements, which were invariably sent (and replaced from the division reserve). This constant summoning of unneeded reinforcements—what were needed were better tactics by the troops already there—further clogged the already overtaxed roads but also made the front lines three times as thick with infantry as they should have been, making fat targets for the German machine guns: "No better progress

The Germans dug an extensive system of underground caverns and tunnels—hundreds of meters in length—into the ridges of the Giselher (shown here after its capture) and Kriemhilde Lines. This view of the cliffs north of Vauquois shows the stairs and paths to the entrances of the German dugouts inside the heights. Thousands of German troops could shelter safely inside the dugouts and defend the trenches on the crest of the heights with good protection from American artillery fire. (National Archives)

made, more casualties caused." Geiger marveled at the "general slowness" of everything: "It was due to the newness of the units engaged and a considerable amount of bad leadership." He noted that on the previous day, as the AEF had struggled to untangle itself from its exertions of September 26, more American officers had been canned by Pershing than had been killed or wounded by the enemy. Nothing seemed to work: "The reason we were two hours at 35th Division headquarters was that my American companion was trying to call up Army headquarters on the phone. We finally left after failing in the effort."[5]

Lack of artillery became the standard excuse for inaction. Units would simply stop and say they couldn't go on without artillery support. Others, promised tanks, would decline to advance if the fragile machines didn't appear. Even as an ardent armor advocate, Lieutenant Colonel Patton had to concede that tanks, which were always falling into ditches or breaking down (like Patton's on September 26), must be treated as a mirage: "It is respectfully submitted that infantry should progress as if tanks were *not* present," even when they were. First Army's chief of staff, General James McAndrew, scolded the American infantry for its overreliance on artillery. It would assuredly have been better had the US artillery showed more dash, but its virtual disappearance from the firing line shouldn't have immobilized the infantry, which had rifles, machine guns, one-pound guns, and mortars. Years later, S. L. A. Marshall, who fought in the Meuse-Argonne as a combat engineer, would study US infantry in World War II and conclude that only about 25 percent of the troops actually fired their rifles in battle. Here in World War I, the situation was proving no different. Seasoned troops had used their rifles effectively in the Marne salient; untried ones hardly used them at all. "Too little use was made of the rifle and all of the infantry weapons," McAndrew fumed. "The infantryman doesn't use his rifle enough; he's too prone to leave the whole matter of fire superiority to the artillery. This is not in accordance with American tradition or doctrine." American machine guns were also curiously silent. Some fired, "others served no purpose beyond furnishing targets to the enemy."[6]

Paradoxically, the Americans were too strong to advance. There were now 750,000 American troops crammed into the narrow Meuse-Argonne sector. If the US First Army had been placed in line with its artillery and trains, the entire eighteen-mile front would have been covered to a depth of one mile—eighteen square miles of infantry and guns pointed at the Germans. If they'd lined up, they'd have stretched five hundred miles from end to end. These American troops and trains stepped all over themselves and trod their three roads into swamps. A French colonel attached to American headquarters told his hosts, "You used too many troops, twice as many as the French would use for such an operation. It's impossible to supply that number with food and to move ammunition to the infantry and artillery. Even *French* staffs couldn't have solved that problem," a problem that had been made all the worse by the hasty transfer of so many units from Saint-Mihiel to the Meuse-Argonne sector in the days before the battle jumped off. "Saint-Mihiel was simple; this is difficult because it requires *continuing* effort."[7]

On September 28, French president Raymond Poincaré had attempted to visit the US First Army at the front and had been stuck in traffic for hours before giving up and turning back. The next day, Prime Minister Georges Clemenceau followed the disappointed Poincaré into action, resolving to bull through the AEF's traffic jams to see the Americans and tour Prussian crown prince Wilhelm's legendary bunker at Montfaucon. Clemenceau too came up short. He drove from Pershing's headquarters at Souilly and was immediately engulfed by traffic—chiefly advancing troops of the 1st Division and withdrawing troops of the 35th, but also forage trains, ammo trucks, and ambulances. So bad were the American roads—rutted by artillery, crowded with supply convoys, snarled with units converging from Saint-Mihiel—that the French premier gave up in disgust. Noting his disgust, the Doughboys either surrounded his car, lifted it in the air, spun it around, and sent him back—"He was just another goddam politician blocking a lifeline with a black limousine"—or watched sullenly as the premier turned back toward Souilly. Accounts of the incident differed, but it was unquestionably an embarrassment for Pershing. Clemenceau's chief of staff met with Pershing as the fiasco unfolded and "read clearly in his eyes that, at that moment, he realized his mistake. . . . The American Army was literally struck with paralysis because 'the brain' didn't exist, because the generals and their staffs lacked experience."[8]

Sometimes the roads were blocked by the French. Captain Thomas Barber, repairing the road between Esnes and Montfaucon on September 27—"the traffic creaking, bumping, crawling along," his engineers filling holes, bracing bridges, and pushing out stuck trucks—was amazed to see a French truck stop in the middle of his sector. "Ça ne veut plus marcher," the Frenchman muttered. (She won't go.) Barber watched the scene unfold: "The typical Frog driver, stuck and glad to remain stuck till rescued." He watched the French driver produce a bottle of wine and a loaf of bread and sit down to eat on the step of his cab. "The battle made no difference to him; the fact that he was blocking the slow, steady stream of supplies that was making the success of the battle possible, never occurred to him." Confirming first that the truck contained no explosives, Barber and his unit squatted, lifted it, and toppled it into the ditch. "The Frog retired cursing, and the traffic resumed its uninterrupted course."[9]

Working on the roads, Barber had a front-row seat to the unending spectacle of skulking Doughboys—the large number of men who deserted the front under all manner of fraudulent excuses. At Cuisy on September 29, Barber's road crew saw a steady flow of skulkers going to the rear along the road, eyes low, all muttering that they'd lost their units. The Doughs called such men "shell-hole rats," troops who'd lost their nerve, gone to ground, and then stolen back to the safety of the rear. They "became conveniently lost and as conveniently found themselves when the show was over," a major in the 1st Division added. That major always took a large number of shirkers for granted, relying throughout on that "certain number of men who can be depended upon, as a general thing, to begin and end all military operations." With German shells playing along the road, Barber watched an angry brigadier general emerge from his tent, seize a rifle from a soldier, and force a ragged band of skulkers to turn around and return to the front. Barber was unimpressed: "It struck me as a very remarkable performance as the skulkers merely went round and back by another route, but at least it seemed to afford the old gentleman considerable satisfaction."[10]

Dos Passos described the march of American infantry up these roads, through a "shattered skeleton of woods, torn camouflage fluttering from the trees, the ground and road littered with tin cans and brass shell-cases, trees festooned with strand upon strand of telephone wire." The Doughs passed elements of what Dos Passos dubbed the great "middle army" that labored day and night to keep the roads serviceable, then a staff car stuck on the side of the road, full of American general staff officers swigging booze from a thermos "with the air of Sunday excursionists." One of them, "a little lieutenant with a black mustache with pointed ends," called to them, "They're running like rabbits, fellers; they're running like rabbits." The unit emitted a "wavering cheer" and marched on, singing:

> *O ashes to ashes*
> *An' dust to dust*
> *If the gas-bombs don't get you*
> *The eighty-eights must.*

Breasting a steep hill, they passed a battery of French 75s, the Frenchmen seated on logs in pink and blue shirtsleeves, smoking and playing cards. One Doughboy expressed his annoyance to John Andrews—Dos Passos's alter ego in the novel—that the French gunners were resting while the Americans marched to the front. "Tell 'em *we're* advancin'," he says to Andrews, the only French-speaker in the outfit. "Are we?" said Andrews, taking in the state of the roads and the crush of stalled vehicles before and behind them. He then called to the French gunners: "Dites-donc, les Boches courrent-ils comme des lapins?" (Tell me, are the Boche running like rabbits?) One of the Frenchmen looked up from his cards and laughed. Andrews conveyed his answer to the squad. "He says they've been running that way for four years."[11]

While Pershing struggled to advance, the British First and Third Armies, led by the Canadians, broke through the Canal du Nord defenses of the Siegfried Position while Rawlinson's Fourth Army assaulted the heart of the Hindenburg Line—the Saint-Quentin Canal and Tunnel complex. The canal, thirty-five feet wide and fifty feet deep, was a moat along the western face of the Siegfried Position. Among Rawlinson's assault troops were two US National Guard divisions: the 27th Orion Division of New York and the 30th Old Hickory Division, drawn from Tennessee and the Carolinas.

In Flanders, Plumer attacked in a driving rain up the ridge above Ypres that had cost Haig so dearly in the 1917 Passchendaele Offensive only to be retaken by the Germans in the spring. Three hundred thousand British troops had died in the salient, and Plumer lost many more, but the German Fourth Army yielded the ridge and fell back. There was progress everywhere, tempered with "an air of immense desolation, a deep sense of vast, irretrievable waste," and Haig's staff chief, General Herbert Lawrence, reviewed the casualties and predicted that this would be the last offensive the British army could undertake in the war. British infantry numbers were at a critical low and couldn't (or wouldn't) be reinforced.[12]

The Tommies would not have been encouraged by the proficiency of their two American divisions. Pershing had warned Haig not to assign these units intricate missions like this: "I beg to remind you that these divisions have not as yet been trained with their artillery and are of course inexperienced." Haig went ahead and used them as assault troops anyway. The 30th Division did well—becoming Haig's favorite American division—but New York's 27th Division fell on its face. Its commander, Bronx-born forty-three-year-old General John O'Ryan, was one of those National Guard commanders, like New England's Clarence Edwards, whom Pershing distrusted but couldn't remove for political reasons. Like Edwards, O'Ryan was revered by his troops—who gave the division its punning nickname "Orion" and called themselves "O'Ryan's Roughnecks"—and protected by the Democrats, who needed New York Irish votes in elections.[13]

O'Ryan, the army's youngest division commander, had never impressed Pershing in training, and this was his first real test. The two US divisions had each been given four thousand yards of front facing the main Hindenburg Line fortifications. On September 27, the two American divisions had been ordered to align themselves with the British corps on either side, so that they could all advance behind tanks and a rolling barrage on the twenty-ninth. "Aligning" involved eliminating German outposts in order to make a straight line, one thousand yards from their objective. The US 30th Division ground forward to take up its prescribed position. O'Ryan's 27th Division hardly budged, thwarted by a belt of German outposts that the British division it had relieved had left intact. This didn't bode well. The Americans were supposed to advance briskly on September 29 to seize the three-mile-wide Scheldt Canal railroad tunnel, which they'd then use as a bridge to get their tanks and infantry across and drive the Germans off the opposite bank, permitting British troops to cross the canal itself and scramble up its fifty-foot banks.

When the offensive began on September 29, the Orions tried again to reach the start line (and fall in behind the tanks and creeping barrage) but were again stopped cold by the three German strongpoints they had wrestled with two days earlier: the Knoll, Guillemont Farm, and Quennemont Farm, all manned by German sacrifice units wearing bulletproof armor. The New Yorkers found themselves effectively marooned one thousand yards behind the barrage line. The barrage, never adjusted for this American failure, fell as planned at 5:30 a.m., stood for four minutes on the start line, then advanced at a rate of one hundred yards every four minutes. The plan was for all units—the British III Corps on the right, the British IX Corps to the left, the Americans and Australians in the center—to advance on a twelve-mile front, gain 1,100 yards, and cross the Scheldt Canal. Without the lagging Orions in support, the Old Hickories were hit with machine gun and artillery fire from the flank and slowed.[14]

Many of the forty tanks accompanying the US 27th Division were destroyed by German shells on the starting line; those that lurched ahead were disabled by a forgotten British minefield, then picked apart by Mauser antitank rifles and antitank guns. The antitank rifles were the standard German Mauser fitted with a fat six-foot-long barrel that rested on a bipod and fired armor-piercing slugs the size of a cigar. They'd punch through the three-quarter-inch armor of the tanks, obliterate any crew they struck, exit through the rear bulkhead, and mangle the tank engine on the way out. The few tanks that ground forward to the objective were stopped at the tunnel by concrete forts. Not surprisingly, tank crews that survived the ordeal were deemed "shaken and in need of pulling together."[15]

One veteran recalled the carnage: The attacking Doughboys went down "like pins in a bowling alley." Every shell hole he passed or dived into was filled with dead, wounded, or terrified Americans. "What a thin line there is between a hero and a coward," the future New York congressman Captain Hamilton Fish reflected. "If there is such a

Two American divisions joined the British assault on the Siegfried Position of the Hindenburg Line on September 29. The Americans drew one of the bloodiest tasks, seizing the Scheldt Canal railroad tunnel, which the Germans had fortified with steel, concrete, artillery, and machine guns. The faces of these men of the US 30th Division—National Guard from Tennessee and the Carolinas—show a mixture of fear, shock, and relief as they rest in the ruins of the German position after the ordeal. (National Archives)

thing." The Doughboys who got through were at least as shaken, overwhelmed by German resistance that boiled out of the subterranean caverns hewn into the walls of the tunnel and the banks of the canal. The American rookies failed to mop up. When the Australians came forward to "pass through" the struggling Doughboys, they encountered a unique situation: a line of frantic American troops, all of their officers killed or wounded, firing at a line of German defenders, who were, in turn, being fired at from the other direction by a surprised line of Americans beyond the canal who hadn't noticed, or wanted to notice, the Germans nested inside the complex when they passed over.[16]

Allied aviators flying overhead and peering down had never seen anything like it in the entire war: from Bellicourt east to Beauvoir, parallel lines of, respectively, Australians, Germans, Americans,

Germans, and then Americans, all blazing away at each other. The Australians finally passed through the Old Hickories—who'd receive more Medals of Honor than any other division in France—on the night of September 29. O'Ryan's 27th Division hadn't advanced beyond the line where its barrage had started. German prisoners took no comfort from this; they noted that despite their difficulties, the Americans still "fought like wild men." The British, war correspondent Charles Repington observed, were "all much amused by the Australian criticism that the Americans are good in battle but terribly rough." For the Diggers to call the Americans rough was "regarded as the best of compliments."[17]

Hindenburg immediately grasped the significance of the hammering, synchronized Allied offensives. In a meeting at Spa with Foreign Secretary Admiral von Hintze on September 29, the day Rawlinson breached the Saint-Quentin Canal and Clemenceau was expressing disgust with American progress in the Meuse-Argonne, Hindenburg told Hintze to "sue for an immediate peace." Two days later, Hindenburg reminded Hintze of the urgent need for an armistice before the German army broke. The German army had always wielded political power, and Hindenburg had no qualms about *ordering* the chancellor and foreign secretary to arrange an end to the war. If they didn't, he would.[18]

After a two-day pause to regroup and plug in new officers in the Meuse-Argonne, Pershing issued stirring orders for all of his divisions to press on. As a coldhearted AEF analysis later put it, "The tactics of these operations were not especially difficult. It was mainly a matter of frontal attack adopted to overcome the German method of retreat, which in turn was the extensive use of machine guns." American guns should have pulverized the German machine-gun nests, but they couldn't get up the muddy, crowded roads to get within effective range of the German positions. "If our artillery preparation was sufficient, the infantry advanced without much trouble. If it wasn't, they had a great deal of trouble and frequently didn't advance at all." Nearly every problem the Americans had was caused by "bad roads, few roads, congested roads, narrow roads, etc.," the analysis glumly concluded. Colonel George Marshall groped for a silver lining. Given the ravages of the weather, American vehicles, and German shellfire, what little was being accomplished on the roads had to be accounted "a miracle of achievement."[19]

The Allies angrily dissented. Already Foch, Pétain, and Haig were condemning the lack of *any* progress in the US sector in what was supposed to be a general advance by *all* of the Allied armies. In the American sector, no one seemed to be advancing. Around Exermont—a village in the gap between the second and third German lines of defense—where the boundaries of the US I Corps and V Corps touched, liaison was so lacking that the two American divisions that reached the place *withdrew* from it after suffering heavy casualties from German machine guns. As usual, the American artillery didn't appear, settling for ineffective barrage fire from deep in the rear areas. The exasperated Doughs began to take matters into their own hands, straggling independently away from the firing line and toward the rear. The British observer General Wagstaff was in the area and noted the astonishing fact that straggling was so widespread and leadership so slack that the strength of an entire twenty-eight-thousand-man American division essentially "disappeared" from the front line on September 29.

Wagstaff noted that hapless American officers were being canned in the midst of battle and that Pershing was having to cannibalize his own headquarters to find adequate replacements. He had to send his own trusted G-2, or chief of intelligence, General Dennis Nolan, to take over the 28th Division's 55th Brigade. Nolan, who'd coached the Army football team to a 6–1 record in 1902, would have difficulty getting wins with this brigade. The Doughboys recoiled in fear and loathing and sang sharp-edged tunes: "The Captain is a bloody funk / He's yellow sober and worse when drunk / The Adjutant, he's a son-of-a-B / And the biggest dud in whole Arm-ee." Worse than the perplexed officers on the scene were the ones in the safe billets far to the rear: "Oh, Colonel Jinx was a hell of a guy / He stayed in Toul while his men marched by." Still worse were the generals: "Oh, the C.O. wants a Croix de Guerre / For sitting around in an office chair."[20]

Poring over reports from the front, Pershing's headquarters staff were thunderstruck. Two US divisions, the 91st of V Corps and the 35th of I Corps, had retreated from Exermont, a critical place where I Corps, advancing through the Argonne, and V Corps, advancing through Montfaucon, joined. Both divisions reported that they were isolated, "in the air," with their flanks exposed, when they actually had each other on their flanks. They just didn't know it. As Clausewitz had written: "In war, the novice is only met with pitch black night."

General Cameron's V Corps noted the extreme difficulty of coordinating attacks by even neighboring divisions like these two. American units would refuse to advance unless they were assured that their neighbors were advancing. If not, they'd retreat. It didn't help that they were being sent against all-but-impregnable positions. When the commander of the US 91st Wild West Division ordered his brigades to take Gesnes on the twenty-ninth "regardless of cost," the officers heard the order read aloud incredulously. Gesnes was up a steep, bare hill, every inch of that hill covered by German machine guns and artillery, the village itself guarded by squat concrete pillboxes, the flanks of the slopes secured by more machine guns.

Staring at the killing ground from the Bois de Cierges, the officers knew they'd never make it. "Our losses would be terrible," a captain objected. "To hell with the losses," another captain shrugged. "*Read the order.*" To avoid being canned and "blooeyed," the officers attacked and suffered 50 percent casualties—most of the terrified Doughs never even seeing a German, just hearing the "weird croon" of their machine guns and the cries of hundreds of men being shot down—before ebbing back to the Bois de Cierges. They'd failed because of their casualties and because the divisions to the right and the left had not kept up, exposing the troops that did make it as far as Cierges to fire from three sides. A wounded runner of the 91st Division recalled the hell of the triage hospital behind the lines—men raving with shell shock ("Some were laughing; some were crying, while some were swearing") and a row of twenty operating tables, all occupied and bathed in the "nauseating smell of blood, mixed with ether. . . . Mangled arms, legs, heads and bodies. Some limbs had been shot off; some were taken off." Men who'd gone over the top yelling the 91st Division's battle cry—"Powder River, let 'er buck"—fell silent in pain and terror. Struggling to make sense of the tragedy before him, General George Cameron limply recommended that, in the future, whenever that might be, "a spirit of helpfulness and generosity towards others" be inserted into postwar training.[21]

Britain's Major Geiger, still circulating behind the American lines, found no helpfulness or generosity anywhere. Despite a promising operational situation—massive American forces arrayed against thin German rear guards—an inexplicable panic raced through the American ranks and command posts. Geiger overheard a colonel raving that his regiment of 3,500 men had been reduced to 500 effectives, as if he were at Rorke's Drift or the Little Bighorn, not in a relatively quiet French pasture. "Probably less than one-quarter of those 'missing' are actually casualties," Geiger commented. The rest were simply men who'd quit, yet "there are not enough proper leaders to stop them." Geiger reported that Pershing's scolding headquarters was canning large numbers of US officers—junior and senior—but took note of the obvious: "It is open to question if their successors will prove a great improvement as there is a total lack of tried officers at present."

At Foch's headquarters, British general Charles Grant confirmed that such had been Pershing's desire to "have an American battle and an American victory" that the moment the attack had begun on September 26, the Americans had dismissed the French officers who'd been sent to advise them, including staff officers of the French Second Army, "who knew all the back areas intimately and had men available to mend the roads and improve the communications." Pershing now asked for them back. "The truism is confirmed," a withering French report concluded. "An army cannot be improvised."[22]

Pershing's floundering start in the Meuse-Argonne had squandered precious time. The German commanders in this sector, Marwitz and Gallwitz, had suspected that the attack on Montfaucon might be a feint to conceal a bigger attack farther east by the veteran American units still at Saint-Mihiel. They now saw that it wasn't and poured in reinforcements. By September 27, four new German divisions had moved into the trenches around Romagne to oppose the American advance. Three days later, six more German divisions had pulled in. The US offensive, so promising when this sector was quiet and lightly defended, now appeared hopeless. The Germans had arrived in force, well armed, well fortified, and smoothly supplied by tactical railways behind their concrete defensive barriers. Pershing had advanced eight miles, then stalled. His open battle, briefly tasted, had reverted to trench warfare.[23]

Wasted time also meant that the Allies would probably not end the war before winter. George Marshall noted that the Germans only had to hold out till the snows fell to prolong the war and perhaps break the increasingly fractious Allied coalition. In AEF headquarters, they recognized that this "marked the crisis of the battle, the enemy in his last prepared defensive position struggling desperately to withstand our assaults until the inclemency of the weather could force us to suspend major operations until the following spring." The short days and heavy rains of a French winter would make it hard to continue operations. It would be impossible to get ammo and supplies forward, and the weakened men wouldn't stand it, "seldom dry, on water-soaked ground, and constantly under fire." If the Germans could hold out till winter, who knew what months of inactivity and acrimony would do to the already-strained Allied coalition?[24]

On September 29, the US 35th Division attempted again to push across the Exermont ravine and into the teeth of the Kriemhilde Line, only to be driven back. Each time the Doughs attacked, the *put-put-put* of German machine guns would start again and the attacking waves would fall, fling themselves to the ground, or shrink backward. "The attack just slowed, sickened and died," a participant observed. "The leading waves flattened, eased into the nearest cover, and started firing and digging in. We in the support waves followed their example." This wasn't the behavior of assault troops. Sergeant Slim Triplet observed that when ordered to press the attack on the German guns, the men of his company "creaked to their feet with all the vim and enthusiasm of the inmates of a nursing home," muttering things like, "Well, here we go again," "Here goes nothin'," or "Here today and gone tomorrow."

Those attacks too were shot to a standstill immediately. One man started forward feverishly reciting scripture: "A thousand may fall at my side, ten thousand at my right hand, but the arrow that flies by day will not come near me." Triplet saw the man killed, dully intoning: "He was wrong." In just three days of combat, the Kansas-Missouri National Guard Division lost over six thousand men.[25]

With no supplies making it forward, ammunition ran short. Triplet recalled crawling between American corpses to take their belts and bandoliers. He was sawing with his knife at the bandoliers of one body—torn open by two belly wounds—when the body stirred and looked at him. Triplet recoiled in horror: "He was light clay–colored, eyes barely open." Everyone in the front lines was famished, subsisting on captured German food, cabbages dug from the fields, or rations plucked from the pockets of corpses. A soldier in the 32nd Division described an obsessive search for food—men roving into other division sectors to steal, it being "a law of the army to respect the rights of a soldier when in possession of an article," no matter how he'd procured it. But if the soldier let the item out of his sight, possession would no longer be respected: "Nothing would be taken from an individual by force, but that didn't prevent it being stolen from him once his back was turned."[26]

Every soldier memoir described constant thieving and counter-thieving—a man might secure a ten-pound tin of corned beef, but if he set it down and looked away, it'd be gone in an instant. Water was as hard to procure as food. Water pooled in every shell hole on this rain-soaked battlefield, but none of it could be considered safe since both sides were firing so much poison gas. Triplet recalled asking his platoon leader for permission to scrounge for food and water, and the lieutenant, a weekend warrior from the heartland, thoroughly out of his depth here, wrung his hands and struggled to hold back tears: "My boys, my poor boys. What shall I do?" Even that decision exceeded his capabilities, and shortly the starving men were driven back by well-aimed German artillery anyway—gas mixed with shrapnel and high explosive. Dozens of men were cut down, and Triplet paused to examine a friend who'd taken an instant-fused 77mm German shell in the hip. Nothing remained of him but a leg loosely attached to a faceless torso. Beside him lay two others of the platoon—one shot in the lungs, the other with a foot torn off. "Try to get stretcher men up for us, Sarge," they called faintly. Cold and pneumonia would kill them both, Triplet predicted as he moved away.[27]

Still mired in the space between Montfaucon and the Argonne, strung out on a three-mile front from the Aire River to Eclisfontaine, facing German strongpoints at Montrebeau, Montrefagne, and Hill 272, the men of the 35th Division felt the weight of despair. The German 5th Guard Division and the German 52nd Division had moved in opposite them: "fresh, first-class divisions." Walking behind the lines, Triplet met with two Red Cross officials in starched uniforms and gleaming leather. They asked to see a German helmet Triplet had picked up near Exermont; it was holed in the front and back where the killing round had ripped through, and it bore the coat of arms of the German 5th Guard Division. One of the Red Cross men examined the helmet, exulted over the blood smeared inside—"This is one Kraut they can write off the roster!"—and then offered Triplet a half dollar for the souvenir. Triplet let the coin slip through his fingers, handed the helmet to the Red Cross man, and strode away, damning "that sanctimonious, philanthropic, bloodthirsty son of a slut thinking he could buy a helmet full of Hun brains with his profit from ten packs of Spearmint."[28]

Red Cross men were liked about as much as Y-men by the troops. The KC—Knights of Columbus—who appeared along roads to hand out cigarettes to the passing troops, were noted for their unhelpful political views. Based among the New York and Boston Irish, the Knights of Columbus hated the Republican Party and the British Empire and weren't shy about saying so—lecturing the Doughs of any unit they met on the sins of the British or the errors of Teddy Roosevelt—which was obviously inconvenient in *this* war with *this* army, which, for the most part, admired TR more than any other politician.[29]

George Marshall described vicious waves of combat for the Exermont ravine, which sat on the threshold of the Kriemhilde-Stellung. Positioned on ridges on the flanks of the ravine, the Germans blasted back every American attempt to push through. At US First Army headquarters, Pershing's staff noted that "the principal difficulty was the lack of understanding by the junior officers of regrouping their units at every opportunity." There were no veterans of major warfare in the American ranks, as Marshall put it, "to assure the rank and file that their experience was typical of a battlefield." Junior officers and NCOs, in other words, were as undone by the German defensive fire as the enlisted men.[30]

John Dos Passos, who served in the Ambulance Corps, described what this pandemonium felt like in his novel *Three Soldiers*. Chris Chrisfield, lost in a wood—possibly this very Fôret de Montrebeau— meets with a lieutenant, "red hair, pink and white face, gold bar on the collar of his shirt," swinging his arms wildly, trying to find his missing platoon. The lieutenant, panicked and shamed, rushes off, splashing recklessly through puddles, crying, "Where's the artillery? That's what I want to know. Where the hell's the artillery? No use advancing without artillery." He hasn't gone far, Chrisfield answers from behind him, when German machine guns open up all around them "in a sudden gust," answered only by the "whip-like sound" of the American rifles. Chrisfield darts one way, the lieutenant another. Chrisfield finds himself in a hamlet of demolished white houses; in the street he collides with another Doughboy who is racing back and yelling, "The barrage is moving up!" "What barrage?" "Our barrage, we've got to run, we're ahead of it." The American guns, silent when the German machine guns were blazing, were now opening up at the very moment that the American infantry had conquered the space. It didn't take a man of Dos Passos's sensibility to register the irony. No wonder Doughboys said that they "felt safer under a French barrage" than an American one. They run for their lives, passing the red-haired lieutenant Chrisfield had met in the woods, now leaning against one of the wrecked houses, "his legs a mass of blood and torn cloth." As they race past the lieutenant, they hear him shouting: "Where's the artillery? That's what I want to know; where's the artillery?"[31]

On September 30, Colonel Marshall found himself having to move 140,000 American troops in and out of the front line to relieve the worst-hit divisions. The Germans, out of reservists of any age and entirely dependent on the annual draft for replacements, didn't have this luxury. A doleful memo from Hindenburg on September 30 advised German regiments that had been reduced to four hundred men or fewer—a common occurrence by this stage—to stop requesting replacements (there were none) and instead to dissolve their third battalion and use whatever men (and horses) it contained to beef up the other two. Only "last surviving sons"—who were sent home when the next to last was killed—were going to make it out of this cauldron alive, or so it must have seemed.[32]

The wind was raw and the rain cold and torrential, adding to the misery. Fires that drew artillery were never permitted on either side of the lines, so the troops shivered constantly in wet uniforms. The Germans suffered from the cold as much as the Americans, an Austrian lieutenant writing of little else in his diary: "The heavy rain did not stop a minute and soaked us through and through" (September 30) and "Rain, rain, and rain again" (October 1). Gallwitz mentioned it throughout his diary. On October 1: "A gloomy fall morning to begin the last quarter of 1918. . . . God has not given us a Bismarck to relieve these hard times and all of the beautiful words, medals, and encouragement have come too late." Indeed, the news for the Germans on October 1 was ghastly: ten thousand prisoners lost to an American army that already outnumbered Gallwitz between the Argonne and the Meuse. To the west, the Allies had retaken the fortified quarries of the Chemin des Dames and breached the Siegfried-Stellung, where they crossed the canal and took Saint-Quentin and twenty thousand more German prisoners. Gallwitz recalled that all talk now was of a retreat to a new Antwerp-Meuse Line, his army group in the Meuse-Argonne the critical "pivot" for the move back from the Hindenburg Line to the new one.[33]

The kaiser, having replaced Hertling as chancellor with his moderate cousin Prince Max of Baden, now named a Socialist, Friedrich Ebert, state secretary of the interior. With curdling hypocrisy, the kaiser, who'd resisted liberalization to the bitter end, now lauded Prince Max and Ebert as "men who possess the trust of the people."

Though ordered to seek an immediate peace on the basis of the Fourteen Points—"Max ist Pax" (Max equals Peace), they were saying in Berlin—Prince Max discovered that neither Hindenburg nor the kaiser seemed actually to have read Wilson's points. They refused to relinquish Alsace-Lorraine or their conquests in the East, both American preconditions for peace talks even to begin.[34]

Hindenburg now spoke bluffly of "fighting to the last man." The kaiser's new finance minister challenged the field marshal, indicating that such sacrifice might be expected of a crack army battalion, but not of a complex nation of sixty-eight million. Clearly the revolution in Germany—prodded by hardship and the Russian overthrow of the tsar—had begun. To the Allies, the change of government in Berlin suggested that the Germans were in the midst of a political crisis that might cost them the war. The German army had yielded 270,000 prisoners and four thousand guns since July 18, and now the kaiser was losing control of his country. Foch, who'd been demanding one hundred divisions (four million troops) from the Americans, met with President Wilson's representative on the Supreme War Council, General Tasker Bliss, on October 3 and told him that he wouldn't need four million Americans after all. The two million Americans who were already in France or on ships to Brest and Saint-Nazaire would be enough.[35]

All eyes turned again to the US Army striking at the pivot of the German withdrawal. If Pershing could break through the Kriemhilde Line and cross the Meuse River in force, the German plan to winter behind the Meuse and prolong the war would be ruined. The revised American plan was to use fresh divisions, as Marshall put it, "to give a new impulse to the advance" (that was nowhere advancing) beginning on October 4. Captain Harry Truman, commanding a battery of field artillery in the 35th Division, was preparing to rotate out of the front line when a runner dashed into his position with a message from an American balloonist who'd spotted a German counterattack gathering on the flanks of an isolated infantry battalion. Truman read the message, sprinted a hundred yards to a knoll, saw the Germans

A veteran who saw Captain Harry Truman's battery of 75mm field guns in action in the Meuse-Argonne never forgot the sight: "Everything clockwork, setting fuses, cutting fuses, slapping shells into breeches and jerking lanyards before the man hardly had time to bolt the door. Shell cases were flipping back like a juggler's act, clanging on the tin hats of the ammunition passers, the guns just spitting fire—spit, spit, spit." Here, gunners of the 1st Division fire in support of their infantry near Exermont. (National Archives)

assembling in the distance, and began calling back ranges and providing bearings.

The runner, watching the scene unfold, never forgot it: Truman's battery responded, "everything clockwork, setting fuses, cutting fuses, slapping shells into breeches and jerking lanyards before the man hardly had time to bolt the door. Shell cases were flipping back like a juggler's act, clanging on the tin hats of the ammunition passers, the guns just spitting fire—spit, spit, spit." The Missouri Doughboys threatened by the German counterattack were invisible to Truman, beneath him on the slope of the knoll on which Truman and the runner stood. But he knew they were there. Across the field before them came the Germans, emerging from trees, which the runner recalled still had their golden autumn leaves. Intent on killing, the Germans tramped forward, bent double, light machine guns held with shoulder straps on their hips. Truman, peering at them with binoculars, called new coordinates to the battery, and the runner remembered the sight as shells landed in the German skirmish lines, blasting squads of infantry, "whole legs . . . flying through the air."[36]

That same day, Captain Thomas Barber, still repairing the road around Cuisy, met the commandant of a battalion of French light tanks returning along the road from Montfaucon. Barber asked the French officer how it was going. The Frenchman professed astonishment at the conduct of the AEF: "In four years I've never seen the like of this. Your men are all over the terrain, fully exposed to the Boche." Had the Germans had more artillery in position, the casualties would have been catastrophic. As it was, they were merely devastating, thousands killed and wounded for little gain. The French officer also recounted frequent incidents of skulking. "They tell your men to advance; they say the Boche are there; they do not advance. I am sent up to lead them with my tanks. There are no Boche in front of them. They see me coming. They cry—'The Boche! The Boche!'—throw down their guns and run!" He reflected for a moment, then added kindly: "They are green troops; we would once have done the same."

Dramas like these bought plenty of time for the exhausted frontline divisions to be replaced with fresh units from the corps and army reserves. Busloads of troops were cautiously sent forward with ration carts and small-arms ammunition. Everything else—artillery and ammo columns—had to be sidetracked to make room for the arriving and departing troops and casualties. Barber noted that the already-calamitous traffic problems became even worse. The main front-to-rear road at Montfaucon was blocked completely on October 1, with trucks lucky to advance one hundred yards in an hour, and they'd been crawling like this for days. Barber saw American wounded coming back, crammed into empty ammo trucks under a steady rain. "The wounded were in a deplorable condition; half-starved and burning with fever." The only water they got was what drivers could scoop out of roadside ditches. There was no straw in the trucks, and few blankets or coats. "They were being bumped along at this incredibly slow pace hour after hour, with no hope of relief. Some of them were screaming, out of their head with fever, and there was a good deal of groaning and yelling."

Barber found himself walking along the road, faster than the crawling trucks, when a man stuck his head over the side of a truck: "Captain, we are in awful trouble here, will you help us?" Barber stood on the wheel, looked in and never forgot the sight: the floor of the truck was two feet deep in wounded men, all tangled together as if they'd been thrown in over the side, some unconscious, most semiconscious, sharing a few coats and blankets. In the middle was a green, rotting corpse, all tangled with the living wounded and stiff as a board. "Dead and living all stank," Barber recalled. They'd been inching along this road for two days, long enough for the man to die and begin decomposing. Barber collared a passing soldier and together they climbed into the truck, extricated the corpse, and heaved him over the tailboard: "We swung him a couple of times and slung him off the road. He hit the bank and turned a cartwheel without bending; so stiff he was."[37]

Foch's staff chief, General Maxime Weygand, descended on Pershing's headquarters at Souilly on October 1 with a proposal to reinforce the French Second Army with two American divisions—the 77th and the 28th—and insert it into the Argonne between Gouraud's Fourth Army and Pershing's First Army. Everyone assumed that the idea had originated with Clemenceau, to get Pershing moving. Pershing took it personally: "I will not stand for this letter which disparages myself and the American Army and the American effort." The attacks on Pershing's independence had resumed, the Allied governments and armies trying to drive a wedge between General Pershing and President Wilson to lay hands on the US Army. Pershing was losing weight and looked haggard and gray. He was desperate for a victory and hoped he'd get one from his best divisions, which were now rotating back into line.[38]

The US 1st Division arrived in the Exermont ravine after juddering up the roads from the rear. Getting off their buses, the veterans of the Big Red One passed the withdrawing troops of the 35th Division and said things like, "What's the trouble around here? Anything need fixin'?" They had, as their commander said, "a peculiar pride of service and a high state of morale" compared to other units. The Germans feared them and nervously followed their deployments. A lieutenant of the 1st Division recorded what his men saw as they picked their way through mud and shell holes to relieve the 35th Division: "Splintered trees, machine-gunned knee high, and dead bodies of fallen Germans and horses." The same shuttle-bus process was used to relieve the 79th and 37th Divisions, which went back and were replaced by the 3rd and 32nd Divisions. The retiring 79th Division, a witness wrote, "looked more like a defeated force than a victorious one," most of the men afflicted by shell shock, "eyes sunken with a dead look." A soldier of the 32nd Division remembered making room for the retiring men of the 37th Division, who'd been hit hard first taking Montfaucon and then pressing that attack north into Cierges. "They were muddy, haggard, unshaven, all showing signs of utter weariness"—and one of them called out to the boys of the 32nd Division, most of whom were replacements from Michigan and Wisconsin, "Better make your peace with your Jesus, fellows, before you go up there." They heard him in silence, knowing it was true. "It's our time to be fed into the bloody mill," one remarked.[39]

The 28th Division, having lost 6,149 killed and wounded and 1,200 to the flu, was finally relieved by the 82nd Division on October 7. The 82nd's commander was fifty-seven-year-old General George Duncan, who'd been sacked as commander of the 77th Division on the Vesle. Duncan was the rare American general in the war given a second chance, chiefly because he'd threatened to enlist as a private in the army if sent home to the States. Duncan looked anxiously at his new command. The troops had been sleeping in the open on wet ground and subsisting on raw meat and potatoes for twelve horrid days. They looked anything but fresh.[40]

Near Cuisy, Captain Barber continued his roadwork, watching the relieving divisions move up and taking cover from German barrages. After one of them, he and his second in command emerged

As US divisions rotated out of the front line in the Meuse-Argonne, they were, a witness recalled, "muddy, haggard, unshaven, all showing signs of utter weariness." As fresh troops passed them going to the front, the exhausted Doughs would yell things like, "Better make your peace with your Jesus, fellows, before you go up there." Here, men of the US 28th Division, reduced by 6,149 killed, stream gratefully out of the line for a rest. (National Archives)

among a string of horses tied to some bushes. One of them had had a leg sheared off below the hock by a shell splinter. Blood flowed from the stump and the horse nickered miserably. "Go over and kill that horse," Barber ordered. The lieutenant strode over and placed his Colt .45 against the star on the horse's forehead and fired. The horse fell at the report, but then staggered back to his three hooves and stood there quivering, blood-drenched, staring at his tormentor. The lieutenant went white as a sheet, took the horse by the nose and fired again into his head. The horse fell a second time, then climbed back on its three good legs, staring dully at the lieutenant. Barber yelled, "For God's sake, stick it in his ear and *kill* him!" He did, this time. Barber decided that he'd never in his life seen a man so shaken. "His morale was completely shattered."[41]

When the Big Red One relieved the hard-luck 35th Division, they too were most struck by the shattered morale of the Kansas-Missouri National Guardsmen. Parts of the 35th Division had fought valiantly, advancing six miles across German killing fields. Other parts of the division had fought less well. General Peter Traub's brigades had simply abandoned mountains of supplies: surgical stores, food, stretchers, rifles, machine guns, cartridges, and stacks of shells. In one location alone, relieving troops from the Big Red One came across 4,000 rounds of 155mm, four lots of 75mm, nine tons of oats, five tons of hay, 600,000 rounds of Chauchat ammo, 350,000 rounds of .30-caliber, 1,000 mortar rounds, and seven tool wagons filled with picks and shovels. "No attempt was made to invoice or even account for any of this property," a 1st Division accountant indignantly scribbled. Everywhere they went inside the 35th's old perimeter, the men of the 1st found discarded rifles and ammo and dead horses. Every foxhole and dugout was crammed with jettisoned supplies: quarters of beef, canned bacon, tins of salmon, corned beef, and loaves of stale bread. There was so much food that the troops of the 1st Division were still munching their way through it when they resumed the attack at last on October 4. The 35th Division had simply walked away from its massive ammo dump at Baulny.

Troops of the 1st Division found 120 horses of the 35th Division left tied to a picket line south of Charpentry and forgotten. They'd been gassed in the meantime and hung dead in their traces. Another team of eighty-six horses—left harnessed to their guns and wagons by Doughs who'd fled—had all been butchered by shrapnel and shell fragments. Beside the horses were abandoned wagons filled with blankets and coats. Officers of the 1st could find no officers of the 35th to coordinate the handover of the sector. "The men said they didn't know where their officers were." Another group of men from the 1st Division happened on a clearing fringed with bushes that infantry of the 35th had used for cover. Inside, they found no men but three hundred rifles, several Browning heavy machine guns, pistols, ammo, grenades, full packs, and even helmets, with the insignia of the 35th Division. The men had all too obviously just removed everything that impeded flight and run away from the Germans. Seething, I Corps's inspector noted: "This is *exactly* what one expects of a National Guard division."[42]

In an American war effort that was balky everywhere, this National Guard division from the heartland vied for balkiest. Its disgrace wouldn't sit easily with the political ambitions of its members. A chief criticism of the American military system, even before the war, was the weakness of the National Guard: the troops were poorly trained and gently disciplined by officers elected by their troops or appointed by the state governor. The attack of the 35th Division having failed, Missouri's governor, Henry Allen, would counterattack in February 1919, appearing before the House Rules Committee in Washington with testimony from the men and officers of the Missouri National Guard to accuse Pershing of not feeding his troops and then sending them against German artillery and machine guns without artillery and machine guns of their own, to say nothing of tanks and aircraft or even grenades, trench mortars, or field telephones, the last to call off friendly fire, which, when the American artillery had appeared, had been the frequent result. "The infantry was several times caught by our own barrage." The poor victims, Governor Allen charged, "lay for 48 hours without receiving attention." The army wondered if the ambition of some of the canned Missouri National Guard officers to run for Congress might have something to do with this sally. In its own defense, the army pointed out that the 35th was the only division to demand a public inquiry despite its middling casualties— sixteenth-highest of thirty divisions engaged in the war—and then dusted off all of its reports from the relieving 1st Division to prove that, in fact, the 35th Division had not only been armed and fed but had left its arms, food, wagons, and horses to the enemy.[43]

That unpleasantness lay in the future. In the present, in the dense Argonne Forest, General Robert Alexander's 77th Division continued its attacks to locate and destroy German batteries using the cover of the woods to fire into the exposed flank of units like the Big Red One relieving the 35th Division in the Aire Valley. Since the forest extended for miles above and below Montfaucon, the Germans couldn't be maneuvered out of it until the Americans had pushed at least as far north as Grandpré, an elevated citadel of the Kriemhilde Line, guarded by the stream and swamps of the Aire and carved into machine-gun and battery positions. Of course rapid progress by Gouraud's French Fourth Army west of the forest would have maneuvered the Germans out, but Gouraud, awaiting American progress to facilitate his own, was not exactly bounding ahead. General Alexander observed that French inactivity west of the Argonne made his job inside the forest far more difficult, as the French west of the woods were supposed to advance, outflank the Germans, and propel the 77th Division forward. "The French made no move to carry out their part of the program," Alexander later wrote. As a result, the fighting in the Argonne was far more vicious than it should have been, as beleaguered Doughboys, sniped at from every direction, fought in small groups. Attempts to get field artillery forward foundered in the traffic, mud, and trees. "Hell is not paved with good intentions but with mud," one wit cracked.[44]

Pershing described the misery: "In the chill rain of dark nights our engineers had to build new roads beyond no man's land and build bridges. Our gunners put their shoulders to wheels and drag-ropes to bring their guns through the mire." To maintain any semblance of a forward-moving line, ground had to be held once taken. If not, the Germans would infiltrate machine-gun units into the gaps, fire into the American flanks, and press the line back. The 77th Division's famous Lost Battalion, which would shortly go missing in the Argonne, was never actually lost. It simply pushed through the German line—severing its communications to headquarters—and refused to back out, its commander, Captain Charles Whittlesey, choosing to hold his ground (and communicate with headquarters by carrier pigeon) rather than retreat to safety. It was easy to see why, when Whittlesey's superiors, desperate to placate Pershing, were issuing orders like this: "If I find anybody ordering a withdrawal from ground once held, I will see that he leaves the Service."[45]

General Wagstaff, head of the British mission in Pershing's headquarters, wrote a secret assessment on September 30, based on notes he'd made while observing the US First Army in action. "The attack was made by new divisions, none of them had a proper fight except the 33rd on the right, who did the best, although the 91st, a fine lot of Westerners, did well the first day too. The 79th were sticky and the 28th and 77th made a hash of the wood fighting." III Corps's commander, General Robert Lee Bullard, said that the problem with New York's 77th Division was that they were all city boys who lacked the ability to find their way around in the dark; they "showed a talent for getting lost." That wouldn't have been the case with the 91st Division, draftees from the wide-open spaces of Washington, Oregon, California, Montana, Wyoming, Utah, and Idaho. And yet all infantry units had problems in woods, as the 90th Alamo Division, newly arrived from Texas, reminded its commanders. Troops (and officers) tended to spread out, losing contact with each other, and all tended to walk parallel to features of the ground, regardless of the direction. The only reliable way to advance on the right track was with the compass, which few were good at, even officers. The compasses malfunctioned anyway because of all the shell splinters lying around, which queered the magnetic bearings.[46]

Haig, Pétain, and Foch, who had no need of compasses to find their way around their familiar headquarters, wondered just what the Americans were doing in theirs. Pershing wasn't advancing at all. Major Gerald Geiger, another British liaison officer, relayed the deflating news that he'd been given by Pershing's staff on September 30:

> There has been no attack today. . . . They will not be ready for at least three days. . . . This is entirely due to road congestion and the impossibility of getting munitions forward. Raw divisions will not go forward unless protected by a barrage. If the assistance of divisional artillery is considered sufficient, they ought to be able to go on four days from now, but if corps and army artillery are needed, a twelve days' delay is likely. Road control is bad because it is under divisions, not the higher formations. This has led to an entire disregard of orders. It is a chaotic state of affairs. . . . An elaborate scheme on the French system is being hatched at G.H.Q., but it will not begin working till the spring![47]

14

MEUSE-ARGONNE: ROMAGNE

Anyone staring from the wet, cold, foggy American lines toward the wooded ridges of the Kriemhilde-Stellung on October 1, 1918, would have supposed that even spring 1919 was too optimistic for an American breakthrough here. One of Pershing's officers, who'd observed the Battle of the Somme in 1916, wondered if this push wasn't ending just as tragically: "My mortal fear was that we too must have our Arras and Passchendaele and fight on through 1919 until we numbered our mourning mothers and wives by hundreds of thousands."[1]

Hindenburg's plan, to hold the exhausted British and French in check on the Antwerp-Meuse Line and defeat the American attempt to smash its pivot, seemed achievable. The British and French were stalled and critically low on infantry and officers, and the Americans were stuck in the mud. Pershing had unwisely packed a quarter of a million assault troops into a space just twelve miles wide that had been preregistered by the Germans for stunningly accurate artillery and machine-gun fire, and the results were gruesome, Pershing already needing ninety thousand replacements to bring his depleted divisions back up to strength. All the Germans needed at this stage was time.

German trenches, revetted with logs, in the Kriemhilde-Stellung at Bantheville. This was just the visible summit of a fighting position that extended deep underground in concrete dugouts and tunnels, where the German defenders sheltered from the cold, wet weather, and American fire. (National Archives)

They'd fought against time in the spring and summer—to win before the Americans arrived in force. They now fought *for* time—to drag the Allies through another winter of casualties, disease, and disappointment. If they could hold out on the Antwerp-Meuse Line, they might collapse the bickering Allied coalition and secure the mild peace they needed. Meanwhile, Haig and Lloyd George were at war with each other, Haig visiting London in October to tell the War Cabinet "that the Government should say what they could do for our Armies, and that if they could not, or would not, do much, they should stop the war." Anything could happen, as a Rumanian prince quipped to the journalist Charles Repington at a lunch in London: "The Boches have tried their utmost to win it for four years and have not succeeded and the Allies have tried their hardest to lose it and have similarly failed. Who then can tell who will *win*?"[2]

The Germans had fallen back only as far as the Kriemhilde-Stellung, which they defended not as an organized trench system but as an improvised zone of combat snaking through the Meuse-Argonne's rolling hills, wooded heights, and elevated villages: a deep area of interlocked combat positions. German tactics for this endgame were wholly defensive, based chiefly on machine guns and artillery, not infantry counterattacks. By now German manpower had become too precious, and the object was simply to kill French, British, and American attackers until they broke. They'd kill plenty of Americans here. The US 32nd Division was ordered to assault the center of the Kriemhilde-Stellung, on the northern edge of the Bois de Bantheville. The 1st Division drew the broken hilly country between Exermont and the Bois de Romagne, which rolled along a chain of two-hundred-meter-high heights named—with military aridity—Hills 272, 269, and 240. They each provided the Germans with clear observation and fields of fire. Officers would recall advancing toward the Kriemhilde Line in bloody leaps, digging in, and then forcing their men to their feet in the night to make them run in place to ward off hypothermia. The 42nd Rainbow Division was charged with breaching the line at Hill 288 and the Côte de Châtillon, key knobs that dominated this broad stretch of country. Having already bled heavily in the Marne salient, the Rainbows would face even stiffer resistance here. They were a tough unit, known for some of the foulest mouths in the Army: "Fuck you, and if you got any sisters, fuck them too," being a typical salutation of the division's New York Irish.[3]

The US 77th Division resumed its halting advance through the Argonne. Major Charles Whittlesey, a battalion commander in the 308th Infantry Regiment, probed north on October 2 with 670 men. Whittlesey, a thirty-four-year-old graduate of Williams College and Harvard Law, was part of a larger operation to seize the German army's Palette Pavilion, a fortified complex that swept the southern

Argonne with fire and fired into the flanks of French units trying to advance up the valley of the Aisne west of the forest. A week of combat (and skulking) had cut Whittlesey's battalion strength in half. On October 3, he realized that he hadn't been part of a broad advance but that his seven weak companies—down to 650 men—had passed through a gap in the German lines and were now marooned in the rear of the Germans, near the road from Binarville to Apremont, in a gully near the Charlevaux Mill. Ringing them were German mortars, machine guns, riflemen, and flamethrowers. Here was a perfect example of why ground could not be yielded to the Germans. They used every gap and bulge in the line to surround advancing American units and fire into their flanks. So it went for Whittlesey's Lost Battalion, which was encircled, mortared, and machine-gunned in a small pocket of forest. One day into the ordeal, the battalion had already suffered 222 casualties, including 82 dead. Whittlesey, totally surrounded, had six homing pigeons, which he now employed to seek help, sending them flapping back to American headquarters with news of his predicament.[4]

Fortunately for Whittlesey, Pershing was preparing to resume the offensive—suspended after the protracted and messy struggle for Montfaucon—even as the major went missing. As long as the American lines remained frozen, Whittlesey would remain lost. Once they advanced, he'd be found. Pershing had ordered a resumption of the American offensive on October 4. He aimed at the Kriemhilde Line, from Grandpré at the top of the Argonne through Romagne and over to the Meuse Heights, the positions he'd vowed to seize on the first day of the offensive over a week earlier. V Corps, which had been mauled and demoralized in its push up to Montfaucon, was entirely replaced: General Beaumont Buck's US 3rd Division relieved the 79th; General William Haan's 32nd Division replaced the 37th; the 91st Division was designated corps reserve. Pershing ordered "lessons learned" from Montfaucon hastily disseminated to all units. American divisions would have to show more initiative and operate across corps boundaries when necessary. The 4th Division of Bullard's III Corps had left the 79th Division of Cameron's V Corps to its fate, explaining that it hadn't been authorized to use Cameron's roads. Pershing deplored these excuses, which reeked of peacetime routines. In war, results were all that mattered. Liaison between infantry and artillery had to be improved. Infantry commanders had to stop cramming reinforcements forward, which led to crowding and panic. It would be better to send them obliquely at a German flank, or not at all.[5]

On October 4 the Americans renewed their attack. Harried by Foch, Pershing mercilessly drove his generals to accomplish the impossible—break through hardened German positions with frontal assaults. He expressed his "great dissatisfaction with the progress of the attacking divisions." To the Doughboys, it must have seemed like a cruel joke, voiced by a faraway château-general more concerned with his reputation than their lives. In fact, Pershing was undergoing a personal crisis. Blocked by Gallwitz, vilified by Clemenceau, undermined by Foch, patronized by Haig, maligned by his own whispering generals, he was nearing his own breaking point, his staff alarmed at his appearance: stooped, shrunken, his hair turned gray, his face sallow and lined. During one drive between the front lines and his headquarters in early October, Pershing suffered a nervous collapse witnessed by his aides, sobbing to his dead wife: "Frankie, Frankie, my God, sometimes I don't know how I can go on."[6]

A veteran compared Pershing's situation to that of a fullback who, having broken through the line of scrimmage, runs into the linebackers, the briefest thrill of escape succeeded by a crushing tackle. III Corps followed the Brieulles-Cunel road, V Corps took Gesnes, and I Corps advanced two miles among the wooded hills of the Argonne and Aire Valley. In these places, the German linebackers met the American fullbacks and stopped them cold. III Corps's 4th Division took three days to cover just a mile to the Bois de Fays. "I've never seen so many dead," a disbelieving private wrote of the experience. "Here is where it takes willpower to go on and face death."[7]

Death lurked also on the 4th Division's flank, where General Adelbert Cronkhite's US 80th Division fought to take the Bois des Ogons. Each of his attacks was shot down, German counterbarrages wiping out whole waves of men the moment they rose to advance. Sick with fear and inadequately trained, Cronkhite's men failed to hug their barrages closely, giving the Germans time to emerge from cover to kill them. Survivors were stricken: one historian began his account of the battle, ninety years later, with the story of a private in the 80th, a sunny thirty-four-year-old family man, who returned home to Virginia a zombie—a sleepless, speechless stranger to his wife and children till he drank himself to death. The field messages exchanged by American artillery during these actions, which ducked in and out of gullies and woods, revealed the difficulty of combining arms in terrain like this. "I directed HILT to thicken the barrage by putting more of his 75s on it, to make it solid for 800 yards," one artillery officer signaled back to headquarters. "Nothing's been done by HILT. At 1:45 DENVER called and said shots were falling in Bois de Fays. I called HILT and said don't get in there with your fire." There were Doughboys there. "He said he wasn't in the woods and in view of the reports there was nothing to do but cease firing. I told him he must <u>not</u> cease firing, but continue fire on the line north of the Bois de Ogons. That was three hours before he called me and told me he hadn't fired a shot."[8]

Rifts like this, opening between the confused American battery commanders, gave the Germans a respite and explained the frequent Doughboy complaints that they weren't given artillery support. Cronkhite despaired and pleaded with Bullard to call off the attack on the Bois des Ogons. Bullard's reply showed how Pershing kept the line moving forward by appealing to the fears and ambition of his generals. "Give it up and you're a goner," Bullard warned Cronkhite. "You'll lose your command in twenty-four hours." A lieutenant in the 80th Division estimated that all of the officers in his company by this time were "nerve-shattered . . . or on the verge of it." No matter—Cronkhite attacked again, and took the wood. He'd lost hundreds more men but saved his command—a sordid transaction familiar to every general in the war. "If this had lasted much longer," a private in Cronkhite's division noted from the damp woods, "we would all have been crazy." He remembered staring horror-struck at a row of

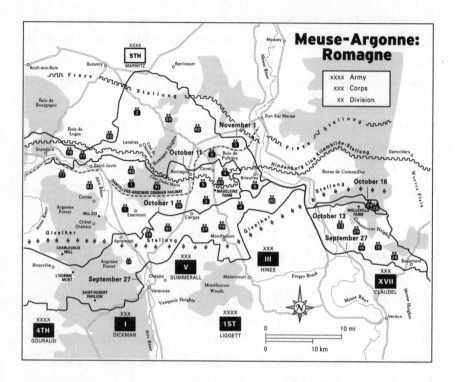

dead Germans gassed to death near Nantillois: "Expressions on their faces showed that they had been gassed and died in agony. Many still had their masks on and had been mowed down by machine gun fire. Their coat collars were torn open in their struggle for breath, and they had turned a dark purple from the effects of the gas. Some were burnt from the mustard gas, lying in shell holes as though scalded by boiling water."[9]

To Cronkhite's left, V Corps's 3rd Division was driven back from its objective, the Bois de Cunel. The division's light artillery sprayed the German positions without effect: "You can't make a siege gun out of a 75," a Doughboy cracked. The American guns here, firing shrapnel at Germans in bunkers, had all the impact of a little boy windmilling his arms, or so said a witness. The 3rd Division commander, General Beaumont Bonaparte Buck, didn't survive the reverse. Pershing visited his headquarters, noted the demoralization and the gaping holes left by skulking and casualties, and then relieved Buck and sent him home to Mississippi with a colonel's rank. The demotion couldn't have been easy to swallow, the AEF's own intelligence allowing that "the Germans had prepared these positions to hold" and manned them with fresh troops, the first-class reserves they'd been keeping for the final struggle. The fighting stalled at Cunel and raged day and night, the Germans firing flares and patrolling aggressively in front of their positions to thwart surprise attacks.[10]

The lines along the Kriemhilde-Stellung were so close that the Doughboys could hear the Germans talking inside their positions and the Germans could hear the Americans; if they overheard someone order, say, Private Kolchak to fetch some grenades, the Germans in the Bois de Cunel would yell, "Hey you, Cupjack, pring dose krenades over here!" The slopes and woods rang with taunts, the Doughboys slandering the kaiser, the Germans the president. The villages of Cunel and Brieulles had to be seized in order to take the last of the "American Army First Objectives," push the salient deeper into the German lines, and force the Germans out of the Argonne. With the Germans and Americans so close, infantry commanders sometimes had to cancel protective barrages and go in with bayonets, as some exchanges between American batteries made clear: "They're going to try to rush the M.G. nests in the Bois de Cunel with bayonets and want our people notified."[11]

Sometimes everyone became confused—an airplane would drop a message to corps artillery warning of a big German troop concentration, the corps artillery would insist that troops in that location must be American, and then someone else would appear to say that, whoever they were, they were already being fired on by American artillery. Pershing ordered Claudel's French XVII Corps to attack on its five-mile front east of the Meuse to divert the German artillery there and relieve the pressure on his men west of the river, but the poilus made no progress. Pershing was stunned by the German resistance; this was "some of the hardest fighting of the campaign, with the enemy striving to hold every foot of ground." The American sector was so narrow and crowded and roads so scarce that the German positions couldn't be bypassed. They had to be taken, as they "were of vital importance to the continuation of the general advance."[12]

The US 3rd and 32nd Divisions attacked again in the center of the American line on October 4, launching five unsuccessful attacks on the Bois de Morine, which was not taken till the next day. The Germans were enfilading the valley south of Romagne so densely with artillery and machine guns that troops couldn't even attempt to cross it in daylight. "The Germans had held this ground for years," Corporal John Barkley recalled. "They knew it down to the smallest furrow." With flanking artillery and machine-gun fire—and little American artillery support—it was bloody work getting forward anywhere. American guns would open fire and then stop because they'd run out of ammo or couldn't be hauled up the primitive roads fast enough to assist the infantry with direct fire.[13]

The Germans, their supply lines functioning smoothly, would use their machine-gun screens to halt American attacks on ground already graphed by the German artillery, which would then open up on the crouching, frozen Doughboys. If the Doughs were trying to follow a rolling barrage into the German lines, the German machine gunners would fire into the Americans until they stopped and lost contact with the protective barrage. "Every minute's delay subjects our troops to destructive hostile artillery fire," General Hunter Liggett raged to the generals of his I Corps. "Employment of all arms and all means available must be developed to the fullest extent." The Doughboys, their logistics still a mess, were attacking with a derisory fraction of their artillery, machine guns, and flamethrowers, or even the smaller weapons they had available stored in crates and wagons behind the lines: trench mortars, one-pounders, and the newly arrived Browning Automatic Rifles (BARs).[14]

For now, the Doughboys took German positions with brute force. Barkley's battalion was under regular fire from a concealed big-caliber German gun on its left front. The cannon would fire from behind a camouflage screen, kill Americans, fall silent, then fire again. No one could locate the mystery gun. At dusk on October 3, the eve of the renewed push, Barkley finally sighted the flash and went to his major, asking permission to take out the gun. "Get a patrol together," the major said. "Kill the outfit. Don't come staggering back with them.

We don't want any prisoners." In this tortured landscape, patrols like this were as likely to be shot by their own men—who were "apt to shoot first and ask questions afterward"—as by the Germans. The men in Barkley's patrol crawled up to the gun emplacement with four grenades each and found it hidden in a deep excavation, shrouded in camouflage netting. It was a 105mm howitzer. They threw in their grenades, killed the crew, and then disabled the piece by packing rocks down the muzzle with a pick handle and throwing the clearing rod into the woods. It was only by these individual fights that the battle progressed, copse to copse, hill to hill, wood to wood. Barkley armed himself differently in that atmosphere of "close fighting." He swapped his rifle for a Winchester sawed-off shotgun and went forward with a pistol, thirty-five rounds of ammo in clips, a trench knife, and grenades.[15]

In the Argonne Forest, the plight of Major Whittlesey's Lost Battalion became increasingly hideous, the Americans barely concealed on the slopes of a deep ravine, the Germans dropping grenades on them, wounded Doughboys screaming "Mama, mama, mama" as they bled out, Whittlesey bravely rallying his thirsty, hungry, exhausted men and soundlessly crying himself to sleep at night. On October 5, Whittlesey sent one of his last precious pigeons to call in artillery fire on the fringes of his own position. One of his platoons vanished under this curtain of fire. This was hardly surprising. Trying to hit Whittlesey's besiegers without hitting Whittlesey's men was, as a veteran put it, like "a battery in the Hollywood Hills striving to shell the unseen spectators in the Los Angeles Coliseum without injuring two football teams playing between the fifteen-yard lines on the field."[16]

As Whittlesey struggled to survive in his patch of the Argonne, he would have heard the bloodiest day in the history of the US 2nd Division—already savaged once in Belleau Wood—playing out on the Blanc Mont Ridge west of the Argonne Forest. Although the Allies criticized Pershing for the slow speed of his advance, he at least had advanced six miles. Hung up by the Blanc Mont—a scarred, steeply rising ridge overlooking the flat country of Champagne—French

Fourth Army commander Henri Gouraud had only gone three. He was hardly advancing on the edge of the Argonne, prompting a fierce rebuke from Foch to Pétain: "Yesterday, 3 October, we witnessed a battle that was not commanded, a battle that was not pushed, a battle that was not brought together and in consequence a battle in which there was no exploitation of the results obtained." The French, Bullard remarked at this time, "were fighting warily, with little offense, without the élan for which they have always been famed. They were weary now." The poilus were either frightened recruits or old veterans with stripes on their sleeves for multiple tours and wounds. "They faced the enemy, but they faced him without heart." They "put no push into their attacks." As an army, the French had all bought into Pétain's simple formula: "Le feu tue" (Firepower kills). The French wouldn't storm positions with infantry. They would grind them up with artillery or wait for someone else to storm them.[17]

Gouraud was supposed to have pushed the Germans off the Blanc Mont and back to the Aisne, helping Pershing to get past the obstacle of the Argonne and through the Kriemhilde-Stellung, but instead the French army commander remained stuck fifteen miles south of the Aisne. This was, as the Marines of the 2nd Division noted, "the Champagne sector, which was one of the last of the old German lines," the other original lines having been freely relinquished by Hindenburg to improve his position. The Blanc Mont—a line of buttes running in a southwesterly direction down to the Suippe River—had so much tactical value that it couldn't be improved upon. The Germans were here to stay; if the Blanc Mont fell, they'd have to pull back from the outskirts of Reims—a ruined ghost town that had been raked by German artillery since 1914—and its vital roads and rail yards. In fact, they'd have to pull all the way back to the Aisne, a retreat of twenty miles, as little of the terrain behind the Blanc Mont was suitable for defense. The Blanc Mont massif glowered over the region; towns and villages beneath it had been abandoned by their French inhabitants, used for a time as billets by the Germans, and then, as the Americans and French approached, subjected to the usual vengeance: houses burned and booby-trapped. The kaiser had stood atop the Blanc Mont in July to observe the launch of his abortive Peace Offensive.[18]

The French infantry were no longer reliable attacking troops; they were by now, one American veteran noted, "taking every care to stay alive, with habitual skill." The African American 93rd Division that Pershing had entrusted to Gouraud *did* attack, one of its regiments suffering 33 percent casualties, inspiring a Tin Pan Alley ditty about their exploits with the refrain, "Instead of picking melons off the vine, you'll find 'em picking Germans off the Rhine." But not just yet. Gouraud summoned the US 2nd Division to take the Blanc Mont by storm. The French, having assaulted the place in years past, had no appetite for it this year: the green and golden slopes of the Blanc Mont had been scoured to a bare chalky white by years of shellfire; hence the name, "White Mount." Two German divisions held the crest of the mount and its neighboring heights, their trenches scraped from the chalk rock and reinforced with concrete. General John Lejeune resolved to attack the flanks of the position across what he called the "hideously battle-scarred country"; his Marine brigade would take the left flank, his army brigade the right flank. If successful, they'd converge on the summit, smashing down the principal barrier to the French Fourth Army's progress.[19]

Attacking in some sectors without artillery support, the 2nd Division lost a heartrending six thousand killed and wounded. Marines and Doughboys overheard anguished phone conversations between battalion commanders, who were ordered to assault the German positions, and their superiors behind the lines, who needed to show "progress" to keep their commands. An army private felt he owed his life to one of these conversations, which went like this:

> It was obvious that the man on the other end of the line, probably the brigade's executive officer, wanted him to do something that the major was violently opposed to. "You don't understand," he pleaded. "The Germans have occupied that area in strength. If I take my battalion there right now, they'll be slaughtered." Then

the headquarters talked for a while. And the major answered them. "I don't give a damn about the map that you have. I've just been there. It's loaded with Boche. I'll lose half my men going in and the other half trying to hold." More talk from headquarters. It was obvious the major was getting nowhere. Finally: "Look, you can remove me from command, you can court-martial me, hell, you can even shoot me. But I'm not ordering the first battalion into that spot until we can clear those Germans out." Then he hung up. Oh my God, we were almost in tears. The poor guy probably ruined his career, but every enlisted man within the sound of his voice wanted to cheer. He was quite a man![20]

Lejeune, notorious for his imperious manner, felt compelled to keep sending the attacks, to break the German defenders and push through. In a long career, the general had never seen a place so desolate—villages and woods gouged from the surface of the earth and shattered debris everywhere. Things that had been lost in previous battles for the ridge were churned to the surface by this one: artillery, machine guns, rifles, helmets, uniform scraps, partly buried horses, and human body parts—"most gruesome of all, arms and legs thrust out of the torn soil," along with "unrecognizable human faces, thrown up to the surface of the ground by exploding shell." Lejeune's command post, named "Wagram" by the French, "was not a home, but a horror," pervaded at all times by the stink of the battlefield and its newly exhumed dead. The Americans now began layering new dead over the old. One witness recalled "the increasing trail of crumpled brown figures" and the "raw smell of blood" on the battlefield. Some of the Marine battalions lost half of their officers. "The afternoon of the 4th of October 1918 was by far the bloodiest and worst day of the war," one of the Marine battalion commanders who survived the fray reported. Everyone in the unit knew that hard fighting was ahead, "but no one dreamed of what the next few hours were to bring."[21]

As the Americans scrambled up the steep ridge, German machine gunners nested in villages like Saint-Étienne and others infiltrated behind the attacking Americans so that they were effectively surrounded and "receiving galling fire from three directions." The French, who'd failed to take the ridge in three days of fighting before the 2nd Division took over, were now supposed to advance on Lejeune's left, supporting his attacks toward the crest. The poilus retreated instead, exposing the Americans to fire from four sides. "We need support on our left flank," a US company commander frantically signaled. "The French have not come up and our left is in the air." Lejeune recalled one French division that did come up—the 170th—but when he attempted to use it, he was told that "it could be used for defensive purposes only, and not under *any* circumstances for offensive purposes."[22]

It was through unheroic arrangements like this that Pétain and Foch glued the cracked French army back together, but at what price? Without the Americans, how would the demoralized poilus have attacked and *won* anywhere? Unsupported on the left, Lejeune's brigades veered to the right—Germans on their left and rear pouring in fire from machine guns and field artillery. The Marines and Doughs charged ahead and took the summit, rushing into the teeth of those chalk stone trenches. A third or more of the men and officers in every company were gunned down. "No one but those present will ever know or appreciate what the battalion went through during the charge up this hill," a Marine major noted. The last German position alone had contained sixty-five machine guns, angled to cover every inch of rising ground. "We shot the tar out of the Boche," the major muttered after seizing the ridge and repulsing the last of the desperate German counterattacks.[23]

The French arrived in the afternoon to mop up after the Americans had taken the ridge. Their casualties hadn't been negligible—in bastions of the Blanc Mont like Essen Hook, Lejeune counted more than one hundred French corpses in a two-acre lot—but the US 2nd Division had been the spearhead, clearing the field for Gouraud all the way to the Aisne. Pétain called it "the greatest achievement of 1918" and tried to spread credit for its capture from the Americans, who'd done it, to the French general commanding their corps. The Marines replied in kind, taking the British classic "Mademoiselle from Armentières" and giving it a sour new verse: "The General won the Croix de Guerre / But the son of a bitch wasn't even there." The Germans were in no doubt of who'd taken it. One of them gave himself up on October 3 and said: "The Americans have a reputation for irresistible courage." Advancing to relieve the 2nd Division on Blanc Mont, a Doughboy of the 36th Division halted to let a convoy of wounded pass. He never forgot the sight. "Hell, it was filled with wounded Doughboys going to the hospitals—must have been hundreds of them. And they were moaning and crying. Poor devils, must have been shot up bad. As we got closer to the front, I kept wondering if I was going to be one of them."[24]

Back in the Meuse-Argonne, the Big Red One attacked at dawn on October 4, preceded by tanks and a rolling barrage. The 1st Division took Montrebeau by 7 a.m., then struck across the Exermont ravine and into the defenses of the Hindenburg Line's Kriemhilde-Stellung. One lieutenant recalled picking his way across the eerily silent ground overlooked by the hulking German positions when suddenly, without warning, the German fire descended and killed or wounded half of his company at a stroke: "Streaks of screaming red and yellow . . . a smash-bang, and it seems to tear everything loose from you." Four men around him were killed instantly by a shell burst, "cut down to a pile of horrid red guts and blood and meat." He stared in disbelief: it reminded him of a "Christmas hog butchering back on the Texas farm."[25]

The fighting *was* like a butchering, the US 1st Division's battalions, in echelons of two companies, advancing and digging in on a line running northwest of Exermont and south of Hill 240. German field guns, firing into ground they'd measured for defensive fire, destroyed forty-four of forty-seven Allied tanks, killing or wounding more than 80 percent of the tank crews. The 1st Division would fight for a week, losing a stupefying 9,400 killed and wounded to advance four miles. "We were simply in a big black spot," a platoon leader recalled. The artillery fire was excoriating: "The intensity of it simply enters your heart and brain and tears every nerve to pieces."[26]

On October 5, the 1st Division took Hill 240 with grievous casualties from machine guns and artillery, both hitting the Doughboys with direct fire from front and flanks. Attempts to push into the space north of Hill 240 failed, the Germans halting the 1st Division's pursuit after they'd gone just five hundred yards. "The enemy machine gunners held their posts until actually bayoneted," the dazed commander of the 18th Infantry Regiment reported as he moved his command post into Exermont, which had finally been cleared. One Doughboy, examining positions captured by the 1st Division, expressed astonishment: "The enemy had machine gun bunkers made of concrete, and their dugouts were framed in concrete, with electric lights and telephones. It was amazing that human flesh could endure what had been inflicted on the Big Red One in capturing these positions."[27]

The Doughs, an officer in another division observed, "had in their own minds given up hope of surviving and their psychology was unconsciously that of sentenced men to whom every day was a reprieve." With supply lines blocked, artillery ineffective, and the men reduced to clubbing their way through the German lines, General Hanson Ely, commanding a brigade of the 2nd Division, remarked that it had become a war of remnants: "Battles are won by remnants, remnants of units, remnants of material, remnants of morale, remnants of intellectual effort." Those remnants who'd survived October 4 tried again on October 5 to push through dominating lines of German machine guns in the Bois de Boyan and the necklace of woods around it, the 1st Division suffering more "extremely heavy casualties." Officers would be busy for months afterward recommending men for decorations, their citations, like that of Lieutenant Samuel I. Parker of the 28th Infantry Regiment, describing the escalating madness of the combat in the Meuse-Argonne, where the Germans refused to give ground: "Lt. Parker showed total and absolute disregard for personal danger by walking up to a German Machine Gun which fired directly at him while he advanced toward it for a distance of 150 yards, and killed the gunner with his pistol." The neighboring 26th Infantry Regiment had the same problems, trying to break through elements of the German 52nd Division, then the 5th Guard Division, both first-class units. Zero hours had to be repeatedly postponed to get rolling barrages out in front of the Doughboys, the barrages hardly denting the well-sheltered German positions.[28]

American machine guns, detached in their own battalions, often failed even to reach the infantry because of the German machine guns already in place: "We have enemy machine guns directly in front and machine gun crossfires from our left flank," the commander of a machine-gun company trying to reach a battalion of the 1st Division messaged. "We cannot get in touch with the Infantry." Infantry officers would charge, regroup, message back their casualties, and then, to guide their groping artillery, sketch their forlorn position in red—"line for counter-attack"—surmounted by blue massifs picked out with blue crosses, each representing a German cannon or machine gun. They hardly needed to add captions like this: "Slope facing us is lined with guns." The US 1st Division's quality was remarkable—pulled together from recruits and replacements, like every other division, it nonetheless had a unique esprit de corps. General James McAndrew, Pershing's chief of staff, praised the Big Red One "for a clean record some of the oldest regiments of the European armies cannot boast—of never having failed to take and hold their objectives on time throughout all the engagements of this war."[29]

Late on October 4, President Wilson received a German diplomatic note in Washington requesting armistice terms on the basis of the Fourteen Points. Initially relieved—their own advances had stopped and they saw no easy way forward against shortening, more stoutly defended German lines—Clemenceau and Lloyd George became alarmed when Wilson, instead of consulting them, withdrew to ponder the German note. Clemenceau now bitterly referred to Wilson as "Jupiter."[30]

The British and French had been carping about American progress in the Meuse-Argonne, but theirs too had stopped. Emerging behind the Hindenburg Line after breaking through the Siegfried-Stellung between Arras and Péronne on September 29, they found themselves with few surviving tanks and eight essentially useless cavalry divisions that couldn't pursue the Germans, even with air support, because of the danger presented by German rear guards with machine guns and artillery. Each Allied step forward under the same pelting rains that were torturing Pershing in the Meuse-Argonne brought new logistical difficulties, for the ground behind them had been desolated by combat and the ground in front by the retiring Germans. Supply trucks stuck in the mud and starving mules and horses died in harness. French and British officers, mainly young and inexperienced now that their elders had been killed, didn't know how to fight their units forward in open warfare. What little training they had was in the slow rhythms of trench warfare.[31]

On October 5, battling on the right flank of the Big Red One for the center of the Kriemhilde Line around Romagne, the US 3rd Division finally took Hill 253 while the 32nd Division took Gesnes and then the Bois de la Morine. The fighting was savage. Private Horace Baker of the 32nd Division remembered vividly the terror felt by the men when platoon leaders selected five-man patrols to walk forward and locate concealed German machine guns. Such patrols were routinely wiped out, and one from Baker's platoon was annihilated on October 6, except for one man, who came flying out of the fog "scared almost to death." He was a recent immigrant, completely unintelligible in any language, able only to pantomime that his patrol had walked into a machine-gun nest. "I don't believe I ever saw anyone in a worse fix from fear than this man was, every muscle of his body was twitching spasmodically and spots chased each other over his face." Baker took all this in from his foxhole and opened his Bible for solace. A soldier passed and muttered: "While you are praying, remember to ask for peace and a return to the States by Christmas."[32]

That would be a tall order. On Hill 253, Corporal John Barkley of the 3rd Division recalled being clubbed to the ground during a German counterattack when a panicked Doughboy landed on top of him crying (in a Brooklyn accent), "Where in hell's the rear?" The New Yorker vanished into the darkness, but Barkley was trapped as night

fell—"There were parties of Germans prowling over the battlefield"—
and so he crawled into a shell hole in the midst of the carnage. The
experience would be etched in his mind forever: "The night all around
was filled with cries, groans and curses. In English. In German. In
languages I didn't know. Cries for water, for help, for death. Once I
heard one boy ask another if he had any chewing gum. . . . Another
boy babbled over and over for hours it seemed to me, 'What is this war?
What's this war for? What is this damned war?'" Crossing through
the woods before dawn the next morning to find a way through the
German lines and back to his division, Barkley and a buddy stumbled
upon a common-enough sight: "In a little hollow we came upon the
bodies of an American sergeant and six privates laid out in a row. It
looked as if they'd been disarmed, lined up and shot. Their pockets
had been ripped open."[33]

To rescue the Lost Battalion and clear the Argonne without
the expected French help on the left, I Corps commander General
Hunter Liggett directed George Duncan's 82nd Division to cross
the bulge created by the 1st Division's push through Exermont, then
strike west across the Aire on a pontoon bridge and into the Argonne. General Duncan, whose career had nearly been destroyed
two months earlier by a false diagnosis of syphilis, now planned to
destroy Germans. He'd rescue Whittlesey and what remained of his
men, clear the fortified complexes at Le Chêne Tondu, Hill 223,
and the village of Chatel-Chéhéry, and cut the German Decauville
railway that snaked alongside the Aire as far south as Apremont,
manning and supplying the German positions in the Argonne. He'd
also drive out the German guns in the woods, which were raking the
French to the west and the Americans to the east. The venture was
risky; the 82nd Division's flanks would be exposed as it approached
the Argonne, and there were no proper march routes inside the forest—just tangled woods and the odd path here and there covered by
German guns. There'd also be no artillery support. The 82nd, like
every division, couldn't get its guns forward through the traffic jams
behind the lines. The men, who marched all night in gas masks because the ground was slicked with mustard gas, would have to defeat

the Germans with only their rifles and the odd trench mortar and light machine gun.[34]

Early on October 8, Corporal Alvin York advanced with the 328th Infantry Regiment on the left flank of the 82nd Division. The battalions of the regiment were stopped cold by German machine guns on Hill 223. Those guns had never been mopped up and now shattered every American attack with well-aimed hundred-round bursts. The German positions in the heights west of Chatel-Chéhéry, a concealed line of machine guns strung between Hills 180, 223, and 244, swept the river bed below, forcing the Doughboys to attack up what was essentially a cliff overhanging the valley road. Sergeant Harry Parsons, Corporal York, and a squad of thirteen men, finding a gap in the cliff, marched past the left flank of Hill 223 and into its rear. They and two other small combat teams were infiltrating the heart of a German division arrayed between the Aire and the Argonne. The staff of a German battalion headquarters, sitting down to breakfast, saw the approaching Americans, ditched their plates, and bellowed the alarm. German machine gunners on the hill, hearing the commotion behind them, turned around to destroy the American flanking column. As the German gunners depressed their guns to rake the Doughboys, Corporal York, originally a conscientious objector who'd refused to break the commandment against killing, braced himself on a tree trunk and opened fire with his US-modified Lee-Enfield rifle. "Every time a head done come up, I knocked it down," York recalled.[35]

When the Germans finally located York, they launched a counterattack toward his position. York killed the charging column of men from back to front, six men and an officer, the officer, leading the charge, the last to fall. York later explained that if he'd worked front to back, the ones at the rear would have had time to take cover and work around his flanks. York then scanned the height for machine gunners and began "splitting skulls" again. By now he'd killed at least twenty Germans while his eight surviving men lay in cover behind him, their rifles leveled at the captured German major and his headquarters detachment. The German major, who'd worked in Chicago before the war and spoke English, finally stood and ordered the Germans around him to surrender. Eighty more Germans came down with their hands in the air.

York hugged the major close and marched him along the hill with his Colt .45 pressed against the back of the German's head. Every time they came into view of a German machine-gun nest, the major would blow his whistle and order the position to surrender. Germans would emerge from the grass and descend with their hands up. They weren't so much demoralized as unsure as to how many Americans had infiltrated their position. Commanding a half platoon, York single-handedly killed 20 Germans and took 132 prisoner. "Well, York," the general in command of York's brigade later exclaimed, "I hear you've captured the whole damned German army." York replied with habitual modesty: "No sir, I only have 132." York was promoted to sergeant and awarded the Medal of Honor. Pershing called him the outstanding civilian soldier of the AEF. Foch called York the outstanding soldier of the entire war. York and his fellows had finally wrested Le Chêne Tondu from Gallwitz, permitting the US First Army to take another big step north.[36]

With Duncan's 82nd Division inside the wood, the Germans fled, and Major Whittlesey—described by journalist Damon Runyon as "a tall, lean-flanked fellow with a funny little smile"—was finally rescued and promoted to lieutenant colonel that night; of his Lost Battalion, only 191 of 670 troops emerged from the Argonne. Like York, Whittlesey would receive a Congressional Medal of Honor for his heroic leadership. He was a model civilian soldier. He'd been among the first to volunteer for the Plattsburg camp and had led his unit through a ghastly ordeal. The men had been trapped under German fire in a narrow oval at the foot of a cliff for several days. The symbolism of the rescue was powerful, one contemporary speculating that if the Germans had destroyed or captured the battalion, the event might have been as scandalous and demoralizing to the American public as Custer's defeat at the Little Bighorn.[37]

But relief at the rescue of the Lost Battalion was quickly followed by wrath. After the Lost Battalion had been recovered—minus 479 casualties—and the line advanced beyond its scarred position, General Robert Alexander, commander of the 77th Division, asked for a staff officer from I Corps headquarters to investigate the 306th Field Artillery Regiment for the "wild firing" during this episode that had probably exterminated one of Whittlesey's platoons. Using one of his six carrier pigeons, Whittlesey had requested 155mm shellfire on the surrounding Germans, and many believed that the barrage had fallen disastrously short. This was a curious parenthesis in what had been and remained an unruly battle filled with friendly-fire deaths. Lieutenant Colonel James Gallogly was assigned the task. Joined by a French chemist, Lieutenant Adrian Leclerc, he hiked around Whittlesey's old position and dug into the fighting pits and craters. They were looking for shell fragments and fuses to determine whether German or American ordnance had killed the New Yorkers.

Gallogly and Leclerc stood in shell holes to determine their newness and whether they'd been excavated by German 77s or American 155s. Leclerc studied the fuses lying scattered about and pronounced them "unquestionably German." The artillery officers under investigation sighed with relief, hastening to add that such mistakes were exceedingly rare, requiring gross errors in the settings for range and deflection that no battery commander worth his salt would authorize, even in the heat of battle, when settings were rechecked after every fifth shot. Poor Whittlesey, an austere New Englander, would bear the burden of the Lost Battalion for the rest of his life: calls for patriotic speeches, whispers that he shouldn't have advanced so far, whispers that he should have withdrawn from the exposed position, letters from his men describing their own anguish since the war. Just three years after the armistice, in November 1921, he killed himself—leaping off a ship sailing from New York to Havana in the middle of the Atlantic Ocean.[38]

Against dogged German resistance, the 1st Division paused several days to regroup, then renewed the attack on the Kriemhilde Line on October 9, suffering more heavy casualties in the woods and along the Fléville-Sommerance road, but they pushed through almost to Sommerance that evening, finding no Germans there the next morning. Fog, clinging to the wet, dripping ridges, caused regular misidentifications and accidents. "We were front company of support battalion," a lieutenant scribbled back to headquarters, "heavy fog, saw figures through it & thought it was 2nd battalion. Found later they were Boche." The army habit of grouping machine guns in their own battalions instead of just giving them to the infantry continued to slow progress: after losing a third of his company and three platoon leaders taking a wood near Sommerance, a company commander sent a runner sprinting back to battalion headquarters: "Can I have two Machine Guns to protect my flanks? There is nobody but Boche in front of me."[39]

Straggling, a massive problem for the AEF throughout this short, sharp campaign, was never officially quantified but showed up in field messages where the fighting was hottest. In its attacks near Sommerance on October 9, a company commander of the 1st Division's 18th Regiment reported back: "Objective reached. Approximate casualties: 37 enlisted, 17 are known casualties; the rest I believe are stragglers." The eighty men left in his company found what shelter they could in a sunken road as they awaited the second phase of the attack in the afternoon, when they'd be expected to relieve the battalion in front of them to press the attack on the Germans. German machine-gun fire from the valley north of Fléville kicked up dirt and sod along the rim of their shelter. Somehow, between midmorning and early afternoon, while the company commander looked for any sign of the battalion that was supposed to be in front of them and tried to correct a pending barrage that, if not precisely aimed, would exterminate his unit, the company lost another ten men, not casualties, stragglers. "I can only find 70 men," the commander plaintively messaged, "I have no officers." Stragglers, of course, were men who slunk away into the woods until the fighting had passed, quite easy to do on the bosky ridges of the Meuse-Argonne, especially when all of the platoon leaders had been killed.[40]

The French denounced the Americans for their carelessness; the Americans denounced the French for their caution. "French Staff officers do not understand American formations," an American staff colonel later wrote. US formations were designed "to penetrate the enemy line and defeat him." That was one reason why US casualties were so heavy compared with French in this phase. The French, as events on their slow-moving front demonstrated, "sacrificed the offensive spirit to the necessity of protecting the troops." Similarly, the French criticized the Americans for not entrenching everywhere, like the French. "The French authorities have again failed to take into consideration the American spirit," the colonel continued. "American troops at rest resent continuous employment in digging successive lines of trenches. Troops," he concluded, "must be either laboring troops or fighting troops." As for French complaints about American liaison with neighboring French divisions, he noted: "Much of the difficulty in cases where American and French troops are side by side has been due to the failure of French troops to *advance.*" That was certainly the case here, where the French wouldn't reach the Aisne at Mouron until October 9, well behind schedule. That failure condemned the Lost Battalion to its agonies in the Argonne but also left a powerful flanking position in German hands. With their French-facing flank secure, the Germans could remain in the forest until both salients, the French to the west and the Americans to the east, joined at the top and forced the Germans to evacuate the Argonne.[41]

In those first days of October, the faltering American push in the Meuse-Argonne collided with the hardened bunkers of the Kriemhilde Line and stalled again. Progress had been tortuous. In more than a week of combat, the Americans had gained just six miles. They'd taken the German second position (Giselher-Stellung) and its bastions of Varennes, Apremont, Montfaucon, and Cierges. The three US corps commanders—Liggett, Cameron, and Bullard—now strung their line through those blasted villages and over to the Meuse at Brieulles, where the line fell away to the south in deference to the unsubdued German guns on "Corned Willy Hill" (the Borne de Cornouiller) and the Consenvoye Heights—the four-hundred-meter-high Côtes de Meuse commanding the east bank of the river. "Congratulate you on getting back the Bois des Ogons," Bullard wrote his frontline officers along the Meuse. "Now order your men to dig in there, put in MG's, thin the front line and stick. Organize a good alert protective barrage for them and let them know that you have." Holed in on the slopes of the German-held ridges, the Doughboys kept their heads down and prayed hard. If a man lit a cigarette and the match was visible, German shells would arrive immediately. Private Horace Baker recalled a conversation that swirled around him as the troops awaited their next push. "Yes sir, I prayed while I was up there and am not ashamed of it," one man said. "Yes, and I prayed not only for myself but for the others too," another man said. "I guess I was selfish," another Doughboy chimed in. "I only prayed for myself." On they went around the group, each man certifying his reliance on prayer. There was only one atheist in these foxholes: "I never thought of it," one man said.[42]

To wreck the German pivot, the Americans would have to "stick" here at all costs, then cross the Meuse to take the heights on the other side. Those heights—Consenvoye, a cross-river extension of the Giselher-Stellung, and "Corned Willy Hill," a cross-river extension of the Kriemhilde-Stellung—not only prevented Pershing from advancing his right flank; they guarded a vital line of communication up to Sedan and indeed to Hindenburg's left flank in France. General Henri Claudel's French XVII Corps, charged with the capture of those positions, was making as little progress as Gouraud's army on the other American flank. Like Gouraud, Claudel asked for American troops to storm the Meuse Heights. Amid the unending bloodshed, there was cause for hope. The continuous pressure, west to east, of Haig, Pétain, and Pershing had driven Hindenburg to seek an armistice. The Americans alone had chewed up sixteen German divisions, for which there were no replacements. But the going here at the vital pivot was tougher than anywhere. The Germans fought to the bitter end, rarely giving themselves up, the French and British general staffs confirming that the ten American divisions serving under Haig and Pétain took more prisoners than Pershing's twenty divisions in the Meuse-Argonne.[43]

Pershing's failure to break swiftly through the Hindenburg Line had broad strategic consequences. Clemenceau spoke with British general Edward Spears early on October 4 and grumbled that all thought of an expanded Allied campaign to crush Bulgaria and thrust into Austria-Hungary in 1918 would have to be shelved and all attention fixed on the Western Front "now that the Americans are not giving us the help we are entitled to expect of such good troops." Indeed, the Tiger wanted to uproot the eight French and British divisions in the Balkans and ship them back to France, to insure against American failure and cover the soaring, apparently irreplaceable casualties of the Entente: 600,000 British casualties since March 1918, 520,000 French. For the British, the loss of infantry was becoming critical. Clemenceau, who was again calling for Pershing's head, menacingly added, "This situation will not be allowed to last long."[44]

Colonel George Marshall detected more than just military analysis here. The French and British, who resented Pershing's independence, now saw an opportunity to destroy the American's reputation and, as Marshall put it, "break up our army and employ our young men in their own." They'd always wanted amalgamation; now, given Pershing's struggles, Paris and London felt that it was finally within reach. Their "poisonous touch reached even the President of the United States," and this was important, because if Generalissimo Foch ordered Pershing to distribute his divisions among the British and French armies, Pershing's only recourse would be an appeal to President Wilson to overrule Foch. Insulated in Washington against the harsh reality of the war—particularly harsh for the AEF because it was so unprepared—some of President Wilson's advisers were ready to fault Pershing, who insisted that "no one can visualize the war who has not seen it," who hasn't "been brought into harsh contact with practical realities" on a daily basis. Major Robert Bacon, a former US ambassador to France and now American liaison officer with the BEF, arrived at Pershing's headquarters in early October to request additional American divisions for service in British corps. This was the thin end of the wedge. Fearful of postwar American influence and prestige—and determined to substitute American assault units for their own—Paris and London were striving to annex American troops and minimize American laurels, "to weaken," as Marshall put it, "Mr. Wilson's powerful position."[45]

Pershing soldiered on, compartmentalizing the increasingly strident criticism—from Allied armies and governments, from influential Americans in Paris and London, and from senior officers inside his own army, men who, Marshall ruefully noted, unfailingly "bucked up" when Pershing was around but then "relapsed into further depths of despondency after his departure." Marshall reflected that "we were in much the same situation as Grant's army in the Wilderness campaign," when Grant, pushing on Richmond in 1864, had suffered heavy casualties and similar levels of condemnation. Many of the Doughboys joined the chorus. Austere and aloof, rarely among the troops because of his immense responsibilities, Pershing was never popular with the rank and file. There was, one who knew him wrote, "a warm human personal Pershing," but "this quality in him appeared less and less frequently as he became absorbed in the machine he created and drove; and in the lapses, the smile the more quickly faded, the hand drew back more quickly behind the gray stone wall of his West Point training." Casualties evacuated to a Bordeaux hospital spoke angrily of Pershing's leadership and the bungled fighting in the Argonne. An officer sent to interview them reported that "the men said that the American disaster at Argonne Wood was the result of bad officering. Companies were bunched together and were easy victims of Boche machine-guns. Two of the men quoted a chaplain as saying: 'Someone will be held accountable for the officering here.'"[46]

On October 9, the US 3rd Division attacked the Tranchée de la Mamelle, the piece of the Kriemhilde-Stellung running east-west along the open ridge southeast of Romagne. The 32nd Division pushed into the low hills at the foot of the Côte Dame Marie; the 1st Division took Hill 272, then the Côte de Maldah and Hill 263. The top of Hill 272 was wooded along the crest and a third of the way down the forward slope. The edge of these woods sheltered German machine guns, which traversed the bare meadow crossed by the hunkering, staggering 1st Division. Once into the dark woods, officers told the Doughs simply to "shoot the hell out of anyone that doesn't talk English well and quickly." Private Horace Baker recalled being pinned down in a shallow ditch. One anxious Doughboy kept peeping over the top to see what he could of the Germans, until a sniper bullet struck him between the eyes: "He jumped down, ran a short distance, and dived headlong into a hole, kicking the air as he went." A medic crouched over him, pronounced him dead, and walked away. A private in the 32nd Division watched as his company commander, bleeding from a shattered leg, coolly smoked a cigarette: "Don't mind me," the lieutenant grimaced. "I'm not hurt much." He pointed to other wounded men and said, "Give them the best you've got." That was leadership: a platoon leader promoted to company command and leading the troops with such courage. The men fought for officers like this, and the Germans found that they could never rest against the Americans; the Doughboys fought day and night, always pushing their patrols into the German positions to snipe, throw grenades, and look for unguarded openings.[47]

German divisions in the Kriemhilde Line reported crippling casualties of their own, several companies of the 5th Guard Division reduced to just ten men by the relentless American attacks. Other weakened divisions, their companies down to fifty or sixty men, were rushed back into the line without rest to stem the American advance. A young twenty-two-year-old second lieutenant named Erwin Rommel found himself in command of a battalion here, so many officers having been killed. "Fresh" German divisions no longer connoted German counterattacks. The new German tactic was increasingly this: the infantry huddled in trenches behind a screen of machine guns, lunging forward to fire from between the machine guns whenever the Americans attacked and then withdrawing back to their trenches. Private Horace Baker of the 32nd Division happened on a German machine-gun nest near Cierges that had been snuffed out by American infantry: "Around the hollow lay three dead Germans with features distorted and bloated. The sight filled me with loathing and disgust. Here had been a machine gun nest and the Boche gunners had stayed to the death. Brave must have been the Yanks who surrounded the nest and killed the gunners in an open field."[48]

Whenever the leaden skies cleared, American planes continued to dump propaganda leaflets to coax German surrenders. German officers initially ordered the men to ignore the leaflets. When the men read them anyway, the officers began paying the men to collect the leaflets and turn them in. Many stuffed them in their pockets instead, later passing them around their dugouts and even mailing them home. One German veteran remembered an American leaflet that his unit found particularly demoralizing: "You're fighting for the Kaiser. We're fighting for you. Think this over for yourself."[49]

All of the Germans noted American carelessness—"reckless to the point of foolishness," as one German officer put it. The Dough-boys were the only troops at this stage of the war who would leave cover to attack machine guns in the open. Indeed, American veterans, like Corporal John Barkley, would note in their memoirs that the chief distinction between experienced and inexperienced Doughboys was that new troops hurried everything (and were usually killed), while those with combat experience proceeded carefully, locating the Germans, assuring their flanks, and using cover. Old-timers like Lieutenant Hervey Allen's Corporal Maginn would urge their rook-ies forward like this: "A battle is gamble enough. Thir's no need for takin' extra personal risks." Few of these men knew the difference between a low crawl and a high crawl. Maginn made sure that they did. "Keep yer tail down. Wiggle. Wiggle's the way to Berlin. If ye act like a hound diggin' out a fox, ye'll die from behind." Too many of the Doughs, Allen confirmed, did die that way. Their own machine guns, firing just overhead, "shot their sterns off." Those who had NCOs as seasoned and helpful as Maginn were lucky. By now, most veterans were too tired to coach the replacements or pay any attention to them at all. Doughboys from the hardest-hit divisions interviewed in the hospital in October all agreed that although the French were "slow fighters" and needed the Americans to "set the pace," they much pre-ferred attacking with the poilus "because the French knew *where* to go and the Americans 'just went.'"[50]

Whenever the Doughboys finally took a German position, step-ping over their own piles of dead and wounded, they rarely bothered to suppress their desire for revenge. Discipline in these fights was hard to uphold because the units were improvised—men from different units

By October 1918, the Allies were taking more and more school-aged German prisoners, "built," as one Doughboy put it, "more like girls than men." Many of them wept with terror when captured. This boy, Karl Lungen, looks pleased to be captured and offered an American cigarette. (National Archives)

jumbled together, high on adrenaline—and the officers were either dead or hesitant replacements. Corporal Barkley of the 3rd Division described a fight in a stone quarry near the Bois de Naulemont that the Germans had used as a fighting position. When he and forty others took it, the men, strangers from five different battalions, wanted to kill the only German left alive, a teenaged boy, "crying like a baby, built more like a girl than a man." "Kill the yellow son-of-a-bitch," the Doughboys growled, advancing on the German. Barkley had to level a shotgun at the gang to extricate the boy and place him safely in a prisoner detail outside the quarry.

The men held the quarry overnight against German counterattacks and then received a chow detail the next morning, led in by six officers. The officers—"all replacements, not a front-line officer in the lot"—tried to organize the men, all combat veterans, who ignored them. One of the officers raised his voice and somebody yelled from the back of the quarry, "Sit down before you get knocked down!" The officer drew his pistol, but then, noting the hot faces and overstrung nerves, slid it back in the holster. "I'll put you under arrest," he quavered. "Horse collar!" several voices yelled, which was southern slang for *pussy*. One of the sergeants in the quarry took the officers aside and said: "The men have been through too much to be expected to click their heels every time stripes are flashed in front of them. Leave the men to me, there won't be any trouble." Later the new officers left; one of them was killed by a German sniper as he emerged from the mouth of the quarry. Barkley watched indifferently: "He had been at the front just long enough to get his boots muddy."[51]

On October 8, President Wilson, who'd received the German note requesting armistice terms four days earlier, finally answered the Germans, without consulting the Allies. Did the Germans truly accept the Fourteen Points? he asked. He added that America couldn't concede an armistice while the armies of Germany and Austria-Hungary still occupied territory in France, Belgium, Luxembourg, and Italy. In the following days, the French and British governments protested the lack of consultation; German U-boats sank a passenger liner off the Irish coast, killing civilians; and German troops, withdrawing toward the Meuse, ravaged the country behind them. Ludendorff, convalescing since his nervous breakdown on September 28, was all too clearly back in the saddle, as the methodical German devastation of the ground before the Antwerp-Meuse Line indicated.

By pulling back to the Meuse, Ludendorff would reduce his front and liabilities from 250 miles to 150 miles. That would free up seventy German divisions, which he could break up to bring his remaining divisions up to full strength. Of course, shortening his own lines would shorten Allied lines too, but by demolishing the entire infrastructure of occupied France and Belgium behind him, Ludendorff was making any renewal of the Allied attack, if an armistice broke down, vastly more difficult. Wilson's tone hardened. He sent another note to the Germans on October 14 informing them that, in view of their continuing "acts of inhumanity, spoliation and desolation" on land and sea, his good offices were no longer available to them. They'd have to look to Foch and the army commanders for armistice terms. One American general was reminded "of a policy expressed 2,000 years ago: 'It is not the custom of the Roman people to accept terms from enemies in arms.'" Would this be Wilson's policy too?[52]

The last German units evacuated the Argonne Forest on October 10. The 82nd All-Americans—the division had recruits from every state—took Cornay on October 10 after a four-day struggle. With the Germans dug into the hilltop village and its eroded cliffs, the Doughs had crawled up the slopes, littered with dead, to fight house-to-house. On the opposite end of the line, Bullard had ordered the 33rd Division to cross the Meuse and attack the Consenvoye Heights and the Borne de Cornouiller on October 8. Those right-bank positions, which had been raining mustard gas shells down into the marshes on the left bank of the river for two weeks, had to be taken to advance the line and open the door to an attack on Sedan along both banks of the Meuse. German and Austrian guns on the heights had cost the 4th Division six thousand casualties and had held it to daily gains of five hundred yards or less. The US 33rd Illini Division would attack in concert with the two American divisions east of the river in Claudel's XVII Corps—the 29th Division, National Guard from New Jersey, Maryland, and Virginia, and the 26th Yankee Division.[53]

The operation was wretchedly coordinated. The 33rd Division built two pontoon bridges in the night but then crossed the Meuse in broad daylight, offering clear targets to the German and Austrian gunners. The French 18th Division hardly attacked; the US 29th Division was shot to a standstill at the base of the Consenvoye Heights; the US 26th Yankee Division was held up at Molleville Farm. A platoon leader in the 29th Division recalled his first sergeant handing him binoculars—"Here, Lieutenant, you'll need these glasses, I won't"—and then running away, accompanied by much of the unit. Such desertions, the lieutenant mused, had become "a routine preceding every attack" in this and every other American division. A soldier in the Yankee Division, exploring a captured German dugout near Molleville Farm, found another soldier of his unit who'd been missing for two days: "I know that this war is nearly over," the man sobbed. "I've been through the whole thing and have never been a coward before. But I'll admit that I'm one now. I want to go back to the States and I know that if I go over the top again, I will be killed."[54]

Nearly four thousand men of New England's 26th Division had already fallen in the Meuse-Argonne, and the ground around these two Yankees was littered with still more. Wounded Doughboys, struck down by invisible German guns, pleaded for water, then watched helplessly as German gas shells plopped into their woods and clearings and finished them off. German positions like these on the Meuse Heights faced American commanders—and enlisted men—with tragic choices. They had no flanks; those were secured by other machine guns echeloned in depth and breadth. Without tanks and heavy artillery, the Americans could only attack with the infantry and try to lose as few men as possible. The lack of progress by the 26th Yankee Division—owed in part to fraternization between the New Englanders and the Germans opposite them, men on both sides apparently agreeing to drag their feet till an armistice—gave an outraged Pershing the pretext he needed to relieve General Clarence Edwards, the darling of New England, whom Pershing finally succeeded in sending home to train new recruits.[55]

Still, the Doughs had gained a foothold in the heart of Gallwitz's critical Maas-Ost group sector on the right bank of the Meuse. On October 8, they killed and wounded enough Austrians to persuade the rest—four thousand men, half the strength of the Austro-Hungarian 1st Division—to surrender Hill 371, cast away their machine guns and grenades, and yield the vital resistance line above Consenvoye, opening the door at last to an American advance to Sedan on both banks of the Meuse. "Like wild tigers, the Americans and French jumped on us and swallowed us up; to resist was impossible," one of the Austro-Hungarian officers rather too glibly reported. The Austrians—and the German units around them—had been ordered to prevent at all costs an American passage to the east bank of the Meuse. They'd failed. All of the fight was going out of these men, the Austro-Hungarian 1st Division reporting that the demoralization of its cold, wet, hungry troops may only have been exceeded by that of the Germans around them, "whose attitude showed no desire to resist or fight any longer."[56]

American barrages of mustard gas had sunk enemy morale to the breaking point, an Austrian officer morosely confiding, "My troops can't leave their masks on all day, especially when they are badly burned in all the unprotected areas." Gas casualties on the Meuse Heights accounted for more than half of German and Austrian casualties on any given day. The Austrian officer's company surrendered en masse and marched in the rain all day and night to the rear, where they were herded into a prison cage and, to their delight, given blankets by the well-supplied Americans. They were glad to be alive; many prisoners never made it to the rear. ("Do you know what our colonel told us before going into the Argonne?" Dos Passos's Andrews confides to a Y-man who has come to visit him in the hospital. "The more prisoners we took, the less grub there'd be; and do you know what happened to the prisoners that were taken?") These Austrians made it back alive and were even more delighted by the grub; indeed, much of the Austrian lieutenant's war diary is filled with memories of the American rations, which were scarce in the front lines and lavishly supplied in the rear: "Breakfast, Heavens, lovely white bread, a piece of which even in peacetime is better than our cakes. Also, meat and vegetables, jam, and coffee with kick to it. Lunch, this priceless bread, a large piece, meat stew and coffee. Afternoon nothing to do. Supper, meat and vegetables, and that lovely white bread again. It is a royal time the Americans give us."[57]

It was easy to see why American captivity was prized. By now, the daily rations for German and Austrian frontline troops were pitiful—thin slices of bread and salami, a handful of grits, and a potato or two. (Rear echelons were getting even less.) Tin was so scarce that canned rations had run out. Horses were being fed straw suitable only for bedding—so sour and reedy that even the famished horses ate it reluctantly. When those poor animals inevitably perished, they were fed to the troops, the Austrians detailing special units to rove the battlefield and butcher horse carcasses. Merchants in the cities of the Central Powers were pressured to donate cigarettes to an army that craved tobacco now more than ever. Food was so scarce that the

Austro-Hungarian general staff was sending out detailed instructions to its divisions in France on how to gather chestnuts, acorns, and beechnuts "now that the leaves are falling."[58]

The US First Army now found itself sprawled across ninety miles of front, which was four or five times the frontage normally spanned by an army on the Western Front. Pershing lacked the staffs to subdivide his vast army, but he would have to. With more than half a million combat troops, First Army was too large for a single headquarters to control. Pershing knew that if he didn't create another American army, Foch would resume his efforts to grab as many US divisions as he could on grounds, this time, of "efficiency." On October 12, Foch's staff chief, General Maxime Weygand, arrived at Souilly with an impertinent letter from the generalissimo relieving Pershing of command of the US First Army and replacing him with French general Auguste Hirschauer, who was to distribute six hundred thousand Doughboys between his Second Army and Gouraud's Fourth. Pershing was to go to the quiet sector around Pont-à-Mousson to do essentially nothing.[59]

The brazen move—certain to alienate Pershing—had been forced on Foch by Clemenceau. France had lost 175,000 casualties since mid-August and was effectively out of replacements. "I would be a criminal," Clemenceau wrote Foch, "if I allowed the French army to wear itself out indefinitely in battle without doing everything in my power to make the [Americans] fulfill the military role for which they are destined." Pershing, Clemenceau fulminated, "must resign himself to obedience."[60]

Many of the Doughboys might have preferred French command. American casualties—driven to astonishing levels by crude frontal assaults, desertion, and the flu—were so high that Pershing had begun breaking up seven of his own newly arrived divisions to bring the rest up to strength. He found that he needed ninety thousand replacements to make good the losses thus far. Clemenceau, who'd been pushing for weeks to get Pershing canned for the American's "invincible obstinacy," wanted to grab those seven US divisions before Pershing could strip them. This might be the perfect opportunity to annex the American army, disgrace its commander, and minimize American influence at the peace conference, which all assumed was imminent. To head off the threat and commit his entire strength before Clemenceau and Foch could pluck it away, Pershing split the US First Army in half on October 12. He gave the eastern half—five divisions, 176,000 men—to Bullard and called it the US Second Army. He entrusted the western half, a slimmed-down US First Army—fourteen divisions, 390,000 men—to Liggett. Bullard would spread the attack eastward to the Moselle and push on Metz, Thionville, and the Briey mines. Liggett would crack the Kriemhilde Line, conquer the Meuse Heights, and drive on Sedan along both banks of the Meuse. Bullard's III Corps was turned over to the famously laconic General John Hines, a 1st Division alumnus, known as "the best linguist in the A.E.F.—for he could be equally silent in all languages, including English."[61]

Pershing named himself commander of this new "Group of American Armies." Now an army group commander, he was fully the equal of Pétain and Haig and, like them, junior only to Foch. He now faced thirty-two German divisions with eight in reserve, Hindenburg having continually reinforced the Meuse-Argonne sector to defend his pivot through Sedan and Mézières. Pershing continued to sack inefficient officers, whom Marshall called "calamity howlers." Marshall mentioned unnamed "officers of high rank . . . who lost the will to conquer and took an exceedingly gloomy view of the situation." Pershing's changes effectively named one of those officers: George Cameron was removed as commander of V Corps and replaced by the 1st Division commander General Charles Summerall. Summerall could be counted on to drive his superiors as relentlessly as his subordinates, Harbord recalling that Summerall had earlier pressed the need for more artillery on Pershing "as nearly to the limit of courtesy as I have ever seen an officer go and escape unrebuked." Summerall was an American Mangin, a general who attacked, led from the front, and never flinched at even the most appalling casualties. The Doughs admired him anyway. Summerall, a war correspondent observed, had an aura reminiscent of Stonewall Jackson's: "He could deliver an exhortation to make men cry and curse and beg to get at the Germans."[62]

For his part, General Cameron had buckled under the strain. The mobile, maneuverable all-arms division was the workhorse of the war, the corps essentially a "brigading unit," a "skeleton" organization to swap fresh divisions in for tired ones. The stresses of the two levels of command were altogether different. The division commander had to fight and maneuver on a small section of front till exhaustion; the corps commander had to keep the combat by multiple divisions going across a broad front, sustaining all units—the originals plus replacements—while preserving mobility, "the last condition," as the French liked to say, "always hampered by the other two." Cameron, whose entire corps had been beaten in the initial advance toward Montfaucon, gave out. Given command of the 4th Division as a sop, he never forgave the humiliation. Offered a last-minute promotion before his retirement six years after the war, he refused it: "I have consulted my family and we are all agreed that the suggested [promotion] means nothing to us."[63]

If nothing else, the Americans in the Meuse-Argonne were succeeding in what Haig called a "wearing-out battle." But like Haig's Tommies, the Doughs were wearing themselves out too. When Liggett took command of the US First Army from Pershing on October 16, he was struck by its fragility. Morale was low because of the frontal assaults and the massive, avoidable casualties. With his cruel insistence on "push" at all costs, Pershing had ripped the guts out of many of his units. An estimated one hundred thousand men of the First Army's fourteen divisions were classed as "stragglers," roving behind the lines, hiding out, stealing food from supply dumps, and trying fearfully to survive the war. Thousands more lay dead. A private recalled constantly stepping over olive-drab figures who looked asleep until you noticed the frost on their hair and clothing—"These were sleeping the last long sleep of the ages." He thought of their homes: "Many a mother's heart would break when the news would be flashed to distant America."[64]

The three weeks after October 10 were the grittiest of the war, the Germans throwing in the last of their first-class divisions to hold their vital pivot and the three American corps measuring their daily advances in yards. The stresses were big and small. On the big end, Summerall inaugurated his command of V Corps with a testy reminder to his generals: "Division commanders must employ the infantry in such a manner as to avoid serious losses." Officers were still ordering frontal attacks in massed formations, exposing the Doughboys "unnecessarily to machine gun and artillery fire." Divisions that had been expected to fight for three or four weeks were being consumed in a few days by these tactics and casualties. What little momentum they had would ebb away as the lacerated division was relieved and the new division came up.[65]

On the small end, an American scout recalled entering a dugout near Cunel to get orders from his sergeant when a heavy shell burst outside and something sailed down the entrance. The two men raised a candle and saw that it was an amputated arm in an olive-drab sleeve. Someone else had witnessed that isolated horror, a burly enlisted man outside, one of the 3rd Division's new replacements, who now lurched into the dugout, eyes flashing, "making a horrible noise in his throat, half howling, half moaning." He ran till he barged into the scout and continued till he hit the wall, crushing the scout against the earthen wall with all of his weight, howling into his face and foaming at the mouth. Another soldier was summoned to remove the crazed man— "For God's sake, throw him out, this is battalion headquarters, there's work to be done!"—but the soldier couldn't be moved, and he collapsed weeping on the floor, putting his head in his arms. When two men succeeded in removing him from the dugout, he ran around in circles, shrieking, until he finally veered off toward the German lines, where everyone supposed he was killed. This was shell shock.[66]

The US 3rd Division reported that the Germans were so stretched by the synchronized Allied thrusts on the Western Front that "they are endeavoring to stop our advance by rushing all detachments of new units into the line immediately. No attempt is made to put in complete divisions, and in no case have we found more than one regiment of the new division identified." Two captured officers of the German 3rd Guard Division reported that they'd been ordered to fight to the last man, and that the "last man" was to go back, after the massacre, and report that his regiment had been annihilated. Any other outcome—surrender or retreat by more than one man—was deemed criminal. The German army was in its death throes. It was running out of men. What men remained were scattered in concealed strongpoints that dominated the rugged terrain. Most American intelligence reports contained the daily refrain, "The enemy's front lines cannot be definitely established."[67]

The weather worsened as the days wore on, Marshall observing that "it always seemed that the battles were inextricably connected with cold and rain, and mud and gloom." The front now straggled along the face of the Hindenburg Line, from Grandpré at the top of the Argonne Forest through the Romagne Heights and Cunel in the center—the most redoubtable section of the Kriemhilde-Stellung— to the east bank of the Meuse, where the still-unsubdued Borne de Cornouiller anchored the position, showering mustard gas on Pershing's right-wing division—the 33rd Illini—and causing its end of the line to curve back to the south, the exact opposite of the direction required.[68]

On October 11, the 42nd Rainbows relieved the spent 1st Division in the space below the Romagne Heights. The thousand-man battalions of the Big Red One had been reduced to 250 men by German fire. Wild Bill Donovan, now a lieutenant colonel in command of a regiment in the Rainbows, recalled passing a 1st Division aid station as his men trooped into line through "a stew of dead Boche and Americans." Donovan's Doughs gawked at the blood-smeared discarded stretchers and piles of torn, reddened uniforms, all from US troops—"the cast off of the dead and wounded." As they retired, the survivors of the 1st Division looked "hollow-cheeked, pale and silent, dazed and bewildered." One of them, a seventeen-year-old corporal, later remarked: "It seemed to me then as though the dead were luckier than I was." He had witnessed men thrown away in futile attacks, mercy killings, the murder of prisoners, and too many corpses indifferently robbed and dismembered to count. None of it affected him anymore: "I was too numb. To me, corpses were nothing but carrion."

Like butchers, these cold killers of the Big Red One had stabbed a bloody gash in the German front. A division that had known nothing of war a few months earlier now, as Summerall put it, "had met and defeated the flower of the great Prussian Army." In the days since it had relieved the faltering 35th Division, the Big Red One—referred to by awestruck staff officers as the "Immortal Division"—had chewed up elements of eight first-class German divisions. The 1st Division's field messages reflected the courage and confidence of its men. Ordered to take an indomitable position, an officer would scribble in reply: "O.K., we'll get thru if such a thing is possible." Usually they would. Once ground was taken and cleaned of German machine guns, it wouldn't be given back, the phrase "This position will be held at all costs" recurring in most reports.[69]

On the First Army's left wing, the US 77th Division attacked Saint-Juvin on October 13. General James McRae's 78th Division—newly arrived National Army recruits from upstate New York and New Jersey—advanced beside the 77th and attacked Grandpré across the Aire River. Little was expected of this untried division, still less because Grandpré was a natural fortress overlooked by the fortified Bois de Bourgogne and protected by the Aire, which branched into two streams here as it neared the Aisne, making two swampy river barriers to cross under fire, not one. The Germans had to cling to this place. Grandpré and the Bois de Bourgogne were a wall between the Americans and Gouraud's French Fourth Army, blocking a general advance toward Sedan.

On October 13, Pershing traveled to Bombon, a village near the old Marne salient, where Foch had moved his headquarters from Sarcus. There, Foch and Weygand derided the American effort as tactfully as they could, to which Pershing answered that he was engaged against Marwitz's twenty-six divisions, with eleven more in reserve, in the most difficult terrain on the Western Front. Pershing was grinding the Germans down, but his troops were also being ground down. "We are not advancing rapidly because the Germans are fighting by echeloning machine guns in depth. The Germans could hold up *any* troops Marshal Foch has at his command," Pershing protested.

Foch affected to be unimpressed. "Every general is disposed to say that the fighting on his front is hardest," Foch interrupted. "I myself only consider results." Pershing coldly concluded the meeting: "I will continue my attacks until the Germans give way." He had thwarted the penultimate Allied attempt to amalgamate the American forces.[70]

In this phase of the battle—the last half of October—the French, having lagged around the Argonne, now raced ahead and were generally several miles in advance of the Americans to their right. The French hadn't suddenly become bolder—they were crossing expendable ground, whereas the Americans were on unexpendable ground, trying to bash through the Bois de Bourgogne and the ridges running from it eastward to the Meuse: Sivry-lès-Buzancy, Champigneulle, Imécourt, Saint-Juvin, Ravin-aux-Pierres, Le Mort Homme, and the Bois des Loges, "a series of ravines, like a giant corrugated iron roof, thick enough to conceal machine guns and to protect the defenders from detection by artillery, yet thin enough to give them murderous fields of fire."[71]

Pulling back the shoulder facing the French, the Germans were leaning in with the other shoulder against the Americans. Once in possession of the Bois de Bourgogne, the US First Army would finally be in direct contact with the French to their left. The Germans doubled down to defend the wood and hold the line of the Aire River—fifty feet wide and six feet deep—as well as its terraced bastions of Saint-Juvin and Grandpré on the right bank. Liggett hoped that General Joseph Dickman's I Corps on the left would draw dwindling German reserves to the Aire and make the job of the 42nd Division, assaulting the center of the Kriemhilde Line, easier. I Corps's appraisal of the fighting in mid-October was numb: "No material advance in any way proportionate to the objective was made in these days during which the objective remained the same."[72]

On October 14, I Corps's 77th Division took Saint-Juvin and V Corps struck into the Kriemhilde Line. General Joseph Dickman's I Corps on the left had made the deepest penetration and was two miles farther into the German position than Charles Summerall's V Corps in the center and five miles farther advanced than John

Hines's III Corps on the right, which still tailed away to the south to lessen the impact of German barrages from the Borne de Cornouiller. Dickman's surge into Saint-Juvin captured tons of German matériel that Marwitz had failed to evacuate in time: "A large dump containing steel bars, 3 million feet of lumber, boilers, standard gauge railroad equipment, box cars, and a small narrow gauge locomotive in good condition." Two days earlier, the German government had sent a note to Washington requesting negotiations, and President Wilson had rebuffed it, recognizing it for what it was—a ruse to buy time to evacuate material like this, reorganize the German army, and replace the five thousand guns Hindenburg had lost thus far.[73]

Still clinging to most of the Kriemhilde Line, the Germans reverted to killing Americans. They manned the front line with machine-gun and sniper nests, which spat devastating fire at every American patrol. German harassing fire was steady—shrapnel, high explosive, phosgene, and mustard gas exploding in the American trenches, foxholes, and roads. German aircraft, in groups of three to fifteen, flew over American lines, shot down observation balloons, reconnoitered, adjusted artillery, liaised with the infantry, and dropped propaganda leaflets on the AEF, quoting Germany's peace proposals and Wilson's negative reply. To prevent surprise attacks, the Germans fired flares continuously and thrust outposts out in the night, then drew them back to the resistance line before dawn. German infantry would approach American outposts, shout "*Kamerad!*" and raise their hands in surrender. When Americans rose to accept their surrender, they'd be fired on from the flanks. A corporal in the 77th Division, who'd trained in the British sector, never forgot advice from a British drill instructor that came in handy here: "'And I'll tell yah bloody Yanks another thing,' he'd say. 'If the Boche comes out with 'is 'ands up yelling '*Komerad*,' give 'im the bayonet in 'is bloody balls. Sure as 'ell 'e's got a potato masher in one of those 'ands.'"[74]

Pershing struggled to put the best face on a dire situation that was dire in part because of his own witless tactics. "Our dogged offensive was wearing down the enemy, who continued desperately to throw his best troops against us, thus weakening his line in front of our Allies and making their advance less difficult."[75]

On October 14, the US 32nd Division, National Guardsmen from Michigan and Wisconsin, took Romagne, but the Côte Dame Marie, a rugged escarpment west of Romagne blocking the American advance, still held out. The *côte* looked invincible. Crescent-shaped, facing south, with fortified knobs on each end of the crescent, it funneled attacking troops onto bare slopes swept with preregistered German fire. Private Horace Baker of the 32nd Division recalled that the men were given eight minutes to prepare to attack. Looking up at the German positions, his first thought was: "I may have only eight minutes to live." When he attacked, running crouched toward Romagne, a voice in his head intoned: "And this is a battle, this is a battle; I'm a participant in a battle."[76]

Unable to flank the position, Summerall's V Corps attacked it frontally. The 42nd Rainbow Division advanced on a five-mile front to the German wire at Landres-et-Saint-Georges. There it was stopped, enfiladed from the Côte de Châtillon—another elevated position just behind the Côte Dame Marie. The men battled here for days under heavy rain: "We were miserable, soaked to the skin without winter underwear or overcoat, with only one soaked blanket." Half the men in any given unit were sick, hardly able to move around. They all dug holes and lay facedown in the mud with their packs on and their helmets laid lengthwise over their head and neck to block shrapnel. Amid all the horrors, one New York soldier remembered something a friend told him as they lay in that cold mud under heavy fire. He'd been talking about his girlfriend at home, expressing his longing for her between blasts. His friend, sodden and terrified, finally blurted out: "Listen, and listen good. Never trust a woman, and that's the truth."[77]

On October 13, Summerall met with General Douglas MacArthur, who commanded a brigade of the 42nd Division, and notoriously said: "Give me Châtillon, MacArthur. Give me Châtillon, or a list of 5,000 casualties." MacArthur just as notoriously replied: "If this Brigade doesn't capture Châtillon, you can publish a casualty list of the entire Brigade with the Brigade Commander's name at the top." Tragically, this was how the US First Army operated. Flayed by Allied criticism and Pershing's vehemence, generals vied to outdo each other in their offensive zeal. ("Generous son of a bitch, ain't he?" one Doughboy muttered when he heard of MacArthur's willingness to accept 100 percent casualties.) Yet even a general as ambitious as MacArthur had qualms. Years after the war, MacArthur recalled the fear and tension in the lines: "I can see them now—forming grimly for the attack, blue-lipped, covered with sludge and mud, chilled by the wind and the rain." Here as elsewhere, the Doughboys attacked without sufficient artillery support. They had their 75s at the front, but nothing heavy to breach the acres of German barbed wire strung across the approaches to strongpoints. And so one Rainbow battalion after another approached the wire, seeking a way through, only to be mown down by German machine guns behind the wire and on the heights of the Côte de Châtillon. New York's Shamrock Battalion, which led the initial assault on October 14, got hung up in the wire and was shot to pieces, German planes circling overhead to bomb the New Yorkers and direct artillery fire on to them.[78]

Engineers sent forward to blast holes through the wire met the same fate. American air cover in the war was generally pathetic. General Billy Mitchell, who commanded Pershing's Air Service, tended to deride missions like close air support and reconnaissance, preferring to function as an "offensive arm" and bomb faraway German "strategic" targets like the factories around Metz instead of the nearby "tactical" ones. During three days of combat, Wild Bill Donovan, commanding a regiment in MacArthur's 84th Brigade, darted between his men in exposed positions, urging them forward and not stopping even when shot in the leg by a machine gun on October 15. "Donovan is one of the few men I know who really *enjoys* a battle," the Rainbow's beloved chaplain Father Duffy testified. One private in Donovan's unit recalled finding the colonel in the thick of the fighting near Landres-et-Saint-Georges: "He was sitting in a shell hole, cool as a cucumber, while his barber tried to shave him with a straight razor." The barber's hand shook like a leaf, as shells were falling everywhere and the valley was

Lieutenant Colonel "Wild Bill" Donovan, shown here with the stripes of the Distinguished Service Cross and the French Croix de Guerre, was, as the Rainbow Division's chaplain put it, "one of the few men I know who really enjoys a battle." Donovan would receive the Medal of Honor for his heroic conduct in the Meuse-Argonne but, with habitual modesty, would insist that the award belonged not to him "but to the boys who are resting under white crosses in France." (National Archives)

carpeted with killed and wounded. Donovan gave his orders calmly, betraying emotion only once, when he stopped to say: "Oh my God! What a waste of lives. What a waste! What a waste!"[79]

In Romagne, Private Horace Baker of the 32nd Division saw nothing but madness as he dug in beside a cemetery and stared at the crucifix while he dug: "I could not think but how great a travesty on religion this war was. Here we Americans were fighting Germans to liberate the French people, and all three nationalities worshipped the same Christ, but there were murderous shells shrieking within a few feet of the image of the Prince of Peace." The 32nd Division had taken Romagne and breached the Kriemhilde Line at its midpoint, but the division's assault battalions had lost six thousand men and were all but destroyed in the process. As many men had probably skulked as attacked, division orders for the push containing this glaring line: "The skulkers have skulked. The quitters have quit. Only the man with guts remains." Most of the men with guts would be cut down. In three weeks of action, Baker's company had lost 162 of its 246 starters, along with its company commander (leg shattered by a shell), his replacement (a bullet through the liver), and then his replacement too (shot in the wrist). The master sergeant was shot in the groin—the most feared wound of all. With little supervision—a lieutenant sent to them as a replacement was so frightened that he hid in a dugout and never emerged—Baker's company, the private observed, "stayed intact by pure Americanism and patriotism." None of the dead here would have to be moved. Romagne would become the US Army's massive Meuse-Argonne Cemetery after the war. Forty thousand Doughboys were buried there, making it what it remains to this day: the biggest American military cemetery in Europe. For years afterward, a Doughboy recalled, it would be a destination "for thousands of brokenhearted and weeping American parents and other relatives of the slain."[80]

To Baker's left, struggling up the heights of Romagne through ankle-deep mud, Donovan was wounded with the Rainbows: shot first in the knee, then by a second burst of machine-gun fire that shattered the tibia. The Germans on the Côte de Châtillon aimed low, to hit men in the legs and feet, pitch them to the ground, and then hit them in the head. With his usual good fortune, Donovan avoided that fate. Sick with the pain, he continued to lead the assault for five hours, receiving the Medal of Honor for his valor. When finally evacuated on a stretcher, Donovan passed Father Duffy and said: "Father, you're a disappointed man. You expected to have the pleasure of burying me over here." Even in severe pain, Wild Bill remained the coolest man on the Western Front.[81]

Progress was so slow that late on October 15, Summerall, never known for his light touch, descended on the headquarters of General

Michael Lenihan's 83rd Brigade, which was making as little headway against Landres-et-Saint-Georges as MacArthur's 84th Brigade was against the Côte de Châtillon. Summerall canned Lenihan as well as a regimental commander and his staff. They were, Summerall growled, "mentally defeated"; they lacked "push." With this example before him, MacArthur, whose 84th Brigade had already lost three thousand men to no apparent effect, left his sheltered headquarters and took a place in the front line. What did he have to lose? If he failed, he'd be "blooeyed" like Lenihan, which, for a man like MacArthur, was as good as dead. He personally led a regiment of Iowa National Guardsmen up Hill 288, muttering to a Doughboy: "If this is good, I'm in it. And if it's bad, I'm in it too." It was bad, of course, MacArthur somehow emerging unscathed from an attack that suffered 65 percent casualties taking the entrenched, wired, heavily manned position on the crest of the hill.[82]

Even in possession of Hill 288, the Rainbows still had to clear the even more formidable Côte de Châtillon—the central bastion of the Kriemhilde-Stellung. After the war, a German veteran shuddered at the memory of fighting the Rainbows: "They were always advancing and acted more like wild men than soldiers." Not all were wild men. The division's ammo carriers were Pawnees from Oklahoma, and as the fight intensified on the Côte de Châtillon—a mile north of Hill 288—some of them refused to carry ammo forward across slopes swept by German fire. One Doughboy recalled his buddy aiming his rifle at the cowering Pawnees and ordering them to bring mortar bombs—they refused. "I guess they figured they were going to die anyway and stood a better chance with Tom than the German artillery."[83]

Summerall, at least as bloodthirsty as Pershing, refused to believe that the Rainbows had still not taken the Côte de Châtillon. Father Duffy, who ministered to the fallen, was struck by the callous cruelty of commanders like Summerall: "Since 1915, no commanders in the [British and French] armies would dream of opposing to strongly wired and entrenched positions the naked breasts of their infantry." American commanders did. They exalted "push" over all else. "There has been," Summerall scolded V Corps on October 15, "a tendency to exaggerate losses and casualties." Unable to correct the defects of training, supply, and doctrine that were causing these problems, Summerall blimpishly banned the use of certain phrases in reports or even casual conversation, phrases like "all shot to pieces"—"held up by machine gun fire"—"men all exhausted"—"suffered enormous losses." Starting now, Summerall ordered, "officers and soldiers are forbidden to use such expressions in official messages, reports, conversations or discussions."[84]

Having sacked General Lenihan and a regimental commander in the 83rd Brigade, Summerall paused to examine the other regiment—from Ohio—only to be reminded by its brave commander that he was asking, if not the impossible, the near impossible: "No man can take fatigue out of men who have been living in water-filled holes in the ground with no overcoats and but one blanket, seeing their comrades killed by shellfire or dying from pneumonia." Summerall backed off, for the moment. His admonishing gaze traveled again to MacArthur, still hung up between Hill 288 and the Côte de Châtillon. With relief and disgrace imminent—the whole operation described by one furious officer as an "abortion"—MacArthur repeated his vow to take the position or "lose 6,000 dead." Late on October 16, MacArthur personally led a reconnaissance up the hill to the German wire and scrambled back the only survivor. Like Patton, he always saw divine intervention in his narrow escapes. "It was God," MacArthur insisted. "He led me by the hand, the way he led Joshua." The Rainbows finally wrested the Côte de Châtillon from the Germans on October 17. While American artillery and the focused fire of sixty machine guns scoured the ridge, a flanking column of Alabama National Guardsmen infiltrated through a gap in the German wire and fired into the flank of the five hundred German defenders on the summit, while MacArthur's main body attacked their front. The Doughs threaded through the German dugouts, lobbing grenades inside to blast out the occupants. The Germans finally yielded the position. "We've got the hill, and a lot of these God damned Heinies as well," a Doughboy yelled to his company commander as they drove the last of the Germans off the ridge.[85]

To MacArthur's right, the 32nd Division cleared most of the Bois de Bantheville on October 18. It had been brought up to strength with troops from the US 39th Division, which, instead of being deployed as a unit, had been broken up for replacements for the scarred divisions at the front. The 89th Division relieved the 32nd and mopped up. "We had all of death but the dying," an exhausted Doughboy mused as he marched back for a rest through rain and slush. The villages they passed were ruins, usually swarming with American engineers and labor battalions quarrying the bricks and stone to shore up the First Army's perpetually sinking roads.[86]

The US 2nd Division, which had replaced its casualties from the battle for the Blanc Mont and left Gouraud's army to join Liggett's, relieved the exhausted Rainbows to begin the advance on Marwitz's last defensive line: the Freya-Stellung. Wherever the 2nd Division and its Marine Brigade went, Doughboys, always resentful of the disproportionate press coverage given to the Leathernecks in the war, would search its columns for Marines and yell: "Hey Marine, go home and tell your mother you're a soldier." Or the Doughs would yell: "Who's winning the war?" The Leathernecks would yell back, "The Marines are!" And the Doughboys would yell back, "Then what the hell are *we* fighting for?" It was the only levity there was in this scourged landscape.[87]

Commanding the relieving 2nd Division, General John Lejeune made his headquarters in recently conquered Charpentry—"a ruined town in a flat valley with high, steep hills around it, in a sea of mud." Pershing called this parade of horrors under the German guns "a trying period." He may have been right in concluding, in his own defense, that "there doesn't exist on the Western Front a more villainous piece of ground than that conquered by the troops of the V Corps in October 1918." Units that were relieved marched south in the direction of Montfaucon, grateful to be alive. Filing to the rear, a soldier of the 42nd Division recalled that they passed the V Corps heavy batteries behind Exermont that had killed Rainbows with friendly fire. The passing troops of the 42nd Division cursed the gunners; some hurled their rifles at them, others broke ranks, ran over, and attacked the gun crews with their fists.[88]

One Doughboy remembered stopping to rest, looking around for something to sit on, seeing nothing more promising than a dead German, and then indifferently sitting down on the corpse. After the mayhem he'd experienced, it seemed like the most natural thing to do. He then began walking back with his unit in the rain, making room for combat wagons loaded with American dead. He and his companions stepped off the road to let a whole convoy of dead soldiers pass—mule-drawn trucks fourteen feet long, four feet deep, and four feet wide, each loaded to the top with corpses packed so tight that "it seemed to me that not another leg or another arm could have been crowded into them." The rain pelted down and the mules staggered in the mud and a body tumbled off one of the wagons. The waiting Doughboys stooped to lift up the dead American and cram him back on the wagon: "He was a young fellow. His back was so stiff you couldn't bend it." Dead Germans were left where they fell or thrown into holes hastily dug by black labor battalions, one German to a hole, his helmet perched on top. The Germans would have to sort them all out after the war. The Doughboys fell in beside an American officer also walking back toward Montfaucon. He'd been supervising an African American burial detail: "They're all right in the daytime," he said, "but we had a hell of a time keeping those niggers up there after dark. They were scared half to death at night. If we didn't watch them every minute they'd pile all the Germans they could see into one shell hole. Then they'd fill it in, stick one helmet on top of it, and call it a day."[89]

15

MEUSE-ARGONNE: BARRICOURT

The war's lengthening casualty lists hardened the mood in America. Teddy Roosevelt, reeling from the death of his son Quentin in France, gave a speech on October 15, mocking President Wilson's call for "peace without victory" and the president's plan for a League of Nations. Roosevelt scorned such idealism—"resting the peace on a scrap of paper"—and demanded harsh terms and "permanent preparedness" instead. If the American people, Roosevelt argued, continued to accept Wilson's "high-sounding phrases of muddy meaning," they would be "cheated out of the right kind of peace." TR judged the Fourteen Points "silly and mischievous," bound to "allow German militarism to survive." Roosevelt was hands down "the No. 1 man among the Doughboys," a soldier recalled. Most of them contrasted the twenty-sixth president's firmness with the twenty-eighth president's "pussyfooting." It was "because we grew up with him," a veteran said of TR. "He seemed to embody everything we were fighting for." Roosevelt now called on Americans to vote Republican in the midterm elections, to elect a Senate that would reject or amend any peace treaty devised by Wilson. "Send to

Washington public servants who will be self-respecting Americans and not rubber stamps."[1]

Wilson, meanwhile, campaigned for a "Democratic sweep" in the House and Senate. Only this, the president argued, would strengthen his hand against vengeful Allies and bellicose Republicans, who said things like, "Let us dictate peace by hammering guns, not clicking typewriters." The November 1918 midterms, coinciding with the end of the war, would stun Wilson, returning Republican majorities to both houses. The Democrats had never been firmly seated; they had gained control of Congress and the White House only because of the Taft-Roosevelt rift in 1912. Now that the Republicans were united again and the Democrats restored to their normal condition of minority party everywhere but the South, the GOP stormed back to win 240 of 432 seats in the House and 49 of 96 seats in the Senate. Having picked up 26 seats in the House and 5 in the Senate, Roosevelt and the Republicans vowed to "beat Germany to her knees," set aside Wilson's "kid gloves and fine phrases," and impose a hard peace.[2]

The Allies estimated that by mid-October 1918, one-fifth of the German army was sick with the flu. Germany's allies were collapsing, succumbing to casualties, the costs of the war, and the exhaustion of their peoples. By October 15, Germany was down to just twenty-five reserve divisions; the Allies, buoyed by the Americans, had eighty-eight. Major Paul Clark, Pershing's liaison to Foch, reported near unanimity in the generalissimo's headquarters that the Germans were finished. "Weygand and the Staff here consider that the enemy is beaten, and that it is only necessary to maintain the pressure here to get any terms that the Allies desire." The great French industrial city of Lille, which had been in German hands since 1914, fell to the Allies on October 18, and Weygand's deputy credited the American thrusts on the Marne and the Meuse with having loosened up the front in Lille and everywhere else: "I tell you Clark, we owe an unspeakable gratitude to you Americans for it is due to you that the Allies, not the Boche, are the victors." The war, he predicted, would be over in a month, certainly by Christmas. General Maurice Duval, chief of Foch's Operations Bureau, agreed, adding that physically the

Germans might continue the war—falling back to a shortened line connecting Antwerp, Brussels, Namur, the Meuse, and Metz—but that the "rapidly increasing American Army" made German defeat in 1919 certain. The kaiser would get better terms now than later.[3]

Hindenburg and Ludendorff wanted those mild terms but, watching the bloody, tortured progress of the Allies, saw no reason to beg for them. In the three weeks since the breaching of the Hindenburg Line in the British sector, the Allies in the west had crept forward only as far as Bruges, Lille, and Cambrai, this against a German army that had lost over half of its guns and whose divisions were down to a handful of weak battalions. Hindenburg now planned to rest and restore his army behind the Meuse barrier—there were six hundred thousand military-aged men still available in Germany—or yield it after a bloody struggle and resume his withdrawal toward the Rhine, gradually dissolving the Allied coalition through illness, cold, casualties, and time. Coached by Hindenburg, the German chancellor, Prince Max of Baden, replied to Wilson's note of October 14, which had referred the Germans to the Allied military authorities for armistice terms. The German army, Prince Max objected, would need firm guarantees that the Allies would not try to increase *their* military power during an armistice and would need additional time for the newly constituted German government to secure authorization for an armistice from the Reichstag.[4]

The Germans, a dejected Haig assured London on October 19, were far from beaten. They were still mounting "considerable opposition" and were "not ready for unconditional surrender." The French, Haig grumbled, "had not really been fighting latterly," and the Americans were "ill-equipped and half-trained." British efforts were doomed by "diminishing effectives." Far from recommending a knockout blow, Haig now advised a speedy termination of the war, demanding nothing more of the Germans than Alsace-Lorraine and occupied France and Belgium. If the Germans retired back to the Meuse and the Rhine in a fighting mood, Haig said, they'd stand there "with the courage of despair." Haig saw no point in this. "Why expend more British lives—and for what?" Lloyd George, sensing military opportunity in the event of a German collapse, now found himself in the unusual position of being more aggressive than Haig. He feared, however, that Haig's gloom implied weakness in the BEF: "If the Commander-in-Chief is tired out," the prime minister said, "what must the Army be?"[5]

Pétain too hesitated to go on and cautioned that if the Allies demanded the return of Alsace-Lorraine, the Germans would continue the war. The French commander would be satisfied with German withdrawal to the Rhine and the return of French and Belgian rolling stock. The "lost provinces" could remain lost as far as Pétain was concerned. Foch, of course, had no qualms about fighting on. He thought the lenient recommendations of Haig and Pétain "not drastic enough." He wanted to drive the Germans across the Rhine and pursue them there, with Allied bridgeheads on the east bank of the river. Only then could the Allies credibly threaten to destroy German towns if the Germans dared break an armistice. A British officer in Foch's headquarters detected a weird and dangerous continuity between Foch's prewar teachings that "moral force" could trump firepower and his views now: "Marshal Foch believes that the enemy consider themselves beaten, and it is the moral side now that will give the material results later on."[6]

In fact, only the Americans were making progress and displaying "moral force" of the kind trumpeted by Foch. The initial Allied surge in August and September had stalled. In the north, the Belgians and Plumer's British Second Army had staggered to a halt in the mud. Plumer's troops were still on the crests of the Passchendaele ridge, busily repairing their roads and merely looking at the Germans in the distance. Echeloned below Plumer, the armies of Horne, Byng, and Rawlinson had spent their strength breaching the Siegfried Position of the Hindenburg Line and battling through its deep zones of forts and barbed wire. By mid-October, despite a chaotic German retreat, they had pushed only as far as Cambrai and Saint-Quentin. "The British infantry are the finest in the world," a French general had said a century earlier. "Fortunately there are not many of them." Now, of course, the French wished that there were.[7]

Haig's staff chief had warned that the assault on the Hindenburg Line might be Britain's last battle, and so far, it was. The French and British were stopped, unable to pursue or even replace their casualties. Each army had lost well over half a million men since March. Unlike the Germans, neither army had trained in open warfare. They were good at rehearsed attacks on prearranged objectives but, as the British official history put it, were "practically devoid of real tactical sense" once committed to the open field with fluid opportunities. Passivity, of course, suited General Pétain perfectly. He had always intended merely to follow the British and American attacks forward, and now, with both armies on the flanks stopped or faltering, the French stopped too, for, as one historian put it, "Marshal Foch was surely far too much of a patriot to intend his aggressive exhortations to apply to his own countrymen."[8]

Applying them even to the aggressive Americans was becoming difficult. US divisions landing at France's Atlantic ports were being broken up to replace the huge losses in the divisions already at the front. Pershing was having to revamp his plans and tactics to focus his shrinking army on "bite and hold" operations. He'd now narrow his front, bull his way into Gallwitz's line, kill as many as he could, invite counterattacks, and then kill some more. Pershing confirmed that he was engaged against thirty-eight German divisions on the Meuse-Argonne front and insisted that, far from doing nothing to facilitate the Allied advance, the Doughboys had "materially assisted operations elsewhere by attracting this force to the American front." British and French military intelligence reacted indignantly to Pershing's suggestion that their offensives had been aided by his. On October 19, they effectively wrote off Pershing's AEF as a fighting force: "It is felt that in insisting on the premature formation of large American armies, General Pershing has not interpreted the altruistic wishes of the American nation, and that he has incurred a grave responsibility both as regards unnecessary loss of life amongst his troops, and in the failure of the operations."[9]

All too clearly, with winter descending, London and Paris had resumed trying to get Pershing fired. They still wanted his troops for themselves, but they misunderstood the real reason for the latest pause in American operations. It had nothing to do with Pershing, who was focused on political and diplomatic activity, and everything to do with General Hunter Liggett, who'd formally taken over the US First Army on October 16. Pershing, as usual, had been all for exploiting the breach of the Kriemhilde Line and pushing ahead at once. Liggett, far more attuned to the actual condition of the AEF after its ordeal on the Kriemhilde Line, understood that, thanks to Pershing's profligacy with men, there was little to push with. Nine of the First Army's seventeen divisions had been crippled by casualties. More than one hundred thousand skulkers hid behind the lines, often having to be bombed out of their hiding places by MPs with grenades. "It was essential," Liggett reflected, "to gather up the army as a team." Pershing's insistence on "push" had bled the army white. Liggett, a far better operator than Pershing, wouldn't make the same mistake. He now placidly and unapologetically devoted two entire weeks to resting and restoring the First Army, bringing up its guns, and readying it for the sort of methodical, careful, devastating attack that the Allies had been conducting for two years and that Pershing had neglected in his haste to advance.[10]

Liggett had good reasons for slowing the pace, which were, of course, the same reasons applied every day on the Western Front by the French army, but none of that mattered to Clemenceau, who saw Liggett's pause as yet more evidence of American perfidy. On October 21, Clemenceau exploded in a letter to Foch. If Liggett's army were placed in column of route, by squads and batteries, it would have snaked for a thousand miles, the distance from New York to Chicago, and yet it was barely moving against three dozen weakened German divisions. Thirty-six German divisions was a lot, of course, but Clemenceau had been a tendentious journalist before he'd become a tendentious politician, and he could make a case for anything. Clemenceau was so angry at the slow progress of the US First Army that he actually advised Foch to write directly to President Wilson to get Pershing moving. "The crisis of the American army continues due to the invincible obstinacy of General Pershing. . . . Since the gains of the first days, they have hardly moved. The American troops are not unusable, they are unused." Clemenceau raged on: "You don't have to be an engineer to see that the immobility of your right wing has robbed your otherwise promising operation of momentum. Persuasion is not working. If Pershing won't obey your orders, you can appeal to President Wilson." Although Clemenceau feared an ugly rift if Foch went over Pershing's head, he concluded: "I think the time has come to speak directly to Wilson."[11]

Far from being "unused," the Americans continued to fight to straighten their lines even as Liggett paused to concentrate his artillery. With Hines's III Corps still lagging behind Dickman's I Corps and Summerall's V Corps, Hines now took aim at the heights of Cunel, which overlooked the zone from Romagne to the Meuse and was a natural rallying point for Germans retiring from the Kriemhilde Line. General John McMahon's 5th Division took Cunel and the key woods on October 17—the Bois de la Pultière and the Bois des Rappes. McMahon, a notorious dimwit who needed forty-five seconds to sign his name and had actually slept though the Saint-Mihiel offensive, seemed shattered by horrors he now woke to witness with his own eyes.[12]

Instead of digging in, McMahon retreated. "Why?" Pershing demanded. "The men were tired," McMahon answered. "Probably it was the division commander who was tired," Pershing snapped. He canned McMahon on the spot, sending him home to command an army post in Kentucky and promoting General Hanson Ely of the 2nd Division in his place. With grim indifference to the heavy casualties that had undone McMahon, Ely retook and held the objectives, opening the way north to the last German line: the Freya-Stellung. Foch sent a telegram to Pershing praising "the valor of his command." But the men under Pershing's command were sickened by death and fear. A thirteen-year-old private in the 5th Division, who'd lied about his age to enlist, despaired of what he'd seen in the Bois des Rappes: "Men torn to pieces, men I'd been talking to a few moments before. . . . Never had there been anything to compare with the ugly viciousness of what my eyes were seeing."[13]

Though the pause and detached operations drove Foch and Haig to distraction, they were the essential prelude to winning the war. Certainly no one else was winning it, or even in position to win it. Only the Americans were. Ignoring their critics, Pershing and Liggett massed a force of sufficiently experienced divisions for a renewed offensive on both banks of the Meuse beginning on October 28. The 89th and 90th Divisions had been brought up from Saint-Mihiel for what Pershing hoped would be the final push. The 1st Division, which had suffered 9,400 casualties in the brawling around Exermont and the Bois de Romagne, was returning to the front line early. So many men had been lost that all leaves in the Big Red One had been canceled so that the brutalized survivors could train the thousands of replacements who'd been hurried forward. For the recruits, some of whom had never fired a rifle, attack formations were sketched on chalkboards, but for most of the rookies tactics would boil down to this: "Here, Green, you follow Smith, and keep abreast of Jones over there." What Green would do when Smith and Jones were struck down or vanished in the fog was anyone's guess.

The 1st Division's new commander, General Frank Parker, "the ablest combat leader of the war," according to Summerall, reminded the men that they were the army's "First Assault Division," that they'd taken all objectives in each of their four battles, that they'd never surrendered an inch of ground to the Germans (and had here taken twelve miles of German ground), and that they'd captured a hundred Germans for every man they'd lost to Marwitz's prison cage. If unit pride alone wouldn't drive a last effort, Parker offered a winter in warm barracks: "It may be that a few more weeks of hammering will cause the collapse of the Central Empires and relieve us from many months of the discomforts of a winter's campaign."[14]

Parker ordered regimental commanders to "equalize" their devastated companies by shifting men between them and adding replacements as quickly as they arrived. The US 2nd, 77th, and 5th Divisions, rested and restored, were returning to the fight, as was the 80th Division. French artillery, engineering, and technical units were being withdrawn and replaced with American ones. All the while, Pershing was scouring his army for the best field officers and slotting them into the critical commands without regard for rank or seniority. He gave a brigade in the 5th Division to a major. MacArthur and several other one-stars were advanced to two-star rank, MacArthur taking command of the 42nd Rainbow Division for the attack on Sedan. It was the only way, and it took the kind of bureaucratic courage that had earned Pershing the sobriquet "the Iron Commander," the War Department having decreed an end to promotions "lest the sedentary generals at home have to fight to keep their wartime rank when confronted by homecoming combat temporaries." Pershing ignored the stupid decree. There was a war on. In the meantime, Pershing's "detached operations" straightened the line of departure for the final all-American thrust. "Like Kipling's ship," Colonel George Marshall recalled, "the army had found itself, and was crouching for the final spring." Marshall was referring to Rudyard Kipling's short story of 1895, "The Ship That Found Herself," in which the parts of a trawler on the voyage from England to America bicker with each other for most of the trip before merging into a single cooperative voice as they approach New York. The same process of assimilation was smoothing the rough edges of the AEF.[15]

On October 23, the US III and V Corps rested at the level of Bantheville. From this date until November 1, the Americans made no attempt to advance. Though Clemenceau seethed at their immobility, it was owed in this case to the immobility of the French Fourth Army, which Gouraud pronounced unable to resume its own advance until November 1. That suited Liggett just fine. Pershing's casualties had been so high that Liggett needed every available hour to fit replacements into the ravaged units and impress upon his field officers the need for more prudent tactics. During the respite, a corporal in the Rainbows walked through an aid station in Sommerance and was struck by the courage on display. The place was "crowded with the brave lads who have lost limbs or jaws or other organs yet they do not even groan, they simply smoke their cigarettes and stay silent."[16]

At home in the United States, fifty-eight-year-old General Leonard Wood blamed the heavy American losses on Pershing. Wood's case was an interesting one, proof of the maxim "The silent soldier is endowed with merit, the talky soldier mistrusted." Wood was a friend of Teddy Roosevelt and had been army chief of staff under President Taft. He'd been a logical choice to command the AEF but had been passed over by Wilson because of his loose tongue, his habit of exchanging indiscreet letters with Lloyd George, his Republican connections, and his advocacy for the Plattsburg "preparedness" camps, which the Democrats viewed as elitist and harmful to the already-functioning system of National Guards. Wood had become so suspect to Wilson that when the general finally wangled a command in France—of the embarking 89th Division—the president had relieved Wood of command at the port of embarkation and sent him back to Kansas. Now an indignant Wood added his fire to the already heavy barrage on Pershing. "Skillful leadership," Wood insisted, "attains the result through maneuver, infiltration and the proper use of the resources of modern war. Unskilled leadership arrives at results through enormous and unnecessary losses; losses which take not only the edge off the fighting blade, but soon wear it out."[17]

That much was true, but it made no allowance for the desolation of the Meuse-Argonne sector, the impossibility of maneuver there, or the lack of "skillful leadership" below the thin crust of Pershing's best officers. The problems only multiplied as the foul weather worsened. The AEF had lost forty thousand horses since Saint-Mihiel; they'd been killed by poison gas and enemy fire, but mainly by exhaustion— pulling guns and wagons through the slurry of the roads behind the US First and Second Armies. This slowed everything down, as guns and caissons, lacking horses, had to be towed by a dwindling number of trucks or men. Marshall recounted the exertions of the 6th Division, which lacked so many draft animals that the sodden, miserable Doughboys had to put themselves in harness and pull the division's vehicles over twenty-four miles of broken ground.[18]

Americans wounded at the tip of the spear often had to be evacuated a hundred miles or more to reach a hospital bed. In the meantime, they'd have to be selected for care at a forward triage station—and not consigned to death or gangrene—then be evacuated on the shoulders

Americans wounded at the tip of the spear often had to be evacuated 100 miles or more to reach a hospital bed. Here, a wounded American officer receives first aid while anxious comrades look on. Note the German prisoner waiting to carry the officer's stretcher. (National Archives)

of stretcher-bearers through shell-swept woods, then placed in mule ambulances to slop through the mud till they reached a solid road, where they'd be loaded onto trucks for the long, juddering drive to a hospital. To these agonized Doughboys, the war must have seemed far from over.[19]

In the last days of October, the Americans captured German "Instructions for Company Commanders"—dated September 28—that read: "An enemy crossing of the Meuse is to be prevented absolutely. Should he get across, he is to be thrown back into the Meuse at once; he must not get a foothold on the right bank of the Meuse under *any* circumstances." With the British and French armies closing on Givet (the same Meuse crossing that Hitler would struggle to seize during the Battle of the Bulge in 1945) and Pershing and

Gouraud thrusting toward Sedan and Montmédy, the Germans were holding their last line.[20]

The omens for Liggett's impending assault on the Freya-Stellung were far better than they'd been when the army had hunkered under German fire in the Exermont ravine or on the forward slopes of the Kriemhilde Line. III Corps on the right had gained the wooded hills north and east of Cunel. On the left, I Corps had cleared the Germans from the Argonne and carried the line beyond the northern bank of the Aire. In the center, Summerall's V Corps had punched through the fearsome Romagne Heights. While waiting for Gouraud, Liggett massed his guns for the next assault. For the first time since the initial thrust a month earlier, the preliminary US bombardment would be suitably massive. With every available gun brought forward on First Army's wretched roads, then packed hub to hub behind the attacking divisions, the American artillery would be able to grind the fields of German barbed wire into dust (along with entire villages, like Landres-et-Saint-Georges), kill or drive away German defenders, and allow the infantry to assault the Freya-Stellung with good chances of success.[21]

Angered by the German diplomatic note of October 20, which disdained serious armistice discussions, President Wilson dispatched a third note of his own, which arrived in Berlin on October 23. Having hoped that the moderate Prince Max would make a difference, Wilson now saw that he wouldn't. If the United States was going to have to deal, Wilson wrote, "with the military masters and the monarchical autocrats of Germany now, or if it is likely to have to deal with them later in regard to the international obligations of the German Empire, it must demand not peace negotiations but surrender." Trying to make a difference, Prince Max met with the kaiser, who was in Berlin when the note arrived. Max blamed this latest collapse of negotiations on Ludendorff's "breach of privilege"—the general's arrogation to himself of powers that belonged to the kaiser and the chancellor. Of course the generals had been breaching privilege since before the war—Germany being, as Mirabeau had famously said of Prussia over a century earlier, "not a state with an army but an army with a state"—but now the crisis was so extreme that even the notoriously tentative kaiser would have to act. Germany's military situation might have stabilized on the Meuse, but Wilson's latest note had unleashed a torrent of revolution in Germany as a hungry, war-weary people rightly blamed the "military masters and monarchical autocrats" for their plight. Riots broke out in Germany demanding abdication and peace. Cornered, Kaiser Wilhelm II summoned Ludendorff on October 26 and coldly forced the general's resignation. His successor would be the army's fifty-one-year-old director of railways, General Wilhelm Groener.[22]

For Liggett's November 1 push, the German defenses again had the advantage of exceptional terrain. The Germans deployed opposite the V and III Corps on the high Barricourt Ridge, which curved in a northwesterly direction. This ridge thoroughly dominated the ground to its south and west. It also covered the vital German lines of communication north and northeast to the Meuse at Sedan and Stenay. Woods atop the crest concealed German batteries and reserves. Hill 253, before this ridge, was the forward combat position, a natural switch line that allowed the Germans to attach that hill, an unsubdued bastion of the Kriemhilde-Stellung, to the Freya Line. High ground north of Landres-et-Saint-Georges gave the Germans good observation over the terrain the Americans would have to cross. The reverse slopes of those heights gave excellent opportunities for the favored German tactic: a machine-gun defense echeloned in depth. Every inch of the rugged country would be swept by fire. The ground was so valuable that when the Germans had lost it briefly to attacks by the 79th and 5th Divisions, they had then counterattacked to retake it. Now it was strewn with dead men of the US 3rd Division, some of them cut down in wave formation where they'd left the woods and walked into German machine-gun fire. Pershing shuttled between his headquarters and the front to see the battlefield and objectives with his own eyes and finalize preparations. Lejeune recalled Pershing blowing past him in a black sedan at seventy miles per hour in the last week of October: "We caught a glimpse of General Pershing." The Iron Commander always cleared the road ahead and traveled at full speed—with a backup car—to save time and elude German artillery.[23]

The Germans were tired; not only were they not getting leaves or even rests behind the lines, they were being kept in battle readiness at all times, which was exhausting. The men had to be ready to fight in fifteen minutes or less; horses had to be kept saddled around the clock. Men slept with their boots on, awakened at all hours by various alarms. Austrian replacements arriving here increasingly refused to replace. Ordered into line in the last days of October, the Austro-Hungarian 25th Jäger Battalion balked. The officers cajoled and threatened; the men were unmoved: "We are worn out; we can do no more. We need rest." Who could blame them? The Germans they were replacing greeted them thus: "Why are you here? Why are you prolonging the war?"[24]

On October 24, American military intelligence noted that "for the first time in the history of the war the enemy now has not one division in reserve on the Western Front which has been out of battle for more than a month." The Germans, in other words, had no fresh troops. They couldn't rest and restore units anymore. Every man was constantly needed at the front. A month earlier the Germans had possessed twenty divisions that had been rested for a month or more. In the intervening weeks, all twenty had been committed, six against the Americans and fourteen against the French and British. That day in Vienna, the socialist *Arbeiter-Zeitung*, no longer fearing Habsburg press controls, threw in the towel: "Every day 10,000 Americans cross the sea, adding 300,000 troops to the Allied army every month. . . . The Americans send over fresh troops while the Germans can only oppose them with old poorly-fed soldiers who have fought through four years of war. Do the people wish to continue the war under such conditions?"[25]

On paper (and in the papers), the Allies were definitely winning, but not on the Meuse, where the Germans stood fast. Following events from his exile in Camp Funston, Kansas, General Leonard Wood felt certain that the war would go on and on and on. Even if the Ottoman Empire and Bulgaria were knocked out, leaving Germany and Austria "surrounded and reduced to a defensive war, this does not necessarily mean a war soon to be over," Wood surmised. "If they are united and fight for life, it is going to be a long hard struggle; for manpower will not be exhausted for years." Knock the Germans out *now*, Wood insisted. They were like a "wobbling ring fighter." A brutal punch had to be landed: "Don't stop to give him breathing time."[26]

The entire German army was indeed wobbling, as the diary of a German lieutenant in Belgium made clear. In Namur, he saw hordes of German stragglers, "gray throngs who, according to their story, are looking for their units, who trail around from one office to the next (at meal time) and who ask only one thing, *not* to arrive at their destination." Attempting to board a train from Belgium to Germany on October 23, the German officer was shoved aside by "an immense and brutal mob" of soldiers. He eventually boarded the train through a window, the soldiers "savagely shoving and shouting taunts," none of them saluting the officers. Once the train was moving, the men shouted the old barrack-room joke, "Put out the lights! Out with the knives! Three men to fight for blood!" This time they meant it. Mockery of German generals circulated loudly through the cars, "sneering laughter" rewarding the jokers: "Hindenburg is like the sun," one soldier shouted. "He rose in the east and he is going down in the west." The field marshal had risen to fame in 1914 by obliterating a Russian army at Tannenberg. Four years later, his sun was all too obviously setting here. The German lieutenant, by now quaking—"If you called them out they'd jump at your throat"—marveled at the degree of savagery attained by these frightened, demoralized troops. "Ludendorff, Hindenburg, nothing and nobody is sacred to this gang," he scribbled, noting that the jabbering, malevolent men fell silent only when the train stopped for an air raid. With Allied planes gliding overhead, looking and listening for targets, the dark, momentarily hushed train "resembled a beast which seeks to escape the butcher by making no movement." The German lieutenant hardly needed to add, "Alas, this is no longer our army of 1917!"[27]

Even with victory at hand, the Allied coalition continued to fray under the pressure of casualties and disappointment. A report on October 25 from Haig's liaison in Foch's headquarters to General Henry

Wilson in London suggested that Foch still intended to snatch Pershing's army away from the American commander at the first opportunity. "Marshal Foch gave an indication of his intention to modify the distribution of the American army, but he gave no precise information as to what he had decided to do in this respect. He left it to be inferred that the concentration of the American army under the command of General Pershing would not last much longer." This was music to Henry Wilson's ears. The imperial general staff chief described the AEF commander thus: "So stupid, so narrow, so pigheaded." Major Paul Clark, the American liaison in Foch's headquarters, asked Colonel Jacques de Chambrun, France's liaison in Pershing's headquarters, why the French and British were so hostile to Pershing. "Pershing," Chambrun replied, "is the biggest man that this war has produced," but "if the war stops now the French and the French government will not give the American effort and General Pershing the appreciation that they merit." Why not? Clark pursued. Because, Chambrun said, "Clemenceau doesn't like him, the French Staff doesn't like him. Only Pétain likes him." Pétain and Pershing were similarly austere, and they shared a headquarters in Souilly. "But *why* don't the French government and the staff like Pershing?" Clark persisted. "Why that's easy," Chambrun concluded. "Because you are foreigners; the French have never traveled and the French army officer has traveled even less than the civilian."[28]

Chambrun was doubtless being polite, diplomatic, and evasive. America's allies—victory in sight—were suffering buyer's remorse and would spend the rest of the war, what remained of it, talking down the American contribution to victory. If victory could really be had in 1918, then the Europeans might still take credit for it. They knew America had saved them, but they deplored the political cost and its vast ramifications. The "transatlantic people" so coveted by the French and British in 1917 had become the transatlantic power so feared by them in 1918. The world would never be the same again. Here was a new power that, in just its first year of war, had spent more money than Britain had spent in three years of war, had registered twenty-four million men for the draft, and had trained and shipped two million of them to France. Having sunk these costs, weathered Ludendorff's offensives, and breached the Hindenburg Line near its vital pivot, Washington seemed in no particular hurry to end the war now. The Americans would have three million battle-ready troops in France by April 1919 for a war-winning blow—three times as many as they had now. London recoiled at the thought, the War Cabinet affirming South African General Jan Smuts's conclusions on October 26: "If peace comes now, it will be a British peace, it will be a peace given to the world by the same Empire that settled the Napoleonic wars a century ago." But if the war continued into 1919, Smuts cautioned, the "center of gravity" would migrate to Washington. The United States would become "the diplomatic dictator of the world."[29]

At a conference of the Allied commanders at Foch's new headquarters at Senlis on October 25, convened to agree on what armistice terms would be offered, Pershing and Foch advocated taking a hard line with the Germans. Haig—worried that the Germans would reject harsh terms and prolong a war for which neither he nor Pétain had sufficient troops—had a dig at Pershing: "The American army is not yet organized, not yet formed, and has suffered a great deal on account of its ignorance of modern warfare." The field marshal then demanded a softer line. To no avail—the armistice conditions went out, Pershing successfully adding the demand for 150 German submarines and an Allied naval occupation of Cuxhaven and Heligoland, Haig weakly objecting: "That is none of our affair. It is a matter for the Admiralty to decide."[30]

Foch's "general battle" idea had been founded on the assumption that huge Allied casualties would be sustained breaching the Hindenburg Line, but then German casualties would be easier to inflict against the lighter defenses behind the line. But the Germans, even in retreat, were still giving as good as they got. Foch, planning to move his headquarters to Épernay to follow the action more closely, insisted that Haig continue to follow orders and press his attacks south of the line Valenciennes-Mons, but Foch's Supreme Command was plainly unraveling. With Haig's staff chief, General Herbert Lawrence, ignoring Weygand's messages, Foch was reduced to sending orders directly to Haig. General Charles Grant, Foch's British liaison, met with Lawrence on October 28 and described the latter's attitude toward Foch as "an impossible one, and the whole attitude of the Staff at G.H.Q. was the same." General Sidney Clive—the British liaison in Pétain's headquarters—told Grant that in Haig's view, "Foch and Weygand were drunk with victory and thought that they could do as they liked at the expense of the British Armies." Grant considered General Lawrence a self-defeating figure, hardly the man to polish off the Germans. "If the war continues," Grant noted in early November, "the position will be a very difficult one," with Lawrence working actively *against* Foch's staff. Of Lawrence, Grant wrote: "It is almost incredible that the chief of the general staff of a victorious group of armies should never have himself believed in victory, and this would not have been possible in any other army but our own."[31]

While Haig and Pétain spun their wheels, Liggett's US First Army straightened its lines for a last push. On October 27, General James McRae's 78th Division had wrested Grandpré from the Germans in a bitter battle that climaxed in house-to-house and rooftop combat. Pershing had expected to take the place on the battle's opening day. He finally had it, a month later. Since relieving the 77th Division two weeks earlier, the 78th had lost five thousand men fighting across the twin channels of the Aire and up the granite cliffs of Grandpré. The fighting in this sector had been as savage as any, day upon day of gas and artillery attacks and failed infantry assaults. But Dickman's I Corps had done its job, seized the western sections of the Kriemhilde Line, and installed itself on the high ground overlooking the Aire Valley. Liggett now had secure flanks and a more or less straight line to continue his attack into the Freya-Stellung.[32]

On October 30, General Dickman advised the three divisions of I Corps—the 77th, 78th, and 80th—that "the pending operation bears a distinct resemblance to the sounding of a gong for what may prove to be the final round of a knockout fight." Rumors of an imminent cease-fire were playing tricks with American morale, no Doughboy wanting to be the last man to die in France. Even the 1st Division, whose motto was "We are the first Assault Division of the AEF," had to take new measures to contain straggling, placing sergeants not where they were needed, at the tip of the spear, but 1,200 meters behind attacking units, to roust the "shell-hole rats" from cover and send them back into the fight. Liggett's staff chief, General Malin Craig, fretted that "the various publications of notes looking to the establishment of an armistice are in their real effect most insidious and calculated to slow up the efforts of all concerned." He ordered his officers to "counteract these insidious effects," which was easier said than done. On the same day, October 30, German officers passed leaflets to their troops that said: "Soldiers! The war is still on, the armistice has not yet come." The weather wasn't helping. Even Colonel George Marshall's stoic memoir recoiled at the incessant rain, mud, and gloom of late autumn in northern France: "The long cold nights, the water-soaked ground . . . the leaden skies of the few daylight hours offered little to cheer the spirits of the men."[33]

Increasing numbers of US frontline troops were coming down with the lethal Spanish flu. Nearly eight hundred thousand Doughboys contracted the flu and forty-seven thousand of them would die of it—almost as many as were killed by enemy action. Transports arriving from the States with the men needed to replace the casualties in the Meuse-Argonne—twenty-six thousand dead and ninety-six thousand wounded so far—were riddled with flu. The youngest, healthiest recruits often died first, as their robust immune systems overreacted to the virus and drowned the men in antibodies. Ships that had already stopped once to let off flu cases in Nova Scotia would arrive at ports like Brest with their dead stacked on the deck, to find freshly dug graves for all of the men who'd died in transit. Some ships had so many flu deaths, easily contracted in the stuffy holds, that the corpses were buried at sea; those that weren't were flung two-deep into long trenches at the port of arrival. Hundreds more would be taken directly from the ships to tent camp hospitals, where they'd be laid under canvas to recover or die. Spanish flu in the fall of 1918 reduced American troop transports to Europe by 10 percent. In the last week of October, the US Army reported nearly three hundred thousand flu cases and four hundred to eight hundred new cases every day. Instructed by President Wilson to travel from Paris to Souilly to meet with Pershing and hear his views on war termination, the always-obliging Colonel House refused to go, saying that if he went he might contract the deadly flu. Back in the States, the army reported 182,591 flu cases in its training camps. Eighteen thousand US troops had already died from the virulent combination of flu and pneumonia. That was more than twice as many men as had died at the Battle of Gettysburg.[34]

Somehow Pershing had to keep the troops going, despite the nearness of the peace, the vileness of the weather, the fury of the flu, and the declining quality of American replacements. Replacements from the South were generally witless but all-American. Many couldn't write their own names, but—the army consoled itself—at least they didn't tolerate the "carping foreign element" embedded in many northern divisions because of immigration. Southern recruits, according to Pershing's intelligence reports, "would tolerate no anti-American remarks." One batch of southern recruits shipped from New York in October beat up all of the "foreign-born draft evaders" on board. These were men who'd tried to escape the draft as conscientious objectors but had been drafted anyway. A Pershing operative noted that the beatings "turned them into rather fair Americans." It was hard to know if he was kidding or serious. Replacements from the West were prized most of all: "They take the usual Western attitude—they don't like to have their peaceful life disturbed by war but since they were in the army they were going to get revenge on the cause of it—the Boche."[35]

Filling out the ranks of his veterans with these new recruits—willing and unwilling—General Liggett sounded the gong, shoving his weary divisions back into the ring for what he hoped was the last round. They marched into position on Halloween for a big push the next morning. Their instructions for this last round showed just how much the young AEF had learned in a month of combat: "Each unit must be made to understand that steady forward progress, any progress on its part, insures the progress of units to right and left. The 75s must follow the infantry within a very few minutes after H-hour.

In October 1918, the AEF estimated that it was missing 100,000 men who were known to be "skulking" behind the lines to avoid battle. Each US division dealt with the problem differently. In the 82nd Division, skulkers were rounded up and marked with a red "Straggler" sign, which they wore till their court-martial. If convicted, they were blazoned with a red "Deserter" sign and sent to prison. (National Archives)

Forward echelons with infantry, rear echelons within a few minutes. Mopping up of concealed dugouts and hidden nests must be thorough. Carriers, transport crews, engineers and road makers—their tasks are as important as that of the combat troops. Liaison between units, superiority of fire—rifle fire—at all times." With the First Army still missing an estimated one hundred thousand stragglers, Dickman and the other corps commanders ordered the deployment of two cordons of MPs reinforced by troops, one just behind the advanced dressing station, the other a mile behind it, to stem straggling. Skulkers were shamed with bold red signs painted on sheet metal and cinched around their waists with wire: "DESERTER" or "STRAGGLER FROM FRONT LINES." All of these measures, it was hoped, would deliver the "scientific knockout blow."[36]

With the British and French attacks farther west advancing slowly, both armies needing (but lacking) an infusion of 250,000 infantry to bring their divisions up to combat strength, Foch urged all of his armies forward, deflecting protests about fatigue and morale with his well-worn maxim: "Victorious armies are never fresh." Taking stock of his fading Allies, Pershing saw that only the US Army could end the war before Christmas. If the AEF broke through the Freya-Stellung, they could race ahead to the Meuse and cut Hindenburg's "jugular": the ten miles of quadruple-tracked railway between Sedan and Mézières that permitted the German army to keep fighting in France. Pershing now instructed Liggett to conclude every order to his corps and divisions with the sentence: "There can be no conclusion to this war until Germany is brought to her knees."[37]

To win the war before year's end, Liggett planned on November 1 to advance Dickman's I Corps from Grandpré to Boult-aux-Bois and Buzancy. I Corps would bash through the Freya Line, flank the Bois de Bourgogne, and join its left wing to Gouraud's French Fourth Army in the nearby Aisne valley and its right wing to Summerall's V Corps in the center. Summerall, advancing from the hard-won Romagne Heights, would strike the heart of the Freya Line, punching through the fortified Barricourt Ridge. If Summerall broke through at Barricourt, the US First Army would be just ten miles from Sedan, clean through the three fortified spines of the Meuse-Argonne, and able finally to advance its guns and bring the railway at Sedan under continuous Allied fire. The Americans wouldn't even have to advance far to fire for effect; the US Navy had delivered four fourteen-inch naval guns on railway mounts to Liggett to begin the destruction.[38]

General John Hines's III Corps on the right would try again to take Brieulles, but only if Hines could outflank and silence the German guns on the Borne de Cornouiller across the Meuse, using the French II Colonial Corps and three US divisions: the 26th, 79th, and 81st. Hines's attacks in the second week of October on the German-held Bois de Fays, Ogons, and Brieulles had been taken in the flank and rear by those German guns across the Meuse. The French colonials,

North Africans from Morocco and Algeria, had already weathered slaughters in Champagne in 1915, the Somme in 1916, the Nivelle Offensive in 1917, and Château-Thierry in the spring and summer of 1918. They now faced yet another on the Borne, described by an American veteran as "barriers the Ice Age seemed to have erected on the Heights of the Meuse northeast of Verdun for the benefit of the Germans 18,000 years later."[39]

Summerall's V Corps prepared to assault the Barricourt Ridge on November 1. One Doughboy ascending the steep Côte Dame Marie, just taken by the 42nd Division, reflected on the toughness of the Rainbows: "It was bad enough to climb the hill, let alone run the Germans off at the same time." The men trudged forward under pouring rain. Though aerial observation was limited by fog and gloom, Air Service photo missions had operated on October 27 and 29, and they had photographed the whole German front to a depth of three miles. This was essential because German engineers used tunnels, camouflage, and concealment to make their fighting fronts appear like a blank wall. Battery positions, machine-gun nests, and routes of circulation had to be discovered, pinpointed, and mapped. On the ground, restless American patrols used German speakers to confuse the enemy, slipping through outposts in the dark by hailing them in German, or greeting and then killing them.[40]

Captured Germans coughed up the information Summerall needed. He was facing at least four quality enemy divisions on the Barricourt Ridge: the 15th Bavarian Division and the German 52nd, 88th, and 28th Divisions. On October 31, Summerall, known for his oratory, addressed the 1st Division. It had been through so much and was being called on one more time. "Men, you belong to a fighting division. You have gone far. You will go farther. You have suffered much. You will suffer more. You have gone long without food. You will go longer. You have faced death. You will face it again."[41]

Liggett had used the two weeks since his last push to bring up artillery concentrations comparable to the massive bombardment of September 26 that had pounded Montfaucon. He had six hundred guns—one for every twenty yards of front, each of which would spit

235 shells into the German lines before the Doughs went over the top. The guns fired for two hours early on November 1—pulverizing a zone eighteen miles wide and a mile deep—and then Liggett's First Army attacked at 5:30 a.m., just as the sun was rising into a clear blue sky. The bombardment was "an elemental cataclysm, like the simultaneous eruption of many volcanoes," Marine general John Lejeune observed. The Doughboys advanced, "leaning on" their rolling barrage as it crept toward the devastated German positions. As was his habit, Liggett sat down with a deck of cards to play solitaire until the first reports came back from the front. The reports, when they arrived, were promising. The assaulting divisions of V Corps—the 89th and 2nd Divisions—had advanced five miles and taken their objectives: Landres-et-Saint-Georges, Saint-Georges, Landreville, Chenery, and the heights of Barricourt, from which German guns had thwarted every previous attempt to pursue beyond the Kriemhilde Line. Stunned German prisoners told their captors that they'd never faced artillery fire like this. The Doughs had advanced behind a four-layered rolling barrage of phosgene gas, high explosive, and shrapnel.[42]

One Doughboy walking along the captured German frontline positions observed "body after body of German soldiers, most of them killed by shell fire." In the machine-gun pits, he saw the corpses of the last defenders. "It was the supreme power of the Artillery, absolute devastation," an awed officer wrote. Passing through ruins of the Kriemhilde and Freya Lines, a major noted their desolation: "Torn to shreds by the American guns . . . drenched with gas . . . the odor of charred things was everywhere as if the earth were still smoldering." In the abandoned German positions that had killed so many Americans, he felt "the hot breath of an unseen, evil power." The ground felt "haunted." Another Doughboy expressed wonderment at this continuing German resistance: "Let us give even the Devil his due . . . 'Fritz' held the world back for months and died game. . . . I disliked the Germans, but I disliked them because I feared them, knowing full well their deadly capability. They had crushed individualism so thoroughly that they had the bravery and determination of insects."[43]

Only General Robert Alexander's 77th Division failed to gain its objectives that day, held up around Champigneulles and Grandpré. Alexander had ordered an enveloping attack on the strongpoints, yet his 153rd Brigade commander, General William Smedberg, had attacked frontally, losing hundreds of men to no effect. Alexander canned the brigadier, notified Malin Craig, Liggett's chief of staff, that he had done so, and was told: "Oh, I wouldn't do that; Smedberg has many very powerful friends and you will hear from it." Smedberg was a West Point graduate and was well-connected in the army and the War Department. Alexander was a "maverick," an officer who had enlisted as a private thirty-two years earlier and worked his way up the ranks. Alexander "blooeyed" Smedberg anyway, bleakly noting in his memoirs, "Since that day I have had ample reason to recognize the cogency of General Craig's warning." Instead of being sent to Blois for "reclassification" and a ship home, Smedberg was given a new brigade in the 32nd Division and permitted to serve a decade longer than Alexander after the war. Armies, like most organizations, feed on connections and patronage.[44]

Lejeune, echeloned ahead and to the right of Alexander with his more successful 2nd Division, recalled hearing the nonstop chatter of German machine guns as they chewed up Smedberg's frontal assaults. German POWs all along the front asserted that American artillery concentrations were this time so effective that they'd been trapped in their shelters and easily overrun and captured. They also marveled at the strength of American assault divisions, like the 89th, which had five officers and 250 men per *company*. By this stage, German battalions didn't have that many men. Some German batteries were so deluged with American gas and shellfire that they'd been unable to fire a shot in return. German officers had been cut off from any communication with their troops, many of whom used this loosening of the reins to surrender.[45]

The US V Corps, spearheaded by the 2nd and 89th Divisions, took Landres-et-Saint-Georges with nineteen tanks—the only tanks the First Army possessed—and pushed through to the ground north of the Bois de Barricourt. The 89th Middle West Division had been

Leonard Wood's unit until President Wilson took it away and gave it to its present commander, General William Wright, who was himself a minor celebrity. Wright had been Pershing's roommate at West Point in his plebe year but had flunked out. President Chester Arthur, prodded by his secretary of state, a friend of Wright's father, then personally commissioned Wright a second lieutenant, prompting an outcry in the Senate and a vote to block the commission on grounds of nepotism. Wright, whose father had been aide-de-camp to George McClellan and Winfield Scott during the Civil War, squeaked through and now was here, facing some of the fiercest combat yet.[46]

Nearly every company in the 89th Division had to overcome ten heavy machine guns. For the first time the Doughboys were colliding with division-strength German reserves, which had been marched up behind the Kriemhilde-Stellung. With thirty-two divisions in line and eight in reserve, the German commanders, Georg von der Marwitz and Max von Gallwitz, took the divisions from their army reserve and subdivided them as needed, wherever the Americans broke through. These German reserves would use local roads, or *pistes*, to rush a battalion or regiment to a threatened point, then use the villages and woods as strongpoints to stop the American advance and throw them back. Allied aerial reconnaissance showed that here, with their backs to the Meuse, ground was so precious that the Germans now dispensed with defense in depth. Each regiment would send two battalions to the front and leave the third close behind. Flushed from their trenches and having no laborers to construct new ones, the Germans now fought from hastily scraped foxholes and shell craters or used woods and terrain. Machine-gun nests were far less likely to be found on crests than far down the reverse slope. These counter-slope machine-gun nests were more survivable and allowed indirect fire against the attackers. Marshall bemoaned the army's continuing lack of tanks to snuff out the German machine guns: "Here was a commentary on the price of unpreparedness to be paid inevitably in human life." America, "the master steel-maker of the world," rode into this climactic battle with just nineteen tanks, not the five hundred required.[47]

One Doughboy witnessed the price in human life at hideously close quarters. Ordered to bury the dead of the US 89th and 90th Divisions, he discovered only pieces of men who had been hacked to shreds by the fire of German machine guns and artillery. "The mutilation and mangling was something terrible." All that was left of one soldier was "a piece of human flesh about twice as large as a man's hand." All that was left of another was "only the legs from the knees down. A shell had made a direct hit on him. Not another bit of his body could be found." The corpses were "torn and horribly mangled. . . . One body had the intestine laying exposed; another had the head split open by a large shell fragment; another had his face shot away in a sickening terrible manner." One corpse clutched a picture of the man's wife and child. The burial party passed the photo around somberly, "as we thought of the fate of the husband and the father, lying cold and stiff at our feet." The Doughboy burying these men, a student at divinity school when the war broke out, paused to contemplate the horror: "Many sad and wistful ears will wait, but will never hear the approach of men who went to war." The carnage depressed him. He knew these men; they'd gone "to their death with a smile and a jest"; they'd done nothing to deserve this fate, "to be deprived of life in this violent manner, away from relatives and friends, and in a distant, alien land."[48]

Finding themselves in a shrinking, alien land, the German infantry and artillery fought like cornered dogs, which was why Haig and Pétain were so reluctant to press their attacks. One of the Marine battalions of the US 2nd Division assigned to attack Saint-Georges and Landres had risen at 5:30 a.m. to attack. To cover them while they formed into waves, their artillery had placed a ten-minute standing barrage just in front of their "jumping-off line." The German artillery immediately countered, and in the ten minutes needed to line up the men, one hundred of the Marines were killed or wounded before they'd even taken a step forward. When the standing barrage began to roll onward, the men followed, encountering German machine guns and artillery in every wood and ravine. Here the village of Chenery had been built into a strongpoint with four 77mm cannon and a checkerboard of machine guns. Three tanks cleaned up the machine guns, and a squad of Marines ran in and captured the battery and its seventy-five gunners. They saw the rest of the garrison, two hundred riflemen, scrambling away toward Sivry.[49]

In their drive to the Barricourt crest, this division and the rest of V Corps captured 360 machine guns, two batteries of 88s, ten 77s, and numerous ammo dumps. With the Barricourt Ridge in hand, Summerall's V Corps had bashed through the heart of the Freya-Stellung and forced the Germans to flee all the way north to the Meuse. On a clear day, the spires of Sedan could be glimpsed from the captured heights. Now US heavy artillery could be brought up to the area around Beaumont to fire on the Sedan railway and interrupt its operations. Reduced by 120,000 casualties in this hellish sector, the American matador was at last playing his blade across the throat of the German bull.[50]

I Corps's 80th Division took Buzancy on November 2, chasing away General Karl von Einem, who'd made his headquarters there during the battles for the Kriemhilde and Freya Lines. The sixty-five-year-old Einem had been German war minister before the war and had advocated successfully for the procurement of machine guns in far greater numbers than the other powers. Now he was gone, fleeing back to Hindenburg's last redoubt behind the Meuse, leaving Buzancy a smoking ruin, his château a pile of rubble. This success, joined to Summerall's victory at Barricourt, ruptured the Freya Line. Lejeune congratulated the men of the 2nd Division for the breakthrough. They'd taken Belleau Wood in June, the Blanc Mont in October, and the Barricourt Heights in November. "Let us press on and destroy the enemy," he urged. Liggett sent General Alexander's 77th Division through the obstacles that had slowed it on November 1 and then north to keep contact with the fleeing Germans.[51]

Liggett wheeled his 78th Division left to Boult-aux-Bois to outflank the German defenders inside the Bois de Bourgogne and join the US First Army to Gouraud's French Fourth Army on the other side of the wood. This they accomplished, meeting Gouraud's right-hand units on the road from Grandpré to the Aisne. Doughboys and poilus were photographed embracing and waving their helmets in the air. The Americans had breached the Kriemhilde-Stellung, the French its extension west of the Argonne, the Brunhilde-Stellung. Gouraud could now cross the Aisne and hasten his pursuit toward Sedan. Dickman's I Corps could advance without threat from German batteries and machine guns in the Bois de Bourgogne. The *bois*, a cornerstone of the German defense, had been rendered uninhabitable by Dickman's massed artillery, which had drenched the wood with forty-one tons of mustard gas. The Germans died at their guns or fled, French villagers later recounting the sight of the shocked rear guards staggering away with their eyes swollen shut and weeping from mustard gas and phosgene.[52]

Hines's III Corps on the right had two missions: to take the easternmost heights of the Barricourt Ridge around Villers-devant-Dun, preventing the Germans there from firing into the flank of Summerall's V Corps, and to take Brieulles. Its own flank, of course, would continue to take fire from the German guns on the Borne de Cornouiller across the river. General Henry Allen's 90th Alamo Division—National Army from Texas and Oklahoma—advanced five miles on November 1 and took its objectives: Aincreville, Doulcon, and Andevanne. This advance by the "Tough 'Ombres," as the 90th was known, unhinged the whole German defense west of the Meuse. General Hanson Ely's 5th Division attacked northeast toward Dun-sur-Meuse to entrap the Germans at Brieulles. Ely lashed together flatboats and pontoon bridges to cross the Meuse and outflank first Brieulles on the right and then Dun-sur-Meuse on the left, wriggling in this way through his end of the Freya-Stellung. He was aided by airpower, German units reporting regular attacks by as many as one hundred low-flying American planes strafing and dropping bombs.

Those Germans also reported that American tactics, though improved in some sectors, remained as careless and unrefined as ever in others. One Bavarian machine gunner posted on a wooded height near Dun, defending the right bank of the Meuse, couldn't believe his eyes when the Americans finally attacked, crossing from Clery-le-Petit in rowboats like "Sunday soldiers." He stared in disbelief, bloodlust mixed with pity. "Never in the entire 35 months that I had spent at the front in this war had I seen such juicy targets." Two of his three machine guns were out of commission—one jammed, one broken. He fired eight thousand rounds with his only functioning gun, till the barrel had to be changed and the water in the sleeve was boiling— shattering the boats, blasting the Americans into the frigid water, and mowing down any Americans who made it across. Another gun to his left opened up, trapping the Doughboys in a cross fire from which there was no escape. That night, the German recalled, was awful—echoing with the agonized cries of the wounded Americans below, pleading for help that the much-reduced Bavarian unit above them couldn't provide. One of the Bavarian veterans reported that his young school-age recruits were completely undone by the experience. They were traumatized by the slaughter they'd inflicted and the searing cries of the American wounded; he saw some of them on their knees praying for forgiveness.[53]

Bullard had said of Ely that he "was ready to fight anyone, anywhere, anytime," and he certainly proved it in this corner of the battlefield, which had inflicted so much misery on the First Army since late September. Across the Meuse, Liggett's French II Colonial Corps and three US divisions—the 26th, 79th, and 81st—continued to pressure the Germans on the Borne de Cornouiller and gird for an all-out assault. If the Borne fell, the US First Army would be able to stream up both banks of the Meuse toward Sedan, threatening an abrupt end to the war. The Germans hated the Moroccans more than any other nationality for their brutality. Knowing that the Moroccans believed that they wouldn't get to paradise if blown up or dismembered, the Germans used *Minenwerfer* wherever the Moroccans appeared, lobbing the big barrel bombs into their trenches nonstop. This made deployments even more dangerous than usual for American units posted near North African troops.[54]

German chancellor Prince Max of Baden had himself contracted the Spanish flu, missing the drama of Ludendorff's dismissal on October 26. When he began to recover on November 3, Germany's situation had worsened considerably. Hindenburg's armies in France, now ably coordinated by General Wilhelm Groener, were still holding the line, but the Austrians and Turks were negotiating for terms with the Allies, Bulgaria had already surrendered, and the German fleet, ordered to sea by Admiral Wilhelm von Scheer to fight an apocalyptic battle with the Royal Navy, mutinied instead. The crews raised red flags, returned to their berths, and then left their ships to fan revolution in the port cities and interior. In Berlin, crowds demanded the kaiser's abdication. Prince Max redoubled his efforts to secure an armistice and head off revolution, dispatching the Reichstag's Catholic Center Party leader, Matthias Erzberger, and a team of negotiators to Compiègne, north of Paris, to meet with Foch.[55]

Even as the Allies fought to terminate the war, the rifts between them widened. Meeting with Pétain's deputy, General Edmond Buat, on November 1, Major Paul Clark heard the general's reservations about the Fourteen Points. "They are so philosophical—so vaguely phrased. . . . What is their practical application? For instance, what does he mean by the phrases 'society of nations' and 'freedom of the seas'? The French people love explicitness and they don't find it in Mr. Wilson's conditions." Captain Charles Freeborn, Clark's deputy, lunched with two of Pétain's adjutants, one of whom declared: "Americans should do the bulk of the police work after the war because France has done much more fighting than the U.S. and has as many dead as there are Americans in France." And yet the Germans had invaded France, not America, and hundreds of thousands of those French dead were owed to the suicidal tactics propagated by Foch himself in 1914. Ambling around Foch's Operations Bureau, Clark was accosted by Colonel Node Langlois:

> Your President is doing the world a bad turn by insisting so much
> on the destruction of the late German Government and by laying
> so much stress on the right of peoples to determine their govern-
> ment. That principle is all right for people who have the qualities
> which justify them in asserting their ability and right to choose
> their rulers, but certainly the Russians, for instance, or the Czechs

or Yugoslavs are not in that category, and Mr. Wilson is helping to unsettle the whole world and throw it into turmoil. Bolshevism asks nothing better, for a world in social disorder is a fertile soil for Bolshevism.[56]

On November 2, Haig's First and Third Armies took Valenciennes, noting a slackening in German resistance. War correspondent Charles Repington reported a surprising lack of celebration—not a flag raised, not a bell rung—as each liberated town fell into Allied hands. Instead there was "a dead, numb, implacable feeling of seeing the thing through." Pershing, who'd lost 150,000 men in the Meuse-Argonne, was feeling numb himself at the scale of the slaughter. On Liggett's front that day, the Germans were forced to abandon Champigneulle opposite I Corps and retreat. American pursuit across open country was now possible, and Tailly, Nouart, and Fosse were taken on November 3. That night, the 2nd Division pushed through the Bois de Belval and closed to within a mile of Beaumont, Lejeune observing that by this stage of the campaign, his troops "by constant practice had acquired night sight and were able to find their way in blackest darkness." They no longer had need of guides and padded silently past their own corps military police without being observed.[57]

Night operations proved essential. They were the only way to move against German machine guns that spewed accurate fire in daylight. They were also dangerous, the Germans leaving all sorts of "field traps" behind to slow the pursuit. At Champigneulle, the Doughboys nearly stumbled over a particularly lethal one: three dozen 150mm shells buried vertically in the road with their noses protruding and rigged to an igniter and trip wire a foot off the ground. Had a sleepy column of troops not seen the device in time, they'd have obliterated themselves and that entire corner of the Ardennes. Night operations often bagged whole German units caught sleeping. One of Lejeune's columns of Doughboys and Marines approached La Forge Ferme near Beaumont in the night and found the fields and barns filled with snoring German troops, all of whom were captured without a shot fired.[58]

The Americans and French had broken the last major barrier shielding the Sedan railway and, in a single day, forced the Germans back a dozen miles to Le Chesne. Hindenburg was compelled to throw in five additional reserve divisions to stem the American advance on November 3. Most of the Germans went back behind the Meuse; the great escape was on. With three British armies and the French First Army now making for Namur and breaching the German defenses on the Sambre-Oise Canal—where war poet Wilfred Owen was killed on November 4—Hindenburg tried to extricate what he could from the shrinking German salient in France, now a sack that Pershing was tying off at the mouth. Or trying to tie off: French progress between the British and American pincers was so slow that more Germans than expected were escaping the pocket. Fugitives from behind German lines described chaos there as the Germans tried all at once to remove artillery, troops, and also able-bodied French and Belgian men for slave labor in Germany. Witnesses who saw the railways, roads, and canals inside the narrowing German pocket noted abandoned dumps of supplies and matériel, jammed roads, canals choked with motionless barges, and the critical railway around Mézières "filled from end to end with a continuous line of German freight trains carrying guns, ammunition, engineering equipment, and other paraphernalia." Chief of staff Wilhelm Groener, the son of a Swabian NCO, who'd inherited his father's fastidiousness, traveled to Berlin and insisted that an armistice be obtained at once. The German army, he warned, was degenerating into a "wild beast."[59]

16

MEUSE-ARGONNE: SEDAN

OBSERVING THE HEADLONG GERMAN RETREAT, PERSHING dispatched an urgent letter to the Supreme War Council, where Clemenceau, Lloyd George, Orlando, and Bliss were weighing the offer of an armistice to the Germans. With remarkable foresight, Pershing saw that letting Berlin off the hook, short of total defeat and "unconditional surrender," would leave the war unfinished and all but assure a future German power grab. Dictate a hard peace to the Germans, he advised. Don't negotiate. The Germans had violated the laws of war, over and over, and to parley with them would "jeopardize the moral position [the Allies] now hold and possibly lose the chance actually to secure world peace on terms that would insure its permanence."[1]

The Allied coalition had been thrown into disarray by the speed of the enemy collapse. Developments that should have taken weeks to unfold—the capitulation of the Habsburgs and the Ottomans, the revolution in Germany, the naval mutiny, Hindenburg's retreat—had happened in *days*, and Allied peacemakers, focused on the fighting, hadn't caught up. Pershing's call for unconditional surrender mirrored a debate in the United States, where Republicans heaped scorn

SONS OF FREEDOM

on the idealism of Wilson and his Fourteen Points. Yet few of the Doughboys shared Pershing's keenness to continue the war. "Heartless wretch to think such, much less speak it," a soldier of the 32nd Division wrote. "A thousand American boys were being killed every day and other thousands injured for life. Who would want *that* to continue?"[2]

The British accepted some of the Fourteen Points but balked at Wilson's call for freedom of the seas at all times, even wartime. How could they accept it? Without the blockade, the Germans would almost certainly have won the war before America intervened. Clemenceau wanted reparations from the Germans, who'd ravaged his country. The Italians wanted territorial annexations in the Balkans that the "new diplomacy" of the Fourteen Points would deny them. Mollified by Colonel House, who chaired a meeting in Paris on November 3 to assure the Allied leaders, with a wink, that the Fourteen Points didn't mean exactly what they said—there could be reparations, there could be secret diplomacy, and the British could blockade—the Allied leaders accepted Wilson's points as the basis of armistice terms that would be offered to the Germans. The Germans, British diplomat Harold Nicolson observed, "accepted the Fourteen Points as they stood; whereas the Allied Powers accepted them only as interpreted by Colonel House." House's last-minute fix, his "hurried and anxious imprecisions," would partly explain the breakdown of the peace later, Nicolson added.[3]

Pershing's call for unconditional surrender was lost in the tumult. Foch, Haig, and Lloyd George already considered the terms the Germans would be offered too harsh and likely to result in a prolongation of the war. There seemed no need to make them even harsher. Moreover, they assumed that Pershing *wanted* the war prolonged to give America, which would have eighty divisions for a 1919 campaign, a bigger hand in the victory. President Wilson too wanted an end to the war. He fumed at Pershing's insubordination in even floating the idea of unconditional surrender without clearing it first with the White House, quashed it, and warned that he might not authorize a US invasion of German territory. Pershing could hardly have been blamed; it was Wilson, after all, who'd spoken throughout the war of "force to the utmost," no "halfway decisions," the "destruction of every arbitrary power." All of that suddenly and inexplicably went out the window. Pershing, Wilson worried, is "glory mad." The AEF commander was a Republican and would be a leading candidate for the GOP presidential nomination in 1920.[4]

General Maurice Duval, Foch's chief of operations, thought that the Allies lacked credible leverage over the Germans for the simple reason that, like Haig, the Allied peoples wanted the war to end at once. "If the Germans contest the armistice terms and try to 'Jew' us down, I very much doubt that the Allies can refuse the German counter-proposition." Many of the French officers opposed the demand for regime change and the confiscation of German colonies as needlessly provocative. Others, like Colonel René de Cointet, chief of Foch's Intelligence Bureau, thought that they couldn't be hard enough: "They are barbarians. They are dirty sons of bitches." Duval seemed to agree; he was recommending an aerial bombing campaign against any German city within range. Cologne was first on the target list, followed by Frankfurt.[5]

The British, guided by Haig's pessimism, quailed at this French anger and vengefulness. Major Reginald Benson, one of Foch's British liaison officers, pronounced London "happy at the outcome. We are willing to have peace, glad to have it." Forced to have it, was more like it. Losses in the British armies closing on the Meuse were mind-boggling. Nearly 70 percent of the men who'd been in the ranks at the start of the Hundred Days in Byng's Third Army had been killed or wounded, and the Germans were still unbeaten. Of his French colleagues on Foch's staff, Benson said: "It seems to me that these fellows here want the war to go on and on so that they can burn up some of Germany, but I don't believe the poilu will fight any more. He has his belly full." Benson worried, not without reason, that if the war continued because of French wrath, the British and Americans would "have to carry it on."[6]

On November 2, the US I Corps joined the suddenly rapid advance to the Meuse. The whole line of the US First Army advanced another three to six miles. Without prepared defense lines—the Doughs had broken them all—the Germans were now simply delaying the American advance to the Meuse. They buried hundreds of land mines on the roads wending north and posted light machine gunners in every wood and ridge between Buzancy and the Meuse. They'd fire at the oncoming American march columns, forcing them to stop and deploy for action, buying time for the engineers behind the Germans to blow up bridges and culverts and crater the roads. On November 3, the Americans penetrated another twelve miles. The big Allied guns could now hit the German railway at Montmédy, Longuyon, and Conflans. Watching the Doughboys advance, Colonel George Marshall remarked the irony that the US 2nd Division stole through the forest at Beaumont to surprise German troops camped in the village, in the same way that German infantry had surprised and overrun French troops in the exact same location in the Franco-Prussian War. The irony was all the greater because, like the French then, the Germans now were withdrawing to Sedan for a last stand, and the Americans, like the Germans then, were pursuing to surround them there.[7]

The Germans were being pressed back on Mouzon, an important station upstream from Sedan on the all-important Meuse railway line. Foch expected the Germans to stand there, on the left bank of the Meuse, before withdrawing to the right bank. A French POW, who escaped from his job on a German truck column, crossed to American lines and reported that the Germans had been unhinged by the speed of the American advance. He'd been at Beaumont on November 2 when orders were distributed for a general withdrawal the next day to Carignan. But at 3 a.m. the alarm was raised and the evacuation ordered immediately, leaving all impediments behind. The French prisoner had observed "total chaos" as German units retreating from the front streamed through the village and the fields around it.[8]

On November 3, Liggett began finally to rub out the German batteries on the Borne de Cornouiller, or "Corned Willy Hill," which had thwarted Hines's III Corps for over a month. With his flanks secured by the German retreat and the advance of Hanson Ely's 5th

Division, Liggett encircled the Borne and attacked its gunners from the flanks. The US 5th Division and French 15th Colonial Division attacked from the west, the US 79th Division from the east. The struggle was vicious, taking four entire days as the French and American infantries fought their way to the summit, seizing it finally on November 7. The Americans lost another fifteen thousand men taking it. A veteran recalled its enduring horrors and notoriety: "Lads returning to the forty-eight states, when asked by their Dads about the Argonne Forest, would say, 'I was never in the joint. But if Mom will leave the room, I would like to say a few words about Corned Willy Hill.'"[9]

Liggett's passage across the Meuse and seizure of the Meuse Heights exposed Hindenburg's left flank in France and opened the way for Liggett's First Army to attack along both banks of the river and for Bullard's Second Army, with two new corps, to attack from Saint-Mihiel across the plain of the Woëvre toward Metz, the Briey iron mines, and the coal and heavy industry of the Saar Basin. Bullard directed his army toward Pont-à-Mousson, where the Prussians had crossed the Moselle in 1870 to encircle and annex Metz. Two massive corps began to move, General Charles Muir's US IV Corps—the 28th, 7th, and 4th Divisions—and General Charles Menoher's US VI Corps. Menoher, who'd yielded command of the Rainbow Division to Douglas MacArthur, now took over a new corps that included the 88th Division and the African American 92nd Division. Menoher had few qualifications other than his loyalty to Pershing; his army career had been mediocre, and even Pershing complained that he lacked initiative. He was certainly not the man to assuage the racial tensions in his corps. The 92nd Division, embarrassed and withdrawn from the Argonne in September, still hadn't recovered. The recruits had been assembled from seven different training camps in the States and had never worked as a unit before arriving in France. White officers and enlisted men attached to the unit refused to salute black officers. Those black officers had other sources of resentment; they'd been sent to France in second-class cabins, not the first-class staterooms reserved for white officers. In France, they were denied admission to white officers' clubs. Soon that would be less of a problem, for Pershing had been steadily reducing the percentage of black officers in the 92nd Division, from 82 percent in September to 58 percent now. Their division commander, General Charles Ballou, was even less effective than Menoher, rated incompetent in every area by Bullard. Ballou set a patronizing tone for the division, rudely reminding the African American troops that "white men made the division and they can break it just as easily if it becomes a trouble-maker."[10]

The US 92nd Division was an experimental unit—the first all-black combat division—and its officers were either inexperienced or as indifferent as the 154 regular army NCOs (presumably not the best and brightest) who'd been pressed into the division. Put into the attack on the Moselle in late October to drive the Germans back on Metz, the division shrank from the assault and retreated. The French, on the flank of the 92nd Division, complained, and an inquiry concluded that thirty black officers had ordered the retreats. Fifty more black officers of the division were investigated for charges of incompetence. Five of the officers involved in the retreats were sentenced to death, sentences that Bullard had commuted and then ultimately dropped. He accused General Ballou of "losing sight of military efficiency in the racial 'uplift' problem that seemed to fill his mind." Here Bullard was mocking Booker T. Washington's racial uplift project, which argued that the apparently immovable obstacles of segregation and voter suppression could be made acceptable only if the American government and business community made real contributions to black progress or "uplift" in education, careers, industry, and agriculture. Both Bullard and "Black Jack" Pershing himself now proved that the US Army was as little interested in "uplift" as any other organ of the US government, which had actually regressed on civil rights since Woodrow Wilson, a southerner, had taken office.

Ultimately, only the Germans were uplifted by the US 92nd Division, whose twenty-seven thousand troops managed to capture only one German soldier in the war. Bullard, a highly developed Alabama racist—"The Negro is a more sensual man than the white man"— naturally intuited that his black troops were indifferent to everything in the war except French women. The 92nd Division had a "rape problem," or so Bullard insisted: fifteen confirmed cases in its short stint in France. Bullard, of course, had a curious way of defining what was rape and what was not; where black soldiers were concerned it invariably was rape, the Alabaman assuring posterity that "it will always be so with Negroes wherever they are in contact with whites." Over Foch's objections, Bullard demanded that the division be sent home immediately after the armistice. It would be the first division to arrive back in the States.[11]

The US III Corps crossed to the right bank of the Meuse on November 5. V Corps approached Sedan, and Dickman's I Corps advanced past the right flank of Gouraud's French Fourth Army, which seemed more concerned to survive the last days of the war than cut the German throat. Liggett moved his best attacking divisions into the front rank to deliver the killing blow and give "fresh impetus." He passed the 42nd Rainbows through the 78th Division and the Big Red One through the 80th. By now, the Rainbows had embodied twenty thousand replacements in the course of their short war; the division, in other words, had been almost entirely wiped out and replaced since its baptism of fire on the Marne five months earlier.[12]

Colonel Marshall, operations chief of Liggett's First Army, recalled meeting with General Fox Conner, operations chief of the AEF, on November 6. Conner excitedly related the German predicament. Hindenburg had begun a *Kriegsmarsch*—redeployment—from all points on his shrinking Western Front back to the right bank of the Meuse, where he hoped to dig in and stop the Allied advance. The German situation, Conner said, had become "critical"; Hindenburg must be given "no pause for reorganization." Heavy guns had been in position since November 4, hammering the only railroad Hindenburg had to supply the German armies backpedaling out of their narrowing salient. The Allies had advanced in every sector and nearly encircled "the great bulge of the Western Front." Conner said that if the war lasted another ten days, the Germans would lose at least a million troops, not from enemy fire but from Pershing's thrust into Sedan, which would cut their only line of retreat and force their surrender.

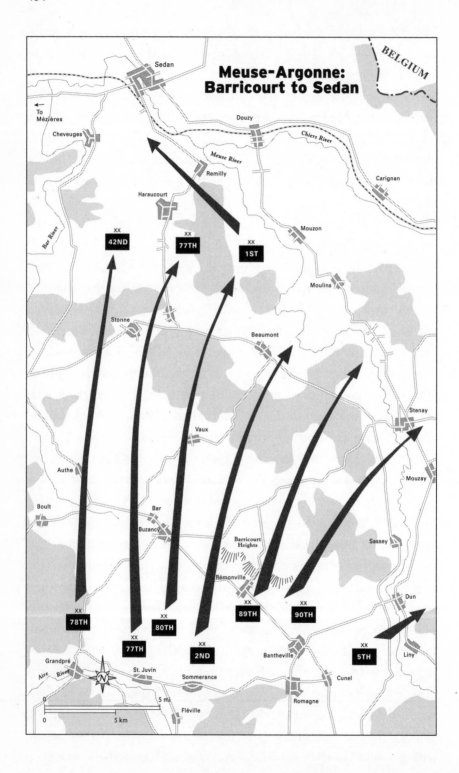

Meuse-Argonne: Barricourt to Sedan

The French had lost in 1870 because the Prussians had surrounded their last army at Sedan and captured it. The Americans were now on the verge of accomplishing the same feat against the Germans.[13]

On November 6, the Germans announced that they were sending delegates to ask Foch for armistice terms. British armies south of the Mons-Condé Canal and the French First Army were thrusting ahead against faltering resistance, and on the Meuse the US 1st Division advanced four miles to seize Mouzon. For the Big Red One, it was a feat of endurance. The division had been called to the front so many times that it was running on fumes. Officers, themselves straining to stay awake, had to shake the men violently after ten-minute halts on the march to wake them. Briefing his three young battalion commanders on the Mouzon operation, Lieutenant Colonel Theodore Roosevelt Jr., commander of the 1st Division's 26th Regiment, turned away for a moment and then turned back to find all three of them fast asleep in their seats. Every farm and village these sleepy men liberated went wild with joy. This area had been under German occupation for four years, and all news had been censored. The locals had had no idea that the Americans were coming. The US 77th and 42nd Divisions also pushed northward. To their right, the US 2nd, 89th, and 90th Divisions also reached the Meuse, where they struggled to entrench in frozen ground that, as one soldier put it, "was hard as granite."[14]

When the German delegates arrived at Foch's headquarters— at 5 a.m. on November 8—the Germans were in full retreat to the Meuse, everyone hurrying to get behind the river and through the bottleneck at Sedan. Gouraud's French Fourth Army continued to lag, yet Foch was determined that the French, not the Americans, would have the honor of liberating Sedan. Having spent the entire fall exhorting the Allied armies to ignore boundaries and harry the Germans everywhere they could, Foch now drew a hard boundary between the French and Americans. He forbade the Americans to take Sedan—even though they were first on the scene—and confined them to a revised sector that ended two miles east of the place. To the French 40th Division would fall the honor of taking Sedan, which had been the scene of France's most humiliating defeat in the Franco-Prussian War. Unconcerned with French sensibilities, Pershing overruled Foch, ordering Dickman's I Corps to take the town: "The honor of entering Sedan shall fall to the First American Army. . . . Boundaries will not be considered binding."[15]

Late on November 6, I Corps's 42nd and 77th Divisions had begun advancing on Sedan; V Corps's 1st Division, at Mouzon, also bent its steps toward the town. Pershing had ordered V Corps to "assist" by keeping pressure on the Germans in its sector, but Summerall, whose motto was "We will go through," wanted the honor of taking Sedan, and he wanted Frank Parker's Big Red One to do it, and so the 1st Division—replenished with eight thousand replacements after the carnage of Exermont—wheeled left and marched across Dickman's supply lines toward Gièvres and Wadelincourt. Covering thirty-five miles in two days of round-the-clock slogging, the men of the 1st Division barged into the space of the 77th Division, losing hundreds of stragglers in the wilderness of wire, mud, and swamps. The 77th Division commander, unaware that Colonel George Marshall had recklessly authorized this detour to reward the 1st Division, expressed shock at the Big Red One's apparition in his midst: "A unit as large as a division cannot move laterally through territory already occupied by other troops."[16]

Oh yes it could. After plowing through the protesting 77th Division, the 1st Division then plowed into the 42nd Division, just across the Meuse from Sedan. Even Clausewitz, who put harebrained measures like this under the rubric "friction of war," would have been astonished at how witless and dangerous it was. Pershing's headquarters, with Marshall's connivance, had suggested the adventure out of sentimentality, without even informing Liggett, who called it a "military atrocity." Parker, Liggett fulminated, was fit to command nothing larger than a regiment. Had a German counterattack gone in while Parker was cutting through the midst of the US I Corps, chaos, rout, and massive casualties would have resulted.[17]

As it chanced, there was only chaos. General Douglas MacArthur, dressed in his trademark nonregulation uniform—floppy cap with the grommet removed, bottle-green tunic, turtleneck sweater, purple scarf, swagger stick, and gleaming high cavalry boots—furiously approached a column of the trespassing 1st Division, which was cutting his supply lines as it had already cut the 77th's, only to be greeted with warning shots and taken prisoner. To the Doughboys of the 1st Division, the Rainbow Division commander's theatrical getup looked more Prussian than American; sputtering with anger, MacArthur insisted that he was in fact commander of the US 42nd Division. "Tell that to the intelligence officer, Heinie," the Doughs growled. Only German officers dressed this way. Seasoned American officers wore enlisted men's uniforms into battle, with their rank insignia pinned in a discreet place or stuffed in their pocket to deceive snipers.[18]

The Americans were now crowding into areas the Germans had held in strength just hours earlier. None of this was easy. The Germans continued to fire perfectly observed, very effective artillery fire from the right bank of the river, killing large numbers of enclosing Americans. As the 1st Division prepared to cross the Meuse at Saint-Aignan, it was warned by the neighboring French 40th Division not to. My guns, the French general said, are already laid and will come down on you "with *le grand precisione*" if you do. The French insisted on the honor of being first into Sedan, and to avoid casualties at French hands (and quiet complaints from the 42nd Division about the 1st Division's freelancing), Summerall reluctantly ordered Parker to back off to the east and quit the "race to Sedan."

But the poilus had no attack left in them. Mirroring the Prussian moves in 1870, the US 89th Division crossed the Meuse and seized Stenay on November 5. Poking around it, an American general was struck by the degree to which it had been Germanized during four years of occupation: "All the streets had been given German names and most of the shops had been given German names. . . . The enemy seemed to think that his frontier had been moved permanently" there. Certainly if the Germans had won the war it would have been. The Meuse, rising in France and emptying into the North Sea, had been the western frontier of the old Holy Roman Empire. The next day, MacArthur's 42nd Division took Wadelincourt, and the 1st Division—defying Summerall's orders—took Cheveuges and then advanced a battalion onto the same height from which Bismarck, Moltke, and Prussian king Wilhelm I had watched the battle of Sedan in 1870. General John Lejeune, attempting to sleep while the 1st Division marched past his 2nd Division headquarters in the night, recorded what they sounded like:

> Nothing could be seen because of the heavy rain and the inky darkness but there was much to be heard. The marching songs the soldiers sang, interspersed with their humorous remarks to each other; the picturesque profanity to which some gave utterance when a wagon found its way into a shellhole, as frequently happened, and the nearest platoon was called on to help the mules pull it out; the shouts of command by the officers, the directions in stentorian tones given by the MPs—to all of these sounds and many more I listened entranced. It was a realistic demonstration of the high spirit of the American troops.[19]

These thrusting American attacks and night marches drove the last Germans off the left bank of the Meuse and into their last redoubt behind the river. On the American right, the entire 5th Division of Hines's III Corps crossed the Meuse on November 6, pushing as far as Brandeville, where they mounted the bluffs overlooking the plain of the Woëvre. The 90th Division crossed at Mouzay, giving Pershing total command of both banks of the Meuse. With Liggett's First Army poised to tie off the sack at Sedan and bag at least a million German troops, George Marshall hailed the "grandstand finish," the "inspiring feat of arms." The Doughboys were moving so fast that many of them had nothing to eat in this phase but cabbages dug from the fields. Marshall only regretted that American citizens at home were so fixated on President Wilson's exchange of notes with the German government and the pending armistice negotiations that they failed to notice this "splendid victory."[20]

In Foch's headquarters, Pershing's liaison, Major Paul Clark, braced to withstand blasts of French anger. The French had wanted to take Sedan to redeem the defeat of 1870 and had tried to keep the Americans out. Colonel Gaston Duffour, chief of the Operations Bureau, wagged a disapproving finger: "You see, Clark, we hear there are evidences of ill-feeling between the French and Americans at Bazeilles, the suburb of Sedan. Each of us wants to take it. It means a great deal to us sentimentally to take it; it was there in 1870 that the Bavarians were especially worthy of the name 'son-of-a-bitch' and it would be an enormous satisfaction to us to take it." He led Clark to the map. "The limits between the French and the Americans are now established *thus*." He jabbed with a finger and told Clark that Liggett must be made to pull units like the Rainbows and the Big Red One back to the southeast and make way for Gouraud.[21]

By now even Clark was losing patience with the French. "They always say 'French and Americans' and never, scarcely ever, say 'Americans and French,'" he observed in his report of the altercation to Pershing. In six days of hard fighting, the US First Army had pushed the Germans over the Meuse between Verdun and Sedan and advanced twenty-five miles. Russian prisoners of war, who'd constructed most of the fortifications in the Meuse-Argonne, took advantage of the ragged German retreat across the Meuse to escape to the Americans on November 6. They told their liberators something that German prisoners had also said: the Germans had captured large numbers of French, British, and Italians, but hardly any Americans. "The Germans fear the Americans more than any other forces on the front," one of the Russians said.[22]

The American assault on Sedan coincided with the arrival of Matthias Erzberger and his delegation of German officials at Foch's railroad car in the Forest of Compiègne. With the army collapsing, the navy in revolt, German dynasties abdicating their thrones, and communists seizing power in Munich, Stuttgart, Frankfurt, Hanover, Cologne, Düsseldorf, Leipzig, and Magdeburg, the Germans needed to end the war at any cost. Foch telegraphed Pershing, Pétain, and Haig and ordered them to keep the pressure on. President Wilson had been crucial in forcing the Germans to the table, refusing to enter into "long conversations" with them and compelling them to seek terms from Foch.

But Wilson failed to include a critical demand: that Germany's military leaders also go to Compiègne, to surrender their swords and taste defeat. By permitting the Germans to send a civilian delegation from a militarized Germany that worshipped the uniform, the Allies carelessly launched the myth that Hitler would later exploit: that the German army had never been defeated in the field, that it had been "stabbed in the back" by "November criminals" such as Matthias Erzberger. The new German government had included a general in Erzberger's delegation to represent the Supreme Command, but Hindenburg, showing where real power lay in Germany, had removed him when the group of delegates transited through Spa, to leave the impression that this was an entirely civilian capitulation. (The German general who remained in the delegation—Detlev von Winterfeldt—remained only because he spoke fluent French.) Pershing was right: the Germans would only grasp the extent of their defeat if the Allies appeared in Berlin—marching "down the *Linden* as an army with banners . . . to let the Germans know who won the war." Shortly after the war, Pershing would tell a friend, "They never knew they were beaten in Berlin. It will all have to be done all over again."[23]

When Erzberger's delegation arrived in the Forest of Compiègne on November 8, Foch received the men in his headquarters train, examined their credentials, and then asked: "What is the purpose of your visit? What do you want of me?" Erzberger quizzically replied that he wanted "proposals of an armistice." Foch replied coldly: "I have no proposals to make." Count Alfred von Oberndorff, who'd been German minister in Sofia until the Bulgarian surrender in September, declared, "We are ready to say that we ask the conditions of an armistice." Even more coldly, Foch replied: "I have no conditions to give you." Clutching Wilson's third note, the one that referred the Germans to the Allied military authorities for terms, Erzberger began to read it aloud. Foch broke in again: "Do you wish to ask for an armistice? If so, say so—formally." Erzberger said so, and Foch's chief of staff, General Maxime Weygand (who would himself be read humiliating armistice terms in this same railroad car twenty-two years later), read the terms. They amounted to a crushing German defeat. Germany would have to yield all occupied territory, including Alsace-Lorraine; deliver the Rhine bridgeheads of Mainz, Coblenz, and Cologne into Allied hands; free all Allied prisoners; and disarm, handing over five thousand cannon, twenty-five thousand machine guns, three thousand trench mortars, 1,700 planes, seventy-five warships, and all of its submarines. The delegation was given until 11 a.m. on November 11 to accept the terms. The Germans asked for a cease-fire while they transmitted the terms to Berlin, and Foch refused. They had three days to accept or reject, and the war would continue in the meantime.[24]

Foch had the armistice terms read to Erzberger's delegation again on November 9; the German delegates were, according to Weygand's deputy, General Pierre Desticker, "completely shattered." The US First Army had successfully crossed Germany's Meuse barrier to threaten Sedan with envelopment. The British armies were over the Sambre-Oise Canal and approaching the Belgian frontier, taking Maubeuge, where the BEF had nearly been annihilated in 1914 before the Battle of Mons. The French First Army had taken the rail hub of Hirson; the French Fourth Army was nearing Mézières. The Allied armies were positioned to surround and capture the German army on the Western Front. General Detlev von Winterfeldt, who'd been German military attaché in Paris before the war, asked again for a cease-fire to consider the terms, and again Foch refused. The delegates explained that they needed the cease-fire to consult with the Reichstag in Berlin and "to save the army from complete ruin." The navy had already dissolved in communist revolution—flying the red flag, purging officers, and banning saluting. The army, the delegates said, was in a similar "state of disorder"; an armistice was needed to save it so that it could be turned against the revolutionary forces in Germany.

Those revolutionary forces had already exploded. Philipp Scheidemann, a minister without portfolio in Prince Max's government, had brushed the aristocratic chancellor aside and unilaterally proclaimed a socialist republic from the Reichstag balcony on November 9. The

German Bolsheviks, known as Spartacists, had seized the kaiser's palace in Berlin nearly a year to the day after Lenin's men had seized the Winter Palace in Petrograd. The thousands of machine guns that the Allies were demanding as a condition of any armistice, the German delegates darkly mooted, might soon be needed to crush the soviet republic sought by the Spartacists. British general Charles Grant, looking over Foch's shoulder at Compiègne, observed, "It is certain that the Germans are more afraid of Bolshevism in their country than of anything else." German acceptance of the Allied terms, he predicted, was inevitable.[25]

After resisting for a week, blaming the revolution on "a few hundred Jews and a thousand workers," Kaiser Wilhelm II abdicated late on November 9, and Friedrich Ebert, the Socialist son of a saddlemaker, became the new German chancellor. Army chief of staff Groener had consulted the German generals at the front, and they'd agreed with near unanimity that their troops would no longer fight for the kaiser or engage in civil war on his behalf. To the men in *feldgrau*, Wilhelm II had become a loathsome figure—a self-serving warmonger and reactionary. On November 10, fearing for his life, the kaiser left army headquarters in Belgium, abandoned his army of three million, and slipped over the Dutch border and into exile. Grant reported shock at the swiftness of the German collapse: only three weeks earlier, Haig's chief of staff, Herbert Lawrence, had told him that there was no evidence that the German armies were beaten or that the Allies could win in 1918. General Sidney Clive, another British liaison in French headquarters, had said the same thing just two weeks earlier, when he'd complained that Foch and Weygand were "drunk with the blood of victory" and pressing on needlessly. Within four months of the last great German offensive, which had nearly reached Paris, the whole German army was retreating and the kaiser had abdicated. It was a stunning turn of events. Haig would later call it "a miracle."[26]

Clark met with the leading men of Foch's Operations Bureau, General Maurice Duval and Colonel Gaston Duffour, on November 8. They were increasingly preoccupied with war termination: how and when to end the war, what additional damage to inflict on the Germans, and what to demand of them—all with an eye to setting up a durable peace that would favor Allied interests. Duval weighed the pros and cons of the spreading German revolution. "Now all of this internal disorder"—the declaration of a soviet republic in Bavaria and the dethronement of the kaiser and crown prince in Berlin—"is great stuff up to the point of compelling the Boche to yield, but we must not have too much of a good thing and I tell you the disorder is contagious and we must not play with fire. We must leave these Boche with enough power to police themselves internally, for certainly we don't want the job of putting their house in order."[27]

The Allies had to strike a delicate balance—weaken the Germans enough to force their surrender, but not enough to fan Bolshevik revolution in Germany. "We must not too greatly wipe out German power; we must leave them the wherewithal to stamp out that evil," added Colonel Louis Paille, who'd headed the French training section attached to the AEF. "It would be a poor joke to win the war and then have Bolshevism swallow us. I want Germany to collapse enough, just enough, but no more."[28]

The French general staff praised the American endgame. "The approach to and cutting of the Sedan railway" had ended the war, a senior French officer observed. That American thrust "had the greatest effect in forcing the Boche to accept an armistice." All of the French officers were dazed by the sudden success, Colonel Duffour declaring that the rushed, thrilling days were like a dream state: "I have to pinch myself to know that I'm awake." Another French colonel wondered what he'd do now: "Well, it's all but finished. What will we do when it's over? After four years of this intense striving, what will we do? Life will seem so tame."[29]

It was anything but tame along the Meuse. For all of the backslapping in Foch's headquarters, the Germans weren't beaten yet. One of the Allied armies would have to finish them off. It would be the Americans. "We'll slip a pill to Kaiser Bill and knock him on his ear," the Doughboys sang as they neared the Meuse, "and when we get von Hindenburg we'll ram him in the rear." Kaiser Bill was

·gone; now it was Hindenburg's turn. On the night of November 9, Pershing ordered the 2nd and 89th Divisions to cross the Meuse near Beaumont. "Make decisive the results obtained," he wrote. Fifty miles to the southeast, the US Second Army began slopping across the muddy plain of the Woëvre toward Metz. Marshall noted that the airwaves around the two American armies crackled with German radio traffic that gave certain proof that Hindenburg's army was dissolving, and perhaps even the German nation. Soldier and sailor councils in the German army and navy—called *soviets*—exchanged condemnations of the war and plans for coordinated action, ignoring orders from the army and the fleet and instructions from the foreign ministry.[30]

On November 10, Hines's US III Corps defeated the Germans at Dun-sur-Meuse—thirty miles upstream from Sedan—and threw a bridge across the river. Engineers lashed bridge sections together, then swam them across the Meuse and fastened them to the far bank, where the 5th Marine Regiment gouged out a beachhead, killing the German machine gunners there. The Germans slumped some more. Hindenburg belatedly informed his troops that the German kaiser and crown prince, as well as the kings of Bavaria and Saxony, had all abdicated, that Ebert was the new chancellor, and that the "bloody struggle was coming to an end." But not yet. He inserted the German army's last intact reserve division on the Western Front to wreck the American bridge and attack at Dun. The place was that important. With it, the Americans could enclose Sedan from both banks of the Meuse and nullify the river as a defensive obstacle. General Lejeune ordered new exertions from his 2nd Division but noted his ambivalence: "I pray God that we may win and end this horrible war by a decisive victory. Many a poor fellow will give his life to his country tomorrow. The men are brave, strong and determined to beat the enemy."[31]

Late on November 10, Ebert's government radioed Erzberger's delegation at Compiègne with coded instructions to sign the armistice. Much time was lost deciphering the message, and the delegates didn't affix their signatures to the armistice document till 5 a.m. That same night—even as the Germans were reading the message that would end the war—the US 2nd Division was crossing the Meuse near Sedan at the Bois de l'Hospice. Engineers again constructed the bridge under heavy fire. Small rafts carrying the bridge flooring were lashed together on shore, and the whole 160-foot-long structure was raised on the shoulders of the men who carried it into the river and swam across to the opposite bank. There were two of these. One was placed in eight minutes, the other in thirteen minutes. At Pouilly, twenty miles upstream from Sedan, Americans on rafts made a bridgehead, and V Corps put seven battalions across in the night. Stenay, seven miles above Pouilly, was enveloped by the US 89th and 90th Divisions against ferocious German machine-gun and artillery fire. Stenay, guarding the approach to Sedan, had been the headquarters of the departed German crown prince Wilhelm. US engineers quickly repaired its fixed bridge, and with more American assault units poised to cross the river, the armistice took effect at 11 a.m.: the eleventh hour of the eleventh day of the eleventh month of 1918. Many of the Doughs resented the last-minute bloody efforts ordered by distant staff officers to cross the Meuse before the armistice: "It was sickening and depressing to hear officers . . . tell of the importance of our gaining a certain ridge or section of ground before the Armistice went into effect. What did these useless killings and injuries mean to officers who had never commanded men in battle, whose entire war experience was a war on paper, where the expenditure of human life was necessary but with which they had no experience, no responsibility, and apparently little sympathy."[32]

A platoon leader in the 89th Division was stunned by the contrasting reactions to the armistice on the two sides of the Meuse. The Americans on the left bank "just gave a sigh. They lay down, some went to sleep; others started writing letters." But on the right bank "the Germans were cheering, laughing, singing, just going crazy." Their bands thundered away—"all these German songs—you know, *dee-boom-boom, dee-boom-boom*, all that brass they use. We were beginning to wonder who the hell had won the thing." Father Francis Duffy, the chaplain of the Rainbows, recalled nothing but grief. "I could think of nothing except the fine lads who had come out with us to this war and who are not alive to enjoy the triumph. All day I had a lonely and aching heart."[33]

Eighty miles to the southeast, Corporal John Barkley was in the village of Culey with the 3rd Division at 11 a.m. Part of the new US Second Army, the Rock of the Marne Division had turned out at dawn, packs rolled, "headed to Metz." As they waited for their trucks, the village erupted in something they hadn't heard since arriving in France: joy. Children raced through the streets; seniors who'd never budged from the chairs in their parlors were suddenly in the streets yelling, "Vive la France! Vive l'America!" "The Frogs are going nuts,'" one of the Doughboys remarked. None of them knew why. A soldier passed and said that the armistice had been signed. "What's an armistice?" Barkley remembered asking. None of the other men in his column knew what an armistice was either. That night the whole village partied, Barkley observing: "French people didn't get drunk often but they were all drunk this time. The children were drunk and the old men and women were drunk and the young people were drunk." They danced and sang all night, shot off rockets and flares, and shouted and cried. The men of Barkley's unit didn't find out what an armistice was till the next morning when the bugles blew and an officer appeared to explain that an armistice was a preliminary treaty of peace. The division's recruits, who'd looked queasily at Metz and its artillery, "went as wild as the French," but the veterans sat still. Peace seemed too good to be true. There had to be a catch.[34]

In Foch's better-informed headquarters, Major Paul Clark enjoyed a riotous lunch on the eleventh. "Lunch," Clark recorded, "a babel of voices, conversation glowed with white heat, the great idea seems to be France victorious, France saved from an ignominious fate." He chatted with General Duval, who'd lost a son in the war. Duval shook Clark's hand warmly and pronounced America France's savior. "We French will feel an eternal gratitude to America, for without your aid we would today be Boche provinces instead of a free people. You came not one hour too soon. We were nearly finished." To Duval, the counteroffensive at Soissons on July 18 had turned the tide in the war:

"Without your troops, the attack would never have taken place" and the Germans wouldn't have been beaten.[35]

General John Lejeune was visiting wounded men in the 2nd Division field hospital after the armistice was announced. He sat beside a sergeant of Marines whose leg had been torn off that morning by shell fragments while crossing the Meuse. The sergeant had known the armistice was imminent. "What induced you to cross that bridge in the face of the terrible machine gun and artillery fire when you expected that the war would end in a few hours?" Lejeune asked. The Marine answered that their battalion commander had induced them with these words: "Men, I am going across the river and I expect you to go with me." The sergeant, a limp trouser leg hanging where his leg had been, added, "What could we do but go across too? Surely we couldn't let him go by himself. We love him too much for that."

Of the hundreds of tragic casualties Lejeune visited, there was one who stood out. One boy, badly mangled by shell splinters, had been on duty in the telephone exchange of an artillery regiment that morning and had been writing down the message, "It is 11 o'clock and the war is—" when a shell tore through the roof and burst, killing his buddy and badly wounding him. Lejeune felt certain that he was looking at the last casualty of World War I. The shell had been fired a second before 11 a.m. and had struck at the exact hour of peace. Returning in the dark to his own headquarters, Lejeune observed Doughboys encamped everywhere beside roaring fires, the first they'd lit since coming to France. Fireworks blazed across the sky from Belgium to the Swiss border. The men, who'd been drenched and chilled to the bone for weeks on end, cheered and whistled; he heard cries like, "It looks like Broadway" and "The lights remind me of home." Lejeune noted that "darkness and the lack of fires were the most pronounced characteristics of the World War." The airplane, observation balloons, and long-range artillery had caused "a reversion to the primitive days when fire and artificial light were unknown." To everyone's relief, the Dark Age was over.[36]

Although the armistice compelled the prompt German evacuation of "the countries on the left bank of the Rhine"—Belgium,

France, and Luxembourg—as well as the immediate surrender of massive quantities of artillery, machine guns, and aircraft, Pershing broke off the combat around Sedan reluctantly. He'd planned next to advance between the Meuse and Moselle toward Longwy with the First Army; the Second Army would attack Briey's rich iron fields, then attack toward Chat-Salins east of the Moselle to isolate Metz. George Marshall had been busy shifting four divisions from the First Army to the Second Army for a massive offensive southeast of Metz to begin November 14.[37]

All of the US divisions had been brought back to full strength with replacements, who were now sailing from America to France in just eight or nine days at sea. Though the new recruits were nothing like the old—"odds and ends of the draft, men who'd been passed over more than once in previous drafts . . . lacking in general intelligence and appearance"—they were certainly better than the last drafts of the German, French, and British armies. All of that work now ended as the Germans surrendered. Pershing informed Secretary of War Baker in Washington that the AEF had achieved its strategic goal: "We cut the enemy's main line of communications, and nothing but surrender or an armistice could save his army from complete disaster."[38]

Before the Germans gave up, Foch had been planning to inflict that "complete disaster" on them. The Americans by now had a million troops in France. The Allied generalissimo told his British liaison, General Charles Grant, that he almost regretted the German surrender: "If the Germans had not signed the Armistice, we would have attacked them in Lorraine on 13 or 14 November with twenty French and six American divisions. The men would have gone like greyhounds as there was nothing in front of them. The Germans had exhausted their reserves and couldn't move a man." Pétain's deputy, General Edmond Buat, who'd sought a cease-fire in November, regretted it four months later, when the paucity of German reserves at the hour of the armistice came into clear focus. "It is with reserves that we make war," and the situation on Armistice Day had been lethal for the Germans, who by then had only 17 fatigued divisions in reserve against 103 Allied reserve divisions. "What a pity the Allied attack for November 14 never eventuated," Buat sighed, too late. "It would have caused a German debacle of tremendous proportions; it would have completely changed the German mental attitude." The Allies would have been able to envelop and destroy what remained of the German army. The Germans would never have been able subsequently to claim—as Ebert and Hindenburg (and Hitler) did—that they had been "*im Felde unbesiegt*" (unbeaten in the field).[39]

Colonel George Marshall agreed: "It will always remain an open question as to what would have been the result of continuing the fighting for another week. Certainly we would have gone straight through the enemy's line, as his last remaining available division, and a tired one at that, was thrown into the battle on the front of our III Corps on the afternoon of the 10th." But, Marshall pointed out, with the discernment that would make him famous, the armistice was almost certainly the best outcome. Had the German army disintegrated, "it would have engaged in guerrilla fighting and terrorized the inhabitants." And a revolution in Germany would have resulted. "We would have had no government to deal with, and we would have had to occupy practically all of Germany, a difficult and lengthy task." Here was the Pottery Barn rule *avant la lettre*—"You break it, you own it." Still, Marshall couldn't help but wonder how history might have unfolded had the Allies "crowned their victory" with a last battle and prevented the Germans from marching home with their arms and flags, boasting that they'd never really been defeated. "Old England," Marshall said, "was much wiser in this matter and demanded the complete surrender of the German fleet, leaving no question in anybody's mind as to the masters of the sea."[40]

Certainly Foch regretted not cutting the German throat. "Sweeping up from the south of Metz, we would have cut all of the German communications and completed the disaster of the German armies," the generalissimo confirmed. It would have been a "terrible catastrophe for them, they would have lost hundreds of thousands of prisoners, practically their whole army." The 1,566-day war had enlivened Foch. He seemed disappointed to have been denied the opportunity to deal the Germans a mortal blow. At British headquarters, Grant reported "a state of subdued joy and bewilderment." Haig, of course, was neither subdued nor bewildered. The four-year war had made him sour. "If the other armies, especially the French, had fought as the British, the result might have been over two months ago," the field marshal groused. Traveling through devastated Noyon, Ham, and Cambrai, Grant met with jubilant French locals. "Fineeshed," they yelled at passing British troops. "C'est fini, n'est-ce pas?" (It's all over, right?)[41]

It was. Even without Pershing's planned coup de grâce, the German army collapsed. Dour German prisoners showed no interest in news of the kaiser's abdication. Their only interest was in having news of the war's end confirmed to them. Discipline broke down utterly, many units reporting "a complete absence of subordination and disciplined organization." In the days ahead, German columns would be spotted marching east with red flags tied to their rifles. Vengeful atrocities were common, the Germans putting French and Belgian villages to the torch as they withdrew. The Germans looted towns as they marched through—stealing livestock, food, money, furniture, linen, copper, and everything of value. They'd then attempt to sell the plunder to the inhabitants of the next village they passed. "Authority of the officers over their men is entirely gone," an American intelligence report noted. German troops threw away their helmets, rifles, and equipment, and defaced portraits of the kaiser. They got drunk and fired their weapons and flares in the air. Refugees reported seeing German troops killing their officers. So many officers were murdered that Hindenburg ordered that all ammunition and grenades be taken away from the enlisted men.[42]

A German army that had grown accustomed to marching only at night was now ordered to march only in daylight, Hindenburg not trusting the men to remain under the control of their officers after dark. A French officer who drove into the midst of the retreating Germans in Belgium noted red flags everywhere—"at the head of columns, on the men's rifles, on the trucks, etc." Belgian women—"mistresses of the officers or men"—followed the columns, lugging bundles. Russians, "apparently used as servants," shuffled alongside. Withdrawing German units were loosely commanded—on the Russian model—by "soviets," councils of one officer, one sergeant, and one enlisted man. These soviets were in full control. Freed prisoners—Russians, French, British, Italians, and Americans—reported that they hadn't actually been freed, just abandoned. They would awake in the morning to find their guards gone. In Brussels, there were scuffles between German soldiers loyal to the Ebert regime and those loyal to the soldiers' soviet—the *Soldaten-Rat*. The scuffles died down when the troops were told that discipline needed to be maintained so that "the Allies could not completely crush Germany." The mutinous troops then pulled together and marched out under German colors mixed with red flags. German officers assured the Belgians when they departed that "the German army was not beaten and that the war was not over." French officers noted signs of "confusion and disorder," but little "open revolt." Hindenburg himself couldn't order a car without the consent of the soldiers' soviet, yet he was ultimately obeyed. The German army would be back.[43]

17

PEACE?

THE AWFUL WAR HAD ENDED AND THE NATIONS AND EM-
pires counted their dead. Eighteen million combatants and civilians had been killed, twenty-four million wounded. The armies of
Germany and Russia had each lost 2 million dead, those of France and
Austria-Hungary 1 million each, Britain's 700,000, Italy's 460,000,
that of the United States 117,000. In his first postwar comments,
Field Marshal Haig judged the Allied victory nothing less than "a
miracle." The Germans, he wrote, had shown how to win wars by superior preparation in 1866 and 1870. They'd done this again in 1914,
and nearly won. They'd been given another chance to win in 1918,
and nearly had. "The word 'miraculous,'" Haig concluded, "is hardly
too strong a term to describe the recovery and ultimate victory of the
Allies."[1]

While most people pondered the miracle of the war's end, the
generals studied the armistice terms. All Allied units were to freeze
in place on the lines of November 11. The Germans would be given
six days to commence their evacuation of France and Belgium before
the Allies came on in pursuit to nudge the Germans over the Rhine.
The Americans needed the week off. They'd run through so many

horses that their armies were effectively immobile. When Pershing hived off a US Third Army from the surplus manpower of Liggett's First Army, he had to strip horses from the other two armies just to equip the new one. George Marshall recalled taking horses from the units not involved in the pursuit and giving them to the ones that were. Hundreds of American batteries and supply wagons then sat forlornly in the countryside or along the roads, unable to move so that the eight divisions of the Third Army could.

The two hundred thousand men of the US Third Army, commanded by General Joseph Dickman, who'd advanced from division to corps to army command in a year's time, set off after the Germans on November 17. General John Lejeune noted that the men of his 2nd Division looked like scarecrows in their torn, filthy uniforms and worn-out shoes, each hauling eighty pounds of gear. But they advanced rapidly under sunless skies and a steady, freezing rain, Lejeune remarking that he'd never seen "a more hardy, vigorous, ruddy-cheeked aggregation of young Americans." Their songs certainly suggested as much: "The 2nd Division is on the Rhine, *parlez-vous* / Fucking their women and drinking their wine."[2]

The Doughs and Marines were to march in prescribed daily stages until they reached the Rhine. Supply was even more difficult than during the last days of the war because the troops were now in no-man's-land—devoid of rails—or the ex-German rear areas, where the railways were still run by Germans, who didn't muster their usual efficiency when it came to supplying the enemy. Plodding along with their borrowed horses, the troops of the Third Army discovered that the Germans had vanished into thin air, releasing their hordes of prisoners behind them. Bands of Russians, Italians, and Rumanians—many armed with cast-off German weapons—roved through the unregulated space.

Colonel Marshall drove into this space to see what was going on. He traversed the Meuse-Argonne battlefield and found the terrain between Montfaucon and Romagne "gashed with shells and sprouting crosses." Forty thousand American dead were being interred in a flat field near Romagne—amid the ruptured Kriemhilde Line. Their graves would shortly become the scene of another ferocious battle, this time in American statehouses and Congress, between lobbyists for America's funeral homes (who wanted the dead returned to the US for burial at public expense) and the diplomatic representatives of France, who wanted them left in French soil to immortalize their sacrifice in the Allied cause. The lobbyists naturally won, and more than 60 percent of the American dead would be shipped home, but the 14,246 who remained in the Meuse-Argonne Cemetery made it the largest American military cemetery in Europe, and one still never visited by any American president.

After surveying the vast graveyard, Marshall drove to Dun, crossed the Meuse on the US 5th Division's pontoon bridge, which had been the target of Hindenburg's last reserve division on November 10, and then continued into the unoccupied zone. Just a mile in, he found the road "filled from side to side with long-bearded, filthy looking Russians." They'd been captured at Tannenberg in 1914 and had been "worked like slaves" in the lines around Verdun and Sedan ever since. "They were so cowed that at the least frown they jerked into a rigid posture." Released French prisoners, "their worldly goods in a handkerchief carried on a stick over the shoulder," tramped day and night through the unoccupied zone, heading home to rapturous, relieved welcomes.[3]

Major Paul Clark, still representing US interests in Foch's headquarters, spoke with a French captain of engineers who had driven to Hindenburg's headquarters at Spa a few days after the armistice to assure radio and telegraph communication between the Allied and German armies. The captain exulted over the German collapse. Prussian efficiency had been swallowed up by revolutionary chaos. Even the official cars of German headquarters had been defaced, the label "Great Headquarters" painted out in red. On the road, German trucks and wagons were painted with red bands or hung with red flags. When the cattle that marched with the German army for food fell dead from exhaustion, famished troopers would swarm around the carcass and carve off hunks of meat with their knives. The railroad cars were crammed with pillaged furniture and clothing. German officers—all showing "distress and exhaustion"—were never saluted. Along the roads, the French officer saw immense quantities of abandoned ammunition, guns, trucks, and wagons. The Germans having lost most of their horses, German vehicles—ammo wagons, supply carts, ambulances—had to be pulled by German troops. The Frenchman saw them, fifteen or twenty Germans to a vehicle, grasping the traces and pulling like mules. At Spa, the Frenchman glimpsed Field Marshal Hindenburg in a hallway: "He looked the worse for the experiences of the last few weeks." Hindenburg's staff regretted the poor communication between themselves and the Allies but said that all of their telegraph and railway personnel had simply walked off their jobs. There seemed to be nothing left but "disorder and dissolution."[4]

On November 19, General Philippe Pétain, who'd rebuilt the French army after the mutinies and conserved its manpower ever since, was made a Marshal of France by a grateful and relieved government. Major Clark attended Pétain's triumphal entry into Metz that day. It was hard to believe that this bastion and rail yard of the German army, seized by the Prussians in 1870 and occupied ever since, was suddenly French again. The boulevards were flagged with tricolors and American flags. Troops of General Charles Mangin's Tenth Army led the celebratory parade, minus Mangin, who'd fallen from his horse that morning. Pétain took post beside the statue of Marshal Ney on Metz's esplanade to receive the review. "I am too moved to speak," he murmured to no one in particular. A flyover by one hundred aircraft nearly ended in spectacular tragedy when one of them clipped a telephone wire and crashed near Pétain. Clark observed that the equestrian statue of Kaiser Friedrich III—who'd ruled for ninety-nine days in 1888 before succumbing to throat cancer and leaving the throne to his son Wilhelm II—had been pulled down, the head sheared off. The two American officers with Clark lugged the 125-pound head to their train as a souvenir. Standing before Metz's magnificent Gothic cathedral, Clark noticed that a German sculptor had given Daniel, set beside Jesus in a frieze twenty-five feet off the ground, the face of Kaiser Wilhelm II. A happy Frenchman had placed an iron chain around Daniel's hands and hung a sign on him in German: "How fleeting is earthly glory."[5]

President Wilson initially agreed to Foch's request that he leave thirty American divisions in Europe until the armistice was converted into a formal peace. The remaining divisions would be raided for replacements until they shipped back to the States. In the meantime, the Doughboys of the First and Second Armies returned to the training areas that many of them had only just vacated to await ships home. Captain Ty Cobb, a chemical warfare officer and one of the most famous baseball players in America, was among the troops who arrived in France too late to fight in the war. One veteran heard an officer say: "I wish the war had lasted long enough for old Ty to go into the Kaiser with his spikes high." The two corps of Dickman's US Third Army were designated "Forces of Occupation in Hostile Territory." The rest stood in reserve. Some ugly intra-Allied spats ensued, with Foch watching American transports taking troops home like a hawk and insisting that the United States maintain thirty *white* divisions, and not try to send white divisions home and leave black divisions in their place. Even in the land of liberty, fraternity, and equality, racial prejudice thrived, as it did in the States.[6]

In December 1918, President Wilson arrived in France to guide the Paris Peace Conference. He and the first lady visited a US Army hospital in Paris; they passed through the wards, shaking hands and expressing thanks and concern to the wounded. When leaving, Wilson asked if he'd been shown everything. Everything but the jaw ward, he was told. What's that? the president asked. It was the ward where men who'd been disfigured were treated. The wounds were so ghastly that nurses there had shorter shifts than anywhere else: faces mutilated by shrapnel, mouths exploded by bullets—men who had to be fed gruel, raw eggs, or gravy through tubes placed directly into their exposed throats or nostrils. Wilson and Edith entered and went down the line, stoically greeting the men, commiserating, and conveying the thanks of the nation. When the president emerged from the ward, he was, a witness recalled, "white as death and his hands trembled. He appeared to stagger. A look of suffering was on his face and he seemed completely crushed." The commander in chief had come face-to-face with a small part of what the Doughs had seen at the front every day.[7]

On Christmas Day, 1918, Wilson left Paris and drove to Chaumont to become the first president in history to review an American army on foreign soil. Wilson had planned to perform the review on the Cheppy road southwest of Montfaucon, where Patton's tanks had battled and the 35th, 28th, and 79th Divisions had overlapped in their tortured progress to the Mount of Falcons. Pershing had planned to have the president review a battalion of veterans from each of those divisions. "Such an occasion," he wrote Secretary of War Baker, "would afford the president the best opportunity he will have to emphasize to Europe, in an address to his own troops as their commander-in-chief, the purposes he had in mind in sending this army to France." That was a fascinating and indeed Clausewitzian statement by Pershing. As war turned to peace, America needed to know *why* it had fought and *what*, in the peace, it would demand as the price of that support. War, after all, is the continuation of policy by other means. What, Pershing prodded, was the American policy that had animated this war?[8]

But first the right troops had to be found. With the entire AEF marching into Germany or returning to its camps and ports and President Wilson impatient to leave France, it was decided that instead of using veterans of the fights at Vauquois and Montfaucon, a "provisional battalion" would be formed from whatever troops were nearby. Thus, Wilson found himself speaking to one thousand freshly arrived recruits, none veterans, from four different New Jersey and Maryland National Guard regiments. Wilson wished them a merry Christmas and assured them that "everyone at home is proud of you." They were "champions of liberty." Even though none of these men had actually fought—let alone fought here—they represented those who had, and Wilson thanked them: "You have put your heart into it, done your duty. . . . Now we are to have the fruits of victory." Wilson assured the troops that as they had done their job in war, he would do his job in peace. "I know what you expect of me."

Speaking to the shivering troops at Chaumont, his breath fogging the air around him, Wilson vowed to guide "the process of settlement," applying the "principles and moral aspects" for which America had fought, to achieve "the high purposes for which the U.S. entered this war: the establishment of peace upon the permanent foundation of right and justice." His policy mirrored the ideas of H. G. Wells, who had authored the line "the war that will end war" in 1914 and whose bestselling 1916 novel *Mr. Britling Sees It Through* had demanded a postwar world "on a different footing," with "an end to the folly and vanity of kings, and to any people ruling any people but themselves," a new "world-republic," a "sane government of the world."[9]

This hallucination was exactly what Wilson now believed attainable. He had a dig at America's allies, who were already gathering in smoke-filled rooms to divide the beaten empires. "This being a people's war, it must be a people's peace." But by what diplomatic mechanism could Wilson implement a "people's peace"? Parading through European cities or barnstorming around America in a train—as Wilson would do—would not budge elected and bureaucratic elites in Europe and the United States, who were dead set against a mild peace and who planned to obstruct or merely wait out the "Wilsonian Moment." Editor Randolph Bourne had predicted the breakdown in consensus even before the US intervention—when Wilson had failed in his efforts to mediate an end to the war—writing in *Seven Arts* that "if the war is too strong for you to prevent, how is it going to be weak enough for you to control and mold to your liberal purposes?" But rational acceptance of reality was never Wilson's strength. The president left the reviewing stand at Chaumont in the afternoon, drove to Montigny for dinner with the officers of the 26th Yankee Division, and then departed for London. It was a flying visit, but he struck all of the key notes of his policy, which would hamstring American interests in the months ahead.[10]

Wilson never tailored his global ambitions to the thrift and pragmatism of America, or to the need to sign a peace treaty before the Allies demobilized and the Germans recovered their nerve. Sailing to France in December 1918 to negotiate the peace, he told his colleagues that the Allies "were beaten when we came in," and he "did not intend to let them forget it." Yet even as he declaimed his grand principles, his instrument of influence and coercion in Europe was shrinking fast. Foch had wanted thirty American divisions in Europe until the Germans signed a satisfactory peace treaty, but Wilson and Congress, sick of the war and its costs and eager to get the Dough-boys home, vowed to reduce their divisions in Europe to twenty in March 1919, fifteen in April, and ten in May. By June 1—before the Germans had even signed the treaty—the AEF would be down to just seven divisions.[11]

While the Americans haggled over troop numbers, the Germans at Versailles haggled over the treaty of peace. They indignantly re-fused to sign the peace preliminaries in May and then again in June 1919. Foch ordered the rapidly demobilizing Americans to prepare for a resumption of the war, to "break the resistance and impose peace." Foch reminded the Allied commanders that hostilities were no longer "suspended" per the armistice but formally resumed because of Ger-man "lapsing of the Armistice." He now ordered an advance on the right bank of the Rhine and an invasion of Germany. Pershing, down to a handful of weak divisions, stared incredulously at his instructions from the generalissimo in June: "Destroy enemy forces and insurgents and take hostages to assure the correctness of the attitude of the in-habitants." Foch's only concession to moderation was to limit the use of poison gas and long-range artillery bombardment, "where possible." Foch ordered preparations for a drive from Mainz, Coblenz, and Co-logne to the "centers of resistance": Weimar and Berlin. He'd make use of twenty-one French divisions, eleven British, seven Belgian, and three American. Pershing recoiled, writing Tasker Bliss, the American representative on the Supreme War Council, that US forces in Europe should be removed from the generalissimo's control and reduced to the lowest possible number to discourage French adventures like this one. Foch, Pershing alleged, "would inevitably follow the desires of his own government," involving America in yet more French battles.[12]

The French had begun to mistrust the Americans as the Paris Peace Conference unfolded in 1919. They loathed the concessions being made to the Germans. In Paris, both London and Washington were distrusted, but in the provinces, a British official in France observed, "the Americans [came] in for the maximum odium." French anger was easy to grasp. Touring the Western Front battlefields with Pershing after the war, Marshall found the ground still stamped with devastation. "Sometimes for miles there is not even a tree." Marshall toured Lens and judged it "the most impressive scene of utter desolation and destruction that I have ever visited. To see a city, a great manufacturing center and mining district, as large as San Francisco, completely leveled to the ground, gives one a better conception of the horrors of war than anything else." For the French, understandably, *any* concession to the Huns after treatment like this was too much. Politician Joseph Caillaux, branded a traitor by Clemenceau during the war, now made a political comeback with his argument that "France was bound to lose by this war, and was bled white by her Allies." Caillaux was at least consistent, as defeatist in victory as he'd been in defeat, and his insinuations, General Edward Spears wrote Churchill in April 1919, "have some appearance of truth in the eyes of the French people." Indeed, they'd be dusted off and reused by Marshal Pétain and the Vichyites twenty years later.[13]

Paul Clark, now a lieutenant colonel, had dinner with his old friend General Duval, Foch's chief of operations, in February 1919. "We Frenchmen are very concerned by the American attitude in negotiations," Duval said. President Wilson seemed intent on securing for the Germans the same rights as other nations, even as Britain and the United States drew down their forces in Europe "in feverish haste, leaving us alone." Duval anticipated the day, not far off, when France would find itself "alone against 80 million Germans, their appetite whetted for revenge." Duval accurately predicted the course of the next war. "Next time if you don't come to our rescue within three months all will be lost. Next time Germany will promptly move to get the port cities along the Atlantic so that you will have no place to land on our shore. The Germans are not docile little lambs," Duval explained. "They only understand *force*." Wilson's League of Nations would do nothing to arrest German aggression. "At best, the League will be like a little child struggling to walk alone; until it proves its efficacy, you Americans should leave an army of 150,000 to stand indefinitely with us in front of the Germans."[14]

But the Americans wouldn't. The last American soldier would be gone within four years. Wilson's Treaty of Guarantee, signed in 1919 by Wilson, Lloyd George, and Clemenceau to fix and guarantee the Franco-German border, would die in the US Senate, nullifying not only the American commitment but the British one too, London having insisted that the costly business of containing the Germans be "an all for one and one for all" arrangement, or no arrangement at all. The British and French were finding Washington to be an oddly reluctant hegemon. Duval finished on a mournful note: "Great Britain and the U.S. are washing their hands of the future and leaving France alone with the League of Nations to protect her against 80 million Germans. The future for France is dark indeed."[15]

It was, if the French were expecting help from America. Congress lost no time in reducing the US military. The Army Appropriations Bill that was to have been $19 billion if the war had continued was slashed to $3 billion after the armistice, and even that was regarded in Congress as a scandalous sum, but irreducible because of the need to feed, house, and transport the AEF back to America over the ensuing ten months. Officers returning home from combat in France were instantly reduced to the rank (and pay) they'd held before deploying to France. Two-star generals were reduced to captains and placed under colonels who hadn't even been in the war. General staff chief Peyton March—still smarting over Pershing's independence in the war—effectively demoted most of Black Jack's protégés, who were nicknamed "BAs," "busted aristocrats," after their reduction in rank. Since the officers who'd served out the war in the States didn't lose their promotions, most of the returning officers assumed that this was all payback—March's belated "swipe at Pershing," as Major Mark Clark, suddenly a lieutenant again, put it.[16]

Returning home from France after the armistice, Secretary of War Newton Baker let it be known that he opposed the formation of an American peacetime army on anything but a voluntary basis.

By February 1919—long before the Germans had signed the peace treaty—77,000 US officers and 1.2 million troops had already been let go. With the Dent Bill, the House authorized an army of two hundred thousand in May 1919, a piece of legislation that also made thirty-nine-year-old General Douglas MacArthur the youngest superintendent in the history of the US Military Academy at West Point. But even two hundred thousand was too much for California's representative Julius Kahn, the chairman of the House Military Affairs Committee. Worried about cost and militarism, Kahn wanted the US Army capped at 125,000, reinforced by a "Swiss-style militia." Congress also hammered the general staff, damning its inefficiency in France. "But then Congress has always been hostile to the general staff," France's military attaché in Washington noted. History had taught the French republic to be wary of the career military's political meddling. The American republic was no less alert to the threat. An attempt in Congress to give Pershing the permanent rank of general failed, pointing again to Washington's suspicion of the uniformed military.[17]

Pershing had sought a peacetime army of 500,000, but Congress set the limit at 135,000 after the war, essentially what it had been before the war. While still in France, Pershing submitted a thirty-eight-page memorandum on the "proposed military policy of the United States" to the military committees of the House and Senate. He had witnessed the price of unpreparedness and now called for a permanent draft, in which American men would be trained for seven months after their twentieth birthday and held in reserve until their thirty-first birthday, with annual two-week refresher courses. Every American would serve, and exemptions would be made only for mental and physical disability and key officeholders and workers. The Marines would be absorbed into the army. The army would adopt German-style territorial organization, with the United States divided into six permanent corps regions and each of the army's eighty-four infantry and twenty-four cavalry divisions (most of them reserve units) assigned to one of them. Pershing considered this essential in order to avoid, as he put it, having once again "to make an army after the war has begun." Cantigny, he reminded his readers, had been the first

American offensive, and even it, a minor push by a single regiment, had not come until fourteen months after the declaration of war. In the future, Pershing warned, America would have to be "ready for the unexpected." If not, Allies would be defeated and removed from the battlefield before the Americans could even arrive.[18]

Pershing's proposals were swallowed up by the larger, urgent drama unfolding at Versailles. President Wilson, there to lead the American peace delegation in 1919, had seen his authority severely eroded by the midterm elections in November 1918. He'd asked the country to make him their "unembarrassed spokesman" in dealings with the conquered Germans, and the country had instead embarrassed him by returning Republican majorities in the House and Senate. In those midterm elections, Republicans had cast Wilson and the Democrats as "Copperheads," like the Peace Democrats of the American Civil War, who'd been too lenient to the Confederates and too eager for peace at any price. Senate Majority Leader Henry Cabot Lodge and the Republicans could thus assail Wilson's idealistic vision of the peace without harm to their own national security credentials. On the contrary, by resisting Wilson's policy for the League and a "peace without victors"—after 117,000 American dead—the Republicans strengthened their image and weakened his.[19]

Wilson's weak position contrasted with the strong, unified position of America's allies. Lloyd George had just been reelected prime minister with Liberal and Conservative support on a platform of making the Germans pay for the war. Although the London *Times* derided the American view that Britain was "out for plunder," it most certainly was. The Allies had contracted $150 billion of war debts to fight Germany, and Lloyd George had won reelection with lavish promises—land for veterans, public housing, and industrial profit-sharing. The money, in a country where the national debt had surged from 24 percent of GDP when the war began to 127 percent of GDP when the war ended, would have to come from somewhere. It wasn't hard to imagine where.[20]

Clemenceau—"Father Victory" to the French public—bore down on the Germans too. When Wilson opposed Italy's plans to annex

Austro-Hungarian and Turkish territory, Prime Minister Orlando left Paris and returned to Rome to secure public reaffirmation of his support and a repudiation of Wilson's policy. With the Germans beaten and in no position to resume the war and the Allies determined to punish Germany, Wilson found himself, as the journalist Elizabeth Shepley Sergeant put it, opposing "nebulous humanities" to Allied realpolitik. "It is a strange thing," Sergeant observed at Versailles, "to see Clemenceau craning a stiff neck to this cloud from the firm soil of *la patrie* and responding with chiseled particularities." She abridged one typical debate to this:

> Wilson: "Our soldiers fought to do away with the old order and establish a new one, which will bring honor and justice to the world."
>
> Clemenceau: "From most ancient times, people have rushed at one another's throats to satisfy appetites or interests."
>
> Wilson: "The balance of power must be replaced with a single overwhelming group of nations, trustees in the peace of the world."
>
> Clemenceau: "With old materials you cannot build a new edifice. America is far from the German frontier."

Against such "chiseled particularities," Wilson found himself helpless. His vision offered mere hope; the Allied vision assured security, or so the Allies imagined. Nor did the president have military or even financial leverage. With two million Doughboys stranded in France's ports of embarkation, Wilson needed British ships to speed the men home. He could hardly afford to be stringent with an ally that literally held the keys to the American car. American agriculture and industry put additional pressure on the president—they'd ramped up production for export to Europe, but when Wilson tried to cut off new credits to pressure the Allies, American producers were stuck with surplus inventory, a fact they made known to the White House. And so instead of calling loans and holding Allied feet to the fire, Wilson felt compelled to prolong the wartime lending in the form of export credits.[21]

At Versailles, Wilson did what he could, successfully insisting that German overseas possessions pass to the victors not as colonies but as "mandates" that would be held in trust and prepared for independence. He also persuaded the Allies to include the League of Nations covenant as Section I of the eventual Treaty of Versailles. This idea, maligned by the Allies in Paris and the Republicans in Washington, was symptomatic of Wilson's increasing alienation. He argued that to "dissect the Covenant from the Treaty" would "destroy the whole vital structure," when in fact the treaty and the League were two separate things, as the Republicans maintained. France and Britain had none of Wilson's idealism about the League, but they thought that it might prove useful in containing a resurgent Germany if the Americans joined. They also had to give at least a symbolic nod to the League, which was hugely popular with many of their voters, who trusted Woodrow Wilson, mistrusted their own statesmen, and fervently desired an end to wars and dueling empires. "We cannot get Wilson to sign the Peace without the League, and if the signature of the U.S. is not on the Peace we shall have to revert to balance of power policy pure and simple, and this will mean war again later on," journalist Charles Repington summarized in March 1919. But would the French and British people even stand for another war, after *this* one? [22]

While he wrestled with the Allies at Versailles, Wilson also wrestled with the Republicans in Washington. To win Republican support for his ideas, Wilson extracted concessions from the other powers, namely, that the League would have to defer in the Americas to the Monroe Doctrine, that the United States could leave the League, that German overseas territories wouldn't simply be annexed by the European powers and Japan, and that the League wouldn't interfere in domestic legislation, such as immigration policy or tariffs.

But the Europeans extracted their own concessions to offset Wilson's demands, most notoriously German "war guilt," reparations, and gifts of German territory to the new states of Poland and Czechoslovakia, which sprang to life on Germany's borders. The world watched as Wilson's "new diplomacy" was steadily vanquished by the old. To drive home the point that security was best sought with old methods, not new ones, France also demanded an American security guarantee—conceded by Wilson, revoked by the Senate—as well as control of Germany's Saar Basin until 1935. The Italians annexed the two hundred thousand Germans of the formerly Habsburg South Tyrol. The Japanese, the focus of prewar American apprehension, seated themselves firmly in China's Shandong province, which they'd seized from the Germans in 1914 and showed no interest in restoring to China.[23]

Edmund Burke, one of Wilson's favorite authors, had said that "you cannot indict a nation," and yet this is precisely what the Allies set out to do. Accepting in theory Wilson's idea of a just peace, the French shrewdly countered that for justice to be done, crime had to be punished, and that the Germans would have to pay for the many crimes they'd committed during the long war. "Justice," as President Poincaré reminded President Wilson, "is not inert; it does not submit to injustice. What it first demands when violated is restitution and reparation."

The Germans winced at the Treaty of Versailles, both its content and the manner of delivery: five days to consider, no amendments allowed, and immediate resumption of the war if not signed. *Vorwärts-Zeitung*, the newspaper of Germany's moderate Socialists, called the final draft presented to the German delegation "a fresh declaration of war. The whole document breathes hate. This means a greater blow to humanity than the war itself." Other German papers called the treaty "a shameful tyranny" and an "absurdity" in view of the hard times that had overtaken Germany since the kaiser's abdication. "I wonder what History will have to say about all this," a German delegate harrumphed to Clemenceau. The French premier, who knew precisely where the war guilt lay in the narrowest legal sense, regarded the German without pity and answered simply: "History will not say that Belgium invaded Germany."[24]

British diplomats awaiting the German decision—to sign or not to sign—arranged a betting pool. Odds that the Germans would sign were five to two in favor. Foch, still the Allied generalissimo, had 750,000 troops on the Rhine ready to advance if the Germans refused. But the German political parties were split on whether to accept the terms. Ebert, elected president of Germany in February, called the Allied terms "unbearable" but was assured (privately) by Hindenburg that the army was incapable of stopping an Allied drive on Berlin. The two socialist parties wavered but favored signing. Erzberger's Catholic Center Party favored signing, as one might have inferred from Erzberger's blasé performance in Compiègne, where he'd plowed through mountains of French food and displayed no sorrow at the German defeat. The National Liberals, representing German big business, opposed signing, as did the Conservative Junkers, who demanded defiance. When Chancellor Philipp Scheidemann's cabinet convened in Weimar and voted, acceptance lost. But how exactly would the Germans resist? Scheidemann declared the "impossibility" of acceptance or resistance, and then unhelpfully resigned with his entire cabinet. It fell to Erzberger and Socialist Gustav Noske, the German Republic's first defense minister, to arrange a new government that would sign and prevent the Allies from invading Germany. The new government was headed by Socialist Gustav Bauer, with Noske at the defense ministry, Erzberger at the finance ministry, and Socialist Hermann Müller as foreign secretary. Bauer and Müller made a last appeal to the Allies for "modifications"—to the war guilt clause and the demand for reparations—but were told that the Allies wouldn't "change another word or comma."

A German newspaper wailed that Wilson's League of Nations, the promised "House of Peace," was being steadily devoured by the "Lion of Hate" and the "Snake of Greed." Without a credible military deterrent, Chancellor Bauer caved, but he demanded that the German Reichstag share the blame and ratify the treaty, which it did on June 20, by a vote of 237–138. The German navy, interned by the British at Scapa Flow in the Orkney Islands, greeted the news by scuttling itself. The sailors hoisted German ensigns and red flags, then opened the sea cocks and knocked the rivets from the watertight compartments. Tirpitz's mighty fleet sank beneath the waves.[25]

Most Americans were more immediately affected by two votes of Congress that day—to end daylight-saving time effective October 26, after bitter protests by American farmers, who were still 25 percent of the population, and to extend wartime prohibition indefinitely, the Senate voting 55–11 to continue the ban on sales of liquor, wine, and beer. With German acceptance of the treaty secured, Secretary of War Baker doubtless recalled a conversation he'd had with Bliss in late 1917. How long will this war last? Baker had asked the general. "Thirty years," Bliss had replied. "Impossible," Baker had snorted. Bliss clarified, "This particular episode will be concluded in a year or two. Then the war will take on a new phase and will be waged . . . with economic weapons until nations rehabilitate themselves and feel a fresh access of strength for another try on the military side. . . . Thirty years would be the normal time for a generation that had the passion to breed this war to pass off the stage and let others come who have a new objective and a new point of view." Foch said much the same thing of the Treaty of Versailles: "This is not peace; it's a twenty years' armistice."[26]

On June 28, Germany signed the treaty in the Hall of Mirrors at Versailles. All of the delegates signed except the Chinese, who refused to sign so long as the Japanese controlled Shandong, the birthplace of Confucius. The next night, Wilson took the train to Brest after signing the controversial Treaty of Guarantee. Foch had insisted that the French border be placed on the Rhine—absorbing the German cities of Cologne, Coblenz, and Mainz—but Clemenceau had agreed to leave the German Rhineland undisturbed if the Americans and British would guarantee France's eastern border against any aggression. Both Wilson and Lloyd George agreed to do so, and the British parliament promptly ratified the treaty on condition that the US Senate ratify it too. Wilson would get a ship at Brest and return home to campaign for Senate passage of his treaties—Versailles with its League Covenant, and the Guarantee.[27]

He'd have his work cut out for him. The same ethnic tensions that had made intervention difficult made peacemaking even more so. Irish Americans hated the treaty's acceptance of continuing British rule in Ireland. Italian Americans deplored Wilson's resistance to Italy's occupation of Fiume and other bits of Austria-Hungary that the president planned to include in the new state of Yugoslavia. German Americans, already enraged by the nation's prohibition of beer sales, were no less angry at the harsh terms meted out to the old *Vaterland*. William Randolph Hearst, who'd complicated the draft with his campaign against "foreign slackers," now complicated peacemaking by damning the League of Nations and its claim on American war powers and resources. Even as Wilson entrained for Brest, California senator Hiram Johnson was denouncing the League of Nations Covenant in a speech to a packed Carnegie Hall. The crowd, assembled by a political action committee named the League for the Preservation of American Independence, hooted and hissed every time Wilson or his League was mentioned. "I will not give up American independence for Woodrow Wilson or anyone else!" Johnson shouted to loud applause.[28]

The Senate majority leader, Henry Cabot Lodge of Massachusetts, first delayed action on the voluminous treaty—insisting that its every word be read aloud to the Foreign Relations Committee—and then set to work picking it apart. Home from France, Wilson took to the rails in September 1919 to barnstorm across America, whip up grassroots support for the treaty, and force the Senate to ratify. But halfway through the trip the president fell ill and returned to Washington, where he suffered a severe stroke on October 2. That was effectively the end of any hope that America would ratify the Treaty of Versailles, the Treaty of Guarantee, and the League Covenant. Confined to the White House, with slurred speech and partial paralysis, Wilson would find it difficult to counterattack Lodge.

Lodge's attacks commenced at once. He reported out the Treaty of Versailles on November 6 with fourteen "reservations," which, taken together, limited America's commitment to the League. The main reservation was the one that worried most Americans, that the League would commit US troops and ships to other peoples' wars. Lodge's reservations required Senate approval of any deployment, a perfectly reasonable (and constitutional) demand that Wilson rejected as "a knife thrust at the heart of the treaty." Wilson's inability to separate his own idealism from the strictures of the Constitution (and the pragmatism of most Americans) would be his undoing. The November 1918 midterm elections had made clear that Wilson's expansive policy was not the policy of the American people, who, as Pennsylvania senator Philander Knox put it, were "impatient with visions and new adventures, and weary of agitation and novel commitments." Wilson essentially denied reality. He'd consent to no changes. The Senate," he said, with an astonishing lack of tact, "must take its medicine."[29]

The president, as lawyers said, was acting *ultra vires*—beyond his legal authority. Many Americans, as one disenchanted Wilson voter put it, viewed him increasingly as an "autocrat." Wilson seemed not to understand that the treaty debate between Congress and the executive was a constitutional one and that Senate consent was required for the treaty to take effect. Naturally, the Senate looked askance at a League Covenant—embedded in the treaty at Wilson's insistence—that was glaringly unconstitutional in that it contained a presidential attempt to commit the United States in some future contingency to war, which was a prerogative vested in Congress by the Constitution. US senators, who took an oath to defend the Constitution, couldn't consent to a transfer of their war powers to the League of Nations. The Constitution would first have to be amended by three-quarters of America's state legislatures to make room in Washington for such an expansive global treaty described by the president as "the last hope of mankind." Citizens, in other words, would have to assent, and there was no time for that now.[30]

The Senate voted down the Treaty of Versailles on November 19, 1919. The first vote, on Wilson's treaty with Lodge's reservations, would have passed had Wilson not instructed Democratic senators to vote against it. The only senators who would have opposed that version were the "Irreconcilables" around Idaho senator William Borah, who rejected the treaty with or without Lodge's reservations. Borah represented Western purists, who feared that any association with foreign powers would inevitably drag the United States into a war as costly and frustrating as the one they'd just exited. Borah was, a reporter wrote, like the "blond country boy of the old-fashioned melodrama who distrusted association with the slick city man."[31]

A second vote, for the treaty without Lodge's reservations, failed when Lodge's Republican "Reservationists" joined Borah's Irreconcilables in opposing the "entangling alliance" threatened by the League.

The Reservationists demanded that the treaty incorporate key "reservations," like undiminished war powers for the Senate, and carve-outs for US strategic interests, like the Monroe Doctrine. Wilson deplored carve-outs; they marred his system. "We ought to either go in or stay out," he scoffed. Wilson also worried that an amended treaty would go down in history as Lodge's achievement, not his. The Treaty of Guarantee, arguably the most useful document Wilson had signed in France, died alongside the Treaty of Versailles. That document had made Washington and London guarantors of France's border with Germany and, if upheld by the Senate, might have given Hitler pause twenty years later.

When the Senate put the treaty with reservations to a vote one last time in March 1920, Wilson petulantly asked Democrats to vote against it, and it failed a third time. Lodge followed with a simple resolution terminating US belligerency in the war, and Wilson vetoed even that. It would fall to the administration of the next president, Warren G. Harding, actually to end the state of war between the US and the Central Powers in July 1921. Harding had won the White House in a landslide with his call for "not heroics but healing, not nostrums but normalcy." That phrase alone stood as a crushing repudiation of Wilson and his policies. Harding pronounced the issue of American involvement with the League "as dead as slavery" and consigned it to "a deep grave." The same fate claimed Wilson in February 1924, a day after he had judged himself "a broken piece of machinery." The Paris newspaper *Le Temps* eulogized Wilson and identified his chief fault: "to love glory, and love to hold the stage alone."[32]

Wilson had gone to Paris in 1918 with no prominent Republicans in his entourage to give it a bipartisan face. His administration and Peace Commission in Paris, dominated by the gray eminence Colonel Edward House and Wilson's second wife, Edith Galt, were notable for their lack of prominent advisers—Baker at the War Department, Lansing at State, Tumulty as chief of staff, Wilson's son-in-law at Treasury, Bliss at Versailles. These were all men who wouldn't overshadow the president. Clemenceau had nicknamed Wilson "Buddha," his entourage "Zero." Cocooned in an echo chamber, enamored of his own impulses and oratory, and increasingly ill with heart disease, Wilson had never bothered to secure broad American support for his vision of a new world order.[33]

The American editor Alfred Holman deplored Wilson's "rainbow-chasing" and ascribed it to the president's "immeasurable vanity and ambition." The whole peace process, Holman concluded, had been absurdly mismanaged. Wilson had prolonged the process at great risk. While the delegates "pottered" around Versailles, the European economy stuttered, Bolshevism spread, and the German spirit, so low at the time of the armistice, when there had been ample US troops to hand, began to revive when there were scarcely any Doughboys left in Europe. In January 1919, open battles erupted on the streets of Berlin as communist Spartacists struggled to take the Reichstag. The rebels entrenched themselves across a dozen city blocks around the Alexanderplatz and captured government buildings, the royal stables, and the telegraph office. The government, defended by Freikorps, the right-wing militias of ex-servicemen like Heinrich Himmler and Ernst Röhm who'd shortly become the storm troopers of the Nazi movement, counterattacked with planes, tanks, poison gas, and *Minenwerfer*. Americans in Berlin fled to the Adlon Hotel, where they sheltered behind a hedge of barbed wire, sandbags, and machine guns. Sixty-year-old General Walther von Lüttwitz, who'd commanded a corps during Operation Michael and now commanded the Freikorps units in Berlin, crushed the Spartacists but opened the door to fascist dictatorship with his unconcealed contempt for democracy and the new German Republic.[34]

Throughout this dangerous crisis, Wilson insisted that a League Covenant (that the US Senate would surely reject) be included in the treaty. America, Holman believed, could be persuaded to continue its close association with the Allies and any nations seeking peace, but would never "refer her individual purposes to a jury of nations, to allow anybody but herself to determine her policies as to sea power and other defensive arrangements." Wilson's real failure was far greater than his unwillingness to compromise on the treaty. He treated statesmen like Lloyd George as rivals, not allies, and failed to make a case, to both parties in America, that the US needed to remain allied to the Allied powers after the war, thus creating a deterrent to future aggressors far more redoubtable than any League of Nations. Wilson created a false opposition between the League and "universal armament," as if there were nothing in between. What lay in between was reality: a generally good and pacific America and its allies who should have been encouraged to enlist in a global security system against communism, as well as any future rogue states like Germany, Japan, or Italy.[35]

Wilson's core belief—that America should sacrifice its "private" national interests to the "public right" of the League of Nations—rebelled against America's conception of itself as a mighty, sovereign, and exceptional nation. His refusal to create a real security architecture with Britain and France on the grounds that it would violate his demand for "open covenants openly arrived at" was ingenuous. His strategic sense had vanished. In December 1918, he described the deterrent potential of the League thus: "It shall operate as the organized moral force of men throughout the world, and that whenever or wherever wrong or aggression are planned and contemplated, this searching light of conscience will be turned upon them and men everywhere will ask 'What are the purposes that you hold in your heart against the fortunes of the world?' Just a little exposure will settle most disputes," he primly assured his audience, ending with the erroneous conclusion that "if the Central Powers had dared to discuss the purposes of this war for a single fortnight, it never would have happened." Of course they *had* discussed it, for far more than a fortnight, in Berlin and Vienna, and then they'd ignited it. Wilson's vanity—defined by Colonel House as his need to be "spokesman of the liberals for the world"—destroyed the sort of workaday, prudent statecraft that would have made America an effective guarantor of international peace and stability. Wilson consistently believed, as a critic wisely concluded, that "verbal righteousness could make up for power orchestration." It couldn't, and it can't.[36]

The death of the treaty stunned the American public. The Senate had twice refused to ratify the treaty in 1919, then refused again in

March 1920. After eight months of debate, the Senate returned the Treaty of Versailles to the president without ratifying it. In each vote, a majority had favored ratification (55–39, 53–38, 49–35), but never the required two-thirds majority. London's *Spectator* marveled at the Senate's powers conferred by the founders: "Any group consisting of one-third of the Senators plus one has a right of veto as absolute as that of any autocrat in the world. As long as the group of one-third plus one hold together they can create an impassable barrier to a treaty." Yet amendments or reservations of a treaty can be made by a simple majority of the Senate, moderating the severity of that veto power. That was an invitation to Wilson to moderate his own extreme views to co-opt the senators forming the antitreaty bloc, but he refused the invitation.[37]

Americans puzzled over the constitutional fact that a simple majority had sufficed to get the nation into war but now a two-thirds majority was needed to ratify the peace. Memphis's *Commercial Appeal* spoke for many when it wrote: "All the blood spilled by our soldiers and all the funds spent by our government will have been for nothing." The *Savannah News* warned that "if the U.S. is forced to submit to another great war, the fathers and mothers of those who have been killed in this war will have no reason to look with benevolence on the men who have blocked the formation of a real League of Nations . . . with American participation."[38]

Those were Democratic papers, all condemning the fact that "a few provincial senators would not sacrifice a little pride or sovereignty to hold the destiny of humanity in their hands," that "the Hindenburg Line—the last redoubt of reaction—has been maintained in the U.S. Senate," that "the soil of the Republican wigwam has been soiled by the blood of the treaty." Without a stout transatlantic connection, Europe would probably plunge back into "that Hell to which the Prussian Beast was trying to lead it." The independent papers were at least as scathing. New York's *Evening Post* jeered that "after surprising the world with our ability to make war, we now offer humanity the spectacle of our surpassing imbecility in the making of peace." Other independent papers considered it "the most humiliating defeat for

American policy in the 140 years of our independence." The war and sacrifices had to be about *something*, yet America had evidently bled and sacrificed for *nothing*. Lodge and the Republicans "have betrayed the dead," wrote the *New York World*. The world had wanted bread in its great crisis, and "America gave them a stone."[39]

Wilson, like the Democratic papers, was offended by the asymmetry of the US Constitution, which—to bind the thirteen colonies together and reassure the small ones that they wouldn't be dominated by the big ones (or by an overweening president)—had given two senators to every state regardless of population. He now regarded a situation in which half of the US population, concentrated in a handful of populous states, was represented by sixteen senators while the other half of the population, spread thinly across the country's empty spaces, had eighty senators. Wilson had won most of the country in 1912 and 1916 and now insisted that he represented "predominant American opinion"—a dubious claim—but the war had changed everything, and Republicans would take back everything but the South in 1920.[40]

Senators were already feeling the change in the wind—a third of them were up for reelection every two years—yet Wilson stubbornly refused to open the bridge over which Republicans might have crossed, that is, to convert the League from a global alliance against war to a more focused mechanism for the application of economic sanctions and international law. It didn't help that Wilson's own secretary of state, Robert Lansing, had declared in Paris that the League of Nations was an abstraction and in need of killing by the Senate, a private declaration that was leaked to the Senate and the press at the climax of the debate. Wilson's vision of the League—a regime of right that would defend the freedom of nations all over the world—wasn't the vision of most Americans, and certainly not that of the Senate Republicans. Entangle America "in the intrigues of Europe," Senator Lodge said, "and you will destroy her power for good and endanger her very existence."[41]

World War I demonstrated America's power for good as never before. When America joined the war in April 1917, the Allies were on the brink of defeat. The capitulation of the Russians, the rout of the Italians, the defeats and mutinies of the French army, and the ruinous British casualties of 1916–1917 had made German victory almost certain. An American general staff study concluded that the hollowed-out BEF had no hope of ever beating the Germans decisively and that Haig's French ally had become "inert." That French inertia never really improved. Despite the legend of Pétain, Americans on the ground in France noted that the inertia "only became worse until the advent of the first American troops, with their accompanying assurance of Encouragement from America." Only US "aid and victory gave France the necessary courage to stem destructive influences."[42]

American casualties—fifty-three thousand killed in battle—had been high for such a short campaign, but the French had lost twenty-two times as many in the war, the British eighteen times as many. And yet all of that Allied bloodshed might have been for naught without the US intervention. Having a stab at what-ifs, the American general staff speculated on how the war would have ended *without* American participation. Without the pressure of an accelerating American deployment, "Germany would never have undertaken the offensives of 1918." French and British armies that had been unable to break the German line on the Western Front when Germany had been fighting with one hand tied behind its back, its army sprawled across multiple fronts, "would certainly have been quite incapable of doing so unaided after their morale had deteriorated and their allies had been either crushed or defeated," as happened to the Russians, Italians, and Rumanians in the course of 1917.[43]

With both hands freed, Germany would have milked all of Europe for the resources it was losing to the British blockade "while the dwindling French and British reserves continued to batter the stone wall of her western defenses and while her submarines starved England into submission." The British blockade, so often cited as the ultimate lever of victory, wasn't. "Expounders of this theory," the American analysts concluded shortly after the war, "would have proved its first victims," given the facility with which the Germans could ransack Eurasia for food and raw materials while parrying weak, diminishing French and British offensives. Without the Americans, the analysis concluded, "England's submission and the defeat of the Allies were assured." It was America—its army, navy, shipping, finance, and industry—that won World War I. "It is important," the report concluded, "that the importance of these facts be established."[44]

Pershing's army, bigger than the British army and nearly as big as the French army at the hour of the armistice, had broken through the most rugged section of the Hindenburg Line and reached the Meuse River at Sedan, a point from which American guns at Carignan could bring the four-track Mézières-Montmédy railroad under round-the-clock bombardment or simply advance to tear up the rails. That American breakthrough deprived the Germans of a third—and indeed the most critical third—of their railways from Germany into France. The four-track section taken by the Americans had carried 250 German trains a day. With it, the Germans had moved five divisions every forty-eight hours; without it, they could barely move a single division. In short, the American thrust deprived the Germans of their ability to supply or move their army. This partly explained the rapid advances of the British and French as the armistice neared; they advanced in many areas less by hard fighting than by desperate German retreating.[45]

Even as the war ended, the American pressure on the vital pivot was relentless, which was *why* the war ended. With the US First Army occupying both banks of the Meuse and commanding the rails at Sedan and the US Second Army scheduled to attack Metz on November 14, Hindenburg had no means to reinforce, withdraw, or provision his army in France. The Doughboys won the war by surrounding the German army in France and Belgium and compelling its surrender.[46]

The Doughboys had performed brilliantly. Everything had been improvised on short notice in a system that amounted to the blind leading the blind. College and graduate school classrooms had emptied when war was declared. Second lieutenants had been commissioned in ninety days. Artillery units had been built from scratch with little training, infantry with even less. An officer in the 89th Division called it "the

Star-Spangled Mess" but marveled at the American ability to make it all right. Edward Streeter, author of the popular Dere Mable letters, the *Willie and Joe* lyrics of World War I, beautifully summarized the American soldier: "That strange mixture of discontent and cheerfulness, stubbornness under discipline and tractability under leadership, sentimentalism and repression, garrulous incoherence." The Doughs were men used to "taking things as they find them. Vaguely understanding. Caring less. Grumbling by custom. Cheerful by nature. Ever anxious to be where they are not. Ever anxious to be somewhere else when they get there. Without thought of sacrifice. Who have left the flag-waving to those at home. Who serve as a matter of course."[47]

Too often the Doughboys were lions led by donkeys, which had been the fate of most armies when they'd taken their first steps in the war. There were brilliant American officers—prodigies like Summerall, who began the war as a lieutenant colonel and rose to corps command—but hundreds of failures too. Pershing performed magnificently in the political side of his job—insisting on an independent US Army—but his military performance, warped by an obsolete fondness for the offensive, was far less magnificent. Liggett emerged the better operational soldier, seeing clearly the way to beat the Germans and spare American lives with prudent tactics and linked offensives. The château of Blois—the notorious seat of the AEF's Officer Reclassification Center—was as feared as the front lines because so many American officers had to be "canned" or "blooeyed" and sent there for reassignment to some humiliating job that didn't require the leadership of men in combat.[48]

American casualties in the short, brutal war were the highest ever, and ever since—thirty-six thousand a month, six times higher than the monthly average in World War II. Even so, the US combat divisions hadn't all been stamped from the same press, as the events of the war had proved and a postwar analysis of casualties confirmed. The 2nd Division, which had battled in Belleau Wood, Soissons, the Blanc Mont, the Barricourt Ridge, and the crossing of the Meuse, suffered the most killed and wounded of any US division: 23,218, edging out the 1st Division's 22,320. The Big Red One suffered the most deaths with 5,142. Pennsylvania's 28th "Bucket of Blood" Division had 3,890 dead, followed by the 3rd Rock of the Marne Division and the 32nd Gemütlichkeit Division from Wisconsin and Michigan, both with more than 3,000 KIAs in the war. That honors were shared by three regular army and two National Guard divisions, one of them filled with German Americans, said much about the reliability of America's citizen-soldiers and immigrants as well as the suppleness of a military organization that had seemed hopelessly inefficient when the war began.[49]

On Armistice Day, ten years after the war, President Calvin Coolidge summarized the American view of Europe. To Europeans, it was remarkable how much Coolidge sounded like Wilson before the war. "We are not interested in their age-old animosities," he declared. He allowed that America had arrived late and unprepared—relying on British transports and British and French matériel—but made a virtue of this fact. America had placed four million men under arms, with six million more registered and available for the draft. "When it was all over, in spite of the great strain, we were the only country that had much reserve power left." America had converted itself into "one mighty engine for the prosecution of the war." Without those vast American reserves and the American blows in the Aisne-Marne salient, Saint-Mihiel, and the Meuse-Argonne, the French, British, and Italians would have been unable to defeat the Germans in World War I. Indeed, after the Russian defeat, they would probably themselves have been defeated. After the war, the Allies, vaunting their own great sacrifices, would downplay or simply ignore the American contribution in a deliberate way that became a historical way—that of the German major who so grossly underestimated Rick Blaine in *Casablanca*. "My impression," Major Heinrich Strasser confides to Captain Louis Renault, "was that he's just another blundering American." Renault regards the major coolly and replies: "But we mustn't underestimate American blundering. I was with them when they blundered into Berlin in 1918."[50]

BIBLIOGRAPHY

ARCHIVES

AUSTRIA
Vienna
HHSA Haus-, Hof- und Staatsarchiv
KA Kriegsarchiv

FRANCE
Vincennes
SHD Service Historique de la Défense

GERMANY
Munich
BKA Bayerisches Kriegsarchiv

UNITED KINGDOM
Kew
UKNA UK National Archives

London
LHCMA Liddell Hart Centre for Military Archives
UKPA Houses of Parliament, UK Parliamentary Archives

UNITED STATES
College Park, MD
NARA National Archives and Records Administration

PUBLISHED SOURCES

Alexander, Robert. *Memories of the World War, 1917–1918*. New York: Macmillan, 1931.

Allen, Hervey. *It Was Like This: Two Stories of the Great War*. New York: Farrar & Rinehart, 1936.

———. *Toward the Flame: A Memoir of World War I*. 1926. Lincoln: Univ. of Nebraska Press, 2003.

Baer, George W. *One Hundred Years of Sea Power: The U.S. Navy, 1890–1990*. Stanford, CA: Stanford Univ. Press, 1994.

Baker, Horace L. *Argonne Days in World War I*. 1927. Edited by Robert H. Ferrell. Columbia: Univ. of Missouri Press, 2007.

Barber, Thomas H. *Along the Road*. New York: Dodd Mead, 1924.

Barkley, John Lewis. *Scarlet Fields: The Combat Memoir of a World War I Medal of Honor Hero*. 1930. Lawrence: Univ. Press of Kansas, 2012.

Belmonte, Peter L. *Days of Perfect Hell, October–November 1918: The U.S. 26th Infantry Regiment in the Meuse-Argonne Offensive*. Atglen, PA: Schiffer, 2015.

Berg, A. Scott. *Wilson*. New York: G. P. Putnam's Sons, 2013.

———, ed. *World War I and America*. New York: Library of America, 2017.

Berry, Henry. *Make the Kaiser Dance: Living Memories of a Forgotten War*. New York: Arbor House, 1978.

Bidwell, Shelford, and Dominick Graham. *Fire-Power: The British Army Weapons and Theories of War, 1904–1945*. 1982. Barnsley, UK: Pen & Sword, 2004.

Boff, Jonathan. *Winning and Losing on the Western Front: The British Third Army and the Defeat of Germany in 1918*. Cambridge: Cambridge Univ. Press, 2012.

Boyd, Thomas. *Through the Wheat: A Novel of the World War I Marines*. 1923. Lincoln: Univ. of Nebraska Press, 2000.

Braim, Paul F. *The Test of Battle: The American Expeditionary Forces in the Meuse-Argonne Campaign*. Newark: Univ. of Delaware Press, 1987.

Bullard, Robert Lee. *Personalities and Reminiscences of the War*. New York: Doubleday, 1925.

Capozzola, Christopher Joseph Nicodemus. *Uncle Sam Wants You: World War I and the Making of the Modern American Citizen*. Oxford: Oxford Univ. Press, 2008.

Carroll, Andrew. *My Fellow Soldiers: General John Pershing and the Americans Who Helped Win the Great War*. New York: Penguin Press, 2017.

Churchill, Winston. *The World Crisis, 1911–1918*. 1931. New York: Free Press, 2005.

Clausewitz, Carl von. *On War*. 1832. Edited and translated by Michael Howard and Peter Paret. Princeton, NJ: Princeton Univ. Press, 1976.

Coffman, Edward M. *The War to End All Wars: The American Military Experience in World War I*. New York: Oxford Univ. Press, 1968.

———. *The Regulars: The American Army, 1898–1941*. Cambridge, MA: Belknap Press, 2004.

Cooke, James J. *Pershing and His Generals: Command and Staff in the AEF*. Westport, CT: Praeger, 1997.

Crocker, H. W., III. *Yanks: The Heroes Who Won the First World War and Made the American Century*. Washington, DC: Regnery, 2017.

Cummings, E. E. *The Enormous Room*. 1922. New York: Barnes & Noble Books, 2006.

Davenport, Matthew J. *First Over There: The Attack on Cantigny, America's First Battle of World War I*. New York: St. Martin's, 2015.

Dickman, Joseph T. *The Great Crusade: A Narrative of the World War I*. New York: Appleton & Co., 1927.

Dixon, Norman. *On the Psychology of Military Incompetence*. 1976. New York: Basic Books, 2016.

Dos Passos, John. *Three Soldiers*. 1921. New York: Barnes & Noble Books, 2004.

Doughty, Robert A. *Pyrrhic Victory: French Strategy and Operations in the Great War*. Cambridge, MA: Belknap Press, 2005.

Eisenhower, John S. D. *Yanks: The Epic Story of the American Army in World War I*. New York: Touchstone, 2001.

Ettinger, Albert M., and A. Churchill Ettinger. *A Doughboy with the Fighting Sixty-Ninth: A Remembrance of World War I*. Shippensburg, PA: White Mane, 1992.

Faulkner, Richard S. *Pershing's Crusaders: The American Soldier in World War I*. Lawrence: Univ. Press of Kansas, 2017.

———. *The School of Hard Knocks: Combat Leadership in the American Expeditionary Forces*. College Station: Texas A&M Univ. Press, 2012.

Fax, Gene. *With Their Bare Hands: General Pershing, the 79th Division, and the Battle for Montfaucon*. Oxford: Osprey, 2017.

Ferrell, Robert H. *America's Deadliest Battle: Meuse-Argonne, 1918*. Lawrence: Univ. Press of Kansas, 2007.

———. *Collapse at Meuse-Argonne: The Failure of the Missouri-Kansas Division*. Columbia: Univ. of Missouri Press, 2004.

———. *The Question of MacArthur's Reputation: Côte de Châtillon, October 14–16, 1918*. Columbia: Univ. of Missouri Press, 2008.

———, ed. *A Soldier in World War I: The Diary of Elmer W. Sherwood*. Indianapolis: Indiana Historical Society Press, 2004.

Fleming, Thomas. *The Illusion of Victory: Americans in World War I*. New York: Basic Books, 2003.

Gallwitz, Max von. *Erleben im Westen, 1916–1918*. Berlin: Mittler, 1932.

Greenhalgh, Elizabeth. *Foch in Command: The Forging of a First World War General*. Cambridge: Cambridge Univ. Press, 2011.

———. *The French Army and the First World War*. Cambridge: Cambridge Univ. Press, 2014.

———. *Victory Through Coalition: Britain and France During the First World War*. Cambridge: Cambridge Univ. Press, 2005.

Grotelueschen, Mark Ethan. *The AEF Way of War: The American Army and Combat in World War I*. Cambridge: Cambridge Univ. Press, 2007.

Gutiérrez, Edward A. *Doughboys on the Great War: How American Soldiers Viewed Their Military Experience*. Lawrence: Univ. Press of Kansas, 2014.

Hirshon, Stanley. *General Patton: A Soldier's Life*. New York: HarperCollins, 2002.

Hodgson, Geoffrey. *Woodrow Wilson's Right Hand: The Life of Colonel Edward M. House*. New Haven, CT: Yale Univ. Press, 2006.

Johnson, Douglas, and Rolf Hillman. *Soissons 1918*. College Station: Texas A&M Univ. Press, 1999.

Johnson, Thomas. *Without Censor: New Light on Our Greatest World War Battles*. Indianapolis, IN: Bobbs-Merrill, 1927.

Kennedy, David. *Over Here: The First World War and American Society*. New York: Oxford Univ. Press, 1980.

Kniptash, Vernon E. *On the Western Front with the Rainbow Division: A World War I Diary*. Norman: Univ. of Oklahoma Press, 2009.

Lacey, Jim. *Pershing: Lessons in Leadership*. New York: St. Martin's, 2009.

Lejeune, Major General John A. *The Reminiscences of a Marine*. 1930. New York: Arno Press, 1979.

Lengel, Edward G. *To Conquer Hell: The Meuse-Argonne, 1918*. New York: Henry Holt, 2008.

Liddell Hart, Basil. *The Real War: 1914–1918*. 1930. Boston: Little, Brown, 1964.

———. *Reputations: Ten Years After*. Boston: Little, Brown, 1928.

Liggett, Hunter. *Commanding an American Army: Recollections of the World War*. Boston: Houghton Mifflin, 1925.

Linker, Beth. *War's Waste: Rehabilitation in World War I America*. Chicago: Univ. of Chicago Press, 2011.

Lloyd, Nick. *Hundred Days: The Campaign That Ended World War I*. New York: Basic Books, 2014.

———. *Passchendaele: The Lost Victory of World War I*. New York: Basic Books, 2017.

March, William. *Company K*. Concord, NY: American Mercury, 1931.

Marshall, George C. *Memoirs of My Services in the World War, 1917–1918*. Boston: Houghton Mifflin, 1976.

May, Ernest R., ed. *The Coming of War, 1917*. Chicago: Rand McNally, 1963.

Millett, Allan R. *The General: Robert L. Bullard and Officership in the United States Army 1881–1925*. Westport, CT: Greenwood Press, 1975.

Neiberg, Michael S. *The Second Battle of the Marne*. Bloomington: Indiana Univ. Press, 2008.

Nelson, James Carl. *Five Lieutenants: The Heartbreaking Story of Five Harvard Men Who Led America to Victory in World War I*. New York: St. Martin's, 2012.

Neu, Charles E. *Colonel House: A Biography of Woodrow Wilson's Silent Partner*. New York: Oxford Univ. Press, 2014.

Palmer, Frederick. *Bliss, Peacemaker: The Life and Letters of Tasker H. Bliss*. New York: Dodd Mead, 1934.

———. *Our Greatest Battle: The Meuse-Argonne*. New York: Dodd Mead, 1919.

———. *With My Own Eyes: A Personal Story of Battle Years*. Indianapolis, IN: Bobbs-Merrill, 1932.

Pershing, General John J., and Lieutenant General Hunter Liggett. *Report of the First Army, American Expeditionary Forces, Organization and Operations*. Fort Leavenworth, KS: General Service Schools Press, 1923.

Pershing, John J. *My Experiences in the World War*. 1931. New York: Da Capo, 1995.

Philpott, William. *War of Attrition: Fighting the First World War*. New York: Overlook, 2014.

Pitt, Barrie. *1918: The Last Act*. London: Cassell, 1962.

Polatschek, Maximilian. "Österreichisch-Ungarische Truppen an der Westfront." PhD diss., Univ. of Vienna, 1974.

Prior, Robin, and Trevor Wilson. *Command on the Western Front: The Military Career of Sir Henry Rawlinson 1914–1918*. Oxford: Blackwell, 1992.

———. *Passchendaele: The Untold Story*. 3rd edition. New Haven, CT: Yale Univ. Press, 2016.

Repington, C. à Court. *The First World War, 1914–1918: Personal Experiences of Lieut.-Col C. à Court Repington*. 2 vols. Boston: Houghton Mifflin, 1920.

Rubin, Richard. *The Last of the Doughboys: The Forgotten Generation and Their Forgotten World War*. Boston: Houghton Mifflin, 2013.

Shay, Michael E. *Revered Commander, Maligned General: The Life of Clarence Ransom Edwards*. Columbia: Univ. of Missouri Press, 2011.

Simmons, Brig. Gen. Edwin H., and Col. Joseph Alexander. *Through the Wheat: The U.S. Marines in World War I*. Annapolis, MD: Naval Institute Press, 2008.

Slotkin, Richard. *Lost Battalions: The Great War and the Crisis of American Nationality*. New York: Henry Holt, 2005.

Smythe, Donald. *Pershing: General of the Armies*. Bloomington: Indiana Univ. Press, 1986.

Stallings, Laurence. *The Doughboys: The Story of the A.E.F., 1917–1918*. New York: Harper & Row, 1963.

Stevenson, David. *With Our Backs to the Wall: Victory and Defeat in 1918*. Cambridge, MA: Belknap Press, 2011.

Streeter, Edward. *Dere Mable: Love Letters of a Rookie*. New York: Frederick A. Stokes, 1918.

Striner, Richard. *Woodrow Wilson and World War I: A Burden Too Great to Bear*. Lanham, MD: Rowman & Littlefield, 2014.

Taber, John H. *A Rainbow Division Lieutenant in France: The World War I Diary of John H. Taber*, edited by Stephen H. Taber. Jefferson, NC: McFarland & Co., 2015.

Terraine, John. *To Win a War: 1918, the Year of Victory*. New York: Doubleday, 1981.

Thomason, John W., Jr. *Fix Bayonets!* New York: Charles Scribner's Sons, 1926.

Tompkins, Jerry R., ed. *The Crossed Hands of God: The World War I Diary and Letters of Eugene William McLaurin*. Eugene, OR: Resource, 2015.

Tooze, Adam. *The Deluge: The Great War, America and the Remaking of the Global Order, 1916–1931*. New York: Viking, 2014.

Trask, David. *The AEF and Coalition Warmaking, 1917–1918*. Lawrence: Univ. Press of Kansas, 1993.

Triplet, William S. *A Youth in the Meuse-Argonne: A Memoir, 1917–1918*, edited by Robert H. Ferrell. Columbia: Univ. of Missouri Press, 2000.

Vandiver, Frank E. *Black Jack: The Life and Times of John J. Pershing*. 2 vols. College Station: Texas A&M Univ. Press, 1977.

Walker, William. *Betrayal at Little Gibraltar: A German Fortress, a Treacherous American General, and the Battle to End World War I*. New York: Scribner, 2017.

Waller, Douglas. *Wild Bill Donovan: The Spymaster Who Created the OSS and Modern American Espionage*. New York: Free Press, 2011.

Woodward, David R. *Trial by Friendship: Anglo-American Relations 1917–1918*. Lexington: Univ. Press of Kentucky, 1993.

Yockelson, Mitchell. *Forty-Seven Days: How Pershing's Warriors Came of Age to Defeat the German Army in World War I*. New York: Dutton, 2016.

NOTES

INTRODUCTION

1. David Stevenson, *With Our Backs to the Wall* (Cambridge, MA: Belknap, 2011), 251.

2. Thomas H. Barber, *Along the Road* (New York: Dodd Mead, 1924), x–xi.

CHAPTER 1: DOG DAYS

1. Elizabeth Greenhalgh, *The French Army and the First World War* (Cambridge: Cambridge Univ. Press, 2014), 78–80, 165.

2. John Terraine, *To Win a War: 1918, the Year of Victory* (New York: Doubleday, 1981), 27.

3. Barrie Pitt, *1918: The Last Act* (London: Cassell, 1962), 32–33; Norman Dixon, *On the Psychology of Military Incompetence* (1976; New York: Basic Books, 2016), 416–436.

4. Basil Liddell Hart, *Reputations* (Boston: Little, Brown, 1928), 103, 127; Terraine, *To Win a War*, 27.

5. College Park, MD, National Archives and Records Administration (NARA), RG 120, NM 91, 84, Box 6704, GHQ, Armies of the North, Feb. 28, 1917, Pétain to Minister of War; Terraine, *To Win a War*, 6–9.

6. Pitt, *1918: The Last Act*, 60–61.

7. NARA, RG 120, NM 91, 84, Box 6704, GHQ, Commander in Chief, May 29, 1917, Pétain to Minister of War.

8. NARA, RG 120, NM 91, 267, GHQ G-3, Box 3112, HQ AEF, Sept. 10, 1917, Maj. Dennis Nolan, extra confidential; Vienna, Haus-, Hof- und Staatsarchiv (HHSA), PA I 898, Geneva, Nov. 20, 1917, Montlong to Czernin;

George C. Marshall, *Memoirs of My Services in the World War, 1917–1918* (Boston: Houghton Mifflin, 1976), 31.

9. Terraine, *To Win a War*, 13, 19.

10. NARA, RG 120, NM 91, 267, GHQ G-3, Box 3113, 682, HQ AEF, Nov. 13, 1917, Lt. Col. Dennis Nolan, "Memorandum on Enemy Effectives"; NARA, RG 120, NM 91, 267, GHQ G-3, Box 3112, Sept. 26, 1917, Col. L. R. Eltinge, Lt. Col. Fox Conner, Maj. Hugh Drum, "A Strategical Study on the Employment of the AEF Against the Imperial German Government," secret; David Stevenson, *With Our Backs to the Wall* (Cambridge, MA: Belknap, 2011), 259–260.

11. William Philpott, *War of Attrition* (New York: Overlook, 2014), 273; C. à Court Repington, *The First World War, 1914–1918* (Boston: Houghton Mifflin, 1920), 2:99; Pitt, *1918: The Last Act*, 5.

12. Terraine, *To Win a War*, 13, 27–28; NARA, RG 120, NM 91, 267, GHQ G-3, Box 3112, Sept. 26, 1917, "A Strategical Study on the Employment of the AEF Against the Imperial German Government," secret; Repington, *The First World War, 1914–1918*, 2:215.

13. London, UK Parliamentary Archives (UKPA), LG/F/163/4/5, Versailles, Jan. 18, 1918, for War Cabinet, Maurice Hankey, "General Outline of a Proposed Scheme for the Employment in the War of Armies Raised by America."

14. Vincennes, Service Historique de la Defénse (SHD), FJ 14N 25, June–July 1917, "Les premieres journées américaines en France."

15. SHD, FJ 14N25, Paris, April 20, 1917, "Considerations génerales."

16. SHD, FJ 14N25, Paris, May 14, 1917, Viviani to Pres. du Conseil.

17. NARA, RG 120, NM 91, 268, GHQ G-3, Box 3108, May 1, 1917, "Confidential, for Use of Officers Only, Not to Be Quoted."

18. SHD, FJ 14N25, Paris, May 14, 1917, Viviani to Pres. du Conseil.

19. SHD, FJ 14N25, Paris, May 14, 1917, Viviani to Pres. du Conseil.

20. From Copenhagen's *Berlingske Tidende*, July 16, 1918; SHD, FC 6N141, EMA 2eme Bureau, Paris, Aug. 2, 1918.

21. SHD, FJ 14N25, Paris, May 14, 1917, Viviani to Pres. du Conseil.

CHAPTER 2: "TOO PROUD TO FIGHT"

1. Vienna, Haus-, Hof- und Staatsarchiv (HHSA), PA IV 59, Munich, March 24, 1917, Thurn to Czernin.

2. US Department of Commerce, Bureau of the Census, *Thirteenth Census of the United States Taken in the Year 1910* (Washington, DC: Government Printing Office, 1913), 194; Vincennes, Service Historique de la Défense (SHD), FC 6N 136, Washington, Aug. 6, 1919, Gen. Collardet to Min. of War, "Situation générale"; HHSA, PA I 897, Washington, Feb. 25, 1915, Dumba to Burián; Barrie Pitt, *1918: The Last Act* (London: Cassell, 1962), 8.

3. George C. Marshall, *Memoirs of My Services in the World War, 1917–1918* (Boston: Houghton Mifflin, 1976), 32; "What German Success Means to America and the World," *Philadelphia Public Ledger*, Jan. 16, 1916.

4. HHSA, PA XXXIII 51, Washington, March 9, 1914, Dumba to Berchtold; HHSA PA I 898, The Hague, July 8, 1918, Hoyos to Burian, "Conversations with Romeo Saccone, New Argentinian General Consul in Amsterdam."

5. HHSA, PA XXXIII 51, New York, Dec. 17, 1914, Dumba to Berchtold; HHSA, PA XXXIII 51, Manchester, NH, Sept. 19, 1913, July 13, 1914, Dumba to Berchtold.

6. London, UK Parliamentary Archives (UKPA), STR/26/2/8a, London, Oct. 12, 1914, Strachey to M. P. Bell, *Chicago Daily News*.

7. UKPA, STR/26/4/10e, Stockbridge, MA, Aug. 9, 1918, F. L. Warren to Strachey.

8. HHSA, PA XXXIII 51, Washington, May 16, 1913, Dumba to Berchtold; UKPA, STR/26/2/8a, London, Oct. 12, 1914, Strachey to M. P. Bell, *Chicago Daily News*.

9. HHSA, PA XXXIII 51, Washington, April 15, 1913, Zwiedeneck to Berchtold; HHSA, PA XXXIII 51, Washington, May 22, 1913, Dumba to Berchtold.

10. *Washington Post*, March 19, 1913; *New York Herald*, March 20, 1913; HHSA, PA XXXIII 51, Washington, March 23 and April 15, 1913, Zwiedeneck to Berchtold; HHSA, PA XXXIII 51, New York, Dec. 17, 1914, Dumba to Berchtold.

11. UKPA, STR/26/4/10c, Stockbridge, MA, Dec. 12, 1918, J. L. Warren to Strachey; Frederick Palmer, *With My Own Eyes: A Personal Story of Battle Years* (Indianapolis, IN: Bobbs-Merrill, 1932), 355.

12. UKPA, STR/26/2/3i, London, Dec. 17, 1915, Strachey to Wood; UKPA, STR/26/2/16c, London, Dec. 1915, Strachey to Mr. McClure of New York.

13. UKPA, STR/26/2/23a, SS *Arabic*, April 13 and May 17, 1915, Henry L. Higginson to Strachey.

14. UKPA, STR/26/4/10e, Stockbridge, Aug. 9, 1918, F. L. Warren to Strachey.

15. "Russia Owes the U.S.A. $188 Million for Delivered War Goods," *Chicago Daily News*, Feb. 12, 1918; SHD, FJ 14N 25, EMA 2eme Bureau, Paris, April 1917, "Note sommaire sur le situation intérieure et extérieure aux Etats-Unis."

16. UKPA, STR/26/4/10c, Stockbridge, MA, Dec. 12, 1918, F. L. Warren to Strachey; UKPA, STR/26/4/10e, Stockbridge, MA, Aug. 9, 1918, F. L. Warren to Strachey; Richard Rubin, *The Last of the Doughboys* (Boston: Houghton Mifflin, 2013), 231; Richard Slotkin, *Lost Battalions* (New York: Henry Holt, 2005), 25; "The President's Solemn Warning to His Fellow Countrymen to Guard Against Any Breach of Neutrality," *Washington Post*, August 19, 1914; Slotkin, *Lost Battalions*, 29–32.

17. UKPA, STR/26/2/18c, London, April 9, 1915, Strachey to Edward Martin, editor of *Life* magazine.

18. UKPA, STR/26/2/18c, New York, April 20, 1915, Edward Martin to Strachey.

19. *Chicago Daily News*, June 11 and 12, 1918; HHSA, PA I, 898, Stockholm, Sept. 22, 1918, Vertraulich to Burian; HHSA, PA I, 898, Versuch Nr. 10, July 22, 1918; UKPA, STR/26/3/1n, London, Jan. 26, 1917, Strachey to Edward Fuller, *Philadelphia Public Ledger*.

20. HHSA, PA I 897, Washington, Dec. 2, 1914, Dumba to Berchtold.

21. "Annual Report of the Secretary of the Navy," *Annual Reports of the Navy Department for the Fiscal Year 1913* (Washington, DC: Government Printing Office, 1914); HHSA, PA XXXIII 51, New York, Dec. 16, 1914, Dumba to Berchtold.

22. UKPA, STR/26/2/15, London, Jan. 22, 1915, Curtis Brown, *International Publishing Bureau*, to Strachey.

23. HHSA, PA I 897, Washington, Feb. 25, 1915, and New York, June 11, 1915, Dumba to Burián.

24. UKPA, STR/26/2/23g, SS *Arabic*, May 17, 1915, Henry L. Higginson to Strachey.

25. UKPA, STR/26/3/1n, London, Jan. 26, 1917, Strachey to Edward Fuller, *Philadelphia Public Ledger*; Robert H. Ferrell, *America's Deadliest Battle* (Lawrence: Univ. Press of Kansas, 2007), 2.

26. UKPA, STR/26/3/1j, Philadelphia, Nov. 2, 1916, Edward Fuller to Strachey; James Carl Nelson, *Five Lieutenants* (New York: St. Martin's, 2012), 9; Robert Lee Bullard, *Personalities and Reminiscences of the War* (New York: Doubleday, 1925), 49.

27. "America and Munitions—A New and Vital Industry—Well-Being Based on War," *The Times* (London), Sept. 9, 1916; *New York Times*, Dec. 10, 1915; HHSA, PA IV 59, Munich, March 24, 1917, Thurn to Czernin.

28. SHD, FC 6N 137, Dec. 4, 1916, "Résumé de déclarations faites par M. Gerrard, Amb. des Etats-Unis à Berlin au moment où il quittait New York pour rejoindre son poste," absolument secret.

29. HHSA, PA XXXIII 51, Washington, Feb. 11, 1913, Zwiedeneck to Berchtold; HHSA, PA XXXIII 51, Manchester, NH, Sept. 19, 1913, Dumba to Berchtold.

30. Palmer, *With My Own Eyes*, 292, 296.

31. SHD, FC 6N 136, Washington, Jan. 21, 1919, General Collardet to War Minister; Nelson, *Five Lieutenants*, 64.

32. Palmer, *With My Own Eyes*, 321; Slotkin, *Lost Battalions*, 27.

33. Robert Alexander, *Memories of the World War, 1917–1918* (New York: Macmillan, 1931), 1.

34. UKPA, STR/26/3/4c, Governors Island, New York, July 8, 1916, Leonard Wood to Strachey; UKPA, STR/26/3/6g, Minneapolis, Nov. 20, 1916, William Edgar, editor of *The Bellman*, to Strachey.

35. "Hughes, in Accepting, Bitterly Assails President Wilson's Foreign Policy: Real Preparedness Is Vigorously Urged," *New York Times*, August 1, 1916.

36. Palmer, *With My Own Eyes*, 309, 316.

37. Palmer, *With My Own Eyes*, 326.

38. "Hughes, in Accepting, Bitterly Assails President Wilson's Foreign Policy."

39. *Washington Star*, Dec. 7, 1915; Woodrow Wilson, "Address of the President of the United States Delivered at a Joint Session of the Two Houses of Congress—December 7, 1915" (Washington, DC: Government Printing Office, 1915); *Washington Post*, Dec. 8, 1915; Kew, UK National Archives (UKNA), FO 115/2126, Washington, DC, Aug. 9, 1916, Spring-Rice to Grey.

40. UKNA, FO 115/2126, Washington, DC, Aug. 9, 1916, Spring-Rice to Grey.

41. Theodore Roosevelt, "The League to Enforce Peace," *Metropolitan*, Feb. 1917; "Colonel Assails Wilson in Maine," *New York Times*, September 1, 1916; UKNA, FO 115/2126, Washington, DC, September 15, 1916, Spring-Rice to Grey; Slotkin, *Lost Battalions*, 32.

42. Earl of Birkenhead, "My Reply to President Coolidge," *Britannia*, Dec. 7, 1928.

43. HHSA, PA I 897, Copenhagen, Nov. 1, 1916, Széchenyi to Burián; HHSA, PA I 898, Stockholm, Feb. 18, 1918, Count Hadik to Czernin; SHD, FJ 14N 25, EMA 2eme Bureau, Paris, April 1917, "Note sommaire sur le situation intérieure et extérieure aux Etats-Unis"; David Kennedy, *Over Here* (New York: Oxford Univ. Press, 1980), 15–17, 319–320; *Christian Science Monitor*, January 26, 1918.

44. "America and Munitions"; HHSA, PA I 897, New York, June 11, 1915, Dumba to Burián.

45. SHD, FC 6N 136, Washington, Oct. 12, 1914, General Vignal to EMA 2eme Bureau.

46. SHD, FC 6N 136, Washington, Oct. 12, 1914, General Vignal to EMA 2eme Bureau.

47. UKPA, STR/26/3/6g, Minneapolis, Nov. 20, 1916, William Edgar, editor of *The Bellman*, to Strachey.

48. Ernest R. May, ed., *The Coming of War, 1917* (Chicago: Rand McNally, 1963), 30–31; SHD, FJ 14N 25, EMA 2eme Bureau, Paris, April 1917, "Note sommaire sur le situation intérieure et extérieure aux Etats-Unis."

49. "Hughes Assails Prosperity of War," *New York Times*, Oct. 14, 1916.

50. UKPA, STR/26/3/6g, Minneapolis, Nov. 20, 1916, William Edgar, editor of *The Bellman*, to Strachey.

51. A. Scott Berg, *Wilson* (New York: G. P. Putnam's Sons, 2013), 427.

52. HHSA, PA IV 59, New York, [Jan. 1917], Dr. Moritz to Julius Bonn; John S. D. Eisenhower, *Yanks* (New York: Touchstone, 2001), 3–4.

53. SHD, FJ 14N26, Washington, Jan. 23 and Feb. 1, 1917, Jusserand to Foreign Minister.

54. J. S. Marcosson, "The Real Woodrow Wilson," *Daily Mail*, Feb. 8, 1917.

55. Kennedy, *Over Here*, 6.

56. Henry Berry, *Make the Kaiser Dance* (New York: Arbor House, 1978), 267, 294.

57. Berg, *Wilson*, 435–440.

58. Adam Tooze, *The Deluge* (New York: Viking, 2014), 65–67; Frank E. Vandiver, *Black Jack* (College Station: Texas A&M Univ. Press, 1977), 2: 675–676; Kennedy, *Over Here*, 20–21; David Trask, *The AEF and Coalition Warmaking, 1917–1918* (Lawrence: Univ. Press of Kansas, 1993), 2.

CHAPTER 3: SLEEPING SWORD OF WAR

1. John J. Pershing, *My Experiences in the World War* (1931; New York: Da Capo, 1995), 78.

2. Vincennes, Service Historique de la Défense (SHD), FC 6 N 142, Washington, July 31, 1917, Maj. Réquin to Minister of War, secret; John W. Thomason Jr., *Fix Bayonets!* (New York: Charles Scribner's Sons, 1926), x; Laurence Stallings, *The Doughboys* (New York: Harper & Row, 1963), 136.

3. Edward G. Lengel, *To Conquer Hell* (New York: Henry Holt, 2008), 77; James Carl Nelson, *Five Lieutenants* (New York: St. Martin's, 2012), 19–20; Robert H. Ferrell, *The Question of MacArthur's Reputation* (Columbia: Univ. of Missouri Press, 2008), 10.

4. Barrie Pitt, *1918: The Last Act* (London, Cassell, 1962), 66; Edward Coffman, *The War to End All Wars* (New York: Oxford Univ. Press, 1968), 43–46; Michael E. Shay, *Revered Commander, Maligned General* (Columbia: Univ. of Missouri Press, 2011), 78.

5. Henry Berry, *Make the Kaiser Dance* (New York: Arbor House, 1978), 184.

6. London, UK Parliamentary Archives (UKPA), STR/26/3/4c, Governors Island, New York, July 8, 1916, Leonard Wood to Strachey; UKPA, STR/26/2/3c, HQ Eastern Dept., Governors Island, NY, Jan. 8, 1915, Leonard Wood to Strachey; UKPA, STR/26/2/3c, HQ Eastern Dept., Governors Island, NY, Oct. 12, 1915, Leonard Wood to Strachey; Robert Lee Bullard, *Personalities and Reminiscences of the War* (New York: Doubleday, 1925), 14; UKPA, STR/26/4/5d, Camp Funston, KS, Oct. 23, 1918, Leonard Wood to Strachey.

7. David Kennedy, *Over Here* (New York: Oxford Univ. Press, 1980), 18–19, 24, 148–149.

8. Kennedy, *Over Here*, 95–96; Ferrell, *MacArthur's Reputation*, 2–3.

9. Kennedy, *Over Here*, 157; Kew, UK National Archives (UKNA), FO 115/2310, Washington, July 19, 1917, Spring-Rice to A. J. Balfour; "Senators Plan to Put Aliens in Draft List," *New York Tribune*, July 18, 1917.

10. UKNA, FO 115/2310, Washington, July 19, 1917, Spring-Rice to Balfour; Lengel, *To Conquer Hell*, 36; Kennedy, *Over Here*, 17, 157; Coffman, *The War to End All Wars*, 64.

11. Richard Rubin, *The Last of the Doughboys* (Boston: Houghton Mifflin, 2013), 235; Kennedy, *Over Here*, 26–27, 87.

12. Richard Striner, *Woodrow Wilson and World War I* (Lanham, MD: Rowman & Littlefield, 2014), 117–121, 129, 147–151; Rubin, *The Last of the Doughboys*, 237.

13. Kennedy, *Over Here*, 24, 75–80, 83–87; Rubin, *The Last of the Doughboys*, 235–236.

14. Rubin, *The Last of the Doughboys*, 241–242; Kennedy, *Over Here*, 60–63, 65.

15. Kennedy, *Over Here*, 150, 155–159, 162; "Partiality Shown to South in Draft, Senators Declare," *New York World*, July 17, 1917; Coffman, *The War to End All Wars*, 70–71.

16. Hervey Allen, *It Was Like This* (New York: Farrar & Rinehart, 1936), 115–116.

17. Edward A. Gutiérrez, *Doughboys on the Great War* (Lawrence: Univ. Press of Kansas, 2014), 48.

18. UKNA, WO 106/534, France, Dec. 6, 1918, Brig. Gen. H. B. Fiske, G-5, "Memorandum for the Chief of Staff, Proposed Military Policy of the U.S., for the Military Committees of the House and Senate"; Stallings, *The Doughboys*, 316.

19. Gutiérrez, *Doughboys on the Great War*, 55; John Dos Passos, *Three Soldiers* (1921; New York: Barnes & Noble Books, 2004), xi–xv; SHD, FC 6N 136, Washington, Aug. 6, 1917, Jan. 9, 1918, and March 8, 1918, Maj. Réquin and Gen. Vignal to War Minister, "Au sujet de la conscription"; Coffman, *The War to End All Wars*, 28–29; Kennedy, *Over Here*, 165–166.

20. UKPA, STR/26/2/3c, London, Jan. 19, 1915, Strachey to Wood; College Park, MD, National Archives and Records Administration (NARA), RG 120, NM 91, 267, GHQ G-3, Box 3114, 695B, May 1, 1918, Pétain, "Memorandum on Instruction of American Infantry Units Attached to Large French Units."

21. SHD, FJ 14 N 25, Paris, May 14, 1917; Berry, *Make the Kaiser Dance*, 390; Coffman, *The War to End All Wars*, 55; C. à Court Repington, *The First World War, 1914–1918* (Boston: Houghton Mifflin, 1920), 2:88.

22. David Stevenson, *With Our Backs to the Wall* (Cambridge, MA: Belknap, 2011), 43–44; John S. D. Eisenhower, *Yanks* (New York: Touchstone, 2001), 16–17; Coffman, *The War to End All Wars*, 8–11.

23. SHD, FC 6N 142, EMA Bureau Special Franco-Américaine, n.d., "L'aide américaine."

24. Albert M. Ettinger and A. Churchill Ettinger, *A Doughboy with the Fighting Sixty-Ninth* (Shippensburg, PA: White Mane, 1992), 2; SHD, FC 6N 142, Paris, March 1918, EMA Bureau Special Franco-Américaine, "Situation génerale de l'armée américaine en mars 1918."

25. SHD, FC 6N 142, Paris, March 1918, EMA Bureau Special Franco-Américaine, "Situation génerale de l'armée américaine en mars 1918"; SHD, Att. Mil. 7N 1716, Washington, Feb. 14, 1916, Col. Vignal to Min. of War, "Démission de secretaire de guerre;" Coffman, *The War to End All Wars*, 16–17; Kennedy, *Over Here*, 18.

26. SHD, Att. Mil. 7N 1716, Washington, Feb. 14, 1916, Col. Vignal to Min. of War, "Démission de secretaire de guerre"; SHD, Att. Mil. 7N 1716, Washington, June 28, 1916, Col. Vignal to Min. of War.

27. Bullard, *Personalities and Reminiscences of the War*, 29–30; SHD, Att. Mil. 7N 1716, Washington, March 21, 1916, Col. Vignal to Min. of War; Robert H. Ferrell, *America's Deadliest Battle* (Lawrence: Univ. Press of Kansas, 2007), 11.

28. Lengel, *To Conquer Hell*, 16–17; Ferrell, *America's Deadliest Battle*, 12; UKNA, WO 106/534, France, Dec. 6, 1918, Brig. Gen. H. B. Fiske, G-5, "Memorandum for the Chief of Staff, Proposed Military Policy of the U.S., for the Military Committees of House and Senate"; Ferrell, *America's Deadliest Battle*, 13.

29. Munich, Bayerisches Kriegsarchiv (BKA), WK 7778/1, 5. bay. Res. Div., GHQ, March 20, 1915, "Gliederung und Verteilung der britischen Streitkräfte Mitte März."

30. SHD, FC 6N 142, Paris, March 1918, EMA Bureau Special Franco-Américaine, "Emploi du Corps Expeditionaire Américaine."

31. UKNA, WO 106/534, France, Dec. 6, 1918, Brig. Gen. H. B. Fiske, G-5, "Memorandum for the Chief of Staff, Proposed Military Policy of the U.S., for the Military Committees of House and Senate."

32. NARA, RG 120, NM 91, 267, GHQ G-3, Box 3112, 681, HQ AEF, Aug. 26, 1917, Maj. Drum, Washington, Sept. 25, 1917, "A Strategical Study on the Employment of the A.E.F. Against the Imperial German Government."

33. SHD, FC 6N 141, Washington, July 25, 1917, Gen. Collardet to Min. of War, "Notes sur les camps d'instructions pour officiers de reserve."

34. George C. Marshall, *Memoirs of My Services in the World War, 1917–1918* (Boston: Houghton Mifflin, 1976), 2; SHD, FC 6N 141, Washington, July 25, 1917, Gen. Collardet to Min. of War, "Notes sur les camps d'instructions pour officiers de reserve"; *New York Times*, Aug. 31, 1917; Stallings, *The Doughboys*, 312–313; Kennedy, *Over Here*, 159–160; Ettinger and Ettinger, *A Doughboy with the Fighting Sixty-Ninth*, 7–8; Berry, *Make the Kaiser Dance*, 416–417; Rubin, *The Last of the Doughboys*, 264–266.

35. SHD, FJ 14N 27, Washington, Aug. 11, 1917, Cdt. Réquin to War Minister.

36. William Philpott, *War of Attrition* (New York: Overlook, 2014), 301–304.

37. NARA, RG 120, NM 91, 267, GHQ G-3, Box 3112, Sept. 26, 1917, "A Strategical Study on the Employment of the A.E.F. Against the Imperial German Government." It was estimated that three hundred thousand to five hundred thousand German reinforcements would suffice to break the Italian line, occupy the Po Valley, and force the Italians to sue for peace, in three to six months.

38. Eisenhower, *Yanks*, 100–103.

39. Frederick Palmer, *Bliss, Peacemaker* (New York: Dodd Mead, 1934), 221.

40. UKPA, LG/F/51/4/72, Paris, Dec. 25, 1917, Lord Bertie to Lloyd George; John Terraine, *To Win a War* (New York: Doubleday, 1981), 25; Robert Doughty, *Pyrrhic Victory* (Cambridge, MA: Belknap, 2005), 402.

41. UKNA, WO 106/534, France, Dec. 6, 1918, Brig. Gen. H. B. Fiske, G-5, "Memorandum for the Chief of Staff, Proposed Military Policy of the U.S., for the Military Committees of House and Senate"; Bullard, *Personalities and Reminiscences of the War*, 25–26.

42. SHD, FJ 14N 26, Washington, Aug. 7, 1918, War Dept., General Orders Nr. 73; SHD, FJ 14N 26, Washington, Aug. 14, 1918, Lt. Col. E. Requin to War Minister; George W. Baer, *One Hundred Years of Sea Power* (Stanford, CA: Stanford Univ. Press, 1994), 79–80.

43. John Lewis Barkley, *Scarlet Fields* (1930; Lawrence: Univ. Press of Kansas, 2012), 40.

CHAPTER 4: "LAFAYETTE, WE ARE HERE"

1. George C. Marshall, *Memoirs of My Services in the World War, 1917–1918* (Boston: Houghton Mifflin, 1976), 3; John S. D. Eisenhower, *Yanks* (New York: Touchstone, 2001), 38, 40.

2. Munich, Bayerisches Kriegsarchiv (BKA), Infanterie-Divisionen, WK 7778/2, 5. bay. Reserve-Div., Nachrichtenoffizier, Heeresgruppe Deutscher Kronprinz, June 8, 1917, "No. 4928, Die Stimmung im französischen Heere"; BKA, Infanterie-Divisionen, WK 7778/2, 5. bay. Reserve-Div., Nachrichtenoffizier der OHL, June 26, 1917, "No. 2493, Die Stimmung im französischen Heere nach Vernehmungen und Gesprächen mit Gefangenen aus den letzten Gefechten am Chemin des Dames"; Robert Doughty, *Pyrrhic Victory* (Cambridge, MA: Belknap, 2005), 360–371, 424–425; Basil Liddell Hart, *Reputations* (Boston: Little, Brown, 1928), 22.

3. Marshall, *Memoirs of My Services in the World War*, 6, 8, 25; Eisenhower, *Yanks*, 42; John W. Thomason Jr., *Fix Bayonets!* (New York: Charles Scribner's Sons, 1926), xix–xx.

4. Marshall, *Memoirs of My Services in the World War*, 12–15, 19; Eisenhower, *Yanks*, 44–45, 53, 56.

5. C. à Court Repington, *The First World War, 1914–1918* (Boston: Houghton Mifflin, 1920), 2:87; Hervey Allen, *It Was Like This* (New York: Farrar & Rinehart, 1936), 10.

6. Henry Berry, *Make the Kaiser Dance* (New York: Arbor House, 1978), 155; College Park, MD, National Archives and Records Administration (NARA), RG 120, NM 91, 267, GHQ G-3, Box 3098, France, June 29, 1918, HQ II Corps, George Simonds, chief of staff II Corps, to commander of 30th Division, "Service of the 30th Division in the Line."

7. Allen, *It Was Like This*, 29; Robert Alexander, *Memories of the World War, 1917–1918* (New York: Macmillan, 1931), 16–17; Elizabeth Greenhalgh, *Foch in Command* (Cambridge: Cambridge Univ. Press, 2011), 336.

8. Edward Lengel, *To Conquer Hell* (New York: Henry Holt, 2008), 52–53; David Kennedy, *Over Here* (New York: Oxford Univ. Press, 1980), 185–186; NARA, RG 120, NM 91, 195, Box 1, Classification Camp Reports, HQ 83rd Division, Le Mans, Aug. 6, 8, 9, 13, 15, 19, 1918, Jas. E. Pollard and George Keppie to Capt. Chas. D. Gentsch, G-2, 83rd Division, "Conditions Among Troops," "Report of Operatives," "MPs in City of Le Mans"; Richard S. Faulkner, *Pershing's Crusaders* (Lawrence: Univ. Press of Kansas, 2017), 563.

9. NARA, RG 120, NM 91, 195, Box 1, Classification Camp Reports, HQ 83rd Division, Le Mans, Aug. 6, 8, 9, 13, 15, 19, 22, 23, Sept. 21, Oct. 29, 1918, Jas. E. Pollard and George Keppie to Capt. Chas. D. Gentsch, G-2, 83rd Division, "Conditions Among Troops," "Report of Operatives," "Classification Camp Report"; Edward Coffman, *The War to End All Wars* (New York: Oxford Univ. Press, 1968), 74.

10. NARA, RG 120, NM 91, 267, GHQ G-3, Box 3101, Mareuil-en-Dôle, Aug. 12, 1918, Col. R. Sheldon to Col. Fox Conner, "Report on 4th Division and 77th Division," secret.

11. George W. Baer, *One Hundred Years of Sea Power* (Stanford, CA: Stanford Univ. Press, 1994), 67–69; Eisenhower, *Yanks*, 60–61.

12. NARA, RG 120, NM 91, 267, GHQ G-3, Box 3120, 734, July 15, 1918, Col. Fox Conner to Maj. Lloyd Griscom; NARA, RG 120, NM 91, 267, GHQ G-3, Box 3112, "Comparative Study of Shipping Data," secret; Kew, UK National Archives (UKNA), WO 106/512, M.O. 1, July 12, 1918.

13. John Lewis Barkley, *Scarlet Fields* (1930; Lawrence: Univ. Press of Kansas, 2012), 50; Hervey Allen, *Toward the Flame* (1926; Lincoln: Univ. of Nebraska Press, 2003), 6.

14. NARA, RG 120, NM 91, 267, GHQ G-3, Box 3112, Sept. 26, 1917, "A Strategical Study on the Employment of the A.E.F. Against the Imperial German Government," secret.

15. NARA, RG 120, NM 91, 267, GHQ G-3, Box 3112, Washington, May 26, 1917, Baker to Pershing, "Command, Authority and Duties in Europe"; Douglas Haig, "The Signal Service," *Fourth Supplement to the London Gazette*, April 10, 1919; Marshall, *Memoirs of My Services in the World War*, 25.

16. UKNA, WO 106/538, Jan. 16, 1919, "Report of General John J. Pershing, USA, Commander-in-Chief American Expeditionary Forces, Cabled to the Secretary of War, Nov. 20, 1918, Corrected Jan. 6, 1919," 2; Eisenhower, *Yanks*, 46–47.

17. Frederick Palmer, *Bliss, Peacemaker* (New York: Dodd Mead, 1934), 204.

18. UKNA, WO 106/538, Jan. 16, 1919, "Report of General John J. Pershing, USA, Commander-in-Chief American Expeditionary Forces, Cabled to the Secretary of War, Nov. 20, 1918, Corrected Jan. 6, 1919."

19. Liddell Hart, *Reputations*, 304; Palmer, *Bliss, Peacemaker*, 222–223.

20. Laurence Stallings, *The Doughboys* (New York: Harper & Row, 1963), 345; Palmer, *Bliss, Peacemaker*, 204–205, 217–219.

21. Vincennes, Service Historique de la Défense (SHD), FC 6N 141, Paris, Nov. 24, 1917, "Rapport de Gen. Hirschauer au sujet de la 1ere Division américaine"; SHD, Bur. Spec. Franco-Américain, n.d., "L'aide américaine."

22. Vienna, Haus-, Hof- und Staatsarchiv (HHSA), PA I 898, Geneva, Nov. 20, 1917, Montlong to Czernin; Repington, *The First World War, 1914–1918*, 2:75–76, 84; John Terraine, *To Win a War* (New York: Doubleday, 1981), 10–13.

23. NARA, RG 120, NM 91, 267, GHQ G-3, Box 3112, 681, HQ AEF, Nov. 14, 1917, "Estimate of the Political and Economic Situation"; NARA, RG 120, NM 91, 267, GHQ G-3, Box 3112, Washington, May 26, 1917, Baker to Pershing, "Command, Authority and Duties in Europe"; NARA, RG 120, NM 91, 267, GHQ G-3, Box 3113, 684A, Dec. 2, 1917, Lloyd George to Robertson, secret; SHD, FC 6N 141, Chaumont, Jan. 5, 1918, Pershing to Clemenceau; John J. Pershing, *My Experiences in the World War*, (1931; New York: Da Capo, 1995), 254–255; Repington, *The First World War, 1914–1918*, 2:130.

24. Liddell Hart, *Reputations*, 271; Lengel, *To Conquer Hell*, 37; Allan R. Millett, *The General* (Westport, CT: Greenwood, 1975), 321–324; Frank E. Vandiver, *Black Jack* (College Station: Texas A&M Univ. Press, 1977), 2:796–797; Michael E. Shay, *Revered Commander, Maligned General* (Columbia: Univ. of Missouri Press, 2011), 141; James J. Cooke, *Pershing and His Generals* (Westport, CT: Praeger, 1997), 19–20; Matthew J. Davenport, *First Over There* (New York: St. Martin's, 2015), 62.

25. Bullard, *Personalities and Reminiscences of the War*, 96–99; NARA, RG 120, NM 91, 1241, Box 46, 201-32.11-16, HQ 18th Inf., France, Jan. 28, 1918, Col. Frank Parker to Gen. Bullard; Marshall, *Memoirs of My Services in the World War*, 138.

26. Marshall, *Memoirs of My Services in the World War*, 22–23.

27. NARA, RG 120, NM 91, 267, GHQ G-3, Box 3100, France, Dec. 17, 1917, Col. Fox Conner to Chief of Staff, "Notes on the Change of Area of 42nd Division and Suggested Action"; NARA, RG 120, NM 91, 267, GHQ G-3, Box 3100, Jan. 1, 1918, Lt. Col. Samuel Gleaves to Col. Fox Conner, "Movement of 42nd Division."

28. BKA, Inf. Div., WK 2468, 4. bay. Inf. Div., Grosses Hauptquartier, Oct. 4, 1917, Hindenburg to all army group commanders and staff chiefs, vertraulich; BKA, Inf. Div., WK 416, 1. bay. Inf. Div., Armee-Oberkommando 3, Feb. 19, 1918, Beilage, "In welchem Rahmen wird sich unsere Währungspolitik nach dem Kriege bewegen?"

29. James Carl Nelson, *Five Lieutenants* (New York: St. Martin's, 2012), 86; John H. Taber, *A Rainbow Division Lieutenant in France*, ed. Stephen H. Taber (Jefferson, NC: McFarland, 2015), 20.

30. Nelson, *Five Lieutenants*, 93–94; Marshall, *Memoirs of My Services in the World War*, 18, 40, 52–53.

31. Woodrow Wilson, "Address of the President of the United States, Delivered at a Joint Session of the Two Houses of Congress, January 8, 1918" (Washington, DC: Government Printing Office, 1918); HHSA, PA I 898, Christiania, Feb. 16, 1918, Hoyos to Czernin; UKNA, FO 115/2432, Washington, Jan. 11, 1918, Spring-Rice to Balfour, "President's Statement of War Aims."

32. NARA, RG 120, NM 91, 267, GHQ G-3, Box 3119, French GHQ, July 3, 1918, Maj. Clark to Pershing, "Military Situation"; SHD, FC 6N 142, Paris, March 1918, EMA Bureau Special Franco-Américaine, "Situation génerale de l'armée américaine en mars 1918."

33. Coffman, *The War to End All Wars*, 49–50; Cooke, *Pershing and His Generals*, 23–25.

34. Robert H. Ferrell, *America's Deadliest Battle* (Lawrence: Univ. Press of Kansas, 2007), 13–14; Coffman, *The War to End All Wars*, 160–163; Robert H. Ferrell, *Collapse at Meuse-Argonne* (Columbia: Univ. of Missouri Press, 2004), 5, 7–8; Cooke, *Pershing and His Generals*, 72; Eisenhower, *Yanks*, 134; Stallings, *The Doughboys*, 177.

35. Terraine, *To Win a War*, 22; Repington, *The First World War, 1914–1918*, 2:329.

36. NARA, RG 120, NM 91, 268, GHQ G-3, Box 3101, "Battle of the Argonne-Meuse," 78th Division Lecture Course, Jan. 3, 1919, Acting Chief of Staff James L. Frink.

37. Berry, *Make the Kaiser Dance*, 165; NARA, RG 120, NM 91, 1241, Box 46, 201-32.16, Oct. 29, 1917, La Marne, 6:00 a.m., CO 3rd Platoon, Lt. Callahan.

38. Marshall, *Memoirs of My Services in the World War*, 20, 24, 61; Taber, *A Rainbow Division Lieutenant in France*, 61; NARA, RG 120, NM 91, 1241, Box 37, 201-32.15, HQ 1st Brig, 1st Div., France, Feb. 28, 1918, Memo No. 9, Lt. Chas. C. Lawrence.

39. NARA, RG 120, NM 91, 267, GHQ G-3, Box 3097, March 21, 1919, "Summary History of the 26th Division"; NARA RG 120, NM 91, 267, GHQ G-3, Box 3098, France, June 29, 1918, HQ II Corps, George Simonds, chief of staff II Corps, to commanding general of 30th Division, "Service of the 30th Division in the Line."

40. Ferrell, *America's Deadliest Battle*, 67.

41. Douglas Haig, "Close and Complete Cooperation Between All Arms and Services" and "The Signal Service," *Fourth Supplement to the London Gazette*, April 10, 1919.

42. Barrie Pitt, *1918: The Last Act* (London: Cassell, 1962), 42.

43. "President's Speech to Congress," *New York Tribune*, Feb. 13, 1918; "President's Speech to Congress," *New York American*, Feb. 11, 1918.

44. Repington, *The First World War, 1914–1918*, 2:136.

45. NARA, RG 120, NM 91, 267, GHQ G-3, Box 3118, 718, Feb. 15, 1918, "Report by Major Paul H. Clark, Liaison Officer French General Head-quarters, of Conversations with French and British Officers"; NARA RG 120, NM 91, 990, Box 6, 1st US Army Corps, G-2, May 16, 1918, "Notes on Recent Fighting."

46. Bullard, *Personalities and Reminiscences of the War*, 103; Alexander, *Memories of the World War*, 32; NARA, RG 120, NM 91, 267, GHQ G-3, Box 3125, 775, AEF GHQ, G-2, Jan. 28, 1918, "Estimate on German Offensives"; NARA, RG 120, NM 91, 267, GHQ G-3, Box 3118, 718, Feb. 15, 1918, "Report by Major Paul H. Clark, Liaison Officer French General Headquarters, of Conversations with French and British Officers"; Douglas Haig, "Close and Complete Cooperation Between All Arms and Services," *Fourth Supplement to the London Gazette*, April 10, 1919.

47. Douglas Haig, "The Length of the War," *Fourth Supplement to the London Gazette*, April 10, 1919; Doughty, *Pyrrhic Victory*, 369.

48. NARA, RG 120, NM 91, 267, GHQ G-3, Box 3118, 718, Feb. 15, 1918, "Report by Major Paul H. Clark, Liaison Officer French General Headquarters, of Conversations with French and British Officers"; NARA, RG 120, NM 91, 267, GHQ G-3, Box 3118, 718, Feb. 15, 1918, "Report of Major Paul H. Clark, Mar. 16, 1918, on Conversations Had at French GHQ," secret.

49. NARA, RG 120, NM 91, 267, GHQ G-3, Box 3125, 772, AEF Advanced GHQ, Trier, April 4, 1919, "Conversation with Col. Von Heye at Treves, April 3, 1919."

50. Eisenhower, *Yanks*, 93–99.

CHAPTER 5: THE KAISER'S BATTLE

1. C. à Court Repington, *The First World War, 1914–1918* (Boston: Houghton Mifflin, 1920), 2:224.

2. Basil Liddell Hart, *The Real War: 1914–1918* (1930; Boston: Little, Brown, 1964), 368.

3. George C. Marshall, *Memoirs of My Services in the World War, 1917–1918* (Boston: Houghton Mifflin, 1976), 61–62.

4. Barrie Pitt, *1918: The Last Act* (London: Cassell, 1962), 47–50.

5. College Park, MD, National Archives and Records Administration (NARA), RG 120, NM 91, 267, GHQ G-3, Box 3118, 718, Feb. 15, 1918, "Report by Major Paul H. Clark, Liaison Officer French General Headquarters, of Conversations with French and British Officers."

6. Munich, Bayerisches Kriegsarchiv (BKA), Inf.-Reg., 15. Inf. Regt., Bundle 13, H.Qu., Feb, 28, 1918, Wilhelm, Kronprinz des Deutschen Reiches und von Preussen. "Leaders must take pains to move infantry forward, not let them hang back, their anxiety is too much; raised in peace, they do not obey '*Auf! Marsch! Marsch!*' automatically. They must be made to—executing orders is a function of discipline. They must be made to understand that the *Feuerwalze* will not destroy all opposition; that they will have to fight during the advance."

7. NARA, RG 120, NM 91, 990, Box 6, 1st US Army Corps, G-2, May 16, 1918, "Notes on Recent Fighting."

8. Marshall, *Memoirs of My Services in the World War*, 62–63.

9. Pitt, *1918: The Last Act*, 70–72.

10. Winston Churchill, *The World Crisis, 1911–1918* (1931; New York: Free Press, 2005), 768.

11. Repington, *The First World War, 1914–1918*, 2:269. Pitt, *1918: The Last Act*, 80–82.

12. Pitt, *1918: The Last Act*, 89–91.

13. Pitt, *1918: The Last Act*, 16–17, 88–89.

14. Laurence Stallings, *The Doughboys* (New York: Harper & Row, 1963), 77.

15. Robert Doughty, *Pyrrhic Victory* (Cambridge, MA: Belknap, 2005), 432–440; NARA, RG 120, NM 91, 84, Box 6704, AEF, G-2, "A Survey of the War 1914–1918: Some Effects of American Participation," secret; Repington, *The First World War, 1914–1918*, 2:262.

16. Robert Lee Bullard, *Personalities and Reminiscences of the War* (New York: Doubleday, 1925), 178; Pitt, *1918: The Last Act*, 95; J. Jellen, "A Clerk in the First World War," *Royal United Service Institution Journal* 105, no. 619 (August 1960): 361–369.

17. Jellen, "A Clerk in the First World War."

18. *New York Tribune*, March 25, 1918; BKA, Handschriftensammlung (HS) 1360, Col. Anton Ritter von Staubwasser, "Das königlich-bayerische Reserve Regiment Nr. 20," 382.

19. NARA, RG 120, NM 91, 267, GHQ G-3, Box 3119, French GHQ, July 18, 1918, Maj. Clark to Pershing, "Military Situation"; David Stevenson,

With Our Backs to the Wall (Cambridge, MA: Belknap, 2011), 391; NARA, RG 120, NM 91, 267, GHQ G-3, Box 3118, 722, April 20, 1918, Maj. Clark to Pershing, "Military Situation," secret.

20. London, Liddell Hart Centre for Military Archives (LHCMA), Grant 3/1, "Notes from a Diary, March 29th to August 1918"; Michael S. Neiberg, *The Second Battle of the Marne* (Bloomington: Indiana Univ. Press, 2008), 2.

21. Marshall, *Memoirs of My Services in the World War*, 75.

22. Marshall, *Memoirs of My Services in the World War*, 82.

23. Vincennes, Service Historique de la Défense (SHD), Bur. Spec. Franco-Américain, n.d. [spring 1918], "L'aide américaine"; Vienna, Haus-, Hof- und Staatsarchiv (HHSA), PA I 898, July 22, 1918, Versuch Nr. 10; John S. D. Eisenhower, *Yanks* (New York: Touchstone, 2001), 115; Marshall, *Memoirs of My Services in the World War*, 79, 82; Bullard, *Personalities and Reminiscences of the War*, 178–179.

24. John Terraine, *To Win a War* (New York: Doubleday, 1982), 24, 45; Eisenhower, *Yanks*, 110; Pitt, *1918: The Last Act*, 106.

25. Pitt, *1918: The Last Act*, 98.

26. NARA, RG 120, NM 91, 267, GHQ G-3, Box 3118, 718, March 26, 1918, Maj. Paul H. Clark to Gen. Pershing, "Military Situation"; David Trask, *The AEF and Coalition Warmaking, 1917–1918* (Lawrence: Univ. Press of Kansas, 1993), 49.

27. Frederick Palmer, *Bliss, Peacemaker* (New York: Dodd Mead, 1934), 254–255; Neiberg, *The Second Battle of the Marne*, 64.

28. Terraine, *To Win a War*, 49; NARA, RG 120, NM 91, 268, GHQ G-3, Box 3111, 12/15/20, Maj. George C. Marshall Jr. to Felix Danbe (from notes made by Pershing's aide de camp, Col. Carl Boyd); Eisenhower, *Yanks*, 114.

29. Repington, *The First World War, 1914–1918*, 2:340; Robert Alexander, *Memories of the World War, 1917–1918* (New York: Macmillan, 1931), 33; Pitt, *1918: The Last Act*, 103, 107–108; Neiberg, *The Second Battle of the Marne*, 73–74.

30. Repington, *The First World War, 1914–1918*, 2:257; Pitt, *1918: The Last Act*, 106–107.

31. Repington, *The First World War, 1914–1918*, 2:262.

32. David Kennedy, *Over Here* (New York: Oxford Univ. Press, 1980), 159, 199–200; Stallings, *The Doughboys*, 311, 319; Eisenhower, *Yanks*, 115.

33. NARA, RG 120, NM 91, 268, GHQ G-3, Box 3104, France, April 26, 1918, Lt. Col. M. A. W. Shockley, Medical Corps to AEF GHQ, "Training Recon of 372nd Infantry [Colored]."

34. NARA, RG 120, NM 91, 268, GHQ G-3, Box 3104, France, May 8, 1918, Col. T. A. Roberts, Cav., "Memo for Chief of Staff"; NARA, RG 120, NM 91, 267, GHQ G-3, Box 3118, 718, Feb. 15, 1918, "Report by Major Paul H. Clark, Liaison Officer French General Headquarters, of Conversations

with French and British Officers"; Repington, *The First World War, 1914–1918*, 2:329.

35. NARA, RG 120, NM 91, 267, GHQ G-3, Box 3118, June 13, 1918, Maj. Clark to Pershing, "Military Situation," secret.

36. NARA, RG 120, NM 91, 267, GHQ G-3, Box 3118, 722, April 8, 1918, Maj. Clark to Pershing, "Military Situation," secret.

37. NARA, RG 120, NM 91, 267, GHQ G-3, Box 3118, 722, March 30 and April 3, 5, 8, 9, 1918, Maj. Clark to Gen. Pershing, "Military Situation," secret; Repington, *The First World War, 1914–1918*, 2:271.

CHAPTER 6: "WITH OUR BACKS TO THE WALL"

1. Barrie Pitt, *1918: The Last Act* (London: Cassell, 1962), 110, 164.

2. David Stevenson, *With Our Backs to the Wall* (Cambridge, MA: Belknap, 2011), 259–260; Munich, Bayerisches Kriegsarchiv (BKA), WK 7778/1, 5. bay. Res. Div., GHQ, March 20, 1915, "Gliederung und Verteilung der britischen Streitkraefte Mitte März"; C. à Court Repington, *The First World War, 1914–1918* (Boston: Houghton Mifflin, 1920), 2:67, 86, 135–136, 174, 222; John Terraine, *To Win a War* (New York: Doubleday, 1982), 30–37; William Philpott, *War of Attrition* (New York: Overlook, 2014), 310–311.

3. BKA, Inf. Div., WK 7778/1, 5. bay. Res. Div., Abteilung Fremde Heere, Jan. 1, 1918, "Mitteilung über die britische Armee Nr. 4: Kampfwert des britischen Heeres," geheim; College Park, MD, National Archives and Records Administration (NARA), RG 120, NM 91, 267, GHQ G-3, Box 3118, 722, April 11, 1918, Maj. Clark to Pershing, "Military Situation," secret.

4. Pitt, *1918: The Last Act*, 117–119, 138; Repington, *The First World War, 1914–1918*, 2:275.

5. Elizabeth Greenhalgh, *Foch in Command* (Cambridge: Cambridge Univ. Press, 2011), 312–315; Frederick Palmer, *Bliss, Peacemaker* (New York: Dodd Mead, 1934), 253–254; BKA, Handschriftensammlung (HS) 1360, Col. Anton Ritter von Staubwasser, "Das königlich-bayerische Reserve Regiment Nr. 20," 390–391; NARA, RG 120, NM 91, 267, GHQ G-3, Box 3118, 722, April 10, 20 and 24, 1918, Maj. Clark to Pershing, "Military Situation," secret; NARA, RG 120, NM 91, 84, Box 6704, AEF, G-2, "A Survey of the War 1914–1918: Some Effects of American Participation," secret; Terraine, *To Win a War*, 51.

6. Palmer, *Bliss, Peacemaker*, 260–261; BKA, HS 2069, Sept. 30, 1918, Maj. von Wenz, "Die militärische Lage"; London, UK Parliamentary Archives (UKPA), STR/26/4/6c, London, March 27, 1918, Strachey to Robert T. Lincoln.

7. Henry Berry, *Make the Kaiser Dance* (New York: Arbor House, 1978), 202.

8. Frank E. Vandiver, *Black Jack* (College Station: Texas A&M Univ. Press, 1977), 2:962; Michael E. Shay, *Revered Commander, Maligned General* (Co-

lumbia: Univ. of Missouri Press, 2011), 136; Edward Coffman, *The War to End All Wars* (New York: Oxford Univ. Press, 1968), 148; Richard Rubin, *The Last of the Doughboys* (Boston: Houghton Mifflin, 2013), 56–57.

9. NARA, RG 120, NM 91, 267, GHQ G-3, Box 3097, July 22, 1918, Col. Fox Conner, "Comments on Conditions in the 26th Division."

10. NARA, RG 120, NM 91, 267, GHQ G-3, Box 3097, April 13, 1918, Maj. Edward Bowditch (301st Infantry) to Col. Malin Craig, secret; Berry, *Make the Kaiser Dance*, 32–33.

11. London, Liddell Hart Centre for Military Archives (LHCMA), Grant 3/1, "Notes from a Diary, March 29th to August 1918"; Palmer, *Bliss, Peacemaker*, 254, 262–263; Robert Lee Bullard, *Personalities and Reminiscences of the War* (New York: Doubleday, 1925), 179.

12. Greenhalgh, *Foch in Command*, 313; Repington, *The First World War, 1914–1918*, 2:261, 275; *New York Tribune*, April 14, 1918; *New York World*, March 12, 1918; Pitt, *1918: The Last Act*, 125.

13. NARA, RG 120, NM 91, 267, GHQ G-3, Box 3118, 722, April 15, 1918, Maj. Clark to Pershing, "Military Situation," secret; Pitt, *1918: The Last Act*, 130.

14. NARA, RG 120, NM 91, 267, GHQ G-3, Box 3118, 722, April 11 and 15, 1918, Maj. Clark to Pershing, "Military Situation," secret; Terraine, *To Win a War*, 51; Maximilian Polatschek, "Österreichisch-Ungarische Truppen an der Westfront" (PhD diss., Univ. of Vienna, 1974), 62–63.

15. George C. Marshall, *Memoirs of My Services in the World War, 1917–1918* (Boston: Houghton Mifflin, 1976), 78–79.

16. Palmer, *Bliss, Peacemaker*, 221, 227, 233; Terraine, *To Win a War*, 31.

17. NARA, RG 120, NM 91, 267, GHQ G-3, Box 3118, 723, May 12, 1918, Maj. Clark to Pershing, "Military Situation," secret; NARA, RG 120, NM 91, 267, GHQ G-3, Box 3120, Col. LeRoy Eltinge, "Notes on the Abbeville Conference, Held May 1–2, 1918."

18. Palmer, *Bliss, Peacemaker*, 229; NARA, RG 120, NM 91, 267, GHQ G-3, Box 3120, Col. LeRoy Eltinge, "Notes on the Abbeville Conference, Held May 1–2, 1918."

19. Stevenson, *With Our Backs to the Wall*, 249; Greenhalgh, *Foch in Command*, 327–329; Pitt, *1918: The Last Act*, 65, 141.

20. NARA, RG 120, NM 91, 267, GHQ G-3, Box 3120, Col. LeRoy Eltinge, "Notes on the Abbeville Conference, Held May 1–2, 1918"; John J. Pershing, *My Experiences in the World War* (1931; New York: Da Capo, 1995), 32–34; Pitt, *1918: The Last Act*, 143; John Lewis Barkley, *Scarlet Fields* (1930; Lawrence: Univ. Press of Kansas, 2012), 56.

21. NARA, RG 120, NM 91, 267, GHQ G-3, Box 3118, 722, May 4, 1918, Maj. Clark to Pershing, "Military Situation," secret; NARA, RG 120, NM 91, 268, GHQ G-3, Box 3088A, Aug. 1, 1918, Lt Col. H.A. Drum, "Considerations

Relating to the Location of the I Army A.E.F.," secret; Marshall, *Memoirs of My Services in the World War*, 86.

22. Kew, UK National Archives (UKNA), WO 106/538, Jan. 16, 1919, "Report of General John J. Pershing, USA, Commander-in-Chief American Expeditionary Forces, Cabled to the Secretary of War, Nov. 20, 1918, Corrected Jan. 6, 1919," 9; John S. D. Eisenhower, *Yanks* (New York: Touchstone, 2001), 120; David Kennedy, *Over Here* (New York: Oxford Univ. Press, 1980), 175.

23. NARA, RG 120, NM 91, 268, GHQ G-3, Box 3101, "Battle of the Argonne-Meuse," 78th Division Lecture Course, Jan. 3, 1919, Acting Chief of Staff James L. Frink.

24. LHCMA, Grant 3/1, "Notes from a Diary, March 29th to August 1918"; LHCMA, Grant 3/2, "Some Notes Made at Marshal Foch's HQrs, August to November 1918"; NARA, RG 120, NM 91, 267, GHQ G-3, Box 3118, 723, May 18, 1918, Maj. Clark to Pershing, "Military Situation," secret; Terraine, *To Win a War*, 53.

25. Matthew J. Davenport, *First Over There* (New York: St. Martin's, 2015), 111–112; Marshall, *Memoirs of My Services in the World War*, 88.

26. UKNA, FO 115/2431, London, Political Intelligence Department, Foreign Office, Monthly Report, June 10, 1918, United States.

CHAPTER 7: BELLEAU WOOD

1. John Terraine, *To Win a War* (New York: Doubleday, 1981), 53.

2. Barrie Pitt, *1918: The Last Act* (London: Cassell, 1962), 136–137.

3. Munich, Bayerisches Kriegsarchiv (BKA), Handschriftensammlung (HS) 1360, Col. Anton Ritter von Staubwasser, "Das königlich-bayerische Reserve Regiment Nr. 20," 391.

4. Pitt, *1918: The Last Act*, 144.

5. BKA, HS 2069, Sept. 30, 1918, Maj. Von Wenz, "Die militärische Lage"; Frederick Palmer, *Bliss, Peacemaker* (New York: Dodd Mead, 1934), 281; Michael S. Neiberg, *The Second Battle of the Marne* (Bloomington: Indiana Univ. Press, 2008), 70; Robert Doughty, *Pyrrhic Victory* (Cambridge, MA: Belknap, 2005), 452–453; Terraine, *To Win a War*, 55; Hervey Allen, *Toward the Flame* (1926; Lincoln: Univ. of Nebraska Press, 2003), 63.

6. Robert Lee Bullard, *Personalities and Reminiscences of the War* (New York: Doubleday, 1925), 204; Palmer, *Bliss, Peacemaker*, 269; BKA, Handschriftensammlung (HS) 1360, Col. Anton Ritter von Staubwasser, "Das königlich-bayerische Reserve Regiment Nr. 20," 413, 437; Vienna, Haus-, Hof- und Staatsarchiv (HHSA), PA I 898, July 22, 1918, "Versuch Nr. 10"; *New York World*, June 2, 1918.

7. The general brought from Salonica was Adolphe Guillaumat. Terraine, *To Win a War*, 56; College Park, MD, National Archives and Records Admin-

istration (NARA), RG 120, NM 91, 267, GHQ G-3, Box 3118, 723, May 28, 1918, Maj. Clark to Pershing, "Military Situation," secret; Pitt, *1918: The Last Act*, 149.

8. NARA, RG 120, NM 91, 267, GHQ G-3, Box 3118, 723, May 28, 1918, Maj. Clark to Pershing, "Military Situation," secret; Palmer, *Bliss, Peacemaker*, 274, 280.

9. NARA, RG 120, NM 91, 268, GHQ G-3, Box 3088A, Aug. 1, 1918, Lt. Col. H. A. Drum, "Considerations Relating to the Location of the I Army A.E.F.," secret; Laurence Stallings, *The Doughboys* (New York: Harper & Row, 1963), 77–78; BKA, Handschriftensammlung (HS) 1360, Col. Anton Ritter von Staubwasser, "Das königlich-bayerische Reserve Regiment Nr. 20," 437.

10. BKA, Handschriftensammlung (HS) 1360, Col. Anton Ritter von Staubwasser, "Das königlich-bayerische Reserve Regiment Nr. 20," 430.

11. George C. Marshall, *Memoirs of My Services in the World War, 1917–1918* (Boston: Houghton Mifflin, 1976), 94, 97; NARA, RG 120, NM 91, 268, GHQ G-3, Box 3088A, Aug. 1, 1918, Lt. Col. H. A. Drum, "Considerations Relating to the Location of the I Army A.E.F.," secret; Kew, UK National Archives (UKNA), WO 106/538, Jan. 16, 1919, "Report of General John J. Pershing, USA, Commander-in-Chief American Expeditionary Forces, Cabled to the Secretary of War, Nov. 20, 1918, Corrected Jan. 6, 1919," 9.

12. NARA, RG 120, NM 91, 1241, Box 46, 201-11.4, HQ 1st Div., Montabaur, Germany, Dec. 18, 1918, Gen. E. F. McGlachlin Jr., "Cantigny Operation, May 28–30, 1918"; Matthew J. Davenport, *First Over There* (New York: St. Martin's, 2015), 154–155.

13. UKNA, WO 106/512, M.O. 1, July 12, 1918, "Notes on American Army"; Marshall, *Memoirs of My Services in the World War*, 96.

14. Marshall, *Memoirs of My Services in the World War*, 97; Davenport, *First Over There*, 263, 269–270, 274; NARA, RG 120, NM 91, 1241, Box 46, 201-11.4, HQ 1st Div., Montabaur, Germany, Dec. 18, 1918, Gen. E. F. McGlachlin Jr., "Cantigny Operation, May 28–30, 1918."

15. *New York Herald*, June 1, 1918; John S. D. Eisenhower, *Yanks* (New York: Touchstone, 2001), 131–132; Donald Smythe, *Pershing* (Bloomington: Indiana Univ. Press, 1986), 128; Marshall, *Memoirs of My Services in the World War*, 96–99.

16. NARA, RG 120, NM 91, 267, GHQ G-3, Box 3125, 771, American Mission French GHQ, Feb. 1, 1918, "Extracts."

17. NARA, RG 120, NM 91, 267, GHQ G-3, Box 3118, 723, May 30 and 31, 1918, Maj. Clark to Pershing, "Military Situation," secret; NARA, RG 120, NM 91, 268, GHQ G-3, Box 3088A, n.d., Lt. Col. H. A. Drum, "Considerations Relating to the Location of the I Army A.E.F.," secret.

18. John W. Thomason Jr., *Fix Bayonets!* (New York: Charles Scribner's Sons, 1926), 5; NARA, RG 120, NM 91, 267, GHQ G-3, Box 3118, 723, May 30 and 31, 1918, Maj. Clark to Pershing, "Military Situation," secret.

19. NARA, RG 120, NM 91, 267, GHQ G-3, Box 3120, 732, French GQG, Feb. 13, 1919, Lt. Col. Paul Clark to Pershing, "The Military Situation," secret.

20. NARA, RG 120, NM 91, 267, GHQ G-3, Box 3118, 723, May 31 and June 8, 1918, Maj. Clark to Pershing, "Military Situation," secret; Stallings, *The Doughboys*, 80–85; Marshall, *Memoirs of My Services in the World War*, 101; Terraine, *To Win a War*, 61–62.

21. Edward Coffman, *The War to End All Wars* (New York: Oxford Univ. Press, 1968), 163–166; David Kennedy, *Over Here* (New York: Oxford Univ. Press, 1980), 129–130.

22. *New York Times*, June 1, 3, and 6, 1918; HHSA, PA I 898, July 22, 1918, Versuch Nr. 10.

23. Allen, *Toward the Flame*, 21; John Lewis Barkley, *Scarlet Fields* (1930; Lawrence: Univ. Press of Kansas, 2012), 57–59.

24. Barkley, *Scarlet Fields*, 58; NARA, RG 120, NM 91, 267, GHQ G-3, Box 3112, Sept. 26, 1917, "A Strategical Study on the Employment of the A.E.F. Against the Imperial German Government," secret. "Germany's best plan seems to be to attack some part of the French line, the loss of which, coupled with the losses inflicted, would have the psychological effect desired."

25. Barkley, *Scarlet Fields*, 58; NARA, RG 120, NM 91, 267, GHQ G-3, Box 3118, June 1 and 8, 1918, Maj. Clark to Pershing, "Military Situation," secret.

26. Eisenhower, *Yanks*, 139; Stallings, *The Doughboys*, 84–85.

27. Stallings, *The Doughboys*, 87; Allen, *Toward the Flame*, 19, 33.

28. NARA, RG 120, NM 91, 267, GHQ G-3, Box 3112, 678, HQ AEF, June 24, 1918, Lt. Col. H. A. Drum to Chief of Staff, "Comments on Attached Tactical Instructions Issued by the Allied C-in-C."

29. Stallings, *The Doughboys*, 88; Thomason, *Fix Bayonets!*, 4–5.

30. Barkley, *Scarlet Fields*, 60–61; Eisenhower, *Yanks*, 136.

31. Barkley, *Scarlet Fields*, 65–69.

32. Henry Berry, *Make the Kaiser Dance* (New York: Arbor House, 1978), 109–110; Stallings, *The Doughboys*, 89.

33. Thomason, *Fix Bayonets!*, 3–4.

34. Thomason, *Fix Bayonets!*, 18–19.

35. Stallings, *The Doughboys*, 92; Thomason, *Fix Bayonets!*, 18–19.

36. NARA, RG 120, NM 91, 1241, Box 54, 202.11.4, "A Brief History of the 6th Regiment, U.S.M.C. from July 1917 to Dec. 1918."

37. Thomason, *Fix Bayonets!*, 9.

38. Berry, *Make the Kaiser Dance*, 110–111; Thomason, *Fix Bayonets!*, 9; NARA, RG 120, NM 91, 1241, Box 54, 202.11.4, "History 3rd Battalion, Sixth Marines."

39. NARA, RG 120, NM 91, 267, GHQ G-3, Box 3118, June 6, 1918, Maj. Clark to Pershing, "Military Situation," secret; NARA, RG 120, NM 91,

990, Box 6, 1st US Army Corps, "Summary of Intelligence, July 4–November 9, 1918"; Thomason, *Fix Bayonets!*, ix.

40. Major General John A. Lejeune, *The Reminiscences of a Marine* (1930; New York: Arno Press, 1979), 255, 258.

41. NARA, RG 120, NM 91, 267, GHQ G-3, Box 3119, French GHQ, July 3, 1918, Maj. Clark to Pershing, "Military Situation"; Eisenhower, *Yanks*, 146.

42. Berry, *Make the Kaiser Dance*, 91.

43. NARA, RG 120, NM 91, 1241, Box 52, 202-32.16, 2nd Div., 5th Marines, June 11, 1918, Field Messages.

44. NARA, RG 120, NM 91, 267, GHQ G-3, Box 3119, French GHQ, July 29–30, 1918, Maj. Clark to Pershing, "Military Situation"; Mark Ethan Grotelueschen, *The AEF Way of War* (Cambridge: Cambridge Univ. Press, 2007), 208–209, 224–226, 235–236.

45. NARA, RG 120, NM 91, 267, GHQ G-3, Box 3125, 777, Chaumont, AEF GHQ, 1919, "Candid Comment on the American Soldier of 1917–1918 and Related Topics by the Germans"; Thomason, *Fix Bayonets!*, 23, 27.

46. BKA, Inf. Div., WK 1480, 3. bay. Inf. Div., Kriegstagebuch, June 14, 1918; Eisenhower, *Yanks*, 146.

47. H. W. Crocker III, *Yanks* (Washington, DC: Regnery, 2017), 94. "Quoi qu'on fasse, on perd beaucoup de monde." Pitt, *1918: The Last Act*, 164.

48. NARA, RG 120, NM 91, 267, GHQ G-3, Box 3118, June 12 and July 17, 1918, Maj. Clark to Pershing, "Military Situation," secret; Palmer, *Bliss, Peacemaker*, 349; NARA, RG 120, NM 91, 990, Box 3, AEF GHQ, Nov. 15, 1918, "Summary History of the First American Army Corps, Extract from the Interrogation by a German Intelligence Officer at HQ of 7th Army of American Prisoners Captured in the Bouresches Sector, June 6–14, 1918"; Stallings, *The Doughboys*, 110–111.

49. C. à Court Repington, *The First World War, 1914–1918* (Boston: Houghton Mifflin, 1920), 2:319; Terraine, *To Win a War*, 53, 61; Pitt, *1918: The Last Act*, 168–169.

50. William March, *Company K* (Concord, NY: American Mercury, 1931), 48.

51. NARA, RG 120, NM 91, 267, GHQ G-3, Box 3118, June 14, 1918, Maj. Clark to Pershing, "Military Situation," secret; NARA, RG 120, NM 91, 267, GHQ G-3, Box 3125, 777, Chaumont, AEF GHQ, 1919, "Candid Comment on the American Soldier of 1917–1918 and Related Topics by the Germans."

52. Lejeune, *The Reminiscences of a Marine*, 262; Stallings, *The Doughboys*, 103–104.

53. NARA, RG 120, NM 91, 267, GHQ G-3, Box 3114, 695B, May 1, 1918, Pétain, "Memorandum on Instruction of American Infantry Units Attached to Large French Units"; NARA, RG 120, NM 91, 267, GHQ G-3,

Box 3118, 718, April 16, 1918, "Observations of General Micheler, Commanding Fifth Army, on the Maneuvers of the 1st Division"; Stallings, *The Doughboys*, 337.

54. Stallings, *The Doughboys*, 105.

55. NARA, RG 120, NM 91, 84, Box 6704, AEF, G-2, "A Survey of the War 1914–1918: Some Effects of American Participation," secret; Lejeune, *The Reminiscences of a Marine*, 295; Eisenhower, *Yanks*, 150; Stallings, *The Doughboys*, 108, 112, 116.

56. London, Liddell Hart Centre for Military Archives (LHCMA), Grant 3/1, "Notes from a Diary, March 29th to August 1918"; UKNA, WO 106/512, M.O. 1, July 12, 1918, "Notes on American Army."

57. BKA, Handschriftensammlung (HS) 1360, Col. Anton Ritter von Staubwasser, "Das königlich-bayerische Reserve Regiment Nr. 20," 389.

58. NARA, RG 120, NM 91, 990, Box 6, 1st US Army Corps, "Summary of Intelligence, July 4–November 9, 1918"; HHSA, PA I 898, AOK, Aug. 20, 1918, "Aus den vertraulichen Nachrichten bis 20. August 1918"; Stallings, *The Doughboys*, 117.

CHAPTER 8: CHÂTEAU-THIERRY

1. College Park, MD, National Archives and Records Administration (NARA), RG 120, NM 91, 267, GHQ G-3, Box 3119, French GHQ, July 6 and 7, 1918, Maj. Clark to Pershing, "Military Situation," secret; NARA, RG 120, NM 91, 267, GHQ G-3, Box 3125, 777, Chaumont, AEF GHQ, 1919, "Candid Comment on the American Soldier of 1917–1918 and Related Topics by the Germans"; Vienna, Haus-, Hof- und Staatsarchiv (HHSA), PA I 898, AOK, Aug. 20, 1918, "Aus den vertraulichen Nachrichten bis 20. August 1918."

2. John Terraine, *To Win a War* (New York: Doubleday, 1981), 72; Maximilian Polatschek, "Österreichisch-Ungarische Truppen an der Westfront" (PhD diss., Univ. of Vienna, 1974), 113–114.

3. Laurence Stallings, *The Doughboys* (New York: Harper & Row, 1963), 114–115.

4. Hervey Allen, *It Was Like This* (New York, Farrar & Rinehart, 1936), 129; Munich, Bayerisches Kriegsarchiv (BKA), Inf. Div., WK 10, 1. bay. Inf. Div., Sept. 13, 1918, "Der Kampf unserer Feinde gegen den deutschen Geist: Eine Kundgebung des General-Feldmarschalls von Hindenburg."

5. John Lewis Barkley, *Scarlet Fields* (1930; Lawrence: Univ. Press of Kansas, 2012), 83; NARA, RG 120, NM 91, 267, GHQ G-3, Box 3118, June 13, 1918, Maj. Clark to Pershing, "Military Situation," secret.

6. NARA, RG 120, NM 91, 267, GHQ G-3, Box 3118, June 13, 1918, Maj. Clark to Pershing, "Military Situation," secret; NARA, RG 120, NM 91, 267,

GHQ G-3, Box 3119, French GHQ, July 2 and 11, 1918, Maj. Clark to Pershing, "Military Situation," secret; Terraine, *To Win a War*, 75.

7. NARA, RG 120, NM 91, 267, GHQ G-3, Box 3118, June 13, 1918, Maj. Clark to Pershing, "Military Situation," secret; Stallings, *The Doughboys*, 114–115.

8. C. à Court Repington, *The First World War, 1914–1918* (Boston: Houghton Mifflin, 1920), 2:267, 369; Major General John A. Lejeune, *The Reminiscences of a Marine* (1930; New York: Arno Press, 1979), 270; Terraine, *To Win a War*, 74; NARA, RG 120, NM 91, 267, GHQ G-3, Box 3119, French GHQ, July 6, 7, 10 1918, Maj. Clark to Pershing, "Military Situation," secret.

9. NARA, RG 120, NM 91, 267, GHQ G-3, Box 3125, 771, AEF GHQ, G-2, Aug. 21, 1918, "Recent Operations in France"; NARA, RG 120, NM 91, 267, GHQ G-3, Box 3120, 732, French GQG, Feb. 13, 1919, Lt. Col. Paul Clark to Pershing, "The Military Situation," secret; Stallings, *The Doughboys*, 121–122.

10. NARA, RG 120, NM 91, 268, GHQ G-3, Box 3101, "Battle of the Argonne-Meuse," 78th Division Lecture Course, Jan. 3, 1919, Acting Chief of Staff James L. Frink; NARA, RG 120, NM 91, 990, Box 9, 1st US Army Corps, G-2, June 27, 1918, "German Infantry Tactics in the Attack"; NARA, RG 120, NM 91, 267, GHQ G-3, Box 3120, 733, French GQG, March 5, 1919, Lt. Col. Paul Clark to Pershing, "Military Situation," secret; Nick Lloyd, *Hundred Days* (New York: Basic Books, 2014), 18–19; Repington, *The First World War, 1914–1918*, 2:339; Stallings, *The Doughboys*, 163.

11. John H. Taber, *A Rainbow Division Lieutenant in France*, ed. Stephen H. Taber (Jefferson, NC: McFarland, 2015), 82.

12. Hervey Allen, *Toward the Flame* (1926; Lincoln: Univ. of Nebraska Press, 2003) 40; Allen, *It Was Like This*, 19.

13. Allen, *It Was Like This*, 60, 86; Allen, *Toward the Flame*, 43–45.

14. Taber, *A Rainbow Division Lieutenant in France*, 84–85.

15. London, Liddell Hart Centre for Military Archives (LHCMA), Grant 3/2, "Some Notes Made at Marshal Foch's HQrs, August to November 1918"; Stallings, *The Doughboys*, 130.

16. NARA, RG 120, NM 91, 267, GHQ G-3, Box 3120, 731, France, Dec. 5, 1918, "Notes on Report Submitted by French High Command to War Department Direct."

17. Allen, *It Was Like This*, 56–57.

18. Allen, *It Was Like This*, 4–5.

19. Kew, UK National Archives (UKNA), WO 106/538, Jan. 16, 1919, "Report of General John J. Pershing, USA, Commander-in-Chief American Expeditionary Forces, Cabled to the Secretary of War, Nov. 20, 1918, Corrected Jan. 6, 1919," 10; Stallings, *The Doughboys*, 131.

20. Barkley, *Scarlet Fields*, 94.

21. BKA, Handschriftensammlung (HS) 1360, Col. Anton Ritter von Staubwasser, "Das königlich-bayerische Reserve Regiment Nr. 20," 442.

22. Allen, *Toward the Flame*, 38.

23. BKA, HS 1360, Col. Anton Ritter von Staubwasser, "Das königlich-bayerische Reserve Regiment Nr. 20," 444; Richard S. Faulkner, *Pershing's Crusaders* (Lawrence: Univ. Press of Kansas, 2017), 569; Barkley, *Scarlet Fields*, 99–101.

24. Allen, *It Was Like This*, 80–81.

25. Barrie Pitt, *1918: The Last Act* (London: Cassell, 1962), 181–182; Albert M. Ettinger and A. Churchill Ettinger, *A Doughboy with the Fighting Sixty-Ninth* (Shippensburg, PA: White Mane, 1992), 122–124.

26. BKA, HS 2069, Sept. 30, 1918, Maj. von Wenz, "Die militärische Lage"; BKA, HS 1360, Col. Anton Ritter von Staubwasser, "Das königlich-bayerische Reserve Regiment Nr. 20," 445; Pitt, *1918: The Last Act*, 182.

27. Allen, *Toward the Flame*, 99; Michael S. Neiberg, *The Second Battle of the Marne* (Bloomington: Indiana Univ. Press, 2008), 109–111; Stallings, *The Doughboys*, 137; Robert Alexander, *Memories of the World War, 1917–1918* (New York: Macmillan, 1931), 63; Repington, *The First World War, 1914–1918*, 2:350.

28. Allen, *Toward the Flame*, 52–53, 67, 183.

29. Lejeune, *The Reminiscences of a Marine*, 369; BKA, HS 1360, Col. Anton Ritter von Staubwasser, "Das königlich-bayerische Reserve Regiment Nr. 20," 448–450.

30. Allen, *Toward the Flame*, 164.

31. NARA, RG 120, NM 91, 990, Box 6, 1st US Army Corps, "Summary of Intelligence, July 4–November 9, 1918"; NARA, RG 120, NM 91, 267, GHQ G-3, Box 3119, French GHQ, July 26, 1918, Maj. Clark to Pershing, "Military Situation," secret.

32. NARA, RG 120, NM 91, 267, GHQ G-3, Box 3119, French GHQ, July 15, 16, 18, 24, 1918, Maj. Clark to Pershing, "Military Situation," secret.

33. NARA, RG 120, NM 91, 267, GHQ G-3, Box 3119, French GHQ, July 12, 13, and 17, 1918, Maj. Clark to Pershing, "Military Situation," secret; Pitt, *1918: The Last Act*, 178.

34. NARA, RG 120, NM 91, 84, Box 6704, AEF, G-2, "A Survey of the War 1914–1918: Some Effects of American Participation," secret.

CHAPTER 9: SECOND MARNE

1. London, Liddell Hart Centre for Military Archives (LHCMA), Grant 3/2, "Some Notes Made at Marshal Foch's HQrs, August to November 1918"; Laurence Stallings, *The Doughboys* (New York: Harper & Row, 1963), 142–143.

2. LHCMA, Grant 3/2, "Some Notes Made at Marshal Foch's HQrs, August to November 1918"; David Trask, *The AEF and Coalition Warmaking, 1917–1918* (Lawrence: Univ. Press of Kansas, 1993), 86.

3. Basil Liddell Hart, *Reputations* (Boston: Little, Brown, 1928), 159; LH-CMA, Grant 3/2, "Some Notes Made at Marshal Foch's HQrs, August to November 1918"; Robert Doughty, *Pyrrhic Victory* (Cambridge, MA: Belknap, 2005), 460; Elizabeth Greenhalgh, *Foch in Command* (Cambridge: Cambridge Univ. Press, 2011), 378.

4. Robert Lee Bullard, *Personalities and Reminiscences of the War* (New York: Doubleday, 1925), 216–217.

5. College Park, MD, National Archives and Records Administration (NARA), RG 120, NM 91, 267, GHQ G-3, Box 3120, 731, Nov. 18, 1918, Brig. Gen. Fox Conner, "Reports Submitted to the War Department in Washington from the French Mission in That City."

6. NARA, RG 120, NM 91, 267, GHQ G-3, Box 3120, 731, France, Dec. 5, 1918, Lt. Col. F. W. Manley, "Notes on Report Submitted by French High Command to War Department Direct"; NARA, RG 120, NM 91, 1241, Box 41, 201-32.7 to 32.8, French 8th Army HQ, March 31, 1918, Passaga, "Memorandum on Attacks in Open Warfare," secret.

7. Nick Lloyd, *Hundred Days* (New York: Basic Books, 2014), 3; Munich, Bayeriches Kriegsarchiv (BKA), HS 2069, Sept. 30, 1918, Maj. von Wenz, "Die militärische Lage."

8. Michael S. Neiberg, *The Second Battle of the Marne* (Bloomington: Indiana Univ. Press, 2008), 132; John Terraine, *To Win a War* (New York: Doubleday, 1981), 78–81.

9. Stallings, *The Doughboys*, 148.

10. Hervey Allen, *Toward the Flame* (1926; Lincoln: Univ. of Nebraska Press, 2003), 34.

11. Henry Berry, *Make the Kaiser Dance* (New York: Arbor House, 1978), 59.

12. H. W. Crocker III, *Yanks* (Washington, DC: Regnery, 2017), 96–97; Edward Coffman, *The War to End All Wars* (New York: Oxford Univ. Press, 1968), 246.

13. Berry, *Make the Kaiser Dance*, 40; NARA, RG 120, NM 91, 1241, Box 50, 201-33.6, France, Aug. 3, 1918, Col. J. M. Cullison to Bullard.

14. NARA, RG 120, NM 91, 1241, Box 50, 201-33.6, France, Aug. 2, HQ 26th Inf., Lt. E. E. Borman, Signal Officer.

15. NARA, RG 120, NM 91, 1241, Box 50, 201-33.6, France, Aug. 3, 1918, Col. J. M. Cullison to Bullard; NARA, RG 120, NM 91, 1241, Box 50, 201-33.6, HQ 2nd Bn., Aug. 3, 1918, Capt. P. N. Starlings.

16. Kew, UK National Archives (UKNA), WO 106/538, Jan. 16, 1919, "Report of General John J. Pershing, USA, Commander-in-Chief American Expeditionary Forces, Cabled to the Secretary of War, Nov. 20, 1918,

Corrected Jan. 6, 1919," 11; NARA, RG 120, NM 91, 990, Box 6, 1st US Army Corps, "Summary of Intelligence, July 4–November 9, 1918"; Crocker, *Yanks*, 95–96.

17. BKA, HS 1360, Col. Anton Ritter von Staubwasser, "Das königlich-bayerische Reserve Regiment Nr. 20," 452–453; Lloyd, *Hundred Days*, 18; Stallings, *The Doughboys*, 194.

18. NARA, RG 120, NM 91, 990, Box 6, 1st US Army Corps, "Summary of Intelligence, July 4–November 9, 1918."

19. UKNA, WO 106/519, HQ 1st Div, 7/27/18, "Report on Operation of First Division South of Soissons, July 18–24, inclusive"; Vincennes, Service Historique de la Défense (SHD), FC 6N 136, Washington, Aug. 6, 1917, Gen. Vignal to Min. of War.

20. Stallings, *The Doughboys*, 151, 161.

21. NARA, RG 120, NM 91, 990, Box 10, 1st US Army Corps, G-2, Aug. 9, 1918, "Study of the Terrain Between the Vesle and the Aisne."

22. Stallings, *The Doughboys*, 152, 169; BKA, HS 1360, Col. Anton Ritter von Staubwasser, "Das königlich-bayerische Reserve Regiment Nr. 20," 450.

23. Stallings, *The Doughboys*, 153–155; Liddell Hart, *Reputations*, 268; Berry, *Make the Kaiser Dance*, 167.

24. NARA, RG 120, NM 91, 990, Box 10, 1st US Army Corps, G-2, Aug. 9, 1918, "Study of the Terrain Between the Vesle and the Aisne"; Berry, *Make the Kaiser Dance*, 281.

25. Berry, *Make the Kaiser Dance*, 32–33, 177.

26. Stallings, *The Doughboys*, 154, 159–161.

27. NARA, RG 120, NM 91, 267, GHQ G-3, Box 3097, Message Center, I Corps, AEF, July 24, 1918, Maj. Scott to I Corps G-3; Stallings, *The Doughboys*, 156.

28. Hervey Allen, *Toward the Flame*, 120, 128–129; Gutiérrez, *Doughboys on the Great War*, 130.

29. "Germans in Retreat from the Marne," *Chicago Tribune*, July 28, 1918; Coffman, *The War to End All Wars*, 250–253.

30. NARA, RG 120, NM 91, 267, GHQ G-3, Box 3097, HQ 1st Corps, Aug. 13, 1918, Maj. Gen. Hunter Liggett to Adjutant General, GHQ, AEF, "Recent Operations 26th Division"; NARA, RG 120, NM 91, 267, GHQ G-3, Box 3118, 719, July 25, 1918, Capt. Herbert C. Bell to Col. Conger.

31. Robert Alexander, *Memories of the World War, 1917–1918* (New York: Macmillan, 1931), 70; NARA, RG 120, NM 91, 267, GHQ G-3, Box 3118, 719, July 25, 1918, Capt. Herbert C. Bell to Col. Conger; NARA, RG 120, NM 91, 990, Box 6, 1st US Army Corps, "Summary of Intelligence, July 4–November 9, 1918."

32. NARA, RG 120, NM 91, 267, GHQ G-3, Box 3097, HQ 1st Army Corps, Col. Malin Craig to Corps Commander, "26th Division."

33. NARA, RG 120, NM 91, 267, GHQ G-3, Box 3097, Épieds, July 27, 1918, Message Center 1st Corps, Maj. Smith to G-3; Allen, *Toward the Flame*, 91–92.

34. George C. Marshall, *Memoirs of My Services in the World War, 1917–1918* (Boston: Houghton Mifflin, 1976), 138.

35. NARA, RG 120, NM 91, 268, GHQ G-3, Box 3088A, July 31, 1918, Lt. Col. H. A. Drum to Col. Fox Conner, secret; Bullard, *Personalities and Reminiscences of the War*, 215.

36. John Lewis Barkley, *Scarlet Fields* (1930; Lawrence: Univ. Press of Kansas, 2012), 109; Stallings, *The Doughboys*, 161–162.

37. William S. Triplet, *A Youth in the Meuse-Argonne: A Memoir, 1917–1918*, ed. Robert H. Ferrell (Columbia: Univ. of Missouri Press, 2000), 187–190; Barkley, *Scarlet Fields*, 105.

38. Barkley, *Scarlet Fields*, 109–110.

39. NARA, RG 120, NM 91, 267, GHQ G-3, Box 3120, 731, Washington, Oct. 7, 1918, Lt. Col. Boussavit, "Extracts from the Reports of the Operations of the American Troops in France, May to August 1918"; Barkley, *Scarlet Fields*, 113.

40. NARA, RG 120, NM 91, 267, GHQ G-3, Box 3125, 777, Chaumont, AEF GHQ, 1919, "Candid Comment on the American Soldier of 1917–1918 and Related Topics by the Germans"; Barkley, *Scarlet Fields*, 108.

41. NARA, RG 120, NM 91, 195, Box 1, Classification Camp Reports, HQ 83rd Division, Le Mans, Oct. 12, 1918, "Classification Camp Report"; NARA, RG 120, NM 91, 990, Box 3, AEF GHQ, Nov. 15, 1918, "Summary History of the First American Army Corps"; NARA, RG 120, NM 91, 267, GHQ G-3, Box 3125, 771, AEF GHQ, G-2, Aug. 21, 1918, "German Morale."

42. Allen, *Toward the Flame*, 155–156.

43. Albert M. Ettinger and A. Churchill Ettinger, *A Doughboy with the Fighting Sixty-Ninth* (Shippensburg, PA: White Mane, 1992), 130; Robert H. Ferrell, *The Question of MacArthur's Reputation* (Columbia: Univ. of Missouri Press, 2008), 45–46.

44. Coffman, *The War to End All Wars*, 77, 80; John Dos Passos, *Three Soldiers* (1921; New York: Barnes & Noble, 2004), 150–151.

45. John H. Taber, *A Rainbow Division Lieutenant in France*, ed. Stephen H. Taber (Jefferson, NC: McFarland & Co., 2015), 24; Allen, *Toward the Flame*, 165, 181.

46. Dos Passos, *Three Soldiers*, 150–151.

47. NARA, RG 120, NM 91, 990, Box 6, 1st US Army Corps, "Summary of Intelligence, July 4–November 9, 1918."

48. Berry, *Make the Kaiser Dance*, 135; Alexander, *Memories of the World War*, 90–91.

49. NARA, RG 120, NM 91, 267, GHQ G-3, Box 3125, 773A, AEF GHQ, G-2, March 18, 1918, "German Code Signals."

50. Allen, *Toward the Flame*, 162–163, 182.

51. NARA, RG 120, NM 91, 990, Box 3, AEF GHQ, Nov. 15, 1918, "Summary History of the First American Army Corps"; Allen, *Toward the Flame*, 98, 138–140; Richard S. Faulkner, *Pershing's Crusaders* (Lawrence: Univ. Press of Kansas, 2017), 584–585.

52. Ettinger and Ettinger, *A Doughboy with the Fighting Sixty-Ninth*, 135.

53. Allen, *Toward the Flame*, 98–99, 121; Ettinger and Ettinger, *A Doughboy with the Fighting Sixty-Ninth*, 132–133; Stallings, *The Doughboys*, 353.

54. NARA, RG 120, NM 91, 267, GHQ G-3, Box 3118, 719, July 25, 1918, Capt. Herbert C. Bell to Col. Conger.

55. Allen, *Toward the Flame*, 149–150; Allen, *It Was Like This*, 125; Barkley, *Scarlet Fields*, 128.

56. Allen, *Toward the Flame*, 46.

57. NARA, RG 120, NM 91, 267, GHQ G-3, Box 3125, 771, AEF GHQ, G-2, Aug. 21, 1918, "German Morale"; Allen, *It Was Like This*, 24, 126–127; BKA, HS 1360, Col. Anton Ritter von Staubwasser, "Das königlich-bayerische Reserve Regiment Nr. 20," 462.

58. NARA, RG 120, NM 91, 990, Box 6, 1st US Army Corps, "Summary of Intelligence, July 4–November 9, 1918"; NARA, RG 120, NM 91, 267, GHQ G-3, Box 3125, 6th Army 2nd Bureau, Aug. 3, 1918, "216th Division Special Interrogatory."

59. NARA, RG 120, NM 91, 267, GHQ G-3, Box 3125, 777, Chaumont, AEF GHQ, 1919, "Candid Comment on the American Soldier of 1917–1918 and Related Topics by the Germans"; NARA, RG 120, NM 91, 990, Box 3, AEF GHQ, Nov. 15, 1918, "Summary History of the First American Army Corps."

60. NARA, RG 120, NM 91, 267, GHQ G-3, Box 3101, Mareuil-en-Dôle, Aug. 12, 1918, Col. R. Sheldon to Fox Conner, "Report on 4th Division and 77th Division," secret; John W. Thomason Jr., *Fix Bayonets!* (New York: Charles Scribner's Sons, 1926), 26–27; Alexander, *Memories of the World War*, 101–102.

61. NARA, RG 120, NM 91, 267, GHQ G-3, Box 3118, 719, July 27, 1918, Capt. Herbert C. Bell to Col. Conger; Allen, *Toward the Flame*, 46–47.

62. NARA, RG 120, NM 91, 267, GHQ G-3, Box 3125, 771, AEF GHQ, G-2, Aug. 21, 1918, "Recent Operations in France."

63. NARA, RG 120, NM 91, 267, GHQ G-3, Box 3118, 719, July 27 and 30, 1918, Capt. Herbert C. Bell to Col. Conger; NARA, RG 120, NM 91, 990, Box 6, 1st US Army Corps, "Summary of Intelligence, July 4–November 9, 1918."

64. Alexander, *Memories of the World War*, 71–72, 126; NARA, RG 120, NM 91, 267, GHQ G-3, Box 3101, Mareuil-en-Dôle, Aug. 12, 1918, Col. R. Sheldon to Fox Conner, "Report on 4th Division and 77th Division," secret.

65. NARA, RG 120, NM 91, 267, GHQ G-3, Box 3120, 731, Washington, Oct. 7, 1918, Lt. Col. Boussavit, "Extracts from the Reports of the Operations of the American Troops in France, May to August 1918"; NARA, RG 120, NM 91, 267, GHQ G-3, Box 3118, 719, Aug. 4, 1918, Capt. Herbert C. Bell to Col. Conger; Horace L. Baker, *Argonne Days in World War I*, ed. Robert H. Ferrell (1927; Columbia: Univ. of Missouri Press, 2007), 12; Allen, *Toward the Flame*, 48.

66. NARA, RG 120, NM 91, 990, Box 1, HQ I Army Corps, Sept. 8, 1918, Lt. Col. F. W. Clark, G-3, III Corps, G-3 Order No. 56.

67. Alexander, *Memories of the World War*, 69, 89; NARA, RG 120, NM 91, 267, GHQ G-3, Box 3125, 771, AEF GHQ, G-2, Aug. 21, 1918, Maj. Stanley Washburn, "Recent Operations in France"; NARA, RG 120, NM 91, 990, Box 3, AEF GHQ, Nov. 15, 1918, "Summary History of the First American Army Corps."

68. NARA, RG 120, NM 91, 990, Box 6, 1st US Army Corps, "Summary of Intelligence, July 4–November 9, 1918"; NARA, RG 120, NM 91, 195, Box 1, Classification Camp Reports, HQ 83rd Division, Le Mans, Sept. 23, 30, 1918, CVL to Capt. Gentsch.

69. Frederick Palmer, *Bliss, Peacemaker* (New York: Dodd Mead, 1934), 231; Stallings, *The Doughboys*, 171; NARA, RG 120, NM 91, 267, GHQ G-3, Box 3092, Paris, Aug. 4, 1918, Fayolle, "General Order."

70. NARA, RG 120, NM 91, 267, GHQ G-3, Box 3120, 730, Aug. 19, 1918, Capt. David Gray, US Liaison Officer, French X Army; NARA, RG 120, NM 91, 267, GHQ G-3, Box 3125, 777, Chaumont, AEF GHQ, 1919, "Candid Comment on the American Soldier of 1917–1918 and Related Topics by the Germans"; Allen, *Toward the Flame*, 48–49.

71. LHCMA, Spears 1/20, Paris, Aug. 5, 1918, Gen. E. L. Spiers to Gen. Sir Henry Wilson (Spiers would change the spelling of his name to Spears in 1918. He was head of the British military mission to the French government); Vienna, Haus-, Hof- und Staatsarchiv (HHSA), PA I 898, Stockholm, Sept. 22, 1918, "Auszug aus den Tagebuch der 11. Sept. 1918."

72. Kew, UK National Archives (UKNA), WO 106/519, "Notes on the Effect of French Counter-Battery Fire," Sept. 4, 1918.

73. NARA, RG 120, NM 91, 267, GHQ G-3, Box 3099, Grand HQ of the Armies of the North and Northeast, August 6, 1918, Pétain, Gen. Order Nr. 116.

CHAPTER 10: THE HUNDRED DAYS

1. Vienna, Haus-, Hof- und Staatsarchiv (HHSA), PA I 898, k.u.k. AOK Ev.B. Nr. 20/56, "Auszug aus den vertraulichen Nachrichten bis 23. Sept. 1918."

2. Nick Lloyd, *Hundred Days* (New York: Basic Books, 2014), 128, 137–138; David R. Woodward, *Trial by Friendship* (Lexington: Univ. Press of Kentucky, 1993), 197–198; Barrie Pitt, *1918: The Last Act* (London: Cassell, 1962),

226–227; C. à Court Repington, *The First World War, 1914–1918* (Boston: Houghton Mifflin, 1920), 2:352.

3. William Philpott, *War of Attrition* (New York: Overlook, 2014), 328–329, 332; Jonathan Boff, *Winning and Losing on the Western Front* (Cambridge: Cambridge Univ. Press, 2012), 29; Major General John A. Lejeune, *The Reminiscences of a Marine* (1930; New York: Arno Press, 1979), 313.

4. College Park, MD, National Archives and Records Administration (NARA), RG 120, NM 91, 267, GHQ G-3, Box 3120, 733, French GQG, March 5, 1919, Lt. Col. Paul Clark to Pershing, "The Military Situation," secret; Repington, *The First World War, 1914–1918*, 2:367.

5. Max von Gallwitz, *Erleben im Westen, 1916–1918* (Berlin: Mittler, 1932), 358. The Germans surrendered Ham, Chauny, Tergnier, and Laffaux on their retreat to Saint-Quentin. NARA, RG 120, NM 91, 1118, V Corps Historical, Box 2, n.d., "History of the Fifth American Army Corps"; NARA, RG 120, NM 91, 268, GHQ G-3, Box 3101, "Battle of the Argonne-Meuse," Division Lecture Course, Jan. 3, 1919, Acting Chief of Staff James L. Frink.

6. Gallwitz, *Erleben im Westen*, 355; Fritz Franek, "K.u.k. Truppen im Westen," *Militärwissenschaftliche Mitteilungen* 62 (1931): 413–414.

7. Lieut.-Col. Charles Repington, "America's Effort: A Tribute, the Campaign of 1918," *London Morning Post*, Dec. 9, 1918.

8. NARA, RG 120, NM 91, 84, GHQ G-2, Box 6704, "A Survey of the War 1914–18: Some Effects of American Participation"; William S. Triplet, *A Youth in the Meuse-Argonne*, ed. Robert H. Ferrell (Columbia: Univ. of Missouri Press, 2000), 159.

9. Vienna, Kriegsarchiv (KA), AOK-Op. Abteilung 557, Vienna, Oct. 2, 1928, "Die öst-ung 35. Infanteriedivision auf dem westlichen Kriegsschauplatz"; NARA, RG 120, NM 91, 990, Box 3, AEF GHQ, Nov. 15, 1918, "Summary History of the First American Army Corps"; NARA, RG 120, NM 91, 267, GHQ G-3, Box 3112, Sept. 26, 1917, "A Strategical Study on the Employment of the A.E.F. Against the Imperial German Government," secret; Gallwitz, *Erleben im Westen*, 285.

10. London, Liddell Hart Centre for Military Archives (LHCMA), Grant 3/2, "Some Notes Made at Marshal Foch's HQrs, August to November 1918"; George C. Marshall, *Memoirs of My Services in the World War, 1917–1918* (Boston: Houghton Mifflin, 1976), 123.

11. "Repington Fears British Will Not Speed Up for 1919," *New York World*, Sept. 12, 1918; Repington, *The First World War, 1914–1918*, 2:370–371; Lloyd, *Hundred Days*, 138–139.

12. Robin Prior and Trevor Wilson, *Command on the Western Front* (Oxford: Blackwell, 1992), 289–292 ("Poussez toujours; il n'y a que ca, tout ira bien, je vous promets"); LHCMA, Grant 3/2, "Some Notes Made at Marshal Foch's HQrs, August to November 1918."

13. Laurence Stallings, *The Doughboys* (New York: Harper & Row, 1963), 196.

14. Shelford Bidwell and Dominick Graham, *Fire-Power* (1982; Barnsley, UK: Pen & Sword, 2004), 131–134; Pitt, *1918: The Last Act*, 197.

15. Lloyd, *Hundred Days*, 67–71; Pitt, *1918: The Last Act*, 204–206; Douglas Haig, "Close and Complete Cooperation Between All Arms and Services," *Fourth Supplement to the London Gazette*, April 10, 1919.

16. LHCMA, Grant 3/2, "Some Notes Made at Marshal Foch's HQrs, August to November 1918"; Maximilian Polatschek, "Österreichische-Ungarische Truppen an der Westfront" (PhD diss., Univ. of Vienna, 1974), 80–81; Pitt, *1918: The Last Act*, 241.

17. Lloyd, *Hundred Days*, 11, 73–74; Pitt, *1918: The Last Act*, 241–242.

18. Hervey Allen, *Toward the Flame* (1926; Lincoln: Univ. of Nebraska Press, 2003), 112–115, 212, 237.

19. Mark Ethan Grotelueschen, *The AEF Way of War* (Cambridge: Cambridge Univ. Press, 2007), 290; Richard Slotkin, *Lost Battalions* (New York: Henry Holt, 2005), 3; Stallings, *The Doughboys*, 198–199; Henry Berry, *Make the Kaiser Dance* (New York: Arbor House, 1978), 347–348; Allen, *Toward the Flame*, 195.

20. Allen, *Toward the Flame*, 231, 269, 278–282.

21. Robert Alexander, *Memories of the World War, 1917–1918* (New York: Macmillan, 1931), 110–117; Allen, *Toward the Flame*, 213–216, 269.

22. John Terraine, *To Win a War* (New York: Doubleday, 1981), 106–112, 119–120; Lloyd, *Hundred Days*, 59–61, 65–67; David Stevenson, *With Our Backs to the Wall* (Cambridge, MA: Belknap, 2011), 260–263; Pitt, *1918: The Last Act*, 206, 222–223.

23. Elizabeth Greenhalgh, *Victory Through Coalition* (Cambridge: Cambridge Univ. Press, 2005), 254; Robert Doughty, *Pyrrhic Victory* (Cambridge, MA: Belknap, 2005), 476–478; Frederick Palmer, *Bliss, Peacemaker* (New York: Dodd Mead, 1934), 331; Terraine, *To Win a War*, 24, 93–95; Pitt, *1918: The Last Act*, 219–222.

24. NARA, RG 120, NM 91, 84, Box 6704, AEF, G-2, "A Survey of the War 1914–1918: Some Effects of American Participation," secret.

25. LHCMA, Grant 3/2, "Some Notes Made at Marshal Foch's HQrs, August to November 1918"; Stallings, *The Doughboys*, 202.

26. NARA, RG 120, NM 91, 267, GHQ G-3, Box 3125, 772, AEF Advanced GHQ, Trier, April 4, 1919, "Conversation with Col. Von Heye at Treves, April 3, 1919"; Marshall, *Memoirs of My Services in the World War*, 125; Stallings, *The Doughboys*, 207; Munich, Bayerisches Kriegsarchiv (BKA), Inf. Div., WK 10, 1. bay. Inf. Div., Sept. 13, 1918, "Der Kampf unserer Feinde gegen den deutschen Geist: Eine Kundgebung des General-Feldmarschalls von Hindenburg."

27. NARA, RG 120, NM 91, 1118, V Corps Historical, Box 5, Chief of Staff, Oct. 14, 1917, "Study on the Eventuality and Forms of a German Withdrawal from the Salient of St. Mihiel."

28. Marshall, *Memoirs of My Services in the World War*, 128, 133.

29. LHCMA, Grant 3/2, "Some Notes Made at Marshal Foch's HQrs, August to November 1918."

30. Marshall, *Memoirs of My Services in the World War*, 124–125, 128.

31. LHCMA, LH IS/2/34, *Reveille*, Feb. 1, 1938, "Mademoiselle from Armentières"; Albert M. Ettinger and A. Churchill Ettinger, *A Doughboy with the Fighting Sixty-Ninth* (Shippensburg, PA: White Mane, 1992), 150; Berry, *Make the Kaiser Dance*, 7, 238, 376, 409–411.

32. David Kennedy, *Over Here* (New York: Oxford Univ. Press, 1980), 186; John Dos Passos, *Three Soldiers* (1921; New York: Barnes & Noble Books, 2004), xiii–xiv, 212–213.

33. NARA, RG 120, NM 91, 195, Box 1, Classification Camp Reports, HQ 83rd Division, Le Mans, Oct. 10, 21, 1918, "Classification Camp Report."

34. NARA, RG 120, NM 91, 195, Box 1, Classification Camp Reports, HQ 83rd Division, Le Mans, Aug. 6, 8, 9, 1918, Jas. E. Pollard and George Keppie to Capt. Chas. D. Gentsch, G-2, 83rd Division, "Conditions Among Troops," "Report of Operatives," Sept. 18, 19, Oct. 1, 1918, CVL to Maj. Gentsch, "Classification Camp Report."

35. Frank E. Vandiver, *Black Jack* (College Station: Texas A&M Univ. Press, 1977), 2:937–938; Stallings, *The Doughboys*, 204; Doughty, *Pyrrhic Victory*, 484–485; Elizabeth Greenhalgh, *Foch in Command* (Cambridge: Cambridge Univ. Press, 2011), 432; John S. D. Eisenhower, *Yanks* (New York: Touchstone, 2001), 186.

36. NARA, RG 120, NM 91, 267, GHQ G-3, Box 3112, 679, HQ AEF, Sept. 24, 1917, Maj. Alfred H. Brooks, Corps of Engineers, "Notes on Mining Industry."

37. Gallwitz, *Erleben im Westen*, 285–286.

38. Marshall, *Memoirs of My Services in the World War*, 137–139.

39. Kew, UK National Archives (UKNA), WO 106/538, Jan. 16, 1919, "Report of General John J. Pershing, USA, Commander-in-Chief American Expeditionary Forces, Cabled to the Secretary of War, Nov. 20, 1918, Corrected Jan. 6, 1919," 13; Gallwitz, *Erleben im Westen*, 361–364.

40. UKNA, WO 106/528, October 1918, "Notes on American Offensive Operations," secret, from information received from French sources; Marshall, *Memoirs of My Services in the World War*, 142–143.

41. Pitt, *1918: The Last Act*, 245–246.

42. Robin Prior and Trevor Wilson, *Passchendaele*, 3rd ed. (New Haven, CT: Yale Univ. Press, 2016), 166–169; Woodward, *Trial by Friendship*, 203; Repington, *The First World War, 1914–1918*, 2:351; Terraine, *To Win a War*, 125–126, 131.

43. Palmer, *Bliss, Peacemaker*, 334; Lejeune, *The Reminiscences of a Marine*, 315–316; Stallings, *The Doughboys*, 211–212.

44. UKNA, WO 106/529, Sept. 16, 1918, "General Wagstaff's Report to D.M.O. Regarding American Operations in St. Mihiel"; KA, AOK-Op. Abteilung 557, Vienna, Oct. 2, 1928, "Die öst-ung 35. Infanteriedivision auf dem westlichen Kriegsschauplatz"; Franek, "K.u.k. Truppen im Westen," 415–416; Marshall, *Memoirs of My Services in the World War*, 65.

CHAPTER 11: SAINT-MIHIEL

1. London, Liddell Hart Centre for Military Archives (LHCMA), Grant 3/2, "Some Notes Made at Marshal Foch's HQrs, August to November 1918"; John H. Taber, *A Rainbow Division Lieutenant in France*, ed. Stephen H. Taber (Jefferson, NC: McFarland & Co., 2015), 111; Hervey Allen, *Toward the Flame* (1926; Lincoln: Univ. of Nebraska Press, 2003), 154; Carl von Clausewitz, *On War*, ed. and trans. Michael Howard and Peter Paret (1832; Princeton, NJ: Princeton Univ. Press, 1976), 119.

2. Max von Gallwitz, *Erleben im Westen, 1916–1918* (Berlin: Mittler, 1932), 371; College Park, MD, National Archives and Records Administration (NARA), RG 120, NM 91, 990, Box 6, 1st US Army Corps, G-2, Aug. 27, 1918, "Intelligence Estimate of the Situation."

3. Vienna, Kriegsarchiv (KA), AOK-Op. Abteilung 557, Feldpost 296, Oct. 3, 1918, k.u.k. 106 I.D. Kdo to AOK; KA, AOK-Op. Abteilung 557, Vienna, Oct. 2, 1928, "Die öst-ung 35. Infanteriedivision auf dem westlichen Kriegsschauplatz"; Maximilian Polatschek, "Österreichische-Ungarische Truppen an der Westfront" (PhD diss., Univ. of Vienna, 1974), 98–101; C. à Court Repington, *The First World War, 1914–1918* (Boston: Houghton Mifflin, 1920), 2:417.

4. NARA, RG 120, NM 91, 990, Box 6, 1st US Army Corps, G-2, Aug. 27, 1918, "Intelligence Estimate of the Situation"; John Lewis Barkley, *Scarlet Fields* (1930; Lawrence: Univ. Press of Kansas, 2012), 135.

5. NARA, RG 120, NM 91, 268, GHQ G-3, Box 3088A, Oct. 19, 1918, Brig. Gen. S. D. Rockenbach, chief of tank corps, to G-3 AEF, "Action of the Tanks Against St. Mihiel Salient Sept 11th to 15th."

6. KA, AOK-Op. Abteilung 557, Vienna, Oct. 2, 1928, "Die öst-ung 35. Infanteriedivision auf dem westlichen Kriegsschauplatz"; Major General John A. Lejeune, *The Reminiscences of a Marine*; (1930; New York: Arno Press, 1979), 327; NARA, RG 120, NM 91, 990, Box 3, AEF GHQ, Nov. 15, 1918, "Summary History of the First American Army Corps"; NARA, RG 120, NM 91, 1241, Box 41, 201-32.7 to 32.8, French 8th Army HQ, March 31, 1918, Passaga, "Memorandum on Attacks in Open Warfare," secret.

7. Lejeune, *The Reminiscences of a Marine*, 322.

8. Kew, UK National Archives (UKNA), WO 106/519, "Notes on Recent Operations No. 3," France, Oct. 12, 1918, AEF GHQ, Gen. James W. McAndrew, chief of staff; NARA, RG 120, NM 91, 990, Box 1, HQ I Army Corps,

Sept. 24, 1918, Gen. Craig to divisional generals, "Feeding, Watering and Care of Public Animals."

9. UKNA, WO 106/519, "Notes on Recent Operations No. 3," France, Oct. 12, 1918, AEF GHQ, Gen. James W. McAndrew, chief of staff; NARA, RG 120, NM 91, 1241, Box 50, 201-33.6, France, HQ 1st Div., Sept. 19, 1918, "Investigation of Movements of 26th Infantry on 12–13 September," Maj. W. R. Wheeler to Gen. Bullard.

10. NARA, RG 120, NM 91, 1241, Box 50, 201-33.6, France, HQ 1st Div., Sept. 19, 1918, "Investigation of Movements of 26th Infantry on 12–13 September," Maj. W. R. Wheeler to Gen. Bullard; NARA, RG 120, NM 91, 1241, Box 50, 201-33.6, France, HQ 1st Div., Sept. 16, 1918, Maj. Whitener to Col. Cullison, "Report on Action of Sept. 12–15, 1918."

11. NARA, RG 120, NM 91, 1118, V Corps Historical, Box 12, IV Corps, Sept. 16, 1918, "Report of Interrogation of German Prisoner of September 16th"; NARA, RG 120, NM 91, 990, Box 10, 1st US Army Corps, G-2, Aug. 30, 1918, "Sector III."

12. NARA, RG 120, NM 91, 990, Box 11, 1st US Army Corps, G-2, September 1918, "Reports of Examination of Prisoners"; Edward Coffman, *The War to End All Wars* (New York: Oxford Univ. Press, 1968), 281.

13. UKNA, WO 106/529, Sept. 16, 1918, "General Wagstaff's Report to D.M.O. Regarding American Operations in St. Mihiel"; NARA, RG 120, NM 91, 267, GHQ G-3, Box 3125, 777, Chaumont, AEF GHQ, 1919, "Candid Comment on the American Soldier of 1917–1918 and Related Topics by the Germans."

14. UKNA, WO 106/519, "Notes on Recent Operations No. 3," France, Oct. 12, 1918, AEF GHQ, Gen. James W. McAndrew, chief of staff.

15. NARA, RG 120, NM 91, 1118, V Corps Historical, Box 5, V Corps, Aug. 9, 1918, "Tactical and Technical Lessons in the Use of Machine Guns Learned During the Spring Offensive of 1918"; Gallwitz, *Erleben im Westen*, 371.

16. UKNA, WO 106/529, Sept. 16, 1918, "General Wagstaff's Report to D.M.O. Regarding American Operations in St. Mihiel"; Henry Berry, *Make the Kaiser Dance* (New York: Arbor House, 1978), 382.

17. NARA, RG 120, NM 91, 267, GHQ G-3, Box 3125, 777, Chaumont, AEF GHQ, 1919, "Candid Comment on the American Soldier of 1917–1918 and Related Topics by the Germans"; UKNA, WO 106/538, Jan. 16, 1919, "Report of General John J. Pershing, USA, Commander-in-Chief American Expeditionary Forces, Cabled to the Secretary of War, Nov. 20, 1918, Corrected Jan. 6, 1919," 13; John S. D. Eisenhower, *Yanks* (New York: Touchstone, 2001), 213; Laurence Stallings, *The Doughboys* (New York: Harper & Row, 1963), 212.

18. NARA, RG 120, NM 91, 990, Box 3, AEF GHQ, Nov. 15, 1918, "Summary History of the First American Army Corps"; Coffman, *The War to End All Wars*, 281; Lejeune, *The Reminiscences of a Marine*, 328–329.

19. NARA, RG 120, NM 91, 1118, V Corps Historical, Box 11, First Army HQ, Sept. 9, 1918, "Interrogation of Hungarian Deserter, 35th Austro-Hungarian Division."

20. NARA, RG 120, NM 91, 1118, V Corps Historical, Box 11, V Corps, Sept. 12, 1918, "Information on the 35th D.A.H., Calonne-Lamorville Sector, Before the Attack, Interrogation of Prisoners of the 63rd R.I. K.u.K"; UKNA, WO 106/529, Sept. 16, 1918, "General Wagstaff's Report to D.M.O. Regarding American Operations in St. Mihiel."

21. KA, AOK-Op. Abteilung 557, Vienna, Oct. 2, 1928, "Die öst-ung 35. Infanteriedivision auf dem westlichen Kriegsschauplatz"; UKNA, WO 106/529, Sept. 16, 1918, "General Wagstaff's Report to D.M.O. Regarding American Operations in St. Mihiel."

22. NARA, RG 120, NM 91, 990, Box 6, 1st US Army Corps, G-2, Aug. 27, 1918, "Intelligence Estimate of the Situation"; NARA, RG 120, NM 91, 990, Box 3, AEF GHQ, Nov. 15, 1918, "Summary History of the First American Army Corps"; David Trask, *The AEF and Coalition Warmaking, 1917–1918* (Lawrence: Univ. Press of Kansas, 1993), 112–113; Marshall, *Memoirs of My Services in the World War*, 146.

23. NARA, RG 120, NM 91, 1118, V Corps Historical, Box 12, V Corps, Oct. 1, 1918, "Interrogation of a Battalion Commander of the 15th Division, 398th Regiment, Captured Sept. 12th."

24. UKNA, WO 106/528, October 1918, "Notes on American Offensive Operations," secret, from information received from French sources; UKNA, WO 106/529, Sept. 16, 1918, "General Wagstaff's Report to D.M.O. Regarding American Operations in St. Mihiel"; NARA, RG 120, NM 91, 1241, Box 50, 201-33.6, France, HQ 26th Inf., Sept. 17, 1918, Col. J. M. Cullison to Gen. Bullard; NARA, RG 120, NM 91, 1241, 210-32.15, HQ 1st Brig, 1st Div, France, Sept. 22, 1918, Brig. Gen. Frank Parker to regimental commanders, "Straggling."

25. UKNA, WO 106/528, October 1918, "Notes on American Offensive Operations," secret, from information received from French sources; Stallings, *The Doughboys*, 217.

26. NARA, RG 120, NM 91, 1118, V Corps Historical, Box 2, n.d., "Comments by the Corps Commander Upon the Operations of the Fifth Army Corps"; UKNA, WO 106/529, Sept. 16, 1918, "General Wagstaff's Report to D.M.O. Regarding American Operations in St. Mihiel."

27. NARA, RG 120, NM 91, 195, Box 1, Classification Camp Reports, HQ 83rd Division, Le Mans, Sept. 18, 27, 1918, CVL to Maj. Gentsch, "Classification Camp Report"; NARA, RG 120, NM 91, 195, Box 1, Classification

Camp Reports, HQ 83rd Division, Le Mans, Oct. 2, 31, Nov. 1, 1918, "Report Conditions at Forwarding Area This Date."

28. Stallings, *The Doughboys*, 214; Polatschek, "Österreichische-Ungarische Truppen an der Westfront," 104.

29. UKNA, WO 106/529, Sept. 16, 1918, "General Wagstaff's Report to D.M.O. Regarding American Operations in St. Mihiel"; LHCMA, Grant 3/2, "Some Notes Made at Marshal Foch's HQrs, August to November 1918"; Gallwitz, *Erleben im Westen*, 375.

30. NARA, RG 120, NM 91, 1118, V Corps Historical, Box 5, AEF GHQ, Aug. 9, 1918, "German Man-Traps Left in Abandoned Terrain."

31. NARA, RG 120, NM 91, 1118, V Corps Historical, Box 12, G.H.Q., 8/24/18, "German Traps and Mines."

32. NARA, RG 120, NM 91, 1118, V Corps Historical, Box 12, IV Corps, 89th Div, Sept. 23, 1918, Gen. W. Wright; NARA, RG 120, NM 91, 1118, V Corps Historical, Box 12, IV Corps, 42nd Div. HQ, Sept. 22, 1918, "Report of the Interrogation of 5 Prisoners."

33. UKNA, WO 106/538, Jan. 16, 1919, "Report of General John J. Pershing, USA, Commander-in-Chief American Expeditionary Forces, Cabled to the Secretary of War, Nov. 20, 1918, Corrected Jan. 6, 1919," 15; UKNA, WO 106/528, October 1918, "Notes on American Offensive Operations," secret, from information received from French sources.

34. LHCMA, Grant 3/2, "Some Notes Made at Marshal Foch's HQrs, August to November 1918"; Marshall, *Memoirs of My Services in the World War*, 148–149; Stallings, *The Doughboys*, 218.

35. KA, AOK-Op. Abteilung 557, Vienna, Oct. 2, 1928, "Die öst-ung 35. Infanteriedivision auf dem westlichen Kriegsschauplatz"; NARA, RG 120, NM 91, 267, GHQ G-3, Box 3125, 772, AEF Advanced GHQ, Trier, April 4, 1919, "Conversation with Col. Von Heye at Treves, April 3, 1919"; Stallings, *The Doughboys*, 219.

36. Trask, *The AEF and Coalition Warmaking*, 22; NARA, RG 120, NM 91, 268, GHQ G-3, Box 3101, "Battle of the Argonne-Meuse," 78th Division Lecture Course, Jan. 3, 1919, Acting Chief of Staff James L. Frink; Stallings, *The Doughboys*, 224.

37. Marshall, *Memoirs of My Services in the World War*, 80, 149; Terraine, *To Win a War*, 135.

38. Gallwitz, *Erleben im Westen*, 377, 381.

39. NARA, RG 120, NM 91, 268, GHQ G-3, Box 3101, "Battle of the Argonne-Meuse," 78th Division Lecture Course, Jan. 3, 1919, Acting Chief of Staff James L. Frink.

40. LHCMA, Grant 3/2, "Some Notes Made at Marshal Foch's HQrs, August to November 1918."

41. Gallwitz, *Erleben im Westen*, 381–390.

42. NARA, RG 120, NM 91, 1241, Box 55, 201-33.6, France, Sept. 18, 1918, CO Co. "H", 28th Inf. to Battalion Comdr., "Loss of Special Equipment."

43. NARA, RG 120, NM 91, 267, GHQ G-3, Box 3097, France, Sept. 15, 1918, 26th Div. HQ, A. Leclerc to Maj. Gen. Edwards; Stallings, *The Doughboys*, 345–346.

CHAPTER 12: MEUSE-ARGONNE: MONTFAUCON

1. College Park, MD, National Archives and Records Administration (NARA), RG 120, NM 91, 84, Box 6704, AEF, G-2, "A Survey of the War 1914–1918: Some Effects of American Participation," secret; Barrie Pitt, *1918: The Last Act* (London: Cassell, 1962), 232–233.

2. George C. Marshall, *Memoirs of My Services in the World War, 1917–1918* (Boston: Houghton Mifflin, 1976), 158–159.

3. Kew, UK National Archives (UKNA), WO 106/528, October 1918, "Notes on American Offensive Operations," secret, from information received from French sources; Lieut.-Col. Charles Repington, "America's Effort: A Tribute, the Campaign of 1918," *London Morning Post*, Dec. 9, 1918; London, Liddell Hart Centre for Military Archives (LHCMA), Grant 3/2, "Some Notes Made at Marshal Foch's HQrs, August to November 1918"; NARA, RG 120, NM 91, 267, GHQ G-3, Box 3119, French GHQ, Oct. 1, 1918, Maj. Clark to Pershing, secret.

4. LHCMA, Grant 3/2, "Some Notes Made at Marshal Foch's HQrs, August to November 1918"; John Terraine, *To Win a War* (New York: Doubleday, 1981), 166; Robin Prior and Trevor Wilson, *Command on the Western Front* (Oxford: Blackwell, 1992), 368–374; Nick Lloyd, *Hundred Days* (New York: Basic Books, 2014), 101–102.

5. Robert Alexander, *Memories of the World War, 1917–1918* (New York: Macmillan, 1931), 156.

6. LHCMA, Grant 3/2, "Some Notes Made at Marshal Foch's HQrs, August to November 1918"; John S. D. Eisenhower, *Yanks* (New York: Touchstone, 2001), 200; Max von Gallwitz, *Erleben im Westen, 1916–1918* (Berlin: Mittler, 1932), 285; Marshall, *Memoirs of My Services in the World War*, 159.

7. NARA, RG 120, NM 91, 990, Box 10, 1st US Army Corps, G-2, Sept. 20, 1918, "Distribution of Troops and Density of Occupation of the Front"; "MacArthur," *American Experience*, PBS, pbs.org.

8. NARA, RG 120, NM 91, 268, GHQ G-3, Box 3101, "Battle of the Argonne-Meuse," 78th Division Lecture Course, Jan. 3, 1919, Acting Chief of Staff James L. Frink; NARA, RG 120, NM 91, 990, Box 6, 1st US Army Corps, "Summary of Intelligence, July 4–November 9, 1918"; Eisenhower, *Yanks*, 203; Laurence Stallings, *The Doughboys* (New York: Harper & Row, 1963), 225.

9. Edward Coffman, *The War to End All Wars* (New York: Oxford Univ. Press, 1968), 301.

10. NARA, RG 120, NM 91, 990, Box 3, AEF GHQ, Nov. 15, 1918, "Summary History of the First American Army Corps."

11. Thomas H. Barber, *Along the Road* (New York: Dodd Mead, 1924), 2, 16; NARA, RG 120, NM 91, 990, Box 3, AEF GHQ, Nov. 15, 1918, "Summary History of the First American Army Corps"; Hervey Allen, *Toward the Flame* (1926; Lincoln: Univ. of Nebraska Press, 2003), 13; Gallwitz, *Erleben im Westen*, 373.

12. NARA, RG 120, NM 91, 267, GHQ G-3, Box 3122, 747, War Office, August 31, 1918, Gen. A. Lynden-Bell to Gen. Wagstaff; Albert M. Ettinger and A. Churchill Ettinger, *A Doughboy with the Fighting Sixty-Ninth* (Shippensburg: PA: White Mane, 1992), 151.

13. NARA, RG 120, NM 91, 268, GHQ G-3, Box 3101, "Battle of the Argonne-Meuse," 78th Division Lecture Course, Jan. 3, 1919, Acting Chief of Staff James L. Frink; UKNA, WO 106/538, Jan. 16, 1919, "Report of General John J. Pershing, USA, Commander-in-Chief American Expeditionary Forces, Cabled to the Secretary of War, Nov. 20, 1918, Corrected Jan. 6, 1919," 15; Marshall, *Memoirs of My Services in the World War*, 157–158.

14. Coffman, *The War to End All Wars*, 314–315.

15. Munich, Bayerisches Kriegsarchiv (BKA), Inf. Div., WK 10, AHQ, 3. Armee, Sept. 23, 1918, "Chefbesprechung."

16. NARA, RG 120, NM 91, 1118, V Corps Historical, Box 5, V Corps, Aug. 16, 1918, "Notes on Recent Fighting."

17. NARA, RG 120, NM 91, 990, Box 13, HQ 1st Armored Brigade, Sept. 21, 1918, Lt. Col. Geo. S. Patton Jr., "Memorandum on Plan for the Use of Tanks"; Eisenhower, *Yanks*, 211–212.

18. William S. Triplet, *A Youth in the Meuse-Argonne*, ed. Robert H. Ferrell (Columbia: Univ. of Missouri Press, 2000), 163–164; Barber, *Along the Road*, 26–29.

19. NARA, RG 120, NM 91, 267, GHQ G-3, Box 3125, 777, Chaumont, AEF GHQ, 1919, "Candid Comment on the American Soldier of 1917–1918 and Related Topics by the Germans"; Barber, *Along the Road*, 26, 97; Gallwitz, *Erleben im Westen*, 390.

20. Stallings, *The Doughboys*, 228; Barber, *Along the Road*, 30–31.

21. Barber, *Along the Road*, 29–32.

22. Mark Ethan Grotelueschen, *The AEF Way of War* (Cambridge: Cambridge Univ. Press, 2007), 324–325; Alexander, *Memories of the World War*, 190; Edward G. Lengel, *To Conquer Hell* (New York: Henry Holt, 2008), 119–120.

23. David Kennedy, *Over Here* (New York: Oxford Univ. Press, 1980), 160–161; Lengel, *To Conquer Hell*, 159–160; Coffman, *The War to End All Wars*, 314–320.

24. UKNA, WO 106/530, British Mission, AEF GHQ, Sept. 30, 1918, C. Wagstaff to P. de B. Radcliffe; Andrew Carroll, *My Fellow Soldiers* (New York: Penguin Press, 2017), 287–289; Robert H. Ferrell, *America's Deadliest Battle* (Lawrence: Univ. Press of Kansas, 2007), 48.

25. NARA, RG 120, NM 91, 990, Box 13, HQ 1st Armored Brigade, Sept. 21, 1918, Lt. Col. Geo. S. Patton Jr., "Memorandum on Plan for the Use of Tanks."

26. Vincennes, Service Historique de la Défense (SHD), FC 6N 141, Sept. 28, 1918, "Rapport du Col. D. D. Pullen to Gen. Rockenbach"; UKNA, WO 106/530, British Mission, AEF GHQ, Sept. 30, 1918, C. Wagstaff to P. de B. Radcliffe; NARA, RG 120, NM 91, 990, Box 13, HQ 1st Armored Brigade, Sept. 21, 1918, Lt. Col. Geo. S. Patton Jr., "Memorandum on Plan for the Use of Tanks"; Ferrell, *America's Deadliest Battle*, 48–49; Gene Fax, *With Their Bare Hands: General Pershing, the 79th Division, and the Battle for Montfaucon* (Oxford: Osprey, 2017).

27. Stallings, *The Doughboys*, 245–246.

28. Lengel, *To Conquer Hell*, 36, 60.

29. Stallings, *The Doughboys*, 241.

30. Robert H. Ferrell, *The Question of MacArthur's Reputation* (Columbia: Univ. of Missouri Press, 2008), 7; Triplet, *A Youth in the Meuse-Argonne*, 160; Stallings, *The Doughboys*, 242.

31. C. à Court Repington, *The First World War, 1914–1918* (Boston: Houghton Mifflin, 1920), 2:392–393.

32. NARA, RG 120, NM 91, 267, GHQ G-3, Box 3099, Sept. 30, 1918, Col. L. J McNair to Gen. Fiske, "Argonne-Meuse Offensive" and "Notes on Recent Operations."

33. Barber, *Along the Road*, xv; Marshall, *Memoirs of My Services in the World War*, 162–163; Alexander, *Memories of the World War*, 37–38.

34. Ferrell, *America's Deadliest Battle*, 67–68; Marshall, *Memoirs of My Services in the World War*, 161; Alexander, *Memories of the World War*, 168.

35. NARA, RG 120, NM 91, 1118, V Corps Historical, Box 2, Nov. 20, 1918, Report of G-2, 5th US Army Corps; Stallings, *The Doughboys*, 271.

36. NARA, RG 120, NM 91, 990, Box 13, HQ 1st Armored Brigade, Sept. 21, 1918, Lt. Col. Geo. S. Patton Jr., "Memorandum on Plan for the Use of Tanks"; Stanley Hirshon, *General Patton* (New York: HarperCollins, 2002), 130–131; Lengel, *To Conquer Hell*, 110–112.

37. Triplet, *A Youth in the Meuse-Argonne*, 173.

38. Stallings, *The Doughboys*, 244.

39. NARA, RG 120, NM 91, 267, GHQ G-2, Box 3125, "German Defensive Tactics"; Triplet, *A Youth in the Meuse-Argonne*, 186.

40. Triplet, *A Youth in the Meuse-Argonne*, 172.

41. NARA, RG 120, NM 91, 267, GHQ G-3, Box 3099, 9/30/18, France, Oct. 4, 1918, Lt. Col. B. F. McClellan, "Memo to G-5: Operations of the 35th

Division (US) Sept. 26th to Oct. 1st"; Ferrell, *America's Deadliest Battle*, 71–72; Triplet, *A Youth in the Meuse-Argonne*, 249–252.

42. Pitt, *1918: The Last Act*, 247–251; Terraine, *To Win a War*, 158–159; Lloyd, *Hundred Days*, 177–178.

43. Lengel, *To Conquer Hell*, 160; Ferrell, *The Question of MacArthur's Reputation*, 15.

44. Marshall, *Memoirs of My Services in the World War*, 172–173; Henry Berry, *Make the Kaiser Dance* (New York: Arbor House, 1978), 94.

45. Eisenhower, *Yanks*, 219.

46. Barber, *Along the Road*, 32.

47. Lengel, *To Conquer Hell*, 100.

48. NARA, RG 120, NM 91, 1118, V Corps Historical, Box 19, V Corps, Oct. 22, 1918, Gen. W. B. Burke, V Corps chief of staff, "Note for Division Commanders"; Lengel, *To Conquer Hell*, 130–131; Eisenhower, *Yanks*, 222–223.

49. Lengel, *To Conquer Hell*, 148.

50. Stallings, *The Doughboys*, 232–233.

51. NARA, RG 120, NM 91, 1043, Box 4, HQ III Corps, Dec. 1, 1918, Hines to Pershing, "The Argonne-Meuse Operations From Sept. 9 to Nov. 11"; Stallings, *The Doughboys*, 233–234.

52. Allan R. Millett, *The General* (Westport, CT: Greenwood, 1975), 404–405; William Walker, *Betrayal at Little Gibraltar* (New York: Scribner, 2017), 156–159, 324–327; Ferrell, *America's Deadliest Battle*, 51–53.

53. Barber, *Along the Road*, 44–45.

54. Lengel, *To Conquer Hell*, 99; Stallings, *The Doughboys*, 235.

55. Eisenhower, *Yanks*, 223.

56. Gallwitz, *Erleben im Westen*, 392–395.

57. SHD, FC 6N 141, "Résumé du Rapport du Gl. Pétain sur les operations de l'Armée U.S. entre Meuse et Champagne, 26–30 Sept. 1918"; UKNA, WO 106/519, "Notes on Recent Operations No. 4," France, Nov. 1, 1918, AEF GHQ, Gen. James W. McAndrew, chief of staff.

58. NARA, RG 120, NM 91, 267, GHQ G-3, Box 3120, 730, Jan. 7, 1918, "Notes Received from Col. LeRoy Eltinge"; NARA, RG 120, NM 91, 267, GHQ G-3, Box 3120, 730, France, Aug. 16, 1918, Pershing, "Instruction on Liaison."

59. Stallings, *The Doughboys*, 247–248; Eisenhower, *Yanks*, 221; Barber, *Along the Road*, 37.

60. Lengel, *To Conquer Hell*, 98–99.

61. UKNA, WO 106/530, British Mission, AEF GHQ, Sept. 30, 1918, C. Wagstaff to P. de B. Radcliffe.

62. Triplet, *A Youth in the Meuse-Argonne*, 193–198, 204, 217.

63. UKNA, WO 106/530, British Mission, AEF GHQ, Sept. 30, 1918, C. Wagstaff to P. de B. Radcliffe.

CHAPTER 13: MEUSE-ARGONNE: EXERMONT

1. College Park, MD, National Archives and Records Administration (NARA), RG 120, NM 91, 1118, V Corps Historical, Box 2, Nov. 20, 1918, Report of G-2, 5th US Army Corps; NARA, RG 120, NM 91, 1118, V Corps Historical, Box 5, V Corps, Oct. 19, 1918, "Summary of Intelligence"; Robert Alexander, *Memories of the World War, 1917–1918* (New York: Macmillan, 1931), 216–217; Thomas H. Barber, *Along the Road* (New York: Dodd Mead, 1924), 23–24.

2. Kew, UK National Archives (UKNA), WO 106/530, British Mission, Sept. 29, 1918, Maj. W. Geiger, secret.

3. Douglas Haig, "Close and Complete Cooperation Between All Arms and Services," *Fourth Supplement to the London Gazette*, April 10, 1919; Major General John A. Lejeune, *The Reminiscences of a Marine* (1930; New York: Arno Press, 1979), 375.

4. Barber, *Along the Road*, 52–53.

5. UKNA, WO 106/530, British Mission, Sept. 29, 1918, Maj. W. Geiger, secret.

6. UKNA, WO 106/519, "Notes on Recent Operations No. 4," France, Nov. 1, 1918, AEF GHQ, Gen. James W. McAndrew, chief of staff; NARA, RG 120, NM 91, 990, Box 13, HQ 1st Armored Brigade, Sept. 21, 1918, Lt. Col. Geo. S. Patton Jr., "Memorandum on Plan for the Use of Tanks"; S. L. A. Marshall, *Men Against Fire: The Problem of Battle Command* (1947; Norman: Univ. of Oklahoma Press, 2000).

7. NARA, RG 120, NM 91, 268, GHQ G-3, Box 3101, "Battle of the Argonne-Meuse," 78th Division Lecture Course, Jan. 3, 1919, Acting Chief of Staff James L. Frink; NARA, RG 120, NM 91, 267, GHQ G-3, Box 3119, French GHQ, Oct. 3, 1918, Maj. Paul Clark to Pershing, "Military Situation," secret.

8. Laurence Stallings, *The Doughboys* (New York: Harper & Row, 1963), 294; Edward G. Lengel, *To Conquer Hell* (New York: Henry Holt, 2008), 183–184.

9. Barber, *Along the Road*, 49–51.

10. Peter L. Belmonte, *Days of Perfect Hell, October–November 1918* (Atglen, PA: Schiffer, 2015), 138; Barber, *Along the Road*, 68–69.

11. John Dos Passos, *Three Soldiers* (1921; New York: Barnes & Noble Books, 2004), 173.

12. Jonathan Boff, *Winning and Losing on the Western Front* (Cambridge: Cambridge Univ. Press, 2012), 36–37; Barrie Pitt, *1918: The Last Act* (London: Cassell, 1962), 236–237.

13. NARA, RG 120, NM 91, 267, GHQ G-3, Box 3112, Aug. 15, 1918, Pershing to Haig; James J. Cooke, *Pershing and His Generals* (Westport, CT: Praeger, 1997), 63–64.

14. "Official Version of 27th's Exploits," *New York Times*, Nov. 8, 1918.

15. NARA, RG 120, NM 91, 267, GHQ G-3, Box 3122, HQ 2nd Tank Brigade, Maj. R. I. Sasse to Lt. Col. H. E. Mitchell; William S. Triplet, *A Youth in the Meuse-Argonne* (Columbia: Univ. of Missouri Press, 2000), 216.

16. Henry Berry, *Make the Kaiser Dance* (New York: Arbor House, 1978), 216–217, 423; Robin Prior and Trevor Wilson, *Command on the Western Front* (Oxford: Blackwell, 1992), 368–372.

17. NARA, RG 120, NM 91, 267, GHQ G-3, Box 3119, Oct. 1, 1918, Maj. Clark to Pershing, "Military Situation," secret; NARA, RG 120, NM 91, 267, GHQ G-3, Box 3092, n.d., "Operations of the 27th and 30th Divisions on the Cambrai-St. Quentin Front with the IV British Army"; John Terraine, *To Win a War* (New York: Doubleday, 1981), 147–148; Edward Coffman, *The War to End All Wars* (New York: Oxford Univ. Press, 1968), 292–297; C. à Court Repington, *The First World War, 1914–1918* (Boston: Houghton Mifflin, 1920), 2:338.

18. Stallings, *The Doughboys*, 295; Terraine, *To Win a War*, 156–157.

19. NARA, RG 120, NM 91, 1118, V Corps Historical, Box 4, AEF HQ, May 26, 1919, Col. C. F. Crain, "Operations of the 79th, 3rd, 32nd, and 89th Divisions in the Argonne-Meuse Offensive, Sept. 26–Nov. 11, 1918"; George C. Marshall, *Memoirs of My Services in the World War, 1917–1918* (Boston: Houghton Mifflin, 1976), 162–163.

20. UKNA, WO 106/530, British Mission, AEF GHQ, Sept. 30, 1918, C. Wagstaff to P. de B. Radcliffe; London, Liddell Hart Centre for Military Archives (LHCMA), LH IS/2/34, *Reveille*, Feb. 1, 1938, "Mademoiselle from Armentières."

21. NARA, RG 120, NM 91, 1118, V Corps Historical, Box 2, n.d., "Comments by the Corps Commander upon the Operations of the Fifth Army Corps"; Lengel, *To Conquer Hell*, 166–172, 191.

22. Vincennes, Service Historique de la Défense (SHD), FC 6N 141, "Résumé du Rapport du Gl. Pétain sur les operations de l'Armée U.S. entre Meuse et Champagne, 26–30 Sept. 1918"; LHCMA, Grant 3/2, "Some Notes Made at Marshal Foch's HQrs, August to November 1918."

23. John S. D. Eisenhower, *Yanks* (New York: Touchstone, 2001), 223.

24. Marshall, *Memoirs of My Services in the World War*, 175.

25. Lengel, *To Conquer Hell*, 188; Triplet, *A Youth in the Meuse-Argonne*, 218, 222.

26. Horace L. Baker, *Argonne Days in World War I*, ed. Robert H. Ferrell (1927; Columbia: Univ. of Missouri Press, 2007), 39; Triplet, *A Youth in the Meuse-Argonne*, 210.

27. John Lewis Barkley, *Scarlet Fields* (1930; Lawrence: Univ. Press of Kansas, 2012), 168; Triplet, *A Youth in the Meuse-Argonne*, 209, 227–228.

28. Triplet, *A Youth in the Meuse-Argonne*, 234; Eisenhower, *Yanks*, 231.

29. John H. Taber, *A Rainbow Division Lieutenant in France*, ed. Stephen H. Taber (Jefferson, NC: McFarland & Co., 2015), 147; Triplet, *A Youth in the Meuse-Argonne*, 234.

30. Marshall, *Memoirs of My Services in the World War*, 167.

31. NARA, RG 120, NM 91, 195, Box 1, Classification Camp Reports, HQ 83rd Division, Le Mans, Oct. 22, 1918, "Classification Camp Report"; Dos Passos, *Three Soldiers*, 178–179.

32. Munich, Bayerisches Kriegsarchiv (BKA), Inf. Div., WK 1876, 3. bay. Inf. Div., Gr. H.Qu., September 30, 1918, Hindenburg to army commanders.

33. NARA, RG 120, NM 91, 267, GHQ G-3, Box 3125, 777, Chaumont, AEF GHQ, 1919, "Candid Comment on the American Soldier of 1917–1918 and Related Topics by the Germans"; Max von Gallwitz, *Erleben im Westen, 1916–1918* (Berlin: Mittler, 1932), 399.

34. Robert H. Ferrell, *America's Deadliest Battle* (Lawrence: Univ. Press of Kansas, 2007), 142.

35. Nick Lloyd, *Hundred Days* (New York: Basic Books, 2014), 195–197; Gallwitz, *Erleben im Westen*, 400; Terraine, *To Win a War*, 161–162; Frederick Palmer, *Bliss, Peacemaker* (New York: Dodd Mead, 1934), 335.

36. Stallings, *The Doughboys*, 239–240.

37. Barber, *Along the Road*, 84–86.

38. Lengel, *To Conquer Hell*, 184–185, 197.

39. NARA, RG 120, NM 91, 1241, Box 46, 201-11.4, HQ 1st Div, France, Oct. 11 and 23, 1918, Gen. C. P. Summerrall; Stallings, *The Doughboys*, 240. Marshall, *Memoirs of My Services in the World War*, 164–165; Baker, *Argonne Days in World War I*, 35–36; Lengel, *To Conquer Hell*, 186–187; Belmonte, *Days of Perfect Hell*, 30.

40. Stallings, *The Doughboys*, 244–245, 296.

41. Barber, *Along the Road*, 100–101.

42. NARA, RG 120, NM 91, 267, GHQ G-3, Box 3099, "Digest of the Reports of the 1st Division on the Relief of the 35th Division on Oct. 1, 1918."

43. NARA, RG 120, NM 91, 267, GHQ G-3, Box 3099, Brest, April 6, 1919, "Memo for General Conner: 35th Division"; NARA, RG 120, NM 91, 267, GHQ G-3, Box 3125, 772, Feb. 20, 1919, Capt. Waldo, G-2, "By Phone from Paris"; NARA, RG 120, NM 91, 1241, Box 46, 201-11.4, HQ 18th Inf., Mogendorf, Germany, Feb. 4, 1919, Lt. Col. H. C. Stebbins.

44. Lloyd, *Hundred Days*, 156; Hervey Allen, *Toward the Flame* (1926; Lincoln: Univ. of Nebraska Press, 2003), 165; Alexander, *Memories of the World War*, 217, 221.

45. UKNA, WO 106/538, Jan. 16, 1919, "Report of General John J. Pershing, USA, Commander-in-Chief American Expeditionary Forces, Cabled to the

Secretary of War, Nov. 20, 1918, Corrected Jan. 6, 1919," 16; Alexander, *Memories of the World War*, 197–198.

46. UKNA, WO 106/530, British Mission, AEF GHQ, Sept. 30, 1918, C. Wagstaff to P. de B. Radcliffe; NARA, RG 120, NM 91, 990, Box 10, HQ 90th Division, Aug. 31, 1918, Col. John J. Kingman, "Passing of Lines, Direction of March, Woods"; Stallings, *The Doughboys*, 199.

47. UKNA, WO 106/530, British Mission, Sept. 30, 1918, Maj. W. Geiger, secret.

CHAPTER 14: MEUSE-ARGONNE: ROMAGNE

1. Frederick Palmer, *With My Own Eyes* (Indianapolis, IN: Bobbs-Merrill, 1932), 375.

2. C. à Court Repington, *The First World War, 1914–1918* (Boston: Houghton Mifflin, 1920), 2:319, 467; Jonathan Boff, *Winning and Losing on the Western Front* (Cambridge: Cambridge Univ. Press, 2012), 53–57; Paul F. Braim, *The Test of Battle* (Newark: Univ. of Delaware Press, 1987), 116, 122; David Trask, *The AEF and Coalition Warmaking, 1917–1918* (Lawrence: Univ. Press of Kansas, 1993), 142.

3. College Park, MD, National Archives and Records Administration (NARA), RG 120, NM 91, 1118, V Corps Historical, Box 2, Nov. 20, 1918, Report of G-2, 5th US Army Corps; Albert M. Ettinger and A. Churchill Ettinger, *A Doughboy with the Fighting Sixty-Ninth* (Shippensburg, PA: White Mane, 1992), 8; Peter L. Belmonte, *Days of Perfect Hell, October–November 1918* (Atglen, PA: Schiffer, 2015), 36.

4. Robert Alexander, *Memories of the World War, 1917–1918* (New York: Macmillan, 1931), 211–212.

5. John S. D. Eisenhower, *Yanks* (New York: Touchstone, 2001), 226–227.

6. Edward G. Lengel, *To Conquer Hell* (New York: Henry Holt, 2008), 301–302, 311.

7. Laurence Stallings, *The Doughboys* (New York: Harper & Row, 1963), 295; Donald Smythe, *Pershing* (Bloomington: Indiana Univ. Press, 1986), 208; Lengel, *To Conquer Hell*, 306.

8. NARA, RG 120, NM 91, 990, Box 19, 181-32-16, Field Messages, Oct. 6, No. 103, from HAROLD; Lengel, *To Conquer Hell*, 1–2.

9. Lengel, *To Conquer Hell*, 202–204, 307.

10. NARA, RG 120, NM 91, 990, Box 6, 1st US Army Corps, "Summary of Intelligence, July 4–November 9, 1918"; James J. Cooke, *Pershing and His Generals* (Westport, CT: Praeger, 1997), 68; John Lewis Barkley, *Scarlet Field* (1930; Lawrence: Univ. Press of Kansas, 2012), 153; Lengel, *To Conquer Hell*, 203, 347.

11. NARA, RG 120, NM 91, 990, Box 19, 181-32-16, Field Messages, Oct. 6, No. 95, from RALEIGH THREE; NARA, RG 120, NM 91, 990, Box 3, AEF GHQ, Nov. 15, 1918, "Summary History of the First American Army Corps"; Barkley, *Scarlet Fields*, 156.

12. Kew, UK National Archives (UKNA), WO 106/538, Jan. 16, 1919, "Report of General John J. Pershing, USA, Commander-in-Chief American Expeditionary Forces, Cabled to the Secretary of War, Nov. 20, 1918, Corrected Jan. 6, 1919," 18–19; NARA, RG 120, NM 91, 990, Box 19, 181-32-16, Field Messages, Oct. 6, No. 103, from DEACON to DAYLIGHT.

13. Barkley, *Scarlet Fields*, 138–139.

14. NARA, RG 120, NM 91, 990, Box 3, GHQ, AEF, Nov. 15, 1918, "Summary History of the First American Army Corps."

15. Barkley, *Scarlet Fields*, 139–143.

16. Richard Slotkin, *Lost Battalions* (New York: Henry Holt, 2005), 338–339; Stallings, *The Doughboys*, 272.

17. Nick Lloyd, *Hundred Days* (New York: Basic Books, 2014), 191–192; Robert Lee Bullard, *Personalities and Reminiscences of the War* (New York: Doubleday, 1925), 243–244; Michael S. Neiberg, *The Second Battle of the Marne* (Bloomington: Indiana Univ. Press, 2008), 30.

18. NARA, RG 120, NM 91, 1241, Box 54, 202.11.4, "A Brief History of the 6th Regiment, USMC from July 1917 to Dec. 1918"; Major General John A. Lejeune, *The Reminiscences of a Marine* (1930; New York: Arno Press, 1979), 342.

19. Mark Ethan Grotelueschen, *The AEF Way of War* (Cambridge: Cambridge Univ. Press, 2007), 252; Richard Rubin, *The Last of the Doughboys* (Boston: Houghton Mifflin, 2013), 264; Stallings, *The Doughboys*, 318–319, 356; Lengel, *To Conquer Hell*, 194–195; Lejeune, *The Reminiscences of a Marine*, 348.

20. Henry Berry, *Make the Kaiser Dance* (New York: Arbor House, 1978), 104–105.

21. Lejeune, *The Reminiscences of a Marine*, 348.

22. Grotelueschen, *The AEF Way of War*, 260; Lejeune, *The Reminiscences of a Marine*, 353.

23. NARA, RG 120, NM 91, 1241, Box 54, 203-33.6, HQ 1st Bn, 5th Marine Regiment, July 6, 1919, Maj. Leroy P. Hunt, "Account of Experiences 1st Bn 5th Regt Marines on Oct. 4, 1918, During the Engagement of Blanc Mont Ridge"; John Terraine, *To Win a War* (New York: Doubleday, 1981), 163–164; Lejeune, *The Reminiscences of a Marine*, 363.

24. London, Liddell Hart Centre for Military Archives (LHCMA), LH IS/2/34, *Reveille*, Feb. 1, 1938, "Mademoiselle from Armentières"; Stallings, *The Doughboys*, 287; Berry, *Make the Kaiser Dance*, 299; Lejeune, *The Reminiscences of a Marine*, 364; NARA, RG 120, NM 91, 267, GHQ G-3, Box 3125, 777,

Chaumont, AEF GHQ, 1919, "Candid Comment on the American Soldier of 1917–1918 and Related Topics by the Germans."

25. Lengel, *To Conquer Hell*, 216–217.

26. Edward Coffman, *The War to End All Wars* (New York: Oxford Univ. Press, 1968), 321–322; Grotelueschen, *The AEF Way of War*, 135–140; Eisenhower, *Yanks*, 232.

27. Ettinger and Ettinger, *A Doughboy with the Fighting Sixty-Ninth*, 155.

28. Hervey Allen, *It Was Like This* (New York: Farrar & Rinehart, 1936), 127; H. W. Crocker III, *Yanks* (Washington, DC: Regnery, 2017), 98; NARA, RG 120, NM 91, 1042, Box 6, HQ 28th Infantry, Germany, Jan. 4, 1919, "Recommendation for Distinguished Service Cross."

29. NARA, RG 120, NM 91, 1241, Box 49, 201-32.16, Oct. 5, 1918, CO MG Co. attached to 2nd Bn. 26; NARA, RG 120, NM 91, 1241, Box 46, 201-11.4, AEF GHQ, Jan. 20, 1919, McAndrew to Parker; NARA, RG 120, NM 91, 1241, Box 49, 201-32.16, Oct. 5, 1918, 7:10 p.m., 3rd Bn. 26th Inf., Maj. Frasier; NARA, RG 120, NM 91, 267, GHQ G-3, Box 3125, 772, AEF Advanced GHQ, Trier, April 4, 1919, "Conversation with Col. Von Heye at Treves, April 3, 1919."

30. Barrie Pitt, *1918: The Last Act* (London: Cassell, 1962), 258.

31. Terraine, *To Win a War*, 180–181.

32. Horace L. Baker, *Argonne Days in World War I*, ed. Robert H. Ferrell (1927; Columbia: Univ. of Missouri Press, 2007), 45–46.

33. Barkley, *Scarlet Fields*, 144–145, 148.

34. Cooke, *Pershing and His Generals*, 108.

35. NARA, RG 120, NM 91, 990, Box 3, AEF GHQ, Nov. 15, 1918, "Summary History of the First American Army Corps."

36. Stallings, *The Doughboys*, 298–302.

37. Alexander, *Memories of the World War*, 229–231; Slotkin, *Lost Battalions*, 342, 374; Grotelueschen, *The AEF Way of War*, 322; Stallings, *The Doughboys*, 298–302.

38. NARA, RG 120, NM 91, 267, GHQ G-3, Box 3101, HQ I Corps, Oct. 12, 1918, "Report of Investigation of Alleged Wild Firing by the 306th Field Artillery on Hill 212, France October 6–7, 1918"; Slotkin, *Lost Battalions*, 380.

39. NARA, RG 120, NM 91, 1241, Box 46, 201-32.16, Oct. 9, 10:45 a.m., Lt. Canby, Co. A 18th to Bn. Comd. 1st Bn. 18th; NARA, RG 120, NM 91, 1241, Box 46, 201-32.16, Oct. 9, 9:40 a.m., Co. A 18th to Bn. Comd. 1st Bn. 18th.

40. NARA, RG 120, NM 91, 1241, Box 49, 201-32.16, Oct. 9, 9:40 a.m., Lt. Canby, Co. A 18th to Bn. Comd. 1st Bn. 18th; NARA, RG 120, NM 91, 1241, Box 49, 201-32.16, Oct. 9, 1:10 p.m., Co. A 18th to Bn. Comd. 1st Bn. 18th.

41. NARA, RG 120, NM 91, 267, GHQ G-3, Box 3120, 731, Dec. 1, 1918, Col. J. N. Greely, "Notes on Report Submitted by French Authorities to War Department Direct"; NARA, RG 120, NM 91, 990, Box 3, AEF GHQ, Nov. 15, 1918, "Summary History of the First American Army Corps."

42. NARA, RG 120, NM 91, 990, Box 19, 181-32-16, Field Messages, Oct. 5, 1918, No. 90, from EMERSON ONE, signed Bullard; Baker, *Argonne Days in World War I*, 50.

43. BNA, WO 106/528, October 1918, "Notes on American Offensive Operations," secret, from information received from French sources.

44. LHCMA, Spears 1/20, Paris, Oct. 4, 1918, Spears to Wilson; Elizabeth Greenhalgh, *Foch in Command* (Cambridge: Cambridge Univ. Press, 2011), 450–453; Terraine, *To Win a War*, 129, 180; Boff, *Winning and Losing on the Western Front*, 41–44.

45. George C. Marshall, *Memoirs of My Services in the World War, 1917–1918* (Boston: Houghton Mifflin, 1976), 163, 174, 176; Repington, *The First World War, 1914–1918*, 2:94, 459; Coffman, *The War to End All Wars*, 174–175.

46. NARA, RG 120, NM 91, 195, Box 1, Classification Camp Reports, HQ 83rd Division, Le Mans, Nov. 3, 1918, "Classification Camp Report"; Marshall, *Memoirs of My Services in the World War*, 174, 176; Palmer, *With My Own Eyes*, 344.

47. NARA, RG 120, NM 91, 267, GHQ G-3, Box 3125, 777, Chaumont, AEF GHQ, 1919, "Candid Comment on the American Soldier of 1917–1918 and Related Topics by the Germans"; Baker, *Argonne Days in World War I*, 61–62.

48. NARA, RG 120, NM 91, 990, Box 6, 1st US Army Corps, "Summary of Intelligence, July 4–November 9, 1918"; Rubin, *The Last of the Doughboys*, 312; Baker, *Argonne Days in World War I*, 52.

49. NARA, RG 120, NM 91, 267, GHQ G-3, Box 3125, 777, Chaumont, AEF GHQ, 1919, "Candid Comment on the American Soldier of 1917–1918 and Related Topics by the Germans."

50. NARA, RG 120, NM 91, 267, GHQ G-3, Box 3125, 777, Chaumont, AEF GHQ, 1919, "Candid Comment on the American Soldier of 1917–1918 and Related Topics by the Germans"; Allen, *It Was Like This*, 124; NARA, RG 120, NM 91, 195, Box 1, Classification Camp Reports, HQ 83rd Division, Le Mans, Oct. 3, 1918, "Classification Camp Report."

51. Barkley, *Scarlet Fields*, 183–189.

52. Pitt, *1918: The Last Act*, 260–262; Terraine, *To Win a War*, 177–178; Alexander, *Memories of the World War*, 220.

53. Stallings, *The Doughboys*, 301.

54. Lengel, *To Conquer Hell*, 298–300, 363.

55. Frank E. Vandiver, *Black Jack* (College Station: Texas A&M Univ. Press, 1977), 2:975–976; Michael E. Shay, *Revered Commander, Maligned General* (Columbia: Univ. of Missouri Press, 2011), 170–171; Coffman, *The War to End All Wars*, 330–331; Grotelueschen, *The AEF Way of War*, 190–191; Stallings, *The Doughboys*, 303.

56. Vienna, Kriegsarchiv (KA), AOK-Op. Abteilung 557, k.u.k. 1. Infanteriedivisionskdo, Oct. 14, 1918, "Schlaagfertigkeitmeldung"; KA, AOK-Op.

Abteilung 557, k.u.k. 1. Infanteriedivisionskdo, "Wochenmeldung für die Zeit vom 14–21 Oktober 1918"; Maximilian Polatschek, "Österreichische-Ungarische Truppen an der Westfront" (PhD diss., Univ. of Vienna, 1974), 107–110; Fritz Franek, "K.u.k. Truppen im Westen," *Militärwissenschaftliche Mitteilungen* 62 (1931): 421–423.

57. NARA, RG 120, NM 91, 267, GHQ G-3, Box 3125, 777, Chaumont, AEF GHQ, 1919, "Candid Comment on the American Soldier of 1917–1918 and Related Topics by the Germans;" KA, AOK-Op. Abteilung 557, k.u.k. 1. Infanteriedivisionskdo, Oct. 23, 1918, "Gaserkrankungen"; John Dos Passos, *Three Soldiers* (1921; New York: Barnes & Noble Books, 2004), 204.

58. KA, NFA 105, Oct. 1918, "Merkblatt zum Sammelm und Aufbewahren von Bucheckern"; KA, NFA 105, Oct. 26, 1918, Maas-Gruppe-Ost, "Einrichtung und Dienstanweisung des Munitions-Sammelstabes."

59. Robert Doughty, *Pyrrhic Victory* (Cambridge, MA: Belknap, 2005), 494–496; Vandiver, *Black Jack*, 2:972, 976.

60. Terraine, *To Win a War*, 200–201.

61. Stallings, *The Doughboys*, 323–324; Terraine, *To Win a War*, 200–202; Lengel, *To Conquer Hell*, 95, 311–312.

62. Vandiver, *Black Jack*, 2:976; Lengel, *To Conquer Hell*, 212; Marshall, *Memoirs of My Services in the World War*, 176–177; Thomas Johnson, *Without Censor* (Indianapolis, IN: Bobbs-Merrill, 1927), 257.

63. NARA, RG 120, NM 91, 267, GHQ G-3, Box 3120, 732, French Army GHQ, Jan. 17, 1919, "Instructions for the Commanders of Army Groups"; Cooke, *Pershing and His Generals*, 150.

64. Lengel, *To Conquer Hell*, 360–361; Baker, *Argonne Days in World War I*, 53.

65. NARA, RG 120, NM 91, 990, Box 3, AEF GHQ, Nov. 15, 1918, "Summary History of the First American Army Corps."

66. Barkley, *Scarlet Fields*, 157–159.

67. NARA, RG 120, NM 91, 1118, V Corps Historical, Box 19, V Corps, Oct. 14, 1918, "From G-2, 5th Army Corps"; NARA, RG 120, NM 91, 1118, V Corps Historical, Box 19, V Corps, Oct. 10–11, 1918, "Summary of Intelligence."

68. Marshall, *Memoirs of My Services in the World War*, 32.

69. NARA, RG 120, NM 91, 1241, Box 46, 201-11.4, HQ 18th Inf., Oct. 19, 1918, Lt. Col. C. A. Hunt, "Reports on Recent Operations of 18th Infantry"; NARA, RG 120, NM 91, 1241, Box 46, 201-11.4, HQ 1st Div., France, Oct. 11 and 23, 1918, Gen. C. P. Summerrall; Belmonte, *Days of Perfect Hell*, 135–136; Lengel, *To Conquer Hell*, 327.

70. Stallings, *The Doughboys*, 323–327.

71. NARA, RG 120, NM 91, 990, Box 3, AEF GHQ, Nov. 15, 1918, "Summary History of the First American Army Corps"; Lengel, *To Conquer Hell*, 376.

72. NARA, RG 120, NM 91, 990, Box 3, AEF GHQ, Nov. 15, 1918, "Summary History of the First American Army Corps."

73. NARA, RG 120, NM 91, 990, Box 6, 1st US Army Corps, "Summary of Intelligence, July 4–November 9, 1918"; NARA, RG 120, NM 91, 267, GHQ G-3, Box 3119, Oct. 16, 1918, Maj. Clark to Pershing, "Military Situation," secret.

74. Berry, *Make the Kaiser Dance*, 346.

75. UKNA, WO 106/538, Jan. 16, 1919, "Report of General John J. Pershing, USA, Commander-in-Chief American Expeditionary Forces, Cabled to the Secretary of War, Nov. 20, 1918, Corrected Jan. 6, 1919," 19.

76. Baker, *Argonne Days in World War I*, 62.

77. Ettinger and Ettinger, *A Doughboy with the Fighting Sixty-Ninth*, 167; Berry, *Make the Kaiser Dance*, 319.

78. Robert H. Ferrell, *The Question of MacArthur's Reputation* (Columbia: Univ. of Missouri Press, 2008), 23.

79. Robert H. Ferrell, *America's Deadliest Battle* (Lawrence: Univ. Press of Kansas, 2007), 123–125; Ettinger and Ettinger, *A Doughboy with the Fighting Sixty-Ninth*, xxiii, 156, 160–161; Ferrell, *The Question of MacArthur's Reputation*, 25; Lengel, *To Conquer Hell*, 329.

80. Rubin, *The Last of the Doughboys*, 314; Lengel, *To Conquer Hell*, 336; Baker, *Argonne Days in World War I*, 67–69, 73, 79.

81. Douglas Waller, *Wild Bill Donovan* (New York: Free Press, 2011), 26–27; Ettinger and Ettinger, *A Doughboy with the Fighting Sixty-Ninth*, 164–165; Ferrell, *The Question of MacArthur's Reputation*, 23, 39; Lengel, *To Conquer Hell*, 340.

82. Ferrell, *The Question of MacArthur's Reputation*, 39–40; Lengel, *To Conquer Hell*, 339–340.

83. NARA, RG 120, NM 91, 267, GHQ G-3, Box 3125, 777, Chaumont, AEF GHQ, 1919, "Candid Comment on the American Soldier of 1917–1918 and Related Topics by the Germans;" Ettinger and Ettinger, *A Doughboy with the Fighting Sixty-Ninth*, 165.

84. Lengel, *To Conquer Hell*, 354.

85. Ferrell, *The Question of MacArthur's Reputation*, 42–43, 48, 54–55, 58–59; Lengel, *To Conquer Hell*, 355, 371–372.

86. Baker, *Argonne Days in World War I*, 1, 77.

87. Berry, *Make the Kaiser Dance*, 114.

88. NARA, RG 120, NM 91, 1118, V Corps Historical, Box 2, n.d., History of the Fifth American Army Corps; Ettinger and Ettinger, *A Doughboy with the Fighting Sixty-Ninth*, 166; Lejeune, *The Reminiscences of a Marine*, 377.

89. Barkley, *Scarlet Fields*, 203–205.

CHAPTER 15: MEUSE-ARGONNE: BARRICOURT

1. Henry Berry, *Make the Kaiser Dance* (New York: Arbor House, 1978), 133.

2. Richard Slotkin, *Lost Battalions* (New York: Henry Holt, 2005), 377–378; David Kennedy, *Over Here* (New York: Oxford Univ. Press, 1980), 233–244;

Richard Striner, *Woodrow Wilson and World War I* (Lanham, MD: Rowman & Littlefield, 2014), 164–165.

3. College Park, MD, National Archives and Records Administration (NARA), RG 120, NM 91, 267, GHQ G-3, Box 3119, Oct. 18, 19, 23, and 28, 1918, Maj. Clark to Pershing, "Military Situation," secret; NARA, RG 120, NM 91, 267, GHQ G-3, Box 3120, 733, French GQG, March 5, 1919, Lt. Col. Paul Clark to Pershing, "The Military Situation," secret.

4. John Terraine, *To Win a War* (New York: Doubleday, 1981), 184; Barrie Pitt, *1918: The Last Act* (London: Cassell, 1962), 262–264; Terraine, *To Win a War*, 186–187.

5. Nick Lloyd, *Hundred Days* (New York: Basic Books, 2014), 227; Terraine, *To Win a War*, 188–191; David R. Woodward, *Trial by Friendship* (Lexington: Univ. Press of Kentucky, 1993), 214.

6. London, Liddell Hart Centre for Military Archives (LHCMA), Grant 3/2, "Some Notes Made at Marshal Foch's HQrs, August to November 1918"; Robert Alexander, *Memories of the World War, 1917–1918* (New York: Macmillan, 1931), 265; Frank E. Vandiver, *Black Jack* (College Station: Texas A&M Univ. Press, 1977), 2:981.

7. Pitt, *1918: The Last Act*, 258–259.

8. David Stevenson, *With Our Backs to the Wall* (Cambridge, MA: Belknap, 2011), 239–240; Pitt, *1918: The Last Act*, 253–254; Terraine, *To Win a War*, 179–180; Lloyd, *Hundred Days*, 188–189, 191–192, 275, 277.

9. Kew, UK National Archives (UKNA), WO 106/528, Oct. 19, 1918, Gen. J. P. Du Cane to Gen. Henry Wilson; UKNA, WO 106/528, October 1918, "Notes on American Offensive Operations," secret, from information received from French sources General John J. Pershing and Lieutenant General Hunter Liggett, *Report of the First Army, American Expeditionary Forces, Organization and Operations* (Fort Leavenworth, KS: General Service Schools Press, 1923), 78.

10. Edward G. Lengel, *To Conquer Hell* (New York: Henry Holt, 2005), 360–361.

11. Vincennes, Service Historique de la Défense (SHD), FC 6N 141, Paris, Oct. 21, 1918, Clemenceau to Foch; NARA, RG 120, NM 91, 268, GHQ G-3, Box 3101, "Battle of the Argonne-Meuse," 78th Division Lecture Course, Jan. 3, 1919, Acting Chief of Staff James L. Frink.

12. NARA, RG 120, NM 91, 990, Box 6, 1st US Army Corps, "Summary of Intelligence, July 4–November 9, 1918."

13. Laurence Stallings, *The Doughboys* (New York: Harper & Row, 1963), 338–339; Robert H. Ferrell, *America's Deadliest Battle* (Lawrence: Univ. Press of Kansas, 2007) 109–111; Lengel, *To Conquer Hell*, 347–348.

14. Peter L. Belmonte, *Days of Perfect Hell, October–November 1918* (Atglen, PA: Schiffer, 2015), 142.

15. NARA, RG 120, NM 91, 1241, Box 41, 201-32.15, HQ 2nd Brig, 1st Div, France, Oct. 21, 1918, Capt. Samuel W. Marshall, "To Commanding Officers 26th and 28th Infantry"; NARA, RG 120, NM 91, 1241, Box 46, 201-11.4, HQ 1st Div., France, Oct. 19, 1918, Maj. W. R. Wheeler, Memo No. 169; NARA, RG 120, NM 91, 1241, Box 46, Oct. 29, 1918, Gen. Parker, "Memorandum to Members of the 1st Division"; Stallings, *The Doughboys*, 351; Marshall, *Memoirs of My Services in the World War*, 178–179.

16. Robert H. Ferrell, ed., *A Soldier in World War I* (Indianapolis: Indiana Historical Society, 2004), 96; Lengel, *To Conquer Hell*, 384–386.

17. London, UK Parliamentary Archives (UKPA), STR/26/4/5d, Camp Funston, KS, Oct. 23, 1918, Leonard Wood Strachey; Frederick Palmer, *With My Own Eyes* (Indianapolis, IN: Bobbs-Merrill, 1932), 342; James J. Cooke, *Pershing and His Generals* (Westport, CT: Praeger, 1997), 57–58; Vandiver, *Black Jack*, 2:802–804.

18. Marshall, *Memoirs of My Services in the World War*, 180, 182, 192.

19. Albert M. Ettinger and A. Churchill Ettinger, *A Doughboy with the Fighting Sixty-Ninth* (Shippensburg, PA: White Mane, 1992), 172.

20. NARA, RG 120, NM 91, 1118, V Corps Historical, Box 5, V Corps, Oct. 23, 1918, "Summary of Intelligence."

21. Ettinger and Ettinger, *A Doughboy with the Fighting Sixty-Ninth*, 169; Lengel, *To Conquer Hell*, 386.

22. Pitt, *1918: The Last Act*, 263–264.

23. NARA, RG 120, NM 91, 1118, V Corps Historical, Box 2, n.d., History of the Fifth American Army Corps; John Lewis Barkley, *Scarlet Fields* (1930; Lawrence: Univ. Press of Kansas, 2012), 164; Major General John A. Lejeune, *The Reminiscences of a Marine* (1930; New York: Arno Press, 1979), 373.

24. Vienna, Kriegsarchiv (KA), AOK-Op. Abteilung 557, Oct. 23, 1918, "Feldjägerbaon Nr. 25."

25. NARA, RG 120, NM 91, 1118, V Corps Historical, Box 5, V Corps, Oct. 24, 1918, "Summary of Intelligence"; *Arbeiter-Zeitung* (Vienna), October 24, 1918.

26. UKPA, STR/26/4/5d, Camp Funston, KS, Oct. 23, 1918, Leonard Wood to Strachey.

27. NARA, RG 120, NM 91, 990, Box 3, AEF GHQ, Nov. 26, 1918, "Last Days of the German Army: From the Diary of a Lieutenant of the 3rd Guard Artillery."

28. NARA, RG 120, NM 91, 267, GHQ G-3, Box 3119, Nov. 1, 1918, Maj. Clark to Pershing, "Military Situation," secret; UKNA, WO 106/528, Oct. 25, 1918, Gen. J. P. Du Cane to Gen. Henry Wilson; Stevenson, *With Our Backs to the Wall*, 249.

29. Vienna, Haus-, Hof- und Staatsarchiv (HHSA), PA I 898, Christiana, October 19, 1917, Hoyos to Czernin; Woodward, *Trial by Friendship*, 214.

30. Terraine, *To Win a War*, 193–196; Lengel, *To Conquer Hell*, 381–382.

31. LHCMA, Grant 3/2, "Some Notes Made at Marshal Foch's HQrs, August to November 1918"; William Philpott, *War of Attrition* (New York: Overlook, 2014), 328.

32. Stallings, *The Doughboys*, 331–332.

33. NARA, RG 120, NM 91, 1241, Box 41, 201-32.15, HQ 2nd Brig, 1st Div., France, Oct. 25, 1918, Capt. Samuel W. Marshall to Commanding Officers 26th, 28th Infantry, 3rd MG Battalion, "Stragglers"; NARA, RG 120, NM 91, 990, Box 3, AEF GHQ, Nov. 26, 1918, "Last Days of the German Army: From the Diary of a Lieutenant of the 3rd Guard Artillery"; Marshall, *Memoirs of My Services in the World War*, 175.

34. NARA, RG 120, NM 91, 195, Box 1, Classification Camp Reports, HQ 83rd Division, Le Mans, Oct. 3–31, 1918, "Classification Camp Reports"; SHD, FJ 14N 27, Washington, October 11 and 24, 1918, Col. Collardet-Jusserand to Min. of War; Richard S. Faulkner, *Pershing's Crusaders* (Lawrence: Univ. Press of Kansas, 2017), 587; Coffman, *The War to End All Wars*, 84; Stallings, *The Doughboys*, 344.

35. NARA, RG 120, NM 91, 195, Box 1, Classification Camp Reports, HQ 83rd Division, Le Mans, Oct. 8, 30, 31, Nov. 1, 1918, "Classification Camp Report."

36. NARA, RG 120, NM 91, 267, GHQ G-3, Box 3092, France, Advanced HQ 1st Army Corps, Oct. 30, 1918, Gen. Malin Craig, "Coming Operations."

37. Stallings, *The Doughboys*, 344, 353–354.

38. Stallings, *The Doughboys*, 342–343.

39. NARA, RG 120, NM 91, 1043, Box 4, HQ III Corps, Dec. 1, 1918, Hines to Pershing, "The Argonne-Meuse Operations From Sept. 9 to Nov. 11"; Stallings, *The Doughboys*, 356–357.

40. NARA, RG 120, NM 91, 1118, V Corps Historical, Box 5, V Corps, Nov. 7, 1918, "Summary of Intelligence"; Baker, *Argonne Days in World War I*, 96.

41. NARA, RG 120, NM 91, 1118, V Corps Historical, Box 2, n.d., History of the Fifth American Army Corps; Belmonte, *Days of Perfect Hell*, 144.

42. Mark Ethan Grotelueschen, *The AEF Way of War* (Cambridge: Cambridge Univ. Press, 2007), 270; Ferrell, *A Soldier in World War I*, 96; Lejeune, *The Reminiscences of a Marine*, 377–378, 383; Stallings, *The Doughboys*, 347.

43. Hervey Allen, *Toward the Flame* (1926; Lincoln: Univ. of Nebraska Press, 2003), 140; Jerry R. Tompkins, ed., *The Crossed Hands of God* (Eugene, OR: Resource, 2015), 56, 68–69; Ferrell, *America's Deadliest Battle*, 132; Lengel, *To Conquer Hell*, 391.

44. Alexander, *Memories of the World War*, 273–274.

45. NARA, RG 120, NM 91, 1118, V Corps Historical, Box 2, n.d., History of the Fifth American Army Corps.

46. Berry, *Make the Kaiser Dance*, 384; Lejeune, *The Reminiscences of a Marine*, 386.

47. NARA, RG 120, NM 91, 1118, V Corps Historical, Box 5, V Corps, Oct. 26, 1918, "Present Tactical Disposition by the Enemy"; Marshall, *Memoirs of My Services in the World War*, 183.

48. Tompkins, *The Crossed Hands of God*, 56, 68–69.

49. NARA, RG 120, NM 91, 1241, Box 54, 202.11.4, "A Brief History of the 6th Regiment, USMC from July 1917 to Dec. 1918."

50. NARA, RG 120, NM 91, 1118, V Corps Historical, Box 5, V Corps, Nov. 1, 1918, "Summary of Intelligence"; Lejeune, *The Reminiscences of a Marine*, 379.

51. Lejeune, *The Reminiscences of a Marine*, 390; Alexander, *Memories of the World War*, 280.

52. NARA, RG 120, NM 91, 990, Box 3, AEF GHQ, Nov. 15, 1918, "Summary History of the First American Army Corps"; Stallings, *The Doughboys*, 352; Ferrell, *America's Deadliest Battle*, 138.

53. Munich, Bayerisches Kriegsarchiv (BKA), Handschriftensammlung (HS) 2180, "Skizze zu den Kämpfen bei Dun, Oct.–Nov. 1918."

54. Berry, *Make the Kaiser Dance*, 421; Stallings, *The Doughboys*, 353–354.

55. Pitt, *1918: The Last Act*, 264–265.

56. NARA, RG 120, NM 91, 267, GHQ G-3, Box 3119, Nov. 1 and 4, 1918, Maj. Clark to Pershing, "Military Situation," secret.

57. C. à Court Repington, *The First World War, 1914–1918* (Boston: Houghton Mifflin, 1920), 2:475; Lejeune, *The Reminiscences of a Marine*, 375.

58. NARA, RG 120, NM 91, 990, Box 6, 1st US Army Corps, "Summary of Intelligence, July 4–November 9, 1918"; Lejeune, *The Reminiscences of a Marine*, 391.

59. NARA, RG 120, NM 91, 990, Box 6, 1st US Army Corps, "Summary of Intelligence, July 4–November 9, 1918"; NARA, RG 120, NM 91, 990, Box 3, AEF GHQ, Nov. 15, 1918, "Summary History of the First American Army Corps"; Terraine, *To Win a War*, 219–220.

CHAPTER 16: MEUSE-ARGONNE: SEDAN

1. John J. Pershing, *My Experiences in the World War* (1931; New York: Da Capo, 1995), 366–367.

2. Richard Striner, *Woodrow Wilson and World War I* (Lanham, MD: Rowman & Littlefield, 2014), 161–162; Horace L. Baker, *Argonne Days in World War I*, ed. Robert H. Ferrell (1927; Columbia: Univ. of Missouri Press, 2007), 140.

3. Geoffrey Hodgson, *Woodrow Wilson's Right Hand* (New Haven, CT: Yale Univ. Press, 2006), 188–191.

4. John Terraine, *To Win a War* (New York: Doubleday, 1981), 216–217; David R. Woodward, *Trial by Friendship* (Lexington: Univ. Press of Kentucky, 1993), 212–214; David Trask, *The AEF and Coalition Warmaking, 1917–1918* (Lawrence: Univ. Press of Kansas, 1993), 157–158; Laurence Stallings, *The Doughboys* (New York: Harper & Row, 1963), 344; Striner, *Woodrow Wilson and World War I*, 161–162.

5. College Park, MD, National Archives and Records Administration (NARA), RG 120, NM 91, 267, GHQ G-3, Box 3119, Nov. 5, 7, 1918, Maj. Clark to Pershing, "Military Situation," secret.

6. Jonathan Boff, *Winning and Losing on the Western Front* (Cambridge: Cambridge Univ. Press, 2012), 36–37; NARA, RG 120, NM 91, 267, GHQ G-3, Box 3119, Nov. 8, 1918, Maj. Clark to Pershing, "Military Situation," secret.

7. NARA, RG 120, NM 91, 990, Box 3, AEF GHQ, Nov. 15, 1918, "Summary History of the First American Army Corps"; NARA, RG 120, NM 91, 990, Box 6, 1st US Army Corps, "Summary of Intelligence, July 4–November 9, 1918"; George C. Marshall, *Memoirs of My Services in the World War, 1917–1918* (Boston: Houghton Mifflin, 1976), 185.

8. NARA, RG 120, NM 91, 1118, V Corps Historical, Box 5, V Corps, Nov. 1 and 7, 1918, "Summary of Intelligence"; NARA, RG 120, NM 91, 1118, V Corps Historical, Box 2, n.d., "Comments by the Corps Commander upon the Operations of the Fifth Army Corps."

9. Stallings, *The Doughboys*, 358–359.

10. Robert H. Ferrell, *The Question of MacArthur's Reputation* (Columbia: Univ. of Missouri Press, 2008), 15; James J. Cooke, *Pershing and His Generals* (Westport, CT: Praeger, 1997), 70; Edward Coffman, *The War to End All Wars* (New York: Oxford Univ. Press, 1968), 72, 318–320.

11. Robert Lee Bullard, *Personalities and Reminiscences of the War* (New York: Doubleday, 1925), 295–298; Lengel, *To Conquer Hell*, 427–429.

12. Marshall, *Memoirs of My Services in the World War*, 188; Ferrell, *The Question of MacArthur's Reputation*, 6–7.

13. Marshall, *Memoirs of My Services in the World War*, 188–189; Trask, *The AEF and Coalition Warmaking*, 163.

14. John H. Taber, *A Rainbow Division Lieutenant in France,* ed. Stephen H. Taber (Jefferson, NC: McFarland, 2015), 132; Peter L. Belmonte, *Days of Perfect Hell, October–November 1918* (Atglen, PA: Schiffer, 2015), 147, 158.

15. Marshall, *Memoirs of My Services in the World War*, 189.

16. Alexander, *Memories of the World War*, 293–294.

17. Robert H. Ferrell, *America's Deadliest Battle* (Lawrence: Univ. Press of Kansas, 2007), 141; Belmonte, *Days of Perfect Hell*, 162–163; Coffman, *The War to End All Wars*, 352; Trask, *The AEF and Coalition Warmaking*, 164–165.

18. Thomas H. Barber, *Along the Road* (New York: Dodd Mead, 1924), 30; Stallings, *The Doughboys*, 362.

19. Alexander, *Memories of the World War*, 300; Major General John A. Lejeune, *The Reminiscences of a Marine* (1930; New York: Arno Press, 1979), 392.

20. Marshall, *Memoirs of My Services in the World War*, 190–192; Stallings, *The Doughboys*, 347; Lejeune, *The Reminiscences of a Marine*, 393.

21. NARA, RG 120, NM 91, 267, GHQ G-3, Box 3119, Nov. 8, 1918, Maj. Clark to Pershing, "Military Situation," secret.

22. NARA, RG 120, NM 91, 267, GHQ G-3, Box 3125, 777, Chaumont, AEF GHQ, 1919, "Candid Comment on the American Soldier of 1917–1918 and Related Topics by the Germans"; NARA, RG 120, NM 91, 267, GHQ G-3, Box 3119, Nov. 8, 1918, Maj. Clark to Pershing, "Military Situation," secret.

23. Stallings, *The Doughboys*, 355, 365, 374; Terraine, *To Win a War*, 220–221.

24. Barrie Pitt, *1918: The Last Act* (London: Cassell, 1962), 265–267; Nick Lloyd, *Hundred Days* (New York: Basic Books, 2014), 252–254.

25. London, Liddell Hart Centre for Military Archives (LHCMA), Grant 3/2, "Some Notes Made at Marshal Foch's HQrs, August to November 1918"; Terraine, *To Win a War*, 224–225.

26. LHCMA, Grant 3/2, "Some Notes Made at Marshal Foch's HQrs, August to November 1918"; Terraine, *To Win a War*, 214, 226–228.

27. NARA, RG 120, NM 91, 267, GHQ G-3, Box 3119, Nov. 8, 1918, Maj. Clark to Pershing, "Military Situation," secret.

28. NARA, RG 120, NM 91, 267, GHQ G-3, Box 3119, Nov. 8, 1918, Maj. Clark to Pershing, "Military Situation," secret.

29. NARA, RG 120, NM 91, 267, GHQ G-3, Box 3119, Nov. 8, 1918, Maj. Clark to Pershing, "Military Situation," secret.

30. Henry Berry, *Make the Kaiser Dance* (New York: Arbor House, 1978), 407; Frank E. Vandiver, *Black Jack* (College Station: Texas A&M Univ. Press, 1977), 2:985; Marshall, *Memoirs of My Services in the World War*, 196.

31. NARA, RG 120, NM 91, 1043, Box 4, HQ III Army Corps, Dec. 1, 1918, Gen. Hines to Gen. Pershing, "Report of Operations, Sept. 9 to Nov. 11, 1918"; Munich, Bayerisches Kriegsarchiv (BKA), Inf. Div., 1. bay. Inf. Div., Nov. 10, 1918, Hindenburg, "Ansprache des Divisions-Kommandeurs"; Belmonte, *Days of Perfect Hell*, 144; Lejeune, *The Reminiscences of a Marine*, 382, 400.

32. NARA, RG 120, NM 91, 1118, V Corps Historical, Box 2, n.d., History of the Fifth American Army Corps; NARA, RG 120, NM 91, 1118, V Corps Historical, Box 2, n.d., "Comments by the Corps Commander Upon the Operations of the Fifth Army Corps"; Ferrell, *America's Deadliest Battle*, 147.

33. Berry, *Make the Kaiser Dance*, 386; Andrew Carroll, *My Fellow Soldiers* (New York: Penguin Press, 2017), 318.

34. Barkley, *Scarlet Fields*, 214–215.

35. NARA, RG 120, NM 91, 267, GHQ G-3, Box 3119, Nov. 11, 1918, Maj. Clark to Pershing, "Military Situation," secret.

36. Lejeune, *The Reminiscences of a Marine*, 405–406.

37. NARA, RG 120, NM 91, 1241, Box 46, 210-11.4, HQ 1st Div., Nov. 16, 1918, Maj. Thos. Gowenlock; Marshall, *Memoirs of My Services in the World War*, 195–196.

38. Kew, UK National Archives (UKNA), WO 106/538, Jan. 16, 1919, "Report of General John J. Pershing, USA, Commander-in-Chief American Expeditionary Forces, Cabled to the Secretary of War, Nov. 20, 1918, Corrected Jan. 6, 1919," 20–21.

39. NARA, RG 120, NM 91, 267, GHQ G-3, Box 3120, 733, French GQG, March 5, 1919, Lt. Col. Clark to Pershing, "Military Situation," secret.

40. Marshall, *Memoirs of My Services in the World War*, 203–204.

41. LHCMA, Grant 3/2, "Some Notes Made at Marshal Foch's HQrs, August to November 1918."

42. NARA, RG 120, NM 91, 1118, V Corps Historical, Box 5, V Corps, Nov. 18, 1918, "Summary of Intelligence."

43. NARA, RG 120, NM 91, 1118, V Corps Historical, Box 5, V Corps, Nov. 12–19, 1918, "Summary of Intelligence"; NARA, RG 120, NM 91, 267, GHQ G-3, Box 3120, 731, Nov. 24, 1918, Capt. Chas. Freeborn to Lt. Col. Paul Clark, "Trip to the Belgian Capital"; NARA, RG 120, NM 91, 267, GHQ G-3, Box 3120, 731, Nov. 17, 1918, Maj. E. E. Farman, "Report of French Officers Returning from Spa"; BKA, Inf. Div., 1. bay. Inf. Div., Nov. 12, 1918, Hindenburg to army commanders; Taber, *A Rainbow Division Lieutenant in France*, 139.

CHAPTER 17: PEACE?

1. Douglas Haig, "The Length of the War," *Fourth Supplement to the London Gazette*, April 10, 1919.

2. Major General John A. Lejeune, *The Reminiscences of a Marine* (1930; New York: Arno Press, 1979), 417–418, 425; Henry Berry, *Make the Kaiser Dance* (New York: Arbor House, 1978), 410.

3. George C. Marshall, *Memoirs of My Services in the World War, 1917–1918* (Boston: Houghton Mifflin, 1976), 202–206; Kyle J. Hatzinger, "'If ye Break Faith': The World War I Foundations for Commemorating America's War Dead," (PhD diss., Univ. of North Texas, 2019), 56–58, 75–77, 169–172.

4. NARA, RG 120, NM 91, 267, GHQ G-3, Box 3119, Nov. 17, 1918, Maj. Clark to Pershing, "Military Situation," secret.

5. NARA, RG 120, NM 91, 267, GHQ G-3, Box 3119, Nov. 20, 1918, Maj. Clark to Pershing, "Military Situation," secret.

6. NARA, RG 120, NM 91, 268, GHQ G-3, Box 3088A, France, Nov. 16, 1918, Pershing to Liggett, confidential; NARA, RG 120, NM 91, 268, GHQ G-3, Box 3104, France, AEF GHQ, Nov. 23, 1918, March to Pershing, confidential; Laurence Stallings, *The Doughboys* (New York: Harper & Row, 1963), 373.

7. Andrew Carroll, *My Fellow Soldiers* (New York: Penguin Press, 2017), 320–321.

8. NARA, RG 120, NM 91, 268, GHQ G-3, Box 3105, Nov. 29, 1918, Pershing to Adjutant General, for Secretary of War, confidential.

9. James Carl Nelson, *Five Lieutenants* (New York: St. Martin's, 2012), 144–145.

10. David Kennedy, *Over Here* (New York: Oxford Univ. Press, 1980), 52; NARA, RG 120, NM 91, 268, GHQ G-3, Box 3105, "Address of Woodrow Wilson, President of the United States, to U.S. Troops at Humes, France, Dec. 25, 1918."

11. Kew, UK National Archives (UKNA), WO, 106/541, Capt. Henry Wolfson, secret, July 23, 1919, "Strength Report, American Forces in Germany"; Richard Striner, *Woodrow Wilson and World War I* (Lanham, MD: Rowman & Littlefield, 2014), 174.

12. NARA, RG 120, NM 91, 268, GHQ G-3, Box 3091, AEF GHQ, May 2, 1919, Pershing to Bliss; NARA, RG 120, NM 91, 268, GHQ G-3, Box 3091, Paris, May 20, 1919, Foch to Pershing, "Directives pour le Haut Commandement seul"; NARA, RG 120, NM 91, 268, GHQ G-3, Box 3091, Allied GHQ, June 19, 1919, Foch to Pershing, secret.

13. London, Liddell Hart Centre for Military Archives (LHCMA), Spears 1/20, Paris, April 6, 1919, Spears to Viscount Duncannon; Marshall, *Memoirs of My Services in the World War*, 229.

14. NARA, RG 120, NM 91, 267, GHQ G-3, Box 3120, 732, French GQG, Feb. 24, 1919, Lt. Col. Paul Clark to Pershing, "Military Situation," secret.

15. NARA, RG 120, NM 91, 267, GHQ G-3, Box 3120, 732, French GQG, Feb. 24, 1919, Lt. Col. Paul Clark to Pershing, "Military Situation," secret.

16. NARA, RG 120, NM 91, 267, GHQ G-3, Box 3125, 771, AEF GHQ, G-2, Dec. 8, 1918, "They're Starting Home"; Edward M. Coffman, *The Regulars* (Cambridge, MA: Belknap, 2004), 224–225; James J. Cooke, *Pershing and His Generals* (Westport, CT: Praeger, 1997), 26; Berry, *Make the Kaiser Dance*, 170.

17. NARA, RG 120, NM 91, 267, GHQ G-3, Box 3125, 773, General Staff, May 13, 1919, "By Phone from Paris"; Vincennes, Service Historique de la Défense (SHD), Att. Mil. 7N 1717, Washington, March 8, 1919 and May 19, 1919, Gen. Collardet to Min. of War; Coffman, *The Regulars*, 233–235.

18. UKNA, WO 106/534, France, Dec. 6, 1918, Memo for the Chief of Staff, "Proposed Military Policy," prepared by G-5, signed by Pershing.

19. Richard Slotkin, *Lost Battalions* (New York: Henry Holt, 2005), 377–378; Kennedy, *Over Here*, 233–244.

20. "The Essentials of Peace," *The Times* (London), Dec. 6, 1918.

21. A. Scott Berg, ed., *World War I and America* (New York: Library of America, 2017), 629–631; Kennedy, *Over Here*, 333–334.

22. C. à Court Repington, *The First World War, 1914–1918* (Boston: Houghton Mifflin, 1920), 2:500.

23. Kennedy, *Over Here*, 358–360.

24. NARA, RG 120, NM 91, 267, GHQ G-3, Box 3125, 773, AEF GHQ, G-2, Paris, June 17–20, 1919; Barrie Pitt, *1918: The Last Act* (London: Cassell, 1962), 281; Striner, *Woodrow Wilson and World War I*, 180.

25. NARA, RG 120, NM 91, 267, GHQ G-3, Box 3125, 777, Chaumont, AEF GHQ, 1919, "Candid Comment on the American Soldier of 1917–1918 and Related Topics by the Germans."

26. NARA, RG 120, NM 91, 267, GHQ G-3, Box 3125, 773, AEF GHQ, G-2, Paris, June 17–20, 1919; Frederick Palmer, *Bliss, Peacemaker* (New York: Dodd Mead, 1934), 212–213.

27. NARA, RG 120, NM 91, 267, GHQ G-3, Box 3125, 773, AEF GHQ, G-2, Paris, June 29, 1919.

28. NARA, RG 120, NM 91, 267, GHQ G-3, Box 3125, 773, AEF GHQ, G-2, Paris, June 22, 1919, L. J. Maxse, "Too Much Wilson"; Kennedy, *Over Here*, 360.

29. Kennedy, *Over Here*, 362.

30. UK Parliamentary Archives (UKPA), STR/26/4/10e, Stockbridge, Aug. 9, 1918, F. L. Warren to Strachey.

31. Striner, *Woodrow Wilson and World War I*, 193.

32. Kennedy, *Over Here*, 362.

33. Robert A. Doughty, *Pyrrhic Victory* (Cambridge, MA: Belknap Press, 2005), 494.

34. NARA, RG 120, NM 91, 267, GHQ G-3, Box 3125, 772, March 8, 1919, Col. Conger to Col. Moreno, "By Phone."

35. UKPA, STR/26/4/16, London, March 27, 1919, Alfred Holman to Strachey.

36. David R. Woodward, *Trial by Friendship* (Lexington: Univ. Press of Kentucky, 1993), 220; Striner, *Woodrow Wilson and World War I*, 60, 132, 136, 166, 176, 190.

37. UKPA, STR/26/4/10e, Stockbridge, Aug. 9, 1918, F. L. Warren to Strachey.

38. SHD, FC 6N 136, Literary Digest, April 3, 1920.

39. SHD, FC 6N 136, Literary Digest, April 3, 1920.

40. UKPA, STR/26/4/10e, Stockbridge, Aug. 9, 1918, F. L. Warren to Strachey.

41. NARA, RG 120, NM 91, 267, GHQ G-3, Box 3125, 773, AEF GHQ, G-2, Paris, June 22, 1919; SHD, FC 6N 136, Literary Digest, April 3, 1920; Striner, *Woodrow Wilson and World War I*, 226.

42. College Park, MD, National Archives and Records Administration (NARA), RG 120, NM 91, 84, Box 6704, AEF, G-2, "A Survey of the War 1914–1918: Some Effects of American Participation."

43. NARA, RG 120, NM 91, 84, Box 6704, AEF, G-2, "A Survey of the War 1914–1918: Some Effects of American Participation"; Robert H. Ferrell, *America's Deadliest Battle* (Lawrence: Univ. Press of Kansas, 2007), 148.

44. NARA, RG 120, NM 91, 84, Box 6704, AEF, G-2, "A Survey of the War 1914–1918: Some Effects of American Participation."

45. NARA, RG 120, NM 91, 84, Box 6704, AEF, G-2, "A Survey of the War 1914–1918: Some Effects of American Participation," secret.

46. NARA, RG 120, NM 91, 84, Box 6704, AEF, G-2, "A Survey of the War 1914–1918: Some Effects of American Participation," secret.

47. Berry, *Make the Kaiser Dance*, 375–376; Thomas H. Barber, *Along the Road* (New York: Dodd Mead, 1924), xiv; Edward Streeter, *Dere Mable: Love Letters of a Rookie* (New York: Frederick A. Stokes, 1918), http://www.gwpda.org/wwi-www/DereMable/Mable.htm.

48. Robert Lee Bullard, *Personalities and Reminiscences of the War* (New York: Doubleday, 1925), 113.

49. NARA, RG 120, NM 91, 1241, Box 46, 201-11.4, HQ 18th Inf., Mogendorf, Germany, Feb. 4, 1919, Lt. Col. H. C. Stebbins; Lejeune, *The Reminiscences of a Marine*, 445; Albert M. Ettinger and A. Churchill Ettinger, *A Doughboy with the Fighting Sixty-Ninth* (Shippensburg, PA: White Mane, 1992), x.

50. Earl of Birkenhead, "My Reply to President Coolidge," *Britannia*, Nov. 30, 1928.

INDEX

MATIAS WAWRO

GEOFFREY WAWRO is the author of *A Mad Catastrophe*, a *Financial Times* Best History Book of 2014. He is also the author of five other books, including *Quicksand* and *The Franco-Prussian War*, and is a professor of history and director of the Military History Center at the University of North Texas. Wawro lives in Dallas, Texas. For more information, visit https://geoffreywawro.weebly.com.